PENGUIN BOOKS

A HISTORY OF CONTEMPORARY ITALY

Paul Ginsborg was born in London in 1945. He graduated in history from
Queens' College, Cambridge, in 1966 and was a Research Fellow there
from 1968 until 1971. For the next six years he was Lecturer in History at
York University. From 1977 to 1980 he lived in Italy and taught at the
University of Turin. In 1980 he returned to England to take up a Lecture-
ship in Politics at Cambridge University and a Fellowship at Churchill
College. In 1991 he was appointed Reader in European Politics at Cambridge. His present post is Professor of Contemporary European History
in the Faculty of Letters and Philosophy, University of Florence. His previous publications include *Daniele Manin and the Venetian Revolution of
1848–1849*, which also appeared in Italian.

From the reviews of the Italian edition, published by Einaudi:

'A history of contemporary Italy that one reads as if it was a novel. It
combines the pathos of a traveller's memoirs with the rigorous
documentation and popularizing skills of the Anglo-Saxon school'
– Anna Maria Guadagni in *L'Unità*

'From now on, Ginsborg's work will form the basis for every serious
discussion of the period' – Gian Giacomo Migone in *L'Indice*

'Controlling with enormous skill an endless number of sources, Ginsborg
offers us . . . a deeply convincing vision of Italy . . . A book of
considerable documentary value, and as fascinating as a novel'
– Agazio Loiero in *Il Messaggero*

A History of Contemporary

Italy

SOCIETY AND POLITICS
1943–1988

PAUL GINSBORG

PENGUIN BOOKS

For Vittorio

PENGUIN BOOKS

Published by the Penguin Group
Penguin Books Ltd, 27 Wrights Lane, London W8 5TZ, England
Penguin Books USA Inc., 375 Hudson Street, New York, New York 10014, USA
Penguin Books Australia Ltd, Ringwood, Victoria, Australia
Penguin Books Canada Ltd, 10 Alcorn Avenue, Toronto, Ontario, Canada M4V 3B2
Penguin Books (NZ) Ltd, 182–190 Wairau Road, Auckland 10, New Zealand

Penguin Books Ltd, Registered Offices: Harmondsworth, Middlesex, England

First published 1990
5 7 9 10 8 6

Printed in England by Clays Ltd, St Ives plc
Filmset in Monophoto 10/11pt Palatino

Contents

Preface

ITALY IN 1943 was little changed, outside of its major cities, since the time of Garibaldi and Cavour. It was still predominantly a peasant country, of great and unspoiled natural beauty, of sleepy provincial cities, of enduring poverty, especially in the South, of rural culture and local dialects. It was also a country in terrible crisis. Mussolini's desire for imperial expansion had led to the invasion of Italy both from the north, by the Germans, and from the south, by the Allies. The very integrity of the nation state, which was less than eighty years old, was called into question. As one British officer in Italy commented at the end of 1943: 'Collectively, they [the Italians] are to us a beaten people who live in squalor and have made a mess of their country, their administration and their lives.'[1]

Forty-five years later, Italy has been transformed out of all recognition. It has become one of the most economically powerful nations of the world, with a Gross Domestic Product more or less equal to that of Britain. It has undergone an extraordinary process of enrichment, urbanization and secularization. The peasant cultures of the previous centuries have not disappeared altogether, but they have been replaced overwhelmingly by a single national urban culture. There has been an unprecedented migration of country dwellers to the cities, and of southern Italians to the North. During the years of the Republic, Italy has witnessed the most profound social revolution in the whole of its history. This great transformation is the principal protagonist of this book.

Italy has been transformed, but the continuities in its history are not easily set aside. While charting the country's dramatic passage to modernity,

I have tried to keep in mind certain themes and issues which have been constants in Italian history at least since the Risorgimento: the incapacity of the élites to establish their hegemony over the classes that lay below them; the weakness and inefficiency of the state; the strength of the Catholic church in Italian society; the class consciousness of significant sections of Italian urban and rural workers; the special political role of the *ceti medi*, the middle classes of Italian society; the enduring problem of the South.

There is one other theme upon which I have tried to concentrate in particular. It is that of the relationship between family and society. Attachment to the family has probably been a more constant and less evanescent element in Italian popular consciousness than any other. Yet the question of how this devotion to family has shaped Italian history, or been shaped by it, has rarely been posed.

The few scholars who have ventured on to this terrain have been disparaging in the extreme about the social role of the Italian family. They have placed the emphasis firmly on Italian familism, i.e. the accentuation of exclusive family values and actions. In the late 1950s the American sociologist Edward Banfield achieved notoriety with his denunciation of the 'amoral familism' of the peasants he had studied at Chiaramonte in the Basilicata. For Banfield the extreme backwardness of Chiaramonte was due to 'the inability of the villagers to act together for their common good, or indeed, for any good transcending the immediate, material interest of the nuclear family'.[2] More recently the Italian anthropologist, Carlo Tullio-Altan, has extended Banfield's judgement both geographically and chronologically. For Tullio-Altan, the exaltation of the family and the distrust of collective action are to be found in virulent form as far back as the fourteenth and fifteenth centuries, in the family diaries and correspondence of Tuscan writers such as Leon Battista Alberti. Familism, for Tullio-Altan, has been one of the great banes of modern Italy: 'In most of Italian society, in both the North and South, there prevailed, and there still prevails, the moral viewpoint of the individualistic Albertian family, with its disastrous social consequences. This is the true and profound root of national *qualunquismo**.'[3]

Any visitor to Italy, whether in the 1950s or the 1980s, let alone the 1440s, would immediately recognize what Banfield and Tullio-Altan are trying to describe. Yet I would like to suggest that the relationship between family and collectivity is almost certainly more complex and less one-sided than they would have us believe.

---

*Qualunquismo is a denigratory term which derives from the short-lived political party, L'Uomo Qualunque (see pp. 99–100). It is not easily translatable, but means, in broad terms, a lack of any sense of social responsibility and an 'I'm all right, Jack' attitude.

By way of an introduction to this theme, I would like to quote briefly an extraordinary life story recounted to Danilo Dolci in Palermo in 1949. 'Gino O.' was an orphan turned pickpocket, who spent his teenage years in various reform institutions, and then joined the Communist Party in 1943. He soon became a leading member of the Palermo Communist federation. He told Dolci of two events in 1949 which epitomize the variable and complex nature of the relationship between family and society. On the first occasion he went to the national congress at Mantua of the Federbraccianti (the rural labourers' trade union). There he was moved to tears by the speech of a woman delegate from the province of Lecce, in the deep south-east of the country. Asking pardon for not being able to speak Italian, she declared: 'Until they give us the land, and as long as my little ones walk around with bare feet, I won't ever tire of fighting side by side with my woman friend, and I don't give a damn for the beatings we get from the police.'[4] In this case, as is obvious, family deprivations were a prime mover to involvement in collective action.

By contrast, 'Gino O.' went in the same year to one of the many land occupations of the great estates in Sicily, at Marineo:

Here I received a hard political lesson, from a practical point of view. Because while I, having read about the collective farms in Russia, exhorted the peasants to cultivate the land collectively, they instead proceeded straight away to split it up and work it individually. They concentrated on marking out their portion with a belt or some stones or the reins of a mule, just as when people get on a train they rush to occupy a seat, throwing their hat or bag or newspaper on to it. To me such attitudes seemed strange and I called over a peasant to tell him that it was not the right way to do things. He replied: 'Excuse me, comrade Gino: if I work my plot with a mule, and next to me there's someone without one, it's only fair that when it comes to harvest time I should have much more to take home than him.'[5]

Here too, the lesson seems clear: the deep-rooted individualism of southern peasant culture was far stronger than any abstract appeal to families to pool their resources.

Individualism and solidarity, family and collectivity: I have tried to mark out the changing nature of these relationships in the forty-five years of Italian history since the fall of Benito Mussolini.

Lastly, I would like to draw the attention of readers to the geographical divisions which I have used in this work (see the map on p. 427). Following the lead of the sociologist Arnaldo Bagnasco in his book *Tre Italie*,[6] I have tried to trace Italy's social and economic development with reference to three major geographical areas: the North-West; the Centre and North-East (often referred to as the Third Italy); and the South, mainland and islands. These divisions, of course, are far from perfect; in purely historical terms it would be better to talk not of three Italys but of three hundred. None the less, a tripartite division does seem a more effective way of describing the reality of contemporary Italy than the old North–South divide. In the statistical appendix Giulio Ghellini and I have added a fourth dimension, and have treated Lazio as a separate entity because of the special statistical weight of the city of Rome within that region.

Very many people, especially in Italy, have helped me in the preparation of this book. I am deeply grateful to them all, but I must make special mention of those who have read and criticized in detail major parts of the manuscript: Luigi Bobbio, Stephen Gundle, Norman Hampson, Bob Lumley, Luisa Passerini, Claudio Pavone, Anna Rossi-Doria. Each of them has made invaluable comments, but none of them bears any responsibility for the final version. I must also thank the Leverhulme Foundation, the Nuffield Foundation and Churchill College, Cambridge, for financial assistance. I am very grateful to my colleagues in the Faculty of Social and Political Sciences at the University of Cambridge for much support and encouragement; I am especially indebted to John Barber and John Dunn. I have to thank Marcello Flores for his constant friendship and for advising me on various problems of historical interpretation. Over the past three years, Ayşe Saraçgil has helped me in innumerable ways; together, an unlikely Anglo-Turkish Italian-speaking team, we have tried to understand something about the country which has become her home. Neil Middleton first encouraged me to write on contemporary Italy; at Penguin, Peter Carson, Caroline Robertson and Esther Sidwell have helped me a very great deal. Finally, I would like to thank Vittorio Foa, who has been the formative influence in the making of this book and to whom I dedicate it, with very great affection.

Churchill College, Cambridge
March 1989

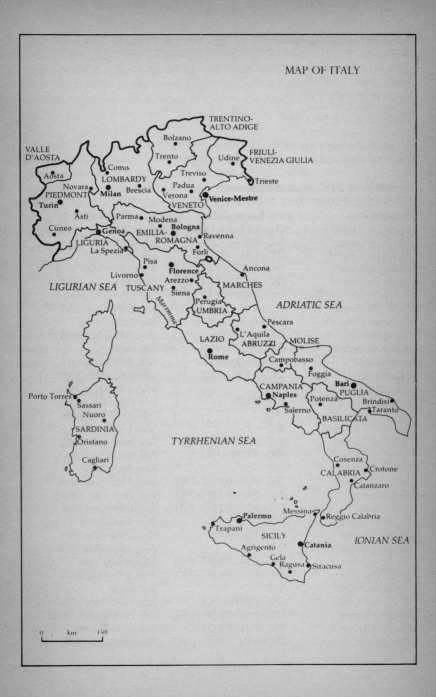

MAP OF ITALY

Presidents of the Republic

Enrico De Nicola, 1946–8
Luigi Einaudi, 1948–55
Giovanni Gronchi, 1955–62
Antonio Segni, 1962–4
Giuseppe Saragat, 1964–71
Giovanni Leone, 1971–8
Alessandro Pertini, 1978–85
Francesco Cossiga, 1985–

Presidents of the Council of Ministers

Ferruccio Parri	anti-Fascist parties	June–Nov. 1945
Alcide De Gasperi	DC–PSI–PCI and others	Dec. 1945–July 1946
Alcide De Gasperi	DC–PSI–PCI–PRI	July 1946–Feb. 1947
Alcide De Gasperi	DC–PSI–PCI	Feb.–May 1947
Alcide De Gasperi	DC–PSDI–PRI–PLI	May 1947–May 1948
Alcide De Gasperi	DC–PSDI–PRI–PLI	May 1948–Jan. 1950
Alcide De Gasperi	DC–PSDI–PRI	Jan. 1950–July 1951
Alcide De Gasperi	DC–PRI	July 1951–June 1953
Alcide De Gasperi	DC	July 1953
Giuseppe Pella	DC	Aug. 1953–Jan. 1954
Amintore Fanfani	DC	Jan. 1954
Mario Scelba	DC–PSDI–PLI	Feb. 1954–June 1955
Antonio Segni	DC–PSDI–PLI	July 1955–May 1957
Adone Zoli	DC	May 1957–June 1958
Amintore Fanfani	DC–PSDI	July 1958–Jan. 1959
Antonio Segni	DC	Feb. 1959–Feb. 1960
Fernando Tambroni	DC	March–July 1960
Amintore Fanfani	DC	July 1960–Feb. 1962
Amintore Fanfani	DC–PSDI–PRI	Feb. 1962–May 1963
Giovanni Leone	DC	June–Nov. 1963
Aldo Moro	DC–PSI–PSDI–PRI	Dec. 1963–June 1964
Aldo Moro	DC–PSI–PSDI–PRI	July 1964–Feb. 1966
Aldo Moro	DC–PSI–PSDI–PRI	Feb. 1966–June 1968
Giovanni Leone	DC	June–Nov. 1968
Mariano Rumor	DC–PSI–PRI	Dec. 1968–July 1969
Mariano Rumor	DC	Aug. 1969–Feb. 1970
Mariano Rumor	DC–PSI–PSDI–PRI	March–July 1970
Emilio Colombo	DC–PSI–PSDI–PRI	Aug. 1970–Jan. 1972
Giulio Andreotti	DC	Feb. 1972
Giulio Andreotti	DC–PSDI–PLI	June 1972–June 1973
Mariano Rumor	DC–PSI–PSDI–PRI	July 1973–March 1974
Mariano Rumor	DC–PSI–PSDI	March–Oct. 1974
Aldo Moro	DC–PRI	Nov. 1974–Jan. 1976

Aldo Moro	DC	Feb.–April 1976
Giulio Andreotti	DC	Aug. 1976–Jan. 1978
Giulio Andreotti	DC	March 1978–Jan. 1979
Giulio Andreotti	DC–PSDI–PRI	March 1979–July 1979
Francesco Cossiga	DC–PSDI–PLI	Aug. 1979–March 1980
Francesco Cossiga	DC–PSDI–PRI	April–Sept. 1980
Arnaldo Forlani	DC–PSI–PSDI–PRI	Oct. 1980–May 1981
Giovanni Spadolini	DC–PSI–PSDI–PRI–PLI	June 1981–Aug. 1982
Giovanni Spadolini	DC–PSI–PSDI–PRI–PLI	Aug.–Nov. 1982
Amintore Fanfani	DC–PSI–PSDI–PLI	Dec. 1982–April 1983
Bettino Craxi	DC–PSI–PSDI–PRI–PLI	Aug. 1983–June 1986
Bettino Craxi	DC–PSI–PSDI–PRI–PLI	Aug. 1986–April 1987
Amintore Fanfani	DC	April–July 1987
Giovanni Goria	DC–PSI–PSDI–PRI–PLI	July 1987–March 1988
Ciriaco De Mita	DC–PSI–PSDI–PRI–PLI	April 1988–May 1989

Chapter 1
Italy at War

A T MIDDAY on 9 September 1943, a young Scottish prisoner of war, Stuart Hood, walked out of his prison camp near Fontanellato di Parma, on the Emilian plain south of the Po. It was the time of the maize harvest. It was also the day after the armistice had been declared between the Italian king, Victor Emanuel III, and the Allies. All over northern Italy the Italian guards were opening the gates of the prison camps to allow men to escape, as best they could, before the Germans arrived.

Hood has left us this description of the Emilian peasantry at work in the late summer of 1943:

In September the cobs make an orange heap on the barn floors. The stalks stand brown and skeletal in the fields, hung with tattered, parchment leaves. The men walk through this insubstantial jungle and clear the land for ploughing . . . In the barns women and children, old men and vagrants, sit round the piles and strip the cobs. Dry, they will stuff the peasant mattresses. The men in the fields heap the stalks and set them ablaze . . . each field is shut in, fenced off by willows, by the vines looped from trunk to trunk, and by the poplars. This is a landscape lush and claustrophobic . . . completely dominated by the sky.[1]

It was not a landscape that offered much security for escaped prisoners. Hood took to the hills and wandered southwards for the next three months, working as a casual labourer, living off peasant hospitality, half-hoping to meet the front line as the Allies swept up the peninsula. In November he crossed the Apennines and came into Tuscany, where, so it seemed to him, 'life had greater ease, promised more than mere labour'.[2] By the beginning of December he was in the hills above Prato, to the north-west of Florence.

There he encountered the partisans for the first time. His contact was a man called Franco, who had worked in the wool mills of the valley until the dust and fibre from the machines ruined his lungs and forced him back to the hill village of his birth. Franco was thirty-five and remembered the time when the local Fascists had destroyed the workers' organizations in the valley, remembered 'his father dosed with castor-oil and tied in a sack, like a calf ready for the market, to lie in his own filth and weakness'. What struck Hood about Franco was that 'he was not *un pur*. He was spendthrift with a hint of the spiv and a spiv's love of little conspiracies . . . The old looked on him with suspicion. His clear and open aim was to destroy life as they knew it – to break the bond that held the peasant to the soil and to the landlord, to liberate the women from superstition, drudgery, the tight, merciless circle of their lives.'[3]

Franco took Hood eastwards to where the partisans had encamped, high up on Monte Morello. They were a very mixed bag. Lanciotto, their leader, was a butcher from a village near Florence, a communist who knew little doctrine but wanted to fight the Fascists. Totò, a mechanic, was also a communist. From him Hood learned of Antonio Gramsci and of the then leader of the party, Palmiro Togliatti, who broadcast from Moscow under the assumed name of Ercole Ercoli. There were other ex-prisoners of war – two Yugoslavs and two Russians. One of the Russians, an industrial worker from Moscow, told Hood that the Italians were not real communists but were only playing at it. Many of the rank and file of Lanciotto's band were local teenagers who had taken to the hills to avoid the Fascist call-up. They were frightened, and with good reason, because if caught they were likely to face a firing squad.

Over the Christmas period they waited. On a clear day, writes Hood, it was possible to see Florence,

the squat dome of Santa Maria del Fiore and Giotto's campanile. It gave edge to our isolation to think of the morning life of the city, the offices, the shops, trams, fiacres, the dressmakers and the shoemakers, the little workshops and the long factory sheds. It gave us, too, a sudden shock of insecurity to see how close we were to the city, to the barracks, the fortress, police headquarters, the *Ortskommandantur*.[4]

On 3 January 1944, the partisans, having moved camp, were unexpectedly attacked by the Fascist militia. The latter, better armed and more numerous, soon gained the upper hand. The partisans' machine-gun jammed and the barn which had served as a refuge soon became a death-trap. The only possible escape was up the hillside towards a crest some 300 yards away. Hood ran and got away with nothing more than a scratched wrist, but he and one of the Yugoslavs were the only two to escape with their lives. A family from a nearby village then saved Hood from imminent recapture and probable death by hiding him for a time in the top room of their house. Much later in the year, after linking up with other partisans in southern Tuscany, Hood was finally to rejoin the Allied forces at Siena.[5]

Politics and War, 1943–4

To understand the complex situation in Italy at the time when Hood was with the partisans of Monte Morello, we need to look back for a moment to the last years of the Fascist regime. Mussolini's decision to enter the Second World War on Hitler's side proved fatal for Italian Fascism. Had Mussolini stayed out of the war, it is difficult to see how internal pressures would have brought down his regime any faster than they did Franco's in Spain. But the Duce was far too committed to his 'brutal friendship'[6] with Hitler and too avid for the spoils of war to resist intervention. An ill-equipped soldiery, spurred on by promises of a short and glorious campaign, entered a struggle which Mussolini defined as being that of the 'poor and populous nations' against 'those who hold a monopoly on all the riches and gold of this earth'.

As is well known, disaster followed disaster. The Italian armed forces were humiliated in Greece and Africa, and the fortunes of war swung slowly in favour of the Allies, with von Paulus's surrender at Stalingrad and Montgomery's victory at El Alamein.

At home, the consensus in favour of the regime, already on the wane, crumbled in the wake of Allied aerial bombardment, food shortages and steeply rising prices. Sections of the industrial working class were the first to express open discontent. On 5 March 1943 workers at the Rasetti factory in Turin staged a prolonged stoppage inside the factory. The police were called in and ten of the strikers arrested. Some form of protest also took place at FIAT Mirafiori on the same day. On 7 March stoppages at work spread to nine factories in the city.[7] The workers' demands were primarily economic, involving equal compensation for the ravages of bombardment and the high cost of living. A small number of Communist militants, encouraged by the news from Stalingrad, were in the forefront of the agitation. By the end of the month many workplaces in the northern cities had seen some form of strike action, with some 100,000 workers involved in all. In April the employers and the government announced substantial concessions. The strikes, the first ever of their kind in Fascist Europe, made a profound impression both in Italy and abroad. Mussolini told the Fascist leaders that their movement had been put back twenty years, Hitler said he could not understand how such disobedience had been permitted, Radio London praised the Turin workers for daring to affirm their rights as human beings.

No other class in Italian society manifested its discontent so openly or so massively, but the erosion of support for Fascism was widespread. The families of small peasant proprietors and sharecroppers, so courted by the Fascists in earlier times, were badly hit by conscription, high taxation and the regime's control of grain prices and consumption. As a result, they turned increasingly to the black market. In the cities the real wages of white-collar workers declined drastically. Shopkeepers found it impossible to obtain stock, unemployment was rife in the consumer industries and leading members of the capitalist class began to distance themselves from the regime.[8]

On 10 July 1943 the Allied armies landed in Sicily. On the 19th, Rome was bombarded for the first time. Hitler, at his meeting with Mussolini at Feltre, refused to assign any more troops to the defence of southern Italy. General Ambrosio, chief of the Italian general staff, tried to get Mussolini to tell Hitler that he was withdrawing from the war. Instead at Feltre the Duce sat in dejected silence, barely comprehending Hitler's monologue in German.

At this point the Italian king, urged on by his generals, decided that the monarchy and the traditional Italian state could only be saved by severing immediately all ties with the Fascists. The ageing Victor Emanuel had been a mediocre king. In the early 1920s he had willingly backed the Fascists, but he harboured no love for Mussolini, who had constantly upstaged him in the following twenty years. The king knew that he had to act to prevent his dynasty being damned in the eyes of the Allies and swept away by pressure from below. He therefore plotted the dismissal of the Duce, confident that he could count on the army and sections of the police and bureaucracy.

The cue for the palace revolution was provided by the meeting in Rome on 24 July 1943 of the Fascist Grand Council, the supreme body of the Fascist party. Leading Fascists like Dino Grandi and Roberto Farinacci had grown increasingly critical of Mussolini's handling of the war effort, and now demanded that he should share power with them and the king. They entered the Grand Council meeting in some trepidation, fearing a violent response from Mussolini. Grandi claimed that he took in two hand-grenades, and passed one to Cesare De Vecchi under the table. After nine hours' discussion a motion critical of the Duce was passed by nineteen votes to seven. Mussolini decided that the best course of action was to underplay the event, and told his friends that he regarded the vote as meaningless.

He had reckoned without the king. While the Fascist hierarchs had little real power to unseat Mussolini, the king had. On 25 July an unsuspecting Duce went for his weekly interview with Victor Emanuel. In halting tones the king asked Mussolini for his resignation and told him that he had already taken steps for Marshal Badoglio to replace him. As a dazed Mussolini emerged on to the steps of the Villa Savoia, he was bundled away into an ambulance and later placed under arrest. Those Fascists who remained loyal to him were taken completely by surprise and failed to organize any resistance to the army units which had moved in to control Rome. Twenty-one years after the march on Rome, Mussolini, who had seemed impregnable in the late 1930s, now fell to the same king who had first summoned him to power.

The confused and dramatic period which followed the fall of Mussolini, from 25 July until 8 September 1943, has gone down in history as the Forty-five Days. In that time the full significance of the king's action became apparent. Instead of Fascism being overthrown by popular revolt, it had been destroyed by a coup from above which preserved the control and freedom of action of the traditional ruling élites in Italian society. Victor Emanuel's 'pre-emptive strike' was to condition the whole balance of power in Italy in the following two years.[9]

The Forty-five Days began with a series of enormous popular demonstrations celebrating the end of Fascism. Fascist insignia and inscriptions were torn from the walls of public buildings and monuments. Fascist headquarters were stormed and burned down. At Milan 4,000 workers of the Innocenti factory marched through the city carrying placards demanding an immediate end of the war. At Genoa women distributed red carnations to the soldiers.[10]

These demonstrations met with a brutal response. The king and Marshal Badoglio were determined to maintain a military dictatorship, but beyond that they were unsure of how to move. On the one hand they wanted peace, not least because they knew that without it they were likely to face an insurrectionary movement founded on the fraternization of troops and civilians. On the other, they were paralysed by fear of Germany. Their eventual response was to play for time when none existed. Secret negotiations with the Allies went ahead painfully slowly; at the same time the Germans were promised that Italy would not desert them. At home, many of the first free demonstrations in post-Fascist Italy ended in tragedy. In Bari twenty-three people were killed and seventy injured when the army opened fire on the crowd in Piazza Roma. Outside the Alfa-Romeo factory in Milan machine-guns were trained on the exits to prevent workers from leaving the factory to join their colleagues in the streets. In mid-August, when the workers of Turin and Milan went on strike to demand an immediate peace and an end to the alliance with Germany, the authorities agreed to release political prisoners but also responded with more bloodshed and a massive wave of arrests.

The uneasy interlude of the Forty-five Days was ended on 3 September 1943 by the signing of the secret armistice between Italy and the Allies. The terms were severe, amounting to unconditional surrender, and Italy was not allowed to become one of the Allies. Instead she was to be granted the strange status of 'co-belligerent'.

Worse still, while the king hesitated throughout August, the Germans had been pouring troops into Italy. Any chance of saving at least central Italy from occupation was lost in these vital few weeks. By the beginning of September the Allies were willing to organize an airborne landing north of Rome to try and secure the capital. But they needed Italian military help for this tricky operation, and when General Maxwell D. Taylor arrived in Rome he found little more than an evasive Badoglio awaiting him. Eisenhower, incensed by Italian procrastination, abandoned any plans for Rome, concentrated his forces for the landing at Salerno, south of Rome, and made public the armistice on 8 September, much too early for the Italian authorities.[11]

In a famous radio broadcast of that same day, Badoglio was forced to announce the signing of the armistice. He told the Italian armed forces to cease fighting the Allies, but left them with no other precise instructions, except 'to react to eventual attacks from whatever quarter'.[12] The royal family then abandoned the capital in considerable haste and made for Pescara, on the east coast. There they boarded a corvette which arrived off Brindisi in the early afternoon of 10 September. The king had no idea if the city was in the hands of the Germans or not. Fortunately for him, Nazi troops had already withdrawn, and he was able to go ashore safely. 'The little king and the old marshal', as Brigadier-General Holmes mockingly described them,[13] had not even managed to bring a typewriter with them to Brindisi. Badoglio's first letters to the Allies were written in longhand, and a typed copy was then made by the Allies and returned to Badoglio for his own use. The flight to Brindisi had hardly been an honourable or courageous action, but it had served the invaluable purpose of keeping the royal person and authority intact, and of opening the way for the creation of a 'Kingdom of the South'.

While the king fled the army dissolved. Badoglio's ambiguous radio announcement was a fitting end to the Italian high command's performance in the Second World War. Rank-and-file soldiers streamed out of their barracks and began to make for home before the Germans could stop them. More than half a million, though, were made prisoners and deported to Germany.

However, if the general pattern was one of total decomposition, the September armistice also marked a watershed in Italian history. At the blackest moment in the whole history of the unified state, with the peninsula invaded from both north and south, there are innumerable testimonies to a new spirit being born among certain, as yet very restricted, minorities of the Italian population. On the Greek island of Cephalonia the Italian garrison of nearly 10,000 men held a plebiscite and refused to surrender to the Germans; 9,600 of them lost their lives. The king had left Rome to its fate but this did not prevent sections of the army and part of the civilian population from attempting a desperate resistance. An estimated 600 Italians were killed before the Germans took the capital. In the other major cities there was no organized fight against German occupation, but isolated individuals seized the chance to prepare for the long hard battle that they knew was to come. It was in these days that Lanciotto, the leader of Hood's partisan band on Monte Morello, loaded a truck full of arms from the local barracks and drove off into the hills. And it was in the afternoon of 10 September, as the first German outriders entered Turin, that the Communist organizer in the city, Andrea Romano, furiously pedalled an ice-cream cart full of guns towards a safe hiding-place. With the arrival of the Nazis the first stage in partisan war, which Henri Michel has called the 'refusal to submit', had come into being.[14]

By the middle of September 1943 Italy was cut in two. South of Naples were the Allies and the Italian king, who finally declared war on Germany on 30 October. To the north were the Germans. In a brilliant parachute action they had managed to rescue Mussolini from his prison high up on the Gran Sasso, in the mountains of the Abruzzi, and take him back to Germany. He soon returned to Italy at the head of a puppet republic of the North, which had its capital at the small resort of Salò, on the western shore of Lake Garda. Salò was chosen because it was felt that both the person and the authority of the Duce would have more chance of surviving there than in the great working-class cities of Milan and Turin. The government of Salò enjoyed nominal control over the whole of northern Italy, but the ageing and dispirited Mussolini was now little more than a useful figurehead for the Germans. It was they who gave the orders, and amongst the first of these was the rounding up and deportation to extermination camps of as many of the Italian Jews as they could find.[15]

As the terrible shadow of Nazi rule fell over northern Italy, the Resistance came into being. Guido Quazza, the foremost authority on the subject, has divided Italian anti-Fascism into three strands.[16] The first was the traditional organized anti-Fascism of those who had always opposed Mussolini, who belonged to political parties which had been declared illegal in Italy and who had suffered trial, imprisonment and exile for their convictions. The second was formed by the spontaneous reaction of many young Italians who had been brought up under Fascism but who felt, as the author Franco Fortini did, that after 25 July it was not a new life that was beginning but life itself. The third, with which we have already dealt, was the anti-Fascism of the Fascists, of those who had always supported the regime but now deemed it advisable to abandon the sinking ship.

The first strand – that of organized political anti-Fascism – was dominated by the Communists. Their aims and strategy will be dealt with at the beginning of Chapter 2. Suffice it to say here that they were the political party which had suffered most under Fascism but which had kept intact none the less. Many of their leaders – Antonio Gramsci, Umberto Terracini, Gian Carlo Pajetta – had been sentenced to very long prison sentences by the Fascist special tribunal. Some, like Gramsci, had not survived the ordeal. Yet the party managed to keep a semblance of organization going inside Italy, to maintain cells in the most important factories, and to provide the majority of the more than 3,000 Italians who fought for the republic in the Spanish Civil War. For the young worker or artisan who wished to oppose the regime in the thirties or early forties, the Communist Party was the likely point of reference. In the early days of the Resistance the Communist formations, which were called the Garibaldi Brigades, comprised more than 70 per cent of the partisans.

Next in numerical strength came the 'Justice and Liberty' Brigades of the Action Party (Partito d'Azione). This organization, which took its name from Giuseppe Mazzini's party during the Risorgimento, was founded only in July 1942. It drew together various groups of radical and democratic anti-Fascists, including that of Giustizia e Libertà, which had been founded in Paris in 1929 by Carlo Rosselli, Emilio Lussu and Alberto Tarchiani. In 1937 Rosselli and his brother Nello were assassinated in France by a Fascist secret agent. The Action Party was composed initially of young men and women from the Italian professional classes, many of whom, like Ugo La Malfa and Ferruccio Parri, were to become major figures in Italian post-war history. They were committed to establishing a new democracy based on greater local autonomies and, while accepting the framework of capitalism, they wanted to correct its distortions and injustices. Their programme of January 1943, the object of heated discussion between moderates and radicals within the party, talked of the need to establish a republic, nationalize major industries, safeguard the middle classes, split up the great agrarian estates and give workers shares in company profits.[17]

The Socialists (PSIUP) were at this time only a shadow of the great party of the early 1920s. They had been far less successful than the Communists in keeping contacts amongst the working class. The party, under the leadership of Pietro Nenni, was characterized by a high level of theoretical debate but scarce participation in the early months of the Resistance. Their political declaration of August 1943 talked the language of revolution, of 'the workers' socialist republic', and of 'leading the proletariat to the conquest of power'.[18] In reality the party contained a great number of ideological positions, ranging from the cautious reformism of the Turin section of the party to the young revolutionaries grouped around Lelio Basso in Milan.

The other two major anti-Fascist parties, the Liberals and the Christian Democrats, contributed almost nothing to the early months of the Resistance, but were active in the various anti-Fascist committees which came into being after 25 July. The Liberals, the traditional party of the Italian bourgeoisie, wanted a return to the pre-Fascist state. The Christian Democrats, about whom much more will be said later, were still in the process of formation.

These parties, all of whom were numerically very weak at the time of Mussolini's fall, were completely outflanked by the action of Badoglio and the king on 25 July. They were forced to play a subordinate role during the Forty-five Days and it was only after the king's flight that they emerged into the limelight. On 9 September they formed in Rome the National Committee of Liberation and called upon the Italian people to join them in the Resistance against the Nazis. During the autumn clandestine committees were set up in all the regions under German occupation, and in January 1944 the central committee in Rome invested the Milan committee with extraordinary powers of government in the North. From this moment the Milan committee, which now became the supreme organ of the Resistance, took the name of the National Committee for the Liberation of Upper Italy (CLNAI). The anti-Fascist parties, though profoundly divided over general ideological issues and the thorny question of the monarchy, managed to preserve a precarious unity of action in these early months.

If we turn from organized anti-Fascism to the mass base from which it recruited, to the second of Quazza's categories, the spontaneous or 'existentialist' Resistance, we see that nearly all the first partisan bands were as mixed in composition as was that which Hood joined on Monte Morello. Some partisans, like the subject of Fenoglio's *Il partigiano Johnny* (the outstanding novel of the Italian Resistance), felt as they took to the hills the historic importance of their choice: '[we were] to oppose Fascism in every way, in the name of the authentic people of Italy, to judge and to execute, to decide both civil and military affairs ... so much power was intoxicating, but the consciousness of the just use we would make of it was more intoxicating still'.[19] Others, very young, went to escape the call-up of the Republic of Salò — more in desperation than in hope. There were many escaped prisoners of war, a significant section of middle-class radical youth and, as the months passed, an increasing number of workers, often fleeing from persecution and arrest in the factories.

By the end of 1943 there were about 9,000 partisans. The casualty rate was extremely high because many of the bands, often led by ex-army officers, made the mistake of trying to fight pitched battles which usually

16

ended, as with Hood's band, in disaster. Partisans or their sympathizers were treated with the utmost savagery by the Nazis and the blackshirt troops of the Republic of Salò. In September 1943 the Germans committed their first atrocity against the civilian population, reducing the village of Boves in Piedmont to ashes, burning alive many of its inhabitants. In spite of reprisals of this sort, and in the face of every difficulty, the partisan movement grew to 20,000–30,000 members by the spring of 1944.

Italian Society in the Early 1940s

The peninsula had thus become the site of prolonged warfare, both between invading armies and between the Italians themselves. At this point we need to ask what Italy was like at this time, to describe its different patterns of work and of family life, its divisions in regional and class terms, its inhabitants' reactions to the dramatic problems posed by the war. With national state authority having dissolved, two occupying armies and three Italian governments (Mussolini's Republic, the CLNAI, the Kingdom of the South) claimed the obedience and allegiance of the Italians. In this unique situation, every citizen was faced with crucial moral and political choices, on which their lives and those of their families might well depend.[20] Here, for obvious reasons, it is not possible to examine every reaction to these dilemmas, nor to describe every region, city and social class; what follows is a sample, an attempt to sketch in broad terms the nature of Italian society before and during the war.

a. LABOUR AND CAPITAL IN THE NORTH, 1943–4
In a country where well over 40 per cent of the active population was engaged in agriculture, Italy's industrial heartland was narrowly situated in the triangle formed by the three great cities of Turin, Milan and Genoa. Let me concentrate on Turin. At the beginning of the war the city had over 600,000 inhabitants, of whom nearly a third were employed directly in industry.[21] The numerical preponderance of the working class was thus very marked, as was the pre-eminence of the FIAT company as the city's largest employer.

Working-class families in Turin in the late 1930s and early 1940s were nuclear in structure, but each family was isolated in formal terms only, for kinship networks were very strong.[22] Family units tended to be quite large, with three or more children each. In spite of legislation on compulsory education and the employment of minors, both boys and girls still went to work while very young, at ten or twelve years of age. The women, employed in tailoring shops or textile factories, would continue to work until they got married, when they would assume the tasks of running the household and rearing the family. The ambition of most men, having served as apprentices and sometimes attended night school, was to enter the factories as skilled operatives. The hours were long, usually ten and often more, with real wages lower in 1939 than they had been in 1921. Working-class families ate little meat and a great deal of minestrone and polenta. There were few luxuries: a good bicycle took three years to buy on hire purchase of 10 lire a month.[23]

In the working-class quarters on the periphery of the city – Borgo San Paolo, Barriera di Milano, etc. – a very particular relationship between family and collectivity had developed in the period 1910–20. The families who populated these districts had usually emigrated from the surrounding countryside at the turn of the century. There was little upward social mobility. Housing usually took the form of flats in tenement blocks, with long balconies on each floor looking inwards on to a communal courtyard. Here, every morning, 'all the alarm clocks would go off almost at the same time'.[24] In these courtyards and districts, isolated from the rest of the city, a strong sense of community flourished: 'In San Paolo everyone knew everyone else . . . We used to sit outside our doors, on chairs and stools, chatting away.'[25] Allegiances developed between families as well as amongst kinfolk. They were based on a complex system of favours and exchanges, and on a social network which was almost exclusively confined to the neighbourhood.[26]

Solidarity also derived from and contributed to a shared political culture. The years 1910–20 saw the new Turin working class in the forefront of the socialist movement in Italy. Class-consciousness in the city reached its height with the demonstrations in opposition to the First World War, the factory-council movement of 1919–20, and the Piedmontese general strike of April 1920. At the workplace and in the cafés the menfolk talked socialist politics as a matter of course: 'On a Sunday they played cards in the taverns . . . At the end of the day, when it was time to settle the debts, 6–8 lire were left over . . . and with the agreement of all the money went off to *Avanti!*'[27]

So strong a sense of community could also be suffocating. For the younger generation the socialist norms of their parents (and especially their fathers) were often experienced as oppression as much as liberation. The Fascist period did not entirely destroy the social patterns and structures described above, but it rendered them much less universal. Fascism entered the working-class quarters both as cudgel and as hidden persuader. With the socialist networks and organizations destroyed, families turned in on themselves. All the oral testimonies bear witness to the *silence* that descended on the working-class districts. Resistance was confined to certain symbolic gestures: the wearing of a red tie or braces on May Day, the scrawling of slogans in the lavatories at work.[28]

However, Fascism was more than mere repression. For the younger generation, Gribaudi has argued, it represented a sort of release: social and geographical mobility increased, as did the integration of working-class youth into the life of the city as a whole. New myths – sport, consumer goods, modernism – replaced the old ones. So too did new leisure-time activities: the traditional games of bowls, rides on the backs of trams, Sunday picnics, games of cards in the cafés, were challenged by the organized pastimes of the cinema, the football match, the cheap outings by train offered by the regime. The city expanded. Lingotto, the new working-class district dominated by the giant F I A T factory of the same name, was populated by families of more recent immigration. Here the socialist subculture had never existed, and many of the characteristics of a modern working-class suburb were already to be found – few amenities or meeting-places, a strong sense of alienation from the environment, families more closed within themselves.[29]

If we turn from Turin to Milan, we find many of the same characteristics, but Milan, with over a million inhabitants, was much less a one-company, one-class city. It had become the commercial and financial capital of Italy, and this meant that the middle strata of urban society, as well as white-collar workers and those employed in the service industries, were much more numerous than in Turin. None the less the industrial working class at Milan was far from insignificant; by the last years of Fascism there were nearly 130,000 metalworkers, most of them working for large concerns like Pirelli, Borletti, Falck and Marelli. Some idea of the condition of the Milanese working class can be gleaned from the housing statistics of the Fascist period. The census of 1931 found that 260,000 Milanese were living in a state of 'grave overcrowding'. The working class of the city (44.5 per cent of the total) were forced to live in 30.6 per cent of available accommodation. Under Fascism the city's housing stock decreased by an estimated 133,000 rooms, as popular quarters in the centre of the city were cleared to make way for offices and luxury flats. On the periphery, in the rapidly expanding industrial suburb of Sesto San Giovanni, an official report of May 1942 talked of nearly 7,000 people living in cellars, stables and garrets.[30]

Genoa, the same size as Turin, was an important steel, shipbuilding and engineering centre. The significant expansion under Fascism of the public sectors of industry was particularly noticeable in the city, where I R I (the Institute for Industrial Reconstruction) controlled the Ansaldo company, which employed 30,000 workers. Genoa was also the most important port in Italy. In 1941, at a time when maritime trade had been seriously reduced by the war, 23,000 sailors and 8,000 dockers still found work from the port's activity.[31]

Although never subject to the saturation bombing employed by the Allies against Germany, the cities of the industrial triangle suffered very severely during the war years. By August 1943 air raids on Turin had already caused 1,175 deaths and 1,615 wounded. In Milan in the same period more than 230,000 people were made homeless.[32] Women and children were evacuated *en masse* to the rural areas near the cities. Camilla Cederna, later to be the journalist responsible for the resignation of President Leone, was a young woman in Milan at this time:

In the late afternoon we too helped to swell that river of people which was heading for the countryside. There were those who had a specific destination, and those who with their children and some blankets were going to spend the nights in the open fields on the periphery of the city. It was a doleful exodus, characterized by a frenetic disorder. The bags attached to the handlebars made the bicycles lean over dangerously, the sidecars of the motor bikes were overladen with goods, there were carts full of children being pulled along by hand, vans propelled by pedal, horse and carts, and even frail old grandmothers sitting in the prams of their grandchildren.[33]

The men usually stayed in the cities, but with shifts in the war industries reaching eleven and a half hours each, they had little time to rest or be with their families.

The labour market in 1943 and 1944 presents a complex picture. On the one hand there was extensive unemployment in all those sectors which were classed as 'inessential' to the war effort – textiles, construction, food products, etc. On the other, those employed in heavy industry, in spite of longer working hours, military supervision and increased rhythms of production, found a unity and strength which they had not known in the Fascist decades.

Many factors contributed to this latter process. The workforce had become more concentrated as war production led to the expansion of the larger factories at the expense of the small and medium-sized ones. Wage differentials had become less marked as price inflation brought a general equalizing downwards. Above all, the proletariat itself was less stratified than before. The standardization of jobs on the production line was partly responsible for this. But so too was a chronic shortage of skilled labour, brought about largely by German demands for factory workers in return for coal and iron. In 1943 in a major factory like FIAT Mirafiori at Turin, with over 12,000 workers, skilled men were in a majority in only four shops out of twenty. Most of the workforce consisted of the lower category of semi-skilled labourers. This greater homogeneity of those employed in heavy industry, when allied with the strength that came from being in the vital sector of war production, formed the material background to the extraordinary strikes of March 1943.[34]

German occupation from September 1943 onwards brought an added dose of terrorism and repression. Workers who were suspected of organizing resistance were arrested and frequently deported to German labour camps. But the Nazis were quite unable to impose their will simply by force. They sorely needed the production from the Italian factories to bolster their war effort and were forced to make concessions to a working class which was not going to be frightened into silence.[35] Often the authorities threatened to dismantle the machinery of the major factories and transport it to Germany where production would proceed undisturbed. Such threats rarely achieved their purpose. The workers responded with strike action and, *in extremis*, with sabotage of the machinery in question.

The enormity of German reprisals encouraged more than one sector of the labour movement, and more than one party in the committees of national liberation, to argue in favour of a policy of limited resistance while waiting for liberation at the hands of the Allies. This *attendismo*, as it came to be known, had its roots in a humanitarian desire to limit bloodshed as far as possible, but it was roundly condemned by the majority of the movement, and by the Communists in particular. They argued that after the Fascist débâcle the Italians would only recover their sense of self-respect and national dignity if they fought against the Germans without offering any truce at all. They also refused to have anything to do with Mussolini's attempts to woo the working class by proclaiming an advanced programme of 'socialization' of the factories under the control of the Republic of Salò.[36] Only a tiny percentage of workers voted in the elections for the internal factory commissions which Mussolini had established, and clandestine 'committees of agitation' carried on the independent organization of workers' action.

Thus in spite of the Germans' presence, strikes and other disruptions of production continued throughout the winter of 1943–4. If the Fascist period had dissolved a compact workers' culture, the war years went a long way to recomposing it. The dramatic events of 1943–5 – occupation, bombardment, the mass strikes, the networks of resistance – created a new era of collective action. They also gave rise to a myth of solidarity which was to be as potent and enduring as that of the Blitz in London. Gaetano Salvemini looked back to this period as one of growing exaltation, as if the Five Days of Milan (the famous urban insurrection against the Austrians in March 1848) was being relived, but not in one city and not for five days.[37] This was certainly one element of what was happening. But there was also another, much more terrible, which was that of civil war. Even in the working-class quarters of Turin families had different allegiances; old scores were settled and vendettas waged, both during the war and immediately after it.[38]

As the Resistance grew in the northern cities, groups of urban terrorists, the Gappisti (Gruppi di Azione Patriottica), started to plant bombs and assassinate Fascist and Nazi soldiers. In Genoa, after the killing of a German officer on 14 January 1944, eight political prisoners were shot at dawn on the 15th. All the factories in the city came out in protest, but were forced back to work on the 20th without any of their demands being met. Arrests, deportations and forced flight to the hills decimated the ranks of the local committees of agitation.[39]

In March 1944, a year after the first major wave of strike action, a new and even more impressive protest spread through occupied Italy. This time the slogans of the strikers were more political, demanding immediate peace and an end to war production for Germany. The numbers involved exceeded the most optimistic forecasts; 300,000 workers came out in the province of Milan. In the city itself tram workers struck on 1 March, and were only forced back on the 4th and 5th by a terror campaign against them. The strike spread beyond the industrial triangle to the textile factories of the Veneto and the central Italian cities of Bologna and Florence. Women and lower-paid workers were in the forefront of the agitation. At one time or another in the first week of March hundreds of thousands of workers downed tools.

The strike was not without its negative aspects. Because the demands had been more political than economic, many workers felt that they had risked a lot — 2,000 of them had been deported — but gained nothing. Before the strike there had been much talk, especially in Communist leaflets, of the imminence of a general insurrection and the probable intervention of the partisans. Nothing of the sort happened and the workers returned to the factories with the bitter realization that they had to face many more months of German occupation. None the less the strike achieved an international resonance.[40]

Little or nothing is known of the conditions and attitudes of the other strata of urban society in these years. There is evidence that in March 1944 the lower grades of white-collar workers made common cause with the strikers, and at FIAT Mirafiori only 20 per cent of technicians and clerks voted in the elections for the Fascist internal commissions. On the other hand, considerable sections of the petty bourgeoisie and the bourgeoisie continued to support Mussolini. At Milan the Fascist prefect Piero Parini appealed to the citizens for a loan of a thousand million lire for 'the Milan of tomorrow'. In spite of the fact that the CLNAI warned that the loan would not be repaid by the 'liberation government' at the end of the war, many Milanese contributed and the money was collected in under three weeks.[41]

We know slightly more about the industrialists. As it became increasingly clear that the Axis powers were facing defeat, the major Italian capitalists began to lay plans for the post-war situation. They were anxious, for obvious reasons, not to offend the Germans. But they were equally worried that at the end of the war the working-class movement might make them pay dearly for any excessive collaboration.

Few responded to this tricky situation by going as far as Agostino Rocca, the managing director of Ansaldo's at Genoa. In August 1943 he distributed to all his managers a copy of the Soviet constitution, to which he had added approving comments. Under the Republic of Salò, Rocca insisted on his managers having the right to remain apolitical, and was actually arrested for his anti-Fascist activity.[42]

Most industrialists preferred instead to play an intricate double game, which achieved its most sophisticated version in the activities of Giovanni Agnelli and Vittorio Valletta, respectively president and managing director of FIAT. In April 1944 the vice-president of FIAT was sent on a dangerous mission over the Alps to communicate to Allen Dulles that the geographical position of Italy and the low cost of its labour constituted an 'interesting opportunity' for the United States. FIAT transmitted to the Allies the production requests of the Germans and secretly agreed with them what levels would be acceptable. At the same time Valletta was careful not to upset the Germans or Fascists, and did little to save the anti-Fascist militants in his factories. In April 1945, when the partisans went to arrest him for collaboration, they found an English officer at his villa, waiting to present a safe-conduct pass on his behalf.[43]

b. SHARECROPPERS IN CENTRAL ITALY

Let us turn now away from the cities to the vast world of rural Italy. In the central Italian regions of Tuscany, Umbria and the Marches, where the principal agricultural products were grain, olive oil and wine, most peasants were sharecroppers. Sharecropping, in simple terms, was the system by which the landowner provided the farm, the peasant family the labour, and the expenses and the crop were shared between the two. The system had many other distinguishing features: sharecropping families lived not in villages but in farmhouses directly on their land; their contracts were annual, but in practice were usually renewed for many years without difficulty; the landlord was not a distant figure, but took an active interest in the running of his farms; the relationship between him and the sharecropper was a direct and paternalistic one, based, as Pazzagli has written, on the profound subjection of the peasant to his landlord, but also on the lord's care and protection of his sharecroppers.[44]

All these features combined to make of central Italian sharecropping (*mezzadria*) a model renowned for guaranteeing social harmony in the countryside. Over the centuries, the *mezzadri* were considered a privileged caste, to be contrasted with those peasants who enjoyed no security on the land – the *pigionali* of Tuscany, the *casanolanti* of the Marches, the *casengoli* of Umbria. A considerable literature grew up in praise of sharecropping; foreign visitors, even as late as the Second World War, gave glowing accounts of what they saw. Doubtless the reality, seen from the peasant side, was not all that idyllic. The *mezzadro* had to perform a series of personal services and favours to the landlord, who exercised considerable power over the peasants' life: marriages in the family could not take place without his consent, nor could the sharecroppers work off the estate without his permission. Security on the land was also not as great as myth and landlord literature would have us believe. None the less, the traditional sharecroppers of the 'Third Italy' (sharecropping also predominated in some provinces of the Veneto and Emilia-Romagna) were certainly better off than the landless labourers of the northern plains or the impoverished peasantry of the South.[45]

Families in the sharecropping regions had more members per household than in any other part of Italy. Numbers in these families were directly related to the security enjoyed on the land and the size of farms. Families were usually multiple and vertical in structure, in the sense of having more than one married couple and more than two generations living under the same roof. By way of example, let us take the family of 'Federico P.', a sharecropper living in the early 1930s on a farm of some thirty-five acres on the plateau land above Gubbio in northern Umbria.[46] The family consisted of eleven people: Federico and his wife Emilia, seven sons and daughters, one daughter-in-law (the wife of the eldest son), and one grandchild of three months. The whole family lived in a single and quite spacious farmhouse of two storeys, and all but a very small part of their time was dedicated to the farm and to household tasks. Families of this sort had had even more members (as many as twenty to thirty) in the nineteenth century, but all observers noted a marked numerical decline by the 1940s.[47]

The male head of the family, called *capoccia* or *reggitore* or *vergaro* depending on the region, ruled over the household in patriarchal and authoritarian fashion: 'As long as I am alive,' the sixty-two-year-old Federico P. was fond of repeating, 'I alone give the orders, and when I am dead it will be my sons who will do the same.'[48] The *capoccia* was in sole control of the family's money and took all the responsibility for relations between the family and the outside world. However, his was not the sole authority. The *massaia*, the senior female figure and usually his wife, also exercised considerable power, especially (as was to be expected) within the domain of the household. Here the other women of the family were at her beck and call. Power relations of this sort led over time to resentments and deep tensions, especially between the *massaia* and her daughters-in-law.[49] The sharecropping family thus presented a united and much admired face to the outside world, but it was one based on notable subjection, particularly of the in-laws and of the younger generation, a subjection that could continue well into middle age.

In the work patterns of the family it was noticeable how hard women worked, both in the fields and at home. Emilia, the forty-eight-year-old wife of Federico P., the *massaia* of this family, worked an estimated 500 hours per year more than any other member of the family. Household tasks were very numerous and time-consuming: fires had to be lit and maintained, food prepared, water brought into the house. Washing, including the landlord's clothes and linen, was a long and laborious task. So too was cleaning, given the constant presence of animals in the household. At Easter, in preparation for the priest's visit and blessing of the farmhouse, 'there is not a single object, starting from the glass in the windows, which is not carefully inspected, washed or polished'.[50] Women would also spin, weave and help in the production of brooms, chairs, ropes, farm tools and raffia work, all of which the family would use, exchange or sell.

It might be expected, given the dispersed nature of the farmhouses and the families' binding internal structures, that the degree of contact and cooperation between them would be very limited. In other words, here one might expect Tullio-Altan's Albertian familism to reign supreme, or to find confirmation for Marx's famous remarks on the peasantry being a sack of potatoes, isomorphous entities without contact between them. This was only partly the case. In central Italy families had developed a rich network of exchanges and mutual aid; typical of these was the *aiutarella*, the exchange of labour between families at crucial moments in the agricultural calendar, such as at threshing time.[51]

No practice epitomized better the frequent contact between families than the *veglia*. On winter evenings, usually from the beginning of November onwards, families would gather in the stables of the farmhouses, to play cards and games, to knit and to mend, to listen to and tell stories. Participation in the *veglia* was not segregated family by family. Rather, as Mugnaini has shown for Castellina in Chianti, it involved rotating hospitality and a complex system of visiting, with young people for instance seeking each other out in farmhouses where they were more certain of a welcome.[52]

The countryside was also populated, even as late as the 1930s, by significant numbers of wanderers: friars and nuns living off charity, rag-and-bone men, gypsies, hawkers, beggars. Not all these, not even the friars and nuns, were sure of a welcome from the sharecropping family. But some were given food and allowed to sleep in the hay; others were given a little oil; and in return they brought news of what was happening from far around.[53]

The traditional world of the central Italian sharecroppers was not, therefore, totally isolated nor devoid of community. It was, though, very static. In his report to the Houses of Parliament on conditions in northern and central Italy, published in 1839, Sir John Bowring recounted that in Tuscany 'I had occasion more than once to see four generations inhabiting the same cottage; but the last had not added a particle of knowledge to the ignorance of the first.'[54] However, from about 1880 onwards conditions began to change rapidly. Increased competition from American grain and the tariff war with France pushed the landowners towards a more commercial agriculture and a more systematic exploitation of their peasants. Security of tenure diminished, as did the size of farms. The *mezzadri*, already suffering under the heavy burden of taxation imposed by the unified state, grew increasingly indebted. In 1902 the Tuscan *mezzadri* went on strike for the first time ever, and another wave of agitation followed in 1906. The *mezzadri* were no longer a privileged and protected caste of peaceful rural dwellers, but were ever more open to the ideas and models of the nearby cities.

After the Great War, with the turmoil and tragedy that it produced,[55] the agitations of the *mezzadri*, like those of the industrial workers of the North, reached their height. In July 1920 the Tuscan sharecroppers forced a 'Red Pact' upon the landowners, which effectively won for the peasants security of tenure, an end to indebtedness and a voice in the running of the estates. However, their triumph was shortlived and the blackshirt squads soon set about restoring 'normality' to the countryside.

The coming of Fascism saw peace imposed on the sharecropping regions, but the regime did little more than paper over the cracks that had appeared in the system. The indebtedness of many sharecroppers, among whom we must number the family of Federico P., continued to grow. Fascism's formal commitment to sharecroppers' rights, as embodied in the Sharecroppers' Charter of 1935, was accompanied by measures which aggravated their lot. The 'battle for grain' interfered with the peasants' choice of crop variety to meet the needs of his own family; the compulsory assignment of grain and other products to the *ammassi*, the state granaries and food stores, was deeply resented.[56]

The war years reopened the fissures in central Italian rural society. War production and mobilizations on the home front forced the regime to break the artificial barriers with which it had tried to keep town and country separate. Peasant labour flocked into the cities. After 8 September 1943 the flow went in the other direction. Suddenly, the world of the sharecroppers was not populated by passing friars and hawkers, but by many thousands of ex-soldiers, escaped prisoners of war, fleeing Jews, former political prisoners, and later those who had refused the Fascist call-up. Furthermore, as government authority weakened in the countryside, the sharecroppers found it easier to avoid consigning their grain to the *ammassi*, and to have recourse to the black market instead. The time-honoured relations between city and countryside had been reversed. The sharecropper found himself with the power to decide who to help, who to supply and on what terms. It was, as Absalom has observed, a world turned upside down.[57]

The great majority of the sharecropping families took the crucial decision to help those who were on the run. In doing so, they risked fierce reprisals. As early as 16 September 1943 the Fascist authorities announced on the radio that all those harbouring ex-prisoners of war would be punishable under the provisions of German martial law.[58] The peasants acted as they did from a mixture of motives. Undoubtedly, they expected the Allies to arrive soon, and it made good sense to aid the side which was going to win. Extra hands helping in the fields were also not to be scorned. But there were other, less calculating reasons, connected with the peasants' dislike of a regime which had turned Italy into a battleground, and with their own desire, as they expressed it afterwards, 'to do good' (*fare del bene*), and 'to live as true Christians' (*vivere da cristiani*).[59] Of course, not all the peasant families took the same decisions. Some lay low and wanted nothing to do with either side. Others, a very small minority by all accounts, informed on those who were helping the escaped prisoners and later the partisans (there were considerable monetary rewards). Hood's Franco was denounced by someone in his own village; he was deported to the concentration camp of Mauthausen and was one of the very few to survive and return.[60]

In the autumn of 1943, most partisan bands soon found a *modus vivendi* with the sharecroppers. They encouraged them not to consign their produce to the *ammassi*; some of the bands also came to ingenious agreements with them over the question of supplies. The partisans would pay for that part of the peasants' produce which they needed, but would leave a receipt saying they had confiscated it all. The peasants were then free to dispose of the remainder of their produce as they saw fit. The partisans, especially the Communists, also promised that at the end of the war the liberation government would pass legislation ensuring that the land would pass into sharecropping hands.[61]

By contrast, the Fascist authorities further alienated the sharecroppers. At the end of 1943 they insisted that given the shortage of grain, every producer should immediately consign to the state granaries fifteen kilos of grain per head and ten kilos per hectare (one hectare = 2.471 acres). All those who failed to do so would be refused the permit entitling them to have their grain milled. In early 1944 word also spread that the Germans were demanding extra agricultural labour for Germany, and that

100,000 rural workers from Tuscany alone were to be selected and deported. The first peasant demonstrations were not slow to follow. In February 1944, at Carmignano, north-west of Florence, sharecroppers gathered in the piazza of the village, declared a general strike and refused to move until the authorities distributed milling permits to everyone. Partisans flanked the demonstrators to protect them.[62]

c. THE RURAL SOUTH

In 1936 59 per cent of the active population of the Mezzogiorno (the southern half of Italy) still worked the land for a living. Manlio Rossi-Doria, one of the foremost of southern agronomists, has divided the agrarian South of the time into two basic types: the first, the fertile 'tree-covered' South, was characterized by an intensive agriculture dedicated to vines, olives and fruit trees. The second, the 'naked' South, was a land of pasture and of the extensive cultivation of cereals.[63]

The dense foliage of vines, olives, and lemon and orange trees which formed the typical landscape of the 'tree-covered' South was to be found only in certain zones: notable among these were the Terra di Bari, the Terra d'Otranto (the southernmost parts of Puglia), and the rich volcanic region surrounding Mount Etna in eastern Sicily. Though constituting less than a tenth of the agrarian Mezzogiorno, these areas were inhabited by nearly 50 per cent of its population. Some of the land was in peasant hands, but there was also a significant number of modern capitalist farms employing wage labourers on a regular basis. The standard of living of the peasantry was generally much higher than in the interior, but the coastal strips suffered from chronic over-population, a chaotic system of marketing and the division of the land into too many smallholdings. When the harvests were good and trade flourishing, the 'tree-covered' South could just about support its abundant population. But in times of depression a significant part of the peasantry was reduced to destitution.

By way of contrast with the central Italian sharecropping family of 'Federico P.', let us examine the family of a day labourer (*jurnaturu*) in the 'tree-covered' area of eastern Sicily in the same period.[64] The orange-producing agro-town of Lentini, in the extreme north of the province of Siracusa, had around 16,000 inhabitants in 1931. Well over 80 per cent of the male workforce were rural labourers. Lentini's agrarian economy was a mixture of the intensive cultivation of oranges, for which it was famous, and the extensive cultivation of cereals in the land furthest from the village.

Labouring families in Lentini were nuclear in structure and much smaller than in the sharecropping regions of the Centre. In 1931 the family of 'Alfio' (who refused to allow any photograph to be taken) comprised five members: Alfio himself, aged 37; Lucia (Ciuzza), his wife, aged 34; two daughters, Maria (Maruzza) aged 16, and Carmela, 8; and one son, Salvatore (Totò), aged 13. Another daughter had died of pneumonia at the age of seven in 1928. All members of the family suffered from malaria, as indeed did most of the population of Lentini.

Alfio's family lived in primitive conditions in two ground-floor rooms with a small adjacent stable, which housed the family mule and chickens. They had very few possessions apart from some rudimentary agricultural tools. Except for the central streets, the roads of Lentini were unpaved and without drains. Where Alfio's family lived, the road became an 'evil-smelling muddy mess' in winter and a dust pit in summer.[65]

Pastimes were minimal. For the women there was little more than the Sunday stroll and a visit to the cinema on the major feast days of the year. Men frequented the cafés and the social club (*dopolavoro*) instituted by the regime, where the radio was a major attraction.

The inhabitants of Lentini were not regular church-goers. The clergy had little influence over the population, the sacraments were not strictly observed and many of the men worked on Sundays. None the less there was, as in so many villages and towns of the South, a profound attachment to the local saints and a mass participation in the major events of the religious calendar. These latter were the principal social occasions of the town. In the nine days preceding Christmas Eve, for example, the women and some of the men would gather in front of the small shrine of each district; music would be played on the pipes and violins, and the carols and prayers of Christmas would be intoned by all present.[66]

The life of the members of Alfio's family, then, was markedly different from that of Federico P.'s. They lived not on the land but in an overgrown village where 80 per cent of the population were like themselves. They were not self-sufficient peasants. Alfio had no stake in the land, no farmhouse of which to be proud, no close relationship with landowner or parish priest. The standard of living of his family was markedly inferior to that of Federico's.

If we turn now to the second of Rossi-Doria's types, the 'naked' South, which comprised nine tenths of the agrarian Mezzogiorno, an immediate distinction must be drawn between the plains on the one hand, and the hills and mountains on the other. The plains, menaced by both aridity and malaria, were used for cereals in summer and pasture in winter. Large landowners or tenant farmers controlled nearly all the land. The peasants were landless labourers, living in large villages or agro-towns much like Lentini. Early in the morning in the local piazza the landlords' *caporali* ('corporals') would usually hire men on a casual basis, for a day or a week. The peasantry enjoyed no stability on the land and precious little remuneration. The southern plains with this type of agrarian economy were to be found mainly in or near the coastal zones – the Roman Maremma, the great Tavoliere of Puglia, the plain of Catania in eastern Sicily, the desolate flats of parts of the Sardinian coast.[67]

The second part of the 'naked' South comprised nearly all the poverty-stricken hill and mountain regions. Beyond the *corona*, the small amount of irrigated land surrounding the village, stretched vast undulating fields of corn, with hardly a single isolated house or tree to break up the landscape. In the summer these fields, golden and brown, seemed to the untrained eye all part of one great estate. But in the spring they were transformed into a complicated patchwork of different shades of green, which betrayed where the work of one man stopped and that of another began.

Ownership of the land was more multi-form than on the plains. In the mountains, where the forests had been largely destroyed, the peasantry had carved out smallholdings from the rocky soil. Between 1880 and 1930 their poverty-stricken economy had only survived thanks to widespread emigration. On the plateaux of the interior, with their great fields of corn, large and medium-sized estates were most common and peasant property rarer. In Sardinia the world of the shepherd and that of the peasant were almost totally distinct.

The hill plateaux region was the heartland of the *latifondo*. The word *latifondo* means large estate, and these were certainly still very common, consisting for example of up to 80 per cent of all cultivated land in Sicily. But the word *latifondo* has come to mean as much a distinct system of agrarian relationships as it has the mere physical presence of large estates. In the *latifondo* system of southern Italy the peasant was not established securely on a piece of land which he and his family owned or at least cultivated from generation to generation. The peasant was rather a man constantly in search of land and work. He would gain enough for his family to live on (the women rarely worked in the fields) in at least three different ways: cultivating his own property, usually very small in extent; renting annually strips of land, often far from each other, from different *latifondo* proprietors; working as a seasonal labourer on the great estates.

The poorest stratum, and the great majority, of the peasants in the *latifondo* zones were thus *figure miste* (of mixed character): proprietors, sharecroppers and labourers rolled into one. The very nature of their work, dispersed and without guarantees of continuity, explains the absence of farmhouses and the existence of the large agro-towns of the southern interior. From these towns every day before dawn the peasants would set out for work, carrying their agricultural implements with them. Often they had to walk many kilometres before reaching the plot of land which was theirs to cultivate for a year. They returned home after dusk.

As for the women, the head of the cooperative of Pietropaolo in the Crotonese (south-east Calabria) had this to tell Giovanni Russo in 1949:

The women are above all slaves: a woman is really on the lowest rung of the social scale. The heaviest physical tasks fall to her; when her man returns from work, she is the one who follows him, barefoot, carrying the weights that cannot be put on a mule. She is the one who has to collect water from the well, to gather acorns for the pigs, to collect faggots for the fire. By the age of thirty she is already an old woman.[68]

The land in the *latifondo* areas was of poor quality, suffering from erosion, from lack of irrigation in the summer, from the top soil being swept away in the torrential autumn rains. Most landowners had consistently neglected their properties, so that they declined in quality every year. Agricultural techniques had remained extremely primitive, the hoe still being the principal work instrument. With the peasants' unceasing search for land, the numbers of sheep and cattle had decreased, reducing the amount of fertilizer available and thus the productivity of the soil.[69]

Under the *latifondo* system the agrarian contracts agreed between landlord and peasant were the worst in all Italy. They were of great complexity and varied widely from region to region, from inland Sicily to the Crotonese and Basilicata, and indeed within these regions themselves. Contracts were nearly always on an individual level, often unwritten, and bitterly contested. In general, and it is a gross generalization, contracts stipulated that the peasants would not receive more than 25 per cent of the crops. Interest rates were extremely high, and the peasants who rented strips of the *latifondo* found themselves in permanent debt.[70]

At the end of the Fascist period the standard of living of the peasantry of these regions was desperately low. Practically the whole of the family budget went on food — bread, pasta, beans, a few vegetables, hardly any meat or wine. In the whitewashed agro-towns of the interior, families and their animals lived in one large windowless room, which served as kitchen, bedroom and stable all in one. The living conditions of the peasants moved Rossi-Doria to outrage: 'These are things which are well known, repeated by every one, but they are things which we must never tire of shouting from the roof-tops, because decades go by, regimes pass away, thousands of millions of lire are spent on superfluous schemes, and eight million Italians continue to live in those houses which are not houses, to the eternal shame of a country which proclaims itself to be civilized.'[71]

As for the landowners, they displayed extremely hidebound attitudes towards both agricultural production and landlord–peasant relations. Absenteeism predominated, with the running of the estates left to tenant farmers or to local farm managers (*fattori*). In Sicily there were often two or more middlemen standing between peasant and landowner.[72] Investment was minimal; income from the great estates was used either for conspicuous consumption in the cities, or else to acquire more land. The *latifondi* survived for as long as they did because the absolute subjection of the peasantry ensured certain economic essentials: elasticity and responsiveness to the market, deriving from the constant mobility of peasant labour; the lion's share of the crops, guaranteed by the inequity of agrarian contracts; reasonable productivity per hectare, at least by national standards.[73] Immediately after the Second World War, the Calabrian Baron Galluccio declared proudly that his estates brought him 40m lire from grain and the same again from small beans (*favette*): 'With 80m lire annually I live extremely well, and the rest of my land I choose to leave uncultivated, in order to hunt on it.'[74]

One other piece of historical detail must be added. In the late eighteenth and early nineteenth centuries the southern peasantry had been deprived of what they took to be their rightful part of the old demesne lands. As first the barons and then non-noble landowners usurped more and more of the common land, the peasants lost their rights to gleaning and pasturage, and of access to the forests. In 1806, under the rule of Joseph Bonaparte, it was decided that the peasantry should be systematically compensated for these deprivations by assigning to them one quarter of the land that had previously been open to common rights usage. This promise of land was like a diamond ingrained in the collective consciousness of the peasantry. In the face of endless obstruction and litigation, they rose up to claim their share of the land at frequent intervals between 1820 and 1860. Not even with Garibaldi's conquest of the South in 1860 was agrarian reform carried out.

Thus the formation of the Italian state in no way provided justice for the southern peasant; quite the opposite. Usurpations of the remaining common lands continued throughout the late nineteenth and early twentieth centuries, accompanied by massive peasant emigration. In the 1930s, when the late Carlo Levi was exiled as an anti-Fascist to the village of 'Gagliano' in Basilicata, he described the peasants' attitude to the state as follows:

What had these peasants of Gagliano to do with power, government and the State? The State, whatever form it might take, meant 'the fellows in Rome'. 'Everyone knows,' they said, 'that the fellows in Rome don't want us to live like human beings. There are hailstorms, landslides, droughts, malaria, and . . . the State. These are inescapable evils; such there always have been and there always will be. They make us kill off our goats, they carry away our furniture, and now they're going to send us to the wars. Such is life!'[75]

In the western Sicilian countryside a habitual reply to the question 'How are you?' is '*Cuntrastamu*', 'We are resisting.'[76] Some families obviously resisted better than others, but it took only a small calamity – the death of a mule, the division of a property, the illness of one of the men – to drive a slightly better-off family back to the direst poverty. From the bitter experience of many battles fought and lost, of many promises made and never kept, of emigration and of war, the southern peasantry had developed a philosophy which mixed fatalism, solidarity and distrust.

The Communist Fausto Gullo, who was to become Minister of Agriculture in 1944, told the Chamber of Deputies in 1950 that in his part of Calabria 'all the folk-songs are laments, there is not a single popular song that has a sense of joy about it; they are all pervaded by a most profound sadness, by a harrowing melancholy which sometimes borders on despair'.[77] From this harshest of realities, the peasants sought refuge and aid not only in the adoration of local saints, as at Lentini, but in a widely diffused pagan religiosity. The various cults of the South, from the *tarantismo* ('dance of the spider') analysed by Ernesto De Martino to the 'festivals of the poor' described by Annabella Rossi, were different expressions of an autonomous culture, separate from the structure and social doctrines of the Catholic church. This was a world which offered the possibility of trance and release, of mass pilgrimages and miraculous cures.[78]

Side by side with these attitudes there also lay a long, evanescent history of solidarity amongst the southern peasants. There *were* structures in their lives which favoured this solidarity. The most important was undoubtedly the *paese* (the village or agro-town) itself, with its concentration of so many families in similar conditions, its absence of social mobility, its networks of street and district loyalties, its links of kinship and *comparaggio* (the conferring on a close friend or leader in the community of the status of godfather to one's children). In the 1940s, when the labourers of Eboli descended from the town to work in the malarial plain below it, they did so in groups based on neighbourhood and kinship loyalties, groups which were accepted and respected by some of the *caporali*.[79] There had been moments in the agrarian history of the South when whole towns had risen up, indeed when collective action had spread through entire regions. The great protest movement known as the Fasci Siciliani of 1893–4 had been one such moment. Another had been on the Tavoliere plain after the First World War, when the anarcho-syndicalists established there an extraordinary level of solidarity and class-consciousness amongst the labourers.[80]

However, there was another pattern which overlaid that of solidarity, both in the *latifondo* areas and elsewhere. If the *paese* brought the *latifondo* peasants together, their work took them apart. The peasants were in constant competition with each other for the best strips of land on the *latifondo*, and for what meagre resources were available. Vertical relationships between patron and client, and obsequiousness to the landlord, were more important than horizontal solidarities. As Bevilacqua has written for the period 1880–1920: 'The peasant classes were more at war amongst themselves than with other sectors of rural society; a war which fed off a terrain of recurring and real contrasts, both economic, psychological and cultural.'[81]

That such attitudes triumphed can only be understood in the context of a society which was dominated by distrust. Here it is not possible to trace the historical origins of such a phenomenon.[82] Suffice it to say that the weight of the past, when combined with the failures of state authority after 1860 and the disastrous peasant–landlord relations outlined above, produced a society where *fede pubblica* (civic trust) had been reduced to a minimum: *'chi ara diritto, muore disperato'* (he who behaves honestly comes to a miserable end) was a noted Calabrian proverb.[83]

In this context, it is important to mention the presence of the Mafia in the Sicilian countryside, especially in the *latifondo* areas of western Sicily. The term *mafia* first appeared in an official document of 1865, and it was a phenomenon to be found from then on in both an urban and a rural context. Mafia, as Gambetta has argued recently, is primarily an agency which offers guarantees or more generally protection in a context characterized by widespread distrust. In Sicily it was never a single organization, but rather a series of competing groups or 'families' living in unstable equilibrium with each other. The services they offered were the maintenance, by means of violence, of monopolies of one sort or another.[84] In rural western Sicily the monopoly to be safeguarded was that of land. Here in the nineteenth century the *gabellotti* (tenant farmers) had increasingly taken over the land from the absentee landowners, and the first *mafiosi* were those who offered an armed protection against any threat to *gabellotto* power.

However, the Mafia was not merely a secret association protecting the class interests of the rural élites. It was also a vehicle for social mobility. The Mafia, and its less well known equivalent, the 'Ndrangheta in Calabria, have tended to flourish in rural areas with an active middle class.[85] For these rural *ceti medi*, to become a *mafioso* was a way, albeit fraught with danger, of acquiring status, power and wealth. Furthermore, the services the Mafia and 'Ndrangheta offered tended to create local loyalties in the face of outside interference. In the absence of effective state authority, it was necessary for all ranks of society to have protection of one sort or another. In this context, as Franchetti wrote in 1876, 'the distinction between a damage avoided and a benefit gained is up to a point artificial'.[86] The Mafia offered protection against bandits, against rural theft, against the inhabitants of rival towns, above all against itself.

In the period from 1918 to 1926, some of the southern peasants managed to acquire land for the first time. Even so, in no region of the South did peasant property become more than 10 per cent of the whole.[87] During the Fascist decades the southern rural population, like their counterparts elsewhere in Italy, suffered from higher taxation, falling agricultural prices, the system of the *ammassi* and the 'battle for grain'. But their most severe affliction was the restriction on emigration. This traditional safety-valve was severely damaged by the tightening of the American immigration laws and by the world economic depression. In the mountain areas the subsistence economy quite simply could not cope with the extra mouths it was required to feed. Everywhere in the South, intense pressure built up on the scarce resources of families; a pressure that after the war was to become an explosion.[88]

One other aspect of Fascism's policies in the South must be mentioned. In the early years of the regime, Mussolini, intolerant of any authority in Sicily except his own, attempted to stamp out the Mafia. The prefect of Palermo, Cesare Mori, accordingly rounded up and imprisoned many hundreds of low-ranking *mafiosi*. But Mori's blitz could not change the relationship between state and society, and the members of the rural élites donned the black shirt as an alternative form of protection. In 1929 Mori was relieved of his post, and the basic structures of Sicilian society remained unchanged.[89]

In the South, the declaration of war in 1940 eased temporarily the pressure of population on the land: an estimated million men were conscripted. But by 1943 the situation in the southern countryside had become critical in other ways. The amount of grain allowed to the peasantry for their own consumption had been decreasing year by year. The shortage of manpower resulted in a rise in wages for agricultural labourers, but this was eaten away by inflation and the spread of the black market. Many essential goods become unobtainable. Mass protests of the peasantry became more frequent, particularly in the Basilicata, the poorest region on the southern mainland. One of the peasants' most consistent demands, itself an indication of their plight, was for sturdy shoes for work. By 1943 a pair of shoes of this type cost 1,000 lire, more than six times their pre-war price.[90]

The Anglo-American invasion of the South brought an end to Fascism. It did so at cost of the lives of many thousands of Allied soldiers who died in the battles to liberate the peninsula. Sadly, it is difficult for the historian to escape the conclusion that Allied social and political policy was found wanting in many respects. The Allied military government (AMGOT) printed on the back of their banknotes a list of the four freedoms that they were bringing to Italy – freedom of speech and of religion, freedom from want and from fear. The list was in English (so as to save the inhabitants from corruption, wisecracked Tommy Trinder), but the real effect of the issue of so much Allied money was a drastic increase in the rate of inflation. The supplying of foodstuffs to the local population was rated a low priority, and was then carried out with an inefficiency and corruption that provoked the later criticism even of the official British historian of these events.[91]

Above all, the arrival of the Allies did not bring with it any greater social justice. Official policy was summed up by the catch-phrase: 'Keep existing administration and temper defascistization with discretion.' What this meant in most localities was the dismissal or internment of the Fascist mayor, the retention of the local *carabinieri* and the enlistment of the aid of the conservative church hierarchy. In Sicily the Allies turned out to have some sinister friends. Leading members of the Italo-American Mafia like Lucky Luciano used AMGOT as a means of returning to their former hunting-grounds. In general, Allied military government ensured the southern rural élites a painless transitional period from Fascism to Victor Emanuel's ultra-conservative Kingdom of the South. The Allies professed to be above politics, but the effect of their policies was to consecrate the social status quo, based, as we have seen, on the most ruthless exploitation of the rural poor.[92]

In a situation which got worse, not better, with liberation, the southern peasantry became increasingly desperate. Widespread protests spread through the rural areas in the winter of 1943–4. The slogans shouted by the demonstrators were nearly always of the same kind: 'No more grain for the authorities', 'No more taxes', 'We want bread subsidies', 'We want salt', 'Out with the Fascists'. Some of the demonstrations turned into open revolt. In December 1943 at Montesano in the province of Salerno, peasants and *carabinieri* fought a pitched battle for three hours. Eight demonstrators were killed and ten wounded. The first occupations of the land date from this period, with peasants in Sicily, Basilicata and Calabria taking over parts of the *latifondi* which the landowners wanted to keep for pasture.[93]

d. NAPLES

With over a million inhabitants in 1941, Naples was the largest city of the South. It was a city of the most strident contrasts between rich and poor. Alongside a small number of its citizens who lived in luxury apartments overlooking the famous bay, there existed a large stratum of impoverished professional families, a significant class of clerks and petty civil servants, and a vast mass of unemployed or underemployed poor. There was little industry; services of one kind or another provided what work there was. Families were much larger here than among the southern rural poor. In the belly of the city, as Serao called it, nearly a quarter of a million people lived in 50,000 *bassi*, ground-floor and basement dwellings with no windows and with doors which opened directly on to the street. In the *bassi*, 'space is so restricted that people are born and die there side by side; the toilet, with a flowered curtain around it, is right next to the stove and pans, and the floor is made of paving stones, exactly the same ones you find in the streets'.[94] In the *bassi* the women made gloves and worked lace until the bad light had destroyed their eyesight. As for the men, Allum has made a list of some of the typical occupations of the Neapolitan slum economy: *spiccia-faccende* (helping to get documents through the intricate bureaucratic machinery); *accotta a vanni* (pedlars of used clothing); *arriffatori* (operating a personal lottery); *petrusinari* (selling parsley and basil); *borsaiolo* (pick-pocket).[95]

In September 1943 the Germans briefly occupied the city in the aftermath of the armistice. They immediately ordered all able-bodied men between the ages of eighteen and thirty-three to report for compulsory labour service. Only 150 did so. When the Germans began to round up men indiscriminately, the city rose in revolt. For four days Naples was the scene of bitter street fighting. On 30 September, with Allied troops fast approaching, the Germans withdrew, leaving 162 dead Neapolitans and a trail of destruction and terror.

The period of Allied occupation of the city, lasting from September 1943 to December 1944, was an unmitigated disaster. Severe bombing of the area near the port had left 200,000 Neapolitans homeless, and in the autumn of 1943 there was very little water and the sewers did not function. With the connivance of many levels of army command, an estimated 60 per cent of merchandise unloaded in the port disappeared on to the black market. By July 1944 only 3.4 per cent of the goods in Naples were available in the form of rations to the population. The city acquired a face of degradation and disease that it had not known since the great plagues of the seventeenth century. Most of the poorer women were forced into prostitution, and severe epidemics of typhus and venereal disease afflicted both the civilian and military population.

An Allied report of 28 September 1944 described the fate of many young children in the city:

Wartime conditions, bombing, evacuation, the death of parents etc., has led to an extraordinary increase of waifs and strays in the streets of Naples. Many hundreds of urchins, their ages varying from six to sixteen, roam the streets, and the following offences are daily becoming more numerous: pimping, prostitution of minors, acting as 'fences' for stolen goods, etc . . . On 10 August 1944 in his appeal for support for the order of St Mary of Ransom for the Redemption of Slaves, which concerns itself with the welfare of young girls, Father Ovidio Serafini wrote: 'It is known that in the Pace Hospital alone, 4,000 diseased have been examined and of that number at least half were minors. There is the same proportion in all the other hospitals of the province and in the region. With respect to our own work, it is very sad to see little girls ill and pregnant, at thirteen and even twelve years of age, unconscious of their condition, continuing to play with dolls, ignorant of their state and their ruined future.'[96]

Italy in 1944 was thus a country where all the apparent certainties of the Fascist period – the bombastic cult of the nation and of its leader, the quest for autarchy and empire, the unceasing emphasis on the moral, physical and cultural regeneration of the Italians – had been shattered by the horrors of occupation and of war. The brutal expansion of the Fascist regime had been forced back upon itself; Italy had become Abyssinia. Bombardment, famine and the clatter of tanks replaced the mass rallies, the school gymnastic displays, the dulcet tones of Beniamino Gigli transmitted on the state radio.

Not since Napoleonic times had the whole peninsula been transformed into a battleground, and the effects in 1943–4 were infinitely worse than in 1796–9. In the South the British and Americans were greeted as liberators (as indeed they were), but all the ambiguities of this liberation were soon revealed, and not only to the Italians. Harold Macmillan, that shrewdest of all contemporary Tories and Allied High Commissioner in southern Italy in 1944, wrote later that the Italians had had 'the dual experience of being occupied by the Germans and liberated by the Allies . . . It was difficult to say which of the two processes was more painful or upsetting.'[97] Without doubt, the German occupation was more terrible in both intention and effect, but at least in the North the issues were clear cut. While in the South the struggle against deprivation and social injustice had no chance of linking with a Resistance movement (was it possible to resist liberation?), in the North and Centre the working-class movement, sections of the peasantry and the partisans were soon united in a single cause. It was upon them that hopes of Italian regeneration would rest.

Chapter 2

Resistance and Liberation

*A*S THE protracted drama of wartime Italy unfolded, it became clear that three forces were going to dominate the country – the Allies, the Communists and the Christian Democrats. It is necessary to look at each of them in some detail, for their respective strategies determined to a large extent the future aspect of the peninsula.

The Allies

From the summer of 1943 onwards the Allies, and the British in particular, staked their claim to Italy. Control of the Mediterranean was traditionally a strategic aim of the British, and the Americans acquiesced to the British desire to be the senior partner. As for the Russians, the Allies quickly excluded them from any direct control over the fate of the peninsula. In spite of angry protests from Stalin, ideas for a joint commission of the three great powers to decide the terms of the Italian armistice were rapidly abandoned. Force of arms now decided all – the Allies in the west, the Russians in the east. When Churchill met Stalin at the Kremlin in October 1944, they successfully carved up Europe between them. There were some countries, Yugoslavia and Greece especially, where the issue was not clear cut, but there could be no doubt about Italy. Churchill told Stalin *en passant* that he had no great respect for the Italian people. Stalin agreed that 'it was the Italian people who had thrown up Mussolini', a remark that hardly belonged to any known class analysis of the origins of Fascism.[1]

The British were therefore the predominant external influence in Italy, and a résumé of their attitudes does not make comforting reading. Churchill had been an erstwhile admirer of Mussolini, congratulating him on one occasion for the way in which 'he had raised the Italian people from the Bolshevism into which they were sinking in 1919 to a position in Europe such as Italy had never held before'. The British Prime Minister much regretted that the Duce had chosen the wrong side: 'he never understood the strength of Britain, nor the long enduring qualities of Island resistance and sea-power. Thus he marched to ruin.'[2]

Churchill's main preoccupation in Italy was to preserve what he called 'traditional property relations' from the threat of rampant Communism. He wanted the king, or at least his son Umberto, to remain in power. He was not interested in eradicating Fascism from the Italian state apparatus, and was content, as Pavone has written, 'to offer immunity in return for obedience'.[3] In Churchill's eyes, Victor Emanuel and Badoglio were the best guarantors of the continuance of the traditional social order and also the most compliant interlocutors the British were going to find. Churchill had little time for the Italian anti-Fascists. He dismissed Benedetto Croce, the distinguished philosopher, as 'a dwarf professor', and in February 1944 made a famous and insulting speech in favour of the monarchy and against the CLN (Committee of National Liberation): 'When you have to hold a coffee-pot, it is better not to break the handle off until you are sure you will get another equally convenient and serviceable, or at any rate, until there is a dish-cloth handy.'[4]

Beneath the contempt there lay a strong punitive streak. Churchill always maintained that it was now up to the Italians to 'earn their return ticket' to the company of the civilized nations of the world. However, it was not the task of the British to help them on the way. Early on in the Allied occupation the monetary exchange rate was permanently fixed at 400 lire to one pound sterling, a crippling devaluation of the lira which made any revival of the Italian economy doubly difficult. The 'return ticket' was clearly going to be very expensive. The British Board of Trade would not hear of American plans to aid Italian industrial reconstruction, maintaining that any revival in Italian textiles would threaten the Lancashire cotton industry. The Foreign Office was worse still. Alexander confided that Eden was 'almost psychopathic' about Italy, and in August 1944 the Foreign Office Research Department submitted a paper suggesting that Italy should remain under British control until her people had learned from the British how to behave in a democratic fashion.[5]

Only the British diplomats in Washington, Macmillan, and many of the British soldiers actually in Italy provided any counterpoint to this unpleasant anti-Italian (as opposed to anti-Fascist) chorus. Macmillan wrote to Eden in September 1944: 'Sometimes they [the Italians] are enemies: sometimes they are co-belligerents. Sometimes we wish to punish them for their sins: sometimes to appear as rescuers and guardian angels. It beats me!'[6]

The deficiencies of British policy were clearly shown up by the rather different American attitudes. The Americans too lost thousands of men in the battle for Italy, especially during the nightmare of the Anzio bridgehead. But on the major issues their positions were consistently less hostile than those of the British. They refused to accept that the king and Badoglio spoke for the whole of the Italian people; they treated the anti-Fascists of the CLN with some consideration; and most important of all, they realized that the rapid growth of the Italian Communists was not altogether disconnected from the desperate living conditions then prevailing in Italy. In Washington in June 1944 Henry Morgenthau Jr expressed this growing American concern, albeit in a somewhat simplistic fashion: 'The whole problem consists,' said Morgenthau, 'in the fact that we have been too idle in confronting the question of what we've been giving to eat to these folk.'[7] After Churchill and Roosevelt met in September 1944, the American administration took a series of unilateral initiatives: it opened a system of credits for Italy to cover the Amlire being spent by American troops, arranged for Italy to receive benefits from UNRRA (the United Nations Relief and Rehabilitation Administration) and tried to ensure a greater supply of foodstuffs for the peninsula.

It would be wrong to interpret these measures as the opening gambits in the American strategy to become the major point of reference, economically and politically, for post-war Italy. That was only to come later. But the difference between the two Allies at this time can perhaps best be summed up by the catch-phrases that they used for their policies in Italy. The British proclaimed their intention to 'prevent epidemics and disorders', the Americans to 'create stability and prosperity'. There was no doubt which was more far-sighted.

As the Allies made only slow progress up the peninsula, one problem came to preoccupy them increasingly – that of the Resistance. At first they had paid little attention to it, advising the Italian partisans to concentrate purely on acts of sabotage. But as the number of partisan brigades grew, and the major role of the Communists became apparent, the Allies, particularly the British, became apprehensive. The creation of a large partisan army, dominated by left-wing ideology, was an obvious threat to the conservative hegemony which the British intended to exercise over the whole process of liberation.

Contemporary events in Yugoslavia and Greece did little to reassure them. Late in 1943 the British switched their support in Yugoslavia from Mihailovic's Cetniks to Tito's Communist partisans in the hope that Tito would be more effective militarily. He certainly was, but he also relentlessly pursued his own aim of establishing a Communist state in Yugoslavia. By the end of 1944 it was clear that the British had lost political control of his actions.

The Greek situation developed in an opposite, if equally dramatic fashion. In December 1944, after the Greek partisans had liberated Athens, the uneasy truce between Communists and Monarchists disintegrated into civil war. Here the British decided that immediate military intervention was called for, and an expeditionary force was dispatched to Athens to support the Monarchists. By 11 January 1945 the Greek Communists were forced to sign an armistice and evacuate the capital.

The British wanted neither the Greek nor the Yugoslav experience — the one permissive, the other repressive — to be repeated in Italy, a country more firmly designated to their control than either of the other two. This fear of Communist intrigue united all the British leaders, and most of the Americans as well. As Macmillan wrote later, 'we had to get control of these movements right from the start'.[8] Allied strategy with regard to the Resistance was therefore to minimize its role as far as possible, and on no account to allow partisan action to lead to unpredictable political consequences.

The Communists

In March 1944 Palmiro Togliatti, the leader of the Italian Communist Party, returned from Moscow to Italy. Togliatti, fifty-one years old in 1944, was the son of a schoolmistress and a petty clerk; he had been with Gramsci in Turin after the First World War, and was one of the founders of the Italian Communist Party in 1921. After the rise of Fascism he had taken refuge in Russia, where he rapidly rose to become the Vice-Secretary of the Comintern. Astute, cautious, cultured and disdainful, Togliatti was a born survivor, a quality that stood him in good stead in the Moscow of the 1930s. While obviously a loyal supporter of Stalin, Togliatti had the great merit of thinking creatively and strategically in an international Communist movement noted for its dogma and fideism.

On his arrival in Salerno, Togliatti outlined to his comrades, amidst a certain astonishment and some opposition, the strategy which he intended the party to pursue in the near future. The Communists, he said, were to put into abeyance their oft-expressed hostility to the monarchy. Instead, they were to persuade all the anti-Fascist forces to join the royal government, which now controlled all of Italy south of Salerno. Joining the government, Togliatti argued, was the first step towards realizing the overriding objective of the period – national unity in the face of the Nazis and the Fascists. The main aim of the Communists had to be the liberation of Italy, not a socialist revolution. Togliatti made this explicit in the instructions he wrote for the party in June 1944: 'Remember always that the insurrection that we want has not got the aim of imposing social and political transformations in a socialist or communist sense. Its aim is rather national liberation and the destruction of Fascism. All the other problems will be resolved by the people tomorrow, once Italy is liberated, by means of a free popular vote and the election of a Constituent Assembly.'[9]

This last phrase revealed Togliatti's commitment to re-establishing parliamentary democracy in Italy. Unlike Tito, he had no intention of making the dictatorship of the proletariat the short-term aim of his party. Nor was his objective the simple restoration of a parliamentary regime on pre-Fascist lines. It was, rather, what he chose to call 'progressive democracy'. The exact content of this phrase remained deliberately vague, as inscrutable as the face of the Sphinx, as Hobsbawm has remarked. In general terms, it was meant to convey a form of state that involved more direct popular participation than did a normal parliamentary democracy. The working class would become the leading political force in the country and would carry through a series of major reforms. These would include the destruction of all residues of Fascism, a radical agrarian reform and action against monopoly capitalism (but not against all capitalism as such).[10]

In order to achieve 'progressive democracy', a wide coalition of both social and political forces would be necessary. Togliatti insisted that the unity of the war years should, if possible, be continued into the period of reconstruction. This grand coalition was to embrace not only the Socialists, but also the Christian Democrats (DC). In a speech in Rome in July 1944 he characterized the DC as a party which had in its ranks 'a mass of workers, peasants, intellectuals and young people, who basically share our aspirations because like us they want a democratic and progressive Italy'.[11]

National unity, progressive democracy, a lasting coalition of the mass popular parties – these were to be the cardinal points of Communist strategy. In trying to explain these choices, it is important not to overstress either the originality or the autonomy of what has come to be known as 'the turning-point of Salerno'. Togliatti's formulations, in reality, were broadly in line with the theses adopted by the Comintern at its seventh congress in July 1935. In the wake of the obliteration of the German workers' movement by Hitler, the seventh congress abandoned the previous disastrous policy of characterizing the mass social-democratic parties as 'social Fascists'. Instead it gave full support to the creation of popular-front governments, based on the alliance of all democratic parties, to combat the Fascist menace. This was the policy which had been pursued by the Communists in Spain, and Togliatti's programme was the logical application of it for Italy.

In 1944, the parameters of Italian Communist Party strategy were also determined by the needs of the Russian war effort. The Russians at this time were extremely impatient for the Allies to relieve German pressure in the east by opening a second front in France. They therefore wanted to avoid any issue which might lead to a souring of relations between the Great Powers. Any attempt by the Italian Communists to pursue an independent policy similar to that of Tito would thus have been most untimely. On 13 March 1944 the Russians recognized Badoglio's government, implicitly confirming the assignment of Italy to the British sphere of influence.

The strategy and needs of the international Communist movement thus shaped Togliatti's choices to a great extent. However, much of what he proposed also derived from the specific Italian situation and from the material and intellectual evolution of the Italian party.

In the first place, the Communist leadership considered the possibility of social revolution to be firmly ruled out by the presence of the Allied army in Italy. Unlike in Yugoslavia, the Allies controlled half the peninsula and were marching steadily northwards. The P C I had little doubt that if the partisans tried to seize power in the north they would be rapidly crushed by Allied troops. To attempt an armed socialist insurrection, argued Togliatti, was tantamount to suicide.

Given the fact that Italy was firmly under British influence, the Italian Communists felt that they were moving to a certain extent on foreign territory. For twenty years they had been branded by the Fascist regime as devils incarnate, and the British were hardly more tenderly disposed towards 'rampant Bolshevism'. Any rash move, any adventurist proclamation in favour of immediate insurrection, argued the Communists, would lead to a new dark age of illegality for their party.

Such attitudes were reinforced by a defensiveness born of two decades of defeat. When Togliatti returned to Italy, he brought with him the bitter experience of having witnessed the physical destruction of the workers' movement in Italy in the 1920s, the Nazi liquidation of the German Communist Party in the early 1930s, the long-drawn-out and infinitely bloody defeat of the Spanish Republic. In reflecting on so terrible a sequence of events, Togliatti was able to make use of the theoretical writings of Antonio Gramsci, who had died in 1937 after many years of imprisonment. In 1944 Gramsci's Prison Notebooks were still unpublished, but Togliatti had had access to them in Moscow.

Gramsci's prison writings were fragmentary in form, constrained by censorship and capable of more than one interpretation. None the less they offered a highly original reflection on socialist strategy in the West. In broad terms, Gramsci argued that as the relationship between state and civil society differed between East and West, so too western revolutionaries had to adopt a revolutionary strategy which was distinct from that of the Bolsheviks in the Russian Revolution: 'In the East the state was everything, civil society was primordial and gelatinous; in the West there was a proper relationship between state and civil society, and when the state trembled a sturdy structure of civil society was at once revealed.'[12] In the West, therefore, a 'war of movement', a direct assault upon the state, was doomed to failure. Instead Western Communists had first to pursue a long 'war of position' in civil society, a protracted struggle which would require 'infinite patience and tenacity'. In this 'war of position' the working class had gradually to establish its hegemony — its moral, political and cultural leadership — over other sections of society. It had to create a 'historic bloc' of social forces in counter-position to those of the capitalist class. It had, to put it at its simplest, to prepare for power.

Gramsci never stated that the 'war of position' would render an eventual revolutionary seizure of power unnecessary. But he did think that the long-term success of any such revolutionary moment would necessarily be dependent upon the outcome of the prior struggle for hegemony. He also insisted that in the lengthy process of creating hegemony, a centralized revolutionary party, 'the collective intellectual', would be the prime mover in organizing, coordinating and leading the anti-capitalist forces in society.

It is probably fair to say that Togliatti both learned from and adapted Gramsci's theoretical reflections. The 'war of position', the struggle for hegemony in civil society, the building of alliances around the working class, all these became cardinal points in the 'Italian road to socialism'. But Togliatti's interpretation of this framework was very much his own. In the creation of alliances, Togliatti stressed not only social alliances, those built from the bottom upwards (very much the emphasis in the Prison Notebooks), but also political alliances from the top downwards, of which that with the Christian Democrats was to be the most controversial and difficult. In addition, Togliatti's desire to win over the *ceti medi* made him appeal to a far wider range of social forces than that which Gramsci probably envisaged. The distinction between 'monopoly' capitalism on the one hand, and potentially 'progressive' small businesses on the other, was very much Togliatti's. So too was the insistence on the long march not only in civil society but in the state apparatus as well, with its concomitant electoralism and the occupation of positions of power in local and national government. Gramsci had said little on this matter in the Prison Notebooks, but his political practice had been devoted to trying to create alternative forms of workers' aggregation and power, not to the conquest of the existing state apparatus. Finally, Togliatti postponed any possible connection between 'war of position' and 'war of manoeuvre', until the latter was eventually to disappear.[13]

Togliatti's adaptation of Gramsci was probably at its most successful in the crucial area of the party. Right from the start, Togliatti put great emphasis on transforming the Communists from a small vanguard group into a mass party in civil society. 'For every bell-tower a Communist party branch' was the campaigning slogan during the heady months of 1945 when literally hundreds of thousands of Italians joined the party. Togliatti wrote at this time:

In both urban neighbourhoods and villages, the Communist sections must become centres of working-class life, centres where all comrades, sympathizers and independents can go, knowing that they will find there a party and an organization which is interested in their problems and which will give them guidance. They should know that they will find there someone who can direct them, who can give them counsel, and if necessary can make sure that they have a good time.[14]

It is a matter of debate whether Gramsci would have approved of the hierarchical and undemocratic structure which Togliatti chose for the new party. But there is little doubt about the clarity and dynamism with which Togliatti built a mass Communist political culture in Italian society.[15]

Any historical critique of Communist Party strategy must begin by paying tribute to its many positive aspects. The PCI avoided any extremist temptations and refused to lead the working class into an impossible revolution. Any insurrection in the north would, in all probability, have divided the country and have been brutally suppressed by Allied troops. A whole generation of militants would have been decimated and the working-class movement put back by many years. Such a disaster would also have led to the considerable postponement of Italy regaining her national independence.

In addition, Communist insistence on national unity proved an invaluable contribution to the partisan fight against the Nazis and Fascists. At a time when the efficacy of many national Resistance movements was seriously impaired by internal political divisions, the Communists' contribution to unity cannot be underestimated. In the short term, Togliatti's decision to enter Badoglio's government ended the political isolation and impotence of the anti-Fascist forces of the CLN. Togliatti's was a political initiative in the true sense of the words, in that it placed the Communist Party at the centre of the political stage and forced everyone else to react to it.[16] His strategy secured the legality of the PCI, created the conditions in which the mass party could be built and meant that Communists occupied certain key ministries, like that of agriculture, during the war years.

However, such achievements were gained at a price high enough to cast some doubts on the general validity of the strategy. In practice, national unity in the fight for liberation became for the Communists an objective to be placed not just *above*, but *to the exclusion of*, all others. The policy of liberation first, 'progressive democracy' second, was fatally misconceived. It meant that at the very moment when the partisan and workers' movement was at its height, when the 'wind from the North' was blowing most strongly, the Communists accepted the postponement of all questions of a social and political nature until the end of the war. All the critical problems concerning the specific nature of post-war Italy – the relations between capital and labour, the nature of the new state, the extent of social reform – were put into cold storage. But it was not possible to freeze history in this fashion. While the Communists postponed in the honourable name of national unity, their opponents acted, decided, manoeuvred and, not surprisingly, triumphed. The king, Badoglio, the Allies, the church hierarchy, the southern landowners, the northern capitalists, every one of them continued to pursue their objectives with all the means at their disposal.

Of course, any determined Communist policy of pursuing social and political objectives *at the same time as* the war of liberation would have encountered stiff opposition. The dangers involved were considerable. But, as Quazza has pointed out, by risking hardly anything in 1944–5, the Communists took a great and in the event unjustified risk on an unknown future.[17]

The criticism to be levied against the Communist leadership, therefore, is not that it did not make the revolution. That was an impossibility. Rather it is that their two-stage strategy – liberation first, social and political reform second – caused them to dissipate the strength of the Resistance and of worker and peasant agitation. As a result, they were completely outflanked by the Allies and by the conservative forces in Italian society.

Both the strengths and the weaknesses of the Communist position are revealed in the consequences of their entering the monarchist government. While this action broke the isolation of the CLN and secured the legitimacy of the PCI, it also proved a most welcome and unexpected gift for their opponents. At a stroke the legitimacy of the Kingdom of the South, previously bitterly contested by the democratic parties, was unreservedly accepted. The substance of this concession was greater than might at first appear. It marked the first stage in that long-term conservation of state institutions and central bureaucracy which was to prove so fundamental a stumbling-block to any serious reform in contemporary Italy. Badoglio and the Allies had already laid the groundwork in the South for this 'continuity of the state', as it has come to be called. The basis was now there for its extension to the whole of the peninsula. The vague Communist formula of progressive democracy, based as it was on a mistaken belief in the neutrality of state institutions, was to be quite inadequate as a check to this structural 'wind from the South'.[18]

The Christian Democrats

The role of the Christian Democrats in 1943–5 was certainly a subsidiary one when compared to that of the Allies or the Communists. The DC played little part in the Resistance and often had only a token presence on the Committees of National Liberation. However, many of the foundations for its later supremacy – the backing of the Vatican, the emergence of an outstanding leader in Alcide De Gasperi, the development of its support amongst both the highest and lowest echelons of Italian society – date from this period.

The Christian Democrat Party was founded at Milan in September 1942 at the house of the steel magnate Enrico Falck. The previous mass Catholic party, the Partito Popolare, had ceased to exist in 1926, killed off by internal dissensions, Fascist repression and the Pope coming to terms with Benito Mussolini. The founding group of the DC consisted of a few old Popolare leaders and a number of Catholic anti-Fascists headed by Pietro Malvestiti. They were soon to be joined by members of the Catholic Graduate Association, among whom were Aldo Moro and Giulio Andreotti.[19] The early programmes of the DC were founded on an appeal to those Christian values which alone could reconcile human conflict: 'Controllers and controlled, guardians and guarded, governors and governed must all feel themselves responsible before the supreme Creator and Moderator of all things. Social conflicts cannot be resolved without that sense of fraternity which is the moving force of Christian civilization.'[20]

Fraternity went hand in hand with the defence and encouragement of small peasant property and small business. In the new Italy, the proletariat was to be 'dissolved' into a nation of property holders. At the same time the early pronouncements of the D C reflected the growing wave of lower-class militancy. Workers' participation in industry, reform of the *latifondi*, even a generic opposition to the 'imperial ambitions of plutocratic capitalism' were all, at least on paper, part and parcel of the D C credo. They were to be eagerly seized upon by the P C I as proof of the progressive nature of the new Christian party.

Alcide De Gasperi, sixty-two years old in 1943, had been the last general secretary of the Partito Popolare. His family came from the Trentino (in the extreme north of Italy). He had been educated at Vienna University and before the First World War had been a Catholic deputy in the Austro-Hungarian Parliament (Trento was still part of Austria at that time). When Mussolini banned all opposition in 1926, De Gasperi did not seek to oppose Fascism actively, but was scarred by its violence none the less. First he was kidnapped in the Val Sugana by a local Fascist squad who subjected him to a mock trial before letting him go. Then the Fascist state staged the real thing in 1927, sentencing De Gasperi to four years' imprisonment, of which he served sixteen months.

During the 1930s De Gasperi was employed in the Vatican library and during this period wrote a regular international column for the review *L'Illustrazione Vaticana*. Forcella's analysis of these articles reveals how much De Gasperi considered the principal political battle of his lifetime to be that between Christianity and Communism. In 1934 he rejoiced in the defeat of the Austrian Social Democrats who 'were de-Christianizing and fanaticizing the young of their country, and using political power to destroy the Family and suffocate the Faith'.[21] The German church, according to De Gasperi in 1937, was correct in preferring Nazism to Bolshevism.

Such attitudes were tempered from 1943 onwards by De Gasperi's genuine anti-Fascism and adherence to parliamentary democracy. However, his organic anti-Communism was never abandoned, but merely put in abeyance. During the struggle for liberation, when his own party was in its infancy and the Communists dominated the factories and the Resistance, De Gasperi saw the advantages and the necessity for cooperation. But he always considered this collaboration to be an unnatural state of affairs, a forced cohabitation, and not, as Togliatti would have liked, a lasting alliance.

De Gasperi rapidly became the undisputed leader of the Christian Democrats. Aloof, dignified and statesmanlike, he was able to steer a judicious middle course for the DC, resisting both conservative Vatican pressure and the more radical Christians on the left of his party. Unrivalled as a political tactician, his great political intuition was a lesson learned from his Popolare days: namely that in twentieth-century Italy a moderate and Catholic party would triumph not in the sphere of activism, but at the ballot-box.

Of course, electoral success depended greatly on the attitude of the church hierarchy. Pope Pius XII, who succeeded Pius XI in 1939, at first adopted an Augustinian attitude towards politics, maintaining that there was no possible convergence between the city of man and the city of God. As Galli has observed, since the city of man was always imperfect, Pius could conveniently argue that the particular degree of imperfection reached by the Nazi and Fascist regimes was of little importance.[22] The privileges granted to the Catholic church by Mussolini in the Lateran agreements of 1929 therefore far outweighed any temporal outrages perpetrated by the regime.

From 1943 onwards Pius had to change his mind. With Italy invaded and in ferment, the papacy was forced to reflect on future relations between church and state: above all the Lateran Pact had to be safeguarded. At first Pius XII thought in terms of a repetition of Franco's Spain – a strong, undemocratic Catholic regime. But as the power of the Resistance and the democratic parties grew, the Vatican moved cautiously, and not without misgivings, towards De Gasperi's Christian Democrats.

The support of the Vatican, dating from the liberation of Rome in the summer of 1944, transformed the DC from a talking-shop into a mass party. Catholic Action swung its more than two million members behind the new party. At the same time the parish clergy received instructions to speak out in favour of the DC. In a country where so much of popular culture and belief was indissolubly linked with the Catholic church, the Vatican's overt espousal of the Christian Democrat cause contributed enormously to De Gasperi's eventual primacy in Italian politics.[23]

So too did the organizations founded by the DC with the scope of entrenching the new party in Italian society. The most important of these was the Coldiretti, the Catholic association of peasant proprietors founded by Paolo Bonomi in October 1944. The association ably exploited the traditional hostility of the southern peasant to the state, and warned them that under a Communist regime all land would immediately be nationalized. At a time when the PCI's attitude to smallholders remained ambivalent, Bonomi set about recruiting with great energy; the Coldiretti had 349 sections by the end of 1944, and nearly 3,000 one year later.[24] The foundation of the ACLI, the Association of Christian Workers, also dates from this period. Conceived as a network of Catholic working men's clubs, the ACLI at first grew more slowly than the Coldiretti, but was to spread very rapidly from 1946 onwards.

At the same time as the DC was putting down these roots amongst peasants and workers, certain sections of the capitalist class were also beginning to look to it as the party of the future. This was far from a linear process. The Liberals, not the Popolari, had been the traditional party of big business, and the DC had yet to prove itself the true representative of capital. However, a few key figures had already decided to throw in their lot with De Gasperi. A significant example is Giuseppe Volpi, who combined in his person the three worlds of financial, industrial and agrarian capital. Venetian landowner, president since 1938 of the giant insurance company Assicurazioni Generali, holder of considerable assets in the chemical and electrical industries, Volpi had occupied leading positions in the Fascist state. He judiciously resigned these in the summer of 1943 and then, in 1944 and 1945, gave twenty million lire to various Resistance organizations. His contact with them was Pietro Mentasi, one of the 'new men' of the Christian Democrats. The DC was the party of the future, and Volpi was not alone in realizing it.[25]

The interplay of force and strategy between Allies, Communists and Christian Democrats had a number of critical consequences for the thirteen months between the return of Togliatti in March 1944 and the final liberation of the whole peninsula in April 1945. In the first place, in spite of the rapid growth of an armed Resistance movement dominated by the left-wing parties, socialist revolution was not on the agenda. The presence of the Allied armies imposed a veto that it would have been more than foolhardy to ignore. The British, twice bitten by partisan movements in Greece and Yugoslavia, grew more and not less intransigent about Italy as the war drew to a close. Only the most casual or propagandist of interpretations can afford to ignore this basic fact.

However, if the question under examination is not revolution but reform, the discourse becomes a very different one. If there is a single, recurrent, almost obsessive theme in the political history of post-war Italy, it is that of the need for reform and of the failure to achieve it. In this respect the years from 1943 to 1945, though adverse in so many ways, offered possibilities that were unrepeatable. The old order in Italian society had been shaken to its core by military defeat and subsequent invasion. The rural poor, goaded beyond restraint by the hardships of the war years, demanded an end to their centuries-old oppression and the reform of the whole system of land tenure and agrarian contracts. The mass strikes of the northern working class were not simply anti-Fascist and democratic in inspiration. They derived from the material conditions of the workers, their cold and hunger, but also their abject housing, their exploitation on the assembly lines, their powerlessness at their places of work. For them the fight against the Nazis and the struggle for a new dignity as human beings, both at home and in the factories, went hand in hand. Above all, many thousands of Italians joined the Resistance not just to liberate their country, but to transform it. They intended their sacrifice (for the mortality rate was extremely high) to be for a new Italy, founded on the principles of democracy and social justice. As the twenty-four-year-old Giaime Pintor wrote to his brother in November 1943, three days before being killed by a German mine: 'In no civilized nation today is the separation between vital possibilities and actual conditions so great: it is up to us to bridge this gap.'[26]

This immense desire and potential for reform remained almost entirely unrealized. The Allies were in no small part responsible for this. They sought out the most pliable and conservative of interlocutors, even if they were tainted with twenty years of support for Fascism. The British were not interested in reform, but in restoration. So too, naturally enough, were the king and Badoglio. Their coup of 25 July 1943, in spite of the subsequent disaster of 8 September, still left them in control of the whole of the southern half of Italy. The two-year existence of the Kingdom of the South insulated the Mezzogiorno from developments in the north, isolated the protests of the southern peasantry, ensured the continuity of the Fascist bureaucracy and suffocated the fragile forces of southern democracy.

However, some of the responsibility for the historic failures of this period must also lie with the left-wing parties, and the dominant PCI in particular. Concerned to establish their own legality, placing national unity above all else, unwilling to disobey Russian requests not to provoke the Allies in Italy and sceptical of their real bargaining power, the Communists chose to play a waiting game. To do so brought many fruits, but social reform was not to be amongst them.

Parties and Politics in the Summer of 1944

On 22 April 1944 representatives of the parties of the Committee of National Liberation, with the exception of the Action Party, followed Togliatti's suggestion, entered Badoglio's government and swore allegiance to the king. Togliatti himself became one of five ministers without portfolio. Some days earlier Victor Emanuel had been told by an Allied delegation that it would be better for the future of the monarchy if he gave way gracefully to his son Umberto. Victor Emanuel dutifully went on the radio to tell the nation that he would retire to private life (but not abdicate) on the liberation of Rome.

After the protracted German resistance at Monte Cassino, the Allied armies finally entered Rome on 4 June 1944. Rome, unlike nearly every other major Italian city, did not attempt an insurrection before the Allied arrival. A major reason for this was the terrible massacre which the Germans had carried out at the Ardeatine caves on 24 March 1944. After a brigade of the Roman urban partisans had blown up 32 German military police, the Germans shot 335 prisoners in reprisal. The Roman Resistance was not to recover from this blow.

With the liberation of Rome came a change of government. At first sight, this appeared a significant victory for the democratic parties. The CLN forced Umberto, who had become Lieutenant-General of the kingdom on his father's retirement, to put Ivanoe Bonomi in Badoglio's place as President of the Council of Ministers. Bonomi (not to be confused with Paolo Bonomi, the founder of the Coldiretti) was the president of the CLN and an old anti-Fascist liberal. Churchill was absolutely furious at this independent initiative of the CLN. Fuming against 'this extremely untrustworthy band of non-elected political comebacks', he obtained the specific consent of Stalin to replace the new government should the need arise.[27]

In reality, he had little to worry about. Bonomi was almost as hostile to innovation as were the British themselves. He realized the necessity of establishing clearly the main features of the new Italian state *before* the north was liberated and the Resistance could bring its weight to bear on the choices of central government. In this sense Bonomi was very much the precursor of De Gasperi.

Bonomi in fact presented a greater threat to reform than Badoglio had done. At least under Badoglio the principal adversary had consisted only in the traditional southern agrarian élites. The state apparatus had been non-existent. But with the liberation of the capital, Bonomi was able to set going again the extensive and cumbersome central administration, without changing its character or purging its personnel. The central bureaucracy, a formidable bulwark against future reform, was resurrected with hardly a murmur from the left-wing parties.[28] Instead they concentrated nearly all their attention on the institutional question, on the mechanics of the future choice between republic and monarchy. But in so doing they mistook form for substance, for the real restoration was going on under their very eyes.

At the time, neither the Socialists nor the Action Party managed to present any significant alternative to Communist Party strategy. The Socialists, mindful of how much the split of 1921 had weakened the working-class movement in the face of Fascism, were officially committed to unification with the PCI at the earliest opportunity. Former disasters thus led them to attenuate what criticisms they had of Communist policy. In the North they were very much the junior partner. Nenni knew that in the country as a whole the Socialists would probably command considerable electoral support, but the party was far more divided and disorganized than the Communists.[29]

The Action Party was strong in the armed Resistance but weak in Italian society. It too suffered greatly from internal division. Its left wing was acutely aware of the stakes that were being played for in these years. As one of them wrote, as early as February 1944: 'The liquidation of Fascism cannot stop at the visible manifestations of the regime, but must tackle, *from this moment onwards*, its economic and structural roots.'[30] But this was a minority opinion in a minority party. The Azionisti contributed greatly to the Resistance, but were quite unable to build any mass following in either city or countryside.

In general, the reasons for Communist hegemony of the left lie at least as much with their own attributes as with the failings of their opponents. The P CI benefited from their outstanding record of resistance during the Fascist era, but even more from being the Italian representatives of Communist Russia. Russia's charisma in this period cannot be over-stressed. Tens of thousands of Italian workers looked to Russia for their model and to the Red Army for the decisive contribution to the creation of Communism in their own country. Stalin was a working-class hero, Togliatti his trusted emissary in Italy.[31]

The Communists also gained greatly from their internal unity. There were differences. Many of the rank-and-file members of the party, especially the partisans, remained perplexed about the adoption of 'progressive de-mocracy' as their end aim. But they interpreted this as essentially a tactical move on Togliatti's part, to ensure the immediate legality of their party. They were convinced that once the Allied troops had left, the revolutionary goals of the P CI would once again be proclaimed. They were quite wrong, but this double-think, or *doppiezza*, as it came to be called, this confusion of strategy for tactics, was fundamental in reconciling class aims with the leadership's insistence on compromise.[32]

The Growth of the Resistance and the Winter Crisis of 1944

By the summer of 1944, according to the conservative figures of the Fascists, the numbers of men and women in the Resistance had grown to more than 82,000. Of these 25,000 were in Piedmont, 14,000 in Liguria,

21,600 in the Veneto, 17,000 in Emilia and Tuscany, and 5,000 in Lombardy. Very few of those who had been in the original partisan bands were still alive one year later, but the strength, fighting ability and organization of the Resistance developed by the month.

In some areas where the partisans had gained complete control, they set up their own republics: that of Carnia in the north-east, with 150,000 inhabitants, Montefiorino in the central Apennines with 50,000 inhabitants, Ossola in the extreme north with 70,000. In all of these the local CLN combined a return to formal democratic principles with cautious social and economic policies. There was much talk, for instance, of instituting progressive taxation of the rich, but very little was done. Part of the reason for this lay in the agrarian character of the liberated zones, where small peasant proprietors and traditional values predominated. But much of the caution was of Communist choice. Their emphasis on the preservation of national unity necessarily meant the postponement of a programme of social reform. The Communists argued that if a rich landowner was aiding the Resistance financially, he was not to be threatened with expropriation.[33]

At the beginning of August 1944, Tuscan partisans played a major role in liberating Florence from the Germans. After fierce fighting, all the city north of the Arno fell under the control of the Tuscan Committee of National Liberation (CTLN). This was the most independent initiative that the Resistance had so far taken, and led to an immediate and significant clash with the Allied authorities. On the question of appointments, the Allies denied that the Tuscan Committee had anything but consultative powers, and imposed their choice of prefect upon the city. For its part the Committee insisted that an old Socialist, Gaetano Pieraccini, became mayor. Eventually, in spite of their own original preference for a member of the Florentine aristocracy, the Allied Military Government acquiesced in the choice of Pieraccini. The confrontation had been largely symbolic, but was indicative of the real room for manoeuvre afforded the CLNAI by the increasing military strength of and popular backing for the Resistance.[34]

Behind the so-called Gothic Line of German fortifications which held the Allies at bay across central Italy, the partisan struggle was waged with great fury. Expectations of a general insurrection in the north were widespread. The Emilian landless labourers, traditionally in the forefront of Italian peasant protests, refused to consign their grain to the occupying forces and carried on a battle that was anti-German and anti-landlord at the same time.[35] Nazi reprisals in Emilia and Tuscany were of unspeakable savagery. The SS battalion commanded by Major Walter Reder exterminated whole villages. Reder's 'march of death' began on 12 August at Sant'Anna di Stazzema, where 560 men, women and children were massacred, and ended on 1 October at Marzabotto, which lost 1,830 of its population.[36]

In late August the Allies launched a major offensive against the Gothic Line, intending to liberate the Po valley and reach the Balkans before the Russians did. Their advance foundered in the face of tenacious German resistance and in the mud of the Romagna. By mid-October Kesselring felt confident enough to launch a major counter-offensive against the partisan brigades. All hopes of the imminent liberation of northern Italy now disappeared. The partisan republics fell one by one, and the Resistance faced its sternest test as German troops poured into the valleys and hills of Piedmont and the Veneto.

It was at this moment that General Alexander, Commander-in-Chief of the Allied forces, chose to announce by public radio message that no further Allied offensive could be expected until the spring and that the partisans should go to ground till then. Interpretations of this renowned and infelicitous message have varied considerably. Those most charitably disposed towards Alexander have argued that he did not intend to make life more difficult for the Resistance, and that he underestimated the psychological boost that his announcement would give the enemy. Those more suspicious of British intentions point to the international context as the key to Alexander's attitude. The Russians had recently allowed the 'internal opposition' of the Warsaw rising to be crushed by the Nazis and had actually prevented the Allies from sending provisions. The Allied action in Italy, according to this argument, was a subtle tit for tat. The Resistance would be liquidated during the winter and the Allies would then not have the political headache of a left-wing mass movement in the North.[37]

The more charitable interpretation is almost certainly closer to the truth, given that Alexander's motives were clearly military rather than political.[37] However, there can be no doubt as to the effect of his message. The Fascists of the Republic of Salò took new heart; on 16 December Mussolini appeared at the Teatro Lirico in Milan to make his first major speech for many months. The Fascist national guard, aided by German troops, began a systematic manhunt through the hills of the north, terrorizing the peasant populations who had sheltered the partisans and leaving no area untouched. Alexander's message had spoken of the need for the Resistance to 'go to ground'. The problem was that there was no ground left. In the woods of the Langhe, Fenoglio's Johnny, running for his life, encountered a young partisan half crazed with fear and convinced that his only salvation was to hide himself in some metal piping which ran under the nearest road. Johnny warned him of the dangers:

'Days and nights'll go by and there are probably all manner of foul creatures inside that pipe.'

'I don't care, just so long as there aren't any men.'

'But their trucks and artillery will drive right over you. The noise will drive you mad, force you out, and then they'll pick you off easy as pie.'

But he was absolutely convinced of being able to hold out, and crawled in head first while Johnny pushed at his feet until his whole body was hidden.[38]

The terrible winter of 1944–5 saw many members of the Resistance, both from its rank and file and from its upper echelons, lose their lives. The movement did not die because in general it had the great good sense to go down rather than up, to seek salvation in the plains rather than the highest mountains. Slipping through the enemy lines in small numbers, most partisan formations eventually regrouped in the low-lying hills near the great cities, or in the Po valley itself.

However, it was in the context of this bitter struggle for survival that in November 1944 a delegation from the CLNAI went to Rome to seek recognition and help from the Allies. The mission, originally of a technical and military nature, in fact became a political confrontation of decisive importance. It culminated in a document of 7 December which, along with that of 26 December between the Italian government and the CLNAI, became known as the Protocols of Rome. General H. Maitland Wilson, 'imposing and majestic as a proconsul' in Parri's description, agreed to grant the Resistance a subsidy of 160m lire per month, and to afford it 'maximum assistance'. The Allies did not formally recognize the CLNAI, but the partisans were accorded some respectability by becoming the executors of the orders of the Supreme Allied Command. In return, the Resistance leaders made many concessions. They promised that at the moment of liberation they would obey unquestioningly the Allied Commander-in-Chief and hand over to the Allied Military Government 'all authority and powers of local government previously assumed'. Partisan units were to be disbanded immediately and all arms consigned to the Allies. Finally, a regular Italian army officer, General Cadorna, was from thenceforth to be supreme military commander in the north.[39]

The Protocols of Rome marked the substantial political defeat of the Resistance. Even allowing for the adverse military situation and a pressing need for finance, it is difficult to argue that either the timing or the content of the agreement served the long-term interests of the CLNAI. The Allies had not recognized the CLNAI, except in a formal military sense, and certainly not as the government of the occupied North, which had been the consistent aim of the left wing of the Resistance. All possibility of negotiating from a position of strength at the moment of liberation now disappeared. As Quazza has argued, it would have been far better to have waited till the spring before opening negotiations of so vital a nature. At the time there were strong protests from within the partisan movement. The Socialist Sandro Pertini, future President of the Republic, denounced the Protocols as 'the subjection of the Resistance to British policy'. He was not wrong, for the agreement at Rome marked a significant moment in that long passage of events which rendered impotent the 'wind from the North'.[40]

The British were well satisfied. The Greek situation, which in this very period was reaching its climax, dominated and conditioned their thinking with regard to Italy. But in spite of the agreement reached in Rome, the Allies were still worried about what the liberation of the North would bring, and had no intention of encouraging the indiscriminate expansion of the Resistance. In February 1945, Allied headquarters ordered that 'supply [is] to be concentrated largely on non-warlike stores and arms [are] to be supplied on a selective basis for special tasks'.[41]

The negotiations between Allies and Resistance coincided with a governmental crisis which divided the left-wing parties and further weakened them at this critical moment. Bonomi resigned on 26 November, with the clear intention of returning to power with the moderate elements in his government reinforced. To make matters worse, he handed in his resignation not to the CLN, by whom he had been designated, but to Prince Umberto. His actions incensed the Socialists and Action Party, who refused him any further cooperation. Togliatti at first agreed with them, but then decided that a continued Communist presence in the government was more important than any other consideration. On 7 December, the same day as the Protocols of Rome were signed, the second Bonomi government came into being. It was to remain in power till the Liberation. The Socialists and the Action Party were excluded. Togliatti became one of two Vice-Presidents, and De Gasperi took over the key Ministry of Foreign Affairs.

On 26 December 1944, Bonomi and the representative of the CLNAI, the Communist Gian Carlo Pajetta, signed a clarifying document which complemented that already agreed with the Allies. Bonomi did not recognize the CLNAI as the government of the North, but only as the 'organ of the anti-Fascist parties in the territory occupied by the enemy'. The Italian government delegated to the northern committee the task of representing it in the North, and the CLNAI accepted this delegated power. As Candeloro has commented: 'Here too the line which took as its inspiration the continuity of the state prevailed over that which sought a renewal of the state in the course of the anti-Fascist war.'[42]

In this alarming climate of slowly advancing reaction, the Action Party tried to find a new common programme to prevent the total political disarming of the Resistance. On 30 November 1944 they addressed an open letter to the other parties of the Committees of National Liberation. In it they urged the strengthening of the CLNs as instruments of popular democracy and the institution of the CLNAI as a secret government of the North. The task of the CLNs, they said, was to restructure the state and society, and to use all the forces unleashed by the Resistance to destroy the continuity with the old order.[43]

The initiative fell on stony ground. The Communists welcomed the idea of reinforcing the CLNs, which had been part of their policy for some time, but refused to commit themselves to any immediate programme of action and warned that their major objective was increased collaboration between Communists, Socialists and Christian Democrats. The Socialists dismissed the proposals as 'populist' and 'interclassist'. As for the Christian Democrats, they warned that a government based on the CLNs would replace one dictatorship by another, because 'it would not be elected freely by the popular masses'.[44] The Action Party's proposals thus came to nothing, and the Resistance approached the moment of liberation with only one set of guidelines – those stipulated by the Allies at Rome.

The Situation in the South, 1944–5

Events in the South, though not as well known as those in the North, were hardly less dramatic. The southern urban and landed élites did not immediately choose the Christian Democrats as the party to represent them. The Monarchists and Liberals also laid strong claims for their support, as did the separatists in Sicily. The MIS, the Movement for Sicilian Independence, had been founded by Finocchiaro Aprile and appeared at first to be backed by the Allies, who appointed as mayor of Palermo a well-known separatist and large landowner, Lucio Tasca. The separatists' traditional appeal to 'end the exploitation of Sicily by the mainland' won many converts, not only amongst the great *latifondisti* but also among small peasant proprietors.[45]

However, the more the church threw its support clearly behind the DC, the more they came to dominate the politics of the South. In Sicily, the activities of Salvatore Aldisio, who became High Commissioner for the island in July 1944, greatly aided their cause. Aldisio, by skilful use of the wide powers attributed to him, successfully attracted *mafiosi* and landowners away from the separatists, and laid the basis for Christian Democrat supremacy in the island.[46]

Deprivation and repression continued to be the salient characteristics of the Kingdom of the South. On 19 October 1944 troops in Palermo opened fire and threw hand-grenades into a crowd consisting of striking municipal workers and women and children protesting against abuses in the rationing system. Thirty died and 150 were wounded. Further mortalities followed when the authorities tried to recall to arms those who had fled homewards on 8 September 1943. The erstwhile soldiers were supposed to present themselves complete with uniform, mess-tin, spoon and blanket. The Communists approved the attempt, but it was a ludicrous and tragic failure. For the southern lower classes the war was over and any attempt to restart it was generally interpreted as yet another assault by the state on one of the few basic rights they had − the right to exist. Protests were particularly violent in eastern Sicily. Some were led by Fascists or separatists, and at Chiaramonte Gulfi resulted in the lynching of two Communists. In others, probably the majority, local Communists and Socialists, in defiance of the official party line, were at the head of the protesters. At Ragusa a young Communist woman, Maria Occhipinti, was one of the leaders of the revolt and has left us a vivid and convincing defence of her actions. At Comiso an independent socialist republic was proclaimed, complete with its own lawcourt and egalitarian system of food distribution. Government troops quickly and bloodily suppressed these insurrections.[47]

In the countryside a vast and significant protest movement gathered strength in the autumn of 1944. The spontaneous land occupations and village republics gave way to more coordinated protest, which drew its inspiration from the legislation of the Communist Minister of Agriculture, Fausto Gullo. In a series of decrees from July 1944 onwards − the 'Gullo decrees' − he tried to alter the balance of class relations in the rural South. Like the good southern lawyer he was, Gullo presented his proposals as a series of contingent measures of no great significance. In actual fact, his was the only attempt made by any left-wing minister to push for reform at this critical moment in the formation of contemporary Italy.[48]

Gullo's legislation was of great complexity, but its principal aspects may be summarized as follows: the reform of agrarian contracts, so as to ensure that the peasants' share of the produce would always be at least 50 per cent; the granting of permission to take over all uncultivated or poorly cultivated land, provided that the peasants formed themselves into production cooperatives; the establishment of bonuses to encourage the peasants to consign their produce to the state food stores, which had been renamed the *'granai del popolo'* (the peoples' granaries); the proroguing of all agrarian contracts, so that landowners could not get rid of their tenants in the coming year; and, finally, the forbidding by law of any intermediaries between peasant and landowner, so as to rid the rural Mezzogiorno of middlemen like the infamous *gabellotti* in Sicily and the *mercanti di campagna* of Lazio.

This legislation clearly had Utopian elements in it, like the abolition of middlemen, which was unlikely to be realized short of a socialist revolution. However, it provoked a profound response among the southern peasantry, and for two reasons. First, the peasants were deeply legalistic and were accustomed to struggle for justice on the basis of ancient rights. For once, their unending struggles seemed to have been acknowledged by a state which was not their enemy, and which had incorporated some of their demands into its laws. Secondly, the insistence on the peasants organizing themselves into cooperatives and committees in order to benefit from the new laws provided the strongest possible incentive for them to take collective action. Gullo aimed to mobilize rather than demobilize the southern peasantry, to encourage them to link family strategies to collective action, to overcome their fatalism and isolation. It was this quality that gave his legislation a certain streak of genius.

At the same time as Gullo moved through government decrees, Giuseppe Di Vittorio, the Communist leader of the newly reconstituted national trade union organization, the CGIL (Confederazione Generale Italiana del Lavoro), promoted an active and far-sighted trade union strategy. The CGIL had been founded in June 1944 by the Pact of Rome, signed by Di Vittorio for the PCI, Achille Grandi for the DC and Emilio Canevari for the Socialists. The pact stressed the unity of all Italian workers, 'regardless of political opinions or religious faith', and was a significant victory for the policy of cooperation between the anti-Fascist parties.[49]

In the rural South in these months the CGIL concentrated its attention on the plight of wage labourers, and tried to impose two closely connected policies – the *imponibile di mano d'opera* and the system of *collocamento*. The *imponibile* was a contract which obliged the landowner to employ a certain number of labourers in strict proportion to the size of his estate. The system of *collocamento*, on the other hand, sought to regulate the methods by which the labourers were hired. The time-honoured ritual by which the landowners' *caporali* chose their workers in the piazza every morning was to be forbidden. Instead the union wanted the drawing up of official lists of the unemployed, with a system of priority worked out and controlled by the union, based on needs and experience. Thus while the *imponibile* tried to control how many labourers gained work, the *collocamento* intended to establish who they were and on what basis they were offered employment.[50]

The mobilization in the wake of the Gullo decrees and the CGIL's programme was the most extensive and remarkable that had ever been seen in the *latifondo* areas of the South, far exceeding the agitations that had occurred after the First World War. Protest action was to continue for more than three years. In this time the labour movement and the left-wing parties succeeded in linking with the southern peasantry and putting down roots in the South in a way they had never done before. In the past southern rural protest had all too often taken despairing forms of local *jacqueries* or extended banditry, and the working-class movement of the North and the Centre had remained blind and deaf to the class struggle in the South. The militancy of 1944–7 broke these traditions and linked the southern peasants of the *latifondo* areas with regional and national politics for the first time.

By the summer of 1945 a report from the PCI federation of Cosenza (Calabria) told the following story:

Less than a year ago the peasants were completely foreign to us, and to a great extent hostile. But now they are coming to us, trustingly, and in great numbers . . . This is due above all to the extensive action we have carried on in the province for the assigning of uncultivated land and over the question of agrarian contracts. Many peasant leagues have been founded and whereas in July 1944 they had 12,000 members, now they are about 40,000 strong.[51]

In the east of Calabria, as Cinanni reports, there was a seasonal calendar of struggles: in March and April, land occupations for the spring sowing; in June, struggles for the correct division between landlord and peasant of the produce of the land; in September and October, new land occupations for autumn sowing; in November and December, the mobilization of the appallingly paid women gatherers of olives and chestnuts.[52]

The traditional forces in the South opposed this renaissance of collective action with every means at their disposal. Nothing illustrates this better than the incident that took place on 20 September 1944 at Villalba in central Sicily. The village of Villalba was dominated by an old Mafia boss, Don Calò Vizzini, who had returned with the Allies in 1943. His nephew was mayor and secretary of the newly opened Christian Democrat section. In September 1944 the Communist leader, Girolamo Li Causi, and a local socialist, Michele Pantaleone, requested permission to hold a meeting in the local Piazza Madrice.

Don Calò gave permission for the meeting provided there was no talk of the land or the Mafia, and above all provided no peasant came to listen. Li Causi arrived with a small group of miners from Caltanisetta, and set up a table in the square. A professor called Cardamone spoke first, then Pantaleone, who attacked the separatists. After that it was the turn of Li Causi. Carlo Levi has described what happened next:

Li Causi is the most popular man in Sicily. His courage and his person have become legendary. The way he talks touches people's hearts. He speaks with simple words, with knowledge, with love. And so, on hearing his voice, the peasants of Villalba, terrified and hiding, felt an urge which drove them into the prohibited square. Li Causi began to talk to that little, unexpected crowd about the Miccichè estate, about the land, about the Mafia. The parish priest, brother of Don Calò, tried to drown Li Causi's voice by ringing the bells of his church. But the peasants listened and understood. 'He's right,' they said; 'blessed be the milk of the mother who suckled him, it's gospel truth what he is saying.' By so doing they were breaking a sense of time-honoured servitude, disobeying not just one order but order itself, challenging the laws of the powerful, destroying authority, despising and offending prestige. It was then that Don Calò, from the middle of the piazza, shouted 'It's all lies!' The sound of his cry acted like a signal. The *mafiosi* began to shoot.[53]

Fourteen people were wounded, including Li Causi, whom Pantaleone hoisted on to his shoulder and carried out of the square.

The landowners thus showed that they were ready to fight at all costs. Yet their opposition was not the only reason for the difficulties Gullo's reforms were to encounter. All the local Communists' courage could not mask the essential subordination of the southern struggle to Togliatti's overall strategy. As their own historian, Paolo Spriano, has revealingly admitted, the PCI leadership 'encouraged the movement but at the same time wished to avert a radicalization which could become an element of disturbance to the difficult governmental equilibrium'.[54] Such attitudes revealed once again that concord at a national level was the aim to which, in the last analysis, all others had to be sacrificed. But if agreement could be reached at Rome, it was not possible to postpone or smooth over the conflict in the South. If peasant land occupations were met with Mafia bullets, if the enforcement of the Gullo decrees was obstructed at every stage by the prefects and the landowners, then the choice was horribly clear. Either the movement was 'radicalized', to use Spriano's word, or it went to defeat. The political compromises of the PCI at Rome, its unwillingness to risk its alliance with the DC, spelt, as we shall see, disaster in the South.[55]

The National Insurrection in the North, April 1945

Conditions in the great northern cities continued to deteriorate throughout the harsh winter of 1944–5. With temperatures reaching $-11°C$, there was no fuel for heating, little chance of replacing windows blown out in the air raids and very severe food shortages. One correspondent from Milan (Camilla Cederna's mother) wrote to her relatives of her bedroom being 'my nightly fridge', and how she had to get dressed in order to go to bed.[56] There was nothing in the shops except one or two sprigs of yellowing parsley, a few roasted chestnuts and large amounts of a special Salò innovation, a sickly glue which went by the name of 'Roma' cheese. The black market flourished, but its prices were prohibitive for most of the working population. The large number of TB cases in the immediate post-war period is an indicator of the degree of malnutrition suffered during the eighteen months of German occupation.

In the factories there was constant fear that both men and machinery would be shipped off to Germany. On 16 June 1944, SS and blackshirt troops had surrounded four factories in Genoa and forced over 1,500 workers, still in their overalls and clogs, into waiting lorries.[57] A day earlier at Turin the word spread that no. 17 workshop at FIAT Mirafiori – aviation motors – was about to be dismantled and transferred to Germany. The whole workforce came out on strike and refused to go back, in spite of Valletta offering economic concessions if the machinery was allowed to leave Turin. On 22 June an Allied air raid completely destroyed no. 17 workshop. The FIAT workers thus paid a high price for their resistance, but at least the German plans had been thwarted.[58] Elsewhere, workers' opposition was much less successful, and significant amounts of machinery were transported to the comparative safety of the mountain valleys or to Germany itself.

By the winter of 1944–5 mass unemployment characterized the cities of the Industrial Triangle. Partly because of the lack of raw materials, and partly because of widespread sabotage, production and employment figures fell drastically in the first months of 1945. At FIAT Mirafiori the output of lorries dropped to ten per day, compared to an average seventy a day some two years previously. The official number of unemployed in Genoa in January 1945 was 11,871, but the Fascist authorities informed the Germans that the real figure was closer to 40,000.[59] Fear of deportation stopped most workers from registering as unemployed.

Workers' agitations, though continuous and highly damaging to war production, did not again reach the level of March 1944. The increasingly adverse conditions of the labour market were the major reason for this, but so too was the need to preserve unity in the Committees of National Liberation and meet the wishes of the Christian Democrats and the Liberals. In many workplaces the committees of agitation, based exclusively on the shopfloor, were subordinated to factory CLNs, uniting both management and workers.[60]

The urban terrorists of the GAP stepped up their activities in the last months of the war. They were flanked by the SAP (Squadre di Azione Patriottica), groups of ordinary workers who in their hours off work did what they could to prepare the ground for the national insurrection. By the beginning of 1945 the working-class quarters of Turin had become more or less no-go areas for the Fascists and the Germans.

German reprisals against the actions of the Gappisti were always prompt and ruthless. One of the most notorious was that of 9 August 1944, at Piazza Loreto in Milan. The GAP had blown up a German lorry in the city the previous day, with the consequence that fifteen political prisoners, ignorant of their fate, were taken at dawn from the prison of San Vittore and shot in the piazza. Their bodies were then left in the piazza for the whole day, exposed to the August heat, the flies and the morbid curiosity of passers-by.

With the coming of the spring of 1945, it became clear that the partisan movement had survived, depleted but intact, the terrible winter months. Its numbers now grew very rapidly, reaching over 100,000 by the last April of the war. As the Russians closed in on the Third Reich from the east, and the Americans and British from the west, the imminent liberation of northern Italy at last became a reality.

The exact nature of this liberation was the subject of profound disagreement between the Allies and the Resistance. When Ferruccio Parri went south to discuss the matter, he reported that the Allies intended the Germans to surrender to them and them alone. They strongly advised the partisans not to take independent action, and to devote their energies to salvaging as many electrical and industrial installations as possible from the Germans' 'scorched earth' policy. This was not all. At the end of the war, Allied plans were as follows: 'transfer and concentrate partisan units into thirty to forty camps; there, at Allied expense, assist them to rest, revive and re-clothe; consign eventual certificates and rewards in money; collect up all arms. This period to last some three to four weeks, after which the partisans will be sent home.'[61]

The partisans themselves had somewhat different ideas. They agreed with the Allies over the need to safeguard Italy's industrial heritage, but refused to accept a secondary role in the liberation of the North. The Communists and the Action Party in particular pressed ahead with plans for insurrection in the major cities. In so doing, they did not want to counterpose their authority to that of the Allies, or to place social revolution on the agenda. Their aim was rather to demonstrate the real power of the Resistance, and to end German occupation in a way that would not easily be forgotten. On 25 February 1945 Togliatti cabled Longo in the North: 'We must fight for the total annihilation of the German troops in Italy, and against every attempt to hold back the insurrection by sham negotiations for a capitulation.'[62] The insurrection of April 1945 represented the final victory over the temptations of military *attendismo*.

On 1 April 1945 the Allied troops in Italy launched their last offensive against the German lines, aiming to break through to the northern plain as soon as possible. But German resistance was tenacious and on 13 April General Mark Clark warned the partisans that 'the moment for action has not arrived'. However, three days earlier the Communists had already issued their famous direction no. 16, in which their militants were ordered to prepare for insurrectionary action. Between 24 and 26 April, with the Allies still in Emilia, the cities of Genoa, Turin and Milan rose against the Nazis and the Fascists.

German forces in the North were still substantially intact, even if their morale had reached a low ebb. Their commanders planned to retreat towards the alpine valleys of the north-east – Carinthia, Tyrol and the Trentino – where they would be joined by the remnants of the other German armies. Their priority, therefore, was to withdraw from the industrial North as fast and as painlessly as possible, leaving a trail of sabotage and destruction in their wake.

At Genoa, when it became clear that the German General von Meinhold was preparing to evacuate the city, the local CLN decided to bring forward the date of the insurrection and not to await the arrival of the partisans from the mountains. Von Meinhold had some 15,000 troops under his command, and over fifty pieces of artillery deployed on the hills overlooking the city. On the morning of 24 April the insurrection began. Three thousand members of the SAP, aided by many thousands of ordinary citizens, rushed the main public buildings. All telephone lines, water and electricity supplies to the German barracks were immediately cut off, and railway communications in Liguria reduced to chaos. The Germans suddenly found themselves prisoners in the city. Throughout the 24th they attempted to break through the partisan lines at various points, but were forced back after fierce street fighting. That evening von Meinhold threatened to bombard the city into submission unless his troops were allowed to leave unmolested. The CLN refused to compromise.

On the morning of the 25th, the insurgents took the Sturla barracks and stormed the heights of Granarolo, where the radio station was situated. Fighting continued all day, and at 7.30 p.m. von Meinhold surrendered unconditionally. The insurrection did not end there because the German forces concentrated around the port were ordered to resist to the last. It was only on the 26th, after the partisan brigades from the mountains had arrived in force, that the port was taken and its installations saved from destruction.[63]

At Turin, a huge strike on 18 April, involving most of the working population of the city, formed the prelude to insurrection. The local Committee of National Liberation fixed the date of the uprising for 26 April, and the evening before the workers stayed behind in the factories to guard them against possible sabotage. Unfortunately, the intervention of the partisan militias from the surrounding hills — fixed for the morning of 26 April — failed to materialize. The head of the British military mission in Piedmont, Colonel John Stevens, on hearing that many thousands of German troops under General Schlemmer were concentrating to the west of the city, decided it would be better to postpone the insurrection. He circularized this information to the partisan units, throwing many of them into confusion and delaying their arrival in the city.

The population of Turin, and the factory workers in particular, thus had to assume the full brunt of the fighting. On the 26th the battle raged around the factories occupied by the workers — Lancia, Spa, Grandi Motori, FIAT Mirafiori, Ferriere and many others. The workers resisted with determination, and on the 27th the SAP counter-attacked, mopping up the remnants of the Fascist forces, and forcing the Germans to concentrate in the heart of the city, around Piazza Statuto. That night the residues of the German garrison broke through the partisan cordon and reached the *autostrada* heading east. On the 28th the bulk of the partisan brigades arrived in the city. To the west, General Schlemmer abandoned plans to enter Turin and eventually surrendered to Allied troops on 3 May.[64]

Events in Milan were far less dramatic. German resistance was weaker than in the other two cities, and the insurrection proved a comparatively easy task. On the evening of 24 April the 3rd Garibaldi Brigade stormed a Fascist barracks on the outskirts of the city and at the same time fighting began in and around the major factories. These were soon safeguarded from destruction, though only after a fierce struggle at Pirelli. The insurgents gradually took over the city, starting at the periphery and working their way inwards. They coordinated their actions with those of the partisans, and by 26 April Milan was free.

Mussolini had been in the city at the beginning of the insurrection. On 25 April, through the intervention of Cardinal Schuster, he obtained a meeting with the leaders of the CLN. He still hoped to reach some sort of terms, but the CLN was adamant in favour of unconditional surrender. Utterly demoralized, Mussolini left Milan and fled towards the Swiss frontier. By this time he was little more than a prisoner in the hands of his SS escort. Disguised as a German soldier, he joined a motorized column heading northwards, but on the morning of 27 April their path was blocked at Dongo by the 52nd Garibaldi Brigade. The partisans insisted on searching the column before allowing it to proceed; Mussolini was recognized and taken prisoner. The Resistance leaders, ignoring the explicit request of the Allied commanders, immediately ordered Mussolini to be shot. His body, that of his mistress Claretta Petacci, and those of other Fascist leaders, were then hung upside down in Piazza Loreto, the same Milanese piazza where the Germans had left exposed the bodies of fifteen political prisoners the previous summer. After some hours Riccardo Lombardi, the new prefect of Milan, ordered an end to the macabre spectacle.

By 1 May the whole of northern Italy was free. The popular and insurrectional character of the Liberation, which left an indelible impression in the memories of those who had participated, was welcomed in most quarters. In others it caused acute anxiety. There was a terrible settling of scores, with perhaps as many as 12–15,000 people being shot in the immediate aftermath of the Liberation.[65] As for the northern industrialists, they had hoped for a painless transition of power from the Fascists to the Anglo-American authorities. Instead they found their factories occupied, the workers armed, and a period of up to ten days between the insurrection and the arrival of the Allies. Some of the more heavily compromised of them did not dare to wait, and fled to Switzerland. Over the next few months the fear of imminent social revolution remained very strong in capitalist circles. Rocco Piaggio, a leading Genoese businessman, told the Allies in June 1945 that he hoped they would assume the control of the major Italian firms, including his own: 'With some form of Allied ownership and with the corresponding political protection, it would be possible to save something of Italian industry. If not, Piaggio foresaw not only expropriation *per se* but the total and definitive ruin of his business as a result of state intervention.'[66]

The Allies too were worried. In military terms their task had been made easier by the urban insurrections, but they did not welcome the degree of independence with which the Italians had acted. For a politician like Macmillan, mindful of the origins of Fascism, the situation in northern Italy seemed to contain all the ingredients for a totalitarian takeover – mass unemployment, inflation, and the widespread diffusion of arms. Only this time the revolutionary colours would be red, not black.[67]

These fears proved unfounded. All the events, conflicts and decisions of the previous months – Churchill's meeting with Stalin in 1944, the example of Greece, Communist Party strategy, the Protocols of Rome – conditioned and determined the choices open to the Resistance in its hour of glory. On 27 April Ernesto Rossi, in the Action Party newspaper *L'Italia Libera*, called for the CLNs to be developed as 'organs of the new democracy', and for them to form a central consultative assembly to control the government's actions at Rome.[68] But there was little response to this last desperate attempt to find an alternative to what had been agreed in Rome the previous winter. The Communists were quite unprepared to risk a confrontation with the Allies at this stage. For them, the Action Party's proposal, if acted upon, might have put in jeopardy the future independence of the country, the strategy of national unity and their own existence as a party. It might also have damaged the interests of the Soviet Union. At a time when the Allies were in a position to move much further into Germany, Austria and Czechoslovakia than had been agreed upon, the last thing the Russians needed was provocative action by one of the Communist parties in the West.

What is more, the arguments of the Communists found very wide acceptance at the base, amongst the workers who had taken up arms to defend their factories and drive out the Nazis and Fascists. Those who still dreamed of revolution sought refuge in that *doppiezza* to which reference has already been made. The revolution, they argued, had not been abandoned but merely postponed. Once the Allies had moved out and the tanks of the Red Army were ready to move in, the countdown to revolution would begin. And until that time 'progressive democracy' could serve as an excellent tactic, 'a Trojan horse within the bourgeois citadel', as one Milanese worker put it at the time.[69]

The Allies, therefore, had little difficulty in carrying through the programme agreed upon by the Protocols of Rome. They were greeted with genuine gratitude and joy by the population of the North, and were impressed by the degree of order and normality already established before their arrival. Riccardo Lombardi, the new prefect of Milan and member of the Action Party, scored a minor personal victory when he refused to swear allegiance to the Allied military authorities and maintained he was responsible only to the Committee of Liberation. He wrote later that 'relations between ourselves and the Allies were based on mutual respect, never on subordination or servility'.[70] But this was more illusion than reality. The Resistance was never servile in the face of the Allies, but there can be no doubting its fundamental subordination.

Allied liaison officers organized the disarming of the partisan brigades as swiftly as possible. The official British military historian, C. R. S. Harris, has described how this took place:

Every encouragement was to be given to partisans to hold ceremonial stand-down parades, which should appear as being held not by Allied orders, but at the partisans' own wishes . . . The parades were to be conducted with as much ceremony as possible and the commander of the nearest Allied formation was to be present, to take the salute and to supervise the collection of arms. The handing in of arms was to be accompanied, where convenient, by the presentation of 'Certificates of Merit'.[71]

Thereafter heavy sentences were inflicted by Allied military courts on anyone found in illegal possession of arms. In spite of the official cooperation of all the CLN parties, there is no doubt that many weapons were hidden away at this time. In August 1945 Allied soldiers made over fifty raids in Piedmont alone, and on half of them weapons were discovered. By

September they had collected a staggering amount of weaponry, testimony to the real military force of the Resistance at the moment of liberation: 215,000 rifles, 12,000 sub-machine-guns, 5,000 machine-guns, 760 anti-tank weapons, 217 cannon, twelve armoured cars, but only 5,000 pistols.[72]

Though the prefects appointed by the Resistance were not replaced, the Allies made the weight of their authority felt very clearly. They were not prepared to tolerate any initiatives designed to build up the CLNs as alternative sources of power. At the end of July 1945 the Allied regional governor of Piedmont wrote to the president of the Piedmontese CLN warning him that no Committee of Liberation 'has the slightest degree of executive or administrative authority'.[73] At the same time the Allies tried to ensure that economic conditions did not force the northern working class to take to the streets in protest. They agreed to an immediate veto on all sackings and to wages being paid regularly (one third by the employer, two thirds by the government), even to those workers who had nothing to do. This shrewd Allied combination of swift disarming of the partisans, absolute military authority and economic guarantees for the working class, served as an effective antidote to the inebriation of Liberation.[74]

The Italian Resistance, if one does not count last-minute adherents, probably numbered some 100,000 active members, and many thousands of others who helped in some way. Of these 35,000 died, 21,000 were mutilated and 9,000 were deported to Germany – casualty figures far higher than those incurred in regular warfare. After the war the British Hewitt Report came to the conclusion that 'without these partisan victories there would have been no Allied victory in Italy so swift, so overwhelming or so inexpensive'.[75]

The cost in human suffering had been very high. The refusal to adopt the policy of *attendismo* or to limit the Resistance to minor acts of sabotage had meant incurring the full brunt of repression and German reprisals, of which the massacre of the Ardeatine caves and the extermination of the villagers of Marzabotto were only the two most terrible examples. At the end of Eric Newby's *Love and War in the Apennines* (based, as with Hood's book, on his experience as an escaped prisoner of war), the peasant Francesco says, 'We've seen some things here, my friends, we and our children. Let's hope that it will never be like that again.'[76]

The sacrifices of the Resistance were not made in vain. At a time when the Italians were very widely despised and discredited for their acceptance and support of Mussolini's regime, the partisans did much to salvage Italy's tarnished image and give the Italians new faith in themselves. Furthermore, they succeeded in creating a lasting tradition of anti-Fascism. This legacy, while frequently abused by official rhetoric, was of fundamental importance during at least two periods in the life of the Republic, in the early sixties and again in the early seventies.

However, much of what the partisans fought for remained unrealized. Paolo Spriano, the eminent Communist historian, has written that the national insurrection was 'the moment of the great rupture with the past, of a break which opened the way to the active participation of the popular masses in the further political and social development of the country; it was a revolutionary democratic impulse of an unmistakable and lasting character'.[77] But this judgement corresponds more closely to what the partisans *wanted* the insurrection to be rather than what it actually *was*. The Resistance's aspirations to a more direct and socially just form of democracy and state, aspirations shared by most Socialist, Communist and Action Party members alike, were not to be realized. For all their heroism, the forces fighting for change in the years 1943–5 did not succeed in making any such profound break with the past.

Chapter 3

The Post-war Settlement, 1945–8

---

*I*N JUNE 1945, after eight weeks of the sort of protracted inter-party haggling which was to become the hallmark of the formation of a new Italian government, Ferruccio Parri, member of the Action Party and deputy commander of the combined Resistance forces, became Prime Minister. With a government headed by the much loved partisan 'Maurizio', as Parri had been known in the years of clandestinity, it seemed as if the many hopes of the period 1943–5 would yet be fulfilled. The Resistance had come to power. In actual fact, the gap between appearance and reality could hardly have been greater. The next three years, with first Parri and then De Gasperi as Prime Minister, far from witnessing the triumph of the ideals of the Resistance, saw the gradual development on both a national and international level of two vast opposing fronts: the one having its focal point in the employing classes, the Christian Democrats and the United States; the other centred on the working-class movement, the Communists and Russia. This conflict of interests and ideologies, at first masked in Italy by the continued cooperation of the anti-Fascist parties, reached dramatic and decisive heights by the time of the spring elections of 1948. The result of these elections, which were the culmination of the struggles of the previous five years, determined for over a decade the nature of the Italian Republic. 'Do you remember that 18th April,' runs the first verse of a once popular Communist song, 'of the time you voted Christian Democrat, without thinking of tomorrow, or the ruination of your youth?'

The Capitalist Front

The employing classes, particularly of the North, emerged from the war in some trepidation. At first, as we have seen, they thought that only indefinite Allied occupation would save them from social revolution. But quite quickly, as the sincerity of Communist orders for restraint became apparent, they regained their self-confidence. Unlike their French counterparts, the Italian industrialists did not have to answer at the end of the war for a prolonged period of collaboration with the Nazis. Some were more compromised than others, but most had played that careful double-game to which reference has already been made – keeping in with the Germans while supplying information to the Allies and even funds to the partisans. They were also able to benefit from the fact that most sources of energy and industrial plant had been saved from destruction in the last few months of the war.[1]

It would be wrong to present the Italian employers as a totally homogeneous group. Quite apart from the southern landowners, who were a law unto themselves, great differences existed between various sectors of the employing classes. Perhaps the most important was that between large employers and small ones; the structure of Italian industry was characterized on the one hand by a whole mass of small firms and artisan shops, and on the other by a quite extraordinary concentration of capital and production.

The three dominant sectors of Italian industry at this time were hydroelectricity, textiles and food. The first was capital intensive and of recent formation, while the other two were quite the opposite, being both labour intensive and at a low technological level. Those sectors later to be of supreme importance – steel, cars and chemicals – were still in the second rank. In 1938, for example, Italy produced only 50,000 cars.

In the post-war years a gradual division emerged between a conservative majority and progressive minority in Italian industry. The dominant wing, represented primarily by the electrical industry, and by the producers of cement and sugar, were safely ensconced in monopoly conditions of production, and placed financial speculation before investments or productivity. The minority, concentrated in engineering (FIAT, RIV, Olivetti), in rubber (Pirelli) and in steel (Finsider), knew that their survival in a competitive market depended on an extensive programme of reconstruction and rationalization.[2]

However, when confronted with labour and the state, divergences such as these took second place to a fundamental unity of aims. Through the Confindustria (the Italian equivalent of the CBI), which accorded extensive powers to its president, Angelo Costa, the employers presented their objectives with unwavering coherence. Basically, they demanded two essentials from any post-war settlement: that the employer regained absolute freedom of control at the workplace; and that the capitalist class as a whole would not be constrained by state planning introduced by the left-wing parties.

At the workplace Confindustria demanded for its members the right to make redundant as much or as little of their workforce as they chose. In April 1945 the CLNAI had made all sackings illegal and the Allies, as we have seen, supported this move through fear of street riots by armed unemployed workers. The industrialists argued that such an exceptional situation should end immediately, for no serious reconstruction could take place while they were required to pay unproductive labour. Similarly, they would not tolerate any schemes of workers' participation or control. 'Dangerous' and novel institutions like the factory CLN, which in some cases had taken over factories where management had fled for fear of reprisals, were to be wound up as soon as possible. Angelo Costa had very clear ideas on the whole subject: 'A good mechanic or turner could give me advice in his area of specialization, but I cannot see what he has to say to me on financial matters . . . And then there is a fundamental factor: the principle of authority which must perforce be respected . . . Now the concept of workers' control threatens that principle of authority; it is the superior who must control the inferior, never the inferior who controls the superior.'[3] Finally, while the return of free trade unionism in the factories could hardly be prevented, every effort was to be made to limit trade union power at plant level. Confindustria demanded national agreements which would fix rigidly, from the centre, all wages and differentials, and would exclude the possibility of local or factory agitations.

As for the state, it had traditionally been viewed by Italian entrepreneurs with some hostility, as being an institution which had not represented their interests in a sufficiently explicit manner, and for which they were not responsible.[4] Now that one of its principal functions had ceased to be the forcible restraint of working-class demands, the suspicions re-surfaced. Many of Italy's leading employers who had made their fortunes under the state-controlled Fascist economy underwent a dramatic conversion to neo-liberalism. The free play of market forces became the order of the day. As long as state intervention had the connotations of socialist planning – and the contemporary bogy was as much Attlee's Britain as Stalin's Russia – the employers wanted nothing to do with it. The textile baron Gaetano Marzotto made this point forcibly when interviewed in 1946:

DE MARIA: Do you think that if the state established a priori the quantity and type of goods to be produced it would be committing a grave error?
MARZOTTO: But that would be Russian Bolshevism! Can the state bureaucrats do something more than he who knows his own business? . . . The state

should stick to administering justice properly, to some semblance of national defence, to education, and to law and order (which up to now it has been unable to obtain). Once it does these things satisfactorily, it has performed its duties.[5]

Marzotto's minimalist view of the state was particular to the textile barons, who wanted to be free of any restraints at a time when opportunities for exporting abounded.[6] Many employers, especially on the conservative wing, did not want socialist planning, but did want the state to continue to protect their privileged positions on the market. However, all of them, conservative and progressive, urban and rural, shared Marzotto's concern for law and order. Summary partisan justice, illegal land occupations and violent demonstrations of the unemployed all had to be eliminated before peaceful reconstruction could begin.

In substance, then, the employers aimed at re-acquiring that freedom of action and control which had been severely compromised by the new-found autonomy of the working-class movement. The political vehicle to which they increasingly turned for the realization of their aims was the Christian Democrat Party. The DC, it is true, was not the organic party of the Italian bourgeoisie. Even though the Milanese industrialist, Enrico Falck, had been amongst the DC's founding members, many big businessmen looked initially to the Liberal Party (PLI) as the traditional political representative of their interests. The Liberals, however, never managed to adapt to the changed conditions of post-war Italy. Most of their leaders, of whom the philosopher Benedetto Croce was the most renowned, had seen their heyday before the advent of Fascism and thought it sufficient to advocate a return to the liberalism of the first decades of the century. They failed to understand the need for a mass party or the necessity of political propaganda which would reach a wider audience than the bourgeoisie of the major cities. As such they remained a party of restricted élites, and could offer the employing class no electoral guarantees.[7]

The Christian Democrats were exactly the opposite. The essence of their political practice was that interclassism which is the prerequisite for any modern conservative party. Through the support of the church and its lay organization, Azione Cattolica, the Christian Democrats hoped to reach believers of all social classes. Through the Coldiretti and ACLI, collateral organizations which offered efficient insurance, social assistance and legal services, they successfully established a mass base amongst peasant proprietors and Catholic workers. And through their general propaganda they made a special appeal to what one of their leaders, Guido Gonella, called in 1946 the 'heroic and famished middle class':[8] artisans, shopkeepers, white-collar workers, state employees, small businessmen – the urban *ceti medi* of

Italian society. Previously the backbone of Mussolini's support, they had been disoriented by the sudden destruction of the Fascist values of nation and party. While some had profited from the black market, many of them had been badly hit by war inflation. Lower civil servants in the provinces, for example, were in grave financial difficulty. In February 1945, the Allied regional commissioner for the Abruzzi and the Marches reported as follows:

We are here to tidy up the aftermaths of battle and to prepare the Italian authorities to take over from us as soon as possible. But it is not fair when officials on whom we must rely to help us are reduced to penury, and are, in fact, often half-starved. Honest officials – there are some – are now reduced to selling their few remaining personal possessions in order to live, as all their savings are gone. The not-so-honest ones are forced to implement their income by the very means that we claim we are here to abolish. How can they do otherwise?[9]

The great majority of the *ceti medi*, both urban and rural, were deeply antagonistic to Communism or Socialism, which they took to mean the deprivation of their individuality and a levelling downwards in the social scale. What the Christian Democrats had to say appealed much more. The D C reaffirmed Catholic morality, promised to safeguard property, to 'respect and protect every healthy initiative in the field of production and work', to limit the power of the great monopolies and to protect consumers as well as producers.[10]

The party also made a special appeal to family values. During the war families had come under terrible strain as the men had gone away to fight and then to prisoner-of-war camps, women and young girls in the southern cities had, as we have seen, been forced into prostitution and children from the industrial North were separated from their mothers and sent into the countryside to escape the bombardments.[11] The Italian family, as Father A. Oddone wrote in early 1946 in *La Civiltà Cattolica*, had 'undergone deplorable ruination and profanation'.[12] The church and the Christian Democrats therefore put great emphasis on helping families overcome the traumas of the war. Catholic organizations, especially the parish networks, offered a variety of services: direct economic aid, inquiries involving paperwork and contacts to try and reunite separated families, charitable assistance to children.

In April 1946, at the first congress of the D C, Gonella made a stirring and revealing appeal to his party comrades to fight in the public sphere for the future of the Christian family:

An invisible and silent atomic bomb has destroyed the family unit. The family, if it is not already dispersed, is more likely to unite around the radio, which is a deafening and dulling window on the world, than around the domestic hearth . . . It is an illusion, and the women present should understand this better than the men, to try and defend the family from inside the family. The state with its wars will tear away from you your husband or your brother, and atheist education or the corruption of the streets will steal the soul of your child. The family is a fortress which cannot be defended from inside the fortress. Certainly we must build up its internal defences, but we must also issue forth and fight the enemy in open battle.[13]

This attention to family problems cut across class lines and held a special appeal for women. For most women above the age of twenty-five, the desire to return to family life was, as Gloria Chianese has written, 'much stronger than aspirations for radical change, which were felt only by those sectors of women who in some way had participated in moments of [political] struggle'.[14] When it came to the first post-war elections the D C was to reap the benefits of such attitudes, and their own emphases on 'restoring the family to health and morality'.[15]

These, then, were the bases upon which the Christian Democrats were able to build a vast area of consent in Italian society. The social block that supported them was, as we shall see, not free from internal contrasts; but the main tenets of De Gasperi's programme — Catholic morality, representative democracy, anti-Communism, commitment to the capitalist system and a special attention to the *ceti medi* and the family — provided the party with its cohesive force.

De Gasperi's programme came under attack on more than one occasion. The Vatican, for instance, would have preferred a more explicitly right-wing party which did not reject the possibility of a return to authoritarian Catholicism, or at the very least a presidential solution to the constitutional question. And, from the opposite quarter, the left wing of the D C, led by Giuseppe Dossetti, envisaged the D C as an evangelical, reforming and anti-capitalist force in Italian society.[16] De Gasperi, quintessentially a man of the centre, rejected both extremes. The party, he argued, had to remain firmly democratic or it would lose all influence in the North. It had to accept the alliance with left-wing forces as necessary, but not desirable. Above all, it had to realize that its real interests lay in the unequivocal support of the employing class. In a famous speech of April 1947, just as the left was being expelled from the government, De Gasperi told the Council of Ministers:

There is in Italy a fourth party other than the Christian Democrats, Communists and Socialists, which is capable of paralysing and rendering vain every effort by organizing the sabotage of the national loan, the flight of capital, inflation and the diffusion of scandal campaigns. Experience has taught me that Italy cannot be governed today unless we bring into the government, in one form or another, the representatives of this fourth party, which disposes of the nation's wealth and economic power.[17]

On an international plane the 'fourth party' was greatly aided by the rapid decline of the British in the Mediterranean, their replacement by the Americans, and the beginning of the Cold War. Britain had been all but bankrupted by the war; the terrible winter conditions of the early part of 1947 paralysed the country for many weeks, and in February of that year the Labour government informed the United States that it could no longer pay for its troops in Greece or continue aid to Turkey.

As Britain's influence in the Mediterranean waned, so the period of uneasy collaboration between the Great Powers came to an end. Harry Truman, President of the United States since Roosevelt's death in April 1945, had long nurtured the desire to take an explicit stand against what he considered to be Russia's remorseless desire for expansion. The need to replace the British in Greece gave him the pretext for which he had been waiting. In March 1947 Truman outlined his plans for the containment of the Soviet menace, a policy that immediately became known as the Truman Doctrine. The United States was to intervene on a global level against Russian expansionism, primarily by economic means but by political and military ones if all else failed: 'it must be the policy of the United States to support free peoples who are resisting attempted subjugation by armed minorities or by outside pressures ... The seeds of totalitarian regimes are nurtured by misery and want. They spread and grow in the evil soil of poverty and strife. They reach their full growth when the hope of a people for a better life has died. We must keep that hope alive.'[18] Congress was asked to grant $400 million immediately for direct aid to Greece and Turkey.

A few months later George Marshall, the US Secretary of State, announced the beginning of the European Recovery Program (ERP), better known as the Marshall Plan. The reasons behind America's decision to pump aid into Europe were far from purely ideological. At the end of the war three quarters of the world's invested capital and two thirds of its industrial capacity were concentrated in the United States. Unless the American economy could find trading partners and sufficient outlets for its products, it risked a return to the conditions of the Great Depression. Europe was a market of immense dimensions, but its economy and thus its buying capacity had suffered greatly from the ravages of the war. It was therefore essential for America to help in the reconstruction of Europe, thereby creating an international capitalist trading structure in which the American economy could thrive. By the end of August 1947 preliminary estimates had been made: the European Recovery Program was to last four years and receive $29 billion in American assistance.[19]

All this was of the most profound significance for Italy. As early as June 1945 the then acting Secretary of State, Joseph Grew, had written: 'Our objective is to strengthen Italy economically and politically so that truly democratic elements of the country can withstand the forces that threaten to sweep them into a new totalitarianism.'[20] In 1946 the United States, through UNRRA (the United Nations Rehabilitation and Relief Administration), had already been providing the lion's share of Italy's imports. The joint committee created to administer the UNRRA funds in Italy had as its co-chairmen Spurgeon Keeny, the American chief of mission, and Lodovico Montini, a close collaborator of De Gasperi and brother of the future Pope Paul VI. However, American aid to Italy in the early post-war years was dogged by policy disagreements and rivalries between different departments and organizations. Keeny, for instance, who was a New Deal Democrat and favoured cautious planning of the Italian economy and Keynesian spending programmes, ran foul of the liberalism of William Clayton, Assistant Secretary of State, who closed down UNRRA at the end of 1946. It was only to be with the full flowering of the Marshall Plan that the American executive acquired a clearer sense of purpose.[21]

The details of American intervention in Italy, which reached a crescendo with the elections of 1948, will emerge in the course of this chapter. Suffice it to say here that American attitudes and actions, if not free from internal contradictions, strengthened immensely the Italian capitalist class in its battles on the home front. For nearly a century the image of the United States had exercised the most potent influence upon the Italians. They had emigrated there in their tens of thousands. Some had become very rich, nearly all had managed to send money home and even those who returned penniless to the deep South after the crash of 1929 (and whom Carlo Levi met in the village of Gargano) could flash their gold teeth as enduring mementoes of American influence. During the Allied invasion of 1943–5, Italy had had its first direct experience of the American way of life – violent in many ways, but also incandescent with its bonhomie, benevolence and jazz.[21a] Between 1945 and 1948 the myth of America acquired new and even more impressive hues. The New World was voluntarily to pour its gold into the coffers of the Old. Only the United States could and would offer Italy the aid necessary for recovery from the devastations of the war.

The Working-class Movement

By the end of the war working-class living conditions, both in town and country, had deteriorated drastically. In the cities bombardment had left many hundreds of thousands of Italians homeless and basic foodstuffs were in very short supply. In the countryside self-sufficient peasant proprietors and sharecroppers had less to complain of, but landless labourers had often been reduced to penury. The situation in the rural areas was also aggravated by the temporary over-population caused by mass emigration from the cities.

Inflation had rapidly eaten away urban workers' real wages. In national terms the cost of living had multiplied nearly twenty-three times between 1938 and 1945 while wages had gone up by only half that amount. These national statistics mask regional details that are even more dramatic. The southern landless labourers were the poorest section of the national workforce. They fared badly even in comparison with their northern counterparts: in 1947 a rural labourer in the province of Foggia (Puglia) earned little more than half the wage of his counterpart in the province of Milan.

The plight of the unemployed was still worse. At the end of the war tens of thousands of men who had been incarcerated in German work camps or who had been prisoners of war began to return home. They joined all those already in Italy (teenagers, ex-partisans, demobbed Fascists and regular army soldiers) in a desperate search for jobs that did not exist. A bitter conflict of interest arose between this mass of unemployed men and the many thousands of women who had worked during the war and wanted to hold on to their jobs.[22] By 1947 1.6 million Italians were unemployed; in Puglia a third of the agricultural workforce could find no work.

Angelo Fumagalli, in 1945 a foundry worker at the Ercole Marelli factory in the Milanese industrial suburb of Sesto San Giovanni, has left this testimony of working-class life in the North at this time:

Our wages were never enough; it was like being trapped in a narrow cage. If one day you bought something for ten lire, the next day it cost twelve, and then fifteen. To have any room to breathe we had to take action. Strikes began easily in those days: there was no need for leafletting, you just held an assembly, the word went round and off you went . . . The first big battle in the factory was over the canteen, and it wasn't an easy one to win. The bosses didn't want to give in because the canteen was a sort of hidden wage. The prefect had to intervene in the end. For a meal in the canteen you paid thirteen lire: eight for a quarter litre of wine because that wasn't compulsory, two lire for the first course and three for the second – cheese, *mortadella* (Bologna sausage) or omelette. It cost nothing compared to normal prices. Nearly everything was still rationed; oil, butter and sugar were at black-market prices. We used a lot of lard because it was the one product that hadn't disappeared. Meat once a week, on Saturday . . . Our way of life was very simple. We went to work by foot or on bicycle, and after work to the club or back home. Saturday evening or Sunday to the cinema. But we were lucky to have work at all. The unemployed arrived from all over the place; there were demonstrations every day in front of the factories. A whole army wanted to get in, but the gates were too narrow.[23]

If conditions were hard, they were tempered, at least in the North, by the sense of power and position of strength which the workers had acquired during the Resistance. With the internal commissions or the factory CLN playing a predominant part in the running of the factories, substantial changes took place: piecework was abandoned as damaging to the unity of the workforce, rhythms of production were modified to suit shop-floor demands, many leading industrialists, like Valletta at FIAT or Giuseppe Rosini at Ansaldo Fossati, were declared *personae non gratae* and subject to commissions of inquiry. The workers' desire to purge (*epurare*) undesirable elements went beyond mere accusations of collaboration with the Fascists to embrace charges that were of a purely class nature. In the major factories there were many demands to get rid of foremen or managers who were 'undesirables' or 'disliked by the masses'. A typical accusation was that levelled against a *caporeparto* (foreman) at Ansaldo Fossati at Genoa: in the eyes of the workforce he was guilty of 'servile submission to capitalist directives tending to the hateful exploitation of the workers'.[24]

However, it would be a mistake to write of a widespread revolutionary consciousness among Italian workers in this period. Attitudes prevalent in the North were not necessarily to be found in the Centre or the South. The Resistance had been a movement of immense importance in Italian history, but by force of events it had remained a northern phenomenon and a minority movement with regard to the population as a whole. While certain sections of the rural poor (the sharecroppers of Tuscany and Umbria, the landless labourers of Puglia and Sicily) were to rival the northern working class in militancy, vast strata of the working population (the white-collar workers of Rome, the underemployed and unemployed of Naples, the peasantry of the Veneto and much of the South) remained hostile or indifferent to a political appeal based on class lines.

Even amongst the highly politicized industrial proletariat of the northern cities it is difficult to identify a generalized revolutionary consciousness. No spontaneous attempts to create alternative organs of political power, such as soviets or workers' councils, are to be found in this period. While many workers looked forward to a new era of socialism (one old militant from La Spezia recalled that 'in the evenings, when we went to meetings, we talked of how to construct the socialist society, of communism and of nothing else'),[25] the revolution itself was seen as an essentially *external* event, postponed to an indeterminate future. In other words, when socialism came it would come not from inside the workers' movement, but from outside, from the USSR. The experience of the Second World War had accustomed the northern proletariat to seeing Italy's future as decided by conflicts that took place on a world scale. National liberation had come in the first instance from the armies of the Allies. Class liberation would be brought by Stalin's tanks.[26]

In addition, many workers remembered and rejected the 'maximalism' of 1918–20. At that time the socialist leaders had talked incessantly of the imminence of revolution, but had provided the working class with no concrete revolutionary strategy. In January 1946 Antonio Negro, a former revolutionary syndicalist who had joined the Communist Party and become the secretary of the Genoese Camera di Lavoro (Chamber of Labour), warned against history repeating itself: 'It doesn't take much to say: let's socialize all industry and if the money isn't here, we'll get it from where we can, i.e. from those speculators who've got rich from Fascism and the war . . . But it's time to discard the false phrases of street oratory which so damaged us in the years after the First World War. After 1918–19 we managed to chatter our way into Fascism. Is that the way we want to go again?'[27]

Without wishing to distort a complex reality, it is perhaps possible to suggest that there were two dominant elements in working-class consciousness at this time: a desire to reconstruct after the terrible damages of the war years *and* a widespread expectation of social and economic reform. Whether in the agrarian South or in the industrial North, the two themes of recovery and reform went hand in hand. In this context it is interesting to quote the testimony of an anarchist worker from Turin, whom we might expect to have had quite different ideas: 'We'd understood that we couldn't change all we wanted to, and so what we wanted to change was something small but substantial (for example, reduction of wage differentials, the introduction of a proper health system, decent pensions . . .). We thought: if we don't get these things now, we'll never get them. The bosses at that time were afraid of worse things to come, and the workers had more resolution and enthusiasm.'[28] The desire for a shift in the balance of forces between labour and capital, a shift that could open up new perspectives for the working-class movement, was widely felt.

These aspirations found a far less secure political outlet than the Christian Democrats offered the employing classes. On paper the strategy of the Italian Communist Party seemed to respond perfectly to the needs of the working-class movement. The Communists continued to argue that revolution was an impossibility (Allied troops remained stationed in the North until the signing of the peace treaty in 1947), but that reform was not. By maintaining the wartime coalition of the three mass parties (PCI, DC, PSIUP), the Communists hoped it would be possible to carry through an extensive reform programme. As Mauro Scoccimaro, one of the PCI leaders, explained in April 1945, 'progressive democracy' would be achieved by an alliance of class forces which would see the *ceti medi* and a part of the bourgeoisie line up with the working class. The reactionary big bourgeoisie would be isolated, the working class would assume the direction of the reform movement, and the possibility of a return to Fascism would be destroyed from the outset.[29]

As in the war years, so too in 1945–8, it would seem wide of the mark to accuse the Communists of failing to make a revolution. The possibility of revolution was made remote both by objective conditions (the continuing Allied military presence followed by the development of the Truman Doctrine), and by subjective ones (the lack of a widespread revolutionary consciousness). But the chance of achieving significant advances for the working-class movement certainly existed and was to a great extent squandered. If in the period 1943–5 the PCI postponed all social and political reform in the name of national unity and liberation, in the next three years they erred in making the political arena, and in particular their alliance with the DC, the exclusive terrain on which reform would be achieved.

Togliatti was convinced, and his conviction lies at the origins of what can be called an enduring fallacy of PCI strategy, that the Christian Democrats were potentially a progressive force in Italian society. When Camilla Ravera expressed doubts on the subject, he said to her: 'But no, believe me, De Gasperi and I agree on a host of things, from agrarian reform to trade union unity. You'll see, we'll achieve a lot together.'[30] This was not only to misjudge De Gasperi, but to mistake the actual nature of the Christian Democrats. Between 1945 and 1947, while the Communists made concession after concession to keep the alliance intact, the Christian Democrats became ever more firmly the representatives of those forces in Italian society for whom the concept of progressive democracy was total anathema. As Pavone has pointed out, the Communist error is at least partially explained by their commitment, for far too long, to pre-Fascist political models; the Christian Democrats were mistaken for their more ambivalent predecessors, the Popular Party.[31]

The primacy accorded by Togliatti to inter-party agreements, a political practice typical of the years of the Third International, made caution and electoralism the hallmarks of Communist action. Restraint had constantly to be exercised to reassure the Christian Democrats of Communist intentions; numerical gains at election were seen as the principal instrument for shifting the balance of power in Parliament and thus in the country.

As a result, the most powerful weapon in the hands of the left, working-class militancy, was virtually discarded in the major political battles of the time. As Foa has written, 'the constant characteristic of the whole reconstruction period was the separation of a political programme from working-class struggle. Militancy was confined to issues concerning the immediate needs of the workers, while the transformation of the balance of class forces was entrusted to the future parliament and deprived of any instruments other than those of pure propaganda. There was no organic programme of mass political struggle.'³² The Christian Democrats, as we shall see, made the most of their unexpected liberty of action. They procrastinated where they could, diluted where they could not, and waited for the moment when they could govern alone.

In later years many of the PCI leaders – Gullo, Longo, Pietro Secchia and others – admitted their mistake. Gullo recalled that 'we were all under the impression that the wind was blowing in our direction, and that therefore what was not achieved today, would be achieved tomorrow'. Secchia (albeit emarginated from the party by this time) was more specific, criticizing Togliatti 'for too often putting the problem in terms of insurrection or acquiescence. Instead there existed a third way, which was that of making braver use of pressure from the rank and file, for all the risks that entailed.'³³

The PCI also proved far less successful than the DC at attracting to its programme the middle sections of Italian society. Their task was, of course, very much more arduous. The political culture of the Italian *ceti medi* had been a Fascist one, and the Communist offer to them of an alliance with the working class against monopoly capitalism was not one that made much sense on a day-to-day level. In some areas, as among the sharecroppers and artisans of central Italy, the PCI made strenuous efforts and, as we shall see, was rewarded with notable success. In others, as in their slowness in building an organization of peasant proprietors to counteract that of the Coldiretti, the Communists lost the initiative to the DC. Everywhere, though, they faced a seemingly insoluble dilemma, and one which was to dog them in the following decades: either they diluted the socialist content of their programme and thus attracted electoral support amongst shop-keepers, small employers, etc.; or they refused to compromise and risked leaving the working class in isolation and their alliance strategy in tatters.³⁴

At the time, the PCI leadership could seek comfort in the extraordinary growth of their party. By the end of 1945 the PCI had no less than 1,760,000 members. The Gramscian strategy of the permeation of civil society could now become a reality. In August 1947 the Communist leadership sent a confidential circular to all its cadres: 'Every federation or section committee must have exact details of all the organizations existing in its territory: leagues, cooperatives, ex-servicemen's associations, youth groups, women's and widows' associations, sporting, recreational and cultural clubs, circles, games rooms, etc.; collect together, control and direct the comrades who are active in these organizations or who frequent their meeting-places. Give them precise tasks.'³⁵

Communist Party sections became key points of reference in the daily lives of families in many working-class communities. Carlo Ciceri, the first post-war secretary of the PCI at Sesto San Giovanni, recalled later: 'At that time the party at Sesto was everything. Instead of going to the local government offices, people came to us, at the Rondò, for housing, for jobs, for welfare assistance.'[36]

The Communists, like the D C, organized their own collateral organizations. The most significant of these was probably U DI (Unione delle Donne Italiane), which had its own journal, *Noi Donne*, and a vast membership in the post-war period. The P CI tried to counter the D C's activism on the family question with its own, socialist version of the relationship between family and collectivity. The model was that of the Soviet proletarian family, in which, according to the propaganda of the time, there existed a rigid morality, many children, and a new respect for the rights of women; families of equal economic status cooperated for the greater collective good. U DI organized its second congress in 1947 around the slogan, 'For a happy family, for peace and for work'.[37]

However, it was much more difficult for the Communists than for the Christian Democrats to present themselves as the champions of the family. Their opponents, like Father R. Lombardi, whose religious broadcasts earned him the title of 'God's microphone', took great pleasure in pointing out the contradictions in Communist theory on the family. Was a cursory glance at the Communist Manifesto, asked Father Lombardi, not sufficient to discover the real intentions of the Communists? Had not Marx and Engels advocated the abolition of the family? Was the P CI not in favour of divorce, 'the first and gravest step in the dissolution of the family'? In a Communist society, concluded Father Lombardi, 'the children born from free love would be adopted by the collectivity, brought up in communes and educated as future producers for the type of work chosen for them by the authorities'.[38]

If we pass from the Communists to the other major force on the left, the Socialists of Pietro Nenni, we are immediately struck by their substantial subordination to the P CI. Although in the first election after the war the Socialists actually polled more votes than the Communists, they were never able in this period to establish their own political autonomy. There were many reasons for this. With the world increasingly divided in two, it was the P CI which was the official representative of the socialist bloc, and as long as the PSIUP remained pro-Soviet it had little choice but to follow in the Communist wake. In addition, the Socialists were acutely aware of how costly the political splits of the period 1920–22 had been. Nenni never tired of reiterating the importance of the unity of the proletariat, so much so that throughout 1945 and early 1946 there was a serious possibility of Communists and Socialists fusing into a single party.

Nenni himself lacked the qualities of a great political leader. By 1945 he was already a historic figure, renowned for his leadership of the insurrectionary 'Red Week' in 1914, and for his role in the Spanish Civil War. But he lacked the strategic ability of either De Gasperi or Togliatti, whom he greatly admired, and he was unable to hold his party together as a 'broad church' of socialist opinion. At this time he also exalted the 'workerist' nature of the party at the expense of a more careful attitude towards the middle classes. In the party congress of 1946 he launched into an unfortunate tirade against 'the socialism of the *ceti medi* [which is] Bonapartism, Fascism, Hitlerism, all movements inspired by the myth of the nation. The socialism of the *ceti medi* is bourgeois.'[39]

There was certainly a great deal more open and free discussion in the PSIUP than in the PCI, with its Stalinist hierarchies of command and its political orthodoxy. At the twenty-fourth congress of the PSIUP in April 1946 there were no less than three major opposition groups and the leadership itself was far from unanimous. Undoubtedly the most significant of the oppositions was that of Giuseppe Saragat and the group Critica Sociale. At the congress Saragat spoke out in the name of a 'humanist Marxism', but his real frame of reference was European social democracy and the old reformist tradition of Italian socialism, which had had its charismatic leader in Filippo Turati. Saragat warned that the PSIUP had acquired a 'workerist rigidity' which was limiting its appeal and denying it a necessary 'breath of universality'. He said that Nenni's insistence on unity had rendered him 'blind and deaf to the problem of autonomy'. Western socialism had to avoid being subaltern to an authoritarian and undemocratic Soviet model. Looking back, it is very difficult to extricate the possible validity of what Saragat had to say from the later squalid history of the Italian Social Democrats. Yet there can be little doubt that there was both the space and the need within the Italian political spectrum for a force that was anti-Stalinist, social democratic and explicitly reformist.[40]

The debate within the PSIUP was thus a vigorous one, but it became so vigorous that the party was left with too little energy for the outside world. The historian Gaetano Arfé, a member of the youth section of the party after the war, recalls how it 'exhausted itself in a permanent and dilettanteish debate on the great themes of the time: the unity of the anti-Fascist forces as a cage for the working class, the relationship between reform and revolution, democracy and socialism, Stalinism and Trotskyism . . . [Meanwhile] the Communists, and their youth above all, were busy constructing the channels through which to take over the Socialist inheritance of social forces, institutions and methods.'[41]

Apart from the two major political parties, the trade union was the other fundamental vehicle of the working-class movement. The CGIL, as we have seen, united Communist, Socialist and Christian Democrat elements. During its first congress, at Naples in January 1945, the delegates put forward a whole series of radical demands: the nationalization of all the major industries, the establishment of workers' participation in them, the breaking up of the *latifondi*, and the equalizing of wages on a national scale.

The CGIL soon boasted a leader of quite exceptional talent and humanity, Giuseppe Di Vittorio. Born in 1892 of poor peasant stock at Cerignola in Puglia, Di Vittorio began work while still only a child, after his father had died at the age of thirty-three. As a young man he joined the anarcho-syndicalists and was a renowned leader of the landless labourers in Puglia. Later he became a Communist, and fought in the Spanish Civil War. At the Naples Congress part of Di Vittorio's speech was almost the exact opposite of the remarks (reported above) of Angelo Costa, the president of the Confindustria: 'Those who think that all possible wisdom is concentrated only in directors' and governmental offices are starting from an anti-democratic and Fascist principle, by which all wisdom can only come from above ... We (on the other hand) have great faith in the creative and organizational capacities of the popular masses.'[42]

Unfortunately, not even Di Vittorio's charisma and obvious sincerity could mask the reality of the situation. Togliatti had backed the creation of a single union with the laudable intention of strengthening the unity of the working class and drawing the DC into collaborating actively in the defence of workers' interests. In this way, the Communists hoped to accentuate the progressive and popular character of the DC. What actually happened was rather different. In spite of trade union membership being predominantly Communist, each of the three political parties was accorded equal status in the executive organs of the CGIL. Decisions were taken on the basis of mutual consent, and time and again the lowest common denominator – usually the Christian Democrat position – became the official policy of the union. The CGIL thus lacked the necessary autonomy from the political parties and all too often became the extension, on a trade union level, of the alliance strategy of the PCI.

Finally, on an international level, the Soviet Union was as much the point of reference for the working-class movement as the United States was for the capitalist class. Photos of Stalin, cut out from the newspapers, were stuck on to walls and machinery in most factories in Italy. 'Baffone' (walrus moustache), the avenger, would soon be on the move again. But the myth of imminent liberation by the Russians could not hold its own for long against the promise of immediate material salvation from the Americans; for whereas the one was pure illusion, the other was rapidly becoming a reality.

Indeed, in at least two respects the Stalinist model was positively harmful. The belief in socialist revolution as something that was brought from outside deprived the Italian working class of any chance of evolving a revolutionary strategy that was based on their own resources. Under Communist leadership political action was split into three distinct spheres: the immediate day-to-day battles waged by the workers against cold, hunger and penury; the struggle for progressive democracy waged by the party in Parliament; and the revolution itself, an impossibility until Stalin moved. The Communists called themselves a revolutionary party (as did the Socialists), but no overall plan ever linked working people's own activity and organization to the eventual winning of state power.

In the second place, the uncritical and adulatory acceptance of Stalinist dictatorship did little to further the cause of socialism in Italy. Both the Communists and the great majority of the Socialists maintained with blind faith (at least in public) that the Soviet state system represented the realization of socialism. However, enough evidence was already circulating from various sources to cast serious doubts on this assertion. For many members of the *ceti medi*, and not only them, Stalinist Russia appeared instead as a totalitarian regime which eliminated its political opponents, massacred the peasantry and ferociously controlled the private lives of its citizens. If this was socialism, they wanted nothing to do with it. Not by chance did the Christian Democrats put the word *Libertas* at the centre of their political vocabulary and on the crusaders' shield which was the electoral symbol of their party. All Togliatti's attempts to build a 'historic bloc' of social forces around the working class foundered against this ideological barrier. As long as Stalinism was synonymous with socialism, vast numbers of ordinary Italians continued to prefer the capitalist system, for all its injustice.

From the above analysis, the inferiority of the working-class movement compared to the capitalist front emerges unequivocally. In all major respects, in clarity of aims, political leadership and international resources, the two sides were unevenly matched. None the less the employers' victory was not easily obtained, nor was the working-class movement left totally empty-handed. At the time, De Gasperi and Togliatti were recognized as opponents of equal stature. As Stuart Hughes has written: 'Similar in mental agility and even in physical appearance, the leaders of the two great parties faced each other – like two Jesuits, as one of their colleagues put it – with quiet deadliness across the ministerial council table.'[43] We must now chart the unfolding of this extraordinary battle during the various governments of the period, and in the various sectors of Italian life.

Parri and De Gasperi, June 1945 to May 1946

a. POLITICS AND INSTITUTIONS

Ferruccio Parri's government lasted little over five months, from June to November 1945. In that time it gave the constant impression of being unable to cope. One of the major problems was Parri himself. He was courageous, honest and widely respected, but he was no prime minister. Instead of establishing a clear order of priorities, Parri allowed himself to be overwhelmed day and night by administrative minutiae and by ceaseless delegations of partisans and others. In between he would snatch a few hours' sleep on the camp-bed which he had moved into his office in the Viminale. Fearless and decisive as a partisan leader, Parri proved tentative in the extreme as head of a supposedly innovatory government. When Togliatti urged him to initiate immediate agrarian reform, Parri refused on the dubious grounds that the Allies, who remained in control of the North until the end of 1945, would intervene by force.[44]

Behind Parri's personal failure lay the deficiencies of his own party and the left in general. The Action Party continued to be paralysed by the internal division between its socialist wing, led by Emilio Lussu, and the moderate liberal democrats of Ugo La Malfa. Parri himself favoured the moderates. The party also suffered from a shortage of cadres because many of its leading militants, having played a prominent part in the Resistance, chose to return to private life in 1945.

All the party's difficulties and contradictions exploded at the party congress of February 1946. Lussu gained a Pyrrhic victory as Parri, La Malfa and most of the moderates abandoned the congress and the party. Those who remained never recovered from this split, and the party dissolved some months later. Over the next thirty years the Azionisti, with their particular qualities of intellectual integrity and personal courage, were to enrich the ranks of most of the other Italian parties, from the Republicans to the revolutionary left.

The Communists and Socialists did little to remedy the Action Party's weakness. In the Parri government the left (PCI, PSIUP and Pd'A) had a technical majority over the Christian Democrats and Liberals, but it was not one they put to good use. The Socialists had wanted Nenni as President of the Council and regarded Parri as an unsatisfactory and temporary alternative. The Communists flirted for some weeks with the idea of using popular pressure to secure social and institutional reforms, but soon reverted to their favoured objective of alliance with the D C. Both left-wing parties were convinced that as soon as elections were held they would emerge as the majority force in the country. They were therefore prepared to make substantial concessions to the DC and the Liberals to ensure that elections were not unduly delayed. Left-wing ministers behaved with great restraint in order to avoid alienating their Christian Democrat colleagues.

All this played straight into De Gasperi's hands. Sensing the ductility of the left, he gained concessions where he could while still managing to postpone the date of general elections. As Minister for Foreign Affairs he was in frequent touch with the Allies, who intervened to express their desire for local elections to precede national ones. The reasoning was simple: the longer the 'molten lava of 1945', to use Lombardi's expression, had time to cool, the more chance the moderates had.[45] De Gasperi threatened a governmental crisis unless his viewpoint was accepted. General elections were finally fixed for the spring of 1946 – later than in any other country that had been under Nazi occupation.

The most significant casualties of this period were the Committees of National Liberation. The Action Party, and to a lesser extent the Communists, still hoped that the committees could serve as elements of direct democracy in the political structure of the new state. The Liberals, the DC and the Allies would hear nothing of it. At the end of May the Liberal secretary Venerio Cattani warned that democracy could be based only on the 'free, direct and secret vote of every citizen individually considered'.[46] Faced with this opposition Communists and Azionisti quietly abandoned the CLNs, allowing them to become mere consultative organs as a prelude to their eventual disappearance. On 1 September Parri himself delivered what amounted to their funeral oration at the first congress of the CLNAI: 'it is evident that the CLNs must respect the limits of their responsibilities; the responsibility for decision-making belongs to the state and its organs and is not divisible.'[47]

In November 1945 the Liberals decided that the time was ripe to get rid of Parri. They announced their withdrawal from the government, De Gaspari supported them, and Parri had no option but to resign, complaining bitterly of the *coup d'état* that had been organized against him. Neither Communists nor Socialists greatly lamented his departure, for both were already thinking of replacing him with Alcide De Gasperi. It was part of De Gasperi's political genius that he continued to inspire the respect and even the faith of the left, while consistently denying them their objectives. On 10 December he became President of the Council of Ministers, with Nenni as Vice-President, the socialist Giuseppe Romita as Minister of the Interior and Togliatti as Minister of Justice.

The left-wing leaders had backed De Gasperi in the hope of securing a pre-election period undisturbed by further political crises. De Gasperi, however, responded over the next few months with a couple of nasty surprises. He insisted that the question of whether Italy was to remain a monarchy or become a republic should be decided by a referendum and not by the Constituent Assembly. And he demanded that the new Assembly should not have legislative powers, but limit its function simply to the drawing-up of a new constitution. Both these positions were contrary to a specific agreement signed between the major political parties in June 1944.

De Gasperi's motives were fairly clear. He favoured a referendum not because he wanted the monarchy to triumph but because he wished to hide the division that existed between the D C's electorate, who were strongly monarchist, and the party's cadres, who were mainly republican. In an Assembly this division could not be masked, the electorate would feel betrayed and the party risked permanent damage. On the second question, that of the Assembly's powers, De Gasperi frequently stated his fear of the Assembly becoming a 'Convention' on the French revolutionary model, with Nenni or Togliatti as its President. With the political situation still uncertain, De Gasperi preferred all decisions to be taken in the Council of Ministers, where he was the supreme master of the calculated veto, the quiet threat and every form of delaying tactic.

The left were more incensed about the proposed demotion of the Constituent Assembly than about the referendum, for they had high hopes of controlling the majority in the Assembly even if the D C emerged as the largest single party. However, faced with De Gasperi's intransigence, they backed down on both questions. On 25 February 1946 Nenni listed in his notebooks the pressures that were to force him to concede: fear of a ministerial crisis and of violent demonstrations against the delays and diatribes of the government, the risk of monarchist and Fascist provocations, the likelihood of an Allied intervention.[48]

Parallel with these clamorous setbacks for the left, an insidious but even more important institutional process was taking place. During both the Parri and De Gasperi governments the traditional state structure and administration inherited from Fascism was being quietly consolidated. Bonomi had already taken important steps in this direction without encountering serious opposition. In 1945–6, apart from the half-hearted support of the CLNs, the Communists and Socialists showed little interest in the matter. Their undervaluation of its importance derived in part from a mistaken belief in the neutrality of state institutions. For them the major problem was to win power at the elections, not to try to reform the bureaucracy.

As a result, in the years 1945–7 none of the apparatus of the state was called into question. No attempt was made to reform the central administration at Rome, in spite of it having greatly increased in size under Mussolini. No serious critique was made of the many semi-independent special agencies created by Fascism for the purposes of social assistance or intervention in the economy. Finally, no moves were taken to alter the structure or recruiting patterns of the judiciary, even though Togliatti was Minister of Justice throughout this period.

If the apparatus itself went untouched, some attempt was made to purge its personnel. This brings us to the whole question of *epurazione*, which proved so burning an issue at the time. Those who had fought in the Resistance or suffered under Fascism maintained, with some justification, that the activists of the Fascist regime should not go unpunished. On the other hand, to purge the administration of active Fascists meant more or less to close it down, since membership of the Fascist Party had been obligatory for all civil servants. The initial activity of the *epurazione* commissions managed to combine the worst of both worlds, for they tended to incriminate rank and file Fascists while leaving many of its leading exponents untouched. This mode of procedure incensed the mass base of the Fascist administration, who now feared for their livelihood at a time of mass unemployment.

Epurazione proved a disastrous failure. The judiciary itself went untouched, and duly proceeded to discharge as many cases as it dared. Other essential sectors of the state's personnel were also unaffected. In 1960 it was calculated that sixty-two out of sixty-four prefects (the central government's principal representatives in the provinces) had been functionaries under Fascism. So too had all 135 police chiefs and their 139 deputies. Only five of these last had in any way contributed to the Resistance.[49]

Leading Fascists were acquitted on outrageous grounds. Paolo Orano, chief of Mussolini's staff during the march on Rome, member of the Fascist Grand Council, under-secretary at the Ministry of the Interior, went free because the court was unable to establish the 'causal link' between his actions and the destruction of democracy. Renato Ricci was found not guilty because the Salò national guard of which he was commander-in-chief was defined as nothing more than an internal police force.[50]

In June 1946 Togliatti drafted an amnesty that marked the end of *epurazione*. Proposed with humane intentions, the amnesty met with very heavy criticisms. Under its provisions even Fascist torturers escaped justice. A most unfortunate and grotesque distinction was drawn between 'ordinary' tortures and 'tortures that were particularly atrocious'. Using this formula the courts were able to pardon the following crimes: the multiple rape of a woman partisan; a partisan tied to a roof who was punched and kicked like a punch-bag; electric torture on the genitals applied through a field telephone. On this last case the Corte di Cassazione (Italy's highest court at that time) ruled that the tortures 'took place only for intimidatory purposes and not through bestial insensibility'.[51]

At the end of the day the only effective *epurazione* was that carried out by Christian Democrat ministers against those partisans and anti-Fascists who had entered the state administration immediately after the national insurrection. Slowly but surely De Gasperi replaced the prefects appointed by the CLNAI with career civil servants of his own choice. And in 1947–8 Mario Scelba, the new Christian Democrat Minister of the Interior, swiftly purged the police of the significant number of partisans who had joined the force in April 1945.

b. ECONOMIC AND SOCIAL PROBLEMS

If we turn from political and institutional problems to economic and social ones, the first year after the war was marked by relatively stable prices but a very low level of production. Industrial production in 1945 was less than a third that of 1938.

Italy has always suffered from the absence of those natural products – coal, iron, petrol – which are at the basis of industrial development. She thus depends heavily on the importation of raw materials and seeks to cover her costs by intensive exporting. In 1945 there was unanimous agreement on the need to abandon the artificial Fascist pattern of autarky (self-sufficiency) in favour of liberalizing commercial relations and obtaining those imports necessary to get the Italian economy on the move again.

However, while the employers, as we have seen, had a coherent strategy which equated a free-trade economy with the full development of their freedoms as capitalists, the left-wing parties showed a great deal of confusion both in theory and in practice. The Communists and Socialists never seemed able to offer any real alternatives in the economic field. Political and institutional problems, such as elections, inter-party relations, the debate on the Constitution, always took precedence. The left combined a lack of economic preparation with certain dogmas taken from contemporary Soviet economists about productive capital being strangled by financial capital and the imminence of another major world crisis. This poverty of ideas and analysis resulted in a substantial subordination to the neo-liberalism of the employers. Except in purely verbal terms, Communists and Socialists hardly ever succeeded in linking day-to-day problems of reconstruction with the overall objective of a planned economy.

In August 1945 the PCI organized a conference on economic problems. Togliatti, in an important intervention, stressed the role of private industry, made no reference to nationalizations, dismissed the idea of a national economic plan as being Utopian, and urged a fight to make the rich pay their taxes: 'the struggle, therefore, is not against capitalism in general, but against particular forms of theft, of speculation and of corruption'. Daneo has correctly criticized Togliatti's speech as being 'a call for a daily *Realpolitik* in which reconstruction was reduced to the prudent democratic administration of the economy on nineteenth-century liberal lines'.[52]

Such a programme was quite insufficient. The Communist Mauro

Scoccimarro was Minister of Finance in this period, but the real power lay elsewhere, at the Treasury, which remained firmly in Christian Democrat or Liberal hands. The left managed to ensure that food subsidies continued, but none of the other pressing needs of the moment evoked a planned intervention from the government's economic ministries. Housing presented the most glaring example of this failure. In the cities of more than 50,000 inhabitants an estimated 1,200,000 dwellings had been destroyed in the war. During the whole of 1946 only 15,063 habitations were built or reconstructed.[53]

The presence of the left-wing parties in the government in no way gave them control over the direction of the economy. Quite the opposite. A process of spontaneous private reconstruction took place, with reaccumulation directed by that restricted number of very powerful companies which controlled so much of Italy's wealth and industrial production. This business élite, though it continued to profess a horror of state intervention, kept close links with leading personnel of the state bureaucracy and in particular with the Bank of Italy, then in the capable hands of Luigi Einaudi.

The way in which this élite operated, and the inadequacy of its opponents, is best demonstrated by an examination of the two principal monetary problems of the time – exchange controls and the revaluation of the lire.

In the first two years after the war Italian textiles enjoyed a remarkable export boom. The leading firms in the sector demanded free rein to use and sell the foreign currency they acquired without being subject to government control. In March 1946, at a time when a member of the Action Party was Minister of Commerce, a Socialist was Minister of Industry, and a Communist Minister of Finance, the government decided to give the exporters most of what they wanted. They were awarded a prize of 125 lire for every dollar, and 50 per cent of all the foreign currency they gained could be sold freely on the exchange markets.

The effect of these government measures was twofold. By not keeping a strict control of the exchange market the government encouraged widespread speculation. And by allowing half the currency gained abroad to slip out of their grasp, the Council of Ministers abandoned any attempt to steer the economy. As Graziani has explained: 'The foreign currency available should have been administered with parsimony, and directed towards those sectors most in need of aid and most relevant to the resumption of production. Freeing the exchange market, on the other hand, meant leaving the currency in the hands of the exporters, thus renouncing implicitly any control over the nature of Italy's imports, and, in the last analysis, over the whole process of national industrial reconstruction.'[54]

The other vital monetary question, the attempt to revalue the lira, was the work of the Communist Minister of Finance, Mauro Scoccimarro. His plan envisaged much more than the mere changing of the face value of the lira, the substitution of one new lira for every hundred old ones, and thus the elimination of all those surplus noughts which still bedevil the Italian currency. He intended rather to strike a decisive blow against inflation. One of the principal reasons for inflation at the time was the excessive amount of money in circulation – an estimated third more than the economy needed. The excess had been caused by the Allies' indiscriminate issue of Amlire during the war, and by the unlimited credit facilities afforded by the major banks.

Scoccimarro planned to limit the excess by imposing a tax on wealth at the moment when old money was converted into new. The Treasury proposed an indiscriminate 10 per cent levy on all money presented for exchange, but Scoccimarro rejected this as being harmful to the interests of small savers. He suggested a progressive assessment instead, as the first stage of an extraordinary general tax on all wealth. In this way not only would inflation be curbed, but the government would be taxing the richest elements of the nation and using the revenue for the immediate needs of reconstruction.

All this came to nothing. Scoccimarro was impeded at every step. First the Liberals blocked the proposal in the Council of Ministers; then the plates from which the new banknotes were to be printed mysteriously disappeared; finally the Bank of Italy let it be known that it could not distribute such vast quantities of money to its local branches for fear of robberies during transit. Even these bizarre delaying tactics could have been overcome, but the left-wing parties seemed to underestimate the importance of the issue. They chose to avoid a showdown over it, and Scoccimarro was left practically in isolation. In January 1946 the new Minister of the Treasury, the Liberal Epicarmo Corbino, insisted that the whole matter be postponed indefinitely.[55]

The major social battles of the time also saw the labour movement lose ground consistently to the employers. Throughout the Parri government the Confindustria pressed unceasingly for the veto on sackings to be lifted. The trade unions replied that they could not permit mass sackings until some sort of programme of alternative employment was devised. It was a hopeless battle. Faced by mounting accusations that they were sabotaging reconstruction, in January 1946 the CGIL consented to a partial unblocking of the situation. Two hundred and forty thousand workers were to be sacked in February and March, an estimated 13 per cent of the northern industrial workforce. The resistance from the base was intense, and some internal factory committees forced the proposals to be suspended for many months. None the less, during the course of 1946 the number of unemployed industrial workers rose from 750,000 to over a million.

In the same period the employers achieved another of their major objectives – wage agreements at a national level which excluded the possibility of local or factory agitation. National contracts were signed in December 1945 for northern Italy, and in May 1946 for the Centre and the South. These specifically obliged internal factory committees to accept the national stipulations and not seek improvements on their own account.

The CGIL accepted this self-denying ordinance for a number of reasons. In a situation characterized by extreme poverty, especially in the South, and by the presence of a massive industrial reserve army of unemployed, the first priority seemed to be the guaranteeing of minimum wage levels on a national scale. Di Vittorio and the other leaders were afraid that local agreements would accentuate the existing differences between the poor and the poorest, between the North and the South. The working class would be further divided at a time when the difference between employed and unemployed was already an abyss.

Undoubtedly, the national agreements went some way to meeting these exigencies. A single national wage scale for industrial workers was created, which permitted no more than a 14 per cent difference in minimum wages between the richest and poorest regions. The minimum holiday period was increased, and the Italian system of Christmas bonuses – a thirteenth month's wages, to be paid at the end of every year – was introduced for the first time. But the price paid was a high one. The factory organizations of the trade unions, deprived of responsibility or initiative in the process of collective bargaining, declined very rapidly. The employers were left as the undisputed masters of the shop-floor, and their reign of glory was to last throughout the fifties.[56]

The employers' supremacy was confirmed by the trade unions' failure to gain acceptance of one of their most cherished projects – the councils of management (*consigli di gestione*). The councils were created by the CLNAI at the time of the national insurrection. Right from the start they were intended not as instruments of workers' control, but as organs of planning and cooperation between management and employees. The two sides were to be equally represented in the councils, but the chairman was always to be appointed by management. The councils were to be responsible for the general running of the factories and for long-term decisions over investments, productivity, etc.

In practice the councils performed a somewhat ambivalent role. Whereas the internal factory committees (*commissioni interne*) directly represented the workers' interests, the councils of management tended to take on the more controversial tasks in the factory. It was they who guaranteed discipline on the shop-floor, who urged sacrifices on the workforce in the name of reconstruction and who had to choose which workers were to go once the veto on sackings had been lifted.

It might have been expected that management would welcome organs of this nature. Some of them did. At a conference in February 1946 Adelio Pace, one of the directors of Montecatini, Italy's largest chemical firm, had this to say of the councils: 'The concrete results have been: a prompt improvement in the organization of our company, an increased spirit of collaboration on the part of the workers (some of whom have even gone without wine and a second course in the canteen to enable the firm to finance the acquisition of primary materials), and the multiplication of workers' initiative to correct certain deficiencies in the mode of production.'[57] The Confindustria, however, fearing that as long as the left was in the government the councils might be used in some way to threaten employers' prerogatives, maintained an intransigent opposition. In January 1946 it announced that the councils 'would compromise irremediably the efficiency of our economy, prevent the refitting of industry, and contribute to the poisoning of the social peace of the country'.[58] Shortly afterwards, FIAT forced an agreement by which the councils were to have a purely consultative role within the company. In July De Gasperi cited the FIAT agreement as a model to be followed by other firms.

At the end of 1946, Rodolfo Morandi, the Socialist Minister of Industry, tried to introduce a bill to regulate the status of the councils. While leaving power substantially in the hands of the employers, he reiterated the planning role of the councils, which he saw as the embryos of a socialist intervention in the economy. He also made provisions for the minority in any council to request the arbitration of the Ministry of Industry. Not surprisingly, the Confindustria reacted extremely violently, and both Morandi's bill and the councils themselves were soon confined to oblivion.[59]

In the midst of all these setbacks for the working-class movement, the introduction of the *'scala mobile'*, the national scheme of threshold payments, deserves a place apart. The *scala mobile*, introduced in the national contracts of 1945 and 1946, was a system to safeguard workers' real wages against the effects of inflation. Every two months price rises were calculated in relation to the 'shopping basket' of an average working-class family. An increase in the cost of the basket led automatically to a proportional rise in the size of workers' pay packets.

The employers granted the scheme without any real battle having to be waged. They feared the unpredictable consequences of galloping inflation, and viewed the *scala mobile* as an instrument both to protect a weakened and numerically reduced working class, and to guarantee productivity. With hindsight, it is possible to say that they underestimated the system's utility as a permanent defence of workers' living standards. In future years the importance of the scheme was revealed by the repeated attempts made to modify its workings, attempts which were finally crowned with success in the referendum of 1985.[60]

The Republic and the End of the Grand Coalition, June 1946–May 1947

a. THE FIRST ELECTIONS AND THE CONSTITUTION

On 2 June 1946 the Italians finally held their first free general elections for over twenty years. The voters were asked to perform a double duty – to decide by referendum between the monarchy and a republic, and to elect their representatives to the Constituent Assembly. It was a historic occasion, not only for the importance of the issues at stake, but for the fact that women voted for the first time in Italian history.

Less than a month before the referendum, Victor Emanuel III, in a last-ditch attempt to save his dynasty, had abdicated in favour of his son Umberto. But the prospect of a new king was not enough to cancel the memory of the monarchy's involvement with Fascism or the ignominious flight from Rome on 8 September 1943. By 12,717,923 votes (54.2 per cent) to 10,719,284 (45.8 per cent), Italy voted in favour of becoming a republic.

The referendum revealed a dramatic split between North and South. Whereas the North and Centre voted solidly, and in some areas overwhelmingly, for the republic, the South was equally strongly in favour of the monarchy. Nearly 80 per cent of Neapolitans were Monarchists, and only in the poverty-stricken region of Basilicata, the scene of extensive land occupations in 1944–5, did the Republicans poll more than 40 per cent.[61] Without doubt, the very different experiences of the Resistance and the Kingdom of the South go a long way to explain these voting patterns. As Giorgio Amendola wrote at the time: 'There are large areas of southern Italy where everything seems to have remained as it was before, under Fascism; the political and state apparatus has not changed, and power remains in the hands of the same families.'[62] But the roots of southern Monarchism went deeper than this. In Naples in particular there was a centuries-old belief, founded on an earlier historical reality, that the monarchy meant work, subsidies and assistance. The Neapolitans were not prepared to exchange monarchist beneficence, which of course included 'gifts' at election times, for the abstract ideal of the republic.

Umberto at first played for time, claiming that the Republicans only had a majority of *valid* votes, and not of all votes cast. There followed a number of days of high tension in the capital, with rumours of a possible army coup in support of the king. But De Gasperi and the other ministers remained firm under pressure, and on 13 June the 'May King', as Umberto was to be dubbed, flew into exile. A fortnight later the liberal Neapolitan jurist Enrico De Nicola, last President of the pre-Fascist Chamber of Deputies, was elected provisional head of state.

The defeat of the monarchy at the referendum was without doubt the single greatest achievement of the progressive forces in Italian society in these years. Looking back at the débâcle of the years 1945–8, the left-wing protagonists of that time could always find consolation in the establishment of the Republic. De Gasperi told Gonella that people had to be reassured that the republic did not mean wiping the slate clean of the past.[63] He was certainly right. However, the elimination of royal power was no token victory. The king had previously exercised absolute control over foreign and military affairs, and the House of Savoy had always shown scant respect for democracy and a penchant for those who, like Luigi Pelloux and Mussolini, had wanted to destroy it.

The second part of the elections of June 1946 were those to the Constituent Assembly, whose principal task was that of drawing up the new constitution of the republic. The elections at last gave an accurate indication of the relative strength of the three major parties. The Christian Democrats emerged by far the most powerful with 35.2 per cent of the votes and 207 seats in the Assembly. They were followed by the Socialists with 20.7 per cent and 115 seats, and then by the Communists with 19 per cent and 104 seats. The DC, as was to be expected, received strong backing in the rural areas, whereas the PSIUP became the largest party in both Milan and Turin. The results of the elections were a bitter shock for the Communists. They had set their sights on being the leading party of the left, and of obtaining, together with the Socialists, more than half the seats in the Assembly. Neither objective had been achieved.

Of the minor parties, the Azionisti obtained a paltry 1.5 per cent of the votes and seven deputies. The Republicans, who had always refused to swear allegiance to the monarchy, re-entered the political fray with 4.4 per cent of the vote and twenty-four deputies. But the most menacing newcomer was undoubtedly the Fronte dell'Uomo Qualunque (the Common Man's Front), which obtained over a million votes, especially in the South, and returned thirty deputies. The Front had been founded by an obese and extrovert playwright called Guglielmo Giannini. His magazine, *L'Uomo Qualunque*, waged war unceasingly on everything that threatened the 'ordinary Italian': the anti-Fascist government coalition, the Allies, the decrees on *epurazione*, etc. The financial backing for the Front came mainly from local bosses in the South, ex-Fascists who had been refused admission to the Liberal Party and who turned to Giannini for a political outlet. Its popularity derived at least in part from the political diseducation of more than twenty years of Fascism, and from the southerners' traditional hatred of central government. The Front was to lend its name to a new derogatory epithet in Italian politics: *qualunquista*, meaning a digger of one's own garden, a cynic, a potential Fascist.[64]

Over the next eighteen months the new Assembly dedicated itself to drawing up the republican Constitution. The Italian Constitution embodies a fairly standard system of representative democracy, based on two Houses of Parliament, called respectively the Chamber of Deputies and the Senate. The Chamber is elected once every five years by a system of proportional representation based on multi-member constituencies. The Senate, originally elected once every seven years (later reduced to five), is elected on a regional basis through a mixed system of proportional representation and single-member constituencies. The Italian system of proportional represent-ation was an extremely 'pure' one, allowing small parties even with less than 2 per cent of the votes to be represented in the Chamber of Deputies. Such a system had the obvious advantage of safeguarding minorities and accurately reflecting public opinion. However, as was to become ever clearer in the history of the Republic, it encouraged the dispersion of votes and made weak coalition government almost inevitable.

Once every seven years the two houses were to elect the President of the Republic. Without being a mere figurehead, the Italian President has only a certain restricted field of initiative. The Vatican exerted pressure on the D C in favour of an American-style presidency, but all the major parties agreed on the need to avoid an over-powerful president.

Certain articles in the first part of the Constitution, entitled 'Funda-mental Principles', were of quite a radical nature. Article 4, for instance, recognizes 'the right to work' for all Italians. Article 5 encourages local autonomy. Article 42 states that within the limits of the relevant laws private property can be expropriated. Article 46 establishes the right of workers to collaborate in the running of their workplaces.

The importance of these articles, however, was almost entirely vitiated in February 1948 by a decision of the Corte di Cassazione. The Court established a distinction between those parts of the Constitution which were of immediate actuation (*norme precettizie*) and those which were defined as programmatic and thus to be realized only at some indefinite future date (*norme programmatiche*). By this means not only did the innovatory articles remain dead letters, but many Fascist laws and codes in clear contradiction to the Constitution were never repealed. In addition, some of the most important elements in the Constitution were introduced only after very long delays: the Constitutional Court in 1956, the Supreme Council of the magistracy in 1958, regional autonomy and the right to hold referenda as late as 1970.[65]

The work of the Constituent Assembly was distinguished by two crucial battles over civil liberties. The first concerned the relations between church and state. The Vatican was adamant that the Concordat (or Lateran Pact) signed in 1929 between Mussolini and the church should be included unchanged in the Constitution. The Concordat proclaimed Catholicism the official religion of the state, made religious education compulsory in state schools and included a number of repressive measures such as civil sanctions against ex-priests. Up until the last moment the Communists, together with all the other lay parties, maintained an intransigent opposition to this proposal. But on 24 March 1947 Togliatti summoned the parliamentary group of his party and explained that the Communists were to support the Concordat. He argued the necessity of establishing religious peace in the country, and of maintaining a dialogue with Catholics both inside and outside the D C. To the astonishment and (it must be added) disgust of their allies, the P C I, with the one exception of Teresa Noce, duly voted in favour of Article 7.[66]

The second battle was launched by a little known Communist called Giovanni Grilli. He was determined that in Article 29, which deals with the family, marriage was not to be declared indissoluble. Without consulting his colleagues, he presented an amendment to this effect. There was uproar in the Chamber of Deputies, not least from the Communist deputies, who had been instructed by Togliatti not to raise the question of divorce. Grilli remained adamant, the Communists decided not to disown him, and the amendment was passed by the narrowest of margins – 194 votes to 191. This minor but significant victory did not go unforgotten when the full-scale conflict on divorce divided Italy in the first months of 1974.[67]

b. PARTIES AND POLITICS

On July 1946 De Gasperi constituted his second government. As leader of the largest party, his position as President of the Council of Ministers was not in doubt, and he used the election victory to strengthen the Christian Democrats' representation in the government. The Action Party and the Liberals were excluded, Communists and Socialists occupied fewer ministries (Gullo was replaced as Minister of Agriculture by the Christian Democrat, Antonio Segni), and the Republicans were allowed only a very minor role.

De Gasperi was content for the time being to continue the coalition with the left, particularly now that the balance of forces had shifted in his favour. However, just at this moment, as if to confound any linear interpretation of their rise to power, the Christian Democrats entered a period of grave crisis. The prime cause for this was inflation. After a lull in the first half of 1946, retail prices began once again to increase very rapidly. The new wave of inflation had a whole host of causes: above all the monetary policies of the government, especially its lack of control of credit facilities, but also a growing demand for consumer goods and widespread hoarding by wholesalers and industrialists.

The reaction of a significant part of the electorate was to blame the D C. The urban middle classes, unprotected by the *scala mobile*, accused De Gasperi of excessive indulgence towards the left-wing parties. The flames of their discontent were fanned by Luigi Einaudi, the governor of the Bank of Italy. He popularized the explanation that government spending, such as on bread subsidies, was the principal (and not just a subsidiary) cause of inflation.[68] In November 1946, local elections were held in six major cities. The D C suffered disastrous losses. In Rome their vote dropped from 218,000 to 103,000; in Naples they collapsed dramatically from 89,000 votes to 29,000. At the same time the Uomo Qualunque consolidated its positions in the South, polled more votes than the D C in Rome and made significant gains even in the North.

Giulio Andreotti, in a conversation with Antonio Gambino, has recalled the feeling of imminent catastrophe that permeated the D C at this time: 'The older members, fearing history would repeat itself, remembered what had happened to the Popular Party: after the great electoral success of 1921 it had rapidly disappeared from the political scene. The younger members were preoccupied by the party's lack of roots in the country . . . In the winter of 1946 we were all acutely afraid that a sudden change in the political climate would destroy the balance of forces established in the previous spring.'[69]

After the November elections, with their warning signals of the middle class's shift to the right, great pressure was exerted on De Gasperi to break with the Communists and the Socialists. No one was more insistent than the Pope. Pius XII sent Cardinal Montini (later Paul VI) to convince De Gasperi, and on 22 December, during an inflammatory sermon to 200,000 of the faithful in St Peter's Square, he re-launched the ancient battle cry, 'either with Christ or against Christ; or for his church or against his church'.[70]

De Gasperi refused every attempt to cajole him into premature action. The Concordat had not yet been incorporated into the Constitution; the Peace Treaty, which had to be agreed by Russia as well as the Allies, was not yet signed. De Gasperi did not want the coalition to continue any longer than necessary, but he reserved the right to choose his moment to destroy it.[71]

It is in this context that we should view his visit to the United States in January 1947. Cold War legend has it that De Gasperi crossed the Atlantic to receive orders from the Americans to expel the left from the government. The scenario seems improbable. The American relationship to the D C was not, or at least not yet, of the 'command and obey' variety. In Washington, interdepartmental warfare was still the order of the day, U S foreign policy was in a phase of transition, and the Truman Doctrine was only to be announced in March 1947. It was De Gasperi who took the initiative for the visit, not the State Department who summoned him. It is possible that he held secret discussions about the eventual expulsion of the left, but U S officials at this time viewed the Italian situation essentially in defensive terms: the problem was to stop the left winning, not about when to end the government coalition. In any event, De Gasperi was able to return in a blaze of publicity, fortified by a new export–import loan of $100m.[72]

Throughout the second De Gasperi government, the left-wing parties remained in a state of substantial immobility. The Communists continued their extraordinary work of recruitment to the new mass party, and their organizational conference, held in Florence in January 1947, gave fresh impetus and efficiency to the party machine. But the election defeat of June 1946 did not lead to any revision of strategy. In the autumn the P C I launched a 'new course' for the political economy of the country, but the proposals were generic and without effect. The Communists' main preoccupation continued to be their participation in the government and the maintenance of the fragile alliance with the D C.

In retrospect, some of their efforts in this direction seem almost tragically ingenuous. Scoccimarro recounts how the night before De Gasperi left for America, he (Scoccimarro) worked into the early hours of the morning to prepare the estimated budget for the forthcoming year, so that the Americans could see that the finances of the country, while in Communist hands, were being responsibly managed. He then rushed the results of his labours to De Gasperi at the airport, and promised further documentation if the Americans required it.[73] And all this when De Gasperi and the Americans were meeting to discuss how best to defeat the left, not cooperate with it.

The Communists had also to bear another cross – the intricate question of the future of Trieste and its hinterland. The area had a complicated history and a mixed Slovene and Italian population, though Trieste itself was mainly Italian speaking. After the First World War a Slovene minority of some half a million had been forced to live under Italian rule. In 1945, the Yugoslavs, seeking over-compensation for this earlier injustice, wanted to annex all the territory up to the river Isonzo. In April of that year they took over a great part of Venezia Giulia and subjected the Italian population to a harsh regime of occupation. After six weeks they were forced to withdraw or risk Allied intervention.

The PCI found itself in difficulty for a number of reasons. The Yugoslavs were Communist comrades and Stalin himself, at this stage still very much Tito's ally, was backing their claims. The Italian Communists were therefore hardly in a position to denounce Yugoslav chauvinism for what it was. In April 1945 they chose deliberately to mispresent the nature of the invasion of Venezia Giulia, and went as far as to welcome the Yugoslav 'army of liberation'.

On the other hand, blind support of Tito's claims meant leaving the PCI hopelessly exposed to attacks from the Italian right-wing parties. Their newspapers had a field-day in pointing out that while the Communists posed as a national and independent party, at the first real test they revealed themselves the pawns of Moscow and Belgrade. Togliatti, in a series of able and diplomatic interventions, did his best to rebut these accusations. He insisted that Trieste should remain Italian, that its hinterland should go to Yugoslavia and that direct negotiations were the only way to solve the problem. But even his skill could not entirely protect his party from the horns of this particular dilemma.[74]

The second half of 1946 was therefore not an easy time for the PCI, but its difficulties were minor compared to those of the PSIUP. In spite of their electoral success, the Socialists were unable to find any internal harmony or capitalize upon the undoubted support that they enjoyed in the country. At the two extremes of the party it became ever clearer that Saragat was intent on breaking away to found his own social-democratic party, and that Basso wanted to drive him out at all costs. From the wings, De Gasperi and Togliatti both encouraged the split in the Socialist ranks; the former sought a more moderate socialist ally, the latter a PSIUP rid of its anti-Communist elements. On 20 November 1946, Saragat gave an inflammatory interview to the *Giornale d'Italia* in which he attacked the leadership's 'smoke-screen of maximalism and fusionism'.

In a climate of increasing bitterness, the Socialist congress was called forward to January 1947. Nenni sided with Basso, and their motion to congress won the support of two thirds of the party. When the congress began at Rome University on 9 January, the opposition refused to recognize its validity and staged one of its own at the Palazzo Barberini. Sandro Pertini's attempts at mediation were destined to failure; Nenni himself seemed overwhelmed and paralysed by what was happening. A small group of anti-Stalinist revolutionaries, led by Mario Zagari and called Iniziativa Socialista, joined Saragat and his supporters to form the PSLI, soon to become the PSDI (the Italian Social Democratic Party). The new party attracted away from the PSIUP fifty-two of the 115 Socialist deputies to the Constituent Assembly. The split was a major tragedy for Italian socialism. It ensured the subordination of the rump of the PSIUP to the PCI, and condemned the social-democratic minority to a sterile future, in the shadow of the DC and constantly susceptible to Cold War American pressure.[75]

Finally, if we turn away from the parties to the trade unions, we find that the CGIL faithfully reflected the left-wing parties' strategic weakness at this time. In October 1946 the trade union leaders agreed to a six-month wage freeze, without being able to obtain anything substantial in return. There was a vague government promise to control prices, and in August 1946 the prefect of Milan (one of the few remaining CLN appointments) imposed fixed prices on essential goods. Control committees consisting of two policemen and one member of the Camera di Lavoro were to ensure that retailers followed the prefects' instructions. The idea spread to Turin and Genoa, but after a while wholesalers and middlemen refused to distribute goods to the shops, and the black market entered a new golden age. In the absence of an overall plan to control the various stages of the transit of goods from producer to consumer, there was little hope of effective price restraint.[76]

c. SOCIAL STRUGGLES

The summer and autumn of 1946 saw increasing social unrest. Prices and unemployment rose rapidly, as did dissatisfaction with the left's performance in government. In August a 'revolt' of former partisans took place. Outraged by the amnesty, a certain Captain Lavagnino with thirty of his men from the auxiliary police took to the hills above Asti. They were soon followed by four hundred others, and in the next few days the protest movement spread all over the hills of northern Italy. The ex-partisans demanded the revocation of the amnesty, the banning of the Uomo Qualunque, an end to sackings and the creation of more jobs. For a number of days it seemed possible that De Gasperi would send in the army, but frantic interventions by the former leaders of the CLNAI persuaded the partisans to return reluctantly to their homes.[77]

In the cities of the North, a wave of spontaneous action against unemployment and inflation flouted trade union calls for restraint. In July 1946 shops were sacked in Venice, a thousand unemployed workers at Treviso forced the prefect to promise them jobs immediately, and at Brescia workers refused an agreement signed by the local Camera di Lavoro and assaulted the leading industrialist of the city. The movement found its highest expression in Turin, where the internal factory commissions themselves organized a general strike of the whole city. In all these protests women and returning prisoners of war were particularly active.

After the summer, agitations in the North were less intense, but in October thousands of Roman manual labourers, threatened with redundancy, invaded the residence of the President of the Council of Ministers. *Agents provocateurs* were suspected of being amongst the crowd, and bitter fighting broke out between police and demonstrators. Two people died and more than 150 were wounded.[78]

To all this must be added a situation of continuous tension in the countryside. In the South peasant agitations to ensure the enforcement of the Gullo decrees reached their height in the autumn of 1946. Because the struggle was waged on all fronts at once, on agrarian contracts, on uncultivated land, on the *imponibile di mano d'opera* and the *collocamento*, the links between the peasants grew at an astonishing rate, as did their organizations – the Camere di Lavoro, the leagues, the party sections. Between 1944 and 1949, by the most conservative estimates we have, 1,187 cooperatives with a total membership of nearly a quarter of a million took over more than 165,000 hectares of land, mainly in Sicily, Calabria and Lazio.[79]

In spite of this extraordinary mobilization, the movement ended largely in failure. Some of the more radical elements of Gullo's programme, such as the abolition of intermediaries, never received any practical application at all. Even the more moderate decrees on the occupation of uncultivated land and the revision of agrarian contracts gained only localized and temporary successes.

At the heart of this failure, on a political level, lay the hostility of the Liberals and the Christian Democrats. When the Gullo decrees were first under consideration by the Council of Ministers in the autumn of 1944, the D C and P L I imposed a number of crucial modifications. Most importantly, they insisted that the local commissions, which were to decide on the legitimacy of land occupations, were to be composed of the president of the local magistrates' court, a representative of the proprietors and one of the peasants. Thus, unless the local magistrate was unusually enlightened (hardly a common occurrence in the Mezzogiorno), there was a built-in majority against the peasantry. What this meant is brutally summarized in the statistics for Sicily: 987 peasant demands, involving 86,000 hectares of uncultivated land, were accepted by the local authorities; 3,822 demands, for no less than 820,000 hectares, were rejected.[80]

Once the decrees were promulgated, and peasant militancy grew, the D C and the P L I denounced the legislation as inflammatory. In April 1946 the Liberal newspaper *Il Giornale* declared Gullo's decrees 'more deadly than the destruction caused by war, or by military occupations, or by natural disasters ... they are the most lamentable phenomenon for agriculture, and it is not even possible, as one would do for hailstorms, to take out insurance against them'.[81] The Christian Democrats, for their part, were extremely worried that Gullo's popularity might eat into the vast reservoir of southern rural votes on which they were so reliant. They were well aware of how important the Ministry of Agriculture was, and worked hard to replace Gullo with a man of their own party, Antonio Segni.

However, the political opponents of southern agrarian reform would not have triumphed as they did without the ductility of the PCI leadership. As we have already noted, Togliatti welcomed the Gullo decrees and the massive peasant mobilization that followed them, but only so long as they did not place in jeopardy the alliance with the DC. If the peasant movement threatened law and order, questioned property rights or led to a confrontation with the DC over state policy in the South, then the Communist leadership could not be expected to support the reforming zeal of its own Minister of Agriculture.

The full significance of this position becomes clear if we examine the eventual fate of one of Gullo's key decrees – that offering bonuses to the peasantry and reductions of rent in kind in return for the consignment of their produce to the *granai del popolo*. The decree was first declared illegal by local magistrates at Sassari in December 1944. Other local courts, staffed by magistrates who had served twenty years under Fascism, followed suit, and their judgement was confirmed by the Corte di Cassazione in May 1946. These rulings were, of course, crippling. They can hardly be called surprising, until we remember that Togliatti himself was Minister of Justice from June 1945 to October 1946. During his tenure of office he made no serious effort whatsoever to reform the judiciary or purge it of its Fascist elements. In this way the full weight of the 'continuity of the state' bore down upon the southern peasant movement and deprived it of its legal bases.[82]

Finally, it must be noted that the peasants themselves found it difficult to maintain unity. The land that the cooperatives did manage to acquire was not only limited in extent, but of poor quality. The cooperatives had too many members and too little land, so that the average holding was around one hectare per person. Under these conditions, divisions soon became apparent, with the poorer peasants abandoning their plots and being bought out by the richer ones.[83]

In addition, the small peasant proprietors of the South, who were to flock to the Coldiretti, felt threatened by the proposed reform of agrarian contracts, which undermined them in their role of employers of casual labour. Their position, though, was an ambivalent one, since many of them also took an active part in land occupations and in the formation of the cooperatives. Had Gullo's decrees been accompanied by an extensive programme of state aid to the poor and middle peasants, it is possible that the smallholders could have been won away from their traditional alliances to the landowning élite. Gullo did in fact make provision in his legislation for extensive credit facilities to be granted to the cooperatives, but in the event no money reached them from the Ministry of Agriculture. Deprived of funds, the cooperatives were doomed to disintegrate, and the famous fifteen Soviet tractors that eventually arrived in the South in 1949 can hardly have been considered adequate compensation.[84]

In central Italy, in Tuscany, Umbria and parts of Emilia and the Marches, the sharecroppers launched an unprecedented struggle to modify the relationships between landlord and peasant. In May 1945 the representatives of the Tuscan sharecroppers, gathered in Siena, drew up their list of objectives. Among their principal demands were those for a minimum of 60 per cent of the produce, for 'the right of the sharecropper to participate in directing the farm on a basis of perfect parity with the proprietor', for security of tenure, for an end to the obligation to perform free services and to supply 'gifts' in kind to the landlord. They also wanted regular annual settling of accounts (to prevent debts from accumulating), and the landowners to pay for all the damage suffered during the war to farms and livestock.[85]

This was an ambitious and realistic programme, even if it did not correspond to wartime promises of land ownership for the sharecroppers. It was pursued with determination and sensitivity by the C G I L's rural trade union, the Federterra, and in particular by the Communist component within it. Building on bases established during the Resistance, the union quickly built up a very large membership.[86] Its activists went from farmhouse to farmhouse, organizing meetings in the evening, transforming the *veglia* into a political occasion. One trade unionist recalled later the extraordinary advantages of such reunions:

In one of those houses' great kitchens . . . you had the whole family there: the young, the women, the heads of family, the other members. In such meetings there was more active participation and discussion from these junior elements of the family. You have to remember that at that time there was a lot of timidity around, with the exception of the cleverer ones or those most involved politically. So this type of meeting made for a more democratic form of participation because it was traditional, because it corresponded to their way of being together, it was theirs, in a word it was *in casa*.[87]

Thus, far from the public and the private being rigidly separate, the very organization of protest and the exposition of politics took place within the home, with whole families listening and participating.

At work, the movement gave birth to its own organizations, the *consigli di fattoria* (farm councils). The *fattoria* was a feature of the Tuscan countryside in particular. With each estate divided into a number of sharecroppers' farms (*poderi*), the *fattoria* was the centre of production, the group of buildings at the heart of the estate. It housed the large agricultural machines, the vats for the wine, the press for the olives. Here the overall plans for the estate were drawn up, and here too was the office (*scrittoio*) where all the peasants came to settle their accounts. The *consigli di fattoria* were elected peasant councils which aimed to supervise and if possible control these nerve centres of the estates. In spite of the fierce opposition of the landlords, some 1,900 councils were formed in the period 1945–7, and in many cases they took over the running of the farms. The landlords, forced to recognize the councils, tried to limit their membership to the *capocci* (heads of family), but soon younger men became leading members, though very few women did. As the mobilization gathered pace, so the rigid hierarchies of the sharecropping family began to be fractured.[88]

The sharecroppers did not, by and large, take strike action in the post-war period. Damaging the crops or the animals was judged to be counter-productive in a period of national reconstruction and food shortages. Instead they concentrated their forces at a critical moment of the agricultural calendar, threshing time. As threshing was completed on each farm (*podere*) in turn, the peasants, often fifty to a hundred at a time, tried to ensure that the landlord or his agent agreed to 60 per cent of the grain going to the sharecropping family. Each time the peasants' weapons were force of numbers, argument, intimidation, even shots being fired at night towards the landlord's villa. The proprietors complained bitterly that they were being left isolated and without protection. The sharecroppers replied with actions designed to win the sympathy of the population as a whole. The chickens, eggs, rabbits and wine which were due as gifts (*regalie*) to the landowners were donated to local hospitals instead.[89]

After the Parri government had made a number of fruitless attempts at mediation in the dispute, in March 1946 the CGIL requested De Gasperi's personal intervention as President of the Council of Ministers. De Gasperi took three months to make up his mind, but then recommended that the landlords contributed 24 per cent of one year's income towards repairing war damage, and that in 1946 they should add another 10 per cent towards improving the land. However, De Gasperi also stipulated that the habitual 50/50 division of the produce should remain in force, and that the *consigli di fattoria* should be eliminated. Thus, if short-term penalties were inflicted upon the landowners, in the long term the strategic aims of the sharecroppers' movement were firmly rejected. No better example exists of De Gasperi's mediating skill.

The *lodo* (gift of) De Gasperi, as it came to be called, was a watershed in the central Italian struggle. The landowners by and large refused to accept its recommendations (which were not legally binding), with the result that the trade union concentrated on making them do so. At the same time much of the left gave a cautious welcome to the arbitration, pointing to the landowners' resistance as evidence of its progressive nature. The more advanced demands of the sharecroppers, like that of parity of decision-making powers with the landowners, were quietly put to one side. A year later, in June 1947, a semblance of peace returned to the central Italian countryside with the signing of a pact drawn up by Antonio Segni, the new Christian Democrat Minister of Agriculture. The sharecropper was to receive 53 per cent of the produce, and the landowner was to put aside 4 per cent of his annual income for improvements.[90]

The struggle of the *mezzadri* thus ended in substantial, if not total, failure. However, it left a notable legacy. A tradition of collective action and cooperation had been established; family and collectivity had been drawn sharply together; the young had contested the dictatorial power of the old, the countryside that of the city. The Communists benefited most of all, for it had been their militants, working in the Federterra, who had guided and instructed the *mezzadri* in the course of the struggle. The P C I's substantial electoral backing in the central Italian countryside dates from this period.

d. THE DITCHING OF THE LEFT

The overall climate of social unrest both in city and countryside in the second half of 1946 contributed significantly to the difficulty of the choice facing De Gasperi. He wanted the left-wing parties out of the government, but would the country be governable without them? De Gasperi was the first to recognize the restraining role that Communists and Socialists had often played over the past three years. If they were now to be forced into unbridled opposition, the country risked civil war.

On his return from America, De Gasperi reshuffled his Council of Ministers, the Italian equivalent of the Cabinet, forming his third ministry on 31 January 1947. The number of ministers was reduced from twenty-one to sixteen and the left's presence in the government from eight to six. Scoccimarro lost the Ministry of Finance and Nenni lost Foreign Affairs. General elections for the first legislative assembly of the Republic were to be held in October of that year.

It soon became obvious that the Christian Democrats could not afford to wait that long. Their unpopularity grew by leaps and bounds in the first months of 1947. The rate of inflation became even more rapid, reaching the appalling figure of 50 per cent for the first six months of the year. In February the Peace Treaty was finally signed and its details proved a grave blow to De Gasperi's prestige. Italy was to lose all her colonies, including those acquired before the First World War. Reparations totalling $360 million were to be paid to Russia, Greece, Yugoslavia, Albania and Ethiopia. Worst of all, while most of the Istrian peninsula went to Yugoslavia, Trieste itself was *not* to remain Italian, but became a free territory under international supervision.

Popular disenchantment with the D C received dramatic confirmation with the regional elections in Sicily on 20–21 April 1947. Sicily, the Val d'Aosta and Trentino-Alto Adige, because of their particular history or the presence of a large ethnic minority, had been granted regional assemblies and a measure of local autonomy. In the Sicilian elections the Christian Democrats lost nearly 250,000 votes (compared to 2 June 1946), dropping from 33.6 per cent of the electorate to 20.5 per cent. In the major cities their share of the vote plummeted: in Catania they fell from 33.9 per cent to 9.8 per cent. The People's Bloc (Communists, Socialists and Action Party) increased from 21.5 per cent to 30.4 per cent, gaining twenty-nine seats in the Assembly to the D C's nineteen. At the same time Liberals, the Uomo Qualunque, Separatists and Monarchists between them gained thirty-one seats.

De Gasperi now had no choice but to move, and to move fast. The Sicilian elections confirmed his suspicion that the church hierarchy, faced with the continuing presence of the left in the government, was beginning to abandon his party. In these circumstances, the D C risked destruction at the general elections. The Lateran Pacts had been approved on 24 March. Almost everything that De Gasperi had hoped to gain from the anti-Fascist coalition had been realized. It was time for the break.

He was encouraged into action at the beginning of May by two events on an international level. The first was the simultaneous crisis in France, where on 9 May the Communists were successfully excluded from the government for the first time since the war. The second, and more important, was the rapid evolution of American foreign policy. The Truman Doctrine had been declared in March, and the Americans now made explicit their anti-Communism with regard to the Italian situation. Orders were given immediately for modern arms to be sold at nominal cost to the Italian army. On 1 May the United States Secretary of State George Marshall wrote to James Dunn, the American ambassador at Rome, foreseeing the perils of the October election and urging De Gasperi to govern without the Communists.[91]

While Rome waited tensely for the President of the Council to make his move, the attention of the country was suddenly and brutally drawn away from high politics to the world of the Sicilian peasantry. On 1 May 1947 the peasantry of three villages in the province of Palermo met to celebrate Labour Day at Portella delle Ginestre. As 1 May fell only a week after the notable advance of the People's Bloc in the regional elections, they had good cause for jubilation.

Fifteen hundred people gathered in the broad plain near Portella that day; entire families loaded into their gaily painted carts had come for the outing. A local shoemaker, Giacomo Schirò, opened the speeches. Suddenly, from one of the surrounding hilltops, a sub-machine-gun opened fire on the crowd. The peasants threw themselves to the ground, but the firing went on, for perhaps as long as fifteen minutes. The notorious bandit, Salvatore Giuliano, had been hired by the Mafia to remind the peasants of who really held power in the province, elections or no elections. Eleven people were killed and sixty-five wounded.[92]

For a week there was talk of nothing else, with the Communist leader Li Causi making an impassioned denunciation to the Constituent Assembly of the landowners' responsibility for the massacre. Then, on 13 May, De Gasperi resigned. At first it seemed that he had calculated wrongly, for the President of the Republic, De Nicola, gave another venerable anti-Fascist, Francesco Saverio Nitti, the task of forming the new government. Nitti, however, was quite unable to form a parliamentary majority around his candidature. The task returned to De Gasperi, who proceeded to announce that he would form a government of the centre, reliant on the parliamentary support of all the right-wing parties. The decisive vote of confidence took place on 31 May 1947. By 274 votes to 231 the Constituent Assembly confirmed the end of the anti-Fascist coalition.

Confrontation, June 1947–April 1948

a. THE POLITICAL ECONOMY OF LUIGI EINAUDI

De Gasperi immediately postponed the general elections until April 1948. His new Cabinet contained two key appointments: Mario Scelba as Minister of the Interior (a post he had already held since January 1947); and the Liberal Luigi Einaudi as Vice-President of the Council and Minister of the Budget (a new post created specially for him). Scelba was exactly the sort of unflinching conservative the Christian Democrats needed at a time of deepening social and political tension. Under his guidance not only were the police and the Carabinieri purged of former partisans, but they were encouraged to intervene incisively and brutally against all working-class or peasant protests that transcended certain narrow boundaries. Scelba's infamous *celere* (flying squads) were to have a place all of their own in popular recollections of this period.

If Scelba sought to impose law and order, Einaudi promised and delivered far more. In the space of a few months the former governor of the Bank of Italy did what the unfortunate Scoccimarro had always been prevented from doing – he intervened decisively in the economy to bring inflation under control. Not that Einaudi's methods were those proposed by Scoccimarro. Instead of progressive taxation by means of the revaluation of the lira, Einaudi favoured classic deflationary policies. In September 1947 he drastically reduced the amount of money in circulation by freezing 25 per cent of all bank deposits and introducing other credit restrictions. The effect was immediate. Inflation rates slowed down, and the very severe foreign-exchange crisis (the lira's free-market value had fallen from 528 to 909 lire to the dollar between January and May 1947) was brought under control. This was very much what the Americans wanted to see. Ever since April their embassy in Rome had been reiterating that tough internal measures were a precondition for future aid.[93]

Both at the time and later, Einaudi's initiatives aroused a storm of controversy. On the one hand, they were widely acclaimed as having saved the lira and the country; on the other, they were harshly criticized, especially from the left. Certainly, no one could deny the effectiveness of Einaudi's anti-inflationary battle, but the methods he chose also had serious negative consequences. Credit restrictions hit small and medium-sized businesses very hard, and provoked an overall decline in investment and thus industrial production. Employers responded to this severe deflation with extensive redundancies. The autumn of 1947 witnessed the first wave of mass sackings which the factory commissions were unable to prevent or at least modify. By 1948 the average monthly figure for the unemployed was over 2,100,000. The economy as a whole remained severely depressed until mid-1950.[94]

None the less, Einaudi's policies provided much of the material basis for the Christian Democrats' electoral victory in April 1948. The urban middle classes, dependent upon fixed incomes, at last saw an attempt being made to safeguard their standard of living. With the left out of the government and the economy finally being brought under control, the Uomo Qualunque and other right-wing parties found the ground being swept away from under their feet. By the beginning of 1948 the DC had stemmed the electoral haemorrhage that threatened its very existence.

b. THE PCI

The Communists also changed course at this critical moment, but with less satisfactory results. Togliatti had reacted to the left's expulsion from the government with characteristic caution and restraint, hoping that the force of events would convince De Gasperi of his mistake. The Communist leader, however, was not a free agent. In September 1947 the Italian Communists were summoned to the small Polish town of Szklarska Poreba to attend the founding meeting of Cominform. Since the dissolution of the Third International in 1943, no formal organization had grouped together the Communist parties of the world. With the onset of the Cold War, Stalin wanted to reverse this situation and impose a uniform line of intransigent opposition to counter America's newfound aggression. He was also alarmed at the centrifugal forces at work in the international Communist movement. It was time for a new orthodoxy.

At the Cominform meeting the French and Italian parties came under heavy attack. They were accused of having been too conciliatory with the parties of the bourgeoisie and too willing to compromise the interests of the working class in order to remain in government. Longo, for the PCI, defended the party's conduct during the Resistance, but accepted much of the criticism of the PCI's line since the end of the war. Zdanov called the western European parties to order: the world was now divided into two blocs, the great imperialist powers intended to unleash a new war against Russia and the Communists in the West had no option but to oppose these plans uncompromisingly. The era of the anti-Fascist coalitions was over and that of the Cold War had begun.[95]

Togliatti accepted his instructions reluctantly. The strategy of alliance with the DC may have produced meagre results, but for Togliatti it was infinitely preferable to the sort of frontal opposition which had led to so many disasters in the twenties and early thirties. However, much of the party felt a sense of relief at being at last in open opposition to the government. During the autumn a fresh wave of social protest gathered force, and this time Communist militants did not have to play a restraining role.[96]

In September 600,000 landless labourers of the Po valley went on strike for twelve days. The northern plains, the heartland of the landless-labourer leagues and indeed the cradle of Italian socialism, had not until this moment been in the forefront of the post-war rural agitations. One of the main reasons for this had been the deliberate restraint exercised by the Federterra. The great capitalist estates of the Po valley were by far the most productive agricultural region in Italy, and the rural trade union was very reluctant to take any action which might be interpreted as sabotaging national food supplies. In September 1947 the Federterra went on to the offensive. It demanded an eight-hour day, the recognition throughout the region of the *scala mobile*, the *imponibile di mano d'opera* and the *collocamento*, an increase in family allowances and greater security of tenure for tied labourers (*salariati fissi*). By no means all these requests were granted, but the strike was certainly a partial success. It won the eight-hour day, index-linked wage increases and the *imponibile* for normal agricultural working, if not for improving the farms.[97]

The agitations of the autumn of 1947 proved no more than an interlude in Communist Party strategy. Togliatti was deeply opposed to any action that relied heavily on extra-parliamentary pressure in order to force change. While respecting the Cominform insistence on opposition, Togliatti quickly channelled Communist Party efforts away from the mass movements of protest and into electioneering. Preparation for the spring elections became the all-important task. Change would be brought about through electoral victory. In December 1947, despite the misgivings of the Socialist secretary Lelio Basso, Communists and Socialists agreed to fight the elections on a united platform, and founded the Democratic Popular Front.

c. THE 1948 ELECTION

The first months of 1948 were entirely dedicated to the election campaign. Never again, in the whole history of the Republic, was a campaign to be fought so bitterly by both sides, or to be influenced so heavily by international events.

American intervention was breath-taking in its size, its ingenuity and its flagrant contempt for any principle of non-interference in the internal affairs of another country. The US administration designated $176m of 'Interim Aid' to Italy in the first three months of 1948. After that, the Marshall Plan entered into full operation. James Dunn, the American ambassador at Rome, made sure that this massive injection of aid did not go unobserved by the Italian general public. The arrival of every hundredth ship bearing food, medicines, etc., was turned into a special celebration. Every time the port of arrival was a different one – Civitavecchia, Bari, Genoa, Naples – and every time Dunn's speech became more overtly political. Whenever a new bridge or school or hospital was constructed with American help, there was the indefatigable ambassador travelling the length of the peninsula to speak in the name of America, the Free World and, by implication, the Christian Democrats. Often the goods unloaded from the ports would be put on a special 'friendship train' (the idea was the American journalist Drew Pearson's) and then distributed with due ceremonial at the stations along the line. And just in case the message was not clear enough, on 20 March 1948 George Marshall warned that all help to Italy would immediately cease in the event of a Communist victory.[98]

Material aid was accompanied by a well-timed intervention on the crucial question of the future of Trieste. A month before the elections, the United States, Great Britain and France promised that the city would return to Italian rule. They were able to do this because the Free Territory under international supervision had never come into being. Russia and the Western powers had been unable to agree on a neutral governor, and Zone A, which comprised Trieste, had remained under British and American military occupation. The worst clause of the Peace Treaty had thus been reversed at a stroke.

From the States itself the large and predominantly conservative Italo-American community devised all manner of propaganda initiatives in favour of the Christian Democrats. Hollywood stars recorded messages of support, rallies were held, and more than a million letters were dispatched to Italy during the election campaign. The letters all stressed the Communist peril, often contained a few dollars, and were for the most part not even addressed to relatives. On 17 March Cardinal Spellman, in the presence of President Truman, declared: 'And one month from tomorrow as Italy must make her choice of government, I cannot believe that the Italian people . . . will chose Stalinism against God, Soviet Russia against America – America who has done so much and stands ready and willing to do so much more, if Italy remains a free, friendly and unfettered nation.'[99]

If all else failed there was always military intervention. The American government studied various plans of action in the event of the Popular Front's victory. Truman hoped to convince part of the Socialists to destroy the unity of the left, but if this did not succeed there were proposals for encouraging an anti-Communist insurrection, with financial and military assistance to clandestine groups, and for the direct military occupation of Sicily and Sardinia. As it was, the Americans strengthened their Mediterranean fleet, and in the weeks preceding the election their warships anchored in the waters of the main Italian ports.[100]

In the face of all this, the Russians had very little to offer. Indeed, the principal event in eastern Europe in these months, the Communist *coup d'état* in Prague, did a great deal to damage the chances of a left-wing victory in the Italian elections. At the end of February 1948 the non-Communist parties in Czechosovakia tried to bring down the coalition government headed by the Communist Klement Gottwald. The Czech CP responded by mobilizing the base of the party, and armed workers occupied the factories. After four days of great tension, the President of the Republic, Beneš, agreed to constitute a new government with the Communists in a clear majority. A series of purges and arrests followed, and on 10 March the former Foreign Minister, Jan Masaryk, was found dead under a window of his house.

The Italian left-wing press unhesitatingly whitewashed the events of Prague. For *L'Unità* an American plot had been defeated by mass intervention; for *Avanti!* the *coup d'état* was a 'popular victory' and Masaryk had killed himself while in a state of 'mental alienation'. But the rest of the press carried a quite different message: the Czech events were a warning of what would happen in Italy if the Popular Front won, for the Communists were incapable of abiding by the rules of democracy and their victory was but a prelude to dictatorship.[101]

On the home front, the Christian Democrats benefited greatly from the fervent intervention, at every level, of the Roman Catholic church. On 29 March Pius XII told the Romans that 'the solemn hour of Christian conscience has sounded'; Cardinal Siri and other members of the episcopate warned that it was a mortal sin not to vote, or to vote 'for lists and candidates who do not give sufficient assurances of respecting the rights of God, the Church and mankind'; in the local churches the parish priests delivered sermons which were unashamedly electoral addresses for the DC.[102] To provide further support, Luigi Gedda, president of Catholic Action, founded the 'civic committees', local action groups whose principal task was to convince Catholics to turn out *en masse* on polling day and to instruct the illiterate and aged amongst them on what to do once inside the polling booth. By 18 April Gedda estimated that his army was some 300,000 strong.[103]

The Christian Democrats themselves waged a campaign that was both virulent and effective. Their posters featured subjects such as Italian mothers shielding their children from Communist wolves, snakes bearing the poison of 'free love' rearing up to destroy the Italian family, and a giant Stalin trampling underfoot the Roman monument to Victor Emanuel II. To these psychological fears were added material ones: 'Don't think,' proclaimed one DC broadsheet, 'that with Togliatti's speeches you'll be able to flavour your *pastasciutta*. All intelligent people will vote for De Gasperi because he's obtained free from America the flour for your spaghetti as well as the sauce to go on it.'[104]

On no account did the Christian Democrats want to appear exclusively as the party of the employing class. The presence of Dossetti's radical wing within the DC helped to make possible a direct appeal to Catholic workers, and De Gasperi himself, in the course of his election speeches, frequently mentioned the need for fundamental reforms. Shortly before 18 April the Confindustria granted a substantial pay rise to white-collar workers, thus mollifying a section of the electorate which had been unable to defend its standard of living in the previous three years.

As for the Popular Front, its rallies were attended by vast, enthusiastic crowds far superior in numbers to those present at similar occasions organized by the DC. Many of the Front's leaders were confident of victory, but as Pajetta told Gambino at a later date: 'What we failed to understand was that only the majority of the politically active population was with us.'[105] The Front's programme was vague in content, and took little account of economic realities. Thus the Marshall Plan was hastily dismissed as a 'desperate solution' devised *in extremis* by monopoly capitalism. Those sectors of the electorate which the left had to win (at least in part) in order to ensure victory were more scared than attracted by the Front's propaganda and its more vociferous supporters. One Genoese militant has recalled how at Ansaldo just before 18 April 'many comrades ... told the white-collar workers: "You'll see, on Monday [after the elections] we may not even let you into the factory." '[106]

The election campaign ended with a suitable exchange of insults between the two leaders of the opposing camps. De Gasperi accused Togliatti of having the cloven foot of the devil. Togliatti replied that he had no intention of exposing his perfectly normal feet, but that one of them, heavily shod in a studded boot, would be firmly implanted in De Gasperi's backside once the elections were over.

The results belied Togliatti's threat. The Christian Democrats' success exceeded their wildest expectations. They not only recouped the ground they had lost since 1946 but soared to 48.5 per cent of the votes and an absolute majority in the Chamber of Deputies – 305 seats out of 574. Their victory was obtained at the expense of both left- and right-wing parties. In the South they mopped up much of the Monarchist and Qualunquista vote, and in the North they gained directly in working-class areas. Saragat's Social Democrats also prospered in the urban North, and were represented in the Chamber with thirty-three deputies.

The Popular Front obtained 31 per cent of the votes, as against the 39.7 per cent of the Socialists and Communists in 1946. The defeat was not an even one. In the South the Front actually made consistent progress, gaining for example nearly 6 per cent in Naples, whereas from Florence northwards their losses were very heavy. The greatest discrepancy was that between Communists and Socialists. The two parties had not presented separate lists, but had relied on the voters to indicate their preferences. It soon emerged that the Communists, far from losing support, had actually increased the number of their deputies from 106 in 1946 to 140 in 1948. The Socialists, on the other hand, had suffered a cataclysmic decline, passing from 115 deputies to only 41. From this moment onwards in the history of the Republic, Communist hegemony on the left was not in dispute.

Four days after the election, an exultant De Gasperi solemnly declared to the *Corriere della Sera*: 'Our people await a battle against unemployment, an increased dignity of labour, an agrarian reform. All this will be carried out.'[107]

Postscript

In the summer of 1948, as Italy began to be moulded in the image of Christian Democracy, one event rocked the new state to its very foundations. On 14 July an isolated fanatic by the name of Antonio Pallante shot and seriously wounded Palmiro Togliatti as he stood outside the parliament buildings at Rome. When news of what had happened began to spread through the peninsula, shops shut, workers downed tools, and the piazzas filled with angry crowds who interpreted the shooting as the beginning of an onslaught on the left. This was the last insurrectionary moment in post-war Italy. All the frustrations of the previous three years – the restraints accepted by the partisan movement, the failure to achieve reform, the humiliation of mass unemployment, the defeat of the Popular Front – now welled to the surface. In central Italy, at Abbadia San Salvatore on Monte Amiata, a policeman and a *carabiniere* were killed, and the miners took over the telephone exchange which controlled all communications between the North and Centre. At Turin workers occupied the FIAT factories and took sixteen hostages, including the managing director, Valletta. At Venice and Mestre road blocks were set up on the bridge over the lagoon, and workers guarded the chemical factories and oil distilleries.[108]

In one city, Genoa, the protest movement clearly assumed power. A Communist trade union leader from Genoa has left us this account of his 14 July 1948:

The emotional reaction was immense, not only amongst us, but in all the population of the city . . . Neither the internal commissions nor the Camera di Lavoro declared the strike; the factories just stopped work by themselves. I went home, I knew nothing of what was happening, I ate, and then I went out again . . . everyone was aghast, there was war in the air. I rushed to the Chamber of Labour; in the meanwhile the city was slowly grinding to a halt, spontaneously, and there was the great spontaneous demonstration in Piazza de Ferrari, the classic piazza for political meetings at Genoa. The executive committee of the Chamber of Labour then held an extraordinary meeting – the Christian Democrats did not show up – and we decided on a forty-eight-hour general strike in protest. We were just drawing up a list of instructions when news arrived that in the piazza the crowd had got the better of the police and had captured their armoured cars. We were practically in a state of civil war. That evening Genoa was in the hands of the people, so much so that at eight o'clock, if I remember right, the chief of police phoned the ex-partisans' association and said: 'Send me a group of partisans to defend the police headquarters, because I'm completely isolated here.' All the police had fled, the whole lot, it was a terrifying occasion . . . [Later] I received a phone call from Di Vittorio: 'But it's only Genoa that's gone so far!! Have you all gone off your heads?! What's the situation now?' 'Two dead,' I replied; 'there's been shooting all night, it could have been much worse; with all the bullets that have been flying around it's a miracle there are only two dead. There could have been four hundred.'[109]

Was revolution a possibility in this situation? All the Communist leaders replied with an emphatic no, both at the time and later, and it is difficult to disagree with them. The response in the North had not been uniform, and the South, with one or two notable exceptions like the shipyards at Castellamare di Stabia, had hardly moved at all. There were few signs of the army or police deserting, and Scelba had at his disposition 180,000 police and Carabinieri, and the army as well. Gian Carlo Pajetta thought that insurrection was feasible in the North, but that Italy would then have been cut in two. Pietro Secchia, who was in charge of the organization of the PCI at the time, said that an insurrection could have counted on only three major centres – Genoa, Venice and Turin, and that the rest were uncertainly balanced or safely garrisoned by the government. Togliatti himself had no doubts. In 1960 he passed this scathing judgement, which encapsulates his whole political outlook and formation: 'Certainly, an insurrectionary attack – and its inevitable defeat – either in 1946 or 1948 would have suited some comrades very well. No danger of the bureaucratization of the party in that case! And the so-called "revolutionary cadres" could have gone off happily to schools of tactics and strategy in prison or in exile!'[110]

At the time the Communist leaders intervened swiftly to prevent what they considered would have been a tragic mistake. By 16 July they were hard at work persuading their militants to unblock roads, dismantle barricades, release hostages and return to work. By the 18th De Gasperi moved back on to the offensive. A wave of repression swept through those areas which had responded most vigorously to the news of the attempted assassination. A hundred and forty-seven of the inhabitants of Abbadia San Salvatore and its environs were arrested and put on trial. On 15 July many of them had undoubtedly believed that Togliatti had met the same fate as Giacomo Matteotti, who had been murdered by a Fascist squad in June 1924. They thought that a new Fascist era was dawning, and that it was time to fight to the end.[111] In the event they were both right and wrong: there was no return to Fascism, but the battle which had begun in September 1943, and which caused many of them to join the local Garibaldi brigade, had been decisively lost by that summer of 1948.

Chapter 4

The Agrarian Reform

T HE CHRISTIAN DEMOCRATS had not won the 1948 elections on a purely conservative ticket. De Gasperi had stoutly maintained the progressive nature of his party, its awareness of the need for social justice, its desire to overcome the worst legacies of the recent and not so recent past. Even with the left decisively defeated, reform remained a dominant item on the political agenda.

However, behind the generic emphasis on the need for reforms, there lurked a number of complex and fundamental questions: what sort of reform was envisaged, whose interest would it serve, and how was it to be carried out? Widely differing answers to these questions circulated in Italy at the time. The Communists and Socialists, for instance, argued the necessity of what they called 'structural reforms', which would serve to increase the power and organization of the anti-capitalist forces in the country and which would provide important elements in the transition to socialism.[1] Dossetti's followers in the Christian Democrat Party had a different, though almost equally radical view of reform. Their vision of a deeply spiritual and socially just Catholic party was translated into a welcome for the sweeping welfare reforms which the British Labour government had recently carried through. In his speech to the third congress of the DC, at Venice in June 1949, Dossetti said: 'The problem is to insert within the portals of the state that part of the Italian people which is, in a certain sense, the most dynamic.' And here he clearly had in mind what he and Giorgio La Pira called *'la povera gente'*.[2] On the other hand, the majority of the Christian Democrats viewed reform with some suspicion. They supported piecemeal adjustments of the system which would lessen the social tensions inherent in it, but had no desire to question its basic nature.

In the history of Italy since 1943, very few pieces of legislation have ever been graced unequivocally with the distinctive title of reform. One of them was the series of three laws concerning agriculture passed between May and December of 1950. It is to their cause, content and effects that this chapter is dedicated.

Peasant Agitations and Government Responses

a. THE PEASANT MOVEMENT FROM THE GULLO DECREES TO THE KILLINGS AT MELISSA

Fausto Gullo's attempts to reform southern agriculture had not, as we have seen (pp. 106–8), been crowned with success. The new Minister of Agriculture, the Christian Democrat Antonio Segni, himself a wealthy landowner from Sardinia, further undercut his predecessor's legislation in two decrees of September 1946 and December 1947. In particular, Article 7 of the first decree gave the landowners the right to reclaim the land if the peasants infringed the conditions on which it had been conceded. This clause was used by the landowners, once the left had been thrown out of government, to wage an all-out legal offensive against the peasants' cooperatives. Much of the land gained in the winter of 1946–7 was lost the following year.[3]

Segni thus reassured the southern élites, and in the April 1948 elections the D C recouped much of the electoral terrain it had lost in the rural South. However, the problems of these regions remained as pressing as before. Too much of the best land was in too few hands and too many people had no land at all. In the 1954 parliamentary inquest on poverty, 85 per cent of the families classified as poverty-stricken were to be found in the South, with Calabria and Basilicata in the forefront. Per capita income, taking 100 as the national average, was 174 in Piedmont and 52 in Calabria. When the Communists organized a regional assembly in Calabria in December 1949, the peasants were invited to draw up lists of their complaints, on the lines of the 1788 French *cahiers de doléance*. It emerged that 90 per cent of the communes in Calabria had either no school buildings or schools housed in unhygienic constructions; 85 per cent of the communes were without drains and 81 per cent without adequate aqueducts; there was one hospital bed per 1,500 inhabitants, and nearly 49 per cent of the adult population were illiterate.[4]

One great step forward, it is true, had been taken. After 1944, thanks to Allied intervention, DDT was employed extensively for the first time. Whole areas of malaria-ridden coastal plain and marsh, in Sardinia, Sicily, the Tuscan Maremma and elsewhere, were rendered habitable.

However, the other afflictions of the southern peasantry remained unattenuated. In 1949, the peasants' movement, which had already seen one extended cycle of protest between 1944 and 1947, moved on to the offensive again. In spite of the fate of the Gullo decrees, the movement continued to be inspired by a sense of legitimacy that was both ancient and modern. The columns that marched on the *latifondi* in that year often had a copy of the 1948 republican Constitution attached to their banner poles. Article 42 in particular had been learned by heart: 'Private property is recognized and guaranteed by the law which may determine . . . its limits in order to ensure its social functions and render it accessible to all.' Still more potent was that collective memory (to which reference has already been made) of demesne land promised to the peasant communes in Napoleonic times but never assigned to them. Between 1944 and 1947 many occupations of former demesne land had taken place, regardless of whether the land was 'poorly cultivated' or not.

Most of the leaders of the peasant movement and many of its rank and file belonged to the Communist Party. Indeed, the PCI sections in the villages and agro-towns of the rural South were completely dominated by the poorest peasants. This pauperized character of the southern rural party caused considerable concern amongst the national leadership. In April 1947 Togliatti urged in no uncertain terms the cadres from the Messina federation to apply the party's alliance strategy and widen its social base:

For too many of you our sections have become meeting-places only for the poor, for the *miserabili*. The rooms themselves show this: they're squalid, uncomfortable, quite unlike those in our northern sections, in Florence, Turin and Milan, in the capital or in Emilia, where any sort of person is happy to spend an evening there. Here instead the section is a little crowded room, full of the poorest elements of the population. They're constantly agitated, they debate the questions that they have at heart, they say they're hungry and that they need work. All this is healthy, it's a sign of class consciousness, it leads to struggle. However, many other elements are lacking, those who are able to link the poorest with the less poor, with those who have a profession or own a small piece of land.[5]

By late 1949 the Communist leadership was particularly concerned to combat the influence of the Coldiretti in the southern countryside. A special appeal had to be made to peasant proprietors and to small landowners as well. Such strategic considerations meant that land occupations of dubious legality, dominated by poor peasants, preoccupied the Roman leadership and PCI regional secretaries like Mario Alicata in Calabria. The Cold

War was at its height, and the débâcle after the attempted assassination of Togliatti had destroyed any lingering insurrectionary illusions amongst the northern party. Togliatti had no desire for peasant action in the South to present the DC with a pretext for further anti-Communist measures on a national scale. However, the southern militants, especially in Calabria, had a different view of the situation, and were unwilling (and often unable) to restrain the peasant movement once it was under way.[6]

In October 1949 the Calabrian peasantry once again marched on the great estates. National conditions no longer favoured them as in previous years, when the left was still in government, Gullo was Minister of Agriculture and a more socially equitable post-war settlement still seemed a possibility. Yet the mobilization of 24 October 1949 exceeded all the expectations of its organizers. Some 14,000 peasants took part, from the communes in the eastern parts of the provinces of Cosenza and Catanzaro. Entire villages set out in procession, women with their children, some of the men on horseback and the red banners of the Communists often carried next to the portrait of the patron saint of the village. From the slopes of adjoining hills different columns of peasants would wave their banners to each other, as a greeting and as encouragement. When they arrived at the estates of the great landowners, the peasants meticulously pegged out and divided the land, and the work of preparation for sowing could then begin.[7]

Incensed at this latest wave of occupations, a group of Calabrian Christian Democrat deputies left for Rome to request extensive police intervention. Scelba's flying squads were soon on their way to the Calabrian villages. On 28 October one of these squads arrived at the village of Melissa, north of Crotone, where they were quartered for the night in the home of the local landowner, Baron Berlingieri. The peasants at Melissa had occupied an estate by the name of Fragalà, half of which had been assigned to their commune by Napoleonic legislation of 1811. The Berlingieri family, however, had over time usurped the whole of the estate. In 1946 and 1947 the local peasantry had taken over Fragalà, and Berlingieri, as if in recognition of the validity of their claim, offered them one third of the estate in settlement. This the peasants had refused.

On the morning of 29 October 1949 the police arrived on the estate. They tried to force the peasants off the land, but the villagers refused to be intimidated. The police then opened fire. Three people were killed, all of them by gunshot wounds in the back. They were Giovanni Zito, aged fifteen, Francesco Nigro, aged twenty-nine, and a young woman, Angelina Mauro, who died later in hospital. Another fifteen peasants were wounded and there were six arrests.[8]

The killings at Melissa, like Giuliano's May Day attack at Portella delle Ginestre, once again forced the condition of the southern peasantry to the attention of the whole nation. The great newspapers sent their correspondents post-haste to the South. The journalists were appalled by the arrogance of the landowners and the deprivations of the peasants. Vittorio Gorresio, from Turin's *La Stampa*, reported the views of a local historian called Mario Mandalari, who claimed that, on the basis of his research in notarial archives, half a million hectares of demesne land was due to the peasants in the province of Cosenza alone.[9]

Peasant reaction was even more important. In the wake of Melissa, the peasant movement spread far beyond Calabria, and involved practically every region of southern Italy. In the next three months nine more peasants were to die, scores were to be wounded, and several thousand arrested.

It is worth trying to analyse in some detail the forms and significance of this extraordinary mobilization. Land occupations and demonstrations were usually planned and organized in the local Communist section or at the Camera di Lavoro, often on a Sunday. The next day a long procession would set off towards the estate that had been chosen. The following account, one of many, is from Campofiorito in western Sicily. It is of special significance as taking place in a Mafia stronghold:

At the head of the procession were the children in their school uniforms and with bows in their hair, holding little red and tricolour flags. That day it had been decided to close the schools: the whole *paese* was going to occupy the manors [*feudi*] of Giardinello and Conte Raineri. After the children came the women, then the village band in uniform, playing '*A fanfaredda vinciu*', I can still remember how it goes, then the peasants on horseback or on mules, dragging ploughs behind them; then the landless labourers on foot, and then a mixed crowd of students, small proprietors, shoemakers, shopkeepers. The whole village was on the move. I was a primary schoolteacher at the time, I'd just got my diploma.

As soon as the procession moved off, the police and *carabinieri*, in their jeeps and lorries, tried to move into position on road no. 111, which at that time was the principal road through Campofiorito. But the women and children sat down in the middle of the road so that the police couldn't pass, and the procession went on. The long column took short cuts through the fields, it divided into many parts, sometimes we ran, and at the end we linked up again and reached the *feudi*. There we ploughed and sowed the uncultivated land, but they were more symbolic actions than anything else. I remember it was October or November 1949, unforgettable days, an interminable struggle sustained by hundreds of assemblies of the peasant leagues, by meetings in the Camere di Lavoro and in the Communist and Socialist sections of the whole zone of Corleone. We worked like madmen. At Bisacquino there were serious incidents with the police, they arrested Pio La Torre and other comrades. Nothing like that happened to us, but I was cautioned and then charged by the *carabinieri*. Under Article 650 of the penal code I was accused, together with 200 peasants, 200!, of having violated private property.[10]

The occupations in this account were largely symbolic, but in many parts of the South they were intended to be permanent. Both men and women would set to work on the land; often, and especially if the land was already under some form of cultivation, they could expect trouble from the *carabinieri*. In confrontations of this sort, peasant women played a vital role in defusing tension, talking to the *carabinieri* individually to try and convince them of the justice of the peasant cause, surrounding their menfolk in a large circle if it looked as if the police were about to charge, and if all else failed, pretending to faint or have a hysterical fit in order to distract the *carabinieri* and allow the men to escape unharmed.[11]

In the course of these struggles, the balance between different elements of peasant consciousness shifted radically. The habitual distrust, fatalism and individualism of the South were eclipsed by those elements which promoted solidarity amongst the peasants. The core of collective consciousness, the focal point of action was the *paese* itself, with its closed, concentrated formation and its *égalité des pauvres*. Gabriella Gribaudi has captured very well these qualities in her description of 'Velia' at this time ('Velia' is in fact Eboli, a large agro-town in Campania):

The dimension of the *vicinato*, of face-to-face relations, had a fundamental importance; it was the first element of aggregation. Faced with the uncertainties of work, with the particular harshness of life on the plains (the kilometres and kilometres covered on foot or on bicycle, the risk of malaria, the difficult relationship with the landowners), the *paese* was the symbol of peace, of solidarity, of physical rest and recovery, of affections, of friendship. Certainly the reality was less idyllic and much more complicated, but in certain aspects this vision could become a new myth, a new common language, a Utopia based on solidarity to be used in the fight against others. 'Red Velia' in fact.[12]

Communism, as it was interpreted and understood in this context, fused with the Utopian, religious and mystical elements that were so strongly present in peasant culture. However, Communism was an especially dangerous form of mysticism, for unlike *tarantismo* or the extended trance it was to be applied to existing property relationships. An extraordinary and exalted *fede pubblica* was created. The organization and collective action of the peasantry would lead them into a new golden age. 'Why,' asked the party of its militants, 'are the workers in the Soviet Union masters of the factories and the peasants of the land they till? Why have the scourges of unemployment, prostitution and hunger disappeared? Why do women have the same wages as men for the same work? Why does the Russian people enjoy the greatest amount of liberty and the most democratic constitution in the world?'[13] The answer lay in their discipline, their organization, their willingness to fight.

At the same time, Communist egalitarianism attacked at their roots those norms which Banfield was later to dub 'amoral familism'. The political culture of equality drew families together, persuaded them to pool their resources, appealed to elements of generosity and self-sacrifice. Family and collectivity, far from existing as polar opposites, were presented as converging and mutually reinforcing elements of civil society.[14]

It would be all too easy to romanticize this particular moment in southern rural history, to present it rather as the PCI itself presented the Soviet Union to the peasants. In reality it was riven with tensions and dissent, not least because the solidarities that arose at the moment of collective action could not be sustained indefinitely. When the land was occupied, as 'Gino O.' recounted (see p. 3), all attempts to farm it collectively were rejected: 'We tried to institute collective control, but jealousies and dissent broke forth, and the opposition of the old was so strong that we were forced to draw individual lots.' Some families were more numerous and had more resources than others, and went their own way once the occasion arose. Peasant proprietors and the rural poor could only with great difficulty find a unity of purpose. The dominant values of the South were not easily submerged beneath the high tide of collective action.[15]

None the less the peasant movements of 1944–7 and 1949–50 were extraordinary attempts to break the mould of a society riven with distrust. Individualism and solidarity, family and collectivity related to each other in a dramatic mixture of aspirations and delusions. This was the greatest attempt to set familism within a collective context in the rural South. It was also the last.

Although all the regions of the South were involved in some way or other, it was Basilicata, the Abruzzi and Sicily which followed the Calabrian example most forcefully. In December 1949, in Basilicata, an estimated 20,000 peasants occupied 15,000 hectares of land in the countryside around Matera. On 7 December 1949 the villagers of Montescaglioso marched to occupy the Lacava estates. They were led, according to the *carabinieri*, by two women, Anna Avena and Nunzia Suglia. Both were to be arrested and sentenced to two years' and four months' imprisonment. A week after the initial occupation the police suddenly occupied Montescaglioso at two in the morning, cut off the electricity, and began a house-to-house search. The peasants gathered in the main square and tried to march out of the village. A policeman was knocked down and retaliated by opening fire on the crowd; he seriously wounded two people, one of whom, Giuseppe Novello, a landless labourer, died soon after. On the day of his funeral the local prefect finally granted the peasants the right to sow 4,500 hectares of land.[16]

In the Abruzzi, agitation was concentrated in the area of the Fucino basin. The Fucino had been the third largest lake in Italy (after Garda and Maggiore), but had been drained by Prince Torlonia in 1878. In all there were 16,500 hectares of reclaimed land, of which the surrounding villages claimed 2,500 in compensation for the fishing rights they had previously enjoyed on the lake. The latter-day Torlonias had been absentee landowners, keeping their peasants in permanent destitution and doing nothing to improve the productivity of the land.

In February 1950 the landless labourers and peasant renters of the region decided on a novel form of protest – the staging of a work-in or 'strike in reverse' as the peasants called it. This form of action had first been attempted in the South in Calabria, but received its most successful application in the Fucino basin. The peasants marched on to the Torlonia estates and set to work on improving the primitive road network and digging irrigation canals. The police and Torlonia's guards tried to chase them off the land, but the peasants were too numerous and kept reassembling in small groups and starting work again on another spot. They demanded the application of the *imponibile di mano d'opera*, which would have constrained Prince Torlonia to take on hundreds of unemployed landless labourers. In this way the land occupations were linked with one of the basic demands of the rural trade union movement.

On 22 February 1950 a general strike was called in the region to support the work-in. Shops, offices and schools shut, and the local railway stations were occupied. The locomotives were festooned with red and tricolour banners, and with placards which bore the principal slogan of the struggle: *'Via dal Fucino il Torlonia'* ('Out with the Torlonia'). Two days later the government gave orders to the prefect of L'Aquila to sign a decree imposing the *imponibile*. Here, as elsewhere, the landowning class replied with killings and bloodshed. On 30 April at the village of Celano, Torlonia's guards fired directly into a crowd of villagers, killing two of them, Antonio Berardicurti, a Communist, and Agostino Paris, a Socialist.[17]

In Sicily in the first months of 1950 the landless labourers won many thousands of days of work through the successful imposition of the *imponibile*. Land occupations, previously largely symbolic in nature, now saw the peasants ploughing and sowing as on the southern mainland. Li Causi, the Sicilian Communist leader, announced on 12 March 1950: 'In the last two weeks tens of thousands of poor peasants and landless labourers in vast areas of the provinces of Palermo and Messina, and in the plateau areas of the provinces of Enna, Calatanisetta and Agrigento, have been occupying the uncultivated land . . . This movement is without precedent in the history of Sicilian agrarian struggles.'[18]

At Bronte, west of Mount Etna, the peasants had once again occupied part of the extensive estate which the Bourbons had given to

Horatio Nelson in recognition for the part that he had played in the Neapolitan counter-revolution of 1799. In 1860 Bronte had been the scene of one of the most infamous and tragic incidents in Sicilian rural history. The peasants, believing Garibaldi to be their liberator, had risen up and slaughtered the local bourgeoisie who, together with the Nelsons, had deprived them of their promised share of the demesne land. Garibaldi sent Nino Bixio to restore order. The peasant leaders were shot, as was the local lawyer Lombardo, who had been sympathetic to their cause but not their methods. The peasant claims went unheard and the demesne land was not redistributed.[19]

If the South was the area in greatest ferment in the winter of 1949–50,[20] it is important to note that the landless labourers of the northern plains had also taken major strike action, both in 1948 and above all in May and June 1949.[21] One of the poorest areas of the North, and the only one which was to be affected by the agrarian reform, was the Po delta. Here the landless labourers lived in great destitution; many of their dwellings were one-roomed huts made of straw and marsh reeds, with beaten-earth floors. Average annual employment for a male agricultural worker was 114 days per year in 1948. In May 1948 the labourers on the northern banks of the Po, in the area known as the Polesine, had fought a bitter strike battle with the landowners, in which one of the labourers at Trecenta was killed by the police.[22] This local strike ended in victory, but both in the Polesine and elsewhere in the North the degree of tension and of class hostility remained very great indeed.

b. THE DC AND THE REFORM

All this created an alarming and unexpected situation for the Christian Democrats. At first sight their commitment to substantial agrarian reform seemed unquestionable. In 1946 De Gasperi had said: 'Now is the time when the great landowners must make sacrifices . . . We must move towards a new equilibrium, towards another system of landed property that is based upon social justice.' In 1947 he had promised that the South was 'the commitment of honour for the Christian Democrats'.[23] De Gasperi, Segni and others clearly favoured the creation of a stratum of independent peasant proprietors which could serve as a bulwark against the spread of Communism in the South. Their philosophy of 'peasantism', heavily influenced by Arrigo Serpieri's teaching during the Fascist period, was in striking contrast to rural Catholicism's pre-1922 emphasis on peasant solidarity and cooperation rather than on competition.[24]

Yet in the eighteen months between their electoral victory of April 1948 and the killings at Melissa of October 1949 the DC had done absolutely nothing. In May 1948 Segni, as Minister of Agriculture, declared that the great estates would be eliminated. In July of the same year it seemed as if his project for an agrarian reform was ready, but in August it was declared only to be 'in preparation'. By October he announced a simple programme of land reclamation instead, explaining that this was 'one of the many means by which we can reach the agrarian reform'. He added: 'We have pledged ourselves to realize the reform, and we will honour our pledge, but for intuitive reasons the exact way in which we will honour it cannot yet be specified.'[25]

'Intuitive reasons' was DC gobbledy-gook for the opposition of the great landowners within the party. The southern magnates were well represented in the DC's parliamentary group, and had no intention of allowing their property rights to be infringed. However, after Melissa and the peasant protests that followed it, the Christian Democrat leaders could procrastinate no more. They faced a clear choice: either they put down the peasant movement, and that would involve a lot more bloodshed, since there was no way in which the police could simply control a mass protest of such dimensions; or they took on the agrarian wing of their party.

Within the party two groups strongly favoured reform. Angelo Costa, head of the Confindustria and one of the outstanding architects of Italian capitalism's post-war recovery, had no intention of allowing the southern magnates' pig-headedness to jeopardize the social and political stability needed for industrial reconstruction. He and his group therefore exerted great pressure on De Gasperi to abandon the southern landowners to their fate. Dossetti's followers, who controlled as much as a third of the party in 1949, were equally insistent, though obviously for different reasons.[26]

It is also interesting to note that the Americans were strongly in favour of immediate action in the South. The continuing relevance of 'farmer' ideology in the United States meant that post-war American administrations had little patience with large absentee landowners anywhere in the world. During the American occupation of Japan after 1945, General MacArthur had forced through the expropriation of the absentee landlords and the redistribution of the land to the peasantry. In Washington on 5 December 1949, the US Secretary of State, Dean Acheson, called in the Italian ambassador, Alberto Tarchiani, to express considerable displeasure at the situation that had arisen in southern Italy.[27]

Other events were also forcing the vacillating De Gasperi into reform action. On 9 January 1950 Scelba's police opened fire during a workers' demonstration at Modena, killing six people. There was widespread revulsion in the country and in the newspapers at the consistent use of firearms against unarmed peasants and workers. De Gasperi decided to form a new government, this time without the Liberals, whose opposition to agrarian reform was well known. In March he went a step further, re-appointing Dossetti vice-secretary of the party and incorporating other leaders of his group into the government. The way to the agrarian reform was open.

Even so, what finally transpired was not the agrarian reform, but various slices of it. The agrarian interests forced the D C to adopt for the first time what was to be one of their most persistent and unsatisfactory practices: the passing of various 'temporary' measures, with the promise that 'real' reform would follow, which it never did. Thus in May 1950 the first provisions for Calabria (called the *legge Sila*, the Sila law) were approved by Parliament. In midsummer Segni presented his draft of the *legge stralcio* (literally his 'extract' from the agrarian law). This was bitterly opposed by the southern magnates, who produced an 'extract' of their own. After intense party feuding Segni's version was approved by the D C's parliamentary group with 196 votes in favour, but 109 deputies either abstained or absented themselves. The *legge stralcio* was then approved in Parliament on 28 July 1950, with only 210 votes in favour out of a possible 574. It was to apply to the Fucino basin, the Tuscan Maremma, the Po delta and various parts of Sardinia, Basilicata, Campania and, at a later date, Puglia. Finally, on the last day of 1950, the Sicilian regional assembly passed a similar law regarding the reform of the island's *latifondi*.[28]

Content and Effects of the Reform

a. AN OVERVIEW

The principal provision of the three agrarian reform laws – the Calabrian, Sicilian and *stralcio* – was for the expropriation of sections of the great landed estates and their redistribution amongst the peasantry of the regions concerned. The criteria for expropriation were not uniform. The Sila law (for Calabria) stipulated that all 'unimproved' arable land on estates over 300 hectares in size was liable to confiscation. The other two laws preferred to estimate the land principally by value rather than extent. Thus all estates worth over 30,000 lire were to be subject to expropriations, with a sliding-scale system safeguarding the more productive landowners while penalizing the largest ones. In all more than 700,000 hectares were expropriated, with full compensation based on the land's value being paid by the state in the form of government bonds.

The reform boards of the different regions divided the expropriated land amongst an estimated 120,000 peasant families. Two types of property were created: the *podere*, or small farm, designed for those who previously had owned no land at all; and the *quota*, which was meant to supplement the smallholdings of the poorer peasant proprietors. The *poderi* varied in size from three to thirty hectares: in Calabria, one of the principal areas of reform, the average size was only 5.37 hectares, while in Sardinia, where the reform was very limited in extent, the average size was as much as 19.27 hectares. The *quote* varied in size from three to six hectares. All peasants in receipt of land were to pay for it by means of thirty annual payments, after which it became theirs. The reform boards were to help the new landowners through the provision of housing, credit, irrigation and technical advice. Those in receipt of land were obliged to join cooperatives, which, it was hoped, would offset the small size of most of the new farms.

The inadequate nature of the reform laws was almost immediately apparent. In the first place, the landowners naturally tried to avoid expropriation as best they could. Many hastily divided their estates among the members of their family, while those in Calabria made full use of the ambiguous phrase 'unimproved' land. It was often sufficient to have built even the most rudimentary shed, barn or the like for the land to be classified as 'improved' (*trasformato*) and thus escape confiscation. The very provisions of the laws ensured that nearly all land acquired by the peasants was of poor quality. In Sicily, of the 74,290 hectares distributed, 95 per cent was classified as 'inferior' and 'marginal', while only 0.4 per cent was described as 'well-irrigated'.[29]

Worse still, the amount of land confiscated was nowhere near sufficient to meet the peasants' needs. The Sicilian reform board drew up a list of 67,000 peasant families which, in its opinion, were eligible for land allocation. Of these, slightly over 17,000, or 26 per cent, actually received any land. In Calabria the figures were better: 18,902 out of the 25,080 families deemed eligible were given farms or plots. Even so, this left more than 6,000 families out in the cold, and at a village level spelt tragedy and embitterment. The French scholar A. M. Seronde noted that in the commune of Roccabernarda in Calabria 'there remain forty-six families of landless labourers who have obtained nothing and to whom nothing can be given because there is no land left'.[30]

The paltry nature of the reform was accentuated by the fact that a great deal of the land already granted to the peasant cooperatives under the Gullo decrees was now included in the new reform areas. In Calabria, for instance, almost the entire holdings of the cooperatives (an estimated 25,000 hectares) were re-appropriated, and formed a considerable portion of the 76,000 hectares of the new *poderi* and *quote*.[31]

The reform also led indirectly to a great rise in land prices. The major landowners, fearing further expropriations and peasant militancy, put a great deal of land on to the market both before and after the reform. They found willing buyers, both amongst other landowners and the peasants. In an important law of February 1948 the Christian Democrats had made it easier for peasants to acquire property by instituting a system of rural mortgages repayable over forty years and offering other credit facilities. Many of those excluded from the reform felt that, whatever the price, they could not let this opportunity pass by. Between 1948 and 1952 land fever gripped the southern peasantry, and in many areas the price per hectare doubled or trebled.

Finally, mention must be made of the reform boards themselves. From the outset, they were solid enclaves of DC power. There were no peasant representatives, but the southern magnates often managed to get their men into positions of power. In Calabria, a relative of the Marquis of Tropea, one of the great landowners affected by the reform, became president of the reform board.[32] Nearly all the reform agencies, when allocating land, actively discriminated against those who had led the land occupations or who were known as Communist militants.

It is hardly surprising, given this long list of negative factors, that the Communists themselves initially voted against the reform laws. Very soon they changed their minds. When it became clear that not even the letter of the law was going to be observed, the Communists urged their militants 'to fight the application of the law, in order to improve it'. They tried to ensure, among other things, that all those eligible for land actually applied for it, that land allocations were not made on political grounds and that the cooperatives promised by the law became independent entities, run by the peasants themselves. All these were fairly hopeless battles. The Communists had led the peasant agitations, but it was the Christian Democrats who had carried through the reform and who fully intended to operate it in the way they chose.

b. THE CASE OF CALABRIA

In order to follow the long-term evolution of the reform in some detail, it is worth concentrating on one region in particular. Calabria is the obvious choice, both because of the widely varying agricultural conditions of its reform area, and because of Pezzino's recent study of the way in which the Sila law has been applied.

The area affected by the Sila law was not the whole of Calabria but, roughly speaking, the eastern third of it. The area is 573,000 hectares in extent, and can be divided into four distinct geographical zones. The Sila itself is a mountainous region, heavily wooded and used mainly as a summer pasture ground for sheep. A few *latifondisti* owned most of the land. The peasantry, who lived in miserable villages on the edge of the upper plateaux of the Sila, were mainly *terragisti*, renting small strips of the *latifondi* on an annual basis. The hills below and around the Sila were some of the worst agricultural land in Italy. They were of Pliocene clay, liable to erosion and landslides, and over the centuries had suffered from poor farming, torrential rain in the winter and long, arid summers. Here again most of the land belonged to a handful of landowners, while the peasants, whose numbers had significantly increased between 1930 and 1950, lived in utter destitution.

The third agricultural zone was the infamous Marchesato di Crotone, in which Melissa itself was situated. This undulating countryside of clay and sand, stretching down to the Ionian Sea, enjoyed a less extreme climate than the Sila, but suffered from a drastic lack of water. This was *latifondo* territory *par excellence*. In the commune of Cuto 83 per cent of the land belonged to 2 per cent of the population. Cuto's population had grown by 37 per cent in the years 1934–49, and one public water fountain served the village's 9,348 inhabitants. Moneylenders would charge the peasants 50 per cent interest on a loan lent for the seven months of the wheat crop cycle.[33]

The last of the Calabrian areas covered by the reform was the most fertile. In the plains of the Ionian coastline, like the Piana di Sibari, the valleys of the Tacino and Neto rivers, and the rich lands of the communes of Corigliano and Rossano, there existed a thriving agriculture based on olives and fruit trees. But this was also the area where the *latifondi* were least dominant, and where there were significant peasant smallholdings.[34]

Of the 573,000 hectares of the reform area, only 85,917 ha., or 15 per cent, was eventually expropriated.[35] The Communists pointed out that if the Sila law had been rigorously applied, at least another 40,000 ha. could have been confiscated. Of the expropriated land 19.7 per cent was in the Sila mountains, 39.7 per cent in the hills, 30 per cent in the Marchesato di Crotone and only 10.6 per cent in the fertile coastal plains.

On the all-important question of long-term state aid to the new peasant farms, it is clear that a selection process operated from the outset. Whereas the settlements of the coastal areas, a small minority of the new farms, were seen as potential profit makers, the *poderi* of the interior, with an average of little more than five hectares of land each, were not given any real chance of becoming self-sufficient. They were created more to split the peasant movement and to reduce social tension in the countryside than to offer any long-term prospect of successful peasant proprietorship. They were there, as Manlio Rossi-Doria put it, *'per resistere'*, until such time as massive peasant emigration solved the problem by eliminating it.[36]

In its irrigation policy the reform board concentrated mainly on the fertile coastal plains. By September 1964 it claimed to have irrigated more than 8,000 hectares of land, but more than half of this was in the coastal areas, which constituted only one tenth of the total land expropriated. The absence of irrigation works was particularly crippling in the Marchesato, where the very low annual rainfall made irrigation an absolute necessity if peasant farming was to thrive. By 1964 a paltry 594 hectares had been irrigated in the two poorest communes of the Marchesato, Cutro and Isolo di Capo Rizzuto.[37]

In land clearance, in road building and in housing the work of the reform board was more equitably distributed. Spending on house construction, the most expensive single item of the reform board's budget, in fact slightly favoured the Marchesato over other regions. In the absence both of sufficient land per farm and adequate irrigation, it is dubious how far this was justifiable. Visitors to the Marchesato in the 1960s all remarked on the transformation of the area, with its brightly painted new farmhouses, each situated on their own land. But this was largely a façade, for the essential criteria for the farms' viability had not been assured.

Finally, the long-term selectivity of the reform board becomes starkly apparent in its credit policy. In the first seven years of the reform a generous system of credit operated over the whole area affected by the reform. The reform board supplied raw materials, services and tools to meet the peasants' needs. Seed corn was to be repaid, without interest, at harvest time, while other goods could be paid for over a twenty-year period at low interest rates. Many peasants did not make regular repayments, and the board's services were widely regarded as a form of welfare hand-out. However, in the agriculture year 1957–8, a sudden change of policy took place. Credit was offered on much harsher terms and all those who were in debt with the board were refused further concessions. Only those farms which were functioning economically were able to meet the new terms imposed, and few of those were to be found in the interior.[38]

The Calabrian reform, then, evolved in a very different way from that desired by the peasants in 1949–50. A restricted number of new farms, mainly in the plains and the river valleys, received persistent encouragement to join the ranks of small capitalist enterprises. The rest stood no real chance of becoming even self-sufficient. They were aided in a consistent way until the late 1950s and then largely left to their fate. The original assignees, however, did not abandon the land; by 1969 only 10 per cent had done so. Their holdings were insufficient by themselves to provide a livelihood, but were better than nothing and could serve as a fall-back for their families. Henceforth, the major part of family income came from the work in the booming building industry of Cosenza, or else from emigration.[39]

c. OTHER REFORM AREAS

Useful though the detailed picture from Calabria is, it would be foolhardy to generalize from it for the rest of the country. There were reform areas which achieved significantly better results, and others which fared distinctly worse. The Maremma belongs in the former category. In the Maremma an energetic reform board acquired no less than 182,000 hectares of stagnant *latifondi* in an area which extended 200 kilometres along the Tyrrhenian coast between Pisa and Rome, and 40 kilometres inland towards the Apennines. The board chose to satisfy less than 60 per cent of the 32,500 applicants for land, but did create *poderi* which averaged sixteen hectares each. Livestock farming was vigorously encouraged, and over the period 1953–64 its share increased from 10 to 38 per cent of total output in the reform area. With the passing of the years, the farms in the poorer hill areas suffered a fate similar to those in Calabria, but those in the plains flourished.[40]

At the opposite end of the spectrum lies the Sicilian reform, if such it can be called. Corruption was rife from the outset in ERAS (the Sicilian reform board) and land assignment proceeded at a snail's pace. By 1954 only 19,000 hectares had been assigned to some 4,300 families. Land occupations continued well into the fifties, whereas in most other regions they stopped soon after the promulgation of the new laws. The *lotti* into which the land was divided were little bigger than the *quote* elsewhere, and Blok described those in the Corleone district as 'unviable strips'. Grandiose irrigation plans were announced, but by 1966 only 150 of the small earth-dammed hill lakes had been completed, out of the more than 5,000 originally planned.[41]

Though the results in the reform areas varied widely, they did have certain common characteristics. One was the attempt, as in the Marchesato, to move the new peasant owners into isolated farmhouses and hamlets. All the reform boards spent very large sums of money on building farmhouses, often out of materials like cement which were peculiarly unsuited to the climate of the South. The policy was no more than a partial success. By the late 1970s, at the time of the survey carried out by INSOR (The National Institute of Rural Sociology), only 59 per cent of the assignees were still living on the land. The pull of the community, the precarious viability of many of the plots, the possibility of casual labour in the agro-towns during the winter, all worked against the 'farmhouse' mentality of the reform.[42]

Another feature common to most reform boards was an over-powerful and over-numerous bureaucracy. The Sicilian ERAS was the worst offender. It employed 3,000 people, 2,000 of whom worked in the new eight-storey ERAS headquarters at Palermo. Not surprisingly, one third of ERAS's budget in the first eight years of its activity went on administrative costs.[43] Other reform boards were not as bad, but all were valuable sources of local patronage for the DC. They were also un-democratic and authoritarian towards the peasants themselves. The obligatory cooperatives set up by the reform in Calabria were resounding failures. At a post-reform conference organized by the DC, peasant delegates were highly critical of the relationship between reform bureacracy and peasant assignee. As one of them said: 'It should be the peasant owner who seeks the collaboration of the agency and not the agency that acts independently with the peasant owner as its dependant.'[44] In later years marketing cooperatives have flourished, but usually only in the specialized fields of fruit, wine and dairy products, and then as initiatives involving all the peasants of a locality and not just the beneficiaries of the reform.

At the end of the seventies the INSOR survey revealed that out of the original 121,621 assignments of land, 97,400 or just over 80 per cent remained. The numbers of *poderi* had diminished more than the *quote*, while in Sicily more than a quarter of the *lotti* had disappeared. None the less the amount of land farmed had actually increased, from an original 681,617 hectares to 850,235 hectares.[45] Beneath these figures lie a number of discernible national trends. That relating to the abandonment of the poorer hill farms has already been mentioned. Of the farms remaining, a distinction can be made between those of limited acreage, which tend to be farmed by older couples (very often the original assignees), and those which have expanded significantly under young proprietors. In the irrigated areas the younger peasants have developed a dynamic agriculture, based largely on livestock rearing and market gardening. They, unlike their parents, are not the impoverished and militant labourers of the past, but the peasant entrepreneurs of the future.

Conclusion

The Italian agrarian reform has aroused considerable enthusiasm, both from those whose responsibility it was, and from many later observers. When Antonio Segni visited the Fucino basin on 19 March 1950, he told the assembled peasants that the reform was 'the most important act of social renovation since the unification of Italy'. Luigi Einaudi described it as 'a blow from a battering ram'. Corrado Barberis, the director of INSOR, suggests that it is 'perhaps the most important legislative act of the entire post-war period'.[46]

The reform was certainly the first serious attempt in the history of the unified state to alter property relationships in favour of the rural poor. In an interview for the BBC's Third Programme in 1957, Manlio Rossi-Doria, both critic and fervid supporter of the reform, noted how the Italian state had finally found the courage to 'attack the great absentee landowners around whom the forces of southern conservatism and immobilism had always gathered'.[47] He also stressed how great were the problems of the hill and mountain areas of the South, with their poor soils and excess population. No easy solutions existed here.

However, he also pointed out how limited the reform had been, and how much of what had been done in its name, especially in the South, had been done badly. One might go further. Judged by the aspirations of the peasants themselves, by the demands that erupted in the wake of the killings at Melissa, the reform was a bitter disappointment. The expropriated land was nowhere near sufficient to meet their needs, and much of it had already been in their hands as a result of the Gullo decrees. Much of it also was former demesne land to which the peasant communes claimed an ancient and inalienable right. Those fortunate enough to receive a small farm often found, especially in the poverty-stricken inland areas where peasant militancy had been greatest, that there was no way to make the farm self-sufficient, and that the bulk of state aid was increasingly directed elsewhere.[48]

In addition, the laws of 1950 touched only one area of agrarian reform, that of land redistribution. The vital questions of the reform of agrarian contracts, a national plan for land reclamation and the conditions and wages of landless labourers were either not confronted or else resolved to the detriment of the rural poor. Segni's bill governing agrarian contracts, which incorporated some of the demands of the rural trade unions, was first approved by the Chamber of Deputies in November 1950. It then took ten months to reach the Agrarian Commission of the Senate, and after a massive mobilization by the landowning elements in Parliament was quietly put to one side. All the gains made on the question of the *collocamento di classe* (the trade union control over the hiring of landless labourers) were reversed in April 1949, when the leaders of the CGIL reached a most unhappy compromise with the government, embodied in Fanfani's law of that month; this shifted the balance of class forces back towards the landowners, for it afforded the workers' organizations only consultative powers in the hiring process.[49]

The agrarian reform could in no way be described as a 'structural' reform, in the sense of being a step in the transition to socialism. After the hurricane of peasant protest, the confiscation of a limited amount of un-improved land from southern magnates and its selective redistribution to individual peasant proprietors re-established the legitimacy of traditional property relations in the South. It also brought much land that had previously been outside or marginal to the market within its workings for the first time.[50] A process of selection encouraged by state discrimination gradually weeded out the profitable from the unprofitable farms, the young capitalist farmers from the part-timers and the ageing peasant couples.

Above all, the reform broke for ever those attempts at aggregation and cooperation which, for all their limitations, had been the inspiration behind peasant agitations from 1944 to 1950. The land occupations involving the mobilization of whole agro-towns swiftly came to an end, with the exception of those in some areas of Sicily. The cooperatives that had mushroomed after the Gullo decrees ceased to exist. The peasant movement split irrevocably. A hundred and twenty thousand peasant families were henceforth dependent for their existence upon the reform boards; more than a few defections took place from the Communist ranks. The values of solidarity, of self-sacrifice and egalitarianism, the attempts to overcome familism and distrust, developed by the movement amidst all manner of difficulties and contradictions, were firmly emarginated. In the subsequent history of the South, no such attempt to build an alternative political ethos is to be found again. The defeat of 1950 was thus of historic proportions, for it determined the values of contemporary southern life.[51]

This is one way of looking at the reform. There is another, of equal historical significance. The agrarian reform was an important part of an overall strategy for securing Christian Democrat power in the agrarian South. This strategy was not planned and executed according to some preconceived blueprint, but was rather a series of contingent responses which none the less reveal an underlying unity of intent.

The events of 1950, as Villari has pointed out, dealt the death blow to the old agrarian power bloc in the South.[52] The agrarian élites had suffered a series of traumatic shocks in that fateful year: first their traditional dominance, long on the decline, had been jolted to the core by the sustained peasant agitations; then the party upon whom they relied to restore their authority had, in their eyes, betrayed them. In December 1951 the southern notables of the party issued a solemn and public protest against the D C's actions, and many of them turned to the extreme right-wing parties for consolation. Many moved their money out of land altogether, preferring to invest as property speculators in the booming provincial capitals, like Cosenza and Agrigento.

The Christian Democrats, therefore, had to construct a new system of social alliances in the agrarian South, based not so much upon traditional domination of the land as upon control of the resources of the state. Fascist agrarian policy, with its glorification of peasant life and its assistance schemes, provided a model which could be developed and refined. The law of February 1948 on the formation of small peasant property was the first step in this direction. The setting up of a state fund to facilitate mortgage terms for peasant buyers ensured that by September 1956 667,003 hectares of land had passed into peasant hands. To this figure must be added the 700,000 hectares of the land reform itself, with all its attendant funding.[53]

In addition, the DC's collateral peasant organization, the Coldiretti, under the determined leadership of Paolo Bonomi, assumed an ever more central role in administering state funds for the rural areas. In 1949 Bonomi won a fierce battle to take over the Federconsorzi, the state organization which distributed agricultural machines, fertilizer, etc., on a national scale. In 1954, thanks to Coldiretti pressure, the Chamber of Deputies passed a law extending pensions to peasant farmers. A year later the Casse Mutue, small farmers' health insurance agencies, were set up, again under Coldiretti control. Throughout this period Bonomi maintained extremely close links with the Ministry of Agiculture. By 1956, 1,600,000 peasant families were members of his organization. Thus, in response to Communist attempts to unite the peasantry around a programme of cooperation and egalitarianism, Bonomi replied with a Catholic associationism which exalted individual peasant families and their properties, and guaranteed their protection by the state.[54]

Last but not least, in 1950 the government not only passed the agrarian reform laws, but also set up the Cassa per il Mezzogiorno (the state fund for the South). The Cassa was to play *the* decisive role in the long-term economic development of the South, and it will be discussed at length in the next chapter.

It is in this context that the agrarian reform assumes its full significance. To the ideological and cultural leadership provided by the parish network, the DC now added the material basis upon which to found its support. To the Communist thrust from below for fundamental change in the countryside, the DC responded from above with a reorganization and re-formulation of its own making. The agrarian reform can thus be seen as one element in the Christian Democrats' construction of consent, based upon the use and abuse of state power. It is to an analysis of this state, to its structure and operation on a national scale, that we must now turn.

Chapter 5

Christian Democracy in
State and Society

The 1953 General Election

*A*LTHOUGH THE Christian Democrats had won an absolute majority in the 1948 elections (48.5 per cent of the votes had given them 305 seats in the Chamber of Deputies out of a total of 574), their security of tenure was short-lived. By 1951 significant sections of their electorate had become dissatisfied. In the South, the extreme right – Monarchists and neo-Fascists – was again making headway in the major cities, while the rural notables, as we have just seen, turned away from the DC after the agrarian reform. All over the country, the inaction of the ruling party since 1948, its inability to live up to its promises of social justice, was to cost it votes. In the local elections of 1951–2, the Christian Democrat share of the poll fell dramatically to 35.1 per cent. The haemorrhage of votes was even more serious in the South, where the DC gained only 30.3 per cent. The cities of Naples, Bari and Foggia fell into the hands of the extreme right. It began to look as if the national election result of 1948, far from heralding an era of undisputed Christian Democrat supremacy, would prove to be unrepeatable.

Thus as early as 1952 the lack of a stable majority, that problem which has completely dominated the surface of contemporary Italian politics, had already come to the fore. From now on politics, at least at its most obvious level, would be characterized by the continuing spectacle of the Christian Democrats searching for political allies, first in the centre, and then on both the right and the left. A disproportionate amount of the considerable energy and subtlety of the Italian political class was to be devoted to this process. Unstable coalitions were formed and dissolved; governments came and went. Each time the public was subjected to ritual news bulletins, on radio and then television, dedicated to the latest complexities of inter- and intra-party squabbling.

Faced with this prospect, De Gasperi tried to avoid it in a brutally simple fashion – by changing the rules of the game. He and Gonella, the Christian Democrat secretary, argued that the system of proportional representation enshrined in the Constitution was not to be regarded as sacrosanct. They proposed a new electoral law by which any alliance of parties which received one vote more than 50 per cent of the votes cast at a national election would receive two thirds of the seats in the Chamber of Deputies. Thus if a coalition of Christian Democrats, Liberals, Republicans and Social Democrats polled more than 50 per cent of the vote, the DC would be rewarded in all probability, given its numerical predominance within the alliance, with at least 50 per cent of the seats in Parliament. The ruling party was proposing, in mid-term, an electoral device to ensure its continuity in power.

Why did De Gasperi, whose commitment to parliamentary democracy was not to be doubted, adopt a measure which smacked so strongly of gerrymandering? In his later years both external and internal influences had pushed him towards a more conservative stance. He was under strong pressure from the Vatican to ally with the extreme right (the municipal elections in Rome in 1952 provided the most clamorous example of this), and the international tension engendered by the Korean war had confirmed his anti-Communism.[1] The left wing of the DC, having made such notable progress at the time of the agrarian reform, faltered badly in the summer of 1951. Dossetti, despairing of any possibility of Catholic reformism, chose to dissolve his faction in the party and to retire to monastic life. De Gasperi rapidly evolved his concept of 'protected democracy', by which the nascent and vulnerable Italian democratic state had to be preserved from its enemies. The means to this end was a series of exceptional laws aimed at restricting civil liberties, enforcing law and order, and limiting the rights of 'extremists'. The electoral law was the single most important element in this strategy.[2]

The Communist and Socialist opposition waged a fierce but unsuccessful campaign against the law. They immediately dubbed it *'la legge truffa'*, 'the swindle law', and pointed out that it bore more than a passing resemblance to Mussolini's Acerbo law of 1923, by which any party receiving more than 25 per cent of the votes would be rewarded with two thirds of the seats in the Chamber. They also tried to obstruct the passage of the bill through Parliament by every kind of delaying tactic, but eventually it became law.

Everything therefore depended on the national elections of 7 June 1953. The campaign was again fought in the political climate of the Cold War, with the American ambassador, Clare Boothe Luce, issuing dire warnings of the consequences if the Christian Democrats lost. The four centre parties — Christian Democrats, Liberals, Social Democrats and Republicans — formed an alliance which in the previous election had gained 62.6 per cent of the votes. Their victory, and with it two thirds of the seats in the Chamber of Deputies, seemed assured. However, a small group of dissidents from the three minor parties, led by Ferruccio Parri and Piero Calamandrei, broke away to form another electoral grouping, Unità Popolare, which campaigned vigorously against the *legge truffa*. In addition, the Christian Democrats knew that they were bound to lose ground in the Mezzogiorno.

When the results were announced, the centre coalition was seen to have failed by the narrowest of margins: they had gained 49.85 per cent of the votes, and a mere 57,000 votes stood between them and two thirds of the seats in the Chamber. The principal victors were the extreme right. The Monarchists had moved from 2.8 per cent to 6.9 per cent, and the neo-Fascist Movimento Sociale Italiano (MSI) from 2.0 to 5.8 per cent. The left, too, had improved on 1948. Communists and Socialists stood separately on this occasion, with the former gaining 22.6 per cent of the vote, and the latter 12.7 per cent. Taken together, this was an improvement of 4.3 per cent over the Popular Front's performance five years earlier. Unità Popolare had played a tiny but in the event significant role by depriving the centre coalition of 171,099 votes. As for the vanquished, the Christian Democrats went down to 40.1 per cent (48.5 per cent in 1948), and the three small centre parties between them lost 4.3 per cent.

Apart from the dramatic defeat of the *legge truffa*, which was annulled a year later, the elections of 1953 were significant for two other reasons: they marked the end of De Gasperi's political career, and the emergence of the neo-Fascists as a permanent force in Italian politics. De Gasperi had lent all his authority to the election campaign, and now had to pay the price of defeat. His attempt to form a new centre government failed to win a majority in the Chamber, and he gave way to one of his Christian Democrat colleagues, Giuseppe Pella. Little more than a year later De Gasperi died at the age of seventy-three.

As the dominant personality of the decade 1943–53, De Gasperi's stern, moralist and devoutly Catholic character, when combined with his Republicanism and anti-Fascism, were in welcome contrast to what had gone before. To the outside world this tall, stooped and slightly forbidding figure seemed a more than adequate symbol of an Italy that had turned its back on the Fascist past. His qualities as a politician were very great, and his handling of the period 1944–8, during which he outmanoeuvred the left and took the D C to its greatest electoral victory, was little short of masterly.

However, De Gasperi had always talked the language of progress, of social reform and of justice. Judged by these standards, his achievements were more limited. The mandate given to him by the country in 1948 was to a great extent wasted in the following five years, and the D C under his leadership became the party of stagnant centrism and virulent anti-Communism. To hold power in the face of the enemy became almost an end in itself, to which essential reforms were to be subordinated. In early 1952 De Gasperi made these views explicit in a letter to Pius XII:

The alternative is this: either to concentrate around the most reliable and active Catholics a large grouping which can resist the still extremely strong grouping of the enemy; or to create a sort of Christian Labour Party which is more systematic and programmatic and which, by rationalizing method, doctrine and action, would proceed to social reform in a most ample manner. But this second alternative ignores the danger of isolation and the reduction of our forces; and it could incur the risk of our being too weak to defend our supreme civil and spiritual values.[3]

The Catholic and the Cold War warrior in De Gasperi thus triumphed over the reformer. Perhaps only his commitment to Europe and the creation of the Cassa per il Mezzogiorno (see below, pp. 159–62) can be seen as partial counterbalances to the lack of action in other vital fields, as disparate as fiscal reform or the drawing up a new penal code. Neither the *legge truffa* nor the concept of 'protected democracy' were fitting ends to so notable a political career.

The Christian Democrats' losses in 1953 had been the extreme right's gains. While the Monarchists soon split and declined, the neo-Fascists of the M S I were to remain a significant minority in Italian politics. Their votes came mainly from the southern cities, from quarters like Flaminio in Rome, with its history of housing construction under Fascism and its population of clerks who owed their jobs to the past regime. Theirs was a rhetorical nationalism: the question of Trieste was still being hotly debated in 1953, and the M S I also sought to represent all those who had suffered from Italy losing her African colonies. The party leaders came mainly from the second ranks of Mussolini's Republic of Salò. Augusto De Marsanich, the national secretary, represented the 'moderate' wing of the party, and sought a united front of all the right-wing parties against the Communist threat. Giorgio Almirante, who was later to hide his racist past beneath a veneer of respectability, was at this time the leader of the internal opposition which remained more faithful to the Fascist tradition. The M S I's 5 per cent of the vote, much of it inherited from the *qualunquista* movement, served as a constant reminder of the potent appeal that authoritarianism and nationalism could still exercise amongst the southern students, urban poor and lower middle classes.[4]

The Christian Democrats and the State

After the failure of the *legge truffa*, the Christian Democrats held power during the next five years by means of minority governments which relied for their survival on the votes of the small centre and right-wing parties. In some cases Christian Democrats alone formed the membership of the Council of Ministers; in others they allied with the Social Democrats and Liberals, their favoured partners of the time. Neither expedient was satisfactory. Politics stagnated, and the second legislature (from 1953–8) came to be known as the 'legislature of immobilism'. However, this was far from the whole story. The 1950s were in fact the crucial period in which the Christian Democrats laid the foundations of their state system, and by this and other means created a new consensus in Italian society. It is to an examination of these processes that the rest of this chapter is dedicated.

a. THE PRE-REPUBLICAN LEGACY

The state which the Christian Democrats inherited had a number of distinguishing features which were to influence greatly their own mode of governing. In the first place, it was highly centralized. When Italy was unified under the Piedmontese monarchy in the period 1859–70, the local autonomies and regional differences which lay at the heart of Italian history were consciously sacrificed to an all-powerful central bureaucracy. The drive to create a single nation with uniform traditions and laws soon meant that the state earned a reputation for being unnecessarily oppressive and interfering. Decisions, even of very minor importance, had to be taken at Rome, where the key ministries were the Ministries of Internal Affairs, of Finance and of Justice. At local level it was not the elected municipal councils but the agents of central government, the prefects, who held the whip hand.

Secondly, the functioning of the Italian administration was, from its inception, based upon the Germanic principle of the *Rechtsstaat* (the state based upon the rule of law). Under this principle legality was paramount: every activity carried out on behalf of the state had to be set within the framework of administrative law. Thus the history of the Italian bureaucracy is that of the minute regulation of administrative activity through the promulgation of laws, statutes, circulars and internal directives. The system was intended to safeguard the citizen against the arbitrary power of the bureaucracy. In reality, it led to the unparalleled confusion of an estimated

100,000 laws and directives governing the administrator's activity, and to a hierarchical civil service where the lower grades were quite unwilling to take initiatives or move outside the straitjacket of the regulations.[5] As a result, the Italian state was not only centralized but also inefficient.

Thirdly, the civil service soon came to be a breeding ground for clientelism. Secure jobs, favours, the expediting of personal papers through the administrative machinery, all were secured by patrons for clients in return for political fidelity. As early as 1913 Gaetano Salvemini denounced these practices in no uncertain terms. He expressed the hope that one day 'a courageous civil servant . . . will write the biography and the history of the political and bureaucratic careers of protectors and protected; and he will have to illustrate it by describing the relations of kinship, friendship and profiteering clientelism that exist on the one hand between the political and bureaucratic big shots [*gros bonnets*], and on the other the lesser parasites for whom, bit-by-bit, jobs and services are being created'.[6]

In spite of these practices, numbers of state employees do not seem to have increased disproportionately in relation to other European countries. There were clearly areas of clientelistic hiring, but there were also others of understaffing. Nor did the administration grow evenly over time. From a starting-point of some 50,000 state employees after Unification, numbers had reached 126,000 by 1891, and 377,000 by 1910. Much of this latter increase was due to the establishment of autonomous state agencies which administered the railways, telephones and postal services, and the state monopolies of salt and tobacco. Fascism did not at first lead to a new growth. De Stefani's law of 1923 in fact tried to freeze civil service recruitment. However, after 1932, with the 'statization' of primary schools, numbers increased markedly again, reaching 1,140,000 in 1941.[7]

Until the turn of the century the civil service was dominated by northerners, and by Piedmontese in particular. However, this picture gradually changed as the North became industrialized while the South stagnated. Increasingly, the educated youth of the North and Centre looked to the private sector with its high wages, while their counterparts in the South, faced with very poor job prospects, sought the security of the civil service. The universities of Rome, Naples, Palermo and Messina turned out law graduates in their thousands, and often their only hope of a job worthy of their status was in the public administration. By 1954 56.3 per cent of the administrative class in the civil service came from the South, although the southern population was only 37.3 per cent of the national total.[8] Thus the Italian state machine, over-centralized, clientelistic and inefficient, slowly acquired a southern character.

Italy's rulers, even before the Christian Democrats, were well aware of the political importance of this mass of southern functionaries. Mussolini himself had had this to say when rejecting further reform proposals from De Stefani:

> Your suggestions would severely reduce employment in state jobs for graduates from the South, thus damaging the southern white-collar proletariat. These people are very much to be feared: they possess an instinctive genius for propaganda, which has much effect in places where friendship and kinship ties are of the greatest importance . . . We must adopt a policy of maximum job availability in the state bureaucracy unless we want to have on our hands an insurrection of hungry – I repeat, hungry – intellectuals, which would be the most difficult of all insurrections to placate. Besides, it is a duty to take care of them.[9]

Finally, the Italian administration has been characterized by the phenomenon of 'parallel bureaucracies'. From the beginning of the twentieth century, the practice developed of founding government special agencies (*enti pubblici*) which were not part of the traditional ministerial bureaucracy. The state agencies (*aziende autonome*) controlling the railways, etc., briefly referred to above, were the first examples. Instead of a relatively unified structure being created, there grew up instead a whole series of autonomous institutions, all with their own bureaucracies, and all jealous of their own powers and spheres of influence. The reasons for the creation of this administrative jungle varied, some being honourable, others much less so. The need to avoid the dead hand of the traditional bureaucracy certainly figured prominently, but so too did the desire to create separate enclaves of power within the state.

The Fascist period witnessed the greatest growth of these special agencies: 260 were founded between 1922 and 1940. They varied from the giant IRI (the Institute for Industrial Reconstruction) to the social-service agencies which were known as the *parastato* and to the far smaller *enti* which amounted to little more than private fiefdoms. Although reliable figures are lacking for all parts of the administration, it is clear that by the end of the Second World War the parallel bureaucracies were already a formidable element in the baroque structure of the Italian state.[10]

b. THE REPUBLICAN STATE

Leaving aside for a moment the functioning of Parliament and the government, it is worth trying to gain a reasonably clear picture of the major component parts of the Italian state as it existed in the late 1940s. They are as follows: the army and the police; the judiciary; the ministerial bureaucracy; the special agencies including the *parastato*; local government.

In all these areas it is important to remember the substantial failure of *epurazione* and the strong continuities with the pre-Republican state. In spite of their role in the removal of Mussolini in 1943, the military had received a severe battering during the war, and emerged in a very subordinate position compared to that which they had enjoyed in the 1930s. On the other hand, the democratic and innovative spirit of the partisans did not succeed in permeating the armed forces, and no effective reform took place. The Italian military differed from their counterparts in Spain and France: there were no traditions of them having taken over from the civil authorities. Although the Republic was not to be free from the shadow of a military coup, this was not to be a dominant theme in its history.

For some years after the war the Italian armed forces remained a token force with no clear purpose. However, with the evolution of the Truman Doctrine, and especially with the onset of the Korean war, a new (if subservient) role came to be created for them within the context of American global strategy. Italy joined NATO in 1949 (see below, pp. 157–8). In 1950 and 1951, in a climate of increasing war fever, the Italian army was rapidly re-equipped by the United States. In June 1951 Admiral Carney arrived to take control of NATO forces in southern Europe. He set up his headquarters in Naples, and stressed the key role that the Italians could play in the Mediterranean theatre of war. At the same time the Italian government assigned 250 *miliardi** of lire to defence, and raised the period of obligatory military service to eighteen months.

Gradually war fever subsided, but the pattern had been set. From now on the Italian armed forces were integrated into a Cold War vision of European geo-politics. American and NATO bases spread through Italy, providing the military aspect of the all-conquering American model of the 1950s.[11]

The other part of the 'repressive apparatuses' of the Italian state, the police, has historically been divided into two sections: the Carabinieri, who were actually part of the army; and the PS (Pubblica Sicurezza), who before 1945 had had more limited means at their disposition. Under the Republic, and especially once the left had been excluded from government, both corps were significantly increased in size, to some 80,000 men each. The PS, with its new militarized mobile battalions and Scelba's *celere*, acquired equal status with the Carabinieri. Together, they outnumbered the army and formed the largest police force in Europe.

Rivalry between the two corps was very great. Although in broad terms the Carabinieri were supposed to be responsible for the smaller towns and the countryside, and the PS for the cities, in practice their responsibilities overlapped. The result was notable inefficiency and strife. Recruitment, especially for the Carabinieri, came from the poorest classes in

Miliardo is one thousand million, i.e. one US billion. It is here translated as billion throughout.

the South. Isolated from the communities they were supposed to serve (the Carabinieri barracks were the most primitive and inhospitable in Italy), both corps could be relied upon to obey orders, maintain law and order, and if deemed necessary use firearms against the populace.[12]

In the judiciary, too, it was difficult to find many echoes of the democratic and innovative aspects of the Italian Constitution. The judges who had served under Fascism kept their posts, and the Codice Rocco, the Fascist penal code, remained in force. The Constitutional Court, set up as the supreme legal guarantor of the principles of the new Republic, only began to function in 1956. Slowly it revoked some of the previous legislation most in contradiction with the Constitution. Distinct progress was made in the area of civil liberties, but this was a piecemeal and far from linear process. As late as 1961, for instance, the Court upheld Article 559 of the penal code, which punished a wife's adultery more severely than that of a husband, with up to a year's imprisonment.[13]

The judiciary in 1945 was a closed caste, resentful of its low pay, mainly recruited from the southern law faculties, and alien to the values of the Resistance. Through its corporate organization, the Associazione Nazionale Magistrati, it campaigned after the war for greater independence and higher pay. The first of these objectives was realized with the setting up in 1958 of the Supreme Council of the judiciary. The council, whose creation had been envisaged by the Constitution, was a body dominated by judges and in part elected by them. It took over responsibility from the Ministry of Justice for internal discipline and promotions within the profession.

The judiciary vigorously proclaimed its 'apolitical' nature, but its judgements reflected a continuing anti-Communism and lack of sympathy for the organized working-class movement. Two decades were to pass before this conservative mould began to disintegrate.[14]

If we turn now to the executive, it is vital first of all to understand the *general* nature of the relationship between citizen and administration which operated in the first decade of the Republic, and which was not substantially modified thereafter. The bureaucracy did not behave towards the citizen on the basis of the impartial execution of its tasks within clear temporal limits, but rather on the basis of its *discretionary* power. The speed and efficiency, indeed the very realization, of a bureaucratic act depended to a notable extent upon the pressures that the citizen could exert upon the administrator. Naturally, not all citizens were equal or could exert equal pressure. Inducements to bureaucratic action varied, from the relatively innocuous use of contacts to outright corruption. This deformed relationship between citizen and state, with its emphasis on the individual's capacity to trigger discretionary action, was a legacy which became an enduring feature of the republican state.[15]

After the war, the traditional nucleus of the administration, the ministerial bureaucracies, increased their number and size, leading to the overlapping of responsibilities, and the further physical dispersion of the central bureaucracy within Rome itself. The Treasury was undoubtedly the most important locus of power. A section of its central accounting office existed in every other ministry, and its approval was required for all expenditure. This gave it considerable negative powers of procrastination and veto. Indeed, the whole system, based as it was upon the post-Risorgimento values of the ratification and control of executive action, rather than on the speed and transparency of its actions, was bound to result in extensive delays. No public money could be spent without passing through five administrative stages: parliamentary vote of credits; legal verification by the Council of State (the supreme administrative court of the republic); control by the auditors of each ministry concerned; agreement of the treasury; notification of the Court of Accounts.[16]

In June 1949, an article in *Riforma Amministrativa*, the journal of DIRSTAT (National Association of the Executive Grade of Civil Servants), gave a revealing inside account of the central bureaucracy at work. Immense amounts of time and energy were being wasted in calculating employees' salaries. This was a true 'game of riddles', based upon unending distinctions and sub-distinctions. With the archives partly destroyed and partly 'inexplorable', the clerks had to try and deal with hundreds of demands every day for 'documentation', losing precious time in trying to find the unfindable. The numbers of civil servants had increased greatly since before the war, but efficiency had not, because it was taking more time to do the same job. The whole system was based 'on the gigantic movement of papers hither and thither, with so many delays and obstacles that you can imagine how delightful it is for us to work in it'.[17]

If we turn from the ministries to the special agencies and the 'parallel bureaucracies', we enter what a recent commentator, Vittorio Emiliani, has aptly called 'the only real Italian forest'.[18] In 1947 there were 841 *enti pubblici*, without counting those at a local level, and all the evidence suggests that this was a conservative estimate. Amidst this dense bureaucratic foliage, certain landmarks stood out. The autonomous state agencies administering the railways, telephones, postal services and state monopolies formed a distinct group which was more closely tied to the central ministries than was any other part of the parallel bureaucracies. The agencies had separate chairmen, boards of directors and budgets, but the relevant ministers remained responsible for laying down general policy.

IRI (the Institute for Industrial Reconstruction) was also conspicuous for being the largest agency for state intervention in the economy. Founded under Fascism in 1933, IRI was employing 216,000 people by

1948, of whom 160,000 were in manufacturing and only 27,000 in the South. Its principal areas of activity were steel, engineering, shipbuilding, shipping, electricity and telephones. IRI enjoyed considerable autonomy from the traditional bureaucracy, an autonomy reinforced by the fact that it was not governed by administrative law and that the companies it controlled were joint-stock enterprises. IRI maintained a controlling interest in them, but private investors also held shares.

In the immediate post-war period the future of IRI seemed very uncertain. Most liberal economists and businessmen demanded its dissolution and the immediate re-privatization of its companies. However, in the winter of 1947–8, under the leadership of the Christian Democrat Minister for Industry, Giuseppe Togni, a 'new course' was mapped out for it. IRI's engineering and shipbuilding concerns were to be grouped together and rationalized under a new holding, Finmeccanica; full support was to be given to the plans of Oscar Sinigaglia to transform the Italian steel industry; and the financing of IRI's concerns was to be sought increasingly on the private market rather than from Treasury funds. As we shall see, IRI's 'new course' was to have a profound importance both for Italy's public sector and its 'economic miracle'.[19]

A third major area in the forest of *enti pubblici* were the social-service agencies which belonged to the *parastato*.[20] Here too the basic configuration of public bodies had been established under Fascism. There were three major institutions: the National Institute for Social Security (INPS), the National Health Insurance Institution (INAM), and the National Institute for Workers' Compensation (INAIL). INPS, which had by far the largest funds and budget, was responsible principally for old-age and disability pensions, for maternity and family benefits, and for unemployment subsidies (of minimal proportions). INAM, as its name indicated, looked after health insurance, and INAIL insurance against accidents at work.

All three were public bodies enjoying administrative and financial independence while titularly under state supervision. They were supposed, in theory, to provide complete medical, pension and compensation coverage for all dependent workers and their families, but the system was both exclusive and chaotic. The unemployed, and also independent workers like artisans and peasant proprietors, did not form part of it. Those who did found overlapping and inefficient bureaucracies which led to extensive delays. Throughout the history of the Republic, the local offices of these institutions were characterized by interminable queues (or scrums) and desperate arguments over the validity of certificates and documentation.

These institutes were directly responsible not only for insurance but for health care. Here too the standard of service was notoriously low. The very title *'medico della mutua'* (the GP appointed by the social-service institute) had an immediate pejorative connotation. For some aspects of health care the three major *enti* had their own hospitals and infrastructures. For others, work was farmed out to private, often religious, hospitals and organizations. These latter had to sign separate contracts with the three institutions, leading to further problems of administration and accounting.

In April 1947 a parliamentary commission under Lodovico D'Aragona was instructed to draw up a plan for reform. It met 108 times and presented its report in 1948. None of its recommendations were acted upon.[21]

In addition to these major landmarks — IRI, INPS, and so on — there also existed, both in the *parastato* and elsewhere, many hundreds of smaller institutions which became known in time as the *enti inutili* (the useless agencies). These bodies were mainly concerned with welfare, and to a lesser extent with sporting, recreational and cultural activities. Fascism had been a boom time for them, but in general their development had been piecemeal, deriving from charitable, private and religious agencies serving sectional interests. They often duplicated each other, used up significant amounts of state money for little purpose, and survived the period 1943–8 unscathed. Thus EGELI, the agency for administering goods confiscated from the Italian Jews, was still in operation in 1950. So too was ONAIRC, the national organization for assistance to children in frontier regions. Founded in 1919, under Fascism its task had been to 'denationalize' German- and Slovene-speaking children living in the extreme north-east. Parliament finally voted its abolition in 1976, by which time it was receiving over 5bn lire a year from the state. ONOG, the national institute for war orphans, had 120 employees to look after 700 orphans, with a central administrative office block on the Lungotevere in Rome, and an income of one billion lire by 1975. Only 20 per cent of these funds reached the 'orphans', by now adult, while the rest went in employees' salaries and administrative expenses. The list is endless, and we must return to these *enti inutili* when considering the state strategy of the Christian Democrats.[22]

The last part of the Republic's state apparatus was local government. The Constitution had promised the devolution of considerable power to regional governments, but by 1950 only Sicily, the Val d'Aosta and Trentino-Alto Adige had been granted regional assemblies, and it was to be another two decades before regional government was finally extended to the rest of Italy. Without it, there were only two levels of local government: the provinces and the communes, for both of which elections were held once every five years. The provincial administrations had very limited powers and were wholly dependent on the Treasury for funds. The communes were very numerous (7,681 in 1947), and 90 per cent of them had less than 10,000 inhabitants. They enjoyed the normal responsibilities of local government: public health, local transport, the census, local policing, certain social services, etc. However, unlike local authorities in Britain, they had only limited powers to levy taxes and these were woefully inadequate for their purposes. The indebtedness, and thus the subordination, of many communes to central government was to increase with the passing of the years. Furthermore, the powers of control and veto which the prefects, the agents of central government in the localities, had historically held were not diminished under the Republic. All acts of the municipal authorities had to be communicated to the prefect within eight days, and he then had twenty-eight days in which to annul them if he saw fit. He also had the power to dissolve communal or provincial administrations: forty-one communes met this fate in the years 1947–9. In the smaller communes, especially in the rural South, the local commander (*maresciallo*) of the Carabinieri played the role of the prefect.[23]

c. CHRISTIAN DEMOCRAT STRATEGY

Unique amongst political parties in western Europe, the Italian Christian Democrats have remained, ever since 1947, the dominant party in government. The result has been an extraordinary degree of fusion between the Christian Democratic Party and the republican state. Political commentators have used different expressions to describe this phenomenon. Some have talked of the DC 'occupying' state power. Others have referred to the state being 'colonized' by the dominant political party. Others still have referred to the 'symbiosis' between party, government and state.[24] All have grasped the essential element of the *continuity* and *permanence* of Christian Democrat power, with its inevitable consequences for the relationship between party and state.

However, permanence in power did not go hand in hand with unity of purpose. If we examine Christian Democrat strategy as it developed in the 1950s, we see that it is characterized by permanent tensions and conflicts on at least three levels: that of ideology, that of the representation of interests and that of the party's organization.

At an ideological level, traditional Catholic social theory lay uneasily alongside liberal individualism. The Vatican had consistently warned against the effects of industrial society, and the Christian Democrats, especially those who had been part of Dossetti's faction, preached the need to safeguard Catholic values in a changing society. Solidarity (*solidarismo*), charity, associationism, the state's duty to protect the family, the weak and the poor, were constant themes in their propaganda. However, while the DC paid lip-service to these values and ideas, in practice the majority of the party fully espoused the cause of 'modernization'. Here the key themes, strongly shaped by American influences, were the liberty of the individual and of the firm, the unfettered development of technology and consumer capitalism, the free play of market forces. Thus *laissez-faire* ideas of the development of the economy and society clashed with those of Catholic integralism, which emphasized the need for society to correspond to and reflect Catholic values.[25]

A second level of tension was to be found in the D C's inter-classism. The desire to represent the interests of capital, the variegated sections of the urban and rural *ceti medi*, and Catholic workers as well, meant a constant battle over resources and the direction of state action. Here the dangers were twofold: the party could all too easily let the cause of the industrial and financial élites predominate; or it could attempt to serve all interests at once and become dangerously immobile, leaving the state as the sponge that absorbed all the sectional requests of society.

A final insidious element acting against a clear-cut strategy was the factionalism of the party. From the death of De Gasperi onwards the D C evolved in the direction of a party divided into increasingly powerful and well-organized factions. In the 1950s, the dominance of Fanfani's Iniziativa Democratica masked this tendency to some extent, but from 1959 onwards it emerged clearly. Each of these factions rotated around one or more leaders of national importance, was soundly based in at least one region of the country, and demanded its share of governmental power.[26]

As a result of these many layers of division, it is not surprising that Christian Democrat strategy should appear as multiform, and the state which it occupied as a sort of archipelago.[27] The various islands of the archipelago came to serve different interests within the party, either personal, or sectional, or (increasingly rarely) ideological. Different D C notables or their factions came to control key ministries for extended periods of time. Giulio Andreotti, for instance, was Minister of Defence for some seven years, from February 1959 to January 1966. Each national leader and each faction fought hard and long to preserve their power and autonomy in that sector of the state under their control.[28] The character of the Christian Democrats and their longevity in power thus served to accentuate what was in any case a basic feature of modern states, the diffused nature of power within them, and the struggle between their component parts.

To this picture must be added the consequences of coalition government. The small parties of the centre who assured the D C of a parliamentary majority had in turn to receive their own sectors of influence within the administration. The Social Democrats, for instance, gained the presidency of I N P S, the most powerful agency in the *parastato*, in 1949, and were to hold on to it until 1965.[29]

In conclusion, it would be wrong to maintain that the Christian Democrats invented the fragmentation of the Italian state; the parallel bureaucracies had existed long before they did. But they compounded it, for they brought to government a fierce factionalism, an extended class base and a system of inter-party alliances, all of which had to be satisfied from state resources.

Such a system of government had grave consequences for parliamentary democracy as it had been established by the Constitution. At the highest level, the independent power of ministers and heads of special agencies greatly reduced the collegiate role of the Council of Ministers (the Italian equivalent of the Cabinet). The Council met less often than its counterparts in other European countries, sometimes as little as once a month, accumulated long agendas which it could not complete, and thus abdicated a significant amount of its responsibilities to party magnates in their respective fields.

Parliament too played a subservient role. Unlike in Britain, no proper procedure was developed for subjecting ministers to hard questioning about their activities. In the first five legislatures (1948–72) the Chamber of Deputies passed a very high number of laws, an average of three hundred a year, but the great majority of these were of limited importance, catering to minor sectional or even individual interests (an example of the first category, chosen at random, was the law governing the conditions of junior officers in the finance police; of the second, the law funding the centre for the study of the works of the poet Leopardi, the Centro di Studi Leopardiani). Furthermore, nearly all these *leggine*, as they came to be called, were passed not by Parliament as a whole but in parliamentary committees. Here a four-fifths majority was necessary for a law's approval. Extensive horse-trading took place, not only between the parties of the government coalition, but also between majority and opposition. In this way the opposition (PCI and PSI) found a minor channel for representing interests of their own. Any vision of the Republic's Parliament as a great legislative and reforming body rapidly gave way to this more mundane reality.[30]

At the lowest level, the elected local governments saw their limited powers of decision-making overshadowed by government special agencies, like the Cassa per il Mezzogiorno, with their enviable resources and freedom of manoeuvre. As Cassese has commented: 'The republican Constitution passed over the state apparatuses without touching them, because in its articles the nineteenth-century myth of the supremacy of Parliament lived on. But the ebb and flow of administrative history are regulated by other, more concrete means, more closely tied to social than to constitutional history.'[31]

To emphasize the archipelago nature of the DC state and the party's fragmented nature is not to deny it any possibility of concerted action. In reality, the 1950s witness the party strengthening its own resources *vis-à-vis* two forces in society on which it had relied very heavily up to that date – the church hierarchy and private capital. The Vatican had exercised a predominant influence on the DC through the power of its ancillary organizations, especially Catholic Action and Gedda's civic committees, which were the key mobilizing agencies of the Catholic vote at election time. Having clashed bitterly with Pius XII over the choice of political allies for the DC, De Gasperi wanted to make the party more autonomous. In June 1954, at the fifth congress of the DC, he made these views explicit: 'There can be no doubt that in the church's domain our adhesion is loyal and sincere . . . But it is also true that neither faith nor virtue are sufficient for those who work in the field of society and politics; it is necessary to create and foster an instrument which is in keeping with the times, i.e. the party.'[32] At the same congress Amintore Fanfani was elected the new national secretary. A diminutive and dynamic university professor with a Fascist past, the forty-five-year-old Fanfani had, as we shall see, many reasons for following De Gasperi's advice to increase the strength of the party. One of them was undoubtedly to make the party independent of Catholic Action and to channel at least part of Catholic activism into the party itself.[33]

As for relations with the capitalist class, De Gasperi's initial solution to this problem was to work very closely with Angelo Costa, the head of Confindustria; private industry was to look back to the late forties and early fifties as a golden era when its influence upon government was very great. But neither De Gasperi nor those who succeeded him were content merely to serve the dominant economic power élites. They sought instead to increase the financial autonomy of the DC, and to make the party itself a major repository of economic power. The way to do this was through the state – by creating new government agencies like the Cassa per il Mezzogiorno and ENI (the National Agency for Hydrocarbons), by increasing the state's hold on the banking system and by encouraging the growth of the public sector of industry. In this way Dossetti's reformism, on which many of the new generation of leaders, like Fanfani and Moro, had been bred, found a distorted outlet in the increase of the economic power of the state under Christian Democratic control. The stages of this offensive and the nature of the new agencies will be analysed below. For the moment, in order to understand the general strategy of the Christian Democrats, it is sufficient to note that this first wave of government intervention in the economy reached its peak with the creation of the new Ministry for State Holdings in 1956, and with the removal in 1957 from Confindustria of all those companies under control of IRI.

None of this was much to the liking of the more backward sectors of private industry. They felt, quite rightly, that their position as a privileged interest group was being rapidly undermined. The large electrical corporations, in particular, were threatened by the growth of ENI, and saw themselves as prime targets for nationalization. In 1955 a man after their own heart, Alighiero De Micheli, took over from Costa as head of Confindustria. De Micheli resolved to challenge the expansionist DC by creating Confintesa, a union of industrial and agricultural élites. The new organization decided to support its own candidates at election time, either Liberals or right-wing Christian Democrats. At the local elections of 1956 this strategy had very limited success, and in 1958 it failed completely. By the end of 1950s it was therefore clear that the balance of forces between the economic élites and the dominant political party had shifted significantly in favour of the latter.[34]

However, in the economic as in other fields, it would be a mistake to present Christian Democratic strategy as in any way *systematic*. The party was too fragmented for that, and some of its creations, as we shall see, rapidly became quite uncontrollable monsters. The development of state economic power was a haphazard affair, heavily dependent upon factions and personalities. At the heart of the nation's economic life, one institution, the Bank of Italy, preserved an autonomy which would be difficult to explain if the DC's actions were construed as part of a relentless march towards total economic control.[35]

d. THE ITALIAN STATE IN THE INTERNATIONAL CONTEXT

If within Italy the composite and conflicting nature of the DC made its strategy anything but linear, in foreign affairs matters were rather more straightforward. The fundamental choice of a close relationship with the United States was made very early on. It was to be reinforced by the outbreak of the Cold War, and by American aid to the DC during the election campaign of 1948. From the moment that the anti-Fascist coalition split up in 1947, Italy was always destined to form an integral part of the American sphere of influence.

However, within this general orientation, there were major policy questions to be decided: the extent of Italy's participation in American global military strategy, the degree of her autonomy in evolving foreign policy, the amount of independence she could exert on major economic issues like the use of Marshall Aid funds.

After the war, Catholic thinking on international questions was strongly pacifist and in favour of neutrality. But as the world became increasingly divided into two camps, and anti-Communism in Italy reached unprecedented levels, the pressure upon De Gasperi to lead Italy into NATO became very great. At the end of November 1948 the Christian

Democrat deputies met to consider the issue. This was to be one of the very rare occasions for a major debate on foreign affairs within the party. De Gasperi opened the discussion by saying that 'with great anguish' he had decided that it was better to have 'that minimum of defence' which was now on offer than to have nothing at all. He was opposed by Dino Del Bo, representing the trade union wing of the party, who pleaded for Italy to remain neutral; and by Dossetti, whose argument was rather different. Dossetti accepted that it was useless for Italy to be 'an earthenware jar amidst those made out of iron'; he also felt that Italy belonged 'substantially in the ambit of the Western world'. However, he argued strongly that there was no immediate danger to her. The Christian Democrats should concentrate instead on working with other European countries towards a peaceful union outside the context of military alliances.[36]

This internal opposition was gradually undermined in the following months. De Gasperi was much helped by Pius XII's radio message of Christmas Eve 1948. The Pope made it clear that the 'solidarity of nations' was justified in guarding against an external threat: 'A people which is menaced or is victim of an unjust aggression, if it wishes to act in a Christian fashion, cannot remain in passive indifference.'[37] In March 1949 the Chamber of Deputies was asked to debate Italy's entry into NATO. Within the DC a motion favourable to entry gained the approval of the entire parliamentary group, with only three deputies voting against and a score abstaining.[38]

Once in NATO, it would be fair to say that Italy faithfully followed American directives, so much so that in the United States she became known as 'America's most faithful ally', and in certain left-wing circles as the 'Bulgaria of NATO'. Certainly, the degree of independence which the Christian Democrats chose to exercise *vis-à-vis* American foreign policy was minimal. Even issues which had major implications for Italian sovereignty, like the establishment of military bases, seem to have aroused little debate.[39]

On the other hand, on matters relating directly to Italy's political economy, the relationship between the United States and Italy was far from the command-and-obey variety. The direction of the flow of Marshall Aid funds shows this clearly. Between 1948 and 1952 more than $1,400m of ERP (European Recovery Program) funds reached Italy, or some 11 per cent of the total funds granted to Europe. In the Italian case, 80 per cent of the funds were grants in the form of goods, and 20 per cent were loans made available on very favourable terms. The Italian government was also required to set up a counterpart fund (*fondo lire*) equivalent to the sums being received in dollars. This fund was to be used for projects approved by ECA (the European Cooperation Administration), which had been established by the Americans. It has been estimated that Marshall Aid represented some 2 per cent of the Italian gross national product between 1948 and 1952. Judged on a purely quantitative level, it was thus an important but not decisive element in Italy's economic development in these years.[40]

At the height of the ERP programme, Paul Hoffman, the head of the ECA, wrote a 'country study' on Italy. In it he criticized the Italian use of ERP funds. No overall plan had been evolved, certain areas like steel and textiles were being indiscriminately favoured, the public administration had not been overhauled. Throughout the ERP programme American officials working in Italy complained bitterly that the Italian government had not taken any steps to correct the many *lacunae* in the Italian tax system.[41]

Beneath this concerted American criticism lay the reality of the limited control that the US could exercise over the use of ERP funds. Although no major study of Marshall Aid in Italy has yet been undertaken, it would appear that the funds went in a number of different directions. In the first year of the programme the strong accent on grain and coal imports reveals their essential aid character. The textile industry also benefited disproportionately, while until 1950 counterpart funds were used mainly to increase Bank of Italy reserves and maintain the stability of the currency. Thereafter, two different directions seem to have prevailed. One was the increasing use of funds to purchase machinery for state and private industry: FIAT, Finsider (the steel company of IRI), Edison and the thermo-electric companies were amongst the principal beneficiaries.

The other was the use of counterpart funds to do something about the South. Here the dramatic situation in the southern countryside, American concern and Catholic social ideology all played a part. The Cassa per il Mezzogiorno and the agrarian reform boards both became important recipients. The pattern of Marshall Aid spending thus corresponded only in part to American directives, and above all to the mosaic of different interests and opinions within the Italian political and business élites.[42]

Finally, on the question of European economic cooperation, we find a third position which is neither direct subordination to American policy nor the reflection of various internal pressures and lobbies. The United States certainly exerted pressure on all West European governments to move towards economic and military cooperation, but De Gasperi's commitment to European political unity went beyond the mere desire to comply. Like Schuman and Adenauer he came from a frontier region of Europe (the Trentino) which had always suffered from the territorial ambitions of competing nations. In addition, his early political formation had been strongly marked by Catholic internationalism.

De Gasperi supported a political federation of European states for two principal reasons: first because it would help to foster peace on the continent after a half-century dominated by war; and secondly because only economic union with northern Europe would be able to solve the structural problems of Italy's economy – its army of unemployed and the under-development of the South. Just as Mussolini had sought an imperial and Mediterranean solution to Italy's economic problems, so now De Gasperi sought a European one. On 20 January 1950 he wrote to the American Committee for a United Europe: 'It will be necessary to provide for the free movement not only of capital but also of persons; without this the problem of unemployment, one of Italy's gravest actual afflictions, cannot be resolved.'[43]

When the European steel and coal community came into being, De Gasperi and Ugo La Malfa, the Minister for Foreign Trade, pressed for immediate Italian participation. They did so in the face of opposition from the Italian private steel manufacturers, preoccupied by the end of protec-tionism. In spite of the fact that their lobby was led by Enrico Falck, a founder member of the D C, Italian membership of the community went ahead.[44]

In December 1951, a further step towards European unity was taken with the foundation of the European defence community. De Gasperi, heavily influenced by the European Federalist Movement led by Altiero Spinelli, used the occasion to insert into the new treaty a clause which foresaw the construction of a political union alongside the military one.

However, at this point the drive towards European political federation came to an abrupt halt. In France Gaullists and Communists combined to produce a parliamentary majority which refused to ratify the defence treaty. In Italy De Gasperi, as we have seen, fell from favour after the 1953 elections, and his successor, Pella, was no Europeanist. On a European scale the federalist and idealist phase gave way to a 'functionalist' one. European cooperation went ahead, but on a more narrowly economic scale. The Italian contribution continued to be significant, but less dynamic and idealist than under De Gasperi. In March 1957 the E E C finally came into being with the signing of the Treaty of Rome. As Cafagna has written: 'The Europe born of the Treaty was a Europe of markets, not a Europe based on common and progressive social standards, nor a Europe which took the initiative in defining qualitative lines of development within which growth and redistribution could be harmonized.'[45]

e. THE INNOVATIONS OF THE 1950s
The full significance of the creation of the Common Market was only to become apparent in the years of the 'economic miracle'. In the meantime the ruling party's attention was concentrated on the internal formation of the state, and especially on the growth of its own power within it.

It is as well to begin with the traditional, ministerial bureaucracy. In the absence of detailed studies for the 1950s, it is difficult to understand the processes at work in this sector. The upper ranks of the central administration continued to be dominated by southerners who had been trained as lawyers, and who seemed content to trade lack of decision-making powers in return for security. Unlike in many other European countries, there was little osmosis between the administrative and political classes. Instead, Italian senior civil servants remained a closed caste, living an uneasy relationship with the politicians: they needed their patronage but they resented their interference. In the post-war review, *Burocrazia*, senior civil servants argued that they should enjoy the same autonomy as the judiciary. A survey of 1965 showed that more than 47 per cent of civil servants thought that political interference in their activities was excessive. Their response was to seek refuge in a 'legalism' which obstructed the implementation of political decisions. Thus the central bureaucracy was far from being a bastion of impartial and enlightened administration, but it was not simply an enclave of Christian Democrat power either.[46]

The DC seemed both unable and unwilling to change this state of affairs. In 1950 an Office for the Reform of the Bureaucracy was instituted, but little was done to tackle the notorious deficiencies of the sector. No élite training school was set up, as in France, to mould a new generation of bureaucrats. Instead the party gave free rein to the process by which sectional and individual interests became all-important in the civil service, to the detriment both of its corporate power and of the relationship between state and citizen.

In the 1950s Fanfani regulated the pay and conditions of civil servants. He kept basic salaries very low while encouraging individual competition for bonuses, privileges and promotion. The hierarchical elements in the service were accentuated, with career prospects more heavily dependent than before upon personal and political preferences. At the same time different grades and different parts of the administration competed against each other in order to secure purely sectional advantages. There came into being what the scholar Ermanno Gorrieri, himself a member of the DC, was to call '*la giungla retributiva*' ('the remuneration jungle'), a tangled mass of micro-sectional laws and regulations governing pay and conditions. Such a fragmented civil service may have made control easier, but it certainly did not make for good government.[47]

It was, therefore, not in the traditional bureaucracy but in the realms of the special agencies that real innovation took place. While the institutions of the *parastato* and the '*enti inutili*' continued to be significant links in the chain of power, in the public sector of the economy new special agencies of outstanding importance were created. Three in particular stand out: the agrarian reform boards, the Cassa per il Mezzogiorno, and ENI.

The origins and purpose of the agrarian reform boards have already been discussed. They complemented the other great institution created for economic investment in the South, the Cassa per il Mezzogiorno. When the Cassa was founded in 1950, De Gasperi was reported as saying that he had chosen the word 'Cassa' (fund) 'to give to the Italians and above all to the southern Italians the almost physical sensation that there would be considerable sums reserved genuinely for the South, which would be allocated in a consistent and constant flow'.[48] There can be no doubting the force of this flow (more than 1,200bn lire in ten years), but its pattern needs close examination.

Although no history of the Cassa has yet been written, the general lines of its policy seem reasonably clear. The Christian Democrats chose not to put the accent on immediate industrialization, but rather on an extensive public-works programme concentrated in the rural areas. In the first ten years of the Cassa, the principal areas of intervention were irrigation, land reclamation, road building and the construction of aqueducts and drains. Some of the achievements were undoubtedly impressive. Manlio Rossi-Doria, for instance, judged the road-building programme carried out by the Cassa to have been the single most important contribution to ending the South's isolation since the railway construction of the first decades after Unification.[49] Interventions in other areas, like land reclamation, were less successful, but the extent of infrastructural work carried out by the Cassa should not be underestimated.[50]

However, the Cassa's policies had severe limitations. The dominant short-term preoccupation of easing social tension in the countryside coloured the whole pattern of its interventions. No projects were undertaken in any urban area with more than 200,000 inhabitants. In the rural areas the public-works programme offered temporary labouring jobs but little prospect of permanent employment. Southern rural society was effectively frozen for a number of years. Between 1950 and 1960 only 12 per cent of the Cassa's spending was devoted to industrial projects. Such a choice also suited the interests of northern industry, which provided the heavy machinery and materials needed for infrastructural construction.[51]

With the creation of the agrarian reform boards and the Cassa per il Mezzogiorno, a new and dominant political caste came into being in the South, whom Gabriella Gribaudi has called 'the mediators'. These were the local Christian Democrat bosses, the bureaucrats, building speculators and lawyers who were in receipt of funds flowing from central government and who mediated between the state and the local communities. The old landed notables were replaced by this new élite, dependent for its power on local government, the special agencies of the state and the faction leaders who controlled the flows of the Cassa's spending in the 1950s and 1960s – Aldo Moro, Emilio Colombo, Silvio Gava.[52]

The other great innovation in the area of special agencies was the creation of ENI. Its history was in some ways emblematic of the way in which the Christian Democrats have used state power, but in others quite unique. ENI was the child of Enrico Mattei, one of the most interesting Italian public figures in the 1950s. He was born in Acqualunga in the Marches in 1906, the son of an officer in the Carabinieri. In 1919 his family moved to Matelica, and Mattei left school at fifteen to work first as an errand boy, then in a tannery, and then in Milan as a salesman of German industrial equipment. By the outbreak of war he had set up his own chemical company, and after 1943 he became a prominent Christian Democrat partisan. Mattei was a man of few principles and great entrepreneurial skill. Giorgio Bocca has commented acutely: 'The Italian provinces, especially the central ones, have produced other personalities like him: of very limited culture, even ignorant, but endowed with sharp intelligence and a great shrewdness; men who have imbibed as if by inheritance the Renaissance tradition of politics as a ferocious, risky and cynical game set in a populist context.'[53]

After the war Mattei was given charge of AGIP, the state petrol company, which had not been a great success under Fascism. Mattei saved it when methane gas was discovered in large quantities in the Po valley in 1946 and 1949. De Gasperi visited the wells of Cortemaggiore in April 1950 and made the following speech: 'We do not want this undertaking to become, like so many others, more or less dedicated to increasing the wealth of private entrepreneurs or shareholders. Rather, we want it to be an undertaking in which the interests of the world of work and of the working-class are predominant.'[54] With the help of the Christian Democrat Minister of Finance Ezio Vanoni, and of De Gasperi himself, Mattei fought against private business for the exclusive right to exploit the natural resources of the Po valley. He won, and on 10 February 1953 ENI came into existence.

During the next nine years Mattei built up an unparalleled industrial empire within the state sector. The basis of its wealth were the profits from methane gas. Mattei built the pipelines so fast and with such disregard for local authorities that his exploits became legendary, and he himself boasted of having broken 8,000 ordinances and laws.[55] ENI, itself a holding company like IRI, soon diversified through five major operating companies into a bewildering number of activities, including petrochemicals, motels and *autostrade*, synthetic rubber, steel piping, contract engineering and construction, textiles, and nuclear power and research. The technical staff that Mattei hired and trained became so good that they acquired an international reputation. The face of Italy was changed by ENI's activities. At Ravenna for instance, the huge petrochemical works, immortalized in Antonioni's film, *The Red Desert*, transformed the life of the city. All over the peninsula the bright, clean and well-appointed AGIP service stations offered motorists the chance to fill up with Supercorte-maggiore, 'the powerful Italian petrol', which was in fact foreign petrol refined by ENI in Italy. Mattei was a brilliant publicist, and he conveyed the impression, often substantiated in reality, that his products combined Italian creativity with efficiency and technical skill.

ENI was Mattei's private fiefdom and his running of it was a dramatic example of the use and abuse of state power. Clientelistic practices were rife throughout the organization. Indeed, so great was Mattei's 'loyalty' to his own origins that it became a standard joke in the fifties that the initials of SNAM (one of ENI's largest operating companies) stood for *'siamo nati a Matelica'* ('we were born at Matelica'). Public money was used habitually and without scruple to bribe clients and officials.[56]

In September 1953, Mattei was instrumental in founding a new faction within the DC, called Base. It was run by his faithful lieutenant, Giovanni Marcora, who had been a partisan with him. Mattei also managed to make contacts and win sympathy over the whole spectrum of Italian politics. He maintained good relations with Fanfani's Iniziativa Democratica, while at the same time earning the respect of many Socialists and Communists for his opposition to the international oil companies, and his support of anti-colonial struggles. He even established links with the neo-Fascists. When questioned about this he is reported to have replied (and it would have been in character), 'I use the Fascists like I'd use a taxi.'[57]

By the early 1960s Mattei was one of the great Christian Democrat barons and ENI the most dynamic of the government special agencies. The reputation of both was upheld through *Il Giorno*, the group's daily newspaper, which happily combined cynical whitewashing of Mattei's activities with open-minded and well-informed reporting of other issues and events.

However, Mattei was overreaching himself. The weak governments of the time provided no control over his activities, and indeed he increasingly controlled theirs. He became known as Italy's unofficial Foreign Minister, so great were his contacts and reputation abroad. His charismatic activism earned him considerable popularity amongst the Italians, but more than a few enemies at home and abroad. The OAS (the French pro-colonialist secret organization) were reported as having condemned Mattei to death for his support of the Algerian independence struggle; the international oil companies loathed his unceasing attempts to undercut them and reach agreements directly with the oil-producing nations; the Mafia through its American organizations had close links with the oil companies. On 27 October 1962 Mattei was killed when his private aeroplane crashed on a return journey from Sicily to Milan.[58]

Not all Christian Democrat interventions in the public sector were as spectacular as Mattei's. Mention must be made of two other areas where the DC increased their economic power and autonomy – the banking system and the new Ministry for State Holdings. Unlike in Britain, the directors of many of the most important banks were government appointees, and thus the DC was able to exercise control over credit flows with comparative ease. Many Italian banks and saving banks (of which there is a great tradition in Italy) are regionally based, and each DC faction expected to control the major banks in the region or city where it was strongest. New credit institutions were also created alongside the government special agencies: ISVEIMER, IRFIS and CIS, for example, flanked the Cassa per il Mezzogiorno, and were valuable prizes for those who controlled them.[59]

The Ministry for State Holdings came into being in 1956. It was responsible for all the special agencies in the public sector of the economy, especially ENI and the giant IRI, whose companies were taken out of Confindustria a year later. There were different views as to what role the ministry should play: the Republican La Malfa wanted it to be the driving force behind capitalist rationalization; Mattei saw it as the champion of state industry against the private sector; Fanfani viewed it rather more modestly as a new ministerial bureaucracy which could serve the needs, both financial and clientelistic, of the party. In practice, it was Fanfani's conception that triumphed. The new ministry was not to play a major role in guiding the economy, but became instead the mouthpiece for the giant agencies it was supposed to control.[60]

Finally, mention must be made of the attempt to provide an overall plan for the economy, presented in December 1954 by the Christian Democrat Minister of Finance, Ezio Vanoni. The plan, which was intended to cover the decade 1955–64, had three major objectives: full employment, the gradual reduction of the economic gap between North and South, and the elimination of the balance of payments deficit. Vanoni's aim was to encourage growth while ensuring government control of economic priorities, and government intervention to correct imbalances and distortions. He considered a growth rate of 5 per cent per annum to be a necessary but not sufficient condition for the realization of the plan. His scheme received the enthusiastic verbal support of Fanfani and other DC leaders at the fifth congress of the party at Trento in October 1956. It was frequently cited in reply to critics who accused the DC of *laissez-faire* policies.[61]

Vanoni's plan was never realized. Growth rates of 5 per cent were achieved and indeed exceeded, but rational planning of Italy's economic development remained a chimera. There were two principal reasons for this failure. The first was that while Vanoni's plan wanted to set the Italian

165

economy going in one direction, the establishment of the Common Market pulled it in another. Italian entrepreneurs, as we shall see, found that the market offered great possibilities for the production and export of certain goods and not others. This export-led expansion dictated Italian economic growth and distorted Vanoni's projections.[62]

Secondly, the priorities and composition of the DC did not make it the ideal vehicle for decennial economic planning. Politics and planning were bound to clash when the DC's prime concerns were to establish its own power base within the state and to cater to the needs of the different sections of its electorate. Moreover, even if Fanfani had committed himself fully to Vanoni's plan, the party's factionalism and its centrifugal tendencies would have made any coordinated policy difficult to achieve.

f. CONCLUSION

The economist Michele Salvati, no supporter of the DC, has called the Christian Democrat achievement in the 1950s an 'economic and political masterpiece'.[63] If one applies this judgement to the party's activity in the sphere of the state, there are certain elements which tend to substantiate it. At an international level, De Gasperi's wholehearted commitment to America and to Europe, a commitment that has too often been taken for granted, ensured that Italy was the southern European country most integrated into the economic, political and military structures of the West. The fruits of these choices were to become strikingly apparent from 1958 onwards.

At the level of social control, the party's creation of special state agencies enabled it to confront the significant menace of the poor peasant movement in the South. The movement was defused and split; public-works projects spread to every corner of the Mezzogiorno; a holding operation was successfully performed on southern society. Finally, at an élite level, the DC shifted the balance of power between the country's politicians and its economic barons. The public sector of the economy was brilliantly, if unpredictably, expanded; the challenge of the conservative elements in the Confindustria decisively beaten off.

On the other hand, by whatever criteria one might wish to apply, and certainly by those of the Republic's constitution, the form of state that emerged in the 1950s must be found wanting. The deformed relationship between citizen and state, based on the administration's inefficiency and its consequent discretionary power, was the single gravest failing of the republican state. Some commentators have claimed that the DC made a conscious choice to perpetuate this state of affairs. In so doing, they argue, the party increased its own discretionary power and gave freer rein to the new special agencies.[64] But it is difficult to accept that the exasperating malfunctioning of the Italian state or the profoundly unsatisfactory relationship between the civil service and the political élite served the DC's interests, either in the short or the long term. A more convincing explanation would be that the DC lacked both the cohesion and the statecraft to tackle a formidable legacy from the past. Instead, more from weakness than from Machiavellian intent, they allowed the situation to deteriorate further.

In addition, the archipelago nature of the state contrasted strikingly with the democratic principles on which the Republic was founded. A structure of loosely connected centres of power, some of them very powerful and semi-autonomous special agencies, served the interests of faction and coalition more than they did those of responsible government. The elected bodies of the Republic – Parliament and local councils – were consciously bypassed in this type of state construction.

Lastly, clientelism came to be an intrinsic mode of appointment and operation in each of the power centres of the state. This was not, once again, a Christian Democrat invention. Rather, it was an inheritance which most of the party's leaders chose to accentuate as they increased their power within the state's apparatus and the public sector of the economy.

Christian Democracy and Civil Society

Having examined the strategy of the DC in the realm of the state, we must now turn to examine its actions, organization and ideology in civil society. Of course, there is in reality no such neat division between state and civil society; the one has increasingly overlapped with and intervened in the other. None the less a broad division between the two may be of some use in enabling us, in the second part of this chapter, to concentrate on Italian society and the nature of its support for Christian Democracy. In 1963 Aldo Moro was to claim that 'we truly represent and express the national reality in all its complexity, both because of the size of our electorate and because all the typical expressions of Italian society find expression in our policies'.[65] It is worth examining this claim in a little more detail.

a. FANFANI AND THE NEW PARTY

When Amintore Fanfani became secretary of the DC in 1954, he immediately set about revitalizing the party. He was convinced that the electoral failure of 1953 had been due to the party's weakness in civil society, its over-dependence on the mass organizations of the Catholic church and its lack of efficient organization when compared to the Communists. He therefore launched a series of vigorous membership campaigns. In 1955 party membership leapt to 1,341,000, the highest figure since 1945, and this level was maintained over the next three years.

The most significant increases in membership occurred in the South. A special 'Office for the Depressed Zones' was created, financed by a national subscription within the party. A thousand new sections were opened in the Mezzogiorno. Membership in the province of Palermo, for instance, increased from 18,113 in 1952 to 27,835 one year later; by 1959 it had reached 39,057. Very soon the number of DC members in the South far outweighed those in the North. A survey of 1961 revealed some remarkable facts: the DC had nearly three times more members in Foggia than in Florence, and almost as many in Cosenza as in Genoa, Turin and Milan put together.[66]

Behind these figures lay the particular nature of Christian Democrat control in the South, which will be analysed at some length below (pp. 178–81). Suffice it to say here that party membership in the South was artificially bloated; it served principally to increase the representation at national level of certain factions within the party. In 1955 Fanfani had declared war on the local cliques and notables of the South: 'Without a powerful organization, our efforts will be confined to words, especially in the far-flung periphery where the powers of the state are at their weakest and the bravura of the hirelings of Don Rodrigo at its greatest.'[67] In reality, as we shall see, the old clienteles were to be replaced by, or to merge with, the new.

b. THE CATHOLIC CHURCH IN ITALIAN SOCIETY

Both De Gasperi and Fanfani, as we have seen, wanted to render the Christian Democrats less dependent upon the organizations of the church. In the early 1950s tensions had run high between Pius XII and the Catholic political leadership. However, after the historic victory of April 1948, neither party nor church ever seriously considered going their separate ways. Fanfani's attempts to build a mass party could not mask the fact that throughout the 1950s the Christian Democrats continued to rely very heavily on the church's profound permeation of Italian society, and on its explicit political support at election time.

At the heart of the church's activity lay the parish. Whereas fifty years earlier Italian parishes had been, for the most part, somnolent and inactive affairs, by the 1950s they were spilling over with activity. In 1956 69 per cent of adult Italians said that they had been to mass the previous week. Even though the real figure was undoubtedly lower, the great number of masses, confessions and communions in each parish each week testified to the church's vigorous state of health. So too did the number of organizations habitually associated with parish life; not only those of Catholic Action, but also the confraternities, the charitable organizations, the non-secular orders and so on. Furthermore, the parish priest had responsibility for the local nursery schools (in the absence of state provision), for Bible classes, oratories, the parish library and monthly bulletin, and much else besides. As Falconi wrote in 1954, the parish was 'a centre of propulsive action which has no parallel in any other lay organization of the same type'.[68]

Alongside the parishes and closely connected with them were the organizations of Catholic Action. By 1954 Catholic Action could boast no less than 2,655,578 members in Italy, divided between its four sections (men, women, young men and boys, young women and girls). The last of these was by far the largest with 1,215,977 members. The northern bias of the organization was very clear: the Veneto had the largest number of members (239,273), followed by Lombardy with 219,475, and Piedmont with 103,630. The largest membership in the South was in Sicily, with only 63,846.[69]

Catholic Action organized a very wide range of religious and social activities. The male youth movement (GIAC), covering the ages ten to thirty, set itself the following tasks: 'the formation of its members, especially in the areas of prayer, action and sacrifice; proselytizing amongst youths; the preparation of young men for family and social life; the furtherance of a healthy intellectual, physical and recreational education'.[70] Activities included prayer meetings, Bible classes, summer camps and sporting associations. In the adult world of Catholic Action, the stress was laid on proselytizing, on the defence of the family and of public morality, and on the Christian education of children. Cultural activities included a very active network of cinemas, where films approved by the church authorities were shown. By 1954 Catholic Action ran over 4,000 cinemas in the country, of which 2,700 were in the North.[71]

In the field of politics, after 1953 the youth movement of Catholic Action gradually disassociated itself from explicit electioneering, and it was left to Gedda's civic committees to hold high the banner of militant Catholic political activism. They were not found wanting. In July 1949, after the Holy Office had excommunicated all those who espoused Communist, materialist or anti-Christian doctrines, the civic committees launched their 'Religious Crusade for the Great Return of Communists to the Fold'. This coincided with the Holy Year of 1950, which witnessed unparalleled Catholic celebrations throughout Italy. Five years later the committees returned to the attack with their Operazione Semaforo Giallo (Orange Traffic-light Campaign): 'the *red* of Communism blocks our commitment to the creation of a better world'.[72] It was not until the end of the decade that Gedda's crusading anti-Communism began to appear outmoded.

Catholic Action, and the closely linked civic committees, were the most important Catholic lay organizations in society, but they were far from being the only ones. Among the many others was a strong network of Catholic cooperatives, organized in the CCI (Confederazione delle

Cooperative Italiane). Building on their pre-Fascist experience, the Catholics decided after 1945 not to work with the left in a single national organization. At first the CCI was weaker than its left-wing and republican rival, the National League of Cooperatives, but by 1962 it had well over two million members and had overtaken the League. Catholic cooperatives were most widespread in Lombardy and the Veneto, as was to be expected, but also in Sicily (where they built upon the traditions established by Don Luigi Sturzo), in Sardinia, and in Emilia-Romagna. Agricultural cooperatives were the most common, followed by those in the building trade.[73]

No account of Catholic influence in Italian society would be complete without mentioning the church's education and welfare activities. Compulsory religious education, as agreed in the Lateran Pacts, gave the church all-important access to children in state schools. In addition, the POA (Pontifica Opera di Assistenza) organized a large number of educational and recreational institutions. These varied from seaside and mountain camps to kindergartens, to *doposcuole* (afternoon activities for six- to twelve-year-olds), to *case del fanciullo* and *della fanciulla* for teenagers in need of assistance. By 1952 in Naples alone there were 155 *case del fanciullo* catering for 30,000 boys. Overall, and again the statistics are for 1952, the POA offered assistance to one and a half million children and youths, who were aided by 128,350 religious and lay 'collaborators'.[74]

The church was perhaps more present in a citizen's life at times of illness and in old age than at any other period. Over many decades the church had built up an impressive network of hospitals, nursing homes and old people's homes, staffed by various religious orders. In the absence of any state provision for old people, families turned with gratitude to Catholic welfare institutions. Sometimes these institutions extracted a political price for their charity. A petty Christian Democrat boss from Naples told Allum how a major figure in the Neapolitan party had promised to ensure his election: 'He said: "Look here, I will help you", and he told me how many votes he would get me from the old people's home where his wife's sister was the Mother Superior . . . and then he had a son who is a priest . . . thus there would be 400/500 votes there . . . and he could give them to whoever he pleased.'[75]

In conclusion, it is vital to stress that Pius XII demanded, and obtained, strict control by the church hierarchy over this myriad world of Catholic associationism. In January 1950 he told the Italian bishops that 'lay cooperation with the apostolate of the hierarchy cannot be effective and beneficial if great care is not taken to avoid any disturbance in ecclesiastical discipline, and to increase instead its order, force and extension'.[76] The Catholics were an army to be disciplined and directed into every corner of Italian society, an army in which, as Lanaro has written, 'the parish priest was the bishop and the bishop was the Pope'.[77]

c. THE DC'S COLLATERAL ORGANIZATIONS

The Christian Democrats could not hope to rival the vast and long-established network of church organizations which has been described above. Indeed, the DC's collateral organizations, as they have come to be known, were far from its own. They were, rather, Catholic organizations which had three, sometimes conflicting, reference points for their actions: the political party, the church hierarchy and their own autonomous needs as a corporate group.

Of these organizations the most successful and formidable was the Coldiretti, which Paolo Bonomi had founded in 1944 to represent the interests of peasant proprietors. By 1956, as we have seen, Bonomi had built up an extraordinary empire, with over 1,600,000 families as members, and more than 13,000 local sections. Internal democracy was kept to a minimum, but large rallies were commonplace and there were active subsections of the organization such as Gioventù dei Campi ('Youth of the Fields') and Donne Rurali ('Rural Womenfolk'); the latter was involved, amongst other things, in organizing choral gatherings and recitals in dialect, as well as preserving folk traditions.[78] The Coldiretti had an active press headed by its fortnightly magazine *Il Coltivatore*. It also set up training schools for farmers and founded 'I Club dei 3P – Provare, Produrre, Progredire' ('Try, Produce and Progress'). These encouraged sixteen- to thirty-year-olds to learn and employ new farming methods under the guidance of the organization's experts.[79]

The ideology of the Coldiretti was rudimentary but effective. Great stress was laid on the peasant family as a model: 'The rural family, as the reigning Pope has many times taught us, is the cell of a society capable of building a civilization which recognizes the primacy of spiritual values. In the rural family there exists the foundation of a healthy and balanced social order, on which it is possible to construct a political order of secure solidity and persistent equilibrium.'[80] Bonomi also emphasized the necessity for a crusading anti-Communism in the countryside: 'We will not defeat Communism or build a dyke against it by means of public works or polished speeches. We need to galvanize the masses on the basis of precise beliefs, give them awareness of themselves and their responsibilities, call on them to fight. This is what the Coldiretti has done up to now. This is why we have won. We will go on winning.'[81]

The foundations of the Coldiretti's success lay in two overlapping areas: the range of services it could offer peasant proprietors and the benefits it won for them through its influence in the state apparatus, especially at the Ministry of Agriculture. Crucial to the first was Bonomi's successful takeover of the Federconsorzi (Federation of Agricultural Syndicates). This powerful organization existed, as we have seen (p. 140), to bulk buy and sell equipment, fertilizers and machines, as well as to store crops, provide credit and aid farmers in many other ways. Bonomi's control of it enabled him to be the crucial link between northern industry and the small peasant proprietor. It also made him the arbiter of the distribution of Marshall Aid in the rural areas. Thus the material resources of the Federconsorzi, when combined with the organizational network of the Coldiretti, provided Bonomi with the basis from which to dominate the world of rural Italy.

Furthermore, by using its considerable influence in the party, the Coldiretti was able to ensure that the government passed special legislation for peasant proprietors. The establishment of the Casse Mutue, or small farmers' health insurance agency, finally gave peasant proprietors benefits similar to those of dependent workers in the cities. Further victories were won with the granting of old age and invalidity pensions. The category of small peasant proprietors felt, with some justification, that for the first time their interests were being properly represented on a national scale.

Paolo Bonomi was thus in many ways the rural and provincial counterpart of Enrico Mattei. In contrast to Mattei, Bonomi started from society rather than the state, building up a mass organization rather than developing a government special agency. But by the mid-fifties Bonomi, like Mattei, could boast of the slice of the Christian Democrat system which he controlled – his fifty deputies in Parliament and the Ministry of Agriculture in his pocket.

If the Coldiretti catered to peasant proprietors, the A CLI and CISL (Confederazione Italiana Sindacati Liberi) were the Catholic organizations for workers. A CLI had been established in 1944 with the aim of preserving an autonomous area of organization and activity for Catholic workers. With the foundation of a united trade union, many elements in both the DC and the church feared that Catholic workers would be swamped by the Socialist and Communist majority. A CLI therefore dedicated itself primarily in these early years to what it called 'pre-trade union work'. As one of its manuals explained, A CLI's task was to ensure that 'Catholic workers enter into the life of the trade union having already acquired a trade union consciousness which accords with the principles of Catholic social doctrine.'[82]

A CLI's role had to be rethought when the CGIL split in July 1948. After De Gasperi's victory in the national elections and the great strike in protest at the attempted assassination of Togliatti, there was nothing, not even Di Vittorio's mediation, which could hold the CGIL together. The Catholic minority, urged on by the Vatican and the American Federation of Labour, announced its decision to leave, and the Republicans and Social Democrats soon followed. Two years later Italian trade unionism assumed the triple character that it bears today: the CGIL represented Communist and Socialist workers, the CISL Catholics and Christian Democrats, and the UIL (Unione Italiana Lavoratori) Social Democrats and Republicans.

The Catholic world now had two organizations for workers, and the division of tasks between them was the subject of some controversy. Gradually, ACLI tended to concentrate more on social activities, and on the moral and religious education of workers. At the same time it moved closer to the DC, with its leaders heavily involved in the left-wing factions of the party. ACLI continued to grow throughout the 1950s and by the end of the decade had more than one million members. Its *circoli*, nearly half of which had television sets and licences to sell alcohol, served as regular meeting-places for Catholic workers.[83]

As for the CISL, its prospects did not at first look very encouraging. In the summer of 1949, Fanfani, as Minister of Labour, proposed a series of severe limitations on the right to strike, including the banning of all strikes which were judged to be 'political' or 'in solidarity'. These proposals never became law, but they were hardly a good advertisement for the Christian Democrats' attitude to trade unionism, especially with an industrial proletariat as class-conscious as the Italian. Nor did it help matters that the CISL had begun life as a 'confessional' organization with exclusive Catholic tendencies.[84]

However, in the early fifties the CISL under Giulio Pastore evolved a trade union line of its own which gradually won it more support. While never questioning the employers' ownership rights and ultimate control, the CISL, in contrast to the CGIL of these years, put the emphasis on plant bargaining and supported workers' demands for increased pay in return for higher productivity. It also became more of a lay organization, inspired by American models of trade unionism. Both these changes soon won dividends. Starting from its strongholds in the textile industries of the Veneto, and receiving favoured treatment in public industry, the CISL increased its membership, especially amongst young workers, throughout the 1950s.[85]

d. LA FAMIGLIA CRISTIANA

In the Catholic world of the 1950s, no social message was preached with more fervour than that of the sanctity of the Christian family. Of all social institutions, it was the family that most aroused the passion and piety of Italian Catholics. Emilio Colombo, who was to become the longest serving Minister of the Treasury in the history of the Republic, wrote in 1952: 'It is without doubt only Christianity that has a conception of the family so noble as to elevate the union of man and woman to the dignity of a sacrament and to make of their union the symbol of the union of Christ with his church.'[86] Throughout the 1950s the weekly magazine, *Famiglia Cristiana*, had an enormous circulation, reaching more than a million copies by May 1961.[87]

Catholic teaching on the family asserted in the first place the primacy of the family in civil society. This pre-eminence was based on considerations which were both temporal and ethical. The *Enciclopedia cattolica* (published in 1950) explained that 'the precedence of the family over society is above all temporal; the family was the first form of social organization, the first school and the first temple'. Furthermore, in a hierarchy of values, society was subordinate to the family 'since society is a means to assure to the family and through it the individual that which is indispensable for its [the family's] self-realization'.[88] Tullo Goffi made a similar point in his often reprinted *Morale familiare* (1958): 'the family enjoys a pre-eminence over civil society in an ordering of ends ... family duties, founded on piety, love, and unity, are of a superior essence, although less defined and distinct, than social duties, which emanate from Justice'.[89]

As for family–state relations, the main emphasis here was on the need to protect the family from external control. Given the whole history of church–state relations in Italy, such a stance was not surprising. In 1891 Leo XIII had warned in *Rerum novarum*: 'It is a great and pernicious error to think that the state can interfere as it likes in the sanctuary of the family.'[90] More than fifty years later, as the church distanced itself from the Fascist regime, Pius XII echoed these sentiments in his radio message of Christmas 1942. The *Enciclopedia cattolica* was quite explicit: 'the state must recognize the family as it has been constituted by God'.[91] The state's duties were therefore to protect the family and to enable it to 'accomplish its mission'; only if the family failed in this task did the state have the right to intervene. Goffi summed up well: 'In the face of the institution of the family, structured on natural rights, political society must consider itself a servant [*'minestra'*].'[92]

In the relationship between family and collectivity, the Christian family thus had many more rights than duties. It was symptomatic that Goffi dedicated five pages to the duties of the state towards the family, but less than one to those of the family towards society. The family's duties were primarily *internal*, not *external*: great stress was laid on its indissolubility, its piousness, the duty of parents to educate their children in a Christian manner. The overall message was robust and simple: Catholic organizations were the prime defenders of the family, the family took pride of place in society, the principal task of Catholics was to care for the inner, spiritual values and harmony of the family.

Such an ideology, though, was open to attack. It could be accused of catering to familism, of isolating the family from society, of stressing private rather than public virtues.[93] The Catholic theologian Elisio Ruffini has pointed out a series of 'temptations' to which Catholic theology of the family tended to succumb: it accentuated an 'isolationist vision of salvation', in which a sense of community did not extend beyond one's own family; it made use all too often of the catch-phrase of the family as the 'nucleus of society', without bothering to question further the relationship between the two; it preached an idealized and ahistorical view of the family, in which the Holy Family itself was ill-advisedly presented as a model.[94]

However, to characterize Catholic attitudes to family and collectivity only in this light would be somewhat one-sided. If the predominant view of family–society relations was the one outlined above, it is also true that Catholic social teaching had tried to correct the balance and place the family in a wider social context. From the late nineteenth century onwards, with Leo XIII's encyclical *Rerum novarum*, with the teachings of Giuseppe Toniolo and the activities of the Opera dei Congressi, the church had intervened in Italian society more actively than ever before. Catholic associationism flourished, above all in the Veneto and Lombardy. And to this new social impetus was added an 'integralist' view of the Catholic's role in society – the need to make all the institutions of civil society conform to and reflect Catholic values.[95]

This was the context for Gonella's resounding battle-cry at the first congress of the DC – 'the family is a fortress which cannot be defended from within the fortress'.[96] The Catholic family had to be defended itself against the Communist menace and the threats of modern society. It could only do so if it emerged from its isolation.

Above all, the family had to 'know, love and serve' the church:[97] a correct family–church relationship was the essential precursor to that between family and society. The prime mission of the family within the church was to link with and help other Christian families: 'In the Catholic apostolate today there are militant fathers and mothers whose password is "the conquest of the family through the family". Christian families are more than ever meeting in groups from time to time, for three purposes: communal prayer, spiritual and material aid, the study of family problems. Such commitment of the family to the apostolic mission constitutes the progressive victory of a communitarian spirit over individualism.'[98]

There was thus a permanent tension in the Catholic view of the family. On the one hand there was the tendency to stress the family's internal values, its primacy over society, the need to protect it from a hostile world. Such a view had been one of the ideological bases of familism in Italy. On the other hand, there was the desire to overcome the family's isolation, both with relation to the church and to society. It remains to be seen which of these two views was more in harmony with the future development of Italian society.

e. THE CHRISTIAN DEMOCRATS IN THE NORTH AND THE SOUTH

In the 1950s, the way in which families related to the Catholic movement and to the Christian Democrats varied notably between the North and the South of the country. In the North, especially in Lombardy–Venetia, the historic strength of Catholic associationism drew families into a network of activities and organizations which constituted an all-embracing subculture. In the South, by contrast, where associationism of any sort was so much weaker, state clientelism acted as a magnet for individual family strategies.

Care must be taken not to establish too absolute a division between the two parts of the country and the two methods of building consent. Clientelism existed in the North just as Catholic associationism could be found in parts of the South. None the less, there were striking differences. They are best illustrated by contrasting briefly the Christian Democrats in the Veneto with their counterparts in the major cities of the South.[99]

The Veneto was the region where the Christian Democrats, from the 1940s onwards, gained more votes than in any other part of the country. Contrary to common belief, it was not an entirely homogeneous region. Venice itself had a strong secular culture, the CGIL had a solid base among the industrial workers of Porto Marghera, the landless labourers of the Adige and Po deltas continued to organize class-based agitations until well into the 1950s.[100] Rather, it was the 'white quadrilateral', consisting of the provinces of Verona, Vicenza, Treviso and Padua, that was the Christian Democrat heartland. In the province of Vicenza, for instance, the DC gained 62.3 per cent of the votes in 1953, a percentage they increased to 66.6 per cent in 1958.

In these provinces, the Christian Democrats were just one element, and not the most important, in a Catholic world dominated by the ecclesiastical hierarchy. The Venetian bishops were formidable interventionist figures like Monsignor Carlo Zinato, bishop of Vicenza from 1943 to 1971. The subordinate role of the party has led Lanaro to assert that it did not exist at all; Allum has preferred to call it a 'party of ideological identity'.[101] Whatever the label, the important point is that the DC gained its harvest of votes principally because of the massed Catholic forces that stood behind it. In the provinces at election time, the faithful were mobilized on a strong ideological basis: on the need to fight Communism, to protect the family, to safeguard Christian values. As Monsignor Zinato proclaimed shortly before the 1958 elections: 'On their [the elections'] outcome may depend the consolidation, or lack of it, of Christian thought in all sectors of civil life and of the church.'[102]

Families were drawn into an environment in which every social activity rotated around the parish and the associations connected to it. The world of children and teenagers was dominated by membership of the youth organizations of Catholic Action, by Bible lessons on Sunday afternoons, by summer-holiday camps at the foot of the Dolomites, where scout leaders spoke of the communion of man with Nature and of the moral dangers of industrial society. Parents were mobilized politically by Gedda's civic committees. In more peaceful times traditional nationalist and religious values were happily combined in a single Sunday outing, first to the shrine of the Madonna of Monte Berico and then to the First World War cemetery at Asiago.[103]

Families were even mobilized on a street level with the introduction of the *Madonna pellegrina*, first in 1948, the year of the Madonna, and then above all in the Holy Year of 1950. One family in each street was chosen to keep the statue of the Madonna in its home for one week, while neighbours and relatives would come and pay their respects and pray to her. The statue would then be moved to another street and eventually to another village or town.[104]

By 1956, in the rural areas of the Veneto, the Coldiretti were organizing some 200,000 families. That year the regional conference of the organization was held at the Teatro Verdi in Padua:

On the stage were the leaders of the 'great family', with groups in folk costume, and on a tricolour backdrop was painted the emblem of the Confederation: the spade, symbol of toil, and the ears of corn, fruit of the farmer's sweated labour . . . the speaker [Antonio Cittante, president of the regional committee] reasserted the firm desire of the organization to fight Communism in our countryside. He reassured his audience, though, that in the Veneto, except for small areas, Communism was like an exotic plant which died in the attempt to transplant it.[105]

Some care must be taken not to exaggerate beyond bounds the real extent of this powerful Catholic subculture. The Coldiretti organized 200,000 peasant families in the Veneto, but as Cittante admitted there were another 150,000 in the region who had not joined. In the diocese of Vicenza there were 95,000 members of Catholic Action in 1958, but this represented only around 15 per cent of the population.[106] Even in its heyday, and even in its heartland, massive numbers of families were involved only marginally, if at all, in this strongest of Italian subcultures.

If we turn now to the southern cities, we see a rather different process at work. Here the practice developed of using state resources in clientelistic fashion in order to create a mass base tied *materially* to the Christian Democrat Party. In the South, clientelism was more important than ideology, the party more than the bishops, local government more than Catholic associationism.

Fanfani's expansion of party membership in the South was the first step in this process, but the southern cities operated to different time-scales. At Palermo the transformation started early, with Giovanni Gioia, Fanfani's lieutenant, becoming the Palermo provincial secretary in 1953. In Naples and Catania it took longer; not until the early and mid-sixties did state clientelism flourish fully, under Silvio Gava in Naples and Antonino Drago in Catania.[107]

In analysing the workings of this phenomenon, it is as well to concentrate on three areas: the institutional resources available to the party at a local level; the transmission belt along which favours travel and by which clients are linked to their patrons; and the returns which the Christian Democrats can expect from the relationships that they have established.

The first major set of institutions are those *enti pubblici* (public bodies) dependent on local government. There were thirty-five of these in Catania by the mid-1970s, of which eighteen dealt with health, pensions, social security and sickness benefit, eleven controlled public utilities (gas, buses, etc.), five were responsible for public housing and one was a credit institution (the Banca Popolare di S. Agata). The Christian Democrats slowly but inexorably tightened their hold on these as the years passed: in 1950 they had only seventeen directors on the various boards and eight presidents; by 1955 they had thirty-three directors and thirteen presidents; ten years later they could count on no less than seventy-nine directors and twenty-three presidents.[108]

Control of these institutions was used for a variety of purposes which can be broadly divided into the three areas of spending, access to credit and discretionary powers. At the highest level, spending was on major public works, the contracts for which were in the gift of the local council. At the lowest, local government funds could be used to bloat the number of menial local government employees – porters, dustmen, etc. By 1968 municipal employees at Naples numbered more than 15,000, an increase of almost 400 per cent in fifteen years.[109] The control of credit through local banks is self-explanatory. As for discretionary powers, they included those of licensing (building permits, permission to open shops, etc.), the speeding up of papers through the bureaucracy, the acting upon personal recommendations.

These practices can best be illuminated by looking at one sector – local public bodies dealing with health provision and pensions. Local social-insurance and pension offices, once under the control of the party, could be used to service 'external' clients. The favours distributed here were not jobs, but money hand-outs in the form of pensions and other welfare payments. Or else the service performed could be a lesser one, like the acceleration of payments delayed by the offices' habitual inefficiency.[110]

Hospitals had many uses beside curing the sick. Indeed this last seemed a secondary concern in the notorious Vittorio Emanuele Hospital at Catania. The third largest employer in the city, with 1,200 workers, the Vittorio Emanuele was a good example of the entirely politicized public institution. The clientelistic use of the job market, from consultant to cleaner, presented remarkable levels of sophistication. Many jobs were kept deliberately unfilled so that the maximum number of aspirants could be drawn into the net for as long as possible. Once in a job, internal mobility and promotion were more the subject of political preference than of professional competence, as was the final and vital step of being made '*di ruolo*', being given a permanent post.

In extremis, and for electoral purposes, the beds of the Vittorio Emanuele could be filled with perfectly healthy D C voters. In 1963 the president of the hospital, Alfio Di Grazia, a D C senator desperate for re-election, moved in many 'patients' who happened to live in the wrong constituency for his purposes (Catania II), but who were allowed by law to vote in the right one (Catania I) from their hospital beds.[111]

Fixing of this sort went on at every level of local politics: lucrative contracts for housing and redevelopment were assigned to D C building speculators or consortiums dominated by Vatican finance houses, such as the ISTICA at Catania; credit facilities were reserved principally for the politically faithful; jobs in local industry were carefully controlled.[112]

If the use of local government institutions and powers has been well documented, that of central government ministries and agencies has not. As yet we know next to nothing in detail about how central government institutions – the prefectures, the local offices of the ministries, the Cassa per il Mezzogiorno, IRI, ENI – have functioned in the field. This lacuna is all the more grave because their resources were often much greater than those of local government, and the links between centre and periphery are the crucial ones in the D C system.

It is possible to say rather more about the transmission belt along which power and influence travelled. Not all local parties were identical, but the main levels of hierarchy are broadly discernible. At the top end of the transmission belt were the *capi correnti*, the leaders of the different national currents or factions. These were the major figures in the party, those who had been ministers and prime ministers for much of their political life, men like Aldo Moro, Giovanni Leone, Amintore Fanfani, Giulio Andreotti, Emilio Colombo.

Immediately below them came a more numerous group of party magnates or notables. These were senators, long-standing deputies, junior ministers and under-secretaries, heads of government special agencies, etc. Piero Ottone, who was to become editor of *Corriere della Sera*, has described a visit to one such southern magnate in 1965: 'One morning I went to see an Avellinese "notable". It was 9.30. The waiting-room was full of poor people seeking favours, and when he emerged from his office, they all greeted him with the deferential titles of "Excellency", "Honourable" or "Senator". But what struck me was not the titles. It was the "notable's" dress, which was a pair of striped pyjamas. And in his smart pyjamas and slippers, he discussed the problems of Avellino with me for an hour.'[113]

Amongst this group must be placed the big-city party secretaries, who had the vital task of trying to coordinate and control the many ramifications of Christian Democrat power in their localities. Some of them, like Silvio and Antonio Gava in Naples and Ciriaco De Mita from Avellino, having built upon solid local power bases, went on to become national figures in their own right. Others, like Antonino Drago at Catania, remained essentially local figures, dependent on a national faction leader for the flow of central government resources to their city (in Drago's case Emilio Colombo).

City secretaries and party magnates alike were heavily reliant upon the next group in the DC hierarchy – the *'grandi elettori'*. Although there is much overlap amongst all these categories, it is possible to describe the *grandi elettori*, as Allum has done, as influential local figures able to reach more than one group in society. These were the local mayor and councillors, the principal clergy, landowners, businessmen, doctors and lawyers who actively worked for the DC in the area.

Below them came the *'capi elettori'*, the corporals and sergeants of the Christian Democrat army. These were activists who tended to reach single networks, which might be occupational (i.e. building workers), geographical (a popular quarter of the city), or even criminal (as with the Camorra in Naples). Or else the *capi elettori* were section secretaries, men of modest means from lower-middle-class backgrounds who offered services in the neighbourhood – the speeding up of pension claims or applications for local licences – in return for votes. They aspired to become municipal councillors but very few eventually made it.[114]

At this level, kinship was also of great importance for building up a reliable block of votes. A former municipal councillor from a commune on the outskirts of Naples recounted in 1963 that 'politically my family is recognized as DC; between relations and relations of relations we are about a hundred. I, in my following, have always been able to count on all these relations.'[115]

At the furthest end of the transmission belt were the mass of ordinary people who, at one time or another, had become clients by receiving or being promised some form of material aid from the ruling party. Where, as in Catania, Palermo and Naples, families were large and unemployment and misery were endemic, the possibility of even one member of a family gaining access to the lower rungs of the clientelistic ladder was all-important. A municipal job, or one with a local company, was an inestimable prize, for it meant a stable income and pension. Local Communists had to come to terms with clientelism as a fact of life. As one of them recounted in Naples: 'After 1950 ... at the Allocca and Belli companies, you had to pass through the Cardinal, the captain of the Carabinieri, etc. ... We faced up to the blow well, by not accusing the comrades who tried to slip in among the friends of the Cardinal.'[116]

In the southern countryside the Communists had tried to establish a system of values which encouraged families to come together in a collective struggle for a better future. In the southern cities, by contrast, the DC responded with an appeal to more traditional values, and a system which offered individual solutions within a clientelistic framework. In the Catholic North an integralist ideology tried to link the family closely with the organizations of the church and the crusade for a Catholic society. In the South, the family—church relationship was of a different kind: the family fought for its own survival; the church took the form of a protector-saint (San Gennaro, for example); society, if all went well, that of a beneficent political patron.

Finally, what returns could the party expect from the favours it dispensed? At the highest level, the currency of clientelism was money: the *bustarella* (the envelope full of cash) was the businessman's or the property speculator's pay-out in return for the local administrators' attention to his interests. On lower levels the major return was obviously fidelity at election time. However, the matter was not that simple, because the Italian electoral system allows a voter to express his or her preference not just for a particular party but for a specific candidate in the list proposed by that party. Thus at Naples one could vote not just for the DC but for Cappello, No. 7 in the DC list, or for Gava, No. 1. The preference vote is an integral part of the DC state system because it feeds and is fed by the fierce factionalism of the party. An ordinary voter, a section secretary, a *grande elettore* is not just tied to the party but to a group or a personality, who must ensure his or her continuing loyalty. There were, and are, frequent transfers, betrayals and desertions, splits within factions, and realignments of forces. Infighting becomes the order of the day.

The Italy of the Christian Democrats

In the 1950s the Christian Democrats succeeded in establishing a new consensus amongst significant sections of Italian society. The social bloc that supported them was never, except in 1948, an absolute majority in political terms. A very significant minority was utterly opposed to them. None the less, the D C was the *dominant* political force of the time.

The bases of their support were both ideological and material. The 1950s was a decade when the morality of international politics was seen in exclusively black and white terms. De Gasperi had chosen America; even more importantly, America had chosen Italy, and the uncomplicated ideology of the Cold War with its crusading anti-Communism helped strongly to mould Italian public opinion. The Korean war, quite unlike its successor in Vietnam, did not arouse a spontaneous storm of indignation and protest. The image of America had not yet been tarnished, and its popular culture as transmitted across the Atlantic – juke-boxes, pin-ball machines, rock and roll, the films of Marilyn Monroe and James Dean – was the dominant one amongst Italian youth.

At home the church remained the greatest moral force in the land. There existed few doubts in the mind of the ageing Pius XII that it was the church's duty to lead an unyielding campaign against Communism. The Christian family had to be defended, the centuries-old Catholic culture of Italy had to defeat the upstart enemy. As we have seen, Catholic social culture was at its strongest in the 'white' zones of Lombardy and the Veneto, but the vigorous messages emanating from Italian parishes were heard throughout the land. Here too everything was seen in black and white, or rather white and red. The genial stories of Don Camillo had a sound basis in reality. Even the heroes of children's comics were ideologically defined. Catholic Action's *Il Vittorioso* celebrated Easter 1951 with a centre-page story entitled 'Resurrection', based on the parable of the Prodigal Son. At the same time the Communist Party's *Il Pioniere* started a new comic strip entitled 'Scugnizzo', dedicated to the Neapolitan boys who fought and fell gloriously in the battle against the Nazi-Fascists during the Four Days of Naples of September 1943.[117]

Catholicism, Americanism, anti-Communism; together they made an unlikely but formidable base for the ruling ideology. There were plenty of tensions. One frivolous example will have to suffice: in March 1952, *Noi Uomini*, the journal of the men's section of Catholic Action, denounced jazz as 'the cause of spiritual retrogression' and as music 'of a materialist and Dionysiac orientation'.[118] But at a time of Cold War, and in a relatively static society (relative that is to what was to come later), the contradictions could be papered over, or else heroic syntheses attempted, like Fanfani's of 1956.[119]

In material terms, the principal basis of the D C's consensus lay with the state. Here they were innovators, albeit haphazard ones. They made a conscious and successful effort to increase the economic power of the state and its ability to intervene effectively in civil society. This had been the boast of Mussolini, but the Christian Democrats gave substance to his words. They did so, as we have seen, principally through the greatly expanded power of the government special agencies – the Cassa per il Mezzogiorno, Mattei's ENI, and the reorganized state holdings in industry. At the same time, especially in the South, they transformed the previous practices of clientelism, which became no longer the prerogative of the local notable but that of state functionaries and the party hierarchy.

If we try to analyse the nature of the new consensus in class terms, it is possible to see how many different sections of society were successfully drawn under the Christian Democrat umbrella. The interclassism of the DC was no illusion. Many of the traditional elements of big business resented the intrusion of the new economic power of the state, but most businessmen were more than grateful for the Christian Democrats' crushing defeat of the working-class movement. The old southern landed élite lamented their 'abandonment' by the DC at the time of the agrarian reform. Yet for them too there was adequate consolation: generous government indemnities for land confiscated could be successfully invested in the building speculation of the southern cities.

No section of society was courted more than the *ceti medi*. For them, as Pizzorno has written, were reserved 'the caresses and preoccupations of the regime'.[120] The fact that the DC's political allies of the time – the Republicans, Liberals and Social Democrats – gained their votes predominantly from the *ceti medi* served as a further guarantee for them.

Amongst the traditional elements of the *ceti medi*, the care given to small peasant proprietors must by now be obvious. The agrarian reform boards, the law on rural mortgages, the activities of the Coldiretti, the establishment of the Casse Mutue, all these bore witness to an extraordinary degree of attention on the part of the DC and the government. But other traditional sections also fared well. Artisans gained health insurance and pension institutions similar to those of the peasant proprietors. Shopkeepers found that it was easy to obtain licences and keep them, while chain stores and supermarkets were obstructed at every turn. The numbers of those working in the retail trade increased markedly between 1951 and 1961 – from 7.5 per cent of the active workforce to 10.3 per cent. Most of the increase came with the creation of small bars and family food shops, run by husband and wife.[121]

Very little is known about the newer sections of the *ceti medi*, the white-collar workers and technicians, in the 1950s. Civil servants may have resented political interference, but they welcomed the security of tenure assured to them by Fanfani, especially after the uncertainties of the war years. Impoverished southern graduates, Mussolini's 'most dangerous' of classes, found the job market buoyant as central and local government expanded their bureaucracies.

Small businesses flourished, as taxation on their activities was minimal and union power non-existent. The professional middle classes also prospered, and the extensive public-works projects in the South offered considerable possibilities for enrichment. Engineers, architects, lawyers and accountants, provided they kept in with or joined the new city bosses, could look forward to years of lucrative employment and positions of influence.

The *ceti medi*, then, could hardly have had it better. For the working classes the story was obviously rather different. The proletariat of the Industrial Triangle, the workers in the small central Italian factories and the landless labourers all over Italy were the rock bed of the left's support. Yet even here the picture was far from uniform. With A C L I at the height of its popularity, Catholic workers voted solidly for the D C. CISL was undermining the C G I L's support, and not just in the Veneto but in its Lombard and Piedmontese strongholds as well. In the South, public-works programmes and the building boom offered construction jobs to tens of thousands of city unemployed. The first waves of emigration from the southern countryside took place in this period, as peasants from the hill areas moved to the provincial capitals to become building workers. Trade unionism was weak on these new sites; kinship and *clientela* relationships were the dominant ones.

One could argue with some conviction that the D C's support was primarily regional, based on the South and on the 'white' areas of the northeast. There is much in this, but it must be remembered that throughout the 1950s the D C controlled, by means of one coalition or another, practically every major city council in Italy. Nor were all these councils run on southern lines by any means; La Pira's administration of Florence could hardly have offered a greater contrast.

None the less, it is difficult to conclude that the Christian Democrats were *hegemonic* in Italian society. In spite of the various levels of their support, both urban and rural, extending from the core of the *ceti medi* both upwards and downwards, the Christian Democrats could not be said to have imparted an effective moral, intellectual and political leadership to society as a whole.

Probably only in Lombardy–Venetia, where the ideological backing for Catholic values was so much stronger than elsewhere, could it be claimed that this was the case. Even here there were some doubts. In a questionnaire carried out by the A C L I in Vicenza in 1954 amongst predominantly male youth between the ages of fourteen and twenty-six, the consent for the D C was overwhelming. Yet that consent was founded quite narrowly on the values of religion and nation. On the question of social justice and work, the party was often found wanting. As one twenty-three-year-old peasant from Valdagno wrote: '[The DC] defends the values of Man, moral values, but it is still incomplete and feeble on social issues.'[122] Elsewhere, the ideological adherence to the DC was much weaker. Especially in the South, the party was viewed more as an instrument to be used than as representing a set of values in which to believe.

Above all, the Christian Democrats did not manage to create an image of the state with which the ordinary citizen could identify. The citizen was not bound to the state because of its honesty, the services it performed, the liberties it guaranteed, the democracy and justice it had to offer. These were all the myths of the Republic's Constitution. At the best the state was viewed with cynicism, at worst as dishonest and oppressive.

Furthermore, too large a minority, overwhelmingly working-class in composition, remained profoundly alien to the ideology of the ruling political élite. This minority was neither apathetic nor submissive; on the contrary, it was well organized with its own counter-ideology. Anti-Communism might have been an effective rallying cry in the Italy of the 1950s. It was no basis for hegemony.

Chapter 6

Left-wing Politics and the Working-class Movement in the 1950s

F ROM 1950 onwards the deflationist policies imposed by Luigi Einaudi in previous years were abandoned. This was not yet a period of unchecked industrial boom, but rather a time when the employers were engaged, with increasing confidence, in an intense reorganization of their industries. Marshall Aid was channelled towards the major factories, plant was renewed, new technology and more efficient working methods were introduced. While European and international markets were opening up to Italian goods, internal demand was stimulated by the spending programmes of the new government agencies — the agrarian reform boards, ENI, and the Cassa per il Mezzogiorno in particular.[1]

For the working-class movement the first half of the 1950s have come to be known as *'gli anni duri'* (the hard years). The employers launched a prolonged attack on the trade union power that had grown out of the Resistance and Liberation period. Mass redundancies were the order of the day in many major firms. Between 1946 and 1952 approximately 75,000 workers previously employed in companies controlled by IRI lost their jobs. At the same time employers sacked or marginalized leading militants, and when the economic upturn called for a new influx of labour they hired young workers, often from the countryside, who had not experienced the struggles of 1943–7, and who were prepared to accept the speeding up of production and the new organization of labour. There was, as Gibelli has written, 'an attempt [on the part of the major employers] to have done with an entire cycle of working-class struggles which had reached levels of intensity which were both preoccupying and incompatible with plans for economic development'.[2]

Smaller firms, which were very much on the increase in the 1950s, were even freer to impose their own conditions. No unionization meant little control over wage levels, dangerous jobs or insurance payments. As small business flourished, so wage differentials, which had been substantially reduced in the mid-1940s, began to widen again, with a significant bulge developing at the lower end. If the marked increase in piece-work done at home by women (gloves, lace, clothing, toys, etc.) is also taken into account, the change for the worse in the Italian wage structure becomes very marked.[3]

This employers' offensive was linked intimately with a climate of explicit political repression. The dramatic confrontation in Korea heightened political divisions at home, with the Communists and Socialists depicted as the internal enemy and as traitors to the cause of democracy and freedom. Between 1949 and 1951 there was a serious risk that the PCI, the PSI and the CGIL would have their freedoms of organization and assembly limited by law. As it was, police repression and subsequent legal action against left-wing organizations reached heights which were never to be surpassed in the post-war period. The figures for just one province, that of Bologna, for the years between April 1948 and May 1954, record that 773 people were hurt and two killed in clashes with the police. There were 13,935 trials for offences against public order, and 7,531 verdicts of guilty. Of these, 4,729 were condemned for *'invasioni di terreni'* (trespass) but 670 people also went on trial for selling *L'Unità*, the Communist newspaper, on the streets, 1,086 for putting up posters, 338 for attending political meetings and reunions, and 61 for factory occupations.[4]

Grave though these figures are, the most serious afflictions of the working classes were not political repression or the employers' offensive, but mass unemployment and enduring poverty. By 1951 well over two million people were registered as unemployed, but official figures were notoriously an under-representation of reality. Another four million people were also classified as 'marginally employed'. Endemic unemployment had spread from its traditional sectors in the South – the landless labourers of the countryside and the urban poor of Palermo and Naples – to the industrial North itself.

At the same time, a sizeable minority of Italians continued to live in conditions of extreme deprivation. The exact effect and extent of this deprivation were examined in detail by the all-party parliamentary inquest on poverty, which published its findings in fifteen volumes in 1953.[5] One index of poverty was homelessness. In Rome the inquest found that in 1952, 93,054 people were still living in shacks, caves, cellars, etc. Another 9,701 lived collectively in former barracks, schools and camps. Many of the homeless were to be found in the *borgate*, the infamous shanty towns on the extreme periphery of the capital. The *borgate* had been created in the early thirties by the Fascist regime as a 'temporary solution' to the capital's housing problem. Their inhabitants lived as best they could in shacks which lacked any basic amenities, and with epidemics rife amongst their children. The squalor and violence of this environment has been memorably portrayed in Pier Paolo Pasolini's film *Accattone*.[6]

Between 1948 and 1952 the Institute for Popular Housing at Rome received 29,000 applications for dwellings and had been able to satisfy only 1,511 of them. It was reported that in newly constructed flats a very high number of families were seriously in arrears with their rents, and that there had been numerous cases of suicide amongst those who had been evicted for non-payment. The parliamentary inquest on poverty, reviewing these statistics, concluded that the problem could only be resolved by an increase in salaries and wages, or by new initiatives on the part of the state in the field of public housing.[7]

The CGIL and Working-class Struggles

a. THE PIANO DEL LAVORO

In the face of the twin evils of unemployment and poverty, the CGIL responded in these years with a far-sighted strategy known as the Piano del Lavoro (the National Employment Plan). In October 1949, at the second congress of the CGIL, Di Vittorio unveiled the union's plan. It envisaged a public spending programme concentrated in three areas. First, the electricity industry was to be nationalized and new power stations, hydroelectric plants and reservoirs were to be constructed where they were most needed, especially in the South. Second, and closely linked, was the programme for agriculture, which was to benefit from extensive land reclamation and irrigation. Third, the dramatic shortage of houses, schools and hospitals was to be met by an immediate national building programme. In all three areas, special government agencies were to be created to finalize projects and carry through the work. The union estimated that their plan would provide work for 600,000–700,000 people over a period of three or four years. It was to be financed by heavily progressive taxation, but Di Vittorio announced that the working class too would be ready for new sacrifices if the plan was accepted. He also warned the government, in February 1950, to be very careful before 'closing the door in our face and thus forcing the workers to choose the alternative of social revolution'.[8]

The Piano del Lavoro had much to recommend it. As the union was at pains to point out, the capitalist system was not being called into question, and the proposals were moderate and neo-Keynesian in content. They demonstrated the CGIL's ability to override narrowly sectional interests in favour of a comprehensive strategy for the political economy of the country. This ability to think in wider terms was to become something of a hallmark of the Italian trade unions, and was to separate them sharply from most of their European counterparts. The plan of 1949 demonstrated a particular sensibility to the needs of the unemployed and the southern poor. As always, Di Vittorio wanted to link in the same struggle North and South, employed and unemployed, the organized working class and those who belonged to no trade union.

The plan was also intended as a rallying call to action. The CGIL hoped for government approval, but knew that mobilization, direct action and pressure from below were all-important. Over the next two and a half years, from the autumn of 1949 to the early summer of 1952, a series of local struggles, above all in central and southern Italy, tried to ensure the plan's implementation. Unemployed building workers and landless labourers, aided by local union officials, produced schemes for land irrigation and reclamation, for the construction of reservoirs and power stations, and for the opening of disused mines. Sometimes they succeeded in mobilizing whole areas in their support.[9]

However, the Piano del Lavoro, for all its merits, ended in almost total failure. The basic and obvious reason for this was that the government had little reason to accept it. De Gasperi is reported to have dismissed the CGIL's project with a single sentence: 'There are plenty of plans around but it is the cash that is lacking.' Angelo Costa, president of Confindustria, made the political reasons for rejection explicit: 'Even when economic plans which appear constructive are produced, their political aims are so evident that unfortunately true collaboration is not possible, even on those points where there is no apparent conflict of interests.' The die had been cast between 1943 and 1947, when the balance of forces had been different, but when the left had lacked an overall economic strategy. By 1950 the ruling class had no need of offers of collaboration.[10]

It is also true that the plan did not succeed in mobilizing the organized working class. To the unemployed it offered an incentive to action and concrete objectives, but it related less well to the day-to-day struggles of the northern factories. Organized workers came out frequently on strike in solidarity with the unemployed, but the plan was not connected organically to their own needs and wage demands.[11]

In addition, the rural objectives of the plan were somewhat backward with respect to the peasant movement as a whole. While the plan talked primarily of irrigation and reclamation, tens of thousands of peasants were occupying the land and clashing with landowners and police. The moderation of the plan had derived from the need to find a minimum programme to which most landowners might not object, but it was strangely out of key with the class conflict that raged in the countryside in late 1949 and 1950.[12]

Defenders of the plan have made various claims for it. One was Di Vittorio's, who said in 1952 that the DC was forced to react and that 'the Cassa per il Mezzogiorno can call itself the daughter of the Piano del Lavoro'.[13] Another, more common, is that the plan helped the working-class movement to escape from the ghetto to which the Cold War condemned it. The proof of this is taken to be the left's modest electoral success in 1953 and the failure of the *legge truffa*. Both points have some truth in them, but they must not be exaggerated. If the Cassa was the daughter of the plan, one can only say that they did not bear much resemblance to each other. And in 1953, it should be remembered, it was the extreme right, not the left, who took the most votes away from the Christian Democrats.

b. DEFENSIVE STRUGGLES IN THE NORTH AND CENTRE

With the Piano del Lavoro, the largest Italian trade union had tried to take the offensive, but the period was in fact dominated by a long series of defensive actions in many of the major factories. The employers in heavy industry, having announced mass redundancies which the CGIL refused to accept, soon resorted to lock-outs. The workers responded by occupying the factories. There then followed a number of epic struggles which came to be known by the amount of time the occupations lasted. Thus there were the '72 days of Ansaldo', the '82 days of the San Giorgio', the 'nine months of the Ilva of Bolzaneto', etc.

These occupations, much less well-known than those of 1920 or 1945, differed from their predecessors in that they occurred at a time of exceptional difficulty for the working-class movement. Everywhere the workers tried to continue production, and everywhere the work-ins won the sympathetic support of much of the urban population. The occupation committees, dominated by the older skilled workers who had been politically active ever since the Resistance, made every effort to involve workers' families in the occupations, and appealed for backing to local councillors and personalities in the world of culture and entertainment. They also tried hard not to repeat the mistakes of the electoral campaign of 1948, and to win over the white-collar sections of their factories. In this they met with limited success.[14]

These protracted struggles all ended in defeat. The most the workers managed to obtain was that sackings were substituted by suspensions and by voluntary redundancies. At Ansaldo of Genoa an occupation that had lasted more than two months ended with 1,312 voluntary redundancies and 1,417 suspensions. Only a short while then elapsed before management sacked all those who had been suspended.[15]

The overall situation in the country made it very unlikely that there could have been any other outcome. The self-confidence of the employers, the hostility of the police, with whom the strikers frequently clashed in the streets of the major cities, the divisions between CGIL, UIL and CISL, all weighed heavily against the occupations and strikes of this period.

The CGIL did manage to unite substantial sections of the factory working class when it called on them to strike on purely *political* issues – against police brutality, the *legge truffa*, the international commitments of the government. However, it was much less successful at the level of general *economic* analysis. The Italian left as a whole was convinced that the country's industry was in a state of degeneration and had to be saved from the irresponsible actions of the monopoly capitalists. Stereotyping of this sort blinded the CGIL to real developments in the economy. While heavy industry in the public sector was being dismantled, FIAT's car section increased its workforce from 14,635 in 1948 to 18,077 in 1953. In the same period Olivetti's employees grew in number from 5,910 to 8,579. Radically different processes were at work in the various parts of the Italian economy; without a proper analysis of them, the arduous task of achieving united working-class action became more difficult still.[16]

The other ideological element which limited the CGIL's responses at this time was a continuing subordination to Russian models of socialist construction. At political meetings or during the factory work-ins, documentaries on the USSR conveyed the familiar images of socialist realism: heroic and muscular workers handling heavy machinery, women driving tractors, work targets achieved or exceeded by those who followed in the selfless Stakhanov's footsteps. Ostrovsky's novel of 1935, *How Steel is Tempered (Come si temprò l'acciaio)*, circulated widely among trade union militants. These political and cultural models served to foster the belief that *production*, not *control*, was the essence of socialism, so much so that Stakhanovism and Taylorism, with their common emphasis on increased productivity, became easily intertwined.[17]

c. DEFEAT AND SELF-CRITICISM

While in political terms 1953, with its electoral defeat of the *legge truffa*, marked a turn for the better, at a factory level the hardest years for the CGIL were still to come. The number of strikes and the percentage of the workforce which adhered to them dropped continuously. Workers were becoming tired of ritual calls on their political solidarity and were filled with a growing sense of impotence as defeat followed defeat. Many of the new recruits to the factories, from the countryside or from the Veneto, were joining CISL, and the CGIL leadership seemed out of touch with the needs and sentiments of its base.[18]

These were the years in which the employers recouped their rights and powers on the factory floor. The members of the internal commission (the elected committee which represented the workers' interests in the factory) were forbidden to move about the factory during work hours. They were no longer given paid leave for trade union duties, nor were they allowed to put up notices in the factory or have a room in which to meet. Restricted in these ways, the workers' representatives rapidly lost ground to the foremen, who now had a free rein in resolving day-to-day problems at a shop-floor level. Management refused to consult or collaborate with CGIL-dominated internal commissions, and introduced suggestion boxes (*cassette delle idee*) instead.[19]

American interest in, and interference with, the situation in the factories reached remarkable levels. On 4 February 1954 the American ambassador Clare Boothe Luce had a meeting in Rome with FIAT's managing director, Vittorio Valletta. Mrs Boothe Luce declared her displeasure that 'in spite of the great sacrifices made by the USA (to the tune of more than a thousand million dollars), Communism in Italy instead of declining seemed to be making continuous progress'.[20] She went on to talk of the unfavourable impression made on many members of Congress by the enduring strength of the CGIL in the internal commissions, and the small number of votes gained by the CISL and UIL. Valletta sent a secret report to the American diplomats, trying to reassure them. In it he wrote of the efforts made by FIAT management to introduce into the factory each year three hundred new workers who had been 'well trained by the company's professional schools', and who would be the foremen of the future. At the same time 'turbulent elements' had been sacked, and activists against whom there were no precise charges were being confined to the notorious OSR (vehicle spare parts) section of the factory.[21]

American disapproval and the employers' offensive had clamorous effects. When elections were held in 1955 for FIAT's internal commission, the CGIL, for the first time since the war, lost its overall control. This defeat in the largest factory in Italy was quite traumatic for the union leadership. It led them to examine critically their activity and practices over the previous ten years. After much debate a change in direction of profound importance took place, so much so that 1955 can be seen as a watershed in Italian labour history. The centralized bargaining structure, where all wage contracts were decided on a national level, gave way to 'a return to the factory', with contracts to be decided sector by sector and firm by firm. Negotiations were no longer to take place in Rome, but were to depend for large measure on the local strength of the union and the ability of its militants to organize the whole workforce. There was no more effective way of healing the gap between the leadership and the base.[22]

Hardly surprisingly, the employers were not to take kindly to this change in strategy, and it was to be a number of years before the union was able to impose it as established practice. However, even in 1955 there were indications of what was to come. At the Ilva factory at Bagnoli near Naples the 3,700 workers went on strike in August to force the employers to subsidize the works canteen. This sort of strike over local conditions, so common in Britain, was a comparative rarity in Italy. The struggle went on for a couple of months, the CISL tried to come to a separate agreement, which the workforce rejected out of hand, and in the end the management was forced to concede defeat and negotiate a sub-sidy directly with the local CGIL.[23] Victories such as that at Bagnoli were to be few and far between in the second half of the fifties, but the defeat at FIAT turned out to be the lowest point in the CGIL's fortunes.

The Left-wing Political Parties

a. THE PSI, 1949–55

The Italian Socialists have accurately been described as living in hiberna-tion after the débâcle of the 1948 elections. They did field separate candid-ates from the PCI in 1953, and fared slightly better as a result, but otherwise they seemed to have learned very few lessons from defeat. Each year Nenni renewed the pact of unity with the PCI, but in practice unity meant subordination. As the Socialist Venerio Cattani recalled later: 'for at least three or four years only temperamental and organizational reasons prevented us from becoming Communists'. It was not just that the Socialists, once Saragat had formed the PSDI, had become a much smaller party than the Communists. It was also that they lacked any proper independence at a strategic level, so that the invaluable gift of unity on the left was accompanied by the more dubious virtues of uni-formity.[24]

A notable example of this was the 'struggle for peace' which occupied so much of the left wing's time and energy in the early 1950s. The

Korean war had greatly exacerbated fears of an imminent nuclear conflict, and Communists and Socialists alike actively promoted petitions and demonstrations in favour of peace and against nuclear weapons. However, unlike the British peace movement of the early 1960s, the Italian one, heavily dominated by the PCI, was unilateralist only in the sense of declaring that the innocent victim on an international scale was the USSR and that the constant aggressor was the United States. Murio De Micheli's poem in *L'Unità* of January 1951 captures the flavour of the period:

> What flag are you clutching in your hand, Eisenhower?
> Tell us about that child in Korea
> who holding an apple
> cries by the side of his mother murdered by your bullets
> . . . We think instead, with love,
> of the green fields of the USSR, where a shepherd,
> listening to his radio,
> hears tell of new forests and canals.[25]

Norberto Bobbio, the distinguished political philosopher, commented acidly at the time: 'Strange peacemakers, these "partisans of peace". They offer themselves as mediators to re-establish peace between the two contenders. But they announce from the outset and without any reticence that one of the contenders is right and the other is wrong.'[26]

The problem was that Bobbio's own party, the Socialists, had no alternative to offer. The Socialist leadership toyed with the idea of declaring the neutrality of the PSI, a position that would clearly have distinguished it from the PCI, but they then decided on uncritical support for the USSR. The class struggle, they argued, had no sense in a purely national context, and on an international plane there was only one possible point of reference — the USSR. It was for consistently opposing this line that Lelio Basso, probably the ablest intellectual in the party, was gradually marginalized.[27]

Only in 1955, at the Turin congress of the party, did the Socialists begin to debate a possible change of tack seriously. At Turin Nenni launched the policy that was to dominate Italian politics in the 1960s — Socialist cooperation with the Christian Democrats:

We must face and try to resolve in a new way, and as well as we can, the problem of our relations with the Catholic masses, with their party and their organizations. Since the DC has announced a programme of political and social reform, it must now have the courage to do what it says. If it takes this first step on the road to committed planning, the PSI will support the proposed reforms and take its share of the responsibilities involved.

The DC programme to which Nenni referred was, of course, Vanoni's, which disappeared into oblivion shortly afterwards. Lelio Basso warned the party at the Turin congress that the Christian Democrats only intended to 'assimilate new groups which they will bend to suit their own purposes'. Riccardo Lombardi, Milan's prefect in 1945, emphasized that Vanoni's plan 'could only be realized against someone, i.e. by attacking the forces of monopoly capitalism that lie at the heart of the economy'. If the Christian Democrats really intended to do that, then the Socialists would be with them. If not, not. Nenni was undeterred. For him, the period of immobility was drawing to a close, and even if the new path was fraught with danger, it was preferable to following meekly in the wake of the Communists.[28]

b. THE POLITICAL CULTURE OF THE PCI

The early fifties was a hard time for the Communists as well. In August 1950 the Roman federation of the party was raided by the police, and right up until the defeat of the *legge truffa* the Communists feared that they would be victims of persecutions similar to those that had taken place in France in 1952 and 1953, where the number two of the party, Duclos, had been arrested and Frachon, the secretary-general of the CGT, the Communist trade union, had only escaped prison by going into hiding. After the D C's defeat in the 1953 election the P C I leadership felt more secure, and in fact membership of the party reached its highest-ever level in 1954: 2,145,317. However, these figures masked the real isolation of the party in Italian society, where the intense propaganda of the Cold War had stigmatized them as the lepers of the nation. The large membership also could not disguise, as Ingrao has pointed out, the difficulties faced by the mass organizations on which the party depended – the peasants' leagues, the workers' trade union and the red communes of Emilia-Romagna.[29]

This was not a period of innovation in terms of general strategy. The party's perspectives for the transition to socialism continued to be based on political coalition and class alliances. The first of these had been ruled out of court in 1947; the second, with the Cold War at its height, was a more daunting task than ever before.

However, defeat and isolation did not demoralize the party activists. Far from it. The P C I developed a rich network of organizations and activities which bound its members together, as well as encouraging them to seek new recruits in every area of civil society. One of the most important non-party institutions in which both the Communists and Socialists worked were the Case del Popolo (literally 'Houses of the People'). Especially in central Italy and in the smaller towns and the countryside, the Case del Popolo, which traced their origins back to the mutual-aid societies of the late nineteenth century, became focal points of community life. Here meetings and debates were arranged, films shown, children's and sports activities organized. In some of the Case medical centres were set up; in the larger ones, like that of the Due Strade in Florence, there were public baths as well.[30] Many of the buildings which housed the Case had been taken (or taken back) from the local Fascist parties at the end of the war. In 1952 the Ministry of Finance decided that all such buildings were government property and should be sold immediately by public auction. Between 1953 and 1955, in spite of mass protests, many Case del Popolo were closed down in this way. Local militants responded by raising subscriptions for new buildings, which they laboriously constructed themselves, and which came to be regarded as symbols of resistance and solidarity.[31]

Another strong component in Communist political culture, this time linked directly with the party, were the *feste dell'Unità*. From their beginnings in the 1930s as an Italian exiles' stand at the Parisian Communist fête for *L'Humanité*, the festivals became major money-raising events to sustain the PCI's daily newspaper, *L'Unità*. The *feste* varied from modest affairs organized in a local park with barbecues, dancing and games for children, to massive national events, such as that in Rome in September 1948 to welcome back the convalescent Togliatti after the assassination attempt of July. The *festa* was often the most important moment in the local Communist section's calendar, a moment when organizational ability and the capacity to attract large numbers of non-Communists were put to the test.[32]

In addition to the sections of the party and the trade union, there were also collateral organizations to which Communists and Socialists alike contributed. The most important of these were ANPI (National Association of Ex-partisans) and UDI (Union of Italian Women), which had more than 3,500 local circles and over a million members by 1954.[33] The nature and activities of a typical UDI circle were described in *La Voce della Donna* in December 1954. The circle's meeting-place was a ground-floor room in the house of the mother of one of the activists. Here the annual assembly took place, with an opening speech of forty-five minutes dedicated to 'How to educate our children'. There were regular fortnightly meetings, which one committee member described as being 'too political'. On 8 March (Women's Day), the local girls' choir and ballet gave a performance and the trousseaus of the members who were to be married that year were put on display. Other activities included petitions for public housing and for peace, the selling of the journal *Noi Donne*, assistance to older and sick women during the winter months, solidarity with women workers sacked at the local shoe factory, the organization of a children's camp by the sea, bus trips to local museums. The aim of the circle was described by its members as that of 'women's emancipation, which must be the human and political *motif* which animates all our activity'.[34]

The party thus developed a very strong subculture which united its members, gave them an alternative vision of the world, and as in the southern struggles of 1949–50, exalted the values of egalitarianism and solidarity. However, there were also areas of silence, of ambiguity and of mystification in their thinking. One key area of silence was in the party's attitude towards the family. The Communists never elaborated a theory of family and society which could serve as a counterpoint to the very strong Catholic teaching on the subject which has been outlined above. The contradiction to which Padre Lombardi gleefully pointed – that between the PCI's claim to defend the family and the Communist Manifesto's advocacy of its eventual abolition – was not taken seriously or reflected upon. It was not until 1964 that the Communists organized a conference on family and society, and even then there seemed little recognition by the leadership of how important the issue was.[35]

In their propaganda on the family, the PCI and its flanking organizations made certain basic points. They attacked the hypocrisy of the DC which, while idealizing the family, 'had not known how to give houses, or work, or assistance to Italian families. Unemployment, poverty, illness, emigration, lack of dwellings have in fact dismembered millions of families.'[36] The Communists defended themselves against the accusation of advocating free love by citing Lenin's denunciation of it as a 'bourgeois vice'. And they extolled the virtues of the Soviet family, based on monogamy, strict morality and sacrifice for the collective good. But in all this there was nothing which conflicted with traditional Italian views of the family, or which, as Rossanda said at the 1964 conference, 'advanced proposals for a perspective which is not that of capitalist modernization'.[37]

In practice, Communist ideology served to pull families together, to help overcome familism and distrust, to pool resources. But it was also true that the hyperactivism of male Communist militants put their family life at severe risk. Tens of thousands of young, unmarried men had joined the party at the end of the war. By the 1950s most of them were married with small children and the tension between family and politics was considerable. There are many testimonies to this effect. A typical one was that of Waifro G., member of the internal commission of the Magneti Marelli factory at Sesto San Giovanni in 1956: '[Family life was limited] to a small amount of time, to quarrelling with my wife because I had a small child. My wife told me, "Because of your political commitments your child and I are always left here alone." So that was a problem as well, and she wasn't in the wrong.'[38] The party seemed to have no clear idea on the crucial question of the balance and connection between private and public life. The PCI could claim that it defended the family, but the model it presented to the outside world was often one in which the needs of the family were sacrificed to the needs of the party.[39]

In another area, the party's attitude to the Soviet Union, mystification prevailed. In the 1950s the P C I was characterized by its Stalinism. At the most straightforward level this meant a slavish adulation of 'Baffone' himself. In *Rinascita* of 1948, reviewing Stalin's work on the national question (of all things), Lucio Lombardo Radice had this to say: 'Creative Marxist that he is, Stalin is not only a scholar of genius who analyses political and historical problems in the light of Marxist principles; he is certainly this, but he is above all the great revolutionary, the great builder who analyses relations in order to transform them, who studies problems in order to resolve them.'[40] On the occasion of Stalin's seventieth birthday Togliatti wrote: 'The role that Stalin has played in the development of human thought is such that he has earned himself a place which until now very few have occupied in the history of humanity.'[41]

When the news reached Italy of Stalin's death in March 1953, the Communist Party went into mourning. *L'Unità*'s headline of 6 March read: 'The man who has done most for the liberation of the human race is dead.' The party's grief extended to its lowest levels. Natoli has described how in the party sections of the poorest Roman *borgate* photographs of Stalin were surrounded by flowers and candles and local militants sat around as if commemorating a saint.[42]

As well as elevating Stalin into a father-figure of superhuman proportions, the party portrayed the Soviet Union as a society where the problems of democracy and social justice had been definitively resolved. In *L'Unità* of 2 February 1952 Mario Alicata wrote from Russia that 'this is the first country in the history of the world in which all men are finally free'.[43] As late as March 1956 we find Luigi Longo insisting that unemployment had been completely abolished in all the socialist countries, that wages and living conditions were constantly improving and that the ordinary working day was being reduced to seven or even six hours.[44]

However, the most insidious elements of Stalinism were not the aberrant judgements on Stalin himself or the Soviet Union, but the attitudes that permeated the life and activity of the party at home. The tradition of uncritical adulation of leaders was only too easily transferred to Italy, where Togliatti seemed happy to allow absurd tributes to be paid to him by lesser comrades and exaggerated stories of his role in the early history of the P C I to be published in the party press.[45] The habit developed, and even the finest brains in the P C I like Amendola and Ingrao indulged in it, of citing the writings of the historic leaders of the party, Gramsci and Togliatti, as if they were biblical texts to serve as sermons of the day.

The other side of this coin was the propagation by the leadership, and the acceptance by the rank and file, of the political lie. The hallmark of Stalinism in the Third International had been the falsification of history and the propagation of bald-faced lies to justify changes in line or the liquidation of opponents. This too found its place in PCI praxis. While Gramsci and Togliatti became the official founding fathers of the party, Amadeo Bordiga's role was either minimized or vilified. Togliatti, having denounced Tito's politics in the late forties, was quite happy to say in 1964 that all those who denied that Yugoslavia was socialist 'have either forgotten or perhaps have never known the ABC of our social and political doctrines'.[46]

Closely linked to this was the party's attitude to political education. The PCI tried harder than any other party to overcome the legacy of Fascist indoctrination, to organize cadre schools and to educate its militants. It set its members daunting tasks of comprehension. Gino O. recalls that after the war at Palermo, 'I organized reading groups with workers: we began with Marx on historical materialism and on the dialectic. We spent months and months trying to understand. Then we went on to the history of the Bolshevik Party, and to Gramsci's *City of Socialism* [sic].'[47] However, some of what was taught was itself a form of diseducation. The rank and file were reassured with a distorted version of historical reality: capitalism was doomed and incapable of self-regeneration, the Revolution would resolve all contradictions, the Soviet Union was a terrestrial paradise.

The final element that the Italian party took from the Russian one was hierarchical organization and lack of internal democracy. The mass party created by Togliatti adopted the version of democratic centralism which had long been predominant in the Third International. Lip-service was paid to workers' control, to democracy at the base and to the ideal of the Soviets, but real power was concentrated in the hands of the party secretariat, and decisions flowed from the top downwards rather from the base to the leadership. Organized opposition within the party was forbidden and every effort was made to ensure the monolithic character of the party.

c. TOGLIATTI AND SECCHIA

Although Togliatti appeared the undisputed leader of the PCI, he had to face two serious crises in the first half of the 1950s. The first of these came at Christmas 1950. Togliatti was in Moscow, recuperating from an operation, when he was asked by Stalin to leave his post in Italy and assume control of Cominform. Cominform, it may be remembered (see pp. 113–14), had been founded in 1947 as a new attempt to coordinate the international Communist movement and tie the national parties more closely to Moscow. Togliatti did not approve of it and had no desire whatsoever to leave Rome, but it was not easy to say 'no' to Stalin. He therefore played for time and asked that the leadership of the PCI should decide on the matter. Much to his surprise and fury, his comrades voted overwhelmingly for him to go. Amendola explained later the reasons for their decision: 'We believed that the Cold War had reached a crucial point, both at home and abroad. There was the conflict in Korea, the Americans were building NATO bases all along our coasts, at Modena the police had opened fire on workers ... We said yes [to Stalin], even if we knew it would displease Togliatti ... At the end of the day we were Stalinists.'[48] It should also be added that Togliatti was more admired than loved by his colleagues. The older generation in particular, while appreciating his political grasp and intellectual acumen, was often alienated by his sarcasm and arrogance.

Togliatti refused to yield. He temporized further, persuaded Stalin that he needed to return to Italy for the congress of his party, and left Moscow by train as soon as he could. By 1952 the matter had been dropped, but for Togliatti it had been a nasty moment.

The second incident concerned what has come to be known as the Secchia affair. Pietro Secchia had been one of the most prominent Communist leaders during the Resistance, and rapidly rose to become the number two in the PCI, in charge of party organization. His relations with Togliatti were not good. Although Secchia never presented an alternative strategy to Togliatti's, there were serious political differences between them. Probably the most important of these was that Secchia wanted a more tightly organized, Leninist party, with more attention being paid to the working-class core of the PCI. He was also critical of Togliatti's handling of the years between 1943 and 1948, believing that Togliatti had been too willing to compromise with the Christian Democrats.

In July 1954 an extraordinary incident took place which led to Secchia's downfall. Giulio Seniga, Secchia's closest collaborator, disappeared, taking with him considerable sums of party money as well as confidential documents. He later justified his actions as a protest aimed at modifying the party's political line, which he considered to be no longer revolutionary. The actual result of his disappearance was the disgrace of his former patron. Togliatti and the rest of the party secretariat demanded and obtained from Secchia an abject letter of self-criticism, after which he was demoted to party secretary in Lombardy, and then removed from any position of influence. With his downfall, Togliatti no longer needed to fear that any of his colleagues could usurp him. His position as party leader now went unquestioned until his death in 1964.[49]

d. THE PCI AT LOCAL LEVEL: EMILIA-ROMAGNA

In one area of Italy, Emilia-Romagna, the Communists reigned supreme from the end of the war onwards. The 'Red Belt' of central Italy afforded the PCI a quite extraordinary degree of support when compared with the rest of the country. By November 1947 the party had nearly half a million members in Emilia-Romagna, 19.1 per cent of the adult population, organized in 1,272 sections and 11,640 cells. In the elections of June 1946 the P C I and PSI, standing together, obtained more than 66 per cent of the vote, and even at the height of the Cold War were never in danger of losing control. *'Bella regione, l'Emilia,'* Togliatti told a Bolognese audience in 1946, and he went on in what for him were almost lyrical terms: 'The torpor which seems to reign elsewhere disappears here . . .; on the faces of the men and women riding the bicycles that fill your streets one seems to note a pride and satisfaction which are absent elsewhere. One feels that this mass of people is tied to a productive activity which interests and absorbs them.'[50]

Why was Emilia-Romagna so Communist? This was not a region of heavy industry with a large factory workforce, but rather one of small enterprises, artisans, sharecroppers and landless labourers. Before 1860 it had formed part of the Papal States, and the fierce anti-clericalism which derived from the papal abuse of temporal power certainly contributed to the growth of a popular radical tradition. The landless labourers' leagues of the region were in the forefront of class agitation at the turn of the century, and by the time of the First World War an impressive socialist and cooperative tradition had been established. In 1919 the Socialists polled 60 per cent of the vote.

After Fascism had destroyed the rural and urban organizations of the working class, the Communists assumed the Socialist mantle. They were able to do so for a number of reasons. Theirs was the lion's share of the Resistance in the region, with 42,000 out of an estimated 59,000 partisans in Emilia belonging to the Garibaldi brigades. Theirs too was the reflected credit for the contribution of the Soviet Union to the defeat of the Nazis. Perhaps most important of all, theirs was the decision to develop assiduously the party's line on social alliances.

With Emilia-Romagna still predominantly rural, Communist involvement in the sharecroppers' struggle (see p. 108–10) was a key step in this policy. So too was their dedication to the problems of the Apennine peasantry, who were mainly Catholic small proprietors. The local P C I also exercised restraint upon the landless labourers, persuading them to adopt other tactics than the all-out strike so as to keep the sharecroppers and small proprietors on their side. They wished to avoid at all costs a repetition of the events of 1920–21, when the labourers' leagues, by their insistence on the need for the collectivization of land, had alienated the other sections of the rural workforce. As Arturo Colombi reported to the sixth congress of the P C I in 1948, 'it has been necessary to reconcile the interests of different categories, finding again the form of compromise acceptable to all, and thus uniting all rural workers against the employers'.[51] This was a delicate operation which was carried out with considerable skill.

Gradually, the Communists also took over control of the cooperative movement. No region had a stronger tradition of cooperation than Emilia-Romagna, both at the level of production and at that of consumption. Fascism had not destroyed this movement, even though it had tried to subject it to rigid control from above. After the war, cooperation flourished as never before. In the countryside, especially in the provinces of Reggio Emilia and Modena, there were cooperatives for dairy production and wine; in the province of Ravenna, cooperatives farmed large areas of land which they either owned or rented collectively (*le affittanze collettive*); in the cities there were building workers' cooperatives, housing associations and innumerable retail cooperatives. Ex-partisans and young people in general flocked to start up cooperatives of every sort in a spirit of equality and solidarity; associationism was to serve to combat two of the gravest of post-war problems: inflation and unemployment.[52]

In reality, the movement was characterized by its fragmented nature, the poverty of its resources, and a very heterogeneous political leadership. Although thousands of their militants were involved in cooperatives, the PCI at first devoted scant attention to them, tending to dismiss the movement as 'reformist' and as having an erroneous conception of the class struggle. However, in 1947, at the twenty-first congress of the National League of Cooperatives held at Reggio Emilia, the PCI, with the help of the Socialists, took over the leadership of the League. Republicans and Social Democrats were isolated and founded their own organization in 1952; prestigious but 'reformist' pre-Fascist leaders, like the Socialist Arturo Belelli in Reggio Emilia, retired; and the Catholics, as we have seen, had maintained their own confederation of cooperatives ever since 1945.

Communist control of the League of Cooperatives did not lead to any startling theoretical innovations. Instead the political limitations of cooperation and its inadequacy as an alternative to capitalism were repeatedly stressed. In the 1950s the party was also not convinced that the cooperatives had a future, crushed as they were by the power of the great monopolies. However, the Communists made notable efforts to improve the movement's organization, to overcome its fragmentation, and to ensure that the *ceti medi*, both in city and countryside, were not alienated from it. In this they achieved considerable success. By the beginning of the 1960s the cooperatives represented one of the pillars of Communist power in Emilia-Romagna, controlling a considerable proportion of the productive and commercial activity of the region, and employing a growing staff of workers, technicians and managers.[53]

The PCI's search for ever-widening circles of influence in the region also made them try to involve more women in the activity of the party, and to increase the percentage of housewives who held party cards. Paternalism prevailed, and much mechanical signing-up by male comrades of their wives took place. However, the Communist women of Emilia-Romagna had the prime responsibility for certain initiatives which attracted great publicity at a national level. They offered hospitality to poor children from Rome and Naples and from the mountains of their own region, and when the Polesine suffered from heavy flooding, many homeless families found refuge in the houses of PCI militants in the Red Belt.

Finally, the Emilian party extended its alliance strategy to intellectuals and to the business and commercial classes of the cities. The Communist review *Emilia* provided a focal point for political and cultural debate in the region between 1949 and 1954. Artisans, shopkeepers and small businesses were reassured that Communist action in local government would not be directed against them and that their interests would be safeguarded. Sections of the urban *ceti medi* demonstrated their solidarity when workers occupied their factories in protest against redundancies, as at the Reggiane factory in Reggio Emilia.[54]

An element of the Emilian rank and file strongly opposed the 'catch-all' nature of these alliances. Disaffected partisans, ex-Gappisti and militant landless labourers were often impatient with and disillusioned by the caution and concessions of the regional leadership. It was not until well into the fifties that general consent prevailed in the Emilian party.[55]

Bologna, the largest city in the region, became the showpiece of Communist local government. Under the amiable and reassuring leadership of its mayor, Giuseppe Dozza, the city council embarked on an ambitious social-welfare programme. The council had limited powers or funds at its disposal and matters were not helped by the fact that for a time the city's prefect was a general, Carlo De Simone. None the less the council managed to build nine schools, 896 flats, and 31 nursery schools in the decade 1946–56. Eight thousand children received subsidized school meals; new drains, municipal launderettes, and street lighting were installed; public transport and health care improved significantly.[56]

The city council of Bologna never once incurred a deficit in these years, and its efficiency and honesty contrasted favourably with the chaos and corruption in many other parts of Italy. The PCI delighted in presenting the city as a 'free commune', taking a heroic stand as in medieval times against an over-powerful emperor. In 1956 the Christian Democrats persuaded Giuseppe Dossetti to come out of political retirement and stand against Dozza in the municipal elections. In many ways the contest represented the best that both parties had to offer. Hidden beneath the polemics of the time was a distinct convergence on many issues. The DC published a *Libro bianco* on the city; in it the party advocated administrative decentralization and stressed the importance of communal life, themes which without doubt influenced the later Communist establishment of the *quartieri* (city districts) and their councils.[57] In spite of Dossetti's vigorous campaign, Dozza won an overwhelming victory. With increasing confidence, the PCI leadership pointed to Bologna as a model, as a concrete example of how the Communists were beginning to realize the transition to socialism. How much this was really so, and how much the Emilian experience was rather the efficient and humane management of capitalism, is something we will attempt to discuss at a later stage (see below, pp. 295–7).

The Watershed of 1956

After 1956 nothing was quite the same again for the Italian left. The year began with the twentieth congress of the Russian Communist Party in February. Khruschev presented a report to the congress which was divided into two parts. In the part that was made public there was a novel and significant reference to the possibility of different countries arriving at socialism by different means. After three decades of apologetics for Russia and intellectual servility, the way at last seemed open for creative discussion on the transition to socialism. But it was the secret part of the report that was the real bombshell. In it Khruschev denounced Stalin for having carried out the Great Purges, destroyed inner party democracy and created a 'cult of the personality'. 'The man who has done most for the liberation of the human race' was revealed as having created a ruthless dictatorship and committed grave crimes against humanity.

The second part of the report was soon leaked to the Western press and naturally provided a gold-mine for right-wing denunciations of the Communist movement. The PCI at first reacted with extreme reticence, with Togliatti attempting to minimize the importance of the revelations. However, such a line could not hold for long, and Togliatti's considered views on Khruschev's report were finally made known in a notable interview published in the May–June 1956 edition of the journal *Nuovi Argomenti*.[58]

In this interview Togliatti showed how able a thinker and strategist he was. He criticized the Soviet leaders *not* for having made the revelations, but for not having gone far enough. They had limited themselves to denouncing the facts and talking of 'degenerations' in Russian society, whereas what was necessary was to 'confront the difficult theme of an overall political and historical judgement'. What Togliatti wanted was not just the details of the 'cult of the personality', but a convincing explanation of how and why in socialist society Stalin had been able to do what he had done. Such an approach was certainly radical, and went far beyond the reactions of other Communist leaders in the West.

Togliatti also used the interview to introduce for the first time his celebrated concept of polycentrism. As his opposition to the Cominform had made clear, Togliatti had wanted for a long time to increase the freedom of action of individual Communist parties. Khruschev's report gave him his chance. He declared that the international socialist movement was no longer centred solely on the Soviet Union, but was increasingly diffuse and thus polycentric. In June, at the central committee of the PCI, he demanded 'full autonomy for individual movements and Communist parties, and bilateral relations between them'.[59]

However, the interview also revealed that Stalinism was much more than the sum of Stalin's crimes, and that an old leopard does not easily change his spots. Togliatti blamed the Soviet leaders for 'having accustomed us' to the uncritical adulation of Stalin, but this was to avoid admitting his own responsibilities, and to feign ignorance of the crimes committed. Togliatti had been vice-secretary of the Comintern in the thirties, and as such he must have been, at the very least, a witness to the 'cult of the personality' and Stalin's dictatorial powers. To express shock and surprise at the revelations and to reproach the Soviet leaders for misleading the rest of the Communist movement was more than a little disingenuous.

Togliatti also reiterated the intrinsic superiority of the Soviet political system over Western parliamentary democracies. Stalin's actions may have 'limited and in part suffocated' Soviet democracy, but this was 'absolutely not to say that the fundamental framework of Soviet society, from which its democratic and socialist character derives, and which renders it superior to modern capitalist societies, has been destroyed'. Any accusations that the one-party system was *per se* a limitation of democracy were dismissed as poppycock. In any case, claimed Togliatti gaily, many of the nations of the Eastern bloc were not governed by one-party states. In China, for instance, 'a plurality of parties today holds power'.[60]

Togliatti's interview, with its shrewd combination of innovation and dogma, must have helped to calm the troubled waters of his party, but there was no hiding the disquiet and even demoralization of the ordinary members. The mood of the moment was well captured in the interview given to Edio Vallini by Wanda L., a thirty-one-year-old worker in a Milanese confectionery factory, who had been a militant in the party since 1946:

I am not at all in agreement with Khruschev because I ask myself, 'And where were *they* when Stalin was committing all these errors that they say he has committed?' . . . This question of Stalin has shaken me because for years I've quarrelled with all those who said that he was a dictator while now I have to admit to my enemies that they were right. I wonder why, if the party knew it, it didn't say so immediately; as it is, it seems as if it has taken us for a ride . . . I remain convinced that Stalin was truly a genius.[61]

As if Khruschev's revelations were not enough for one year, events in Poland and Hungary, themselves heavily dependent on what had happened at Moscow, greatly increased the ferment in the Italian party. In late June there was a workers' insurrection in the Polish city of Poznan, resulting in thirty-eight deaths and 277 persons wounded. Di Vittorio immediately expressed the solidarity of the CGIL with the Polish workers, but the party frowned upon his initiatives and preferred to toe a line that was close to Moscow's. The insurrectionaries were described as 'criminal elements' and *'provocateurs'*, and Togliatti's editorial in *L'Unità* of 2 July, in which he denounced 'the presence of the enemy' in Poznan, was reproduced in *Pravda*.[62]

In the autumn the Hungarian Revolution led to major dissension in the international Communist movement. In the wake of the Russian armed suppression of the uprising, tens of thousands of militants left the western European parties. The PCI leaders came out unequivocally in support of the Russian invasion. They criticized the errors and injustices of the Rakosi regime that had held power prior to the Revolution, but they went on to denounce the reactionary aims of those who had taken its place and, as with Poland, they falsified the class composition of the revolt.

Within the party's ranks, and especially amongst its intellectuals, furious debates raged over the rights and wrongs of the Hungarian tragedy. Davide Lajolo, the editor at that time of the Milanese edition of *L'Unità*, recalled later how his office had been transformed into a battleground. One day Secchia and Alberganti, the 'two old Stalinists', would arrive shouting 'All power to the Soviet tanks!' The next Rossana Rossanda and Giangiacomo Feltrinelli would bring in a declaration against the Soviet Union and try to enforce its publication.[63] In every party section the fundamental questions of democracy, national independence and the role of the Soviet Union were argued over with an intensity and openness that had never previously been experienced.

The culminating point of 1956, a year which was to be dubbed by Ingrao as 'unforgettable' and by Amendola as 'terrible', came in December, with the eighth congress of the PCI. Various delegates reported on how disconcerted the rank and file had grown during the course of the year. Giuseppe Prestipino from Messina said that no one could deny that thousands of peasants and workers from southern Italy had been won to the party through their belief in Stalin's infallibility, and that it was now no easy task to explain to them that Stalin had been wrong. Valerio Bertini from Florence also reported that many comrades had lost their faith in the party and the Soviet Union and no longer knew what to believe.[64]

The most dramatic part of the congress centred on the interventions of those Communists who had become open dissenters from the party line.

Foremost of these was Antonio Giolitti, deputy for Cuneo and grandson of the famous prime minister. Giolitti made three requests: the establishment of effective liberty of opinion and discussion in the party, within the context of democratic centralism; the recognition by the leadership of the vital import-ance of democratic liberties, and consequently an admission of its error in defining the Hungarian regime prior to the revolution as 'legitimate, demo-cratic and socialist'; and finally the full autonomy of the PCI in its relations with other Communist parties.[65]

This last point was close to Togliatti's own heart, but the other two were anathema to him, and he had no option but to launch an overwhelming counterattack on Giolitti and the other 'revisionists'. The dissenting wing in the party was not strong, and it was easy enough for the leadership to win the consent of the great majority of delegates. Giolitti, Furio Diaz, Fabrizio Onofri and Eugenio Reale were either expelled from the party or resigned of their own accord. In general, the eighth congress and its aftermath must count as a significant victory for the leadership of the party. There *were* mass defections: Amendola has estimated that some 400,000 members were lost between 1955 and 1957. A significant number of intellectuals left the party, of whom the best known were probably the writer Italo Calvino and the historian Delio Cantimori. But the bulk of the party held together remarkably well at a time when some commentators were predicting its imminent and unavoidable decline.

The year 1956 was a watershed for *both* the major parties on the Italian left. If we look first at the PCI, we can see that certain crucial elements in its strategy derive from the crises it had to confront during the course of the year. In the first place, 1956 marked a new phase in the party's relationship to the international Communist movement. Gone for ever was the uncritical acceptance of the USSR as the model socialist state, and of its right to command while others obeyed. Instead the PCI laid claim to its autonomy, no longer regarded itself as confined to a Western outpost, and became more Eurocentric in outlook. The speed with which all this happened should not be exaggerated. Polycentrism was not made explicit for some years, and the degree of Togliatti's agreement with Moscow remained very great. It was not until the great Polish crisis of 1981 that the Russian and Italian parties finally came to breaking-point.

Secondly, there was a gradual shift in the party's position on proletarian and bourgeois democracy. The concept of the 'dictatorship of the proletariat' was not formally abandoned. Indeed, Luigi Longo, in a pamphlet of 1957 attacking Giolitti, stressed that the transformation to socialism under working-class direction necessarily implied 'the reduction and eventual total obliteration of the rights and powers of those forces averse to and hostile towards this transformation'.[66] However, over the years such assertions of Communist orthodoxy became less and less frequent. In their place came the acceptance of the *permanent* value of the political and civil liberties enshrined in parliamentary democracy rather than the mere acceptance of their *tactical* usefulness. Already at the eighth congress Togliatti gave indications of these developments when he stressed the centrality of the republican Constitution of 1947 in the transition to socialism in Italy.

Thirdly, the cultural and intellectual atmosphere in the party underwent a striking transformation. The pedantry, moralism and closedness of the Stalinist years gave way to a more liberal approach, where the category of 'degenerate' was less frequently used with reference to contemporary Western culture and where historical research could escape the narrow confines of party dogma. This process had already begun with the founding of the journal *Il Contemporaneo* in 1954, but it was to be much accentuated after 1956.

Finally, mention must be made of the organizational changes that took place in the PCI. These too had begun before 1956, and Amendola dates the 'renewal' of the party from its fourth organizational congress in January 1955. The older generation in the party, whom Togliatti dubbed the 'satraps', the legendary local leaders and Resistance heroes, were replaced by younger men who had come into the party relatively recently and who were to remain loyal to the leadership during the crises of 1956. The local autonomies enjoyed by the older charismatic militants passed away with them, as did the most rigid forms of Stalinism. As a result, the party became both more centralized and more open to the outside world, characteristics which conflicted with each other and which provided one of the fundamental tensions in the development of the PCI.

Thus the changes in the PCI during and after 1956 were of a major kind, and their full significance will be considered at a later point (see below, pp. 292–3). Perhaps of even greater importance for the next decade of Italian politics was the transformation wrought by the events of 1956 in the PSI. In the local elections of May 1956, the PSI and the PSDI both gained votes, while the PCI fell back for the first time. The Socialists condemned the Russian invasion of Hungary, and when Togliatti tried to liken Russian action in Hungary to its earlier support of republican Spain during the Civil War, Nenni denounced the historical parallel as being completely false. The Socialists' strategic subservience to the Communists had come to an end. In August of 1956 Nenni held a secret meeting with Saragat at Pralognan, in the Val d'Aosta. The two leaders discussed the possible reunification of their parties. Nothing came of the initiative, but 1956 was the first year since the war when the Socialists refused to renew their pact of unity of action with the Communists.[67] Many of those who left the PCI at this time, like Antonio Giolitti, joined the Socialists instead. The two parties drew further apart, and for the first time the PSI set about acting as a free agent.

Chapter 7

The 'Economic Miracle',
Rural Exodus and
Social Transformation,
1958–63

*I*TALY IN the mid-1950s was still, in many respects, an under-developed country. Its industrial sector could boast of some advanced elements in the production of steel, cars, electrical energy and artificial fibres, but these were limited both geographically, being confined mainly to the north-west, and in their weight in the national economy as a whole. Most Italians still earned their living, if they earned it at all, in the traditional sectors of the economy: in small, technologically backward, labour-intensive firms, in the public administration, in a great proliferation of small shops and trades, in agriculture. Standards of living remained very low. In 1951 the elementary combination of electricity, drinking water and an inside lavatory could be found in only 7.4 per cent of Italian households.[1]

Agriculture was still by far the largest single sector of employment. In the census of 1951 the category 'agriculture, hunting and fishing' accounted for 42.2 per cent of the working population, and this figure rose to 56.9 per cent for the South. Apart from the dynamic and prosperous farms on the plains of the Po, Italian agriculture presented a picture of substantial backwardness, with growth rates inferior to those of Yugoslavia and Greece. The 1950s saw a marked increase in the fragmentation of property. In the central areas of the peninsula the time-honoured sharecropping system began to decline rapidly. Young peasants were increasingly reluctant to follow in their parents' footsteps; the landowners found their profit margins and authority diminishing; the buoyancy of the land market encouraged them to sell, most often directly to the sharecropping families themselves. In the South, as we have seen, a similar process of land sales was in operation, and peasants throughout the peninsula benefited from the law of February 1948 which had established the system of rural mortgages repayable over forty years. The effect of these land sales and the agrarian reform was to increase the amount of smallholding property by nearly 10 per cent in the period 1947–55.[2]

This increase in ownership did not lead to a golden age of peasant farming. Rather, the selection process which we have examined in detail for the Calabrian reform area (see pp. 133–5) applied broadly to small farms in the rest of the peninsula. For a minority of new properties, situated in fertile areas and aided by the reform boards and the public works of the Cassa per il Mezzogiorno, the way was open for crop specialization and production for the market; for the majority in the hill and mountain regions there were no such prospects. In these regions, in both the Centre and the South, the peasant holdings were too small, poor and dispersed, and state aid too limited, to make anything more than subsistence farming possible. Thus land ownership, the perennial dream of the Italian peasantry, had become more widespread, but the terms and extent of ownership offered a means to survive rather than to prosper.[3]

For many millions of the rural population there was not even the consolation of a small plot of land. In 1953 the parliamentary inquest on unemployment estimated that 48 per cent of the rural workforce of the South was drastically underemployed, and the figures for the Centre (43.8 per cent) and the Veneto (41.3 per cent) were little better. In the 1950s, as in previous decades, this vast reserve army of labour could find only very partial satisfaction for its work hunger.

One outlet was emigration. This took a number of different forms, the most dramatic of which was emigration overseas, to the Americas and Australia. Between 1946 and 1957 the numbers of those leaving Italy for the New World exceeded by 1,100,000 the numbers of those returning: 380,000 had remained in Argentina, 166,500 in Canada, 166,000 in the USA, 138,000 in Australia and 128,000 in Venezuela. They were for the most part artisans and peasant proprietors rather than landless labourers, nearly 70 per cent were from the South, and by 1957 many of them had settled permanently abroad. In the Calabrian villages, South America in particular was dubbed *'e d'u scuordo,* 'the land of forgetting'.[4]

Another pattern of emigration, of a rather different sort, was that to north Europe. Between 1946 and 1957 the numbers heading north exceeded by 840,000 the numbers of those who came back: France took the lion's share (381,000), followed by Switzerland (202,000) and Belgium (159,000).[5] The emigrants to these countries tended to go for shorter periods, on six-month or one-year contracts, and regarded work abroad as a temporary rather than a permanent solution to their problems.

Within Italy itself, the Industrial Triangle exercised only a limited pull in these years, mainly upon the rural populations of Lombardy, Piedmont and the Veneto. All the major cities and towns of the peninsula attracted a certain influx of rural labourers seeking work primarily in the building trades. There was also a small but significant flow of migrants, mainly rural labourers, from the deep South to other rural areas of Italy – to Tuscany, the Bolognese countryside and the Ligurian coast.

All these movements of population, as well as the increase in peasant land ownership and the work of the reform boards and the Cassa, ensured that the world of rural Italy was not immobile in the 1950s. And yet continuities still far outweighed changes. When in the mid-fifties the American sociologist Edward Banfield went to the village of Chiaramonte in Basilicata, he persuaded one of the peasants, Carlo Prato, to keep a diary for 1955. Prato, who was forty-three and married with two children, managed to find 180 days' work that year. In December and January he was employed on an olive-oil press in a nearby town, sleeping in barracks, working from two in the morning until nine at night and earning three meals, a little cash and half a litre of oil a day. After that he was unemployed until he found a job on a road gang some three hours' walk from his home. In the summer he found decent wages with the major landowners of his village, but in the autumn months he had no work at all and just pottered around his tiny plot of land. The Pratos lived in a one-room house which they owned. In the summer it was alive with flies. There was no drinking water, no electricity, no lavatory. Although the winter at Chiaramonte was cold and wet, Prato's jacket was the only warm outer garment possessed by the family. Prato's wife suffered from permanent ill-health.[6]

The years 1958–63 saw the beginning of a social revolution which was to turn the world of Carlo Prato upside down. In less than two decades Italy ceased to be a peasant country and became one of the major industrial nations of the West. The very landscape of the country as well as its inhabitants' places of abode and ways of life changed profoundly. It is to the origins of this transformation and its first extraordinary years that this chapter is dedicated.

The 'Economic Miracle'

a. ORIGINS

The period 1950–1970 was a golden age for international trade. In that time trade in manufactured goods increased sixfold; the degree of economic integration of the major industrial countries reached new heights; and mass production for mass markets, both internal and external, produced an unprecedented level of prosperity. Fordism (the automated mass production of consumer goods) and consumerism became the twin gods of the age.

How was it that Italy, far from playing a minor role in this great era of expansion, became one of its protagonists? The reasons are many, and there is no general consensus amongst economists as to the order in which they should be placed. Certainly, the end of Italy's traditional protectionism must be considered of prime importance. Whereas Franco's Spain, with an economic structure somewhat similar to Italy's in 1945, remained isolated for many years from the main currents of European trade, Italy, as we have seen, was in the forefront of European economic integration. Many Italian businessmen viewed with unjustified foreboding this sudden exposure to the winds of European competition. In fact, Italy's industry had reached a sufficient level of technological development, and had a sufficiently diversified range of products, to be able to respond positively to the creation of the Common Market. The advanced sectors were of modest proportions, but everywhere in them there were entrepreneurs, engineers, designers and skilled craftsmen ready to meet the challenge.[7]

Even before the 'miracle', some areas were expanding dramatically. In 1953 Vittorio Valletta decided to invest heavily in a gigantic production line for FIAT's latest model. Two years later the age of mass motoring in Italy was heralded by a multicoloured procession through the streets of Turin of brand new FIAT 600s. In the same period fierce competition between ENI, Edison and Montecatini resulted in great advances in Italy's petrochemical industry and in the production of synthetic rubber and fertilizers. And, as we have seen, Marshall Aid, with its influx of American machinery and know-how, had also opened up new horizons for many Italian firms.[8]

The end of protectionism, then, far from signifying catastrophe, revitalized Italy's productive system, forced it to modernize and rewarded those sectors which were already on the move. Italy's capacity to compete was also greatly aided by new sources of energy and the transformation of its steel industry. ENI's discovery of methane gas and hydrocarbons in the Val Padana, and Mattei's importation of cheap liquid fuels (see pp. 163–4), afforded an alternative to imported coal and enabled Italian entrepreneurs to cut their costs. So too did Oscar Sinigaglia's insistence on a modern steel industry under the aegis of IRI. His plan for steel involved considerable state investment in modern steel works at Cornigliano, Piombino and Bagnoli. Here steel was produced from raw materials through the use of blast furnaces. Under Sinigaglia's guidance, Finsider went from strength to strength, and in the 1950s was able to provide much cheap steel for Italian firms.[9]

ENI and IRI thus played a notable role in the origins of the 'miracle'. And while the Italian state cannot be said in any meaningful sense to have planned the great boom, it certainly contributed to it in many ways. Infrastructural works, such as the construction of *autostrade*, served as vital 'external economies' for the private sector. Monetary stability, the non-taxation of business interests, the maintenance of favourable lending rates by the Bank of Italy, all these served to create the correct conditions for the accumulation of capital and its subsequent investment in industry.[10]

Last, but far from least, it is quite clear that the 'miracle' could not have taken place without the low cost of labour then prevalent in Italy. The high levels of Italian unemployment in the 1950s ensured that demand for work far exceeded supply, with predictable consequences in terms of wage rates. The unions' post-war power had been effectively broken, and the way was now open to increase productivity and exploitation. The external free-trade credo of the EEC found its internal counterpart in the freedom of the employer at the place of work. Between 1953 and 1960, while industrial production rose from a base of 100 to 189, and workers' productivity from 100 to 162, real wages in industry fell very slightly from 100 to 99.4.[11] With labour costs as low as these, Italian firms were highly competitive on international markets.

b. DEVELOPMENT

In the period 1951–8, growth in the Italian economy, although considerable, would seem to have been mainly due to internal demand. The rate of increase in the Gross Domestic Product averaged 5.5 per cent per year, but the major investments of the period were less in export industries than in housing, public works and agriculture. International trade had not yet become the motor for the Italian economy.[12]

This picture changes quite dramatically for the years 1958–63. In the first place, growth rates reached a level never previously attained in the history of the unified state, an average annual increase in GDP of 6.3 per cent. Furthermore, investments in machines and industrial plant grew by an average of 14 per cent per annum, as opposed to 6 per cent per annum in the previous seven years. Industrial production more than doubled in the period 1958–63, with the engineering industry and petrochemicals leading the way. Above all, exports became the driving sector behind expansion, with an average increase of 14.5 per cent per annum. The effect of the Common Market was clear for all to see: the percentage of Italian goods destined for the EEC countries rose from 23 per cent in 1955 to 29.8 per cent in 1960 and 40.2 per cent in 1965.[13]

The pattern of what Italy produced and exported changed significantly. Textiles and food products gave way to those consumer goods which were much in demand in the advanced industrial countries, and which reflected per capita incomes far higher than Italy's own: Italian fridges, washing-machines, televisions, cars, precision tools, typewriters and plastic goods were all marketed in extraordinary numbers.

Symptomatic of the 'miracle' was the extraordinary growth of Italy's domestic electric-appliances industry. In the post-war period nearly all the firms that were later to become well-known names in Europe were little more than artisan concerns: in 1947 Candy produced one washing-machine per day, Ignis had a few dozen workers and even Zanussi had only 250 employees on its books. In 1951 Italy was producing just 18,500 fridges. By 1957 this number had already grown to 370,000; by 1967 it had reached 3,200,000, by which time Italy was the third largest producer of fridges in the world, after the United States and Japan. By the same date Italy had also become the largest producer in Europe of washing-machines and dish-washers; Candy was now producing one washing-machine every fifteen seconds.[14]

Behind this transformation lay a number of factors: the entrepreneurial skills of the owners of the new Italian firms, their ability to finance themselves in the early 1950s, their willingness to adapt new techniques and to renovate their plant continuously, their exploitation of the low cost of labour and its high productivity, the absence until the late sixties of any significant trade union organization. Often the new factories were located outside the major cities and in the 'white' regions of the country. Pordenone, in Friuli, became the company town of Zanussi, and its inhabitants identified the transformation of their own fortunes with those of the firm.[15]

The domestic electric-appliances industry was the most dramatic example of the boom in Italian industry and its export potential, but it was far from being the only one. Car production, dominated by FIAT, was in many ways the propulsive sector of the economy. It has been estimated that by 1963–4 some 20 per cent of the total volume of investments in Italy derived from the production choices made by FIAT – not only in the smaller firms which supplied parts, but in the areas of rubber production, the construction of roads, the supply of steel, petrol, electrical goods and so on.[16]

Another major area of expansion was typewriters. With Olivetti in the forefront, and its 'model' factory at Ivrea one of the great success stories of the fifties, the number of typewriters produced rose from 151,000 in 1957 to 652,000 in 1961. The production of plastic materials also increased fifteenfold in the period 1951–61, while the volume of their exports multiplied by no less than fifty-five.[17]

The geographical location of Italy's industrial production expanded beyond the narrow confines of the Industrial Triangle. If Lombardy and

Piedmont still remained the epicentres, industrial Italy now spread southwards towards Bologna and eastwards along the whole of the Val Padana, to reach the Adriatic at Porto Marghera and Ravenna. By 1961, the year of the national census, the number of those employed in industry had already reached 38 per cent of the working population, while those in the tertiary, or service, sector had also increased to 32 per cent. The agricultural sector had declined to 30 per cent of the working population.[18] The balance had shifted decisively, and the way was open for Italy to join the restricted group of advanced industrial nations.

c. IMBALANCES

One of the most striking features of the 'miracle' was its autonomous character. Vanoni's scheme of 1954 had laid plans for controlled economic development which would have taken social and geographical factors into consideration. Instead the boom assumed a trajectory all of its own, responding directly to the free play of market forces, and producing as a result a number of grave structural imbalances.

The first of these was what has been called the distortion of consumption patterns. Export-led growth meant an emphasis on private consumer goods, often of a luxury nature, without any corresponding development in public consumption. Schools, hospitals, public transport, low-cost housing, all items of prime necessity, lagged far behind the startling advance in the production of private consumer goods.[19] The political responsibility for this state of affairs will be examined in some detail in the next chapter. Suffice it to say here that the pattern which the boom assumed (or was allowed to assume) emphasized individual and familial roads to prosperity while ignoring collective and public responses to everyday needs. As such, the economic 'miracle' served once again to emphasize the importance of the individual family unit within Italian civil society.

The boom years of 1958–63 also accentuated the dualism within the Italian economy. On the one hand there was the dynamic sector, consisting of both large and small firms, with high productivity and advanced technology. On the other, there remained the traditional sectors of the economy, labour intensive and with low productivity, which absorbed manpower but acted as an enormous tail to the Italian economic comet.[20]

Finally, and most dramatically, the 'miracle' heightened the already grave disequilibrium between North and South. With very few exceptions, all the sectors of the economy in rapid expansion were situated in the northwest and in some parts of the Centre and north-east of the country. It was there that the capital, resources and professional expertise of the nation had traditionally been concentrated, and it was there that the export firms, both large and small, flourished in unprecedented numbers. The 'miracle' was quintessentially a northern phenomenon, and the most active parts of the southern population did not take long to realize it.

Migration

Antonio Antonuzzo, born in 1938, was the second of five sons in a peasant family from the village of Bronte in eastern Sicily. The Antonuzzo family was not so poor as some of the villagers. They owned a number of farm animals and cultivated a small piece of land as sharecroppers. When Antonio was still very young, his father, 'struck by the wandering spirit of the Sicilians',[21] left for Argentina to make his fortune. He worked there as a stable boy and as a shoe-polisher before returning to Bronte two years later, poorer than when he had left.

Then, in 1950, when Antonio was twelve years old, the whole family migrated to Montino, near Massa Marittima in Tuscany. Three landowners from Bronte had bought an estate there, and promised that the land was rich and that they would sell it off in small farms to the peasants who came with them from Sicily. This fact, the possibility of owning land, was the determining one for Antonio's father. His mother, however, resisted bitterly the idea of leaving Bronte: 'My father then hit my mother twice; that which he had never done in so many years of marriage he did on that occasion. He hit her in the name of Fortune.'[22]

On 28 September 1950 the Antonuzzo family and that of Antonio's uncle, twenty-one people in all, left for Tuscany. At Grosseto station Antonio remembers that 'people stopped to stare . . . not with sympathy or with indifference but with contempt at our caravan of gypsies'.[23] The move to Montino was an unmitigated disaster. The land was poor and the five hectares that Antonio's family managed to buy was mainly woodland. The family became practically destitute and scraped a living as charcoal-burners. As soon as he was old enough, Antonio went to work in the mines at Massa. In the same period the family, having experienced the hostility of the local Tuscan peasants, who were all Communists, decided to join the Christian Democrat Party.

In April 1962, after he had done his military service, Antonio Antonuzzo decided to leave the Tuscan countryside and head for the northern cities. He went first to Legnano where his cousins were, and then, a few weeks later, to Milan. Another cousin, Vincenzo, was living in a room at no. 70 Corso Garibaldi, and offered to let Antonio stay there: 'it was very small, with only one window. The glass had been smashed and there was cardboard in its place. The one electric light was so dim that most of the room was always in darkness.'[24] There was a single bed that the two cousins shared. In Milan for the first time, Antonio felt absolutely desolate: 'it was as if I was in a forest where there was not a single living being'.[25] Using a letter of recommendation from the Christian Democrats at Massa, Antonio soon found work at the Coca-Cola factory in Piazza Precotto. After twelve days he gave in his notice. Immediately afterwards, and again with the help of the DC, he found a better-paid job, at the Alfa-Romeo car factory.

At the end of 1962, after he had saved a little money, Antonio moved his family from Montino to Milan, to a two-room flat he had found in Piazza Lega Lombarda:

On 29–30 December of that year, we went to meet my parents at Melegnano, at the exit of the Autostrada del Sole. When I and my brother Giuseppe arrived, we saw a lorry with a Grosseto number plate. He went over to it and inside the driving cabin there were my mother, my father, and my brother Giovannino. They'd travelled all night, four of them huddled up together inside the cabin of the lorry. There was a lot of snow and it was extremely cold. They were frozen because they hadn't enough clothes on. On the back of our lorry there were all our belongings: six chairs, two double beds, and a very old wardrobe.[26]

Antonio stayed at Alfa-Romeo for the next five years, becoming one of the leading militants at the factory. After that, he left to become a full-time trade unionist in the CISL.

The 'economic miracle' meant much more in the history of Italy than a booming economy and rising standards of living. It meant an unparalleled movement of the peninsula's population. Hundreds of thousands of Italians, like the Antonuzzo family, left their places of birth, left their villages where their families had lived for generations, left the unchanging world of rural Italy, and began new lives in the booming cities and towns of the industrial nation.

a. PATTERNS AND STATISTICS OF MIGRATION
No proper statistics exist to help us document the waves of migration that took place in these years. The records of residence changes are one of the least unreliable indicators, but even here there are grave problems. A Fascist law of 1939, designed specifically to prevent internal migrations and urbanization, trapped the would-be migrant in a Catch 22 situation: in order to change residence to a town of more than 25,000 inhabitants, the migrant had to show evidence of employment at the new place of abode; however, in order to gain such employment the migrant had first to produce a new residence certificate. This absurd law was only repealed in 1961. By then it was being even more widely ignored than most Italian laws, but it had none the less cost hundreds of thousands of migrants quite unnecessary heartache, had weakened their position *vis-à-vis* their new employers and land-

lords, and had placed them in a quite unwarranted position of illegality. It had also, rather more incidentally, falsified all statistics on migration, because many of the pre-1961 migrants only legalized their position after the repeal of the law.[27]

Bearing this preamble in mind, it can safely be said that in the two decades between 1951 and 1971 the location of Italy's population underwent a revolution. Massive migration took place between 1955 and 1963; migration then halted briefly in the mid-1960s, but resumed strongly in the period 1967–71. In all, between 1955 and 1971, some 9,140,000 Italians were involved in inter-regional migration.[28]

The patterns of migration are extremely complex, and no comprehensive study of them has yet been written. Their predominant feature is a massive *rural* exodus in all parts of the peninsula. The figures for immigration to Milan in the decade 1953–63 show for instance that some 70 per cent of the new arrivals were from rural communes. In the north-west the percentage of the working population employed in agriculture fell from 25 per cent in 1951 to 13 per cent in 1964. In the north-east the figures are the most dramatic for the whole country: the percentage of rural workers fell from 47.8 to 26.1 per cent in these same years, 1951–64.[29] The number of women employed in northern agriculture plummeted; figures for Lombardy show a drop from 109,000 in 1959 to 36,000 in 1968.[30] The cities of the Industrial Triangle obviously exercised the greatest pull upon these migrants, but the provincial cities of the North should not be forgotten. These were boom years for Mestre, Padua, Verona, Bergamo, Brescia, Varese, Ivrea and so on.

The central regions of the country witnessed a rural exodus almost as great as that of the north-east, with their agricultural sector declining from 44.3 per cent of the working population in 1951 to 23.3 per cent in 1964. The number of sharecroppers began to fall very rapidly, from 2,241,000 in 1951 to 1,114,000 in 1964. By 1971 less than 500,000 sharecroppers remained.[31] The rural migrants of central Italy tended not to move very far, and to swell the populations of the cities of their own regions rather than those of the North.

The same cannot be said of the southern migrants. The agricultural population of the Mezzogiorno declined slightly less than those of the Centre and the north-east (from 56.7 per cent of the working population in 1951 to 37.1 per cent in 1964), but southern migration was by far the most dramatic because it involved a massive exodus from the Mezzogiorno itself. The migrants were mainly from the poorest agricultural regions, the hill and mountain villages of the South, and the number of small proprietors who left actually outnumbered the labourers.[32]

For many of the migrants the provincial or regional capitals of the

South were a first port of call; for a smaller number, the first move, as with
the Antonuzzo family, was to another rural area in the Centre or North.
However, the magnet of the North was too strong to be resisted for long.
The hopes and plans of the southern migrants were concentrated in two
directions: towards the industrial heartlands of northern Europe, especially
West Germany, and to the expanding cities of northern Italy.

Between 1958 and 1963, net emigration of Italians to northern
Europe totalled 545,000 persons; of these 73.5 per cent came from the
South. Germany rapidly overtook Switzerland as the favoured destination
for Italian emigrants. By 1963 these two countries alone accounted for 86
per cent of Italian emigration to north Europe.[33]

However, the greatest flow of all was towards the northern region of
Italy. In the five years of the miracle (1958–63), more than 900,000
southerners changed their places of residence from the South to the other
regions of Italy. In 1958 the communes of the Industrial Triangle registered
69,000 new residents from the South. In 1962, after the repeal of the anti-
urbanization law of 1939, this number leaped to 203,800 and in 1963
remained at the very high level of 183,000. Similar figures for 1958 show
60,100 new migrants from the South in the central and north-eastern
regions, increasing to 104,700 in 1963. Puglia, Sicily and Campania were the
southern regions which, in absolute terms, suffered the greatest haemor-
rhages of population.[34]

The major cities of Italy were transformed by this sudden influx. The
population of Rome, swollen by immigrants from Lazio, Puglia, Sardinia,
Campania and the Abruzzi, increased from 1,961,754 in 1951 to 2,188,160 in
1961 and 2,614,156 in 1967. Milan, where 70 per cent of the immigrants
were from Lombardy and the Veneto and 30 per cent from the South in the
years 1958–63, increased its population from 1,274,245 in 1951 to 1,681,045
in 1967. At the same time the towns of its hinterland grew very rapidly. By
1968 Monza had a population of 105,000, Cinisello Balsamo 70,000, Rho
40,000. Perhaps most striking of all was the case of Turin, which was smaller
than Milan and Rome, and which had a very high percentage of southern
immigrants, predominantly from the three provinces of Foggia, Bari and
Reggio Calabria. The city itself increased its population from 719,300 in
1951 to 1,124,714 in 1967. Between 1961 and 1967 alone the twenty-three
communes of its immediate hinterland grew by over 80 per cent. So great
and persistent was the flow from the South that by the end of the sixties
Turin had become the third largest 'southern' city in Italy, after Naples and
Palermo.[35]

b. DEPARTURE AND ARRIVAL

Many of the structural reasons which drove the rural populations from the land have already been highlighted in this and previous chapters: the poor quality of the soil in much of the South, the persistence of chronic underemployment and poverty, the widespread ownership of uneconomic smallholdings, the very limited nature of the agrarian reform of 1950. To these must be added a number of factors which relate specifically to the late 1950s. In 1958–9 the holding policy of the agrarian reform boards with regard to the hill and mountain peasantry underwent, as we have seen (p. 135), a profound change. Credit facilities were severely restricted and the peasant owners found that their plots were no longer viable. In addition, the gradual liberalization of grain markets from 1955 onwards meant a marked fall in grain prices; small owners, with their extensive debts and limited flexibility, were the worst affected.[36]

The late 1950s also saw a worsening in the conditions of rural labourers. In December 1958, the Constitutional Court declared the *imponibile di mano d'opera* (see pp. 61 and 114) illegal, and thus removed one of the most important props to rural employment. For example, in the winter of 1956–7 alone, the *imponibile* had ensured more than 186,000 labourers regularly paid work for more than two and a half months each. Increased mechanization and new technology further worsened the prospects of employment for rural labour. The number of tractors increased from 61,000 in 1949 to 250,000 ten years later, and this was the period in which the labour of the *mondine*, the women workers in the northern rice fields, was replaced by the use of weed-killers.[37]

These 'push' factors coincided with 'pull' ones of a compelling nature. First, and most obvious, higher incomes were a near certainty for those who left the land for the cities. At the end of the 1950s both the marginal small proprietor and the rural labourer could expect at least to double their incomes by transferring to the tertiary or the industrial sector.

Wages were all-important. Domenico Norcia, for instance, was working in 1960 in a small village in the Irpinia on a building site funded by the Cassa per il Mezzogiorno. He was earning 500 lire a day; having insulted the foreman he got the sack and promptly left for Germany: 'At that time, 500 lire was not much, but if I had found work for 1,000 lire a day in my village, I would never have gone to Germany, I would never have left.'[38]

However, money was not the only pull. The prospect of regular wages and regular hours of work was deeply attractive to peasants who had always laboured like Trojans at harvest time, but who had little to keep them occupied or in pocket in the winter months. For the young, who were to constitute the majority of the first migrants, the lure of the city was irresistible. In the evenings, in the piazzas of the southern villages, their talk was of nothing else. The television of the local bar transmitted images from the North, images of a consumer world, of Vespas, portable radios, football heroes, new fashions, nylon stockings, mass-produced dresses, houses full of electrical appliances, Sunday excursions in the family FIAT.[39]

The young men, usually single, were the first to go. They were the most dissatisfied, the most ruthless, the most determined elements in the villages. Kinship networks were used to the full to give them some sort of base once they arrived in the North. Antonio Antonuzzo, as we have seen, went to his cousins, first to Legnano and then in Milan. Help was also enlisted from children's *compari*, their godfathers, who sometimes belonged to a higher social class, as well as from in-laws and neighbours.

The southern migrants left on the *treno del sole*, the famous over-crowded train full of suitcases and parcels. It started both from Palermo and Siracusa, linked up at Messina, and travelled slowly northwards through Calabria, Basilicata, Campania, Lazio, Tuscany and Liguria. For the Pugliesi there was the *direttissimo* from Lecce, for the Sardinians the ferry from Porto Torres and the train from Genoa. The *treno del sole* arrived at Turin station every morning at 9.50 a.m., and at the peak periods of migration it was followed by another ten minutes later.[40]

For the immigrants from the rural South the first impressions of the northern cities were bewildering and often frightening. What struck them most were the wide streets full of traffic, the neon lights and advertisement boards, the way the northerners dressed. For those who arrived in the winter, the icy fog which enveloped Turin and Milan was the worst of all; these were cities which seemed not just of another country, but of another planet.[41]

On arrival, those who could went straight to relatives, friends and acquaintances. Those who could not, and there were many in the first years, found a bed in the small hotels (*locande*) near the stations, four or five to a room, sometimes as many as ten or fifteen. The *locanda* usually had a restaurant as well, where the new arrivals could eat, badly, for 250–350 lire. For those who could not afford the *locande* there were only the waiting-rooms of the stations and the empty compartments of the trains. A ticket of fifty lire for a nearby station was usually enough to ensure being left alone for the night by the station guards.[42]

Amongst these first southern immigrants there was a clear distinction between the minority who came from the towns and cities, and the majority from the rural communes. The *cittadini* had more contacts, found jobs immediately, could speak some Italian and were generally less disoriented by city life. They looked down with some contempt at their country cousins, who according to them went around 'with radios round their necks, holes in their shoes and speaking only in dialect'.[43]

c. THE NORTHERN LABOUR MARKET AND THE SOUTHERN IMMIGRANTS

In the years of the 'economic miracle' the balance in the northern labour market tipped for the first time in favour of the workers, as demand slightly exceeded supply. In Lombardy alone the number of metalworkers in industry increased by some 200,000, confirming Milan and its hinterland as one of the great industrial centres of Europe.[44] The growth that took place was both in industry and also in the tertiary sector; in fact for Italy as a whole the tertiary sector grew faster than any other part of the national economy.

The southern immigrants did not usually go straight into the engineering factories. Their habitual starting-points in the northern labour market were the building sites. Often whole groups of workers from the same village or province, specializing in a certain trade, would be hired at the same time. Hours were long, turnover extremely high and safety precautions minimal; in Turin in one month alone, July 1961, there were eight fatal accidents on the building sites. At the end of the working day, it was not unusual to go on to another job in the evening: in Turin, as casual labour in the preparation of the centenary exhibition, Italia '61; in Milan, in the construction of the Metropolitana, the city's new underground railway. As Montaldi wrote: 'From the excavations and tunnels of the Metropolitana there came forth the babble of all the dialects of Italy: *barbe alpine, massacani, garzoni siciliani*.'[45]

In the late 1950s, many southerners found their first jobs, especially in Turin, through the so-called 'cooperatives'. The organizers of the 'cooperatives', usually bosses of southern origin, provided the northern factories with cheap labour and themselves with lucrative rake-offs. The worker would pay an inscription fee to the 'cooperative', and would then begin work without any proper contract, pension provisions or employer's insurance payments. The grateful firm would pay the 'cooperative' a certain sum per worker, of which half or less would find its way into the worker's pocket. The system was a classic way of dividing the workforce, for northern workers found their own bargaining power undermined by the *'terroni'* who were doing the same job for a third of the salary. At their height there were 300 'cooperatives' in Turin alone, organizing as many as 30,000 workers. In October 1960, after widespread protests from the trade unions and the immigrants themselves, the 'cooperatives' were declared illegal.[46]

Conditions in the small and medium-sized factories, even without the 'cooperatives', were very harsh. The working day, with overtime, was rarely less than ten to twelve hours long. Contracts were always short-term, for three or six months, and turnover almost as high as in the building trade.

Prospects for promotion were minimal, with the mass of southerners confined to the lowest category of workers. The very large firms, like FIAT, seem to have done their best in these years to avoid hiring southern labour, preferring instead the traditional reservoirs of the Piedmontese and Lombard countryside.

When the southern women joined their men in the North, they too found a labour market which offered them new possibilities, even if in conditions of great exploitation. Most married women stayed at home, many of them taking on piece-work of some sort, as seamstresses and the like (see also below, p. 244). Domestic service was generally shunned as being 'unsafe', but a significant number of young southern women went to work in factories for the first time. Sometimes this proved a terrible ordeal. Clizia N. from Casoria in the province of Naples went first to work in her aunt's bar at Monza, near Milan, but then got a job making car seats in the Pirelli factory at Brughiero: 'They were all northerners in the factory, all from the same place, and I was the first southerner to work there . . . The first days were terrible for me. When it came to them having to teach me the job, it was as if they were afraid to come near me, as if I was contagious in some way . . . They understood each other and did everything together, and left me out completely. Just as if there was a wall between them and me.'[47]

In other, smaller factories, the female workforce was prevalently from the South. These were often firms operating at the limits of legality, producing plastic goods, television parts, electric lights, shock absorbers, biros, sweets, beauty products, etc. Wages were approximately half those being paid to men, while safety regulations and insurance payments were non-existent. In spite of these conditions, many young southern women liked the experience of factory work as a form of emancipation. They had escaped the male hierarchies of their families and were earning their own money. One of them told Fofi in Turin: 'There are a lot of us all together in the factory, and we feel ourselves to be independent. We are not criticized and no one pretends to try and teach us how to behave. They just pay us for the work we do.'[48]

Of course, the northern labour market did not only offer jobs in factories. Trade and commerce, though we know very little about them, soaked up migrant labour as well, and it was in the shops, bars and restaurants that immigrant children between ten and fifteen years of age found work as errand boys, waiters and cooks' helps. The working day was as long as ten hours, with pay around 3,000 lire a week, one third of what their elder sisters and one sixth of what their elder brothers were making in the factories. Many southerners aspired to open shops or workshops of their own, with southern tailors in particular acquiring a reputation for their reasonable prices and considerable skill. A few became municipal workers, though the ranks of dustmen, postmen, etc., were often the strict preserve of the northerners.[49]

For some, factory work with its noise and repetitiveness was intolerable. One casual labourer and part-time pimp told Canteri at Porto Palazzo in Turin: 'The factory is a prison without air . . . the sun, the fresh air, these are beautiful things, my friend, and when I am dead who will give me back the days that have been stolen from me in the factory?'[50] For others, the great journey northwards ended sadly in petty crime and prostitution. In the early 1960s the wide avenues on the periphery of Milan were lined at night with prostitutes from the South.[51]

d. HOUSING AND SOCIAL SERVICES IN THE NORTHERN CITIES

As soon as they felt able and had saved enough money, the immigrants in the North would tell their families to come and join them. Often their parents, especially if they were aged, were urged to stay at home in the countryside, to be sent money and visited in August. For the immigrant family there then began the drama of finding somewhere to live. The northern cities were absolutely unprepared for such a massive influx, and immigrant families were forced to live in appalling conditions during the years of the 'miracle'.

In Turin, the new inhabitants of the city found lodgings in the basements and attics of the centre, in buildings due for demolition, and in disused farmhouses on the extreme periphery. Racist attitudes were in evidence everywhere, with flats available for renting only to non-southerners. Turin's daily newspaper, *La Stampa*, did nothing to combat this racism, but chose instead to extol the 'civilizing values' of the Torinesi. Overcrowding was worst in the attics in the heart of the city. Here there were at least four or five people per room. The 'rooms' themselves were often no more than a single space divided by curtains or old blankets. Lavatories and washbasins were in the corridors, each one serving the needs of ten families, or at least forty to fifty people.[52]

In the towns of the northern hinterland of Milan, immigrants found a different solution to the problem of housing – the construction of *'coree'*. These were groups of houses built at night by the immigrants themselves, without planning permission, on plots of land that they had purchased with their savings. The *'coree'* took their name, apparently, from their first appearance at the time of the Korean war.

Vito, an immigrant in the mid-fifties from Cavarzere in the Veneto, told Franco Alasia in 1959 how he came to build his house. His story is extraordinary testimony to the individual sacrifices made in the passage from one Italy to the other:

[At Cavarzere] my life was always a tribulation. I have three daughters, there was no work for them, and they remained without hope. I didn't want to send them to become domestic servants. So I alone worked and my wife worked a little in the fields and at harvest time out of ten quintals of maize they gave us three and a half, which was a great help . . . I was a casual labourer in the building trade, and in 1952–4 I worked all year round, 1,200–1,250 lire a day, from sunrise to dusk: that was the way it was and still is in my part of the world. You work not by the clock but by the sun . . . I came to Milan on 18 January 1955. It was windy and snowy and in that weather I began to look for work. I tried five or six firms and they all told me to come back in fifteen days: 'the weather's too bad'. But on the third day I found work with the INGR company of Milan. And there everything went like clockwork, and I was able to send three quarters of my pay back home. I worked eight hours and after that they asked me: 'Do you want some contract work?' 'Certainly,' I replied, because in any case I was used to working from morning to evening.

I slept in the cellars of the houses I was building. The firm gave me permission and I cooked my meals by myself on a camping stove. For two years my life was like that, and that was how I saved enough to buy this bit of land. At first I hadn't even intended bringing my family here, but then I realized that we could all breathe more freely, and there was the possibility for the girls to go to work. And so I made the effort to buy this piece of land . . . It took me a year to build the house. When I'd got enough building material together, I began work at 9, 10, or 11 o'clock at night, because I worked by moonlight and by the light of a lantern . . .

As soon as I'd managed to insulate the boiler and make it waterproof, I brought my family here. Here in the kitchen there was no proper floor. For doors I only had table tops with nails in them. As soon as my family arrived in these conditions, the girls went to work and my wife went to help in a market garden, and we all worked together on the house. And so the family V., after twenty-four years of marriage, finally bought some bedroom furniture, because before at home we all slept together, on straw. And so that is how I have come to belong to the nation of workers, because now if I say I live badly I'd be telling a lie. Now if I want a steak or pasta or anything else I have only to ask. Now when I go to work I take biscuits and fruit in my lunch box. To sum up, everything is going normally, and I have nothing else to say.[53]

In the absence of any programme of council housing, each immigrant family had to cope as best it could. In the *coree*, as well as in other areas of new construction, observers noted how much every family fended for itself. Even the ground plan of the *coree* reflected this atomization. Houses were built to avoid facing each other, if possible without overlooking windows, and for one family only.[54]

Housing was the most dramatic of the problems facing the immigrant, but it was far from being the only one. The health services in the North had been barely adequate even before the immigrant influx; in the early 1960s they were quite unable to cope. Hospitals had insufficient nurses and doctors, with beds spilling out from the wards and down corridors. In Turin there was a sharp rise in the number of cases of infant mortality. The major cities had no structure of social services to speak of; immigrants in need of material and psychological assistance were left in the hands of private and church charities.

The schools became the filter through which a generation of southern children learned Italian and became northerners. Teachers faced a myriad of problems. There were insufficient classrooms for the number of children, and teaching had to take place in two or sometimes three shifts during the day. New immigrant children arrived throughout the school year. At first they understood little of what was being said to them and could express themselves only in strong local dialect. Often they responded with mute hostility to attempts at integration. So great was the difference in standards between North and South that even those who had attended school regularly in the South had to go down one or two classes on arrival in the North. Many southern peasants thought that it was quite unnecessary to send their daughters to school. All missed the 'collective education' of the southern villages and towns. As Fofi wrote, 'The streets and courtyards of Turin were not those of Lucera or Piazza Armerina, and the problems and inadequacies that derived from these environmental and familial short-comings were not to be underestimated.'[55]

Slowly, and it was a question of years not months, the conditions of the immigrants improved. By the mid to late 1960s private firms had built sufficient tower blocks on the peripheries of the northern cities to allow a majority of immigrants to move into a flat of their own. These new working-class quarters were very ugly and often lacked all the basic amenities – shops, libraries, post offices, public transport, parks and facilities for old people. However, compared to what had gone before they were paradise. The new flats had central heating, bathrooms, proper windows and floors; soon their occupants could afford to install televisions, fridges and eventually washing-machines.[56] The terrible period of uprooting and transition seemed to have been worth it; a new life had begun.

e. GERMANY AND SWITZERLAND

No chapter on Italian emigration in the years of the 'miracle' can hope to be complete without a section, albeit too brief, on Italian emigrants in northern Europe. West Germany, with economic growth rates even more startling than Italy's, became very swiftly the country with the largest flow of Italian immigrants. In June 1963, of 800,000 foreign workers in the Federal Republic, 297,000 were Italians, 114,000 Spaniards, 103,000 Greeks and 26,000 Turks. Thirty-seven per cent of the Italians were working on building sites, 25 per cent in metalworking factories, and another 18 per cent in factories of other sorts.[57]

In contrast to the migrants to northern Italy, most Italians in Germany and Switzerland regarded their stay as temporary. They rarely remained more than a year at a time, and even more rarely did their families leave to join them. Indeed, while German managers were full of praise for the adaptability of the southern Italians to factory conditions, and the way they saved their money, they disliked the frequency with which the Italians changed their jobs and returned to their villages, 'for the elections, for earthquakes, for saint days'.[58]

In 1963 the journalist Giovanni Russo visited the village of Castel-luccio, in the province of Foggia, in Puglia. Of the 4,000 inhabitants of the village, 2,000 had left in the preceding four years. The majority of these had made their way to Germany. The local doctor told Russo how and why they had left:

First a young building worker went to Germany because he'd got a contract as a skilled worker. It was he who told the others to come. As very few of them were skilled men they had to organize their own departures. Here there have never been training courses or any assistance from the organs of the state. Nearly all the emigrants left on tourist passports and paid their own way to the North or abroad . . . they had to go because we had no work for them, but they felt on leaving the disinterest and absenteeism of the state.[59]

One of those who left was Donato. Fifty years old in 1963, he had found a job working in the giant Volkswagen factory in Lower Saxony. He was living with twenty-five other Italians in a barrack hut:

I have four sons, a wife and a father to keep. At Castelluccio my land was worth at most 120,000 lire net per year. I had a tiny olive orchard which wasn't worth the blood and sweat that I lost on it. Now I'm earning 96,000 lire net per month. I send 60,000 of this to Italy and I keep the rest for myself . . . The working day is thirteen hours long because we're on piece-work . . . I was treated well when I started in the factory. They took me on as a labourer and began by putting me in the spray shop. I was a peasant and I didn't know anything about anything. My German instructor taught me by sign language and every time I made a mistake he marked an X on a blackboard . . . We Italians spend all our time with each other, without any forms of entertainment, and in the evening after work we go for a walk. But what's the choice? My family must have enough to eat . . .; now I'm working on the first stages of making carburettors.[60]

The Italian emigrants to northern Europe undoubtedly suffered most. For ten months of the year they did little but work very long hours, living in isolation far away from their homes and those they loved. For married men, the strains imposed upon them and their wives were very great, and fathers saw very little of their children as they were growing up. In 1964 and 1965 Don Antonio Riboldi, of the village of Santa Ninfa in the Belice (western

Sicily), went to visit his parishioners who had gone to work in Switzerland. There were more than 500 of them. At the entrance to a public park in a Swiss city he saw the notice, 'No entry for dogs and Italians': 'In those meetings with our emigrants they made me understand the depth of their nostalgia for their villages and their families; many times these feelings were expressed to me in anguishing scenes, but most often simply by the shedding of pent-up tears.'[61] All accounts confirm the bitterness of the Italians in northern Europe. For them the 'miracle' was as much tragedy as liberation.

The South in the 'Economic Miracle'

In 1962 Pasquale Saraceno, one of Italy's leading economists, commented: 'We feel that we are resolving the southern problem more than in any other moment of the history of the unified state.'[62] To some it must have seemed that with mass emigration the problem was not being resolved but liquidated. However, this was not Saraceno's point. He emphasized, rather, that a great deal of investment and income was flowing into the South, with the result that growth rates there (5.7 per cent per annum in the decade 1951–61) were higher than ever before.

What were these new sources of wealth? The Cassa del Mezzogiorno was continuing to invest very significant sums in agriculture, in road-building, in aqueducts and in drainage. In the five years between 1961 and 1965 it also, for the first time, began to spend significantly on industry – some 30 bn lire or 12 per cent of its total budget. By 1973, this figure had risen to 230 bn annually, which made industry, with 30 per cent of the budget, the largest single sector of the Cassa's activities.[63]

Secondly, in 1957 the Council of Ministers announced a decision of great importance: in order to aid the South, 40 per cent of IRI's total investments and 60 per cent of its investment in industrial plant would henceforth be concentrated in the Mezzogiorno. Behind the government's decision lay the pressure of a number of leading southern Christian Democrats, as well as the initiative of Giulio Pastore, who was at that time Minister for the South. For men like Emilio Colombo, the undisputed leader of the DC in the Basilicata, the infrastructural works of the Cassa were no longer enough. It was time for technocratic values to be applied to the South, time for modern industry to disturb the stagnant waters.[64]

Furthermore, certain priority areas of the South (Bari, Brindisi, Cagliari, Salerno, Taranto) were henceforth to be earmarked as 'development zones' (*poli di sviluppo*), while others, smaller and of lesser importance, were to be designated as 'industrial nuclei' (*nuclei di industrializzazione*). Private industry was to be attracted to them by very generous financial concessions offered by the state: 20 per cent of the entire initial investment was to be made available in the form of a non-repayable grant, while 70 per cent could be obtained in a loan repayable over fifteen years with interest of 4 per cent.[65]

Finally, the money sent home by the emigrants constituted an enormous influx of funds into the South. The local doctor of Castelluccio told Russo that at least 800m lire had been sent back to the village in the last five years. Standards of living had improved greatly; sugar and meat were being consumed in much greater quantities, and the number of children afflicted by serious illness had declined markedly. As for public holidays, 'you should see what Easter and Christmas and the feast day of San Giovanni, the saint of the village, are like now, when all the emigrants return *en masse*. It's what we call *"la calata dei tedeschi"* (the descent of the Germans).'[66]

a. INDUSTRY AND THE CITIES

Money from emigrants, public investment in the South and the designation of new development zones were certainly provoking profound changes. At Taranto and Bagnoli near Naples Finsider developed its massive steelworks; at Gela in southern Sicily ANIC, a subsidiary of ENI, built a petro-chemical works which by 1967 had a workforce of more than 2,500; Alfa-Romeo, another state-owned company, opened a new factory at Pomigliano d'Arco near Naples (see below, pp. 289). As for private industry, amongst the most noteworthy new developments were SIR's petrochemical works in Sardinia, at Porto Torres and Cagliari; the Olivetti factory at Pozzuoli near Naples; that of FIAT at Poggioreale in Sicily; and the opening of the giant Montecatini chemical works at Brindisi, an event so different from anything else that had ever happened to the city that it was likened by its inhabitants to the arrival of the Martians.[67] With so much investment and diversification in the southern economy, and with rising standards of living, it looked as if Saraceno's optimism was justified.

However, all was far from well. The siting of some of the development zones was widely criticized, as they seemed to be the result more of successful clientelistic pressure than of rational economic planning. Worse still, the major new industrial plants soon earned the epithet of 'cathedrals in the desert'. They were nearly all in capital- rather than labour-intensive industries, and as such made a limited contribution to the enduring problem of southern unemployment. They also had a limited effect in stimulating the local economies around them. Throughout the 1960s new factories, petro-chemical and steelworks, the most dramatic symbols of the 'miracle' in the South, remained in splendid isolation. The Martians might have landed in Brindisi, but they had not got much further than the outskirts of the city; in the 1960s the traveller in the South passed very quickly from a landscape of factory chimneys to one of semi-abandoned villages.[68]

The major southern cities – Naples, Palermo, Catania, Bari – underwent a marked transformation, but not of the same intensity as that of Rome or of the corresponding cities of the North. If from 1951–61 they had served as magnets for the rural population, in the following decade their population increase was very much less marked.[69]

Naples acquired some elements of a new working class, but industrial development was geographically dispersed over a very wide area. So too was the labour force, which was recruited from the many communes of the Neapolitan hinterland. The new industrial proletariat, above all metal, chemical and electricity workers, was thus much diluted as a political and economic force.[70]

The heart of the city remained much as before. In the early sixties an estimated 800,000 of the population (out of a total of 1,170,000) had no fixed income, and more than 67,000 families (280,000 persons) were officially described as destitute. The long undulating narrow streets of the centre were lined with improvised stalls or tables selling all manner of contraband and other goods – radios, cigarettes, sweets, chewing-gum, lighters, vegetables, clothing and so on. The *bassi* (see p. 36) continued to house a significant proportion of the city's population. Conditions had not improved, but even here the television set, the indispensable *vade mecum* of the 'miracle', had made its appearance.[71]

In both Palermo and Naples small firms in traditional industries like textiles, food, leather and wood collapsed in the face of mass-produced goods from the North. Both cities grew outwards in unplanned sprawls, the victims of unfettered building speculation and the collusion of the municipal authorities (see below, pp. 287–8).

b. AGRICULTURE

Much of the emigration that had taken place from the agricultural zones of the South was unavoidable. The soil was too poor, and the number of mouths it had to support too many, for there to have been any other solution. Even if a proper agrarian reform had been carried through, with widespread land redistribution on a more rational basis, with improvement of agrarian contracts and with extensive state aid to the new landowners, the 'bone' of the rural South would still have had to shed a significant proportion of its population. In 1967, during a conference organized by the Einaudi Foundation, Manlio Rossi-Doria rejoiced in the fact that at long last an alternative had been opened for the peasants of the South: 'We must not lament the fact that they are abandoning agriculture and leaving their villages; on the contrary, we must celebrate, because this means that finally the men of the South will find a way of living worthy of human beings, and not of non-humans as they were in the past.'[72]

There were two problems with this position. The first was that pointed out at the same conference by the Communist Pietro Grifone, Gullo's close collaborator in the late 1940s: 'The southern peasant who left Melissa or Torremaggiore to go to Stuttgart has not gone voluntarily. I have visited them at Stuttgart, these emigrants of ours; they have been constrained and obliged to leave their homes. This is the human, social and economic dimension of the problem.'[73]

The second was that the numbers of those leaving had, by the later 1960s, far exceeded what anyone who cared about the South thought was advisable or necessary. With so many young people leaving, the southern villages risked irreversible decline and degradation. Rossi-Doria himself recognized this, and argued that every effort should be made to stop the haemorrhage of population at a certain point. For the *latifondo* areas of extensive grain cultivation, he proposed the constitution of large peasant cooperatives, each with responsibility for between 600 and 1,000 hectares of land. Such a scheme was no pipe-dream, he argued, because it could be based on the *affittanze collettive*, the tradition of collective renting which had existed in certain parts of the South. Rossi-Doria was convinced that the peasants in these zones, if given sufficient technical assistance and access to modern machinery, would welcome such a solution.

It was too late.[74] The flight from the southern countryside continued unabated, with a higher percentage of small proprietors leaving than any other group. As a result, the number of landless labourers, while declining in overall terms, increased as a percentage of the total rural labour force, as did the number of *casual* labourers within this group. Thus the growth of a peasant proprietor class, which since the 1920s had made much progress against all the odds, was abruptly halted. Instead, the most dependent stratum of rural workers — casual wage labourers, amongst whom were a large number of older men, women and children — increased its relative weight.[75]

Government legislation in these years did little to confront the dramatic crisis of the rural South. On the contrary, the two 'Green Plans' of 1961 and 1966, especially the second, channelled public spending increasingly towards the capitalist farms of the most fertile regions, and left the hills and mountains to their fate. The results of such policies became clear in the national agrarian census of 1970. For the first time since the war, a significant amount of arable land, and not only in the South, had been abandoned; between 1961 and 1970 the total cultivated land surface in Italy declined by $1\frac{1}{2}$ million hectares.[76]

Common Market agricultural policy further emphasized these trends.

In the early years of the EEC, the Italian government and its representatives at Brussels, more than content with the industrial benefits of the Common Market, were willing to compromise on agricultural issues. The Six's rural Europe was born a world of milk, butter, sugar, meat and grain; southern Italy's fruit, vegetables, olives and wine had little place in it. By means of the complicated price-fixing mechanisms of the EAGGF (European Agricultural Guarantee and Guidance Fund), Europe's richest farmers became richer still. Every year the Common Market countries, through the EAGGF, spent $700 for every Dutch farmer, $330 for every French farmer, $220 for every German, but only $70 for every Italian. Of southern Italian products, only olive oil was subsidized on a scale comparable to that accorded the products of northern European farms.[77]

The Third Italy and the 'Economic Miracle'

In the Centre and north-east of Italy social and economic developments differed quite radically from those in the Industrial Triangle and the South. The dramatic and sudden end of the centuries-old system of sharecropping has not yet been studied in any detail. What is clear, though, is that the sharecropping families who acquired land in the 1950s did not, for the most part, find that it brought them prosperity. On the contrary. Often their small farms were not viable economic entities, and they lacked the capital to make essential improvements. Faced with these problems, the ex-sharecropping families did not abandon their new properties. Instead they sought to diversify their sources of income. The older generation was left in charge of the land, which was worked more to meet family needs than to produce for the market. The young went off to seek their fortunes elsewhere, in the towns or cities.[78]

Initially, there was a marked difference between the movements of population in the north-east and the Centre. In the period 1955–61, the Veneto lost over 237,000 of its inhabitants, mainly to the industrial cities of Lombardy and Piedmont. No other region, not even those of the South, suffered so great an exodus in these years. By contrast, those who left the land in the central regions did not, by and large, travel very far. If the Marches and Umbria shed over 100,000 inhabitants between them, Emilia-Romagna's population remained stable, and Tuscany had a net *immigration* of 47,300 inhabitants. In the following period, 1962–71, the patterns in the Centre and the north-east are much more similar. The Veneto lost only 47,300 inhabitants, much the same as Umbria and the Marches, while both Tuscany and Emilia-Romagna attracted immigrants, in the most part from the South.[79]

If initial immigration patterns differed sharply, those of industrialization did not. Both in the Centre and the north-east the decade 1951–61 saw a very marked increase in the number of those employed in industry: in the Veneto, from 32.8 per cent of the working population to 44.0 per cent; in Tuscany from 34.0 to 44.0 per cent. The next decade saw continued growth in these regions, though at a slower rate. In this second period, it was the turn of Umbria and the Marches to increase their industrial employment very rapidly.[80]

The industrialization of the Third Italy was very distinct from that taking place in the great centres of Lombardy and Piedmont. With one or two notable exceptions, like Porto Marghera and Ravenna, it was characterized by small firms employing less than fifty people – and often less than twenty. These firms flourished in traditional sectors like clothing, shoe-making, furniture production, ceramics and leather goods. A significant minority of them were also to be found in the more modern sectors of machine tools and the production of parts for larger metalworking companies. Nearly all of them were highly flexible, adapting swiftly to the market, and increasingly export-oriented.

Geographically, their development also followed a distinctive pattern. The many small and distinguished cities of the Third Italy, once so economically dynamic in the late Middle Ages and the early Renaissance, became the focal points for a new age of prosperity. The merchants of Prato stirred from their slumbers, with remarkable results.[81] Industrial growth was not concentrated in the major cities, but spread amongst these smaller centres and in the countryside around them. The terms 'diffused industrialization' (*industrializzazione diffusa*) and the 'urbanized countryside' (*la campagna urbanizzata*) became widely employed to describe this model of economic growth. City and countryside were linked in industrial districts, usually specializing in a single field of production: textiles at Prato, ceramics at Sassuolo, hosiery at Carpi, footwear at Ascoli Piceno, and so on. The dynamic growth of these districts began with the 'economic miracle', but was only to reach its apogee in the 1970s.[82]

If we return now to the ex-sharecropping families, it is possible to suggest (though much more work needs to be done) that they played a significant role in this remarkable transition. The young men who left the land found work initially as manual labourers in the towns or cities. Soon they decided to try to set up on their own (*mettersi in proprio*). They did so with remarkable success. In 1982–3 a survey was carried out in Bassano (Veneto) and the Valdelsa (Tuscany), both typical areas of diffused industrialization; 50 per cent of the entrepreneurs interviewed had begun their working lives as manual labourers; the great majority of them were first-generation entrepreneurs, around forty-five years old and with no schooling beyond the age of fourteen.[83]

In order to survive and prosper in the early sixties, these entre-preneurs relied heavily on the experience and resources of their families. Although the size of families and their extended character were in rapid decline in these regions, a significant majority of large families remained. In 1961 26.9 per cent of families in the Third Italy were extended ones, while 28.1 per cent had five or more members. If the older generation could be left to look after the land, wives, brothers, sisters and cousins could be brought in to work in the new businesses. Even as late as 1982–3, more than 60 per cent of businesses in Bassano and the Valdelsa were family concerns. Work and family were thus tied closely together, in a climate of economic dynamism, self-sacrifice and rapid social mobility.[84]

Finally, it is worth considering what role, if any, central and local government played in this process. Public industry did not undertake a major investment programme as it did in the South. Central government seems to have taken a permissive rather than a propulsive role. Taxation of the new firms was kept to a minimum and casually enforced. Bureaucratic norms governing firms' activities were widely ignored, as were the social-insurance contributions which they were supposed to pay.

At a local level, the Christian Democrat and Communist administra-tions which dominated these regions did their best, within the limited powers of local government, to aid the new businesses. For the Communists the decline of the sharecroppers as a political force was certainly not to be welcomed, nor was encouragement of the new entrepreneurs easily reconcil-able with the collective socialist values preached in the farmhouse kitchens in the 1940s. However, recourse could always be made to the party's alliance strategy. Small industry continued to be represented as 'healthy' and 'progressive', as a potential ally in the face of the all-powerful monopolies. As for the Christian Democrats, family capitalism of this sort presented them with few ideological problems. Indeed its development closely resem-bled their ideal picture of the modern world. The 'urbanized countryside', with its strong local identities, offered far fewer perils than the streets of Milan.[85]

Changes in Class Structure

The years of the 'economic miracle' saw, as was only to be expected, some radical changes in the employment patterns and class composition of Italian society. Paradoxically, the most notable change on a general level was the sharp decline in the active workforce as a percentage of the total population. In 1951 the active workforce was 42 per cent of the total population; this figure fell to 41.6 per cent in 1961, and 36.3 per cent in 1971. Even allowing for a general tendency to a diminishing workforce in advanced capitalist countries, these figures still compare poorly to those of other European nations: in Great Britain the active workforce was 45.7 per cent of the total population in 1966, in France 40.9 per cent in 1968.[86]

There appear to be two principal reasons why the Italian figures were so low in spite of booming employment prospects in the North and Centre. The first of these relates to the position of women in the Italian labour market. The majority of the women who had been registered as active in agriculture before the rural exodus did not find full employment in their new urban environment. Some, as we have seen, especially the young and single, did go into the factories of the North; most, however, remained at home, and became officially classed as housewives even if they did part-time or piece-work at home.[87]

Secondly, employment prospects in southern Italy continued to be worse than in any other area in the Common Market. As we have seen, the 'cathedrals in the desert' did not create enough new jobs, and the cities teemed with unemployed or those employed on the most precarious of bases. In addition, traditional high birth-rates in the southern cities showed little signs of decreasing. Even if some of the men found work through emigration to northern Europe, large numbers of women and children stayed at home. The employment figures for the South were appalling: the active workforce was 37.5 per cent of the total population in 1951, 34.2 per cent in 1961, and only 31.2 per cent by 1971.[88]

Turning now to the different sections of Italian society, it is evident that the Italian business class underwent considerable transformation. The Confindustria continued as its mouthpiece, dominated by the electrical trusts, suspicious of the Common Market, resentful of the power of state industry, hostile even to the growing independence of the CISL. Beneath this conservative carapace, we know little as yet about the relative weight of the different factions of Italian capital and the changing relationship between them. Some sections which had benefited from the great boom, such as building speculators and dealers in petroleum, shared the ideology of the leaders of Confindustria. Others, amongst them FIAT and the most successful export companies, were perforce more European in outlook, more open to new ideas, more receptive to American influences.[89]

In both private and public industry, the number of managers increased markedly. These were the young lions of the 'miracle', sometimes trained at Harvard or MIT, speaking more than one foreign language, enthusiastic proponents of East Coast ideas of marketing, publicity and the organization of the firm. Mattei's ENI was full of them; so too was the new public industry in the South.[90]

At a small-firm level, and not only in the Third Italy, a whole new generation of Italian businessmen was born. These were men of limited culture and education, but determined and audacious, and they were prepared to travel all over the world in order to build up markets for their products. They were the *nouveaux riches* not only of the major cities, but perhaps above all of the provinces – of Brescia and Bergamo, of Verona and Treviso, of Modena and Ravenna, of Prato and Pistoia. In Vigevano, to take just one example of a smallish town near Milan, Bocca reported in 1962 that there were 900 workshops and factories making shoes; one quarter of all Italy's shoe exports came from Vigevano. The entrepreneurs there talked of their markets in the Congo and in Burma; one had taken his holidays go-karting in the Bahamas, 'whereas his father had gone by bicycle to Casalpusterlengo or Sartisana'.[91]

Of the professional classes, we know next to nothing. In the rapidly expanding Italy of the early 1960s, certain categories of the *liberi professionisti* – engineers, architects, designers and lawyers – undoubtedly increased both their weight in society and their own well-being. So too did new groups which came to the fore at this time: researchers and the upper ranks of technicians in industry, those working in public relations, in advertising and the mass media.

On the other hand, in the absence of social and educational reform, professional jobs in the state sector remained at modest levels. The numbers of teachers, for instance, did not increase significantly before 1964. The myriad of professional jobs associated with an active welfare state – from administrators in the health service to town planners and social workers – was conspicuously absent in Italy. As a result, large numbers of graduates in the humanities continued to have great difficulty in finding jobs which corresponded to their status.[92]

The fastest growing sector of the Italian workforce was the white-collar one. In 1951 there were 1,970,000 Italian white-collar workers, in 1961 2,650,000 and in 1971 3,330,000. In these twenty years, according to Sylos Labini's figures, the white-collar sector increased from 9.8 to 17.1 per cent of the total workforce. Such a growth was in line with developments in all advanced countries, and it was noteworthy that in the private sector Italy's increase in white-collar workers was very modest by international standards (8.9 per cent of the workforce in 1971 compared to 19.3 per cent in France in 1968 and 23.4 per cent in Britain in 1966).

At the top end of the private sector were an increasing number of technical workers employed in the dynamic sectors of the Italian economy – in petrochemicals, in typewriters, in car production. Between 1958 and 1965 in Olivetti the first grade of white-collar workers (which was dominated by technicians) increased its share of the white-collar workforce from 20.5 to 32.8 per cent, while the lowest grades fell from 43.8 to 29.7 per cent.[93] At the lower end of the private sector, the increasingly mechanical and repetitive work of the clerks, as well as their surveillance in typing pools and large offices, increased their sense of alienation and decreased their status. The world of the Italian petty clerk in the 1960s, its routines, petty rivalries and frustrations, was immortalized in Ermanno Olmi's film *Il Posto* (1961).

As for the public sector, much play has been made of its excessively bloated nature. Care must be taken not to exaggerate this phenomenon. In 1951 public white-collar employees were only 4.6 per cent of the active workforce, increasing to 6.2 per cent in 1961 and 8.2 per cent in 1971. Comparative figures for France were 7.3 per cent in 1968 and for Britain 11.2 per cent in 1966. What is striking about the Italian case is the rough numerical parity between the private and public sectors, in contrast with her European neighbours, whose private sectors were numerically much stronger.[94]

In the traditional sectors of the lower middle class, the number of artisans remained much the same over the two decades 1951–71. There was a distinct decline in workshops in traditional sectors, but this was compensated for by the rapid growth of new trades, such as car mechanics and electricians.

The anomalous position of Italian shopkeepers deserves special mention. This sector of the Italian petty bourgeoisie remained a much higher percentage of the workforce than in other European countries – 8.7 per cent of the Italian workforce in 1971, compared to 6.1 per cent in France in 1968 and only 2.2 per cent in Britain in 1966. We have already seen how protective measures passed by successive Christian Democrat governments restricted the growth of supermarkets and subsidized family shops. In the period 1951–71 the numbers of shopkeepers actually increased in Italy from 1,350,000 to 1,700,000, with 150,000 new shops opening in the South, compared to only 80,000 in the Centre, and 120,000 in the North.[95]

As for the industrial working class, their numbers increased steadily, both in absolute terms and as a percentage of the workforce: from 3,410,000 in 1951 to 4,190,000 in 1961 and 4,800,000 in 1971. Building workers increased their numbers by half a million in this same period, and transport workers by 280,000. Industrial and building workers taken together accounted for 22.9 per cent of the workforce in 1951, 29 per cent in 1961, and 33 per cent in 1971. The last figure compared favourably with France's 27.8 per cent in 1968 and Britain's 31.6 per cent in 1966. However, the small-firm nature of much of Italy's industrialization was very clear. By 1971 little more than one fifth of the industrial workforce was employed in firms with more than one hundred employees.[96]

At the bottom of the social scale came the casual labourers, the underemployed and unemployed. Their total numbers, though not their relative weight, declined markedly in the countryside. No longer was there a massive rural reserve army of labour, each member of which could expect to work little more than a third of the year. On the other hand, the problem was far from solved, because much of it had been transferred to the peripheries of the major cities. In the shanty towns of Palermo and Naples, in the *borgate* of Rome and on the squalid outskirts of Milan and Turin, hundreds of thousands of families continued to live in abysmal conditions. Some money was to be gained in the building trade, some from small dealings of every sort, some from petty crime. By the end of the 1960s this section of the Italian population was estimated at 4 million out of a total population of $54\frac{1}{2}$ million. For them the 'economic miracle' might have meant a television set but precious little else.[97]

Culture and Society in the 'Economic Miracle'

The years of the 'miracle' were the key period in an extraordinary process of transformation that was taking place in the everyday life of Italians – in their culture, family life, leisure-time activities, consumption habits, even the language they spoke and their sexual mores. The transformation, of course, was not instantaneous or in any way uniform. As Stephen Gundle has written, 'If cultural unification in accordance with the myths and models of consumer capitalism was the dominant feature of this period, it is important to remember that this process was as much one of superimposition, grafting new habits and practices on to pre-existing forms of consciousness, as one of profound mutations.'[98]

In the twenty years from 1950 to 1970 per capita income in Italy grew more rapidly than in any other European country: from a base of 100 in 1950 to 234.1 in 1970, compared to France's increase from 100 to 136 in the same period, and Britain's 100 to 132. By 1970 Italian per capita income, which in 1945 had lagged far behind that of the northern European countries, had reached 60 per cent of that in France and 82 per cent of that in Britain.[99]

Urged on by the unprecedented expansion of advertising, Italian families, above all in the North and Centre of the country, used their new wealth to acquire consumer durables for the first time. Whereas in 1958 only 12 per cent of Italian families owned a television, by 1965 the number had risen to 49 per cent. In the same period the number owning fridges increased from 13 to 55 per cent, and washing-machines from 3 to 23 per cent.[100] Between 1950 and 1964 the number of private cars in Italy rose from 342,000 to 4.67 million, and motorcycles from 700,000 to 4.3 million.[101] Eating habits changed radically, with more money being spent on meat and dairy products than ever before. In 1962 the sharp-eyed Bocca noticed that even as far south as Foggia most of the food shops had gone over to refrigerated cabinets.[102] The way in which Italians dressed also changed, with women rapidly abandoning the traditional black of the South for mass-produced coats, dresses and stockings. For the first time the majority of Italians were able to afford proper shoes.

These improvements in the standard of living were enormously welcome. However, it must be noted that the Italian model of development, like so many others, lacked the dimension of collective responsibility. The state had played an important role in stimulating rapid economic development, but it then defaulted on governing the social consequences. In the absence of planning, of civic education, of elementary public services, the individual family, particularly of the *ceti medi*, sought salvation in private spending and consumption: on using a car to go to work, on private medicine and on private nursery schools in the absence of state ones.[103] The 'miracle' was thus an exquisitely private affair, which reinforced the historic tendency of each Italian family to fend for itself as best it could.

a. TELEVISION

No innovation of these years had a greater effect on everyday life than television. In 1954, in the first year of its introduction, there were 88,000 licence holders, a number which increased to one million in 1958. By 1965 49 per cent of Italian families owned a television set.[104]

Television, as elsewhere in Europe, was a state monopoly. In Italy this meant that it was controlled by the Christian Democrats and heavily influenced by the church. In the years 1954–6, Filiberto Guala, the candidate of Catholic Action, was the president of RAI and he imposed a severe code of conduct on the nascent television service. Programmes were not to 'bring discredit on or undermine the institution of the family'; nor were they to portray 'attitudes, poses or particulars which might arouse base instincts'.[105] There were regular religious-education programmes, while news and current affairs had a heavily anti-Communist bias. Light music, variety, quiz shows and sports events made up the great majority of RAI's broadcasting time. Typical of this fare was the enormously popular quiz show, *'Lascia o Raddoppia?'*. Compered by Mike Bongiorno, it was the Italian equivalent of 'The 64,000 Dollar Question'.

Attempts to control television's content were nowhere clearer than in the field of advertising. Forced to choose between America's *laissez-faire* inundations and the BBC's total ban, RAI came out with a uniquely Italian form of advertising. Advertisements were grouped together into a half-hour programme called *'Carosello'*, which was transmitted at peak viewing time, just before the nine o'clock news. In each spot, which lasted all of 110 seconds, the product could be mentioned only at the beginning and for five seconds at the end. The rest of the time had to be filled with little stories, cartoons or fairy-tales. As such, *'Carosello'* exercised a great appeal for children, who were introduced in this familial, homely and seemingly innocuous way to the delights of consumerism. Parents became accustomed to sending their children to bed 'after *"Carosello"*'. By 1960, three years after its introduction, *'Carosello'* was the most watched television programme in Italy.[106]

Television, as it became a mass phenomenon in the late 1950s, was a potent weapon in the hands of the Christian Democrats. It was rather more of a two-edged sword for the Catholic church. *'Carosello'* seemed innocuous enough, but the values of the consumer 'miracle' were not consonant with those of the church of Pius XII. In a telegram of 1957 to the Coldiretti, the Pope implored the organization to save the 'traditional Christian aspect' of the rural population, which was being undermined by 'changing times, materialist propaganda and audiovisual communications'.[107] Pier Paolo Pasolini made the same point rather more wickedly:

the Vatican never understood what it should or should not have censored. For example, it should have censored *'Carosello'* because it is in the all-powerful *'Carosello'* that the new type of life which the Italians 'must' lead explodes on to our screens with absolute, peremptory clarity. And nobody can tell me we're talking about a way of life in which religion counts for very much. On the other hand, the purely religious broadcasts are so tedious and so repressive in spirit that the Vatican would have done well to have censored the lot.[108]

Initially, the watching of television in Italy was a collective form of entertainment. With private television sets still the privilege of the rich, the televisions of the bars and cafés, especially in rural Italy, became a focal point of social reunion. In an article in *L'Espresso* of January 1959, M. Calamandrei recounted the experience of the village of Scarperia in the Mugello, north of Florence. Although there were only eleven television sets in the whole village, 91 per cent of the population had watched television at least once: 'Interviewers tell of seeing in the evening (specially on Thursdays at the time of *"Lascia o Raddoppia?"*) peasants, sometimes poorly dressed, come down steep mountain paths, bringing a chair with them and perhaps through the rain, just to watch a television programme.'[109]

In another part of Tuscany, in 1954, the local Christian Democrat authorities gave the Antonuzzo family a television set for the section headquarters that they had founded at Accesa. Antonuzzo recounts how the installation of this set in the village split the local Communists: one half of them, 'the more Stalinist', denounced the new apparatus as 'priest's garbage', and would have nothing to do with it. The other half, in spite of strict prohibitions, went along to watch.[110]

Gradually, the essentially atomizing nature of television asserted itself. As more and more families bought their own sets, the habit of watching television in bars or at neighbours' houses died out. In the new *palazzi* (blocks of flats) on the peripheries of the cities, each family watched television in its own flat. This startling development obviously increased the tendency towards passive and familial use of leisure time, and decreased other more participatory and collective pastimes.

b. LEISURE AND MOBILITY

As television audiences grew, the cinemas entered their long and seemingly unavoidable decline. None the less, cinema-going, especially on Sundays, continued to be a favoured pastime for the Italians. The Italian film industry was extremely productive and attractive in this period; 1960 was the year both of Fellini's *La Dolce Vita* and Visconti's *Rocco and His Brothers*. The first, with its denunciation of the life-style of Rome's *nouveaux riches*, marked a watershed in public statements on Italian society. It provoked furious polemics, earned the condemnation of the church, and was a smash hit at the box office. The second, with its deeply moving and dramatic account of the fate of a southern family in Milan, gave the world an unequalled portrait of Italy in the years of its great transition.

No works of literature rivalled Visconti's *Rocco*. The novel of the period which made the most impact was Tommaso Di Lampedusa's *Il Gattopardo*, set in Sicily during the Risorgimento. In the first twelve months after its publication it sold over 100,000 copies. However, the reading public continued to be much smaller than in Britain or in France, and it was to take some time for the increased literacy of the population to be reflected in book sales. The paperback boom can only really be said to have begun in 1965, the year Mondadori launched its Oscar series.[111] Popular reading matter continued to be dominated by the *rotocalchi* (illustrated magazines), with a marked increase in the number and sales of women's magazines. *Amica*, *Annabella* and *Grazia*, with their new emphasis on consumerism, rapidly achieved mass circulations.

Along with the advent of television, increased mobility was probably the greatest innovation in leisure-time activity. The FIAT 600 was quickly followed by the smaller and even more economical 500. For the *ceti medi* and the upper echelons of the northern working class, Sunday outings by car became a possibility for the first time. Gone for ever were the Sunday trips on the backs of Turin trams of the early 1940s. Instead families travelled by car into the countryside, to the mountains and in the summer to the sea. The amount of paid holidays they took increased slowly but significantly, as did the tendency to travel further afield during them. Italian regionalism, so strong and enduring, began to break down a little as the motorized armies of the 'miracle' hurtled along the new arteries of the peninsula.

c. WOMEN, THE FAMILY AND SEXUAL MORES

What was happening to the family, that pivotal institution of Italian civil society, in these years? The little research that has so far been done shows us that the *size* of Italian families was declining everywhere, but that *types* of family were changing only slowly. In Italy as a whole the average size of the family had declined from four members in 1951 to 3.3 in 1971. The decline, as was to be expected, was most marked in the heavily urbanized north-west, and least in the South. On the other hand, types of family remained little changed. In 1951 nuclear families, composed only of husband, wife and children, formed 55.7 per cent of the total number of Italian families; twenty years later they formed 54.1 per cent. In the same period extended families declined slowly from 22.5 per cent to 16.9 per cent of the total, with percentages for the Third Italy being much higher. Marginal increases in the number of families composed of only one or two persons were also to be noted.[112]

What was certainly true, but hardly quantifiable, was the increased isolation that urbanization brought to each family. For southern emigrants in particular, the absence of collective festivals, of the piazza as a meeting point, of street living and of inter-family visits marked a profound transformation. This privatization in smaller family units seems to have had both positive and negative aspects: on the one hand, as Pizzorno recounts for Rho, near Milan, families were glad to escape from prying neighbours and from the stifling atmosphere of rural courtyards. The privacy afforded by northern urban structures was thus an enormous relief. On the other hand, each nuclear family unit tended to be more closed in upon itself, and less open to community life or to forms of inter-family solidarity.[113]

For the young, urban life offered many opportunities not previously available. If the nuclear family became more sharply and exclusively defined *vis-à-vis* society as a whole, the young found that they enjoyed greater freedoms than previously, both inside and outside the family. Authority structures within the family became less rigid, as did paternal control over the family's finances. At Rho in 1959, a twenty-year-old female clerk recounted how she had dared, after many hesitations, to propose to her father a radical change in family organization. Instead of giving him all her wages (45,000 lire a month), and receiving in return 1,000 lire pocket-money per week, she decided to keep all her earnings and pay only her part in the upkeep of the house.[114]

Outside the home, the young found the constrictions of rural life falling away. There were new freedoms, pastimes and ambitions. Bars equipped with billiard-tables and juke-boxes were important meeting-places; so too were the hundreds of new dance halls. Young men went to football matches; young women went shopping. Together (and there was no higher ambition), they rode the city streets on their Vespas and Lambrettas.

The 1960s also saw a distinct shift in the woman's role within the family. With the new emphasis on house-based living and consumption, more Italian women than ever before became full-time housewives. In the North, it was their responsibility to care for children, who were staying on at school longer than ever before; theirs too was the task of looking after the needs of a husband whose day's work, with overtime and commuting, often amounted to between twelve and fourteen hours. The women's magazines and the television advertisements of the time exalted this new figure of the modern Italian woman, *'tutta casa e famiglia'*, smartly dressed, with well-turned-out children and a sparkling house full of consumer durables.

The percentage of women in the Italian workforce, as we have seen, continued to fall, and was confirmed as one of the lowest in western Europe. This was particularly true for the age group 30–49, who, unlike their counterparts in Britain or the United States, rarely returned to the registered workforce after marriage and child-rearing. Italian women of this age often found part-time jobs, but they tended to be piece-work done at home or in the informal sector (*lavoro nero*), and thus never reached the official statistics.

In the absence of any social history of Italian women in this period, it would be foolhardy to pass categorical judgement on these changes in women's lives. The transfer to the cities undoubtedly gave women greater freedom from traditional family hierarchies and a greater autonomy in a whole number of ways. This was especially true for younger women in the North who were in full-time work. However, the idealized confinement of women to the home in the 1960s served to enclose them in a purely private dimension, and to remove them even more than previously from the political and public life of the nation.[115]

Finally, a word about sexual attitudes. The Italy of the boom was still a society full of taboos about sexual behaviour. The restrictive codes of official morality were deeply intertwined in the South with codes of honour. Sexual mores were to change almost more slowly than anything else in Italy. However, in the early 1960s there were a few signs of a more open approach. Timid discussions of pre-marital sex appeared in some women's magazines, *Oggi* ran a survey on sex education and the radical weekly *L'Espresso* (founded in 1955) even dared to publish an investigation of infidelity levels amongst Italian wives (the infidelity of men seems to have been taken for granted). The first cracks in the official morality had appeared, but it was to be another decade at least before sexual mores underwent any major change.[116]

d. THE DECLINE OF RELIGION

One of the most significant consequences of rural exodus and urbanization was a dramatic decline in the influence of the church. Church attendance had always been strongest in the rural areas and amongst women, especially in the Trentino-Alto Adige, in the Veneto and in some regions of the South. As we have seen, a survey had found that 69 per cent of Italians went regularly to Sunday mass in 1956. By 1962 this number had dropped to 53 per cent. Six years later the Catholic sociologist Silvano Burgalassi found that only some 40 per cent of Italians were regular church attenders. Of these just 6 per cent could be classified as *'devoti'*, in the sense of following closely the church's teachings.[117]

Behind these figures lay other trends which were even more disturbing. Recruitment to the priesthood had fallen off drastically; the diocesan clergy was becoming an ageing body ever less able to cope with a growing and changing population. Worst of all, on the peripheries of the great cities, where the new urban population was most concentrated, church-going had plummeted. In 1968, on the peripheries of cities with more than 300,000 inhabitants, only some 11 per cent of men and 26 per cent of women were attending mass on Sundays.[118] Pasolini's dire warnings of the insidious effects of the new consumer values seemed more than justified.

Another major reason for the emptying churches was the difference between northern and southern Catholicism. In Turin, Fofi found that the southern migrants missed the local customs, patron saints and *feste* of their village churches and could not reconcile themselves to the somewhat barren and arid life of the northern churches. One parish priest in Milan denounced the southerners who 'had been used to living their religion in a totally superficial way, more as magic and bigotry than in a truly Christian manner'.[119] This may well have been the case, but doctrinal purity was hardly likely to attract the migrants back to the fold. In 1957 the radical priest Don Lorenzo Milani lamented the imminent end of popular religion:

For a priest, what greater tragedy than this could ever have taken place? To be free, to have the sacraments, to control the House of Deputies, the Senate, the press, the radio, the bell-towers, the pulpits, the schools; and with all this abundance of means, both human and divine, to gather only the bitter fruit of being scorned by the poor, hated by the weakest, loved by the strongest. To have our churches empty. To see them getting emptier day by day. To know that soon the faith of the poor will be a thing of the past. Does it not occur to you to ask if the persecution of the church could really be worse than all this?[120]

e. BUILDING SPECULATION AND THE
RAPE OF THE LANDSCAPE

The thirty years between 1950 and 1980 saw a catastrophic change in the landscape and cityscape of the Italian peninsula. Many of the historic centres of the Italian cities and towns were modified irreversibly, and their suburbs grew as unplanned jungles of cement. Thousands of kilometres of coastline were ruined as hotels and second houses were constructed without any restraints upon their siting or their density. Woods, alpine valleys, fishing villages, lagoons and islands were polluted, destroyed or transformed beyond recognition. Urban Italy sprawled outwards, unchecked and un-planned. The new face of the peninsula was represented by the suburbs of Rome, Naples and Palermo, by the periphery of Milan, by skiing resorts like Cervinia and seaside towns like Viareggio. All this earned the Italians the reputation of being a nation both incapable of protecting its heritage, natural and man-made, and unable to govern its future.

It is essential to understand that this lamentable state of affairs was not inevitable, but arose from precise political choices. The governments of the 1950s and 1960s decided to allow the maximum degree of freedom to private initiative and speculation in the building sector. This was in line with their actions in every other part of the 'miracle', with the exception of broadcasting, which of course they were only too anxious to control. The ruling parties' point of departure was the town-planning law of 1942, which safeguarded the rights of landowners, made no attempt to tax profits deriving from land speculation and abandoned the idea of any serious government intervention. The law of 1942 made provision for *piani regolatori particolareggiati* (local development plans) to be drawn up and enforced by local communes. The plans would have been an important step forward, but the communes were never granted the resources or powers to put them into operation. As a result they were either never formulated or else remained dead letters.[121]

The building speculators, with money to spend and to corrupt, were left with a free hand. Houses were built, and built fast: 73,400 in 1950, 273,500 in 1957, 450,000 in 1964. But they were built how and where private interest dictated. No provision was made for town-planning, none for parks, landscaping or even adequate parking facilities. Often the *palazzi* were constructed without regard for building norms or safety regulations. The newspapers dutifully chronicled the doleful stories of whole families destroyed by collapsing apartment blocks, of hospitals built without anti-seismic foundations in earthquake zones.[122]

Other aspects of housing policy reflected these same emphases on private rather than public initiative. Very little attempt was made to safeguard the needs of the poorest sections of the community by the creation of a public- or council-housing sector like those of Britain, Holland or West Germany. Between 1948 and 1963 public housing schemes accounted for only 16 per cent of total investment in the construction of houses.

The most notable public initiative was that of the INA-Casa (INA = Istituto Nazionale Abitazioni), a scheme launched by Fanfani in 1949. In the fourteen years of its existence one thousand billion lire was spent, and the scheme constituted a small but significant example of what could have been achieved had government policy been different. In 1963 the INA-Casa scheme was replaced by the GESCAL (Gestione Casa Lavoratori), which became notorious not for building houses but for the corrupt and clientelistic use of its funds. GESCAL was mercifully wound up in the early 1970s. The only other public intervention of note was the IACP (Istituto Autonomo Case Popolari), a scheme which was allowed slightly more local autonomy than the INA-Casa, but which was crippled by its shortage of funds.[123]

Throughout the great building boom of 1953–63, there was often open collusion between the municipal authorities and the building speculators. The 'sack' of Rome, as it came to be called, was dramatic testimony to this. Property developers like the giant Società Generale Immobiliari, whose principal shareholder is the Vatican, were allowed to fill up every available space in the city itself, and then to cover the periphery with apartment blocks of poor construction and even poorer aesthetics. In 1956 the magazine L'Espresso launched a famous inquest entitled 'Capitale corrotto: nazione infetta'. Manlio Cancogni described a visit to the housing department: 'In the offices there are tables, telephones, containers full of files, but no clerks. The clerks who are supposed to work there are hardly ever there. In their place are private citizens who have come to see how their files are getting along. They sit at tables, leaf through registers, take out and put back files as if they were in their own homes.'[124] It was not surprising that by 1970 one house in every six in Rome was 'abusive', i.e. it had been built without any proper permit, and that 400,000 people were living in habitations which officially did not exist.[125]

A New Model of Social Integration?

In October 1947 Marshall McLuhan, writing on American advertising, noted that an American officer in Italy, who was also the correspondent for Printer's Ink, was rather perturbed by what he found there:

the Italians can tell you the names of the ministers in the government but not the names of the favourite products of the celebrities of their country. In addition, the walls of the Italian cities are plastered more with political slogans than with commercial ones. According to the opinion of this officer there is little hope that the Italians will achieve a state of prosperity and internal calm until they start to be more interested in the respective merits of different types of cornflakes and cigarettes rather than the relative abilities of their political leaders.[126]

Put crudely but effectively, this was the majority American view of the social and political consequences of the consumer revolution. Modernization led to increased material prosperity, to an overriding interest in consumer products, to greater individualism. It decreased active interest in politics and excluded the possibility of collective action against the existing order.[127] How far had Italy travelled down this particular road by 1963?

There seems little doubt, as has become clear from the sections above, that the social dynamic of the 'economic miracle' worked to increase the atomization of Italian civil society. The role of the individual nuclear family became even more important than previously. The new urban structures served to isolate families, which were decreasing in size, in small but comfortable living-quarters, and provided few spaces for collective gatherings or community life.[128] Women became the principal target of the new consumerism, and the increased emphasis on their service role within the home intensified their isolation. Cars and television further encouraged an essentially privatized and familial use of leisure time. Thus the 'economic miracle', by linking rising living standards with accentuated individualism, seemed to fulfil the American dream. It had introduced a new model of social integration to Italy.

Such developments were not much to the liking of either of the dominant ideologies in Italy at that time. It was very hard for the Catholics, as we have seen, to escape the conclusion that urbanization equalled secularization. Their traditional bases in the countryside were being destroyed. A declining number of young men wanted to be priests. Worst of all, the Catholic family was under dire attack. It was being undermined, but not by the 'old enemy', the atheists and materialists, the swirling communist snakes of 'free love' depicted on the D C posters in 1948. Rather, it was the American model of consumer society that had revealed itself as the Trojan horse within the citadel of Catholic values. In 1954 Cardinal Siri of Genoa warned of what was to come: 'The mass of goods being produced or being coveted has often put into the shade the good that goes by the name of the "family".'[129] Mariano Rumor, the new secretary of the D C, told the party at its ninth congress in 1964 that 'the family finds itself at the centre of the decomposition of the traditional structures of Italian society'.[130] The A C L I were appalled that the 'family is being bombarded by the insistent hammer blows of advertising pressure, which seeks to transform it into a mere appendix of the distribution chain of industrial products'.[131]

The Communists were hardly more content. The younger generation had little time for the traditional collective pastimes and activities of the Case del Popolo. Participation in the various organizations of the party diminished drastically in the early sixties. Attendance at section meetings fell off; UDI began a rapid decline.[132] Television, consumerism and home-based living were blamed for the new isolationist trends. The values of the 'miracle' were roundly denounced. *'Lascia o Raddoppia?'* was dismissed as 'a cruel game . . . far distant from the life of ordinary people, from the tastes and intelligence of the Italians'.[133] Tullio Seppilli, in an impassioned speech at the 1964 conference on 'Family and Society', urged the party to find the moral force to combat the new, insidious values of neo-capitalism.[134]

It was Pasolini, at a later date, who provided the strongest image of an Italy that was changing for the worse, an Italy where the old values, dialects and traditions were being destroyed for ever. The fireflies, wrote Pasolini, had disappeared: 'In the early 60s, with the pollution of the air, and above all in the countryside with the pollution of the water (the blue streams and the transparent sunbeams), the fireflies began to disappear. The phenomenon was as rapid as lightning. After a few years they were not there any more . . .'[135]

Yet the transformations of the years 1958–63 do not point so categorically in one direction. For millions of Italians the 'miracle' offered a material transformation which can only be called a profound liberation. For the first time the majority of the population had the possibility of living decently, of being warm and well clothed, of eating good food, and could bring up their children without fear of their being malformed or malnourished. 'Vito' from Cavarzere (see p. 226) had good reason to celebrate the fact that he and his family had finally joined the *'nazionalità operaia'* (the nation of workers). The wall which had separated town and countryside, South and North, mass deprivation and relative prosperity, had been breached – not in the way that the Communists or even the Catholics would have liked, but breached it had been.

Furthermore, the processes at work in the 'miracle' were not all atomizing or integrative. Within the family, the old patterns of authority and dominance were rapidly breaking down, if not between men and women, at least between old and young. Urban youth, in particular, was freer than ever before, with the chance to find jobs of their own, to spend their own money, to break out of the tight circles of family lives. This new generation of youth found itself growing up in the great metropolises of the North, at the centre of national life, not in the forgotten villages of the Crotone or the Sicilian interior.

Finally, it was in the factories that the Italian model of modernization most belied any facile expectation of immediate social integration. Whereas in West Germany the workforce of the 'miracle' was deeply divided between German and foreign workers, in Italy the southern immigrants were of the same nationality and enjoyed the same rights as their northern counterparts. Their entry into the northern factories did not produce, as many observers expected, a new era of social peace. On the contrary. A new era of collective action, which was to last nearly twenty years, had begun, and the immigrants were to play the leading role in it.

The Resurgence of Class Conflict in the North

There were many reasons for the new militancy in the northern factories. In the first place, the conditions of near full employment in the North gave the workers a self-confidence which they had lacked since the mid-1940s. Immigrant workers in particular soon discovered that in order to be sure of a job it was not necessary to keep one's head down at all costs. Protest often led to improved conditions. When it did not, and the employer reacted with reprisals, then there was nearly always the possibility of finding a job in another factory.

Secondly, the technological changes of the 'miracle' had transformed the organization of work in the northern factories. In the early 1960s mass production took the form of mechanical, repetitive work executed at high speed with few breaks throughout a very long working day. The *'operai comuni'*, the new mass of semi-skilled workers, reacted strongly against these conditions. As their confidence grew, they demanded changes in work rhythms and pay, and eventually greater control of the work process as a means of combating their alienation.[136]

In addition, the southerners brought particular qualities of dissatisfaction and protest into the northern factories. One foreman in a Turin factory told Fofi: 'the most difficult to deal with are the southerners, because they are the ones who get angry most often and who protest the most; the Piedmontese hold it against me that I've become a foreman, but they are the more tranquil and conscientious workers'.[137] Within a very few years, the initial climate created by the so-called 'cooperatives', with the southerners acting as a bulwark against strike action, had totally changed. Immigrant workers found in the factory a focus for collective action which was denied them in the community. They brought into the factory all their resentment at the conditions which they found outside it, where so little provision had been made in terms of housing, social services, schooling and transport. Far from being the grateful 'guests of the city' as *La Stampa* would have liked, they were highly critical of a society which had forced them to migrate and which gave them so little at a time of self-evident economic plenty. As Michele Dimanico, a worker at FIAT-Spa in Turin, told Lanzardo: 'the

Piedmontese have never had the anger which these uprooted southerners have got'.[138]

In 1962 the national contract of the metalworkers came up for renewal. The unions demanded a reduction in the working week from forty-four to forty hours, and a five- rather than a six-day week. They also sought a lessening of pay differentials, and more freedom for trade union representatives within the factory. The focal point of agitation was Turin. Here over the previous two years a large number of small engineering factories, with predominantly immigrant workforces, had witnessed strikes of differing duration and outcome. Very often there had been no trade union organization in the factories; young southerners had taken the lead spontaneously, gradually persuading the rest of the workers to follow them. Here too there was a new interest amongst young Marxist intellectuals in the transformations which the working class was undergoing, and the possibilities which these offered for a new cycle of workers' struggle. In 1960 the review *Quaderni Rossi* began publication. Its analyses of the new realities of the northern cities, and its attempt to link theory with empirical inquiry, were to have a seminal influence.

The great stumbling-block in Turin was FIAT. Its workforce was the best paid in the city, it contained relatively few southerners, and the workers enjoyed the privileges of the company's efficient social assistance policies. Throughout the fifties troublemakers at FIAT had been isolated and sacked. In 1959 eleven strikes had been called in the different parts of the company, but not one had succeeded. The metalworkers' union desperately needed the FIAT workers to join the agitations, but it seemed impossible to break management's hold over them.

At the beginning of 1962 two fierce trade union struggles took place at the Lancia and Michelin factories in Turin. At Lancia, 2,000 new workers had been taken on in the previous three years, and half of the 5,500-strong workforce were southerners. Amongst the local demands were an end to short-term contract working and a third week's paid holiday. After a month of demonstrations, both inside and outside the factory, intermittent strikes, and sympathetic action from the inhabitants of Borgo San Paolo, the Lancia workers won a substantial victory.

At Michelin the workers waged a bitter and often violent struggle. There were frequent clashes with the police, the occupation of the railway station at Porta Nuova and even a march to the Turin home of the French managing director, Doubrée. Alarming episodes took place of pickets beating up foremen, white-collar workers and scabs. The strike ended after ninety days with no substantial concessions from management.[139]

After these two strikes, the fate of the movement in Turin depended on how the FIAT workers would react to national calls for action. On

13 June 1962, the first day of national strike action, the 93,000 FIAT workers clocked in as usual, in spite of the insults of the 100,000 workers who were on strike at other factories in Turin. Then nine days later, in response to another strike call, the trade union vanguard of FIAT workers, some 7,000 in all, came out; on 23 June, for the first time, the majority, some 60,000, stayed out. A mass strike at FIAT had finally been achieved, and with it the dawn of a new turbulent era in Italian labour relations.[140]

Two weeks later, the FIOM and FIM, the metalworkers' sections of the CGIL and CISL, called a general strike of all metalworkers in Turin. On 7 July the strike was a great success, but outside FIAT Mirafiori and other factories there were violent clashes as pickets blocked off the entrances to the factories, turned over cars and beat up some of the managers. During that morning, however, it was announced that the UIL and SIDA, the FIAT company union, had reached a separate agreement with FIAT management. Incensed by this news, some 6,000–7,000 workers assembled in the afternoon outside the UIL offices in Piazza Statuto, in the heart of the city.

For the next two and a half days, Piazza Statuto became the site of an extended urban riot. An extraordinary series of running battles took place between demonstrators and police. The demonstrators broke windows, threw stones, set up rudimentary barricades and repeatedly charged the police lines. They were armed with slings, sticks and chains. The police replied by driving their jeeps at the crowd, filling the piazza with tear gas and using the butts of their rifles on the demonstrators. The clashes went on late into the night both on Saturday 7 July and Monday 9 July. Pajetta of the PCI and Sergio Garavini of the CGIL tried to persuade the crowds to disperse, but they were ignored and manhandled. Over a thousand demonstrators were arrested by the police, though the numbers charged were far fewer.

When the city had recovered its calm, La Stampa denounced the demonstrators indignantly. The trade unions, the PSI and the PCI all argued that the violent clashes had been the work of agents provocateurs. Diego Novelli, the future Communist mayor of Turin, produced evidence that youths had been given 1,500 lire each and cigarettes in order to go and make trouble in the piazza. However, when those who had been charged came to trial, it was difficult to escape from the disconcerting truth: the great majority of those who had taken part in the riots of Piazza Statuto were young workers, and at least half of them came from the South. Lanzardo's collection of eye-witness testimonies, published in 1979, further confirms this picture. The piazza had been full of young and very young workers, and there had been more than one Communist ex-partisan there as well, helping to organize the crowd.[141]

The trade union battles of 1962 and the events in Piazza Statuto gave notice that any dreams of social harmony developing as a result of the 'miracle' were profoundly misplaced. If on the one hand the boom produced a much greater individualism in Italian society, it was also responsible for the explosive meeting of southern youth with northern labour and Resistance traditions. The subversive tendencies of the Italian popular classes were far from dead.

Chapter 8

The Centre-left, 1958–68

*T*HE SOCIAL revolution described in the previous chapter posed a fundamental challenge to the Italian political class. The country was richer than ever before, but in the wake of the 'miracle', as we have seen, came a series of major social problems which demanded an immediate political response. Would the politicians and institutions of the Republic be capable of meeting this challenge? The pages that follow are an attempt to answer this question.

The 1958 Elections, the Birth of the Dorotei and the Tambroni Government, 1960

The elections of May 1958 produced few surprises and provided good evidence of the essential stability of the Italian electorate. No party gained or lost more than three percentage points. The Christian Democrats increased their share of the poll from 40.1 to 42.4 per cent, as did the PSI, from 12.7 to 14.2 per cent The extreme right declined, the MSI dropping from 5.8 to 4.9 per cent, and the Monarchists from 6.9 to 4.8 per cent. The Communists could only gain 0.1 per cent on their showing of 1953, moving from 22.6 to 22.7 per cent.

However, if all was quiet on the electoral front, it was not within the Christian Democrats. Fanfani was becoming ever more powerful and ever more disliked. After the elections he took on the mantle of both President of the Council of Ministers and Minister of Foreign Affairs, as well as keeping the secretaryship of the party. As Ottone wrote later: 'He [Fanfani] seemed to be the master of Italy.'[1]

At the same time Fanfani began to push for a fundamental shift in the pattern of the D C's political alliances. The governments of the fifties had been weak centrist coalitions, incapable of giving a lead to the country. From the time of the D C's national council at Vallombrosa in July 1957, Fanfani argued that the D C should 'open to the left' and include the Socialists in the government. For Fanfani, a new D C–P S I axis, controlled by himself, would be a firm basis for social planning, for moderate reform and for further public intervention in the economy. It would also isolate the P C I.

So much personal and political ambition was bound to have its repercussions. The Christian Democrat right under Mario Scelba, Catholic Action, the church hierarchy, all were greatly alarmed by the direction of events. Leading members of Iniziativa Democratica, Fanfani's own faction, had also become increasingly critical of his high-handedness and arrogance. Opposition within the party grew rapidly. In January 1959 Fanfani's government fell, and immediately afterwards he resigned as party secretary.[2]

A few months later, in March 1959, a new and powerful faction of the D C came into being. The Dorotei, named after the convent of S. Dorotea in which they first met, were led by Mariano Rumor, Carlo Russo, Emilio Colombo and Paolo Emilio Taviani, all erstwhile members of Iniziativa Democratica. For them, though, the time was not yet ripe for the 'opening to the left', nor had sufficient assurances been offered to either private capital or the church hierarchy. The Dorotei were rapidly recognized as the central faction in the party, and were to dominate the Christian Democrats for the next decade.

In October 1959 the Christian Democrats held their seventh congress at Florence. It was the most important and bitterly contested in the party's short history. Amidst many verbal and some physical clashes, the Dorotei, supported by Andreotti and Scelba on their right and Moro on their left, emerged as very narrow victors over Fanfani and his allies.[3]

Aldo Moro was confirmed as the new party secretary. Forty-three years old in 1959, Moro was a university professor of law from the southern city of Bari. Devoutly Catholic, he was reserved, courteous, but intensely ambitious. At thirty he was a Member of Parliament, at thirty-two under-secretary at the Ministry of Foreign Affairs, at thirty-seven president of the D C group in the Chamber of Deputies. Intellectually able and an unparalleled mediator, he was excessively meticulous and incapable of making decisions swiftly.[4]

Under his secretaryship, the 'opening to the left' was not abandoned but subjected to his particular brand of cautious delay. Fanfani's fall and

Moro's caution thus meant that any possibility of a new politics was postponed, at the very moment when economic conditions were most favourable. In January 1960 the *Financial Times* awarded its monetary 'Oscar' to the Italian lira as the most stable currency of 1959. The time was ripe for clear political leadership, but the DC was not capable of giving it.

The stalemate that followed Fanfani's narrow defeat showed how little idea the new DC leaders had of how to form a working government majority. Eventually, in the spring of 1960 the President of the Republic, Giovanni Gronchi, invited a second-rank DC politician, Fernando Tambroni, to form a new government. Tambroni was a fifty-nine-year-old lawyer and an active exponent of 'law and order' policies. His own press office luridly described him as belonging to 'that virile and masculine bourgeoisie which faces up to social and political problems without dissimulation and above all without fear'.[5] More of an opportunist than anything else, Tambroni was on good terms with some of the leaders of both the PSI and the MSI. However, his government only won its initial vote of confidence thanks to the support of the MSI and the Monarchists. From then on, Tambroni was tarred unavoidably with a right-wing brush.

In June 1960, after the new government had been in power a few months, the MSI announced that it would hold its national congress that year at Genoa. The policies of the MSI leader of the time, Arturo Michelini, had not in general been designed to provoke confrontation. Michelini himself was a respectable businessman who disliked the Fascist street gangs of the North and those who were still nostalgic for the Republic of Salò. He wanted the MSI to become instead a respectable right-wing party in alliance with the Monarchists, sharing in the fruits of local government clientelism and rewarding adequately its mass southern base of petty clerks, traders and artisans. At the MSI congress of 1956 he had had to face stiff opposition, with his opening speech being met with the scarcely edifying cries of 'more cudgels and less double-breasted suits'.[6]

However, Tambroni's reliance on their votes made the MSI leadership less cautious. No one could deny the provocative nature of the choice of Genoa, a city which had been awarded a gold medal for its part in the Resistance. The neo-Fascists added fuel to the flames by announcing the participation at the congress of Carlo Emanuele Basile, the last prefect of Genoa during the Republic of Salò, who had been responsible for the deaths and deportations of many Genoese workers and anti-Fascists.

The reply of the majority of the population of Genoa was not slow in coming. As in July 1948, at the time of the attempted assassination of Togliatti, so in June 1960 Genoa showed itself to be the most insurrectionary of Italian cities. On the afternoon of 30 June 1960 a demonstration of tens of thousands of Genoese marched through the streets. In the evening furious battles broke out between demonstrators and the police. Jeeps were overturned and set on fire, barricades erected, and once again Piazza de Ferrari, the central square of the city, was turned into a battleground. On 1 July police reinforcements were drafted into the city, while for their part the local federation of Resistance veterans set up a permanent Liberation committee, ready 'to take over the government of the city'. In an atmosphere of the greatest tension, the city's prefect, in consultation with Tambroni, decided that the MSI congress had to be postponed. That evening saw spontaneous celebrations in every part of Genoa, with the monument to the Resistance covered in a sea of flowers.

After this débâcle Tambroni made the cardinal error of attempting to assert his authority at all costs. The police were given permission to shoot in 'emergency situations' and were not slow to use their powers on anti-Fascist and anti-government demonstrators. On 5 July, at Licata in Sicily, the police killed one demonstrator and seriously wounded five. Two days later at Reggio Emilia five demonstrators were shot dead and nineteen seriously wounded. The CGIL immediately proclaimed a national general strike, which gained massive support. The police continued to open fire on demonstrators: further deaths followed in Sicily on 8 July, both at Palermo and Catania.[7]

By now deeply alarmed, the Christian Democrat leadership sought to replace Tambroni as swiftly as possible. Moro had called his party 'popular and anti-Fascist'; Tambroni's doings were the antithesis of both. On 22 July Tambroni was persuaded to resign. Fanfani was summoned back to form an interim government composed only of Christian Democrats, supported in Parliament by the Republicans and Social Democrats.

The Tambroni affair established clearly one of the constants in the political history of the Republic: namely that anti-Fascism, especially in northern and central Italy, had become part of the dominant ideology. Any attempt to move in an authoritarian direction, away from the Constitution and back towards the Fascist regime, was likely to meet with a massive and uncontrollable protest movement. The Communists would be at the heart of this movement, but participation in it would by no means be confined to them.

It is worth noting in this context that the demonstrations in Genoa, superficially similar to those in Piazza Statuto in Turin two years later – they were both formed of young workers anxious to have a go at the police – were in fact profoundly different. The Genoese events were linked directly to the Resistance and received their legitimation from it. The rioters in Piazza Statuto, by contrast, bore no such historical mantle. Their protest was part of the new Italy, not the Italy of the war, but that of the 'miracle', and their actions presaged the rebellions at the end of the sixties.

Tambroni's swift demise also established another rule of Italian politics – that the Christian Democrats could not hope to govern with the support of the M S I and the Monarchists. The road to the right was thus definitively closed; that to the left was open but unexplored.

The Foundations of the Centre-left

Over the next two years the Christian Democrats and Socialists inched slowly towards each other. After the local elections of 1960, in which the left made significant gains, the first experiments in centre-left government were undertaken at a local level. Milan, Genoa, Florence and Venice, as well as many smaller localities, all formed centre-left administrations. Often the right wing of the D C and the local prelates greeted the new administrators with angry denunciations and mutterings; at Genoa the conservative Cardinal Siri roared more than muttered. However, the tide was against him and his supporters. The early 1960s saw very significant changes in two crucial areas for Italian politics – United States foreign policy and the leadership of the Catholic church.

a. THE USA AND THE CENTRE-LEFT

With John Kennedy's assumption of the presidency in January 1961 the worst excesses of American Cold War attitudes in Italy, personified in the figure of ambassador Clare Boothe Luce, came to an end. In the spring of 1961, Kennedy sent Averell Harriman to Rome to report on the Italian political situation. On his return, Harriman told Kennedy that he thought the centre-left the only possible political solution for Italy: to obstruct it or to remain neutral would serve only to push the PSI back towards the Communists.[8] Kennedy's special adviser, the historian Arthur Schlesinger, Jr, was of the same opinion. For him, the centre-left would serve two purposes: it would provide Italy with a government more committed to reform and justice, i.e. more in line with the ideology, or at least the rhetoric, of the new incumbent at the White House; and it would serve to isolate the Communists within Italian politics. Throughout the Kennedy years, Schlesinger was to play a very active role in encouraging those in Italy who were favourable to the 'opening to the left'.[9]

However, as in the immediate post-war period, American diplomacy did not speak to Italy with a single voice. At the State Department Dean Rusk remained sceptical of the benefits that would accrue to the United States if the PSI joined the government. He favoured a policy of strict neutrality, as did the US ambassador at Rome, Frederick G. Reinhardt.

Within the American embassy at Rome there were those who

expressed extreme opposition to making any concessions to the Italian Socialists. In a meeting of November 1961, Vernon Walters, the military attaché, advocated armed intervention should a centre-left government be formed. He was supported by members of the CIA office in Rome, including Karamessines, who was later to play an important background role in the Greek military coup.[10]

Kennedy himself was distinctly in favour of the centre-left, but was cautious about supporting Schlesinger too openly. The President had little desire to alienate his Secretary of State on what was, after all, a matter of secondary importance. In June 1961, Fanfani, who had bounced back to the limelight as head of the interim government, was invited to Washington. In private Kennedy told him that the United States would 'observe with benevolence future developments'. For the moment, Kennedy was not prepared to go further. None the less, the absence of an American veto on the centre-left, and the President's 'benevolence', were to be of decisive importance in this new phase of Italian politics.[11]

b. POPE JOHN XXIII AND THE CATHOLIC CHURCH IN THE 1960s

Of even greater significance was the death, in 1958, of Pius XII, and his succession by Angelo Roncalli, Pope John XXIII. As we have seen, Pius XII's long, conservative reign, from 1939 onwards, had witnessed the Catholic church's unceasing intervention in Italian politics and society. Throughout it, Pius had remained an aloof and solitary figure, erudite but incapable of speaking the language of ordinary people. A formidable centralizer, he had chosen not to have any Secretary of State at his side after the death of Cardinal Luigi Maglione in 1944.

The brief papacy of John XXIII (1958–63) provided a very great contrast. Angelo Roncalli was born in 1881 into a poor peasant family from the province of Bergamo in Lombardy. His parents had only the income from three hectares of land (approximately eight acres) with which to bring up thirteen children. In 1909, as a young priest, Angelo Roncalli followed the lead of his bishop, Mgr Radini Tedeschi, in supporting a strike by textile workers in the Bergamasco. The leader of the local Catholic workers' league had been sacked for demanding a reduction in the working day, then ten and a half hours for six days a week. As Roncalli wrote later, 'at stake was the fundamental principle of the liberty of Christian workers to organize themselves in the face of the powerful organization of capital'.[12]

For much of his life, though, Roncalli had no great contact with the world of ordinary Italians. He spent many years as a diplomat, first in Bulgaria and then Paris, before becoming Patriarch of Venice in 1953. Extraordinarily for a diplomat, Roncalli managed to preserve a great simplicity and humility, which emerged fully when he became Pope. His conception of his role was pre-eminently a pastoral one, expressed in a language of such directness and candour as to win him the deep affection of believers and non-believers alike. 'When you go back home,' he told his audience one Sunday in St Peter's Square, 'you will find your children there. Stroke their faces, and tell them that this caress comes from the Pope.'[13]

In many ways Pope John, '*il Papa buono*', was a confirmed traditionalist. He was an old man of seventy-seven when he became Pope, and he brought with him many of the prejudices both of the peasant world in which he had brought up, and of the higher ecclesiastical circles in which he had spent most of his active years. Television, for instance, was anathema to him; it was too 'feministic', and initially he maintained Pius XII's ban on priests from buying sets or watching programmes other than those of religious content. On the other hand, John XXIII had an acute sense of how fast the world was changing, and how important it was for the church to understand this change and adapt to it. 'What is tradition?' he asked the second ecumenical council: 'It is the progress that was made yesterday, just as the progress that we make today will constitute the tradition of tomorrow.'[14]

For the first two years of his papacy, John XXIII trod very carefully. His Secretary of State, Mgr Domenico Tardini, was an old and conservative cardinal, and the Curia was accustomed to continuity, not change. In the field of Italian politics, the church maintained its opposition to a centre-left alliance. In early 1959, the influential Cardinal Ottaviani was in the forefront of the attacks against Fanfani, and in May 1960 the *Osservatore Romano* issued an explicit condemnation of the centre-left. Thus in the critical boom years of 1959–61, the church too had more than its share of responsibility in blocking the formation of a new political majority committed to reform.[15]

However, the summer of 1961 saw the beginning of John XXIII's radical re-evaluation of the role of the church in Italian society and politics. From then on he made it increasingly clear that not only would he view with sympathy the 'opening to the left', but that he wanted the church to abandon that interventionist political role which it had assumed ever since the foundation of the Republic. The civic committees ceased to exist, Catholic Action was confined to spiritual and social activities, and its crusading and anti-Socialist president, Luigi Gedda, was transferred elsewhere. By November 1961, Aldo Moro could state confidently on television, albeit in his habitually coded fashion, that the church hierarchy was on his side.[16]

In the last two years of his life, John XXIII tried to turn the Catholic church in a new direction. His encyclical of May 1961, *Mater et magistra*

('Mother and Teacher'), concentrated on the social teaching of the church. It rejected the free play of market forces, emphasized the need for greater social justice and called for the disinherited to be integrated into the social and political order.[17] In October 1962 John XXIII opened the second ecumenical council of the Catholic church. The first had met in 1870, and John's decision to summon another had been bitterly opposed by those who feared the centrifugal tendencies in the church. In his opening speech to the 2,500 Catholic prelates who had come from all over the world, John XXIII stressed that the church, 'rather than merely reiterating the vetoes of the past, sees the necessity of meeting the needs of the world today, and thus demonstrates the continuing validity of its doctrine'.[18]

Finally in July 1963, Pope John issued his last and most famous encyclical, *Pacem in terris* ('Peace on Earth'). This was a moving plea for international conciliation, based on the neutrality of the church and its refusal to accept the barriers of the Cold War. Its framework could not have been further from Pius XII's insistence on defending the West in a Holy War against the Communist and atheist East. The encyclical was addressed to 'all men of good will', not just to Catholics, and argued the need for cooperation between people of different ideological beliefs. In addition, the encyclical stressed the need for the increased economic and social development of the working classes, the entry of women into public life and the justice of anti-colonialist struggles in the Third World.[19]

The papacy of John XXIII was to have a profound influence on the development of the Catholic church. It also opened a new phase in the relations between church and society in Italy. The integralism of Pius XII gave way to a different conception of the church, based more on its spiritual and pastoral role than on its political, crusading and anti-Communist vocation. The possibility was opened for a dialogue between Catholic and Marxist worlds. At the local level, the era of Don Camillo and his Communist rival, Peppone, forever plotting each other's downfall, was drawing to a close. At the national level, Christian Democrats and Socialists were finally to come face to face.

c. THE PSI AND THE DC, 1960–62

The thirty-fourth congress of the PSI, held in Milan in March 1961, marked a significant victory for Pietro Nenni and those in favour of entering the government in alliance with the DC. Nenni's 'Autonomous' faction gained 55 per cent of the votes, against the 35 per cent of the left, who were led by Tullio Vecchietti, and the 7 per cent of the 'Alternative' faction of Lelio Basso. With Kennedy in the White House, Nenni abandoned his position of strict neutrality between East and West, and made it clear that the PSI was henceforth in favour of NATO. For him and his supporters, it was now a matter of urgency to enter what he called 'the control room' of the state. The state's economic intervention in society had grown notably, the controls themselves had greatly increased in numbers, and it was the Socialists' duty to use them to the best possible effect.

However, all was far from clear in the Socialist camp. The PSI congress of 1961 could not be compared to that of their German Social Democratic colleagues at Bad Godesberg some two years earlier. There the SPD had definitely renounced its Marxist past, preferring henceforth to call itself a popular party and committing itself to reforms within the structure of capitalism.

Nenni, at least verbally, had no such intentions. His strategy, as he insisted at the thirty-fourth congress, distinguished itself from Social Democracy 'because it does not obscure the sense of diversity between bourgeois democracy and socialist democracy; because it does not postulate an insertion into bourgeois society, but is designed to create the civic instruments for the conquest of the state for democracy, and the conquest of democracy for socialism'.[20] In order to win Italy for socialism, he continued, it was necessary to adopt 'the method that peasant wisdom has consecrated in one of the many proverbs of our countryside. If you want to pull down a tree, it is not always a good idea to use a rope. If you pull too hard the rope might break. Better then to dig all round the tree so as to make it fall down. For the moment, the tree that we need to make fall is that of the reactionary and conservative interests in the country.'[21]

Such language may have rallied the party faithful, but it was hardly designed to reassure Nenni's prospective political partners, let alone the more conservative elements in the country. The Christian Democrats were seemingly being offered the same sort of alliance that Lenin had advocated between the British Communists and the Labour Party in 1920; the Socialists were to be the hangman who put the noose around the neck of the Christian Democrats.

In 1961 Nenni's 'Autonomous' faction was the most moderate section of the party. Riccardo Lombardi, the chief Socialist theoretician of the centre-left, supported the 'Autonomists', but he had an even more radical notion than Nenni of what the centre-left should entail. He told the thirty-fourth congress that there existed the possibility of 'conquering the state from the inside', and that the best way to fight neo-capitalism was 'to substitute the absolute criterion of profit with that of collective utility'.[22] Two years earlier he had told a PSI conference that the politics of planning 'could not help but enter into conflict with the structures and superstructures of capitalist power'.[23]

Furthermore, over 40 per cent of the party in 1961 remained firmly opposed even to Lombardi's version of the centre-left. For Vecchietti, as for

Basso, a coalition government with the DC would not lead to the realization of structural reforms, but rather to the integration of the PSI into the already existing political system.

For their part, the Christian Democrats had no intention of allowing the Socialists to push them any further than they wanted to go. The theoretical bases for their alliance with the Socialists were presented at a conference they organized at San Pellegrino Terme in September 1961. The economist Pasquale Saraceno explained how the market, left to its own devices, could not resolve and indeed exacerbated the geographical, social and productive disequilibria that charcterized modern Italy. The state had to intervene by means of economic planning, in order to ensure balanced economic development. The sociologist Achille Ardigò warned that Italy's rapid industrialization threatened the bases of the DC's electoral power: the drastically diminishing number of peasants and rural middle classes meant that the Christian Democrats had to look for a 'new synthesis'. This was to take two forms: at a sociological level, the understanding and eventual political leadership of the new urban social classes; at a governmental level, a new relationship with the Socialists.[24]

The party leaders listened to their intellectuals, but they had their own reasons for seeking an alliance with the PSI. Prime amongst these was the need to find a greater stability both inside and outside Parliament. The centre-left would provide, or so they hoped, a firm majority in the Chamber of Deputies, as well as facilitating the organization of consent in a rapidly changing society. They agreed with Saraceno on the need for greater state intervention, but not necessarily for his reasons. In an ideal world, state intervention might lead to a more balanced and just economy; but even if it did not, there would still be increased power and spoils for the government parties.

Finally, and perhaps most importantly, the DC leadership wanted to ally with the Socialists in order to divide the left. This was the same line of argument that John Kennedy was pursuing, and it was the one which Moro, Fanfani and the Dorotei used with greatest effect against the right wing of their own party. If the Socialists could be weaned away from their Communist comrades, then the PCI would find itself in total political isolation, and the cooperation between Socialists and Communists within the CGIL would be placed in serious crisis.

In January 1962 the Christian Democrats held their eighth congress at Naples. Aldo Moro, as secretary of the party, delivered a famous speech in favour of the centre-left. It was ninety-nine pages long, took over five hours to deliver and was a masterpiece of ambiguity. Moro managed simultaneously to reassure the opponents of the centre-left and encourage its supporters. On the key question of state planning, for instance, he had this to say: 'it is up to the state to install a new relationship with the reality which it has the duty to govern, a new relationship which is capable of bringing the action of our social forces more in line with the progress of Italian society'.[25] No one was quite sure what such passages meant, but politically they were terribly effective. With Moro at the helm, the Dorotei felt reassured. The right-wing Andreotti also gave his blessing to Moro's version of the centre-left, dubbing Moro's speech an encyclical with the title of *Casta connubi* (the chaste marriage partners being in this case the D C and the P S I). Eighty per cent of the delegates at the congress backed the list called 'The friends of Moro and Fanfani'. For a party that had seemed gravely split only three years earlier, this was a notable reassertion of unity.

d. ITALIAN INDUSTRY AND THE CENTRE-LEFT

Certain sections of Italian industry in the early 1960s mirrored the majority of the Christian Democrats in their conversion to the centre-left. Prime amongst them were those large private firms – F I A T, Pirelli and Olivetti in particular – which represented the most dynamic sectors of the Italian economy. For them the attraction of the centre-left was twofold: the advent of central government planning seemed more likely to enhance than to impede the growth sectors of the economy; and the presence of the Socialists in government would, they hoped, help to diminish the growing tensions in the northern factories. The model of the 1950s had served its time. Vittorio Valletta, the managing director of F I A T, was a firm supporter of the Christian Democrat version of the centre-left. When he went to see Kennedy in May 1962, Valletta recommended that if and when the U S A began to support the Socialists financially, it should do so via the D C so that the latter could use the money 'as a lever to extract the cooperation of the Socialist party'.[26]

Public-sector industry was also favourable to the 'opening to the left', though in an equally cautious way. Mattei, the head of E N I, was, as usual, backing many political horses at once, but from 1960 to 1962 his newspaper *Il Giorno* was a consistent supporter of the idea of the centre-left. G. Petrilli, the managing director of I R I, the other giant of the public sector, was a far less independent and less political figure than Mattei. As a solid member of the D C establishment, Petrilli was content to accept what the secretary of the party decided.[27]

A sizeable proportion of Italy's employing class, therefore, was willing to accept a moderate version of the centre-left. However, very influential sectors were not. Confindustria remained firmly in the hands of the electricity trusts, who knew that they were the prime target for nationalization under a centre-left government. In 1961 they succeeded once again in electing a man of their own, Furio Cicogna, to the presidency of the employers' association. The lead that Cicogna gave to the thousands of small employers who looked to Confindustria for guidance was one of intransigent opposition to any 'opening to the left'. He painted a lurid picture of ever-increasing workers' power once the Socialists came into government. On 4 January 1962 the business newspaper *24 Ore* warned small and medium firms that they could be faced 'with a situation similar to that of their Czechoslovak, Hungarian and Chinese colleagues around the year 1950'.[28] The entrepreneurial class, knowing that their profits in the 'miracle' depended on low wages and lack of workers' organization, were not slow to get the message.

The importance of these sectors of the bourgeoisie should not be underestimated. The electricity trusts were very closely linked with the world of Italian high finance, and conservative elements controlled most of the country's newspapers. Their mass base was that provincial bourgeoise which had been one of the chief protagonists of the 'miracle'. Not for the first time in Italian history, crucial sectors of the upper classes turned their faces firmly against a strategy of progress, and against more equitable cooperation with the classes below them.[29]

Reforms and Reformism

As the lines were drawn for what was to be the second great political battle of the Republic (the first being that between Togliatti and De Gasperi in the period 1945–8), one question overrode all others: what would be the precise content of the reform programme to be carried out by the new political coalition?

There were three substantially different answers to this question. The first can best be summarized under the heading of the reforms of the reformists. Its leading exponents were men like the Republican leader Ugo La Malfa, the Christian Democrat economist Pasquale Saraceno, and, considerably less consistently, Amintore Fanfani. For them capitalism was very much to be supported, but steps had to be taken to remedy the deformations and imbalances specific to the Italian model of economic development. What was necessary, therefore, was a series of *corrective* reforms. These would try to tackle perennial problems like the poverty of the South and the backwardness of much of Italian agriculture. They would also attempt to transform the relationship between state and citizen, and to correct the imbalance between private and social consumption. Thus the bureaucracy needed to be made more efficient and purged of corruption, regional government was finally to be introduced and local government was to be overhauled so as to cope with the new needs arising from rapid urbanization.

Provision was to be made for the building of houses and schools, the education system was to be modernized and a national social insurance and health service introduced.[30]

This was an ambitious programme, but its supporters argued that the long economic boom offered a unique historical opportunity. For the first time the objective conditions existed for an enlightened ruling class to carry through the economic and political integration of the lower classes into the nation state.

The second position *vis-à-vis* reforms was very different. Its proponents included all the major figures of the PCI and the PSI, both those who supported the centre-left and those who opposed it, both Togliatti and Lombardi, Nenni and Basso. For them what was necessary was a series not of *corrective* but of *structural* reforms. Each reform, whether it was in the field of agriculture or housing or education, was to be a stepping-stone on the way to socialism. Its efficacy was to be judged by the degree to which it increased the anti-capitalist consciousness of the lower classes and prepared them to become the dominant class. Thus structural reform was not designed to aid capitalism but to call it further into question. As Riccardo Lombardi said, what was being proposed was a '"revolutionary reformism", a process that continually destroys the equilibrium of the system and creates a series of counter-powers'.[31] Structural reforms were, therefore, a series of intermediate objectives which linked capitalism to socialism in a continuous process.

The 'Autonomist' Socialists, and here they differed from the rest of the left, maintained that a centre-left government was the best launching pad for the initial stages of this transition. The centre-left, they argued, would attract all the progressive elements in Italian society. In particular, the 'dynamic' and 'enlightened' elements of Italian capitalism were potential allies of great importance. Since the principal opponents of structural reforms were the monopolies, of which the electricity trusts were the best example, and since the trusts were the sworn enemies of FIAT, Olivetti and the like, there existed an objective basis for an alliance between the working-class movement and 'progressive' capital.

The strategy of structural reform was deeply attractive but Utopian in at least two ways. The centre-left version of it, which is the one that interests us most here, offered no explanation of how the transition would take place from corrective reforms to structural ones. It was possible to envisage a scenario in which progressive forces, both political and economic, might combine with the PSI to combat the most obvious imbalances in Italian capitalist development. However, they would do so in the name of capitalism, and any attempt to pass from what they deemed necessary to what they deemed threatening would, all too obviously, incur their immediate hostility. The alliances of the centre-left, then, were capable only of achieving corrective reform. Nor was it possible to claim, as the Socialists did, that such reforms necessarily increased the political consciousness of the working class and prepared the terrain for structural reform. There was no such automatic link between the two. Indeed, in some situations, as in Britain between 1945 and 1949, reforms of a corrective type had led to a decrease of militancy rather than increased anti-capitalist consciousness. Thus the passage between corrective and structural reform was one which the Socialists, with excessive optimism, left wholly unexplored.

Secondly, and more generally, it was very doubtful indeed whether any structural reform could take place in Italy (or elsewhere?) without precipitating a revolutionary situation. Confindustria and FIAT might be at loggerheads, Fanfani and Scelba at opposite ends of the DC spectrum, but faced with a common threat they could be expected to close ranks immediately. The space for structural reform, as the experience of the Gullo decrees had shown, was very limited indeed. Nenni could talk of the need to dig round the tree of reaction, but it was a misguided metaphor. The 'reactionary' elements of capitalism were in reality but one branch of a capitalist tree; the branch *might* be lopped off, but the roots would be defended at all costs. Thus the vision of a gradual, step-by-step transition to socialism was a pure chimera. At most, structural reform might come at the end of a process of building anti-capitalist hegemony. It could never come at the beginning.[32]

Finally, there existed a third position on the question of reforms, which might best be termed *minimalist*. Its exponents were the Dorotei, and, in the final analysis, Aldo Moro himself. The minimalists paid lip-service to the idea of corrective reforms, sometimes at very great length, but were absolutely not prepared to let the fervour for reformism weaken the unity of the DC or its hold upon the state. For them corrective reforms were a secondary objective, to be welcomed but always to be made subordinate to the needs of the party. The centre-left, in this conception, was not designed to transform the face of Italy, but to transform the PSI, bringing the Socialists into government without threatening the hegemony of the Christian Democrats.

These then were the three views of reform which existed as the long period of the centre-left's gestation finally drew to a close. They were irreconcilable, and the years 1962–8 were to see the clear triumph of only one of them.

The First Centre-left Government, 1962–3

In March 1962, Amintore Fanfani formed the first centre-left government, consisting of the Christian Democrats, the Social Democrats and the Republicans. In spite of the very changed conditions, both internal and external, which have been outlined above, the moment was still not deemed ripe for the Socialists to join the government. However, the PSI abstained from voting against the government, and Nenni made it clear that this qualified form of support would continue provided that three initial reforms were realized before the elections of 1963: the nationalization of the electricity trusts, the institution of a single form of middle school and the formation of regional governments. Fanfani accepted these terms, and in his programme of government read to the Chamber of Deputies on 2 March 1962 he threw in a few other proposed reforms for good measure: reform of the state, economic planning on a national level, agrarian reform and so on.[33]

The economic programme of the government was defined in May of that year in a famous 'Additional Note' prepared by Ugo La Malfa, the Republican Minister of the Budget, as an appendix to the general report on the economic situation of the country in 1961. In his Note La Malfa stressed the need for economic planning in conjunction with the unions as well as industry. The high rates of growth which had characterized the recent performance of the economy were to provide the basis for the provision of efficient social services. Planning would create the necessary balance between agriculture and industry, between the various social classes, between private and public consumption.[34]

The first major political event in the life of the new government did not augur well for its reforming intentions. Giovanni Gronchi had come to the end of his term as President of the Republic, and a furious battle was waged for his succession between Antonio Segni, on the right of the DC, and Giuseppe Saragat, the leader of the PSDI. Communists, Socialists, Republicans and Social Democrats all eventually supported Saragat. A section of the DC left led by Fanfani was loath to back the official DC candidate, Segni, but Moro insisted on party unity and threatened a government crisis unless the Fanfaniani came into line. After nine ballots in Parliament Segni was finally elected, but he had needed the votes not only of the DC but of the Monarchists and neo-Fascists as well. Moro's obduracy thus ensured that the new President of the Republic was not a man committed to reform, but one profoundly suspicious of the consequences of a centre-left government.[35]

However, after this inauspicious beginning Fanfani's government got into its stride. It proceeded, with a rapidity that bore tribute to Fanfani's dynamism, to take the major step of nationalizing the electricity trusts. There were five trusts concerned: Sade, which controlled the distribution of electricity in the Veneto and part of Emilia; Edison, whose operations covered Lombardy, Emilia and Liguria; Sip, for Piedmont; Centrale, for

Tuscany, Lazio and Sardinia; and Sme, which covered the mainland South and Sicily. Sme, in particular, was notorious for its failure to take new initiatives in an area which desperately needed them.[36]

The economic reasons for nationalization were clear enough. Government control of the industry would enable it to fix prices, programme power resources on a national scale and make investments where they were most needed, such as the development areas in the South. The political reasons were even clearer, and probably paramount. The nationalization of the trusts would, it was hoped, destroy that conservative agglomeration of power that lay at the heart of Italian capitalism. Confindustria would be released from its right-wing stranglehold, and the centre-left from the attacks of its most powerful opponent.

The real debate, as so often in these cases, came over the form of compensation to be paid. Guido Carli, the governor of the Bank of Italy, wanted the compensation money to be paid directly to the former trusts, which would remain in being as finance companies. He argued that this was the best way to ensure that men of considerable business expertise would reinvest the money in industry, as had happened at the beginning of the century after the nationalization of the railways. He was opposed by Riccardo Lombardi, who also sat on the parliamentary commission dealing with the nationalization. Lombardi saw no reason to share Carli's optimistic assessment of the trusts' former directors. He wanted the trusts to be abolished completely, and the compensation to be paid after a certain number of years to the tens of thousands of former shareholders. Carli's line offered the guarantee of continuity, but at the price of preserving much of the trusts' former influence; Lombardi's offered the prospect of real change, but with the fear that the compensation funds would be dispersed aimlessly. After four days of heated discussions, during which Carli threatened to resign, continuity won the day.[37]

The nationalization of the electricity industry, as it was presented to Parliament in June 1962, was essentially a corrective reform, an act of 'rationalization' as Emilio Colombo called it. Looking back, no one could possibly judge it to be structural in content, in the sense of representing a pass towards socialism.

The new national electrical company that came into being, ENEL, began a programme of extensive investments, but did not succeed in reducing costs to consumers. As for the compensation funds, it has been estimated that little more than 50 per cent of the 1,500 bn lire paid to the trusts found its way in the end into productive investment. The rest was dissipated in a variety of ways. In economic terms, Carli's battle had thus been fought largely in vain: the small shareholders would probably not have dissipated the funds to any greater extent. However, in political terms the continuing influence of the electricity barons had been ensured.

Two other reforms marked this first phase of the centre-left. The government took a first, timid step towards supervising the activity of the stock exchange by passing a withholding tax on stock dividends. It hoped in this way to make the names of share-owners public knowledge, and thus combat tax evasion and increase revenue for its reform programme.[38]

It also succeeded in instituting a reform that had been dear to the left since the war – the establishment of compulsory secondary schooling until the age of fourteen. In the early years of the Republic compulsory schooling had ended at eleven, and those children who continued into secondary education had been sharply divided in a way similar to the old British system of secondary modern and grammar schools. The extension of the school leaving age and the establishment of a single system of middle schooling were only approved in Parliament after a prolonged rearguard action by the right.

Many middle-school teachers remained hostile to the new law. For them it destroyed the old élite middle schools, it made Latin optional, it threatened discipline. Gradually, they got used to it, and the number of children completing middle school rose slowly over the next decade. For the first time, too, large numbers of girls received some form of secondary education.[39]

At the end of 1962, the reforming impulses of the Fanfani government were abruptly halted. The members of the government, like La Malfa, who were most in favour of reform had become increasingly isolated. On their left, Togliatti had been careful not to appear as automatically hostile to the government's reforming endeavours, and had promised a constructive opposition on the part of the Communists. However, this was a far cry from giving any direct support to the government. In particular, the CGIL, dominated by the PCI and left-wing Socialists like Vittorio Foa, refused to be drawn into La Malfa's neo-corporatist strategy by which the trade unions would accept wage restraint in return for the promise of reforms. CGIL representatives did agree to serve on the national planning commission when it was established in August 1962, but that was as far as they were prepared to go.[40]

On the other flank, the economic and political conjuncture of the second half of 1962 had given rise to a steadily growing tide of panic. Whereas in 1960 only 46 million working days had been lost in strikes, and in 1961 79 million, in 1962 nearly 182 million days were lost. July 1962 had also seen the riots in Piazza Statuto, the responsibility for which was laid by the Confindustria firmly at the door of the 'pro-worker' government. In the North, demand for labour was exceeding supply for the first time ever.

Wages in some sectors were soaring above those agreed in national contracts, and their rate of increase was beginning to exceed that of productivity. The largest firms, still very much on the crest of the boom, felt able to absorb these increased costs and labour difficulties. For the small and medium-sized firms it was a different story. They found themselves in financial difficulty and were not slow to blame the government for their fate.[41]

From the autumn of 1962 onwards the multiple responses to this very changed economic situation became apparent for the first time. As employers passed wage increases on in prices, and as demand for certain manufactured commodities exceeded supply, inflation became a significant problem for the first time since the 1940s. Small and medium industrialists reacted to the situation with an investment strike. What was the point, they argued, in investing at a time of such economic uncertainty, and with wage bills eating heavily into profits? In addition, investors responded to the new withholding tax on stock dividends by shifting significant amounts of capital abroad. The ex-electricity trusts, whose influence in financial circles was untouched, fomented the climate of uncertainty; stock prices fell, businesss confidence drained away.[42]

These were the circumstances which made the majority of the DC call a halt to reform. The Dorotei hastily impressed on Moro the dangers that the party faced if it did not put a brake on Fanfani's activism. Inflation and financial panic were wreaking havoc among the small and medium savers who had always been amongst the strongest supporters of the Christian Democrats. The risk of alienating them as well as the in-dustrialists was too great to be taken. National elections were due in the spring of 1963. It was time to placate, and swiftly.

Moro's loyalty to his party predominated, as usual, over all other considerations, with the result that two vital reforms which were about to be presented to Parliament were struck off the government's agenda. The first of these was the long-awaited institution of regional governments. Regional devolution meant giving more power to the Communists in the Red Belt of central Italy. The DC leadership knew that this was hardly the moment to be seen to be making such a concession.

The second reform was that of town planning, and the way in which it was sabotaged must rank as one of the poorest political decisions in the history of the Republic. Fiorentino Sullo, the reforming Christian Democrat Minister of Public Works, first presented his town-planning bill to the government in June 1962. It represented the first (and the last) real attempt to deal with the problems of land speculation and urban sprawl which have so afflicted contemporary Italy. Sullo's major proposition was that local administrations should issue compulsory purchase orders on all undeveloped land included in a city's *piano regolatore*. They should then provide the basic public utilities (roads, water, electricity, drains), and afterwards sell back the land at a controlled higher price to private individuals. In this way the savage speculation on land due for urbanization would be completely eliminated. In addition, Sullo proposed that the new owners would own only what was constructed on the land, not the land itself, which would continue to belong to the municipalities. The public authorities would thus be able to maintain an element of real control over those who attempted to violate the *piano regolatore*. As Sullo said in an interview of March 1979: 'The state at that time had the resources to carry through the compulsory purchases as we were still in the middle of the boom. We would have been able to safeguard the destiny of our major cities – Milan, Turin, Rome and Genoa.'[43]

Sullo's far-sighted corrective reform aroused the most furious opposition in certain sections of Italian public opinion. In the spring of 1963, the right-wing press accused him of Bolshevik intentions, and of wanting to nationalize the land. On 1 April 1963 *Il Tempo* came out with the headline: 'Eight million heads of families determined to defend their houses.' Faced with this onslaught, Sullo sought the support of Fanfani, who told him that all depended on Moro. Moro responded quite ruthlessly. The building industry, small urban proprietors and *rentiers* were all up in arms, and the elections were less than three weeks away. Sullo offered to abandon the distinction between the ownership of property and of the land. It was not enough. He also asked to be allowed to go on television to explain to the nation the real nature of his proposals. Moro would not hear of it. On 13 April 1963, fifteen days before the elections, Moro, without informing Sullo, published an article in *Il Popolo* in which he declared that the proposed reform was the personal initiative of the Minister of Public Works, and was not the responsibility of the Christian Democratic Party. Sullo had been ditched, and so had the prospect of any effective town planning in Italy.[44]

On 28 April 1963, the Italians went to the polls for the fourth time in the history of the Republic. The Christian Democrats dipped under 40 per cent for the first time, gaining 38.3 per cent of the votes in comparison to the 42.4 per cent of five years earlier. This was a notable drop by Italian standards, but not of the dimensions that some on the right of the party had feared. The chief beneficiaries of the DC's decline were the Liberals, whose consistent hostility to the centre-left earned them an increase from 3.5 to 7 per cent. Further to the right, the Monarchists practically disappeared (falling from 4.8 to 1.7 per cent), while the MSI crept up from 4.8 to 5.1 per cent. On the left, the PSDI was rewarded for its participation in Fanfani's government with an increase of 1.5 per cent (from 4.6 to 6.1 per cent), while the PSI declined marginally (from 14.2 to 13.8 per cent). The real victors on the left were the Communists, who for the first time gained more than a quarter of all votes (22.7 to 25.3 per cent).[45] The reasons for this success were almost certainly not to be sought in their attitudes to the centre-left, but in the social transformations of the years 1958–63. The PCI gained all over the country, but particularly heavily in the immigrant quarters of the northern cities and amongst emigrant workers in northern Europe.

Moro's First Government, 1963–4

The lessons from the elections of 1963 were not very clear. The Christian Democrats had been penalized for the 'opening to the left', but after the Tambroni disaster there was no political alternative available. Aldo Moro and the Dorotei decided that the experiment must continue, but in as moderate a form as possible. Segni, the President of the Republic, therefore asked Moro himself to form the next government, and the Dorotei leader, Mariano Rumor, became the new secretary of the party.

While the attention of most Italians was taken up with Pope John's illness in the last few weeks of his life, Moro conducted lengthy and delicate negotiations for a new centre-left coalition. The Socialists had to be included this time, because they were no longer prepared to give external support to the government. By 16 June 1963 Moro seemed to have succeeded, but that night, which went down in Italian political history as the night of S. Gregorio, the Lombardi faction of the Socialists vetoed his proposals. Once again the sticking point was proposed town planning reform, which Lombardi rightly found extremely nebulous. Nenni, called from his bed at 2 a.m., suddenly found himself in a minority within his party. Moro's web had been broken, and Giovanni Leone was called upon to head a caretaker government until the Socialists could sort themselves out.

This they did, in a manner of speaking, at their thirty-fifth congress in October 1963. Nenni and Lombardi patched up their differences, though Lombardi's speech at the congress was as radical as ever. Basso, Vecchietti and others all spoke against joining the government, but a motion in favour of Socialist participation in the government was passed by a narrow majority by the Lombardi and Nenni factions.

Finally, in December 1963, after a gestation period of more than six years, the Italian Socialists became part of the government. Moro was President of the Council, Nenni his deputy. Among the other Socialist ministers, the most important was Antonio Giolitti, the ex-Communist (see pp. 207 and 209), who now became Minister of the Budget. Lombardi did not take up a ministerial position, and this was a grave error because he was a far more forceful figure than either Giolitti or the ageing Nenni.

Moro's programme, as presented to Parliament, was extremely long and promised everything. Giovanni Malagodi called it aptly 'Short Observations on the Universe'. Moro promised that the establishment of regional government would be a 'primary' task, that reform of the school system would be an 'absolute priority', that reform of housing was 'fundamental', and that agriculture, the imbalance between North and South, fiscal and social insurance reforms, town planning and an anti-monopoly law were all 'priority tasks'. 'If Parliament gives us its vote of confidence,' promised Moro, 'we will realize our entire programme.'[46]

For the Socialists, entry into Moro's government brought tragedy. The left of the party, the large minority at the October congress, refused to vote for the government in Parliament, and faced immediate disciplinary procedures. There may have been room for compromise, but Nenni seemed unwilling to seek it. In January 1964 thirty-eight deputies and senators left the party to form the PSIUP, the Partito Socialista di Unità Proletaria, adopting the name which the Socialists had had in the 1940s. 'In our opinion,' said Lelio Basso in Parliament, 'there is only one thing that cannot be done, and that is to sacrifice the autonomy of the working-class movement, to subordinate its political choices to the overall plan of the dominant class. And it is exactly that overall plan that we now see in the Moro government.'[47] About 30 per cent of the PSI joined the PSIUP but in the trade union movement the damage was greater, as Vittorio Foa, secretary of the CGIL, led some of the best cadres into the new party.

The Socialists had thus split twice in twenty years, once to the right with Saragat in 1947, and once to the left in 1964. This terrible process of fragmentation, even if it finds some sort of counterpart in the French experience of the same period, cannot but reflect poorly on Nenni's qualities as a party leader. In the context of the centre-left, the split weakened notably the already limited contractual power of the Socialists *vis-à-vis* the Christian Democrats. Within the PSI, it also undermined Lombardi's position with respect to Nenni. The veteran Socialist leader may have been pleased about this last point, but the ever-dwindling electoral strength of the rump of the party must have been a constant source of anguish to him.

The first government with PSI participation was a damp squib of the first order. Moro's reforming zeal was limited at the best of times, and a difficult economic situation gave him a cast-iron excuse to procrastinate. With neither inflation nor the flight of capital showing any signs of abating, Guido Carli, the governor of the Bank of Italy, imposed a credit squeeze in the autumn of 1963. At the beginning of the following year, Carli and Emilio Colombo, a duo who were to dominate the political economy of Italy for the rest of the decade, introduced full-scale deflationary measures. These, it was argued, were necessary both to combat inflation and to reduce a balance of payments deficit caused by excessive internal demand. The Colombo–Carli line was, in economic terms, the exact opposite of what La Malfa had proposed in his 'Additional Note' some two years earlier.[48]

Deflation produced its usual consequences. Unemployment rose, with women workers being the first to lose their jobs; many small firms closed or were bought up by larger ones in a complex process of industrial restructuring; consumption was contained; labour's bargaining power was diminished.

The political consequences of deflation were grave. Moro argued strongly that reforms were not possible in such an economic climate, and proposed instead a two-stage policy: first the economy was to be restored to health, which was what the governor of the Bank of Italy wanted, as did the EEC; then, and only then, would the programme of reforms be resumed. Faced with this proposal, Nenni found himself in great difficulty. Having just insisted on going into the government at the cost of splitting his party, Nenni could hardly resign in protest a few months later and thus admit that the scissionists had been right after all. On the other hand, the only alternative was to submit to Moro's logic and accept the postponement of reform.

The Socialists remained in the government. Discussions on reform came and went, but little or nothing was achieved. The bill to reform agrarian contracts, a subject last heard of with Gullo in 1944, sat on Moro's desk for nearly three months. The establishment of regional governments came no closer to taking place. The Socialists waged a long battle for the reform of the Federconsorzi (see p. 140), with the aim of breaking down centralized control and making them genuinely cooperative, but were successfully blocked by the Bonomi wing of the DC. As for town planning, the new minister Pieraccini, of the PSI, prepared a bill that was less radical than Sullo's, but even this was howled down by the right inside and outside Parliament. Pieraccini commented later: 'then, even more than now, the "backward" sector was extremely strong and conditioned the attitudes of the dominant economic and political groups. Thus a battle that was too advanced risked remaining sterile in the sense that it could not find the necessary support in Parliament to overcome the hostility of those groups directly threatened.'[49] Indeed, if the economic crisis was the official reason for postponing reform, it is impossible to escape the impression that major corporate groups – the building industry, the financial barons of the ex-electricity trusts, Bonomi's rural lobby – were the real stumbling block, and that Moro was more than susceptible to their pressure.

In June 1964 Moro resigned after a squabble in Parliament over private education. His six months of power had been marked only by procrastination, in notable contrast to Fanfani's determination and sense of urgency in 1962. Worse was to come.

The De Lorenzo Affair and Moro's Second Government, 1964–6

In the summer of 1964, for the first but certainly not the last time in the history of the Republic, there is considerable evidence of an attempt to subvert the democratic order. Antonio Segni, the President of the Republic, had given Moro the task of forming a new government, but seemed increasingly impatient as negotiations between the parties dragged on into July of that year. Segni's own aversion to the formula of the centre-left and his dislike of the Socialists were no great secret. On 15 July 1964, as part of the consultations between the President and the leading political figures, Segni took the very unusual step of summoning to the Quirinale the head of the Carabinieri, General Giovanni De Lorenzo. The event caused a considerable stir, particularly because on the day before negotiations between the four parties of the centre-left had temporarily broken down.

What were the President and the General up to? The answers, and then only some of them, emerged more than five years later when in March 1969 the government, in the wake of a very vigorous press campaign, was forced to appoint a parliamentary commission of inquiry into De Lorenzo's activities.[50]

General Giovanni De Lorenzo was fifty-seven years old in 1964. With his upright bearing, neat moustache and monocle, he was an archetypal army figure, but he also enjoyed the reputation of being a brilliant and intelligent officer. Of Sicilian origin, De Lorenzo had taken a degree in naval engineering at Genoa university, served on the Russian front in the Second World War and was then active in the partisan movement as vice-commander of the CLN's intelligence office. In 1955 he was appointed commanding officer of SIFAR (Servizio Informazioni Forze Armate), the Italian military secret service. During his time at SIFAR, De Lorenzo built up detailed personal files on leading Italian politicians, including such moderate figures as the Social Democratic leader Giuseppe Saragat.[51]

In 1962 De Lorenzo became commander-in-chief of the Carabinieri, and within a few months of his appointment he had created a modern mechanized brigade where previously there had existed only ill-equipped mobile and horse-mounted battalions. The brigade was armed with American M47 tanks and M113 armoured personnel carriers. As Ferruccio Parri, the former partisan leader and Prime Minister, was to write later, De Lorenzo had formed 'his own little personal army, superior in discipline and efficiency to the rest of the armed forces'.[52]

At the beginning of 1964 De Lorenzo evolved his 'Solo' plan, which bore a striking resemblance to the 'Prometheus' plan used by Colonel

George Papadopoulos to establish military government in Greece in 1967. The 'Solo' plan was basically a counter-insurgency plan which was insurgent in itself. Lists of persons who 'posed a danger for public security' were to be drawn up and provision was to be made for their arrest and detention. The exact names on these lists have never been discovered, but there is little doubt that Communists, Socialists and trade unionists figured prominently among them. At the same time prefectures, television and radio stations, telephone and telegraph offices, as well as the headquarters of certain political parties, were all to be occupied. Under De Lorenzo's plan the Carabinieri were to act alone, without the knowledge or the cooperation of the police or the rest of the armed forces. The parliamentary commission which investigated De Lorenzo's activity was split over its interpretation of the plan: the majority, while admitting the dangerous implications of the plan, stressed its *defensive* nature; De Lorenzo had intended to employ it only in the event of an attack on the institutions of the Republic. The minority was convinced rather that the plan was essentially *preventive* in character; De Lorenzo had intended to strike first, in order to destroy a threat which may or may not have existed.[53]

In June 1964, at the height of the government crisis, De Lorenzo gave orders for the Solo plan to be prepared in detail at a local level. However, his scheming, although obviously dangerous, had that incomplete and in some respects farcical character which has characterized all the plots against the Republic since 1964. The Carabinieri were to act alone because De Lorenzo knew he could not rely on support from the other sections of the armed forces. One mechanized brigade, however up-to-date, was hardly enough to make a coup in a country with the Resistance traditions of Italy. Even within the Carabinieri there were serious doubts about the Solo plan. In Rome and Naples De Lorenzo's immediate subordinates did little to render the plan operational. In Milan General Adamo Markert took things more seriously. As General Remo Aurigo recounted to the parliamentary inquiry: 'I should note that when the division commander indicated that one of the objectives we would have to occupy was the office of the prefect, he included the fact that if the prefect offered opposition, we were supposed to take him into custody, if necessary with pistol in hand. We were all taken aback by this and said to one another: "What do we have to do, carry out a *coup d'état?*"'[54]

It has never been established how much the President of the Republic knew of these goings-on in the Carabinieri barracks. Segni was certainly not interested in a *coup d'état*. He was, however, seriously contemplating an end to the centre-left, the appointment of a 'non-political' government made up of civil servants and perhaps the increase of presidential powers along Gaullist lines. De Gaulle himself, at a reception at the Elysée palace on 1 July

1964, had remarked that Italy seemed to be in the same state as France had been at the end of the Fourth Republic. There was little truth in such a comparison, and Segni was hardly de Gaulle.

None the less, Segni knew that the appointment of a government of 'experts' and a possible increase in presidential power would encounter very strong opposition, both inside and outside Parliament. He wanted, therefore, to avoid another fiasco along the lines of 1960, and to increase the state's capacity to deal with public disorder. This was where De Lorenzo came in.[55]

A trial of strength of such dimensions would have been the gravest crisis that the Republic had faced. It was averted by Nenni and the Socialists, who quickly abandoned all political quibbling. Nenni had no clear idea of what De Lorenzo was up to, but he was afraid of the right, suspicious of Segni and had been in Italian politics long enough to know when danger was in the air. Moro was able to form his second government with the Socialists by the beginning of August 1964. At the same time Nenni, reflecting on the crisis that had just ended, wrote in *Avanti!*: 'The parties and Parliament suddenly realized that they could be bypassed. The alternative ... would have been an emergency government, entrusted to so-called eminent personalities, to persons of technical expertise, to disinterested servants of the state. In Italy today that would have meant a government of the right – fascist, industrialist and land-owning in character. July 1960 would have been nothing in comparison to it.'[56]

As for De Lorenzo, in 1965 he was made Chief of Staff of the Army, one step away from the most important post in the Italian armed services, the Defence Chief of Staff. However, in 1966 the SIFAR scandal broke, with extracts from De Lorenzo's SIFAR file on Saragat being published in a weekly magazine. De Lorenzo was quickly relieved of his command. The parliamentary commission of 1969, although very critical of De Lorenzo, refused to recommend action against him. In the meanwhile, he had been elected to Parliament as a Monarchist, and once there he transferred his allegiance to the neo-Fascists of the MSI. De Lorenzo died in 1973.

The Socialists had averted a major crisis, but they had also been bludgeoned by the threat of it back into Moro's arms, and in conditions not of their own choosing. The programme and composition of Moro's second government were both more moderate than those of its predecessor. Gone were the sweeping promises of barely six months previously, and gone too were the ministers who had represented Fanfani's supporters in the DC and Lombardi's in the PSI. For the first time, the Confindustria gave a cautious welcome to a centre-left government.

Moro's second government lasted nearly three times longer than his first (until February 1966), but achieved just as little. All the reforms which were supposed to be the hallmarks of the centre-left – town planning, housing, regional government, education, economic planning, etc. – were quietly postponed. Moro continued to emphasize the need for a 'two-phase' policy (first stability and then reform), and the Socialists acquiesced reluctantly. They were, to tell the truth, somewhat less reluctant than before. Gradually, the Socialists were shifting their priorities away from structural reform or even 'digging round the tree of reaction', towards the more limited affirmation that their presence in the government was the best defence against reaction. The major task was to ensure the survival of the centre-left. It was the form that now mattered the most, not the content.[57]

As the PSI changed, so the differences between it and the PSDI became less and less apparent. Nenni and Saragat began to talk of reunification, with the hope, perennial to the Socialists, of becoming a major electoral force which stood between the Communists and the Christian Democrats. Cooperation between the two parties received a substantial boost when Saragat was elected President of the Republic in 1964. Shortly after the July crisis, Segni had been struck by partial paralysis, and the fight for his succession, between Fanfani and Saragat, was waged furiously over twenty-one ballots. With the backing of the Communists, Saragat finally emerged victorious. Nenni hailed this as a highly significant victory, the first time that a President of the Republic had belonged to the Socialist camp. Certainly, Saragat was something of a relief after Segni, but his term of office, as we shall see, was hardly to be a distinguished one.[58]

Moro's Third Government, 1966–8

In February 1966, Moro's second government fell, but was immediately replaced by his third. This time there was no threat to democracy, no De Lorenzo lurking in the wings, and Moro was able to reach agreement without difficulty with the Socialists, Social Democrats and Republicans. His third government was to last over two years, until June 1968.

Once again, the government's chief characteristic was its immobility. There was even less excuse for this than previously. The economy was recovering strongly, the balance of payments showed a comfortable surplus, real wages had hardly risen at all and workers' militancy was at a low ebb.[59] It was true that the business classes continued to invest very sparsely, but this could hardly be attributed any longer to the threat posed to them by the centre-left.

Occasionally, the torpor into which Moro had successfully lulled everyone was disturbed temporarily. In July 1966 new high-rise buildings in Agrigento in Sicily, built without planning permission on the hillside overlooking the city's ancient Greek temples, began to collapse and cause a landslide. The public outcry was great, and was reinforced by the terrible floods in Florence and Venice in November of that year. All three 'natural calamities' could have been avoided had the centre-left passed proper laws on town planning and the defence of the environment.

The government responded with Mancini's *'legge ponte'* (bridging law) of 1967, another in the long series of Italian laws which have been presented as stopgap measures preceding a real reform which never materializes. Mancini's law did nothing to help Florence or Venice, nor could it be compared with Sullo's earlier proposals. However, it did establish that private landowners and not the state had in future to pay the costs of 'primary urbanization' (roads, electricity, gas, etc.), and part of the costs of 'secondary urbanization' (schools, parks, etc.). In 1968 two important ministerial decrees also laid down limits to the density of construction along roadsides, and established the ratio between built-up areas and public spaces. All this was then vitiated by a moratorium on the *legge ponte*, postponing it for a year (until September 1968) in order to try and boost the building trade. The result was that 1968 became a bumper year for building permits, as speculators and others rushed to beat the government's deadline. A million permits were granted, and further irreparable damage was done to the Italian landscape.[60]

Apart from this rather less than successful foray into the urban jungle, Moro's government did remarkably little. Pieraccini, the Socialist Minister of the Budget, did succeed in getting an economic programming law passed in 1967, but its provisions were never put into practice. Gui, the Minister of Education, presented a law to reform the universities, but it never came to a vote in Parliament, and was to be swept away by student discontent.

The PSI finally united with the PSDI in 1966, the new party taking the name of PSU (Partito Socialista Unificato). By now the Socialists were very much a party of government. Not only had structural reforms been quietly forgotten, but there was evidence that some parts of the party were becoming as clientelistic and corrupt as the DC. In January 1962 the Socialist deputy Leonetto Amadei had promised Parliament that the turn to the left would mean a 'new morality' in public life, 'a new relationship between the citizen and the state'.[61] But by the end of the decade the first accusations concerning the Socialists' abuse of state power were being made. Giacomo Mancini, the Minister of Public Works and later secretary of the party, came under especially heavy fire.[62]

Conclusion

By 1968 it had become clear that of the three views on reform – the corrective, the structural and the minimalist – it was the minimalist that had triumphed. The various programmes of the centre-left governments bore no relation to their achievements. Few reforms had been passed, and then nearly always in a heavily qualified form: the electricity industry had been nationalized, but in a way which left the ex-trusts with enormous financial power; the withholding tax on stock dividends had been watered down in April 1964; the most that could be managed on the key question of town planning was the 1967 'bridging law', the application of which was promptly postponed for a year. Compulsory secondary schooling till the age of fourteen had been achieved, but the archaic content and organization of secondary and university education had hardly been touched. Pieraccini's law on economic programming sank without a trace. There had been no fiscal reform, no reform of the state bureaucracy, no introduction of a national health system, no reform of agrarian contracts or the Federconsorzi. Even the establishment of regional government, so often promised as an 'absolute priority', had not come into effect. All in all, this was a very unimpressive record.

In seeking to explain why this was so, we need to spend few words on the failure to realize structural reform. Within the centre-left, only Lombardi's faction really believed in structural reform. Lacking the active support of the PCI and the PSIUP, there was no possibility of making the centre-left the initial stage of a transition to socialism. As Basso argued, only the united action of the left, accompanied by massive popular mobilization, could have realized any of Lombardi's dreams. Even then, as has been suggested above, civil war was as likely an outcome as structural reform.

The real question is, rather, why corrective reform was not achieved. Here what is immediately striking is the isolation of the 'Autonomist' Socialists both inside and outside of Parliament. They received initial support from the Fanfani wing of the DC, and rather more consistent support from the Republicans and Social Democrats, but the forces they could muster did not begin to compare with those available to the left in the period 1945–8. The PCI, at this stage, was not prepared to campaign actively on a programme of corrective reforms, and was convinced, rightly, that structural reform and the transition to socialism could not begin from the premise of a coalition with the DC. All the Communists in the CGIL and the majority of Socialist trade unionists agreed with this point of view. By the time the left of the PSI split away to form the PSIUP in January 1964, Nenni's 'army of reform' had been reduced to very modest dimensions.

Even amongst those Socialists who remained committed to the centre-left there reigned considerable confusion. Men like La Malfa, Saraceno and Sullo had a far clearer view of the extent and limits of corrective reform than did Nenni and the Socialists. Indeed, the gap between ideology and action, always a problem in Italy, was macroscopic in the Socialists' case. The Socialists in the centre-left veered between two extremes. At the outset Nenni and his faction insisted, as we have seen, that social-democratic reforms were not worth making. However, the more they trumpeted the less they risked achieving, for the language of structural reform was bound to alienate those progressive elements in Italian society which had given a cautious welcome to the centre-left. For many Italians, the Socialists became synonymous with anti-capitalism, and Nenni's blue beret as potent a symbol as the red cap of the French Revolution. Then, after De Lorenzo, the Socialists rapidly passed to the other extreme. By making it clear that they would stay in the government at almost any cost, they allowed the pressure for reform to dwindle, and the first elements of governmental clientelism to develop in their midst. Lombardi's mountain thus became Mancini's mole-hill.

Outside Parliament, the forces militating against corrective reform proved far stronger than anticipated. FIAT, ENI and IRI had all seemed in favour of a programme of modernization and government planning, but in the period of 1962–8 they exercised no hegemony over Italian capital as a whole. Instead it was the seemingly less powerful elements who predominated: Confindustria and the myriad of small businesses who supported it, the ex-electrical trusts and the financial interests they controlled, the building speculators. Probably these two worlds – those of 'progressive' and 'parasitic' capital – were far less separate than the reformists believed. The Agnelli family was not above land speculation any more than the electricity barons were against investing in modern industry. What is certain is that very considerable sections of the Italian capitalist class did all they could to undermine the centre-left from 1962 onwards. Inflation, the flight of capital, the crisis of the stock exchange and the persistent investment strike were all body blows which La Malfa and others tried to counter in vain. Significant sections of Italy's economic élites once again showed themselves to be short-sighted in the extreme. They were the real saboteurs of corrective reform, ably seconded at a critical moment by an irresponsible President of the Republic and an adventurist commander-in-chief of the Carabinieri.

To combat such formidable opposition, the reformers needed much more consistent support from within the ranks of the Christian Democrats. This was not forthcoming. Moro was no more a committed reformist than the Dorotei were, and he was happiest mediating between conflicting elements in a way that nearly always resulted in immobility. Moro was a master political tactician, but with little sense of the real needs of a rapidly changing country. His governments were long lasting but essentially empty.

There can be few doubts as to the relative merits in this period of the DC's two 'thoroughbreds' (as they were called at the time), Fanfani and Moro. Fanfani was much the less attractive personality, abrasive, arrogant, always convinced he was right, while Moro was reflective, courteous and shy. Fanfani, however, achieved more in his one government than Moro did in his three.

Thus, as Salvati has pointed out, the Italians managed to achieve neither the French nor the Austrian model of modernization. In the France of the Fifth Republic, a strong conservative political leadership, closely allied with the most dynamic elements of French capital, pushed through a modernizing programme based on very high levels of investment. In Austria the Social Democrats, working in close alliance with the trade union movement, both modernized and carried through a series of corrective reforms.[63] In Italy the decade of dynamic economic growth, 1958–68, was a time of missed political opportunity. Corrective reform was not achieved, and the consequences for the social history of the Republic were not slow to manifest themselves.

The State in the 1960s

Far from the 1960s going down as the decade of reform, they saw instead the marked decline of key areas of the state apparatus. The centre-left governments had announced, more than once, their intention of reforming the state along rational, efficient and democratic lines. The state's actual development was in a quite different direction.

a. THE DECLINE OF PUBLIC ENTERPRISE

In the 1950s public enterprise in Italy had, by and large, been a success story. IRI had won the attention and admiration of many economic observers outside Italy. Sinigaglia's plan for steel had been a resounding success and an important element in the Italian 'miracle'. ENI had hardly been run in an exemplary fashion, but no one could deny the entrepreneurial genius of Mattei, or ENI's dynamism while under his control.

This picture changes significantly in the course of the next decade. The major programmes of the 1950s – the development of steel, the building of *autostrade* and the expansion of the telephone network – were coming to an end, without any strategic indication of where state enterprise was going next. At the same time, it became increasingly free of controls. Public enterprise was significantly less self-financing than the major private firms and was heavily dependent on public money, which it obtained all too easily; its various activities were not subject to the scrutiny of any independent body of senior civil servants; its nominal head, the Minister of Public Holdings, was no more than the lapdog of one or other of the DC factions (first the Base and then the Fanfaniani). In the period 1963–72, state industry achieved minimal levels of profitability. IRI's last good year was 1963, after which it showed losses for five of the following nine years. ENI achieved modest results until 1969, after which it too dipped into the red. Other state enterprises showed heavy losses for the whole decade.[64]

Such developments were not uncommon elsewhere in Europe, but in Italy they assumed a pathology all of their own. Political power and industrial management became ever more closely intertwined, with disastrous results. More and more jobs in the state enterprises were assigned not on the grounds of merit or competence but on those of party or factional loyalty. *Lottizzazione*, the practice of dividing among the governing parties the command posts of the public sector, became the order of the day.[65]

Guido Carli, the Governor of the Bank of Italy from 1960 to 1975, declared that this period witnessed the growth of what he termed a 'state bourgeoisie'. This term has been used rather widely and loosely, and excessive claims have been made for the 'state bourgeoisie's' homogeneity and for its political as well as economic dominance. None the less, there was no denying the growth in the number and influence of employees in the state sector, most of them appointed, even in the lower echelons, on the principle of *lottizzazione*. At the top, a new generation of public managers and entrepreneurs, very closely linked with the dominant political parties, not only wielded considerable power but also diverted substantial amounts of public funds into private channels.[66]

The most spectacular example of the sixties' 'state bourgeoisie' was Mattei's successor at ENI, Eugenio Cefis. Sharp-witted, financially competent and blessed with outstanding business acumen, Cefis was also cynical, unprincipled and extremely ambitious. He enjoyed the political support above all of Fanfani and the powerful Dorotei leaders of the Veneto and Trentino (Rumor, Antonio Bisaglia and Flaminio Piccoli). By the mid-1960s, Cefis was no longer content with being, in Piccoli's words, one of the government's best captains of industry.[67] He had set his sights, instead, on the giant Montedison chemical company, which had been formed in 1966 through the fusion of Montecatini and the former electrical company, Edison. The fusion, bitterly opposed on anti-monopolistic grounds by the PCI and by the Lombardi Socialists, gave Montedison control of nearly 80 per cent of the Italian chemical industry and 15 per cent of the European market.

Right from the start the new giant was in serious trouble. It had no

284

clear command structure, much useless duplication of activity and a long tail of unprofitable companies. While president of ENI, Cefis began secretly buying up shares in the Montedison company. By 1968 he exercised effective control, and three years later he left ENI to become president of Montedison. His move was a much contested one. ENI (and thus public) funds had been used in vast quantities to gain control of Montedison, without there being any debate as to the advisability of such a strategy. Montedison itself showed increasing losses in the period 1970–72. Cefis was undeterred. By the early 1970s he stood at the head of a considerable empire, which stretched from Montedison through the ownership of major newspapers, to the financing of political parties and close links with the secret services.[68]

Cefis was the most dynamic and ruthless of the public managers of the sixties, but he was not alone: Raffaele Girotti, Leopoldo Medugno and many others constituted a group which owed their fortunes (and misfortunes) to the interlinking of political power and public enterprise. With men such as these at the head of the public sector, a further reason for the failure of corrective reform becomes apparent. Public enterprise, although nominally in favour of the centre-left, presented no 'progressive' alternative model, and as such could hardly be expected to offer an alternative leadership. The ethos of Cefis or Girotti was little different from that of Edison's Giorgio Valerio. The minimalism of the Dorotei therefore corresponded perfectly to the attitudes of the most powerful public managers. Corrective reform was anathema to them because it called into question the basis of their power, which lay in the interweaving of party political power, private interest and public enterprise.

b. THE ATROPHY OF THE PUBLIC ADMINISTRATION

There is very little empirical research on developments within the Italian bureaucracy in the 1960s. However, it was clear enough that here too the state's physiognomy was not conducive to reform. Putnam's comparative analysis of Western European bureaucrats, carried out in 1973, confirmed some of the alarming characteristics of the upper echelons of Italy's bureaucracy.[69] In Italy, 95 per cent of the senior civil servants had entered the service before 1943. For them 'it was not so much Italian political life as democracy *in se* and *per se* that was uncongenial'. Nearly half of those interviewed expressed reservations about universal suffrage. Suspicion of innovation was endemic.

Closely connected with these attitudes was the growth in the 1960s of two phenomena which were to become major stumbling-blocks to reform: the *'residui passivi'* and the non-implementation of reforms that had become law. The *residui passivi* were sums of money that had been allocated for a certain piece of legislation, but had not been spent in the time allowed for their use. Once unspent, they reverted to the Treasury. The main reason for failure to use allocated funds lay in the complicated juridical and administrative net which 'protected' new legislation. This net ensured, to quote Cassese, that 'procedures became blocked, administrative non-realization of programmes became systematic and the money set aside for their realization remained, to an increasing extent, unused'.[70]

Laws that remained dead letters were part and parcel of the same process. Giorgio Ruffolo was the secretary responsible for economic programming for much of the sixties. He found to his dismay that economic planning could make little headway, not only because of lack of political will, but also because of the inadequacies and hostility of the bureaucracy. The rigid application of different roles and areas of responsibility fragmented any decision-making process; the technical preparation of laws (wording, etc.) often produced baroque constructions which then had to be interpreted by other parts of the state administration and sometimes completely reformulated; the suspicion of senior civil servants was expressed in exasperating delays which amounted to effective vetoes.

Even at an international level, the same defects were glaringly apparent. Italian agriculture, as we have seen, did less well out of the Common Market than its French and German counterparts, but those benefits which were offered to Italy were often left unused. It has been calculated that by the end of 1974, of the grants given to Italy by the orientation section of the E A G G F for structural projects for the decade 1965–74, only 15 per cent had been spent, compared to 37 per cent in France, 53 per cent in Germany and 55 per cent in Holland. Administrative paralysis was the principal culprit, but this in turn depended at least in part on Italian juridical culture. The administration was able to apply only law which had been 'incorporated' into the national legal code. New laws had to be formulated to ratify Common Market regulations, which in other countries of the E E C had been applied directly.[71]

c. THE CONSOLIDATION OF SOUTHERN CLIENTELISM
At a local level, above all in the Mezzogiorno, the decade of the Dorotei saw a much more systematic clientelism than previously, based on the constant appropriation of the state's expanding resources. All over the South, the 'young Turks' of the D C firmly took over the reins of local government. Prominent among them were Antonio Gava at Naples, Giovanni Gioia and then Salvo Lima at Palermo, Antonino Drago at Catania, Nino Gullotti at Messina. Many of them indulged in the rhetoric of renewal. Gioia's campaign slogans in Palermo at the end of the fifties stressed the need for a stricter morality in party and public life, and for an unceasing

struggle against clientelism. Antonino Drago spoke in Catania of the necessity 'for young people to flock into our party sections, bringing with them the purity and enthusiasm of their youth, and their passionate contribution to our debates'.[72] This was the official morality. The actual practice of the new city bosses was, as we shall see, quite another.

These local leaders, most of whom acquired themselves unenviable reputations, were very closely linked with one or other of the major national figures in the DC. Gullotti in Messina was the protégé of the Dorotei leader Mariano Rumor; Antonino Drago, as has been said, received the protection and support of Emilio Colombo; Antonio Gava, before becoming a national leader in his own right, gained vital backing from the major Dorotei figures. However, such links were not confined merely to the dominant faction in the DC. The leaders in Palermo, Gioia and Lima, who earned their city a sad primacy for misgovernment, were both until 1968 major figures in Fanfani's faction. While, therefore, at a national level it is possible to make a distinction, at least in the early 1960s, between Fanfani's commitment to reform and the Dorotei's minimalism, at a local level their mode of practice was identical. If anything, Fanfani emerges with the more tarnished reputation, thanks to the misdeeds of his lieutenants at Palermo.

The Christian Democrats' control of the South in the 1960s derived from four major economic sources: the building boom of these years, the new southern poles of industrial development, the expanding resources of local government and hand-outs from central government funds.

If we look first at the building boom, the pell-mell expansion of the southern cities was a case-study in the triumph of private interests over public needs. The monstrous, unplanned sprawl of cities like Naples and Palermo was founded on the close collaboration between building speculators, proprietors and local administrators. In each of these cities the key role was played by the assessor of public works, whose office has overall responsibility for town planning. At Palermo, dominated as we have seen by Fanfani's faction, two insalubrious figures were assessors of public works in the crucial period 1956–64: Salvo Lima, from 1956 to 1958, after which he became mayor; and Vito Ciancimino, from July 1959 to July 1964.

During the 'golden era' of Lima and Ciancimino, Palermo expanded dramatically towards the north-west. At the extreme north-western periphery the public-works department purchased cheap agricultural land for the construction of public housing, and then provided the major infrastructures – streets, water, electricity, etc. – to link the periphery to the centre. As a result, the land that lay between increased by as much as ten times in value. As Chubb has written, with commendable restraint: 'certain clearly defined property interests were at stake in the areas favoured by the city administration'. When the so-called regulatory plan was approved by the city council in 1959, some six hundred 'variations' accompanied it, all of which tended to increase building density or infringe on land reserved for public use.[73]

Such abuses were common throughout Italy, and southern Italy in particular. Palermo was an extreme case, made even worse by the collusion between city administrators and the Mafia. As the agrarian sector became less important, the major Mafia families moved their attention to the cities, and especially to Palermo. The construction industry and the municipal wholesale markets became their strongholds, and Vito Ciancimino their favoured interlocutor in city government. In 1964 Ciancimino was forced to resign in the wake of accusations by the national anti-Mafia commission. But by 1970 he was back, and for two months in that year he actually became mayor of Palermo. Only in 1975 did the D C exclude him from their electoral lists. Nine years later, in 1984, Ciancimino was arrested as the principal political figure accused by the former Mafia boss, Tommaso Buscetta, of extensive collusion with the Mafia.[74]

Chubb has painted a convincing picture of how the Christian Democrats, through their administrative control of the building boom, were able to maintain the support of the major sections of Palermo's population. At the highest income levels, landowners, real-estate brokers and building contractors worked hand in glove with the city administrators. So too did firms dealing in home furnishings, amassing fortunes through the sale of modern kitchen and bathroom units. The building boom also benefited significant sections of the professional and technical middle class – engineers, architects, surveyors and draughtsmen. It brought prosperity to artisans and small manufacturing firms, especially producers and transporters of building supplies; it offered continuous employment to thousands of skilled and unskilled workers; it provided the *ceti medi* with the real prospect of owning a modern flat for the first time, and the lower classes with the chimera of public housing projects.[75]

Poor Sullo! No wonder his town-planning reform of 1962–3 never saw the light of day. A model of urban development such as Palermo's, even if it involved, as it did, corruption, collusion with the Mafia, unchecked building speculation and the elimination of public amenities like parks, was not one which either Fanfani or Moro was prepared to forgo. Its value as a mechanism for gaining consent on an inter-class basis was too high, and any reform like Sullo's threatened its very being.

The second economic axis upon which the southern Christian Democrats moved was that of the state's selective industrialization of the Mezzogiorno (see pp. 229–30). The new poles of development and the '*territori di sistemazione*' gave the southern bosses access to unprecedented sources of funds and patronage. From 1965 onwards overall planning was centralized in the hands of the Cassa. Little initiative but a great deal of money was transmitted to the various development agencies and local authorities.

It was probably in the heavily subsidized area of small and medium-sized industry that clientelism was most extensive, and the misuse of public money most widespread. At Salerno, for example, development funds were used to cover the costs of bad management and even for purposes quite removed from those for which they had been allocated. Thus credit obtained for developing a firm's technology would be used instead for speculation on the building market. The local political class, through their control of the development agencies, would do their best to ensure that these abuses never came to light. In return, they could expect a substantial cut of the funds in question, and the right to recommend prospective employees to the local 'entrepreneurs'.[76]

As for the larger firms, the room for clientelistic manoeuvre was less because of the sounder technocratic and managerial bases on which they were founded. In them, commitment to the success of the firm was most often the dominant criterion for action. None the less, there were several spectacular exceptions. After intense pressure from Silvio Gava, the leader of the Neapolitan D C, the state-owned Alfa-Romeo firm decided in 1968 to build a new factory at Pomigliano d'Arco, in the province of Naples. The factory proved a major disaster, with soaring construction costs, a faulty production plan, and clientelism rife at all levels. At Alfasud by the mid-1970s the cost of producing each car exceeded by one million lire the price at which it was sold.[77]

The third resource at the D C's disposal in the South was the constantly expanding local government sector. Here, as we have seen (p. 178), the Christian Democrats gradually tightened their hold on all major local institutions, from the savings banks to the hospitals and the public housing authorities. They also made sure that they dominated the new local government institutions of the 1960s – the municipal authorities for aqueducts and transport, the *consorzi* for the development of *autostrade*, etc. Local government employment continued to be one of the linchpins of the clientelistic system. By 1976 in Palermo, no less than 2,500 dustmen and street cleaners were employed by the municipal garbage collection agency, AMNU. The city was divided into eight zones, each presided over by a *capo-zona*, a sort of foreman with dictatorial powers. Each *capo-zona* had around 250 workers under his direct control, and as such was a key figure both for *raccomandazioni* (recommendations for jobs) and for turning out the vote.[78]

The last source of funds in the South were hand-outs to certain restricted groups in civil society. Pensions took pride of place among these subsidies. Although the total value of pensions was lower in the South than in the North, their relative weight was far greater than it should have been, given the low percentage of the adult population in regular employment (see p. 236). In 1975, the South, with 34 per cent of the country's population, received 31 per cent of all pensions, which was about twice the amount it should have received in strict relation to its working population. In the South disablement pensions (*pensioni di invalidità*) figure very highly, as do 'social' pensions (*pensioni sociali*), which are minimum pensions paid to those who have reached retirement age without having paid regular contributions.[79]

Granted all this, the reform of the state, about which so many words were written in the 1960s, seemed an unlikely event, in strident contrast to the established way of governing in the South. Here, as we have seen, little distinction could be made between the Dorotei, the Fanfaniani, or even the Base faction of the party. Colombo's local power in Basilicata, as Fanfani's in Sicily, De Mita's in Avellino, or Moro's in Puglia, all rested on these same bases. As Gribaudi has rightly written: 'How contradictory it was to expect much in the way of the rationalization of the system from a political stratum who had tailored the inefficiency of the state to its own measure, which had built up its strength by monopolizing the public sector, by the mediation between the ancient and the modern, between a traditional world of subsistence and one with wider horizons.'[80]

The Italian Communist Party in the 1960s

As a counterpoint to the above, it may be worth concluding this chapter with a brief assessment of the great outsider in the 1960s – the PCI. In the decade between 1956 and 1966 the Communist Party lost nearly a quarter of its membership, passing from 2,035,000 members in 1956 to 1,576,000 ten years later. Many of the institutions of its subculture, like the rural and small town Case del Popolo, were thrown into grave crisis by the rapid social transformations of these years. Its youth movement declined rapidly, from 358,000 members in 1956 to 154,000 in 1966. The social composition of the party remained fairly stable. Figures comparing 1954 with 1967 show workers at a steady 40 per cent of the party. The decline in the percentage of rural labourers (17.8 per cent in 1954, 10.4 per cent in 1967) and peasant proprietors (16.2 to 12.4 per cent) reflected the great rural exodus of the early sixties. The most disquieting element in these statistics was the gradual ageing of the party – the percentage of pensioners increased from 4.4 to 13.8 per cent.[81] The golden age of recruitment to the party had long since passed. Excluded, *a priori*, from the 'opening to the left', the PCI found itself forced into the somewhat sterile role of a semi-permanent opposition.

None the less, the number of votes that the party received rose slowly but significantly; in 1963, as we have seen, the party exceeded 25 per cent of the poll for the first time. The PCI, despite its political isolation and its inability to recruit youth to its ranks, remained a great force in Italian society. The PCI-dominated cooperative league had two million members, organized in 7,000 cooperatives with 8,000 retail outlets. There were still 200,000 members of UDI (Unione delle Donne Italiane) and the party organized, in one form or another, 1,300 sporting societies and 3,000 cultural and recreational circles. Between 8 and 10 per cent of the Italian press was in Communist hands: *L'Unità* sold more copies than any other daily except *Corriere della Sera*, and it was flanked by important local newspapers, such as *Paese Sera* in Rome and *L'Ora* in Palermo. Thus by the mid-1960s the party, though slimmer than a decade earlier, was organizationally very much intact.

a. THE DEATH OF TOGLIATTI

On 21 August 1964, Togliatti died at Yalta in the Soviet Union, where he had gone to meet Khrushchev. His funeral in Rome was attended by an estimated one million people. Togliatti had led the party through an extraordinarily successful transformation from a small group of militants to the largest Communist organization in the Western world. This creation of the mass party was his greatest achievement. It is true that the circumstances of the post-war period were on his side, but it is enough to look at the fate of the Italian Socialists to understand that there was nothing preordained about the PCI's success. Between 1944 and 1947 Togliatti refused to allow adventurism to triumph in the party. Instead he guided it away from insurrectionary temptations (which would have ended in catastrophe) towards a more painstaking Gramscian strategy: deep-seated entrenchment in civil society and a long 'war of position' were to be the prerequisites for the transition to socialism.[82]

Togliatti also, on more than one occasion, demonstrated a notable capacity for recognizing changing circumstances and past errors, and for adapting the party accordingly. It was Togliatti who responded to Khruschev in 1956 with a more fundamental reappraisal than that of any other Western Communist leader. The dominant themes of his last years were polycentrism, freer intellectual debate and greater cultural liberalism within the party. In the last article he wrote, which has come to be known as the Yalta Memorandum, Togliatti defended the Chinese Communists from instant excommunication from the Communist world, and insisted that the PCI should widen still further its cultural horizons: 'We must become the champions of intellectual freedom, of free artistic creation and of scientific progress.'[83]

Togliatti's achievements were thus very considerable, but it would be wrong to accept the PCI's predominantly a-critical and hagiographical treatment of him. His long experience as one of Stalin's lieutenants made his political praxis, even after 1945, profoundly authoritarian, hierarchical and undemocratic.[84] Working-class politics was always viewed from the top downwards; it was the party leadership who, in the last analysis, decided anything of importance. Autonomous working-class action was extolled, but only within the context of overall party control. The party itself was not a democratic organization but a closely controlled transmission belt. From the Stalinist tradition, too, came Togliatti's willingness to allow a personality cult to grow up around him. All this, when combined with the slavish acceptance of Russian propaganda in the years 1944–56, made it easier to build a mass party based on certain historic myths, but more difficult to convince sceptical Italians that the PCI's view of socialism had much to do with either liberty or democracy.

Above all, by the time of Togliatti's death, there was little to demonstrate that his greatest strategic legacy, the 'Italian road to socialism', really was what it said it was. By 1964 the vision of a gradual and hopefully peaceful transition to socialism, with the working class slowly becoming the ruling class, was open to at least two orders of doubt. One has already been mentioned in the context of structural reform. The key to Togliatti's strategy (as to Lombardi's) was the realization of a series of radical reforms which would open the way to the transition from capitalism to socialism. However, there was very little evidence to show that such reforms could be achieved in Italy without engendering a major confrontation with the ruling élites. The experience of the centre-left had, on the contrary, given ample warning of the capacity and vigour of the conservative elements of the Italian ruling class. They had successfully sabotaged reforms far more moderate than those Togliatti had in mind. In any confrontation with them, the left, enjoying the allegiance of little more than a third of the Italians, was not in a hegemonic position, and was not likely to win.

The second doubt concerned the capacity of the PCI to maintain indefinitely an alternative political vision. The longer the party remained becalmed in the relatively placid waters of the Republic, the more likely it was to be slowly transformed by this experience rather than itself initiate a process of socialist transformation. As the years passed, so the integration of the PCI into the political system became more evident, and its aims and language more limited. The Italian road, therefore, seemed to lead not to socialism but to a choice between two unwanted destinations: either, through an insistence on structural reform, to open confrontation and possible civil war; or, through a slow but consistent process of integration, to the acceptance of a more limited and social-democratic role in Italian society.

b. AMENDOLA AND INGRAO

These dilemmas surfaced in an explicit way in the major debate which took place within the PCI in these years, and which reached its climax with the eleventh congress of the party in January 1966. Luigi Longo, the wartime leader of the northern PCI, took over as party secretary after Togliatti's death, but it was generally recognized that he did so in a caretaker capacity. On either side of him, the left and the right of the party clashed in a more open way than ever before. Giorgio Amendola and Giorgio Napolitano were the leading spokesmen for the right, while Pietro Ingrao came to be seen as the leader of the left.

The two wings of the party had diametrically opposed interpretations of the centre-left and of the lessons that were to be drawn from it. For Amendola and his supporters the 'opening to the left' had clearly been a failure. Reforms had not taken place and the problems of Italian society were too intractable for so small a band of reformists to be able to solve. In Amendola's opinion, a new crisis was imminent. With its arrival, the way would be open for the PCI to make further electoral gains, and stake its claim to govern the country. The PSI would abandon its ill-fated alliance with the DC and move once again towards cooperation with the Communists. In order to show the necessity for unity on the left, Amendola proposed provocatively the unification of the PCI with the PSI. Together, he argued, the two parties would be the core of a real reformist alliance in the country, and one which would carry through the reforms which the centre-left had abandoned. Amendola stressed that the next phase in the history of the Republic would not be socialist but democratic. What was necessary was full employment, better salaries and pensions, and more public spending on houses, schools and hospitals. Amendola still paid lip-service to the transitional nature of this programme (it would have been heresy to have done otherwise), but its actual content was essentially corrective.[85]

Ingrao's analysis of the centre-left was quite different, and more pessimistic. According to him, there was a real danger that significant sections of the working-class movement could be integrated into the system by means of progressive neo-capitalist policies. The material wealth on which such policies could be based now existed for the first time. For Ingrao the real danger for the PCI in these circumstances was not that of permanent exclusion from government, but of slipping gently towards social democracy.

In order to combat these trends, the left of the P CI called for a 'new historic bloc' of social forces based on anti-capitalist alliances within civil society. The Communists were to organize mass struggles for structural reform, and lead the new workers' agitations in the factories. A network of local power centres and of direct democracy had to be created. The cities and provinces of the country governed by left-wing local administrations could be the starting-points for this process, which would lead eventually to new forms of workers' control.

For Ingrao, then, socialism was on the agenda, but only if the P CI reacted energetically and radically to the siren voices of progressive reformism. In order to do so, the party had first itself to become much more democratic. Ingrao criticized the authoritarian and hierarchical nature of the P CI's 'democratic centralism', and called for greater intra-party democracy. A truly democratic P CI would serve as a model for future socialist political organization.[86]

The language of the debate was a carefully codified one, and neither side made their points as explicitly as they have been made above. When the eleventh congress met in January 1966, it soon became obvious that the left was very much in the minority. The leadership made a number of gestures in their direction, and Amendola certainly did not get everything his own way; but on all the major issues – party democracy, the nature and implications of structural reform and the question of alliances – Ingrao's supporters were heavily defeated. After the congress, various leaders of the left were removed from positions of influence. Ingrao himself, though defeated and much criticized, remained firmly committed to the P CI and accepted the majority line.

The left lost the eleventh congress for a number of reasons. They were not, in the first place, an organized group in any way, but rather a mixture of very heterogeneous elements. They had no national structure (factions were strictly prohibited), and their support was very patchy in the country as a whole. Ingrao himself was rather a reluctant leader, and his alternative programme remained very vague at certain crucial points. In at least one way his opposition came late in the day, because workers' militancy had been at its height in 1960–62, and was in the doldrums by 1966.

Above all, the leadership of the party, Longo and Enrico Berlinguer, were much closer to Amendola than to Ingrao, whose policies seemed to them a dangerous departure from Togliatti's middle way. Once the leadership had made up its mind, it was impossible for the left to make progress. All the reins of the party were in the secretariat's hands, all the full-time officers were dependent on it for their livelihood and all the rank and file of the party had been educated to loyalty, not debate. Ingrao and Amendola had both raised important questions, but it was to be a long time before they were answered.[87]

c. EMILIA-ROMAGNA IN THE 1960s

It was only in the Red Belt of central Italy that the Communists held power in the 1960s, and it was here that they could attempt to present an alternative vision of modern politics (see also pp. 200–204). The 'economic miracle' brought striking changes to Emilia-Romagna as to elsewhere in Italy. The percentage of the population active in agriculture in the region fell from 51.7 per cent in 1951 to only 20 per cent in 1971. All the major cities along the Via Emilia, *'la città lineare'*, Reggio Emilia, Parma, Modena, Bologna, Forlì, registered dramatic increases in their population. As elsewhere in the Third Italy, small-scale industrial concerns predominated. Most factories in Emilia-Romagna in the 1960s were metal-works, employing between ten and fifty workers. There were also two centres of specialist production which had acquired international importance: the ceramic works at Sassuolo-Scandiano; and the many hosiery workshops at Carpi.[88]

The Communists' first regional conference, at Bologna in 1959, saw decisive changes in policy and leadership. At the conference Giorgio Amendola argued with great vigour that the Emilian Communists could no longer base their policies upon an agrarian reality that was disappearing before their eyes. Small industry had come to dominate the region, and it was high time to respond with 'new political and social alliances'. This was the view also of the new generation of local leaders, men like Renato Zangheri, Guido Fanti and Umbro Lorenzini. These were young intellectuals and professional men, trained in the party schools, and they gradually replaced the older leaders like Alfeo Corassori, the mayor of Modena, who had been a landless labourer and partisan. Dozza, the much-loved mayor of Bologna, finally made way for Fanti in 1966. This new generation of Communists took over the reins of local government at much the same time as the DC 'young Turks' did in the South, but with rather different results.

Guido Fanti explained their strategy at the regional conference of 1959. Monopoly capital, he argued, exercised a stranglehold over the entire economy of Emilia-Romagna. It controlled prices, credit, and the supply of raw materials and essential machinery. The objective conditions therefore existed for an alliance against it, consisting of nearly all sections of the region's population, *including* the local industrialists and employers.[89] This was, of course, the same line of argument that Lombardi had used on a national scale when appealing to 'progressive capital'.

The alliance between employers and employed, apparently heretical, was justified by a redefiniton of Communist aims. As Fanti and Zangheri wrote later, their ideology was 'to be stripped of its egalitarian element, which had its origin in the struggles of the landless labourers'.[90] This abandoment of economic equality as a prime objective placed the Emilian leaders firmly within the reformist wing of the party. They had little time for Eastern-bloc socialism, and if they still referred periodically to the 'revolutionary force of the Emilian working-class movement', their real interest was in guiding and responding to the rapid process of modernization that was taking place in their region.

In examining their policies in the 1960s, it is probably most instructive to concentrate again on the city of Bologna, which gradually became a Communist showpiece. In 1963 Fanti announced that the municipal accounts would go into deficit for the first time. 'Healthy and honest administration' along Dozza's lines was no longer enough. More money was needed to realize the twin planks of Communist policy: on the one hand to provide subsidies and facilities for local industry and the *ceti medi* in general; on the other to continue Dozza's work of providing Bologna with first-rate social services and cheap and effective public transport. These notably different objectives were pursued with great success in the sixties. Local business and commerce discovered that the Communist administration was far from hostile to them, and that it could do much to ensure good labour relations.[91]

In the field of social services, Bologna by the early seventies had an enviable reputation for efficency and comprehensiveness. Public transport was both cheap and plentiful. As for housing, the municipal authorities made the most they could out of the limited possibilities offered to them by the law no. 167 of April 1962. Whereas in Rome between 1963 and 1968 only 7.4 per cent of rooms constructed formed part of the *'Piani di Edilizia Economica e Popolare'* ('Plans for Economic and Popular Housing'), and in Milan only 15 per cent, in Bologna the figure was 34.7 per cent. At the same time a real effort was made not to exile the working class to the extreme periphery of the city. Indro Montanelli complained bitterly of the ugliness of the new Bolognese suburbs, 'all vomit-coloured cement barracks', but even he had to admit that the worst aspects of chaotic growth had been avoided.[92]

In September 1960 the municipal council divided the city into fifteen neighbourhoods (*quartieri*). The intent was to foster a sense of community throughout the city, and to combat the isolation and alienation so typical of areas of recent urbanization. Neighbourhood councils were set up, though at first they had consultative powers only.[93]

Throughout the 1960s, Communist policies proved highly successful. The PCI constantly increased its share of the vote at local elections: in the province of Bologna from 44.8 per cent in 1960 to 46.5 per cent in 1970; in that of Modena from 44.5 to 48.7 per cent in the same period; in the province of Ravenna from 40.4 to 48.9 per cent. In very many ways it could be said that the objectives of the centre-left were realized not by its exponents on a national scale, but by its Communist opponents on a local one. The humane and moderate reformism of La Malfa, based on inter-class alliance, good labour relations and social-service spending, found its home in Communist Bologna.

However, this was not the interpretation that the local Communist leaders wished to put upon their actions. In 1970 Renato Zangheri claimed that a municipal council like Bologna was an 'instrument of popular sovereignty. It refuses to act the role of executor of choices made within the mechanisms of capitalist development. On the contrary, the commune [municipal council] is the bearer of a vision which is antagonistic to these choices. It promotes, within its sphere of action, decisions and initiatives which are capable of establishing the priority of social needs and consumption.'[94]

Such a claim was a grossly inflated one. There was nothing in the Bolognese Communists' actions, as opposed to their words, to suggest that they had refused to act within the mechanisms of capitalist development. On the contrary, they had accepted it, but had tried, in a way that corresponded closely to corrective reform, to modify its worst imbalances and distortions. Indeed, they could have done nothing else, because the powers and resources of Italian local government were far too limited to permit a truly alternative model to develop on a merely local level.

The Bolognese Communists also made much of their attempts to encourage 'moments of self-government' as they called them, both in the neighbourhood councils and within the social services. In reality, these were no more than moments, carefully controlled by a party federation which was not noted for its internal democracy. The experience of Communist-controlled municipal government remained very far removed from Ingrao's vision of it as the initiator of direct democracy.

All in all, Togliatti was nearer the truth when he said that the Emilian model represented 'a civic cohabitation of a higher kind, in which new forms of content, of understanding and of collaboration are establishd in the interests of all working poeple'.[95] For the Italy of the 1960s that was a notable achievement, in striking contrast to the failure of reformism at the national level.

Chapter 9

The Era of Collective Action, 1968–73

B ETWEEN 1962 and 1968 the governments of the centre-left had failed to respond to the multiple needs of a rapidly changing Italy. They had done both too little and too much, in the sense that they had talked endlessly of reform but had then left expectations unfulfilled. From 1968 onwards paralysis from above gave way to movement from below. There followed a most extraordinary period of social ferment, the high season of collective action in the history of the Republic. During it the organization of Italian society was challenged at nearly every level. No single moment in Italy equalled in intensity and in revolutionary potential the events of May 1968 in France, but the Italian protest movement was the most profound and long-lasting in Europe. It spread from the schools and universities into the factories, and then out again into society as a whole.

The Revolt of the Students, 1967–8

a. ORIGINS OF THE STUDENT MOVEMENT

The material bases of the explosion of protest in the Italian universities are to be found in the education reforms of the 1960s. With the introduction in 1962 of compulsory secondary education until the age of fourteen, the number of school students nearly doubled between 1959 and 1969. A mass education system beyond primary school had been created for the first time. It had grave inadequacies – traditional curricula, a shortage of classrooms and textbooks, a lack of teacher training institutions, etc. – but it did open up new horizons for hundreds of thousands of children from the *ceti medi* and the working classes. Many of them, especially from the middle classes, decided to continue their studies and go on to university. Legislation of the 1960s made this easier: in 1961 access to science faculties was opened to students from technical institutes, and in 1965 entrance to university by examination was abolished. By 1968 the number of university students totalled over 450,000, compared to only 268,000 in 1960. The number of women students had doubled in the same period, but in 1968 still constituted less than a third of the new intake.[1]

This new generation of university students entered a system which was in an advanced state of malfunction. The last serious reform of the universities had been in 1923; little provision had been made since that date to cope with student numbers that had increased tenfold. By 1968 the three universities of Rome, Naples and Bari had 60,000, 50,000, and 30,000 students respectively, while they had been designed for student populations of little more than 5,000 each.[2] There were too few university teachers; worse still, many of them were rarely to be found in the universities. Their obligations amounted only to fifty-two hours of lectures per year, and once they had given these they were free to do what they wanted. Professors who were also doctors, lawyers, architects or politicians were notorious absentees. There were no seminars, no tutorials, and thus almost no staff–student contact. The situation was a little better in the science faculties, but even there most curricula had remained unrevised for years. Most examinations were oral, with a consequent high degree of uncontrolled subjective evaluation. For the Turin students of 1968 oral exams were occasions when 'a policeman dressed up as a teacher spends five to ten minutes in liquidating the accused with a series of questions'.[3]

The decision to allow open access to such a grossly inadequate university system amounted simply to planting a time bomb in it. The position of 'worker-students', as they were called, was particularly difficult. In Italy there were no state grants for students, with the exception of a few scholarships for the academically outstanding. Well-to-do parents paid for their children while they were at university, but by 1968 more than half the student population was having to work as well as study. Many found part-time jobs in the schools; others were salesmen or baby-sitters, or worked in bars and restaurants. It was often impossible for them to attend lectures at all consistently, and in the absence of any other type of teaching they were reduced to studying textbooks at home. Not surprisingly, the number of these worker-students who then failed their oral exams was very high. Failing an exam did not mean having to leave the university; there was no obligatory time within which a student had to graduate. However, demoralization tended to set in and the number of drop-outs was great. In 1966 81 per cent of those with a secondary school diploma went to university, but only 44 per cent succeeded in graduating. The Italian education system thus operated a particularly subtle form of class-based selection: the university was supposedly open to all, but the odds were heavily stacked against poorer students ever getting a degree.[4]

Even with a degree there was no guarantee of a job. Italy had always produced too many graduates, but the situation got steadily worse in the late 1960s and throughout the 1970s. Thus many of the aspirations awakened by the half-baked reforms of the 1960s remained unsatisfied. The sons and daughters of the expanding urban middle classes experienced a series of sharp disillusionments. The schools were overcrowded and full of poorly trained teachers, the universities were an obstacle course of formidable dimensions and society as a whole was unable to guarantee high-status jobs to all those who did emerge from the long and distinctly dark tunnel of Italian education.

These were the material bases for revolt, but there were other, ideological ones of equal, if not greater, significance. Many of the school and university students of the mid and late sixties were less than convinced by the values that had become predominant in the Italy of the 'economic miracle' — individualism, the all-conquering power of technocracy, the exaltation of the nuclear family. Consumerism, too, seemed an ambiguous blessing to some of the Italian younger generation. The chance to play and listen to rock music, wear different clothes and enjoy freedom of movement was obviously welcome, but a minority was appalled by the sixties' obsession with the acquisition of commodities. Aldo Marchetti, who was to be one of the first students expelled from the Catholic university in Milan, recounts how for him '1968' began as he listened to the headmaster of his *liceo* (upper secondary school). The headmaster's optimistic portrayal of the future that awaited his pupils — positions in Italy's modern élite, working in banks, management, science, etc. — contrasted starkly with Marchetti's own half-formed feelings of pessimism and alienation. That generation of *liceo* students were reading Camus, Sartre, Pavese, Baudelaire; their heroes, if they had any, were rebels and outsiders.[5]

Their sense of rejection was able to find fertile support in minority developments in both the dominant ideologies of Italy, Catholicism and Marxism. The pontificate of John XXIII had opened the Italian church to a new ferment of ideas and activities. More than ever before, attention was paid to the need for social justice. In 1967, Don Milani, a dissident Catholic priest, published an extraordinary book called *Lettera a una professoressa*. In it, students from the school of Barbiana, in the village of Vicchio Mugello, north of Florence, documented the class bias of the educational system and the triumph of individualism in the new Italy. The philosophy of Italian education, according to Don Milani's school students, ran as follows: 'Woe betide him who touches the Individual. The Free Development of the Personality is your supreme conviction. You care nothing for society or its needs . . . You also know less than us about your fellow men. The lift is a machine for avoiding your neighbours, the car for ignoring people who go by tram, the telephone for not talking face to face and for not going to other people's homes.'[6] The book rapidly became a cult text for the student movement.

At the same time a revival of Marxist thinking was taking place. Under the lead of Emilio Panzieri, and then of the journal *Quaderni Rossi*, new attempts were being made to relate Marxist categories to the rapid material development of Italy. After the events of Piazza Statuto in Turin, changes in the Italian working class became the major object of analysis. The young *'operaisti'*, 'workerist' intellectuals, who were responsible for these analyses were for the most part outside the traditional left parties. They were few in number, as were the print runs of their publications, but they were to have a disproportionate influence on the student movement. So too did the little journal *Quaderni Piacentini*, which acted as a forum for Marxist ideas on economics and politics, culture and society.

These new initiatives, both Catholic and Marxist, were in no way symmetrical in their influence on the students. Nor indeed were they in agreement between them. But taken together, they provided part of an ideological background in which the values of solidarity, collective action and the fight against social injustice were counterposed to the individualism and consumerism of 'neo-capitalism'.

The year 1968, therefore, was much more than a protest against poor conditions. It was an ethical revolt, a notable attempt to turn the tide against the predominant values of the time. The students, and soon the whole population, had to be prevented from 'interiorizing' the values of a capitalist society. As Guido Viale wrote in 1968: 'The university functions as an instrument of ideological and political manipulation. It aims to instil into the students a spirit of subordination to the powers that be (whoever they may be). It tries to cancel, in the psychological structure of every student, the collective dimension of personal needs. It intends to destroy the possibility of establishing relations with one's neighbour which are other than purely competitive in character.'[7]

This ethical revolt drew inspiration and political identity from the dramatic and unique international conjuncture of the late 1960s. The Vietnam war changed the way a whole generation of Italians thought about America. The American dream of the 1950s was shattered by the newsreels of the napalming of Vietnamese villages in the 1960s and by the example of peasant resistance to the American war machine. One of the most recurrent slogans of '68 in Italy, as elsewhere in Europe, was: 'create one, two, three, many Vietnams'. For Italian youth of this period the 'real' America became another: the anti-war protests on the campuses, the Californian communes and counter-culture, the Black Power movement.

Simultaneously, a new model for the achievement of socialism seemed to have emerged from the experience of the Cultural Revolution in China in 1966–7. In contrast to the hierarchical and centralized Russian version of socialism, which had had its heyday in Italy in the 1940s, the Cultural Revolution was very widely interpreted in Italy as being a spontaneous and anti-authoritarian mass-protest movement. Socialism was to be reinvented from the bottom upwards. Mao had invited Chinese youth to 'open fire on headquarters'; in Italy, too, the time seemed ripe to initiate a 'cultural revolution' from below, against established hierarchies and values.

Finally, events in South America completed the 'Third World' inspirations of the student movement. The death of Che Guevara in Bolivia in the autumn of 1967 provided the Italian students, as it did the French and German, with their single greatest hero. But in Italy the teachings of radical South American priests who sought to reconcile Catholicism and Marxism found a very particular resonance. Not by chance, the first revolts in Italian universities were to be in strongly Catholic institutions.

These, then, were the international influences at work on Italian youth in 1967–8. They formed an extraordinarily potent mixture.

b. THE COURSE OF THE MOVEMENT

Although there had been rumblings of trouble in 1966–7, the real explosion in the Italian universities occurred in the period from the autumn of 1967 (long before the French unrest) until the spring of 1968. In that fateful academic year, the first university to be occupied was that of Trento. Founded in 1962 by Catholic intellectuals on the left of the Christian Democrat Party, Trento was the only university in Italy to have a faculty of social sciences. Its purpose was to train a modern Catholic élite which would analyse and direct the complex processes of transformation that were then under way in Italy. However, in the heady atmosphere of the autumn of 1967, the students rejected totally the role that had been assigned them. Instead, in the course of an uninterrupted series of sit-ins and assemblies, they tried to formulate a Marxist analysis of the role of students in society, couched in terms of the students being carefully modelled and selected products that were to be sold on the intellectual market.[8]

In mid-November, Trento was followed by an even more Catholic institution – the Catholic university at Milan. This private institution (Trento was a state university) had provided the D C with many of its most notable leaders. Here the original cause of the agitation was an increase in fees but, as everywhere, more global questions soon came to dominate the discussions of the student assembly. In response to this first-ever occupation, the rector called in the police to expel the students by force. After their expulsion, the students expressed 'indignation, suffering and deeply troubled human, civil and Christian feelings in the face of the authorities' behaviour towards the occupation'.[9] There were many expulsions, and the disturbances were to continue for some months.

After Milan, on 27 November 1967, it was the turn of Turin. The occupation of the Faculty of Letters in Palazzo Campana was to set the tone for the many other occupations that were to follow throughout Italy. A unifying feature of them all was to be the rejection of Gui's proposals, as Minister of Education, for university reform. Gui wanted to reintroduce restricted entry and to provide three different types of degree, from a one-year diploma through to the full degree course. These ideas of producing rigid hierarchies among the students ran exactly contrary to the students' own emphasis on equality and on the need to reduce the gap between the worker-students and the others. At Turin, teaching, course content and examining came under concerted attack for the first time.

From December 1967 to February 1968 the movement spread throughout the country, until even the sleepiest universities in the provinces and the South were brought into the fray. So too were some secondary schools, especially in the major urban areas.[10] At Turin and Trento students introduced the new tactic of interrupting lectures and forcing professors to confront the issues that were being debated in the student assemblies. Very few of the university teachers were able to cope with this explicit questioning of their authority. In Italy, in contrast to France, no significant part of the teaching body was to side with the students.

The atmosphere of these months, as at all such moments of sudden rebellion, was one of almost magical fraternity. In Milan, in the area around the state university, graffiti appeared everywhere and on everything. Students changed the way they dressed and looked: the men grew their hair and abandoned jackets, ties and sombre-coloured clothes in favour of jeans, beards and red handkerchiefs tied round the neck; the women gave up make-up, dresses and high heels in favour of trousers, jeans, pullovers and boots. In winter everyone wore khaki 'Eskimo' jackets and long scarves.[11]

In February 1968 the movement reached a turning-point with the occupation of the university of Rome. After police had evicted students from the university, the students met at the Piazza di Spagna and decided to try and 'recapture' the Faculty of Architecture, which was isolated in the gardens of the Villa Borghese. There the police baton-charged them, but the students replied in kind. Cars and vans were set alight, forty-six policemen ended up in hospital and an unknown number of students were injured. The next day the pictures of the 'battle of Valle Giulia' were on the front pages of all the newspapers. 'Valle Giulia' was a critical step, because up until that moment the student movement had been relatively pacific. From then on police and students loathed each other, and many of the students adopted the habit of wearing crash-helmets to demonstrations.

The spring of 1968 saw the movement reach its climax and begin to decline. It proved impossible to maintain for long the level of intensity and commitment that had characterized the previous months. In addition, the national elections of May 1968 began to divert attention elsewhere. The movement certainly did not die; there were to be student agitations throughout the 1970s, but they never again achieved the national impact and iconoclastic force of these first few months.

c. THE VALUES OF THE MOVEMENT

At the heart of the student movement lay an irreverent anti-authoritarianism. No hierarchy, authority or centre of power in Italy, and least of all those of the university and the forces of order, was safe from its ridicule. Eugenio Scalfari, who was later to found the newspaper *La Repubblica*, recounted in 1969 the infectious nature of this student disrespect. At the Faculty of Letters in Rome,

they told me of their battles with the police, and it was a pitiless account. There were the policemen heavy with sweat and tiredness, weighted down by their gunbelts and their bags full of tear-gas canisters; and circling round and round them were the students, dressed in their light trousers and teeshirts and plimsolls . . . Recounting all this while continually interrupting one another, they burst out laughing. And I was reminded of all those hours spent in the courtroom [of the SIFAR trial] with those ghost-like judges . . . and that grotesque parade of generals suspected of plotting against the state and now protected by the state so that they could lie with impunity and conceal the truth. I began to laugh too, and we all started laughing, first ten of us, then twenty, then fifty, until the whole hall in the Faculty of Letters was full of that bitter, unjoyful laughter.[12]

However, student rejection of authority went much beyond the most obvious targets. For the first time in the history of the Republic the family came under attack. Minority groups amongst the students, following the lead of their counterparts in northern Europe and America (and strongly influenced by R. D. Laing's writings), denounced the inadequacies the nuclear family. Far from loyalty to the family and the furtherance of it being absolute values, the family was attacked as a source of oppression and evil. As Fiorella Farinelli recalled later: 'By far the best of the graffiti on the walls of my faculty at the university, I remember it absolutely clearly, was this one: "I want to be an orphan." I agreed with it, I photographed it, I took a poster of it back to my home; it was the slogan I liked most.'[13]

Few students went this far, but many rejected the narrow loyalties of the family in favour of a greater commitment to their peer group and to collectivist ideals. Parental advice, with its emphasis on all politics being a dirty game, on the importance of getting a degree and making a career, was scornfully rejected. As for the relationship between family and society, the student movement criticized harshly the modern family's closedness, its distrust of the outside world, its predominant values of material enrichment. Luciana Castellina summarized these criticisms in a well-known article of 1974, where she wrote of 'the exasperated dichotomy between collectivity and family, the latter being conceived of as a lair, a refuge, a system of fortresses where solidarity with one's relatives is the other face of a brutal egoism towards the outside world'.[14]

Some of the students' strongest disdain was reserved for the traditional forces of the left. The Communist Party was dismissed for the most part as an 'integrated opposition', incapable of fighting the system. The PCI's youth movement, the FGCI, made little headway amongst the students, and its representatives were often treated with derision in student assemblies.

If all hierarchies and centres of power were under attack, what was to be put in their place? The movement, of course, had no well-formulated programme, but its underlying principles were clearly discernible. In the first place, direct democracy was, as far as possible, to control the exercise of power. All decisions were to be taken by mass assemblies, and if delegates were elected they were subject to recall as and when the need arose. Students were encouraged to participate directly in decision-making, rather than passively allow their representatives to exercise power on their behalf. The democratic model, therefore, was not that of the Constitution of the Italian Republic, but of the Paris Commune of 1871.

The students tried not only to make political decisions collectively, but also to live their lives in the same way. Communes sprang up in the major cities, though fewer than elsewhere in Europe. It was difficult to find large houses or flats to rent, and in any case many students were forced, for financial reasons, to continue to live with their parents.

The movement was collectivist, but it was also libertarian (and here it differed starkly from Chinese Communism). No central authority was to control individual actions, which were to be allowed as free a rein as possible in the private sphere. Nowhere was this more evident than in sexual relations. The taboos that surrounded sexual intercourse in Italy were systematically broken; sexual liberation became both one of the objectives of the movement and one of its practices.

However, the students' values remained essentially masculine ones. Women experienced considerable ambivalence in their attitudes towards the movement. On the one hand there were the positive elements of new political commitment and an extraordinarily intense sociality; on the other, most women remained subordinate within the movement, unable to express their own needs and desires. Sometimes new oppressions arose in the name of liberation; obligatory sexual liberty was the most notable of these.[15]

While it would be misleading to give a single label to the movement, it would probably be correct to describe it, in broad terms, as Marxist. Marcuse's *One-dimensional Man*, Mao's writings, Marx's own early texts were amongst the books that were most widely read at the time. However, the Italian movement, in contrast to the German, did not seriously preoccupy itself with the elaboration of theory. There were exceptions. Pisa's oft-reworked '*Tesi della Sapienza*' was the most notable example, and in some occupied medical and architecture faculties (notably that of Venice) extended discussions took place on the subjects of alternative medicine and radical town planning.[16] For the most part, though, Italian students were concerned to translate consciousness into action, organization and struggle. During the Turin occupation the student commission on Vietnam quickly abandoned a historical and economic analysis of imperialism in favour of duplicating a chronology of the Vietnamese struggle and reproducing a series of documents of the FLN. At Turin, again, in protest against 'book fetishism' and 'those new members of the massed ranks of neo-capitalism who build altars in their homes and call them libraries',[17] the 'scientific' commission proceeded to cut some books into five pieces for distribution amongst its members. It was not learning that mattered, but action; not individual possessions and family life, but the pooling of resources and collective action.

Finally, it is worth examining in a little detail student attitudes to violence, especially because of what was to come later. The movement was originally peaceful enough, and its apologists have rightly pointed out that it was police brutality within the universities that eventually provoked a response in kind. However, it would be quite misleading to infer from this that the movement was a pacifist one, forced against its will to adopt a violent stance. Violence was, rather, accepted as inevitable and justifiable, and entered almost unquestioned into the values and actions of the movement. The just violence of the revolutionaries – of Mao, of Che and of the Vietnamese – was opposed to that of the capitalists. 'Power comes out of the barrel of a gun';

'Violence in return for violence'; 'War no, guerrilla action yes': these were amongst the most popular slogans of the time.

d. RESPONSES TO THE MOVEMENT

Robert Lumley has rightly characterized one of the initial reactions to '68 as being moral panic. The *Corriere della Sera* usually referred to the student activists as *'Cinesi'* — a term which, as Lumley remarks, 'conjured up the red menace and the yellow peril in one'.[18] The Italian *ceti medi* as a whole were aghast at the rebellion from within their midst. The press and television intoned endlessly against the students, reproving them for their 'anarchism', their lack of respect and their intolerance. Furious battles broke out within families, as sons and daughters rejected their parents' advice and authority, and their very way of living. What made matters worse was that this was not, of course, in any way a purely Italian phenomenon. The European dimensions of the movement recalled the revolutionary waves of 1848–9 and 1918–20. When the French students and workers forced de Gaulle to leave Paris temporarily at the end of May 1968, it looked for a moment as if the whole post-war settlement was being called into question.

For the major force on the Italian left, the Italian Communists, the student movement presented notable problems. The students were clearly anti-capitalist, but they were quite ferociously anti-Communist as well. In June 1968 Giorgio Amendola gave vent to a widespread feeling within the party when he attacked the movement for being irrational and infantile. He called for a 'battle on two fronts', against both capitalist power and student extremism. Luigi Longo, as secretary of the party, had taken a rather different line in May. He admitted that the student movement posed 'a series of problems of tactics and strategy', but asserted that 'it has shaken up the political situation and has been largely positive . . . in undermining the Italian social system'.[19]

One person, however, closely associated with the PCI, did not spare the students his contempt. On 16 June 1968 Pier Paolo Pasolini published a famous anti-student poem in *L'Espresso*. It began as follows: 'Now the journalists of all the world (including / those of the television) / are licking your arses (as one still says in student / slang). Not me, my dears. / You have the faces of spoilt rich brats . . . / You are cowardly, uncertain, and desperate / . . . When, the other day, at Villa Giulia you fought / the police, / I can tell you I was on their side. / Because the police are the sons of the poor. / They come from subtopias, in the cities and countryside / . . .'[20]

In the same issue, *L'Espresso* published a round-table discussion on the poem. Pasolini was there, and in response to criticism from other members of the panel, especially from the trade unionist Vittorio Foa, he replied that his poem had been 'in more than one key at the same time. Thus my ugly verses should be read as if they were dubbed; that is, they are both ironic and anti-ironic.' Foa replied, 'The poem, once published, has its own momentum, and whoever reads it knows nothing of the interpretative canons of its author. Your poem, Pasolini, is published in a determinate society at a determinate moment; a moment in which youth, in spite of your illusions, is in the gravest difficulty (and I am speaking of both students and young workers). In my opinion everything is being done to isolate the youth movement . . . In all this concerted action only the voice of the poet was missing . . . [but] today we are witnessing a revolutionary process, or at least we are aware of its initial but absolutely unmistakable symptoms.'[21]

e. CONCLUSION

Foa was right to emphasize the novelty and subversive potential of the student protests of 1967–8. They had arisen spontaneously, beyond the instigation or control of any of the political parties. In this they differed fundamentally from the great wave of protest of 1945–8; then the PCI had controlled the movement, which for the most part had remained narrowly conformist in ideological terms, with Stalin's Russia as its model. The students of 1968 were broadly Marxist as well, but theirs was a libertarian and iconoclastic reading of historical materialism.

The movement was especially significant because for the first time a substantial section of the Italian *ceti medi* (for it was from these social groups that the students mostly came) aligned themselves on the left. In the rise of Fascism, the students, as is well known, had played a quite different role as the leaders and supporters of the anti-worker squads. The students of '68 also broke with their own parents, most of whom were not Fascists, but had benefited notably from the 'economic miracle' and accepted the values inherent in it. The movement was thus subversive because it challenged directly the model of modernity which had emerged in Italy in the previous years.

The students were certainly not without their faults. They were often presumptuous, arrogant and intolerant. They accepted, all too facilely, the use of violence as a weapon. They did not question, until much later on, the nature of the male values dominant within their movement. Assemblies were often not the models of direct democracy they were supposed to be – speakers holding unpopular views were howled down or were not even allowed to the microphone. It was this that made Habermas, amongst others, fear for a 'fascism of the left'.[22]

The students also never managed to harness protest in order to achieve change. The very nature of their critique and of their organization – radical, decentralized, Utopian – militated against them becoming an effective pressure group for reform. The universities, as we have seen, were desperately in need of reform: students required grants, curricula were ripe for change, new universities were needed in a hurry. But all this was too narrow a perspective for a movement that thought in wider terms. It was the system that needed changing, not a part of it.

However, the Italian students were not so Utopian as to believe that they were going to change the world by themselves. Unlike the bulk of the German student movement, which dismissed the working class as irredeemably integrated, and unlike Marcuse, who put the emphasis on marginal groups as the true revolutionaries, the Italian students never thought for a moment that they were *the* revolutionary class. To their credit they made it clear, almost immediately, that their aspirations to radical change would only make headway if they carried them to the working classes and convinced them of the necessity and viability of their cause. The student movement of 1968, therefore, turned rapidly away from universities, and their possible reform, towards the factories. It was there, they argued, that the decisive battles were to be fought.

The Factory Struggles, 1968–73

a. THE ORIGINS OF THE 'HOT AUTUMN' OF 1969

The Italian students had more grounds for optimism than many others like them who, at various moments in both Italian and European history, had 'gone to the people' in order to achieve profound social change. We have already seen (pp. 250–53) how in 1962 a new phase of tension and radicalism had swept the northern factories and had given rise to the riots of the Piazza Statuto in Turin. The conditions that underlay those events – the rigidity of the northern labour market, the alienation of the unskilled and semi-skilled workers, the anger of the southern immigrants – had not disappeared in the ensuing years between 1962 and 1968. There had been significant changes, but nearly all of them served to increase rather than diminish class conflict.

In the first place migration to the North and Centre from the South had not ceased. Only in 1965–6, as a sort of delayed response to the economic crisis, had there been a sharp decline in the numbers leaving the South. In 1967 net migration from the South to the Centre and North was once again over 120,000 a year (compared to 287,000 in the peak year of 1963). This figure did not fall to less than 100,000 per annum until 1974.

The massive new influx put renewed pressure on the structures of the major cities. It also made the process of assimilation that much more difficult; no sooner had the immigrants of 1958–63 found somewhere decent to live than a new wave moved into decrepit inner-city areas like the Corso Garibaldi in Milan and the Via Garibaldi in Turin. One survey of the Corso Garibaldi in 1969 found many flats without lavatories, some without running water, and landlords willing to let for only six months at a time.[23]

The provenance of this second wave of immigrants differed to a certain extent from that of their predecessors. There was still notable emigration from the poorest rural areas of the South. Piselli, for instance, has shown in her study of the Calabrian hill village of 'Altopiano' that it was not until the late sixties that migration to northern Italy reached its height: 147 families left the village for the North between 1959 and 1966, but 270 between 1967 and 1976. However, large numbers of immigrants were also coming from the more developed areas of the South. There is some evidence too from Turin of a minority of workers, attracted by offers of new jobs at FIAT, returning from Germany, Belgium and France.[24]

Even with the upturn of the economy post-1966, there were clearly not enough jobs to satisfy the expectations of all these immigrants. But the labour market was heavily segmented; this meant that there was still a certain shortage of the kind of labour that the major factories were looking for in 1967–8. FIAT, Pirelli and others wanted young men over twenty-one with a school leaving certificate and some experience of urban conditions. The supply of such labour from Lombardy and Piedmont was drying up, and firms like FIAT for the first time took on a large number of southerners. Priority was given to those returning from northern Europe and to those from the cities and industrial areas of the South. As such, the new cohorts of labour were unlikely to be as deferential as their predecessors.[25]

One other fact concerning the workforce and the labour market needs to be mentioned. The increase in educational opportunities in the 1960s had had a twofold effect: on the one hand, it had taken increasing numbers of young people out of the factories, thus increasing the rigidity of supply in this sector of the market; on the other, it meant that those who did go into the factories were more literate and more aware than previous generations. The hidebound textbooks of the Italian schools in the 1960s were hardly manuals for militants, but the connection between increased literacy and the agitations of the 'hot autumn' is evident.

Within the factories, too, conditions had changed. The major restructuring that followed the crisis of 1964–5 had resulted in increased mechanization and the speeding-up of production lines. The spread of piece-rate working had created further differentials between workers. Foremen had been given greater powers to grant favours and make job allocations. Management control and surveillance was on the increase.[26]

Finally, there can be little doubt that in the 1960s a profound gap opened up between the union shop-floor organizations, such as they were, and the mass of the *operai comuni*. At the Borletti factory in Milan the internal commission was composed predominantly of male skilled workers, many of whom had been at the factory since 1945. The majority of the employees were, by contrast, young unskilled women workers, whose complaints about speed-ups, foremen and piece-working found little sympathy from the internal commission. The *operai comuni* lacked adequate representation. In 1968–9 they responded by taking matters into their own hands.[27]

b. WORKERS' STRUGGLES AND REVOLUTIONARY GROUPS, 1968–9

The first workers' struggles of 1968 took place not in the major Italian factories but in more peripheral areas, both geographically and in terms of production, and above all in factories where the trade unions were traditionally weak. The most dramatic of these first struggles was at the Marzotto textile factory at Valdagno, in the Venetian hills. The factory dated back to 1836, and the Marzotto family had established there a long tradition of Catholic paternalism. In the 1960s the paternalism continued, but was accompanied by a radical reorganization of production. As in so many other factories, time and motion studies led to faster work rhythms, piece-work bonuses were made less accessible, real wages fell and management threatened some 400 redundancies. The trade unions had never been strong at Marzotto, and workers responded to the decline in their conditions with spontaneous protest action. One night in April 1968 the office containing all the new time-charts was broken into and the charts destroyed. On 19 April a demonstration some 4,000 strong, including a high percentage of women, marched through the town. In the main square they pulled down the statue of Count Gaetano Marzotto, the founder of the textile dynasty. The police responded by making forty-two arrests. In the ensuing furore, it was significant that the town council, overwhelmingly Christian Democrat, took the side of the workers, demanding the release of those arrested and the intervention of the government to re-establish social harmony.[28]

Valdagno was an isolated case, but was indicative of a new spirit that was sweeping through the central and northern factories in the spring of 1968. In March the trade unions had called for a nationwide strike in support of the demand for higher pensions. The response exceeded all expectations: in Milan alone some 300,000 metalworkers were involved, and white-collar workers joined the protest in significant numbers.[29] Day by day, events at home and abroad served to increase workers' self-confidence. The huge general strike in France in May 1968, with its brief demonstration of workers' power, made a profound impression in Italy. So, too, did the student movement. Although working-class opinion was divided, some young workers viewed student anti-authoritarianism with considerable sympathy.[30]

From the summer of 1968 onwards the student movement itself underwent a profound transformation. As students abandoned the universities and began picketing outside the factory gates, the movement lost its libertarian and spontaneous character. The accent was now on organization and on the need to lay the bases for a new revolutionary party which would wrest workers' loyalties away from the P CI. Here again, events in France played a major role. For many on the Italian far left, it seemed as if a real possibility of revolution had existed in Paris at the end of May 1968; it had been let slip through lack of coordination and the absence of any political leadership other than that of the ultra-cautious French Communist Party. It was important for Italian revolutionaries not to make the same mistake. What was needed was organization, ideology, discipline and revolutionary strategy.

Thus, from the autumn of 1968 onwards, the Italian new left was born, a left that was really not new at all, but as old as the Russian Revolution itself. Leninism, in one form or another, became the dominant model for nearly all the new groupings; the disagreements which had characterized fifty years of international Communism were now repeated on a miniature scale.

A bewildering number of revolutionary groups sprang up in these months. There were the Maoists of Servire il Popolo ('Serve the People'), with their attention to peasant politics, their fanatical dedication and extreme discipline; Avanguardia Operaia ('Workers' Vanguard'), centred first in Milan, an orthodox Leninist organization, anti-Stalin but pro-Mao; the Movimento Studentesco ('Student Movement'), with its stronghold at the state university of Milan, theorizing on the central role of the students, sympathetic to Stalinism; Lotta Continua ('Unceasing Struggle'), libertarian, irreverent and chaotic, the most innovative of the groups; Potere Operaio ('Workers' Power'), with considerable influence in Turin and Porto Marghera, convinced of its own superiority and of the prime importance of an external vanguard on Leninist lines; last but not least Il Manifesto, a small breakaway group from the left of the Communist Party, mainly intellectuals of some seniority, who were to found a famous and long-lasting daily newspaper of the same title.[31]

The Italian revolutionary groups, taken together, were the largest new left in Europe. Throughout the period 1968–76, they mobilized many thousands of militants in unceasing and exhausting activity, with the aim of creating a widespread anti-capitalist and revolutionary consciousness among the Italian working class. However, the groups were fatally flawed from their inception. In the first place, they were hopelessly and ferociously divided. Ideology was all. Their newspapers and periodicals were full of complex and mostly unintelligible theoretical analysis, much of which purported to establish the greater correctness of one group's political line over another. United action, let alone unification, was rarely achieved.

Secondly, the groups rapidly became mini-versions of the major political parties, with their own hierarchies (almost entirely male), and strutting *'leaderini'* (little leaders). Even Lotta Continua was not immune in this respect. Thirdly, they all accepted a dangerously casual attitude towards violence, adopting contemporary South American and Asian liberation struggles as their models, with little reflection on their applicability or likely consequences in the Italian situation. Lastly, and most seriously of all, the groups were convinced of the imminence of revolution in the West, and of the feasibility of generalizing the experience of some northern factories to the whole of Italy. None of them analysed in depth the nature of Italian society in the late 1960s, or the likely obstacles to the spread of revolutionary consciousness. For the Italian revolutionary groups, socialist revolution was around the corner, and they communicated this urgency and short-term perspective to the many young people, both middle and working class, who came to join them. But this was voluntarism run riot, the mistaking of a dream for reality, and the over-estimation of what activism alone could achieve.

All this, though, was far in the future. From the autumn of 1968 to that of 1969 the groups lived a magical moment, as significant numbers of workers were attracted to their ideas. In these months in the major northern factories, the trade unions frequently found that the initiative had passed out of their hands and into those of rank and file committees which had come into being either spontaneously or through the activity of the groups. The mould of Italian working-class politics, and much else besides, looked as if it was breaking apart.

The agitations in this, the most subversive year of recent Italian labour history, were begun by skilled workers rather than *operai comuni*. They were the workers who had had experience of organizing struggles and who were least likely to be intimidated. But once they had begun a factory agitation, the unskilled and semi-skilled workers very soon took over, and with demands that went far beyond those of the more traditional and skilled sectors.[32]

It was at the Pirelli Bicocca factory in Milan that the pattern of agitation was set for the coming months. The national contract for workers in the rubber industry came up for renewal in late 1967. At Pirelli some 2,000 new workers had recently been taken on. The trade unions at the factory organized three days of strike action in support of the claim, but settled in February 1968 for very modest increases in wages and practically no improvement in conditions. As a result, in June 1969 a group of blue- and white-collar workers at Pirelli, together with members of Avanguardia Operaia, organized the Comitato Unitario di Base (CUB, united base committee), in order to continue the struggle at factory level. The response to the CUB far exceeded the hopes of its organizers. Semi-skilled workers flocked to its meetings in great numbers, the trade unions and the PCI were denounced for their excessive willingness to compromise, and after many months of fierce struggle in the factory the workers won significant gains. The CUB became the model for other base committees in Milan, and the city's revolutionaries began to talk of creating a situation of dual power, in which the CUBs were the embryos of revolutionary workers' councils.[33]

Out of the Pirelli struggles and the others that followed there emerged a series of workers' demands which aimed to transform the relationship between labour and capital in Italy. Objectives varied from those immediately concerning workers' conditions, such as the end of piece-work rates and the slowing down of assembly lines, to others which were far more wide-ranging. Workers insisted that pay differentials between white- and blue-collar workers should be reduced, and that the differences between blue-collar workers should be diminished. One of the most frequent demands was that semi-skilled workers should automatically be promoted to a higher category after a certain number of years. The base committees urged workers not to accept more pay for jobs that were dangerous or constituted health hazards, but to fight instead to control conditions and safety regulations in the factories. They also demanded an end to wage 'cages', i.e. the paying of different rates for the same job in different parts of the country. A skilled engineering worker in the South, they argued, should be paid the same rates as one in the North. After strikes on this issue in the southern provinces of Latina and Taranto, the solidarity shown by northern workers (many of whom, of course, were of southern origin) was so widespread that the trade union leadership was forced to adopt the demand as their own. A successful national struggle was waged on the issue in 1969.[34]

Finally, and most subversively, the worker militants of 1968 and 1969 argued that wage increases should no longer be linked to productivity. Wages, to use the terminology of the time, were to become an 'autonomous factor', not dependent on company profits or the economic situation. The task of the base assemblies was to make sure that the workers received more pay for less work, and thus that the exploitation of workers diminished.

In order to impose these demands the workers invented a whole series of new forms of coordination and struggle. As with the student movement, mass assemblies became the major vehicles of decision-making; workers were urged to participate in person, and not to delegate to trade union leaders the task of directing the struggle. Strikes were organized in new ways. Traditionally, any strike action had been suspended while negotiations were taking place between management and trade unions. Now it continued, often against the wishes of the trade unions. Wildcat strikes became more frequent, assuming novel forms which provoked maximum disruption of the workplace with minimum cost to the workforce. The 'hiccup' strike (*a singhiozzo*) involved a whole factory alternating brief periods of work with others of strike action; the 'chess-board' strike (*a scacchiera*) meant that different parts of the factory, and sometimes even single workers, struck for short periods at different times, so that at any one moment there were some shops working and others not. The emphasis was always on the decentralization of strike action, with workers taking matters into their own hands and coordinating action from the base upwards.[35]

All this was possible because of a new-found confidence on the shop-floor which profoundly disconcerted management. In many factories foremen were no longer able to exercise any authority. Militant workers demanded that the most authoritarian foremen should be moved out of their shops. Often foremen and lower management were threatened with physical violence; sometimes they were beaten up outside the factory by groups of workers (the so-called *pestaggio di massa*).[36]

Finally, mass picketing outside the gates, often with the aid of students, gave way in the course of 1969 (and even more in 1970) to demonstrations inside the factories themselves. A group of workers would down tools, but instead of walking out of the factory, they would begin to organize inside it. Other groups would quickly join them. Within a short space of time all work had stopped, a procession would form, workers would use old oil cans as makeshift drums, slogans would echo through the factory and the demonstration would head for the managing director's office. Sometimes he would make his escape in time; at others he would be temporarily kidnapped and harangued.[37]

The climax of these months of spontaneous action came, as so often in Italian labour history, with the events at FIAT in Turin, in the summer of 1969. Throughout May and June, young workers, mainly from the South, *'selvaggi'* and *'incazzati'* ('wild' and 'outraged') as Lotta Continua called them, led a series of strikes for better conditions at the giant FIAT Mirafiori plant. Action was coordinated by a student and worker assembly which met at the end of shifts in a lecture hall at the university's Faculty of Medicine. At the beginning of July, the national trade unions called for a one-day general strike in protest at the high level of rents in Italy (see below, pp. 323–6). The rank and file of the worker–student assembly was not impressed: 'According to these gentlemen the class struggle takes place only on certain days of the year, as if they were Bank Holidays, and they of course decide when. But we are not going to wait for permission from anyone.'[38]

On the afternoon of the day of the strike, 3 July 1969, an independent demonstration of several thousand workers, both from Mirafiori and other Turin factories, set out from the gates at Mirafiori. The official trade union slogan for the general strike was 'no more rent rises' (*'blocco degli affitti'*). However, the demonstration that left from Mirafiori had a slogan all of its own, destined both to earn it immortality and to send a shiver down the collective spine of the Italian business class: *'Che cosa vogliamo? Tutto!'* ('What do we want? Everything!') The march soon clashed with the police. As in the Piazza Statuto seven years earlier, the demonstrators responded in kind, constructing barricades along the Corso Traiano, and fighting running battles with police far into the night. The 'battle of Corso Traiano', as it came to be called, was followed by mass assemblies in FIAT and other Turin factories, which involved many thousands of workers and students. Tension in Turin ran very high. In contrast to the events in Paris a year earlier, it seemed as if a real alliance, on a revolutionary basis, was being formed between young workers and students. For Guido Viale, one of the leaders of Lotta Continua, the struggle at FIAT represented 'something which was profoundly different and more mature than all the other experiences which have so far taken place in Europe'.[39] A revolutionary process had begun, and the groups were convinced that the autumn of 1969 would see it develop rapidly.

c. THE TRADE UNIONS AND THE 'HOT AUTUMN', 1969–71

The actual development of the famous *autunno caldo* ('hot autumn') of 1969 turned out to be quite different from that which the groups had expected. Lotta Continua talked in November of a 'cultural revolution' taking place in Italy as well as in China: 'The workers are slowly liberating themselves. In the factories, they are destroying all constituted authority, they are dismantling the instruments which the bosses use to control and divide them, they are overcoming the taboos which until now have kept them as slaves.'[40] However, the groups overestimated the depth of the crisis on at least two counts: anti-capitalist consciousness was nowhere near as widespread as they thought, or at least hoped; nor were the traditional loyalties of the working class to the trade unions and the major left-wing parties so easily to be swept aside.

Indeed, the Italian trade unions, showing a notable ability to adapt to changing conditions, succeeded, to use the terminology of the time, in 'riding the tiger' of worker militancy. One of the reasons that they were able to do so was because they managed, with some considerable difficulty, to win a partial autonomy from the control of the political parties. This was true both of the CGIL, and, more surprisingly, of the CISL. In the CGIL leaders like Luciano Lama and Bruno Trentin, while remaining Communists, insisted on having freedom of action in determining trade union responses to events in the factories. Often they went far beyond what the more cautious leadership of the party would have liked. Similarly, the CISL moved away from the tight control of the Christian Democrats. The CISL's metalworkers' section, the FIM, was to be especially prominent in the agitations of the 'hot autumn'. The FIM became the home for more than one Catholic revolutionary, and sometimes acted more radically than the FIOM, the CGIL's organization for metalworkers. As one FIOM activist at the Innocenti factory in Milan remarked rather ruefully in 1972: 'That lot [the FIM] have just discovered the class struggle, whereas we discovered it twenty-five years ago.'[41]

As the trade unions developed an autonomous response to the events of 1968–9 they also moved closer together. Even the UIL, realizing that it risked extinction by remaining a bosses' union, began to make decisions jointly with its larger brothers. The strategy of the trade unions was straightforward. Although a minority of their leaders and members, especially in the FIM, advocated revolutionary syndicalism, the majority wanted to make the trade unions a vehicle for reform. The new demands and forms of struggle that were emerging from the shop-floor were not to be rejected as extremist. Rather, they were to be channelled into trade union campaigns which would ensure permanent victories for labour. The trade unions were to become more powerful, both on the shop-floor and in national politics. Armed with this new strength, they would then force the procrastinating political class to carry through those major reforms which had been promised but not realized by the centre-left governments.[42]

The first step of this offensive came with the national mobilization for the renewal of the metalworkers' contract. In the autumn of 1969 nearly one and a half million workers were called out on strike at one time or another. The factory agitations, which previously had been confined to certain parts of the workforce within certain firms, now spread to all the major metalworking factories in Italy. The trade unions espoused the cause of the *operai comuni*, and the employers were taken aback by the trade unions' aggression and their willingness to use new forms of struggle.

In December 1969, at the end of the 'hot autumn', the new national contract was signed. It represented a significant victory for the trade unions and for the new militancy. Equal wage increases were to be granted to all, the forty-hour week was to be introduced in the course of the following three years, and special concessions were made to apprentices and worker-students. The trade unions also won the right to organize mass assemblies at the workplace. They were to be held within the working day and were to be paid for by the employers, up to a maximum of ten hours in each calendar year. The revolutionary groups denounced the final contract as a 'sell-out', but there was no doubt that a new unity had been created around the platform put forward by the metalworkers' unions. The 'hot autumn', then, for all its later notoriety, was not a further development of the revolutionary trends of the previous year, but rather the reassertion of trade union leadership in the factories.[43]

In 1970 and 1971, the fight for improved working conditions and for greater control at the workplace spread into many other sectors of production. After the metalworkers, it was the turn of chemical and building workers, railwaymen and other sections of organized labour. Agitations spilled out of the major workplaces into the minor ones, and out of industry into the tertiary sector. Many white-collar workers and technicians went on strike for the first time. Public-sector workers – postmen, teachers, hospital workers, civil servants, etc. – also moved on to the offensive. Their objectives were a mixture of corporate self-defence and radical desire for change. They demanded higher wages to maintain the distance between themselves and blue-collar workers, but many of them also fought for greater democracy at their workplaces and for more efficiency in the public services.[44]

Some far-flung parts of the tertiary sector saw strike action for the first time ever. Shopworkers and hotel workers, mainly women, waged bitter struggles for better conditions and for increased trade union representation. Agitations even spread into bars and shops. Here in the heart of the retail industry employers were at best paternalistic and at worst despotic. Between 1969 and 1971 their power was challenged, albeit in a very patchy way, for the first time. Most remarkably of all, some women doing piece-work at home went on strike against the putting-out system which enslaved them. Their protest was short-lived, however, because the suppliers of raw materials simply moved their operations elsewhere.[45]

Labour agitations were thus more widespread than at any time since the war. In itself this was disconcerting enough for the employers. Worse still was the fact that peace did not, as it always had in the past, return to the factories once the major national contracts had been signed. Whereas in France the great strike of May had soon given way to the reassertion of managerial power, in Italy the protests went on and on. The summer of 1970 was a low point, but in the autumn the workforces of the major factories moved on to the offensive again. By now the traditional supremacy of national negotiations over plant bargaining had all but disappeared. The initiative had passed firmly to plant level: in each workplace the trade unions pressed hard and with considerable success for the abolition of lower grades, the transitional nature of the third grade, which was that of most semi-skilled workers, and the establishment of the *inquadramento unico*, the single wage scale for all blue- and white-collar workers.[46]

Plant bargaining proved effective because the unions responded quickly to workers' demands for greater representation and democracy. The winning of the right of assembly during working hours had been the first step in this direction. In the course of 1970 and 1971, first the CGIL and then the other unions went further and approved the introduction of a radical new system of representation, based on the creation of factory councils. The councils were composed of delegates from every shop or department in the workplace. Delegates were elected in a secret ballot by all the workforce, whether trade union members or not, and were subject to recall at any time. The meetings of the factory council were open to all workers. The duties of the councils, as cited in the statute of one of them (GTE Autelco, Milan, October 1970), were as follows: 'to coordinate and elaborate in close liaison with the workers all the trade union activity of the factory (company, sectional and individual problems, political education, plant bargaining); to encourage meetings with other factories and other categories of workers to exchange experiences; to take initiatives to help resolve workers' problems in the factory and in society; to contribute, by means of serious debate, to the elaboration of trade union strategy'.[47]

The councils spread very rapidly. They had many advantages over the old internal commissions: they represented workers' interests more directly, with a greater number of delegates from the workers, and they had more power within the factories and closer links with the trade unions outside it. The employers' associations resisted their introduction for as long as they could, but were forced gradually to accept the inevitable. Many of the revolutionary groups also opposed the councils, though for very different reasons from the employers. The groups argued that a cap was being put on workers' spontaneity, and that the autonomy of 1968–9 was being replaced by gradual incorporation. The polemics between the groups and the trade unions over this issue were bitter and uncompromising.

However, the tide of trade union success was unstoppable. At their height in 1965, the old internal commissions in the metalworking industry had numbered 1,023, representing 552,148 workers. By 1972 in the same industry there were 4,291 factory councils, representing 1,055,592 workers. At the same time trade union membership increased by leaps and bounds. Combined figures for the CGIL and CISL show membership growing from 4,083,000 in 1968 to 5,399,000 in 1972, and 6,675,000 by 1975. In the public sector, the CGIL had a 15 per cent annual growth rate; to take one dramatic example, there were only 4,000 teachers who were members of the CGIL in 1968, but 90,000 by the beginning of 1975.[48]

Only in one area, and probably the most crucial, did trade union strategy fail. The unions had hoped to use their new-found strength to force the government to pass those major reforms on issues such as housing, the health service, the tax system, etc., which affected the lives of every worker. Between 1969 and 1971 they launched major campaigns on these issues; while some succeeded, like that on pensions, the majority ended in substantial failure. But perhaps it is best to postpone the discussion of why this was so until the political and economic mediation of the 'hot autumn' can be examined as a whole (see below, pp. 326–31).

d. THE WORKERS' MOVEMENT, 1971–3

The period from 1971 to 1973 was one of substantial consolidation. With the economic crisis of 1971, and the growth of inflation (see below, pp. 331–2), the favourable economic conjuncture of 1968–9 was seen to have come to a definite close. The maintenance of real wage levels and the defence of jobs now took pride of place in trade union actions, rather than the attempt to change the organization of production. Attack gave way to defence.[49]

At the same time, the impulse towards joint action between the three trade union confederations, while remaining strong, fell short of the target of complete reunification. It was supposed that 1972 would be the year when the three confederations dissolved themselves, and 1973 the year of complete unification. Instead, in July 1972, the trade unions signed a pact which gave birth to the federation CGIL–CISL–UIL. The federal formula suited the unions best, because it allowed for close cooperation while continuing to guarantee their individual autonomy. Total unification had in fact been viewed with some apprehension from both right and left: the right feared that it would be swamped by the numerical superiority of the CGIL, the left that there would be a repeat of 1945–7, when the moderates had successfully vetoed all radical proposals within the old united trade union.[50]

In spite of the general defensive climate of these years, the number of strikes and workplace agitations showed little sign of diminishing. In 1972, nearly four and a half million workers were involved in conflicts at their place of work, and this number rose to 6,133,000 in 1973. Only in 1969 had a greater number of workers been involved in protests.[51]

The climate of permanent agitation and conflict had both its positive and negative aspects. For tens of thousands of Italian workers the late 1960s and early 1970s was a sort of golden era, when they became aware of the power of collective action, and acquired a new self-confidence. Mario Mosca, one of the founders of the CUB at Pirelli Bicocca, remembers 1968 'as the best year of my life. It was the year in which as a worker I felt myself to be a protagonist and the master of my fate. And I continued to have that sensation for the following two years. It was wonderful to be alive.'[52] In 1962 Clizia N. had been, as we have seen (p. 224), a very young isolated worker from the South who had been treated in her first days in a Milanese factory as if she was suffering from an infectious disease. But in the late sixties she began to change: 'I became more of a chatterbox; I began to be able to communicate.' She joined the CGIL and in 1974, at the age of twenty-nine, she looked back with satisfaction on her experience of the 'hot autumn': 'You get a lot out of going to work in a factory. You learn things directly. Not like a housewife who learns things second hand. She can't have the same experience as a woman who works in a factory where you discuss many things and learn a lot. Small things too; but you manage to understand, to learn . . .'[53]

On the other hand, the continuous militancy of these years and the hyperactivity of the most committed workers had very high costs. Domenico Norcia (see p. 221) recalls: 'I continued to be politically active but with tremendous consequences for my family life . . . Sometimes I'd come back from meetings at two or three at night; my wife was at the window, waiting for me and crying. This happened often in 1972 and 1973.'[54]

In addition, workers' agitations in the factories sometimes, though by no means always, culminated in violence against persons. Managers and foremen, as we have seen, were the most obvious targets. However, those who refused to strike were also much at risk. Norcia again recalls one terrible incident at FIAT Mirafiori in the early seventies. The office staff had refused to join a blue-collar strike. A demonstration of some 4,000 workers forced them to leave the offices on pain of physical expulsion. As the office staff finally emerged, they had to run the gauntlet between long lines of jeering workers, who spat at them, kicked them, and humiliated and physically assaulted the terrified women.[55]

At the end of 1972 the metalworkers' contract came up for renewal again. The employers felt stronger than in 1969 and in the new year broke off negotiations, hoping to divide the unions. Their action produced the opposite effect. The first three months of 1973 saw a great resurgence of workers' militancy, which culminated in March with a symbolic two-day occupation of FIAT Mirafiori. Confindustria quickly returned to the negotiating table. The resulting national metalworkers' contract was a further substantial victory for the trade union movement. The single wage scale for blue- and white-collar workers (*inquadramento unico*) was agreed to, and a notable reduction took place in the differentials between the highest and lowest point on this new scale. A novel and striking modification in the working week was also successfully negotiated. Metalworkers were henceforth to enjoy 150 hours per year paid study leave, in which courses were to be organized by the trade unions. The 150 hours' education scheme rapidly spread to other sections of Italian labour. Workers not only studied for higher qualifications, but demanded courses which were extremely varied and markedly political in content. University and school teachers, trade union cadres and workers, came together in an ambitious attempt to realize a minor cultural revolution.[56] By the end of 1973, then, it was clear that the counter-cultural force of 1968–9 was far from exhausted, and that in spite of economic recession the workers' movement was more solidly and militantly established than ever before.

Social Movements outside the Workplace, 1968–73

In these years, collective action aiming to transform existing social and economic relations spread into nearly every part of Italian life. Everywhere, but especially in the Centre and the North of the country, groups of activists challenged the way in which power was exercised, resources distributed, social classes divided.

For the first time, though not in any systematic way, the *modus operandi* of the various parts of the state apparatus was brought into question. New groupings amongst state employees attacked entrenched hierarchies and tried to democratize structures and attitudes. Magistratura Democratica (Democratic Magistrates) was probably the most renowned of these new pressure groups within the state. Under its umbrella, young magistrates and judges, strongly influenced by the intellectual climate of '68, tried to reform the antiquated legal system, to diminish the intolerable delays in the administration of justice, to evolve less class-based forms of justice. The *'pretori d'assalto'* (literally 'the assault guards of local stipendiary magistrates', though in English the two terms seem improbably associated) soon achieved considerable renown. As one of them wrote later:

Hardly a day passed when the members of one of the lowest ranks of the judiciary were not in the limelight. They intervened in every sort of area: from pollution to food additives, from building speculation to surveillance in the factories. Their administration of justice was aimed not, as had always previously been the case, at beggars and thieves, pedlars and petty debtors, but at major economic interests and at leading political and administrative figures.[57]

The revolutionary groups, especially Lotta Continua, also launched initiatives in two previously untouched areas of the state – the army and the prisons. From 1970 onwards Lotta Continua's newspaper contained a regular supplement called *Proletari in Divisa* ('Proletarians in Uniform'). It was aimed at the conscripts who formed the majority of the army, and who had to undergo eighteen months' military service of notable futility and deprivation. *Proletari in Divisa* was distributed clandestinely on a wide scale in the principal barracks of Friuli, Trentino, Alto Adige and Piedmont. Nuclei of activists organized strikes over conditions, and set up liaison committees and political education sessions. They also appeared in uniform and dark glasses at left-wing demonstrations, as symbols of the unity that was hopefully being forged between the proletariat of the factory and that of the army.[58]

Another regular column in Lotta Continua's newspaper was entitled '*I dannati della terra*' ('The damned of the earth'). It contained letters from and information about Italy's appalling prisons. Horrific details emerged of daily life in the prisons: overcrowding, intimidation, lack of exercise, undernourishment and the regular miscarriage of justice were recurring themes. The young criminal, brought up in the shanty towns of Rome and Naples, or on the extreme periphery of Milan and Turin, became for Lotta Continua a potentially revolutionary subject. How far the group gained sympathizers in the prisons is not clear; almost certainly it had less success here than in the barracks.[59]

However, it was in civil society, not the state, that radical alternatives spread most rapidly: 'red' markets, kindergartens, restaurants, surgeries, social clubs, etc., opened (and often shut) one after another. Their aim was to organize social life along quite different lines, which not only challenged the individualism and segmentation of modern urban society, but also superseded the subcultures of the traditional left.[60]

No social movement was larger than that concerned with housing. Tens of thousands of Italians came together, if only temporarily, in a fierce struggle to gain proper accommodation for themselves and their children, and to establish fair rents on a national scale. The way Italy had modernized – rapid urbanization unaccompanied by town planning or adequate housing programmes – could not produce, at least in the short term, a new model of social integration based on contented urban individualism. Instead it gave birth, in the supercharged atmosphere of the years after 1968, to a widespread rank-and-file movement which claimed adequate housing as an elementary right.

The housing struggles were fought in two different areas of the major cities: on the periphery, where the public authorities IACP and GESCAL (see p. 247) had constructed or were in the process of constructing modern apartment blocks; and in the centre, where decaying popular quarters of the city were under threat from property developers.

On the periphery, major rent strikes took place in Milan, Turin, Rome and Naples. In Milan between 1968 and 1970 an estimated 40 per cent of the 100,000 families living on public housing estates went on partial or total rent strike. Their objectives were twofold: to reduce rents to an acceptable level *vis-à-vis* income (not more than 10 per cent); and to put pressure on the authorities to provide adequate services (schools, parks, shops, transport, etc.) for estates that were no more than concrete deserts.

One minor but well-documented example of this latter problem was the case of the phantom post office in the new Milanese quarter of Quarto Oggiaro (population of 7,200 in 1959, growing to 80,000 in 1972). Over the years the inhabitants had waited in vain for a post office: in 1964 the local section of the DC had promised to 'consider' the problem; in 1967 the Ministry of Post and Telecommunications had assured a DC deputy that plans for the post office were at 'an advanced stage', and that building would begin in 'a relatively short period of time'; in 1968 the provincial director of posts announced that 'the preliminary stage' of the necessary paperwork had been completed; in 1970 the regional director of posts announced that various buildings were 'under consideration for the siting of a post office'; in the same year the local DC talked of the post office at Quarto Oggiaro as 'a concrete reality'. By September 1973, there was still no post office, concrete or otherwise.[61] Such failings could not be attributed to malicious discrimination against the quarter; no one's interests were served by such protracted delay. They were, rather, straightforward evidence of the malfunctioning of the state apparatus, of its incapacity in the absence of radical reform to meet the needs of its citizens.

The leadership on the housing estates was normally divided in two: in Milan, for instance, the Unione Inquilini ('Tenants' Union') was a conglomerate that united the revolutionary groups and some elements of the trade unions; SUNIA, on the other hand, was the organization identified with the CGIL and the Communist Party.

On no issue did the two organizations clash more fiercely than on the question of squatting. In all the major Italian cities the revolutionary groups encouraged homeless or poorly housed families to occupy apartment blocks constructed by the public authorities but not yet lived in. Some of these squats assumed massive proportions: in Turin, for instance, in 1974 some six hundred families were involved in the occupation of the new Falchera estate. The P C I denounced the squats because the flats had already been assigned to families high up on the housing authorities' waiting-lists. There was a real risk of a 'war between the poor', of physical clashes between those who were squatting in the flats and those to whom they had been officially assigned. The P C I's position had much to commend it, but in the early seventies at least there was little doubt that squatting produced results. Magistrates quite regularly refused to condone police action in evicting and arresting squatters; and the local authorities, precisely in order to avoid fights breaking out, often found squatters permanent accommodation elsewhere.[62]

In the inner city it was much more difficult for the housing struggles to achieve a satisfactory outcome. Here too, tenants' committees agitated for rent reductions, but their main objectives were an end to evictions, the restructuring of the oldest and most run-down houses, the vetoing of new office-block construction. At the heart of Milan, in the Garibaldi-Isola quarter, a struggle along these lines was waged throughout the seventies. The tenants' aim was to force the local government to intervene. The Milan municipal government, a centre-left coalition, made many vague promises, but the destruction and transformation of the quarter continued inexorably. In the inner city the property speculators' lobby was opposed to any compromise settlements, and it made its weight felt where it mattered most.[63]

Overall, in spite of the mobilization of large numbers of people and some spectacular local successes, it cannot be said that the struggles made any great impression on the housing problem in Italy. Subjective failings, especially excessive factionalism, certainly played their part. But the principal problem was that agitation was for the most part confined to the public sector, where there was some possibility of gaining concessions from local authorities. However, as we have seen, it was the private sector, not the public, that dominated the building industry in Italy. Data on immigrant housing in fifty-five communes of the Milanese hinterland showed, for instance, that in 1971 only 6.4 per cent were living in public housing, while 33.7 per cent lived with relatives or friends and 43.1 per cent lived in private housing.[64] The dominant private sector was a jungle where collective action from the base could be organized only with the greatest difficulty. In such circumstances, the way in which struggle was reflected and mediated through political action became all-important. Only reform at a national level could hope to answer the demand for fair rents, adequate services and decent housing for all.

The Political and Economic Mediation of Collective Protest, 1968–73

a. REFORM

In May 1968 national elections were held. The results, as usual, changed very little. The DC gained 0.8 per cent, totalling 39.1 per cent of the vote; the PCI gained a little more, 1.6 per cent, and reached 26.9 per cent. The principal loser was the new United Socialist Party (PSU), which totalled only 14.5 per cent, 5.4 per cent less than the former PSI and PSDI. The principal gainer was the PSIUP, the left-wing split off from the PSI. The PSIUP, which gained 4.5 per cent of the vote, seemed the party most in tune with the social ferment of the moment.[65]

After the elections, as unrest spread to the factories, it became clear that the sleepy, stable Moro governments of the mid-sixties were a thing of the past. The PSU split into its component parts (PSI and PSDI) again. The twelfth congress of the DC in June 1969 was riven by faction. Eight groupings contested the conference; the largest of them, the Dorotei, managed to gain only 38 per cent of the delegates, and in the autumn dissolved themselves.[66] The DC was more divided than ever, at precisely the moment when calm and clear-headed leadership was most needed. Between 1968 and 1972 there were a series of short-lived governments, mainly centre-left coalitions. Three of them were presided over by the insipid DC politician Mariano Rumor. All of them testified to the nervousness of the politicians in the face of the crisis, and their inability to find a stable formula for government.

However, beneath this perennial image of governmental crisis, certain changes of attitude can be clearly discerned. Both the DC and the PSI, the major coalition partners, were unwilling to turn their backs on the social ferment, or choose the path of simple inactivity and repression. Emilio Colombo, who was to become Prime Minister in August 1970, expressed these feelings well at the end of the national council of the DC in January 1969: 'Where have we fallen short? It seems to me that ... reforming action has marked time so that the structures of civil society have aged badly and the whole fabric has deteriorated. Social forces have not found suitable channels for the expression of their freedom. That is why pluralism ... is actually turning into disorder, with a wave of unrest and sometimes of irrationality.'[67] The DC leaders could not remain insensitive to the pressure for change coming from their collateral organizations, principally the ACLI and the much changed CISL. For the PSI too, now that the PSIUP was barking at its heels, a passive presence in government was tantamount to suicide.[68]

As a result, the period from 1969 onwards saw the politicians mediate collective protest by a sudden increase in reform legislation – patchy, unprogrammatic, insufficient, but distinctly reform. Some of it, to be fair, had been initiated by the centre-left governments of the sixties and only now emerged from the long preparatory tunnel of the state bureaucracy. This was the case with regional government, which was finally introduced in the spring of 1970. Twenty-two years had passed since the provisions for its institution had been written into the Constitution. Fifteen regular regional governments now took their place alongside the five regions which enjoyed a special autonomy (Val d'Aosta, Trentino-Alto Adige, Friuli-Venezia Giulia, Sicily and Sardinia). Each regional government had its own elected council and enjoyed greater powers than those accorded to the communes and provinces. Each region had the right to legislate on all major issues that affected it – housing, health, social welfare, agriculture, etc. – provided that its laws were consonant with 'the framework of national legislation'.

In June 1970 the first regional elections were held. There were no major shifts in voting patterns, but the PSI and PSDI, standing separately, recouped a large part of the losses sustained in the 1968 national election. The most important result was that which the centre and right-wing parties had always predicted and feared – the creation of a Red Belt in central Italy, comprising Emilia-Romagna, Tuscany and Umbria.

The institution of the regions was certainly a major step. So too was the introduction of the right to hold referenda, which had also been included in the Constitution, but came into being only in May 1970. The new law stipulated that a referendum could be held if 500,000 citizens or five regional councils or one fifth of either House of Parliament requested it. No referendum could propose legislation; it could only exercise the negative power of repealing an existing law.

Taken together, the institution of the regions and of the referendum represented a significant shift towards decentralization and towards the ordinary citizen exercising some minimal control over the decision-making process. However, much remained to be done. The gap between representative democracy and the direct democracy advocated by both workers and students remained very great. The regions had insufficient funds and personnel. Furthermore, they were instituted in isolation, unaccompanied by any wider attempt to eliminate the worst practices of Italian public administration. There was thus nothing to stop the regional governments from becoming new repositories for the abuse of power on an intermediate level between the communes and the national government.[69]

These two political reforms were accompanied by a number of social ones. After further mass protests over pensions had followed the demonstration of March 1968, the government agreed, in February 1969, to raise considerably the level of pensions for those who had been in regular work. For a person retiring after forty years of work, the new law guaranteed 74 per cent of his or her average annual wage in the five years prior to retirement. This was a significant victory for the trade unions, though it left unresolved the problem of fair and automatic pension provision for those who could not demonstrate any such regular employment.[70]

Little more than a year later, in May 1970, the Statuto dei Lavoratori (Workers' Charter) became law. Pushed through the Council of Ministers and Parliament with great determination by the Socialist Giacomo Brodolini, the Workers' Charter both reflected and guaranteed the achievements of the 'hot autumn'. The charter consisted of a series of articles laying down the rights of the worker at his or her place of work: the right of assembly, the right to organize trade unions within the workplace, the right to protection in dangerous jobs, above all the right to appeal to the courts against unfair dismissal. In the early seventies workers made considerable use of the charter, and judges, especially in the lower courts and in the Centre and North of the country, frequently found in their favour. Italy at last had a labour law which was not altogether one-sided in its articles and application.[71]

The same year, 1970, also saw the culmination of the long struggle to introduce divorce into Italy. The Socialist deputy Loris Fortuna had first introduced his divorce bill in October 1965. It was moderate in content and laid down careful limitations to the right of divorce. None the less, its progress was, predictably, blocked by the Christian Democrats and subject to fierce attack by the church hierarchy. Gradually lay opinion, much helped by the activities of the LID (the Lega Italiana per l'Istituzione del Divorzio), gathered in support of Fortuna's initiative. In 1969 further proposals by the Liberal Antonio Bislini were incorporated into the bill, and the Communists lent their support. Within the Chamber of Deputies the opposition to the new legislation could count only on the votes of the DC and neo-Fascists. In November 1969, with the LID gathered outside the Chamber of Deputies and the Cardinal Vicar of Rome inviting the faithful to pray for preservation from the plague of divorce, the Chamber of Deputies passed the Fortuna–Bislini bill by 325 votes to 283. There was then a delay of one year while the bill was approved, and further modified, by the Senate. It finally returned to the Chamber to become law on 1 December 1970. Lay Italy had won a notable victory.[72]

No such unequivocal judgement can be passed on the housing reform of October 1971. Once again, housing proved to be a key area where reform foundered on the rocks of entrenched interest and state practice. It is worth taking a little space to try to explain this sequence of events.

In the period 1969–71 the forces pushing for reform in the area of housing and town planning were very much more powerful than at the time of Sullo and the beginning of the centre-left. The principal difference was that the trade union movement had entered the fray. As we have mentioned, the most ambitious part of trade union strategy was the attempt to use the widespread militancy of these years as a lever with which to achieve fundamental reform. This meant that the reformists were no longer a relatively isolated group of politicians as in 1963, but were sustained by a mass movement of considerable proportions.

In November 1969 the trade unions called a one-day general strike on the housing question. It was an enormous success, with hundreds of thousands of workers participating. The unions then began to negotiate directly with the government during 1970 and 1971. Their basic demands were for greatly increased state spending in the public housing sector, the establishment of a fair-rents system for tenants in state-owned housing, and guarantees for the building unions in terms of immediate construction programmes. Negotiations dragged on for many months, interspersed with other regional and provincial strikes called by the unions.

When the law of October 1971 was finally passed, it was given qualified approval by the unions, but in fact met their demands in only a very partial way. The whole system of public housing was simplified and handed over to the local authorities – regional, provincial and communal. Powers were granted to them to expropriate areas necessary for public construction and services, and to pay compensation only at average agricultural prices; large sums of money were assigned for a new public housing programme. However, in practice, and this was the acid test, the law proved impossibly complicated, and there was no overall control over the way in which it was applied (or not applied) in the localities. By January 1974 only 42bn lire had been spent out of the 1,062bn available.[73]

Why were the reformists unable to guarantee effective public housing reform, even when they were at the height of their influence? It would be wrong to accuse the trade unions of Utopianism. Their demands were directed towards the public, not the private, sector, and were for the sort of spending on public housing which had characterized government intervention in many other European countries. Rather, there was a distinct lack of unison between the trade unions and those political parties interested in reform. The parties, including the PCI, resented the trade unions' intrusion into a political sphere – that of negotiations at government level — which they considered to be exclusively theirs. Enrico Berlinguer, the new secretary of the PCI, made these reservations explicit in 1971. As a result, the reformist forces, rather than having a single strategy and leadership, were pulled in several different directions.[74]

In addition, the trade unions were unwilling to link the rank-and-file struggles on housing to their negotiations with the government. The sort of pressure they put on the government was a fairly ritualistic one, consisting of strike action which soon became repetitive and of diminishing potential. The mobilization had no precise objectives on a local level, no forms of action on the housing estates which would have kept the government under constant pressure. The metalworkers' unions proposed such a strategy in February 1971, but the desire for unity at the highest levels of the trade union leadership ruled out action which might have been considered 'extremist'.[75]

However important these failings, they were not the whole story. The reform emerged as a botched job principally because those opposed to it used the instruments of the state more successfully than its supporters. First, when the law was going through Parliament, they introduced so many amendments as to make its application very difficult. Secondly, after the law had been passed, the nature of the central bureaucracy and most of local government made implementation difficult and procrastination all too easy. The reformers, by contrast, had little or no statecraft. Their inexperience of government made them unaware of the probable consequences of certain decisions. Above all, behind their opponents' victory lurked the unpalatable fact that it was the state itself that needed reform before all else. However strong the reformist army, the marshes of the Italian state apparatus could be relied upon to slow or stop its forward march.[76]

The other demands for reform raised by the trade unions, in the fields of health, schools, transport, etc., met with even less success. Various promises were extracted from the governments of the time, but little or nothing came of them.

In the area of fiscal reform, some progress was achieved through the new regime that was introduced in the period 1971–3. For the first time, the principle of progressive income taxation was extended to the whole working population. However, the results made a mockery of the principle proclaimed. While dependent workers had income tax deducted at source, no proper method was introduced of tax collection from the self-employed. From shopkeepers to lawyers, massive tax evasion was the order of the day. As R. Valiani has commented: 'In Italy, as in other industrial societies, there operates the principle of taxation serving redistributive purposes, but with one notable anomaly: that is, redistribution takes place in the opposite direction to the ideal one, since income tax is concentrated in those sectors with the least ability to pay.'[77]

In one field alone, that of investment in the South, the demands of the reformers corresponded, at least in part, with the intentions of an important section of the state's élites. The barons of public industry, ever more powerful at a time when the politicians were weak and divided, had chosen the South as their favoured area for investment, and between 1969 and 1973 gave a further notable impetus to that process of industrialization which has already been described for the 1960s (see pp. 230–31). The share of the Mezzogiorno in total national investments passed from 28.1 per cent in 1969 to 33.5 per cent in 1973. In addition, in 1971 the Cassa per il Mezzogiorno announced a further shift towards industrial investment.

Naturally, the mode of investment did not correspond at all precisely to what the unions demanded. Investment continued in large, capital-intensive plants, principally in petrochemicals and steel. In the mid and late seventies both these were to prove disastrous choices *vis-à-vis* the world economy. The trade unions had demanded instead more varied forms of investment and higher levels of employment. They were not satisfied on either point, but no one could deny the positive, if limited, spin-off for the southern economy deriving from public industry's commitment to it.[78]

b. POLITICAL ECONOMY AND THE EMPLOYERS' RESPONSE, 1968–73

The government's record on reform at this period was amongst the most active in the history of the Republic, a genuine if partial attempt to mediate social protest in a constructive fashion. The same could not be said for the government's economic policies as a whole, nor for the employers' response to the 'hot autumn'.

In terms of the international economic system, the period after 1969 was characterized by increasing signs of strain. In most advanced capitalist countries over-accumulation and tight labour markets tended to push up wages and threaten profits. The break-up of the Bretton Woods system and the dollar devaluations of the early seventies created a climate of financial uncertainty. The student revolt and the explosion of workers' agitations further sapped business confidence.[79]

In Italy, the authorities replied to the wave of wage increases at the end of 1969 with moderate deflationary policies. They hoped in this way to produce an economic situation similar to that which had occurred after 1964: the expulsion of excess labour, a rapid readjustment of the balance of forces in the factories, an increase in productivity and a revival of profits.[80]

Nothing of the sort happened. Deflationary measures served only to discourage further an employing class which had been menaced much more fundamentally than in the period 1961–3. In addition, there were no political signs that the government was firmly behind the employers rather than the working-class movement. In France, as Salvati and Gigliobianco have shown, the decisive victory of the conservative front in the June elections of 1968 had restored business confidence and opened the way for an unparalleled boom in investments.[81] In Italy, by contrast, no such political reassurance was forthcoming and the reformism described above seemed to be oriented in the opposite direction.

In these circumstances the employers did not respond in a uniform manner. State industry and large private groups like FIAT and Pirelli maintained high rates of investment, thereby mitigating in part the generally depressed state of the economy. They also sought to come to terms with the new situation in the factories, seeking to strengthen the trade unions as a counterbalance to rank-and-file organization and action. As Giovanni Agnelli told Eugenio Scalfari in November 1972: 'With profits at zero levels, the crisis will not resolve itself, but may become cancerous, with fatal effects. We have only two choices before us: either direct confrontation to reduce wage levels, or a series of bold and path-breaking initiatives to eliminate the most intolerable examples of waste and inefficiency. It is superfluous to say what our choice will be.'[82]

Most of the private sector responded in more traditional and negative ways. As wage increases were passed on indiscriminately to prices, inflation began to rise markedly. The flight of capital took on menacing proportions; investments slumped dramatically. Most significantly, Confindustria remained firmly in the hands of those who responded to the situation only with prophecies of doom. In 1972 its president went so far as to accuse the trade unions of 'subversion of the country's democratic institutions'. Once again, as at the time of the centre-left, the more open-minded or neo-corporatist elements of Italian capital seem to have been swamped by a wave of conservative hysteria. It was to be 1974 before the die-hard elements in Confindustria were replaced.[83]

In Italy, as in the other Western economies, a mini-boom alleviated matters temporarily in 1972–3. However, in the course of 1973 the Italian situation became critical. The metalworkers' victory meant that real wages showed no signs of decreasing. The flight of capital had intensified. In these circumstances, the authorities decided that they could no longer defend the lira; from February 1973 onwards the Italian currency was allowed to float, and depreciated markedly in the course of the next two years. Imports came to cost very much more, just at the moment when the price of raw materials (and, as we shall see, of oil in particular) was rising very fast. As Gaetano

Rasi has written: 'the devaluation of the lira still appears today not just to have been an unfortunate choice but a mistaken one from the very beginning. The greater severity of Italy's economic recession in 1974–5, when compared to all other Western countries, without doubt has this as its dominant cause.'[84] Italy soon had the highest rate of inflation of all the Western economies. Consumers were hit hardest. Widespread uncertainty and instability ensued.

c. THE STRATEGY OF TENSION

There was one other reply to the 'hot autumn', and it was the most insidious of all. On 12 December 1969 a bomb exploded in the Banca Nazionale dell'Agricoltura in Milan's Piazza Fontana. Sixteen people died, eighty-eight were wounded. Most of the victims were farmers and tradesmen, in from the Lombard plains on a weekly visit to the bank. On the same day two other bombs of the same type went off in Rome, wounding eighteen people.

The police and the Ministry of the Interior immediately announced, with undue haste, that anarchists were responsible. The police then began to round up anarchist suspects; one of them was Pietro Valpreda, a ballet dancer from Rome. He was soon accused, principally on the evidence of a taxi-driver, of being the principal perpetrator of the Milanese massacre. Valpreda was to spend three years in prison awaiting trial, and was only finally cleared of any association with the crime in 1985.[85]

Worse still was the fate which awaited another anarchist, Giuseppe (Pino) Pinelli. A Milanese railwayman, Pinelli was arrested on the night of the bomb attack, and spent the next forty-eight hours in the police headquarters in Milan. On 15 December, shortly after midnight, he fell to his death from the fourth-floor office of the police commissioner, Luigi Calabresi. In the office at the time were the Carabiniere lieutenant Savino Lo Garano, and the police brigadiers Vito Panessa, Pietro Muccilli, Carlo Mainardi and Giuseppe Caracuta. The official version of Pinelli's death was that he had committed suicide. In a press conference that same night the Milanese police chief, Marcello Guida, announced that Pinelli's alibi had proved false, and that he was 'gravely implicated in the organization of the massacre'. Six years later the courts ruled, on the contrary, that Pinelli had been innocent of any involvement in the crime. The truth about how he died has never been established.[86]

Slowly but surely, the police version of anarchist responsibility for the bombings began to disintegrate, and a more alarming explanation began to take its place. Evidence which the police had chosen to ignore pointed not to the anarchists but to a neo-Fascist group based in the Veneto and led by Franco Freda and Giovanni Ventura. What was alarming was not that neo-Fascists rather than anarchists were probably responsible for the bombing, but that Giovanni Ventura was in close touch with Guido Giannettini, a colonel in the SID, the Italian secret service. Giannettini, it then emerged, was not only in the SID, but was a fervent supporter of the MSI, the official neo-Fascist party. Nor was he alone. A most disquieting picture began to emerge of extensive contacts between members of the secret services and extreme right-wing groups. Italian public opinion, alerted by some fine investigative journalism, became ever more convinced that a plot was afoot: a series of bomb explosions and other outrages would sow panic and uncertainty, and create the preconditions for an authoritarian regime. This was the strategy of tension. The colonels had employed it successfully in Greece, and it now looked as if neo-Fascists and sections of the secret services were trying to repeat the pattern in Italy.[87]

At this point, 1970, many sectors of the press and the political opposition called on the government and the President of the Republic, Giuseppe Saragat, to investigate immediately the activities of the secret services. Far from doing so, the highest authorities of the Italian state seemed more interested in a cover-up. On the grounds of national security, the magistrates investigating the bomb explosion in Piazza Fontana were prevented from obtaining access to the secret-service files covering the activities of Giannettini and other officers of the SID. The Corte di Cassazione, Italy's highest court for deciding legal procedures, intervened on no less than three occasions, either to delay the Piazza Fontana trial, or to change its location, or to transfer investigative responsibility from Milan to Rome. The last of these occasions was in 1975, at the precise moment when the Milanese magistrates were interrogating the secret-service chiefs. The trial dragged on interminably. In 1981 Giannettini, Freda and Ventura were sentenced to life imprisonment, but all were later cleared by the Court of Appeal.[88]

One year after the bomb in the bank of Piazza Fontana, another incident served to confirm the turbulence of the extreme right. During the night of 7–8 December 1970, Prince Junio Valerio Borghese, who had commanded blackshirt troops during the Republic of Salò back in 1944–5, attempted a *coup d'état*. This coup had even more elements of farce in it than had the plans of De Lorenzo. Borghese's only troops were a battalion of forest guards and a group of former members of the parachute regiment, led by the future MSI deputy Sandro Saccucci. Borghese succeeded in occupying the Ministry of the Interior for a few hours, but then withdrew without a shot being fired. The incident was only made public the following March. Borghese was clearly an adventurer without much support, but once again disconcerting evidence accumulated of his links with sections of the army and the secret services. In 1974, after endless delays, no fewer than four generals were accused of complicity in Borghese's attempted coup. One of them was Vito Miceli, the head of the secret service. At the subsequent trial all were acquitted.[89]

d. THE SHIFT TO THE RIGHT, 1972–3

At the end of 1971 Giuseppe Saragat's mandate as President of the Republic expired. His tenancy of the Quirinale had not been a distinguished one, and his attitude to the strategy of tension had been equivocal. The PSDI, Saragat's party, had always been very closely tied to American interests. Many commentators suspected that the President thought along the same lines as the CIA: namely, that the activities of the extreme right would serve the salutary purpose of increasing the demand for strong and moderate government.[90]

Saragat stood again for election, as the Constitution entitled him to do, but was supported only by his own party (the PSDI), the Liberals and the Republicans. Fanfani was the official DC candidate, while Socialists and Communists supported the Socialist Francesco De Martino. Once agàin, the country was treated to the protracted spectacle of the political parties' inability to reach agreement. After the twentieth ballot of the members of both Houses of Parliament, the Christian Democrats came up with a compromise candidate, the Neapolitan lawyer and DC politician, Giovanni Leone. On Christmas Eve, 1971, after twenty-three ballots, Leone became President, but only the support of the MSI gave him the necessary majority.[91]

Soon afterwards, the new President, in agreement with the majority of the political parties, decided to call elections in 1972, one year ahead of schedule. This was the first time in the history of the Republic that Parliament had not lasted its full five-year term. The reasons for early elections were both old and new. The parties continued to hope that at least part of the electorate would abandon its traditional voting habits and thus finally unblock the Italian political system. The heightened political awareness and the tensions of the post-'68 years increased the hopes of both left and right. In addition, a new problem had arisen to which the political parties of the governing coalition had no easy solution. After the divorce law had been approved by Parliament, various militant Catholic organizations decided to call a referendum on the issue. They swiftly collected the 500,000 necessary signatures, and the referendum was fixed for the spring of 1972.

However, none of the political parties had any great desire for the referendum. The Christian Democrats, in particular, feared isolation from their traditional lay and socialist allies. Only the MSI would line up with them against divorce. The PCI, for its part, was apprehensive that the

Catholics still had enough influence in civil society to sweep all before them. A clause in the new referendum law, stipulating that a referendum could not be held if Parliament was dissolved, offered a way out. It seemed preferable to hold elections, delay the referendum by at least a year, and then reconsider the situation.

The general elections of May 1972 did mark a shift in voting patterns, but it was in no way decisive. Any hopes that the left might have had proved illusory. The PCI held steady, with 27.2 per cent of the votes, an increase of 0.3 per cent in comparison with 1968. The PSIUP, however, declined dramatically, dropping from 4.5 per cent in 1968 to 1.9 per cent, and failing to elect a single Member of Parliament. The party did not survive this disaster; its majority joined the PCI, while the minority, renaming itself the PDUP, moved towards the revolutionary groups. One of these, the Manifesto Group, also fielded candidates in 1972, but gained only 0.7 per cent of the votes.

By contrast, there was a distinct if limited move to the right. It seemed as if the strategy of tension had paid off. The Christian Democrats, standing on a centre-right platform, held their own with 38.7 per cent of the vote, dropping only 0.4 per cent. The real victors were the neo-Fascists. Having absorbed the tiny Monarchist Party and renamed themselves MSI–DN (Destra Nazionale), they gained 8.7 per cent of the votes, compared to 4.4 per cent in 1968. Under the leadership of Giorgio Almirante, they had fielded a shrewd mixture of candidates. On the one hand, there were senior figures from the military establishment like De Lorenzo and Admiral Gino Birindelli, who had been the NATO commander in the Mediterranean; on the other, there were agitators like Pino Rauti and Saccucci, more closely tied to traditional Fascist theory and action. The MSI–DN was particularly successful in the South, for reasons that will be discussed below (pp. 337–40). The PLI, hardly surprisingly, lost votes to them, and declined to 3.9 per cent.[92]

For the Christian Democrats the lessons of the elections were clear enough. For the first time for many years they formed a centre-right government, presided over by Giulio Andreotti. It consisted of the DC, the PLI and the PSDI. The Liberals came into the government for the first time since 1957, and the PSI joined the ranks of the opposition. The DC set about wooing the MSI's electorate. The new government was anti-workerist in stance, and its most notable action was to offer voluntary early retirement, on extraordinarily generous terms, to senior bureaucrats in the civil service.[93]

However, the shift to the right had not been strong enough either in the country or in Parliament for Andreotti's government to present a stable solution. With the resurgence of the workers' movement in the first months of 1973, Andreotti was forced on to the defensive. The DC, torn by its internal divisions, uncertain how to deal with a worsening economic crisis and a social crisis that seemed unending, veered again towards an alliance with the PSI. Andreotti fell in June 1973, and a new centre-left coalition was formed, presided over by Rumor, and consisting of DC, PSI, PRI and PSDI. The politicians were back to where they had been ten years earlier.

The South, 1968–73

In these years the pattern of social protest and political affiliation in the Mezzogiorno differed radically from that of much of the rest of the country, and it needs examining in its own right. Trade union mobilization and factory agitations had a much more limited impact here than elsewhere. It would be wrong to represent the South as immune from the 'hot autumn': there were worker agitations, and the fight against 'wage cages' in 1969 saw a high level of mobilization in various factories. But industrial workers, concentrated primarily in petrochemicals, steel, shipbuilding, metalworking and transport, were only a small proportion of the South's population, and many of them were also isolated in the 'cathedrals in the desert' which had been constructed in the 1960s. The trade unions made great strides in the early seventies, but the mass of the southern population remained outside their reach and influence.[94]

Southern society, in fact, had changed drastically under the dual impact of emigration and economic development. The rural interior, especially the *latifondo* areas, had suffered most from depopulation (see pp. 231–3), so much so that they had become almost entirely marginalized and passive. Here, too, there were exceptions. In December 1968 at Avola, in the province of Siracusa (Sicily), landless labourers demonstrated for pay and conditions equal to those of their counterparts in nearby Lentini. They set up a road-block outside their village, but police opened fire on the demonstrators, killing two of them and seriously wounding four others. Avola became a national scandal, as urban Italy discovered that the old patterns of southern rural protest and brutal repression were still in operation.[95]

However, the agro-towns and villages of the interior were no longer the centres of collective action that they had been in the 1940s. Some declined irreversibly. Others, as Piselli has shown for 'Altopiano' in the hills above Cosenza in Calabria, changed and accommodated. At 'Altopiano', migrants first bought up land and then built houses on it, as much as status symbols as places of residence. The class structure became more stratified: no longer was the population of the village divided into the small élite of landowners and the mass of the rural poor. Small proprietors, traders, public officials and the professional classes all became more numerous. Rigid family hierarchies broke down; a collective code of conduct was replaced by a variety of different behaviour patterns. Various forms of state assistance, especially pensions, aided the economic life of the village.[96]

Even more striking were changes in the coastal areas and major cities. Here, as Rossi-Doria has written, development was 'chaotic, unstable, precarious, without respect for any order or civic discipline'.[97] Small industries, often linked to agriculture, such as tomato-canning factories, offered less than stable prospects of employment. The building trade flourished, but so too did the system of subcontracting (*appalti*), with the result that few building workers had regular contracts or were protected by safety regulations, and even fewer had trade union representation. A mass of the unemployed or underemployed remained on the extreme fringes of the labour market, exposed to all the inducements and publicity of a consumer society, but without the material means to satisfy many of their basic needs. In the interstices of this vital but chaotic growth, criminal organizations like the Mafia in Sicily and the Camorra in Naples increased their networks of influence and protection. Society was divided against itself. Narrow municipal or corporate or criminal rivalries flourished, leaving little possibility for the sort of solidarities which had typified the 'hot autumn'. The political class of the South, corrupt and clientelistic, presided contentedly over this spectacularly uneven development.

a. THE REVOLT OF REGGIO CALABRIA

Between 1969 and 1973, the South was riven by a series of urban protests, nearly all of which reflected the fragmented nature of its society and the precariousness of its modernization. In the spring of 1969 the town of Battipaglia rose in revolt after the threatened closure of local factories. Two people were killed by the police, two hundred injured, and a police station was sacked by the enraged populace.[98]

The most serious revolt of the period occurred at Reggio Calabria. Promises had been made by various politicians that Reggio would become the seat of the new regional government. However, in the summer of 1970 Catanzaro was chosen instead. The ex-mayor of Reggio, the Christian Democrat Pietro Battaglia, organized a series of strikes and demonstrations, one of which was dispersed with particular brutality by the police. Very soon the situation got out of hand; barricades were erected, the railway station was taken over by demonstrators and all trains between Sicily and the mainland were halted.

The left-wing parties and trade unions, with the exception of PSIUP, called for a stop to what they judged to be an unjustified municipal revolt. However, they were out of touch with the problems and attitudes of the majority of Reggio's population. Behind the protest lay a socio-economic situation of considerable gravity. Not more than five thousand people in the whole of Calabria were employed in large or stable workplaces. In Reggio twelve thousand people lived in squalid shacks, some of which dated back to 1908, the year of a great earthquake there. The retail trade soaked up manpower, but with one shop for every thirty inhabitants there were frequent closures and no security of employment. In these circumstances, the possibilities offered by employment in the public sector were all-important. Reggio, one of the poorest cities in Italy, *had* to become the seat of regional government. So too, for that matter, did Catanzaro, only marginally less poor.[99]

The protests at Reggio continued for over a year. For the period July–September 1970 alone, according to official figures, there were nineteen days of general strikes, twelve dynamite explosions, thirty-two road-blocks, fourteen occupations of the railway station, two of the post office, one of the airport and one of the local TV station; there were six assaults on the prefecture and four on the police headquarters (*questura*); 426 people were charged with public-order offences, three people were killed and more than 200 wounded.[100]

The left, with the exception of the PSIUP and the revolutionary groups, continued to condemn the protests. The neo-Fascists had no such scruples. Reggio had always voted to the right: it had been strongly monarchist in 1946, and the DC had dominated local politics ever since. The MSI now stepped in where the Christian Democrats no longer dared to tread. The neo-Fascist Ciccio Franco soon became the mob leader of Reggio, and in the 1972 national elections at Reggio, the local MSI candidate gained 21,000 preference votes in the city. In many urban areas of the South, the neo-Fascists came to be recognized as the representatives of the marginalized sectors of society, the champions of the deprived in a society of increasing affluence. At Catania, in the local elections of 1971, the MSI gained 21.5 per cent of votes.[101]

The government's response to the revolt of Reggio Calabria was to confirm Catanzaro as regional capital, but to allow the regional assembly to meet at Reggio. In order to aid the plight of the Calabrian unemployed, plans were also announced for the building of a giant steel works at Gioia Tauro, up the coast from Reggio. This was to be most spectacular and disastrous of all the 'cathedrals in the desert'. Part of Gioia's rich agriculture of citrus fruits and olives was destroyed, a major port was constructed in its place, but no steel works was ever built. By the mid-1970s the world steel market had collapsed and there was no point in construction going ahead.

In October 1972 Vincenzo Guerrazzi, whose family came from the province of Reggio Calabria, was one of a thousand Genoese workers from the Ansaldo company who hired a ship and sailed down to take part in a demonstration of solidarity by northern industrial workers with their southern brothers. He and his comrades, some 40,000 in all, marched through Reggio Calabria to the amazement of the local population; some applauded, others jeered. In reality, the two worlds were far apart.[102]

Conclusion

In drawing up a political balance sheet of the turbulent years 1968–73, two questions stand out. The first concerns the hopes and aspirations of the students and young workers who were the protagonists of the years 1968–9. Their stated aim was to effect a revolutionary transformation in Italian society and politics. Judged by these intentions, their actions resulted, to a great extent, in failure. Why was this so?

The second question refers to reform rather than revolution, and to the later period 1969–73: why was it that the progressive forces in Italian society, with the trade union movement at their forefront, were once again able to achieve only a limited response to their demands for corrective reform?

In answering the first question, it is easy enough to provide a subjective explanation, and to ascribe the failure of revolution to the shortcomings of the revolutionaries themselves. As has already been said, the strategy and actions of the revolutionary groups which emerged in 1968–9 were an inadequate response to the demands for political leadership that were coming from the students' and workers' movements. The groups were sectarian, dominated by Third World models of revolution and unable to draw realistic conclusions from the evidence of Italian society. In many ways they reflected the crisis and fragmentation of the revolutionary movement on a world scale. It was difficult to see this crisis in 1968, with Cuba, Vietnam and the Cultural Revolution at the front of everyone's minds. Ten year later it had become clear enough.

However, the failings of the revolutionaries, manifest though they were, were only part of the answer. In 1972 a group of Pirelli workers who had been active in the factory base committee (CUB) wrote a short account of their struggles. In it they listed the necessary phases by which their fellow workers would be won to revolution: 'The worker *must* conceive of himself as a producer and acquire consciousness of his role; he *must* have a class consciousness and become a communist; he *must* realize that private property is a dead weight, an encumbrance that needs to be eliminated [emphases theirs].'[103]

At its simplest level, the problem was that the majority of the Italian working class was unlikely to respond to any of these imperatives. In spite of all the efforts of the militants (and no one could accuse Lotta Continua, for instance, of lack of initiative), the revolutionaries remained small minorities even in the North. Vast sections of Italian society were impervious not only to revolutionary ideology, but even to a modest political awareness. The Garibaldi-Isola quarter in the heart of Milan was, as we have seen, one of the centres of political agitation and housing struggle in these years. Yet a survey of 1971–2 amongst the immigrants of the quarter found that 87 per cent of them had no or very little knowledge of any of the political organizations in the neighbourhood.[104]

In the major northern factories political consciousness was undoubtedly higher. But even in the Centre and the North many areas and workplaces remained untouched by the social protest of these years: this was true of small-scale factories, of most commercial and artisanal concerns, of the areas of peasant farming, of many of the urban *ceti medi*.

The revolutionaries, therefore, who thought that the battle of Corso Traiano was the beginning of a process of revolutionary aggregation found instead that it was the highpoint of subversive action. In the years that followed, only relatively small groups of workers, both blue- and white-collar, were prepared to follow their lead. There are many reasons why this should have been so. In the North and Centre of the country, long-standing loyalties to the traditional parties of the left and to the trade unions made it difficult for the revolutionary groups to make progress. The old pre-1967 student organizations could be swept away without any great difficulty; the same was not true of the CGIL or the PCI. Indeed, when the trade unions decided to 'ride the tiger' of militancy, it became clear that the political space for the revolutionary groups was limited.

It is also true that the objective conditions of young FIAT workers in 1969 were very different from those of most other parts of the central and northern labour force. A 'segmentation' of the labour market had occurred. Labour shortages of certain sorts in the large firms in 1968–9, when combined with the concentration of southern labour in them, gave the workforce of the major northern factories a particular self-confidence and aggression. Elsewhere, especially in the 'industrialized countryside' of the Third Italy, a rather different picture emerges: of involvement in family firms, of a less direct conflict between capital and labour, of a labour force that was regional in its origins.[105]

As for the South, the preconditions for revolt certainly existed. However, as we have seen for the case of Reggio Calabria, the political culture of the urban South, clientelistic and criminal, and the fragmented nature of its society, made it far more likely that protest would find a right-wing rather than a left-wing outlet.

Finally, there is one other hypothesis for why the revolutionary message did not, in the end, achieve a lasting resonance in the Italy of the 'hot autumn'. The student movement and later the revolutionary groups tried to achieve a cultural revolution in the sense of challenging most of the accepted values and institutions of the society in which they were living. In broad terms, theirs was a revolt against authority, against capitalism, against individualism, against excessive consumerism, against sexual repression, even in part against the family. Their ideals, often expressed in the vaguest of terms, and not always adhered to, were those of social and economic equality, of collective patterns of social life, of direct democracy.

However, ever since the 'economic miracle', Italian society as a whole was following a quite different trajectory. As Italy became more urban and more secular, it did not, by and large, move further towards the values which surfaced in 1968, but further away from them. The society that was being formed in the image of the 'economic miracle' was one that accentuated atomization and individualism, as well as further strengthening the family unit. Indeed, the family became *the* basic unit for satisfying needs in contemporary Italy. Italy's modernization, as so many others, was not based on collective responsibility or collective action, but on the opportunities it afforded individual families to transform their lives.

This process was far from complete by 1968. In many ways it had only just begun. It is true that, given the totally unplanned nature of Italy's 'miracle', strong imbalances and contradictions had come to the fore. Hundreds of thousands of immigrants, once they arrived in the North, found nowhere decent to live, no adequate schooling for their children, no proper health care. Many of them also had the sort of work, in large or medium-sized factories, which both accentuated their alienation and increased the possibility of collective action.

However, the *underlying* trends of the period after 1968 were not towards deepening these contradictions but towards their alleviation. Major employers rapidly decentralized production as far as they could so as to fragment the working class and break up the centres of militancy that had emerged in 1968 (see also below, p. 353). Real wages rose significantly, and in spite of inflation were not to decrease for most of the 1970s. Outside the factories, needs were beginning to be met as prosperity increased and family strategies began to pay off. The housing situation was much improved compared to that of the early years of immigration. In 1965 49 per cent of Italian families had had a television, 55 per cent a fridge, and 23 per cent a washing-machine. By 1975 the figures were respectively 92, 94 and 76 per cent.[106]

These figures have not been quoted in order to provide a crudely materialist explanation of the failures of the generation of '68. However, they may form some part of the reason why Corso Traiano proved to be the exception rather than the rule, why rent strikes dwindled away and even why Battipaglia and Reggio Calabria were not, as some militants hoped, the first signs of a generalized southern insurrection.

In this light, the 'cultural revolution' of 1968 emerges as an extra-ordinary but unsuccessful attempt to challenge the predominant values of a rapidly changing society. The movement gained force from the unique international conjuncture of that year; it was aided by the traditions of the Resistance and of working-class militancy; it attracted support because of the dramatic and disorderly way in which Italy was becoming urbanized; but, in the last analysis, it was in direct conflict with the underlying trajectory of Italian modernization.

In May 1968 Rossana Rossanda, one of the leaders of the Manifesto group, wondered 'if the student revolt is the index of a socialist potential that is maturing under the impact of capitalist development, with its consequent moulding and re-moulding of Italian society'.[107] This was a legitimate enough suggestion at that particular moment in time. However, with hindsight, it seems possible that the opposite was true: the long-term trends in Italian society were diametrically opposed to the social and political projects of the generation of '68.

This is not to say that '68 and its aftermath had no influence on the future development of Italian society. Indeed, Italy's path to modernity was never quite the same again. In a whole number of ways, in attitudes to authority, in the openness of the society, in relationships between the sexes, in the subjective value ascribed to politics, the movement left a lasting mark. It was also true that the spontaneous collective action of these years was the prime mover behind the reforms that did emerge.

Yet these consequences were only in small part those which the participants intended or desired. The core values that they held – anti-capitalist, collectivist and egalitarian – were to be rejected; not suddenly, as in France in June 1968, but protractedly, over the course of more than a decade.

If we turn for a moment to the second question, it seems difficult to explain the limited nature of reform in the years 1968–73. The predominant trends in Italian development did not preclude and in many ways cried out for the sort of rationalization which the reformers were demanding. Needs were being met (if not for everyone, everywhere), but institutions and structures were not being modernized, and nor were the worst excesses of unplanned development being checked or curbed. By 1973 a few steps had been taken along the reformist path, but there was no systematic forward march.

How far were the reformers themselves responsible for this failure?

They were certainly not without faults or blind spots. As a movement they were immeasurably stronger than their counterparts in 1963, even though they were without the force of youth, since most young people, on becoming politicized, had posed themselves more global objectives. It is also true that the PCI emerges as the great absentee in these years. Within the CGIL, its militants were mobile and responsive, but as a *political* party the Communists seemed incapable of taking a lead. Jealous of the new-found trade union strength at a political level, often obsessed by the challenge posed by the revolutionary groups to its hegemony of the left, the PCI too often fell back on well-worn political formulas. The Communists were stuck in an uncomfortable half-way house. They wanted to lead the social movements, but they feared that to do so would alienate the moderate electorate and compromise their chances of entering government. The result was a sort of dignified paralysis.

The Socialists did rather better. The strength of social protest in these years gave them a leverage within the government which they had always lacked in the 1960s. Some of the most important reforms of the period, like the Workers' Charter and the divorce law, were in no small part due to the determined action of Socialist deputies.

As for the trade unions, the great protagonists of these years, there is much to be said in their favour. It was they who introduced the factory councils and delegates into Italian workplaces, and it was they who ensured basic democratic rights for workers, such as that of holding meetings during the working day and freedom of movement for their representatives within the factories. Their espousal of the 150-hour education scheme was an outstanding example of a trade union movement looking beyond narrow economic considerations to a broader, cultural perspective of its role. The Italian trade unions attempted to go even further. Their intervention in favour of structural reform was not successful, but at least they had tried to mobilize millions of Italians for better housing and pensions, investments in the South, etc. All in all, this was an impressive record for a mere five years' activity.

However, even the trade unions had a number of blind spots which were to cost them dear. Their efforts were concentrated almost exclusively on the organized working class, and they failed to move out from the factory into society. Their rigid and ritualistic concept of how people could be mobilized in favour of reform was to weaken considerably the pressure they could exert on government. Finally, and most seriously, they were at a loss in the South. It had been one thing to organize the rural labourers of the agro-towns in the 1940s. It was quite another to attempt an intervention in the complex and divided society of the new urban South. Reggio Calabria revealed how weak the Italian trade unions were in the poorest areas of the country.

Not all the responsibility for the limited nature of their success can be placed upon the reformists themselves. Behind the failure to achieve more lay the central problem of the state. By the early 1970s it had become clearer than ever before that the key to reform in society lay with the prior reform of the state. Yet here, in the interstices of the state, matters were getting worse not better, and the politicians seemed incapable of turning the tide.

In the key period from 1970 onwards the public-sector deficit began to increase with alarming rapidity. Two major reasons lay behind this phenomenon. One was the increasing weight, responsibility and indebtedness of public industry. State industry, as we have seen was already in poor shape by the end of the sixties. Then in 1971 GEPI (Gestione e Partecipazioni Industriali) was founded, to bail out and take over an increasing number of uneconomic private companies. GEPI served an important social function, but lacking a radical overhaul the Partecipazioni Statali became an albatross around the government's neck.[108]

The second reason for the growing public-sector deficit was the increase in welfare spending, without a corresponding increase in taxation. Pensions were the largest single item here, the direct result of the reform of 1969. Their extra cost could only have been borne if an efficient and progressive system of taxation had been introduced. The fiscal reform of 1971–3 had fallen far short of this objective.[109]

The bureaucracy was the other major crisis area within the state. The unreformed public administration had acquired a relative autonomy of action which rendered it impervious all too often both to society's needs and to government instruction. The two phenomena of the *'residui passivi'* and the non-implementation of new laws (see pp. 285–6) continued to characterize administrative action in the 1970s. The fate of the housing law of 1971 was paradigmatic of both these phenomena. The state administration could preserve the status quo, but it could be used in the cause of reform only with the greatest difficulty. Indeed, ordinary measures over which there was no political disagreement could easily be sabotaged either by bureaucratic complexity, or by corruption, or by conflicting authorities operating within the administration. Reform of the state was the most difficult of all tasks because of the vested interests involved. Yet without it, any reform programme seemed bound to flounder.[110]

In January 1968 an earthquake destroyed a number of villages in the poverty-stricken valley of Belice in north-west Sicily. Over five hundred people were killed and 90,000 rendered homeless. The President of the Republic, Giuseppe Saragat, immediately promised that the government 'will do everything possible to aid the people made homeless by the earthquake'. Vast sums of money were assigned by Parliament for the reconstruction of the Belice villages. Nine years later, 60,000 people in the valley were still living in the Nissen huts which had been erected immediately after the earthquake. Huge and surreal infrastuctures had been built in the valley – roads that led nowhere, flyovers used only by flocks of sheep, pedestrian walkways with no pedestrians, and so on. Meanwhile, not a single new house had been assigned by the authorities to any of the villagers. The money voted by Parliament had not been spent, or it had been misspent or simply embezzled.[111]

In December, 1975, Don Antonio Riboldi, the parish priest of Santa Ninfa in the Belice, organized the writing of some seven hundred letters by the primary-school children of the Belice to the Senators and Deputies of the Italian Parliament. One of these was from Giovanna Bellafiore to Giulio Andreotti, the veteran Christian Democrat leader. Andreotti replied on 26 February 1976. It is worth reproducing this correspondence as an end-piece to this chapter, not as a personal indictment of Andreotti, but as an example of how the pervasive torpor of the state had triumphed. For a brief moment, for all their failings, the revolutionary groups had challenged this state of affairs from below: organizations like Magistratura Democratica had been small but significant attempts to launch a radical mobilization within the state apparatus. However, the challenge had faltered, leaving the state unreformed and the politicians apologetic but acquiescent.

Santa Ninfa, 16 February 1976

Dear Honourable Andreotti Giulio,

My name is Giovanna Bellafiore. I am the little girl who wrote to you before Christmas, but you didn't reply, which is not right.

I live in a prefabricated hut which is 24 metres square and has only one room. The rain comes in and leaks on the bed, on the wardrobe and on the plates which have been put in the rack to dry. Perhaps you didn't reply because the problem is too hot for you to handle. I beg you to intervene on our behalf, something which no deputy has so far done. Often there is no electricity and no running water in our huts. You Members of Parliament have comfortable houses to live in, with central heating, and you certainly couldn't understand the type of life which we *baraccati* have to live, with no space for anything, no room to study or play, or even for the chairs to put round the table. Do you know that when we eat I sit on my Daddy's and Mummy's bed? In fact the table is almost attached to the bed. If you don't believe my letter I invite you to come and sleep and eat in my house for a week.

Why is no one taking an interest in us victims of the earthquake? I beg you not to throw away this letter because I'm still waiting for a reply, and I beg you to discuss the matter in Parliament with the other *onorevoli*. Yours

Giovanna Bellafiore

Roma, 26 February, 1976

Dear child,

I've received your little letter of 16 February, but I never got the one you said you wrote to me before Christmas. The Belice affair is unfortunately a painful and not easily explicable case of administrative malfunctioning [*procedura*]. The funds for reconstruction were promptly allocated at the time. Three years later a delegation came to Rome and we learnt that there were difficulties over the regulating plans and other town-planning aspects. In 1972, when I was President of the Council of Ministers, I summoned all the mayors of the Belice and I made sure that all the measures that they requested were adopted.

I know that a group of schoolchildren from Santa Ninfa has recently been to Rome and has been able to explain the situation to the country's highest authorities. I hope that this state of affairs will now be resolved. But perhaps it is a good idea for you to ask the mayor of your village to write to me if there is something which I, as a minister and as a deputy, can do. I share your suffering for the inconvenience of makeshift living conditions which should only have been temporary.

With my greetings I am sending you a doll. My children are grown up by now and buying a toy for you took me back for a moment to the time when they were young.

Affectionately,

Giulio Andreotti[112]

Chapter 10

Crisis, Compromise and the 'Anni di Piombo', 1973–80

The D C and the Divorce Referendum of May 1974

THE CHRISTIAN Democrat vote in national elections had remained remarkably stable during the 1960s and early 1970s: 38.3 per cent in 1963, 39.1 per cent in 1968 and 38.7 per cent in 1972. If the traditional rural bases of the party had declined, it had none the less held its own in the new Italy. However, beneath the surface all was not well. The end of the Dorotei's dominance of the party had led to a new and damaging factionalism. In June 1973, at the twelfth congress of the party in Rome, the Dorotei (led by Rumor and Piccoli) could only muster 34.2 per cent of the votes, while Fanfani's faction had 19.8 per cent of the delegates, the Andreotti–Colombo group 16.5 per cent, Base 10.8 per cent, Forze Nuove 10 per cent, and the supporters of Aldo Moro 8.7 per cent.[1]

There were other things wrong as well. Membership was still heavily southern in character, based more on clientelistic necessity than on political conviction. There was low turnover amongst the party's élites, and its parliamentary representatives stayed put longer than those of any other party. Supporting organizations no longer played the crucial role once assigned to them: Azione Cattolica had boasted three million members in 1960; by 1970 its numbers had dropped to 1,657,000 and by 1975 to no more than 635,000. A CLI (see pp. 172–3) had both declined numerically and asserted its autonomy from the party at the same time. CISL had at least grown, but so too had its independence.[2]

Worst of all, the party lacked any strategy when faced with the very changed Italy of continuing collective protest. By June 1973 it was clear that the experiment of Andreotti's centre-right government was not going to work. With difficulty the faction leaders reached a new agreement, the so-called 'pact of Palazzo Giustiniani', signed on the eve of the twelfth congress: the centre-left was to be relaunched, with Rumor as Prime Minister, and Amintore Fanfani was to be recalled as party secretary.

Fanfani intended to strengthen the party organization and public industry, as he had done in the 1950s. However, much had changed since then, and in early 1974 the party was rocked by two major scandals. The first was uncovered by Genoese magistrates, who revealed that petroleum refiners and distributors had been making payments to politicians, above all D C politicians, in return for measures directly favouring their interests. In the ensuing uproar, Parliament hastily passed a law providing for the public financing of the political parties. All parties repre- sented in Parliament were to be funded in proportion to their electoral strength. The measure did little to placate public opinion. Many people were incensed that taxpayers' money was being used in this way, and there was also widespread conviction that private and covert payments to the parties would continue in any case.[3]

The second scandal concerned the activities of the secret services. Here too the work of a young magistrate, Giovanni Tamburino, from Padua, was of crucial importance. Tamburino's inquiries revealed the existence of an organization called the 'Rosa dei Venti', the 'Weathervane', which was coordinating acts of terrorism as a prelude to a right-wing coup. The Rosa dei Venti had members both in the Italian secret services and the armed forces, and appeared to be linked to a supra-national secret-service organization established by N A T O. In October 1974 Tamburino went as far as to order the arrest of General Vito Miceli, the head of the S I D (Servizio Informazioni Difesa), the major branch of the Italian secret service. The Corte di Cassazione hastily ordered Tamburino's inquiries to be transferred to Roman magistrates, who were rather less than vigorous in following up his leads. After a few weeks in detention, Miceli was released. As with the Piazza Fontana bombing, no proper light has ever been shed on the exact composition and activities of the Rosa dei Venti.[4]

Both the petrol scandal and the discovery of the Rosa dei Venti provoked widespread criticism of the D C's political integrity and competence. Then, in the spring of 1974, the thorny question of the divorce referendum returned to the fore. The referendum could no longer be delayed or avoided, and was fixed for 12 May 1974.

Whereas two years earlier the D C had been anxious to shelve the issue, Fanfani now saw it as a chance to relaunch the DC as well as his own political career. Having twice failed to become President of the Republic (in 1964 and 1971), Fanfani abandoned definitively his left-of-centre image. He adopted instead a vigorous traditionalist approach in order to appeal to time-honoured Catholic values. The 1972 election results seemed to him to show the way the wind was blowing. The DC and the MSI, the two parties opposing the new divorce law, had gained 47.4 per cent of the votes between them. It would not need much, argued Fanfani, to tip the balance in their favour.

With little apparent dissent, the rest of the DC leadership fell in line behind Fanfani's initiative. His campaign began with some extraordinary speeches in Sicily. At Enna he made it clear that what was really at stake was the salvation of the Italian family, that 'instrument of progress, guarantor of continuity, fertilizer of the earth, procreator; that hearth which keeps alive ideas and affections, that cradle of the most fervent sanctity'. At Caltanisetta, in front of an audience of swarthy farmers, he went further: 'If divorce is allowed, in Italy it will then be possible to have marriages between homosexuals, and perhaps your wife will leave you to run off with some young girl or other.'[5] This was pretty crude stuff; later in the campaign, Fanfani toned down his interventions and reverted to his professorial style.

The Italian Catholic world as a whole was by no means as convinced as Fanfani of the need for or wisdom of a fanatical campaign against the divorce law. At the highest level, Paul VI chose to remain aloof; his opposition to the law was made clear, but so too, as in his speech of 5 May 1974, was his desire to maintain 'religious peace'. The council of Italian bishops (CEI) took a harder line. On 21 February they stated that 'in such grave circumstances no one should be surprised if priests carry out their mission of illuminating the faithful; and if the latter, aware of their rights and duties, defend the unity of the family and the indissolubility of marriage'.[6] However, there was no shortage of bishops who hastened to add that they regarded the choice as a matter for the conscience of each individual Catholic. Some senior leaders of the CISL went further, and came out actively in favour of divorce; among them were Pierre Carniti and Luigi Maccario. So too did most of the base committees which had sprung up in the late sixties and early seventies.

The pro-divorce camp had its own difficulties. The Socialists and the lay centre parties adopted an unequivocal stance, but the Communist leadership entered the campaign in some trepidation. They were afraid that the Italians were not yet ready for a civil liberties campaign of this sort, and that Fanfani's crude appeals would prove effective. They also did not want to drive a further wedge between themselves and the Christian Democrats at a time when Berlinguer was beginning to propose the need for compromise between the two parties (see below, pp. 354–8). For years the Communists had tried to reassure Italian public opinion that they were as staunch defenders of the family as the Christian Democrats. The referendum laid them open again to the old accusations of seeking to undermine the family.[7]

The result of the referendum of 12 May 1974 showed that both Fanfani and the PCI had misjudged the electorate. The divorce law triumphed by 59.1 per cent against 40.9 per cent. No one had expected so clear a margin of victory. As Italy had modernized and become more urban, opinions and values had changed. For the majority of Italians it seemed both just and sensible to establish the right to end an unhappy marriage. At least on this issue, traditionalist Catholic hegemony had been effectively challenged. The Catholic right had been the first to invoke the referendum mechanism, but it had rebounded on them in a most unexpected fashion.

Economic Crisis

From the autumn of 1973 onwards the advanced capitalist countries experienced an economic crisis which was the most serious since 1929 and which dominated government agendas for the rest of the decade. For Italy it is vital to understand how much the crisis limited the room for manoeuvre and conditioned the actions of all the country's social and political forces. The rapid transformations from 1958 to 1972 had given rise, as we have seen, to major tensions and widespread militancy. Had the economic climate been more serene in the 1970s, this militancy might have won greater concessions and achieved a higher level of political mediation. As it was, no sooner had Italy become one of the great industrial nations of the world than she found herself exposed to the icy winds of recession. The almost simultaneous occurrence of these two elements – transformation and crisis – had the most profound effect on the history of the Republic.[8]

In the autumn of 1973 the OPEC countries decided on a 70 per cent increase in the price of crude oil, as well as a 10 per cent cut in oil exports (later briefly raised to 25 per cent). During the winter of 1973–4, oil prices soared. The long ensuing crisis cannot be ascribed *solely* to the actions of the OPEC countries. As we have seen, a series of major problems had already beset the international capitalist economy before 1973 and had sapped business confidence – the break-up of the Bretton Woods system and the accompanying international financial uncertainty, the dollar devaluations, the explosion in European wage rates, over-accumulation in relation to the labour supply, and sharp decline in profitability. The end of the long boom had thus already been signalled.[9]

However, the oil crisis did play a key role in producing the crash of 1974, which marked the end of a golden era of world trade and the beginning of a decade of stagnation and mass unemployment. The oil price rise raised input costs very greatly, forcing industry to increase its prices and sending profits spiralling downwards. It also transferred to the OPEC countries an estimated \$64 bn or $1\frac{1}{2}$ per cent of world purchasing power. This they neither could nor did spend in the short run. As a result, world demand fell.[10]

In June 1974 Germany's largest private bank, the Herstatt, collapsed. This was the signal for a major slump, but inflation continued to rise. As all the indicators show, 1975 was the blackest year since the war. In the following years, the Western economies were characterized by their stop-go aspect; brief recoveries were followed by brusque halts. The underlining trend was that of 'stagflation', stagnation accompanied by inflation. Prices remained high, profits low, accumulation sluggish. Unemployment rose everywhere as world trade declined. Between 1963 and 1973 the average annual growth of world trade had been 8.5 per cent. In the following decade this figure fell to 3.5 per cent, and the advanced capitalist countries' share fell as that of the newly industrializing nations increased.[11]

How did the Italian economy fare in this unfavourable conjuncture? Various structural problems combined to make Italy, along with Britain, one of the most vulnerable of the Western economies. Her poverty of energy sources had been translated into an over-reliance on oil; in the absence of any national energy policy, oil had come to provide 75 per cent of Italy's energy needs by 1973, compared to only 33.6 per cent in 1955.[12] Her capitalist class had for the most part responded to industrial unrest with investment strikes and the flight of capital. Her governments were notoriously weak; by contrast, her labour movement remained the strongest in Europe, making it next to impossible for increased costs to be met by decreasing real wages.

The Italian economy followed the 'stop-go' pattern of most other advanced capitalist countries: the 'mini-boom' of 1972 and 1973 was followed by the deep recession of later 1974 and 1975, the recovery of 1976, a new decline in 1977 and another moderate recovery in 1978. However, beneath these annual hiccups lay four major trends specific to Italy: a very high and lasting rate of inflation, the growth of the 'black' economy, a limited decline in production and the spiralling public-sector deficit.

Italian inflation remained the highest in the Western world throughout the 1970s. It reached a peak in 1974, but declined very little in the following years. The continuing devaluation of the lira kept Italian goods competitive, but the price to be paid was more expensive imports and even higher prices on the internal market.[13] With the balance of payments in deficit (oil and imports costing ever more), the Italian government was forced to seek a series of international loans, both from West Germany and from the IMF.

At the same time, in line with IMF policy, the Bank of Italy introduced severe deflationary policies and restricted the money supply. A major business recession ensued. Many factories closed (or at least tried to close, as we shall see). Production stagnated; unemployment increased, though only slowly. Problems on the labour market were exacerbated by the lack of work opportunities elsewhere in Europe. In fact 1973 was the first year since the war in which more Italians returned to their country than left it.[14]

The very characteristic Italian response to the recession was to decentralize production as far as possible and to increase the 'black' or hidden sector of the economy. In the Third Italy, as we have seen, there already existed a strong tradition of small-scale production. To this was now added an ever-increasing number of small firms, often illegal, which either performed tasks previously carried out in the major factories or produced goods for the traditional sectors of the economy. The advantages for the capitalist class were manifold: the trade unions had much greater difficulties organizing in small firms and employers could often avoid paying taxes and social-security contributions. The least protected parts of the labour force – women and youth – were frequently employed in the 'black' sector, often on a part-time or home-working basis. So too was family labour.

The 'black' economy, where labour costs were low and profits high, helped to sustain the Italian economy in the midst of the recession. Given its semi-clandestine nature, reliable statistics on the 'black' sector are not to be had: ISTAT, the national statistical office, excluded it from its official figures but estimated that between 1 and 3.5 million people were employed in it; CENSIS, the private social-research institute, put the figure at between 4 and 7 million in 1979, accounting for a staggering 15–20 per cent of the economy. Thus the real state of the Italian economy was more buoyant than official statistics suggested.[15]

Finally, the 1970s saw a continuing rise in Italian public-sector spending. This, of course, was not unique to Italy. The 'fiscal crisis' of the state was to afflict all major capitalist countries by the end of the decade. In Italy, the debts of public-sector industry and the amounts spent by the state on the Cassa Integrazione (the fund for workers made redundant, paying out 90 per cent of previous wages in the first year of redundancy) grew by leaps and bounds. So too, towards the end of the decade, did state spending on education and health provision (see below, pp. 391–3). In 1970 public-sector spending had amounted to 38 per cent of Gross Domestic Product; by 1973 it had reached 43.5 per cent, and by 1982 55 per cent, by which time it was greater than in any other major western European country. Revenue increased more slowly: from 33 per cent of GDP in 1970 to 43.3 per cent in 1982. The public-sector deficit grew correspondingly.[16]

It is worth ending this section by quoting at length the report of one foreign correspondent, Dominick Coyle of the *Financial Times*, for 12 April 1976. This was certainly not one of the better moments for the Italian economy, but Coyle's account does give a very good idea of the economic climate of an unhappy decade:

The lira, meanwhile, has been effectively devalued against the dollar by roughly one quarter over the last three months since the Italian foreign-exchange market was closed down temporarily on 20 January following a major run on the currency . . . the present economic background is one of continuing domestic recession, Italian GNP having fallen last year by 3.7 per cent, the first decline since the Second World War. In crude terms, measuring assets against liabilities, and even making generous allowances for a revaluation of Italy's uncommitted gold reserves, the country is not now on the verge of bankruptcy, it is theoretically bankrupt.

The optimists, and surprisingly there are still many in Italy, point to the capacity of the Italians to overcome crises . . . Oil imports alone this year, assuming no overall increase in usage, will require $2bn in additional exports merely to pay the same bill, and the effects of the lira devaluation are already showing up in domestic prices . . . The authorities have put the main emphasis on monetary measures to try and restore confidence and to counteract the run on the lira. This has pushed up the central bank's discount rate to 12 per cent, and correspondingly, the cost of investment borrowing to all but first-grade bank clients to close on 25 per cent . . .

Interest rates apart, most of Italian industry is now in poor shape. Corporate profitability generally is low or non-existent, and much worse than in 1974 . . . In effect the stop-go cycle has given way to stop-stop, the one exception being the public-sector deficit, which for all practical purposes now appears to be almost totally out of control.

This is what particularly concerned the team from the IMF which was in Italy recently as part of negotiations for a further Italian drawing of $530m from the fund. No one wants to admit officially that the talks have broken down . . .[17]

The Historic Compromise

The major political initiative of these years of crisis came from the PCI. In March 1972, at the party's thirteenth congress, Enrico Berlinguer was elected secretary. He was only fifty at the time, a Sardinian and aristocrat by background, a small shy man of transparent honesty and determination. He certainly did not lack ambition, and as secretary of the party he was to wield nearly as much absolute power as Togliatti had done; but his position in the party was tempered by his aversion to any personality cult. While he took from Togliatti his dislike of rhetoric and the sobriety of his oratory, he lacked Togliatti's aloofness and disdain, and this was to make him more loved by the Communist rank and file.[18]

Berlinguer realized, as did many other leaders of the party, that the PCI's 'dignified paralysis' (see p. 344) of the preceding years could not be allowed to continue. In October 1973, in a famous series of articles in *Rinascita*,[19] Berlinguer launched the concept of the 'historic compromise' between the three major political parties, the PCI, the DC and the PSI.

His starting-point was the need to safeguard against any repetition in Italy of the recent events in Chile, where Salvador Allende's socialist and democratic government had been overthrown by an army coup. In Italy as well, maintained Berlinguer, there was the 'pressing danger of the nation being split in two'; 'we know, and the tragic Chilean experience has demonstrated it once again, how the anti-democratic reaction tends to become more violent and ferocious when popular forces begin to conquer the fundamental levers of power in society and the state'.[20] Ever since 1969, maintained Berlinguer, this tendency had been apparent in Italy. Student and worker militancy had been countered by the strategy of tension, the mobilization of the extreme right and a deteriorating economic situation. The reactionary forces in the country were seeking to create 'a climate of exasperated tension' which would open the way to authoritarian government or at least a permanent shift to the right.

In order to counter these tendencies, Berlinguer proposed a new grand alliance resembling that which the anti-Fascist forces had created in the period 1943–7. Quoting Togliatti on the need for both social and political alliances, Berlinguer insisted that an 'extended and robust fabric of unity'[21] had remained in the country in spite of all attempts to destroy it. This fabric had recently taken on new forms, the most striking of which (although Berlinguer did not mention it specifically) was the drive towards trade union unity.

At a social level, the most important alliance was that of the working class with the various sections of the *ceti medi*, to render them impervious to reactionary appeals. At a political level, it was time for a new understanding with the DC. Socialists and Communists together, argued Berlinguer in a famous passage, could not hope to govern the country, even if they gained 51 per cent of the votes. The Christian Democrats, a party which expressed 'a diverse and quite changeable reality', could be won to cooperation with the left. There was no reason to regard the DC as an 'ahistorical category',[22] permanently on the side of reaction. On the contrary, it had sided with the forces of progress at the time of the centre-left, and had a highly composite social base. Berlinguer concluded: 'The gravity of the country's problems, the ever-present menace of reactionary adventurers, the necessity of opening the way at long last to secure national economic development, social renewal and democratic progress: all these make it ever more urgent and opportune that the forces which group together and represent the great majority of the Italian people reach an agreement which may be defined as the new great "historic compromise".'[23]

There is no doubt that this first version of the historic compromise was primarily defensive in nature. Berlinguer cited Lenin to the effect that revolutionaries had to know when it was best to retreat, as Lenin himself had done at the time of NEP. However, as the debate on the historic compromise unfolded, it became clear that Berlinguer's conception of it was actually extremely ambitious. He presented it, especially after 1976, as a grand strategy in which Communists and Catholics would find a shared moral and ethical code on which to base the political and social salvation of Italy. The Catholic emphasis on solidarity would combine with the Communist practice of collective action to produce a new political order.

This convergence of Catholic and Communist morality in the name of a greater political good was the dominant theme of Berlinguer's life. His own family was founded on just such a compromise, since his wife Letizia was a devout Catholic and his children had been brought up in the Catholic faith. For Berlinguer, the PCI and the DC had a shared interest in preserving Italy from the moral degradation of late capitalism, from 'unbridled individualism, senseless consumerism, economic disorder and the dissipation of resources'.[24]

In his later articles he looked forward to a gradual superseding of capitalism, to the introduction of socialist elements into the economy and to a new order based on austerity, collective values and cooperation. Austerity became the antechamber to salvation. Berlinguer called on the working people of Italy to make sacrifices, and he promised them that these would not be in vain: 'A more austere society will be a more just society, with greater equality, more real freedom, more democracy and more humanity.'[25] Gradually, as the historic compromise forced the ruling conservative groups into crisis, a new historic bloc would emerge, with the working class and its political party as the hegemonic forces in society.

Berlinguer's proposal served two notable purposes. It took the Communists back to the centre stage of Italian politics after years in the wings. It was also to realize, as we shall see, that first defensive intention of its author — the safeguarding of Italian democracy and the insulation of the

D C and the *ceti medi* from authoritarian temptations. Given the explosive nature of the Italian crisis in the 1970s, this was no mean achievement.

However, in terms of Berlinguer's grand design, of the meeting of Catholic and Communist morality on the way to socialism, the historic compromise contained a number of flaws. In the first place, it was based on an idealistic assessment of the Christian Democratic Party. It was all very well to say, as Berlinguer did, that the D C was both capable of change and had changed since 1945, but any sober analysis would have led him to conclude that it had not changed for the better. In 1945, when Togliatti attempted compromise with De Gasperi, the Christian Democrats were a new party, as yet outside the state, and with some radical features to their programme. Thirty years later this was no longer the case. By the early 1970s the D C had occupied and transformed the state, and become *the* capitalist and conservative party in Italy. As such it was the antithesis of Berlinguer's project.

In the second place, Berlinguer's appeal to the Italian population to achieve a more just, more collectivist but more austere society fell for the most part on deaf ears. It was an appeal that was profoundly out of tune with the radical transformations that had taken place in Italian society since 1945. As we have seen, the mass migrations of the late fifties onwards had not been organized on a collectivist basis, nor had they been encouraged and regulated by the state. They had been quintessentially family affairs, with each nucleus seeking to use its own networks in order to survive and prosper in the arduous transition period. In the new Italy, families measured their degree of success in material and consumer terms. Thus any appeal for a new collectivist austerity, from whatever source and with whatever connotations, was bound to be met with incomprehension. For the ordinary Italian, Berlinguer's puritan vision was perhaps to be respected but certainly not to be welcomed.

There was also something distinctly authoritarian and hierarchical about the historic compromise. One of Berlinguer's closest advisers at this time was Franco Rodano, whose own peculiar combination of Catholicism and Stalinism fuelled the attempt to reach agreement exclusively at the leadership level. The expectation was that decisions would then be transmitted downwards to the base of the two great mass organizations of modern Italy. There was thus an open contradiction between aims and means. The historic compromise was supposed to produce greater egalitarianism, direct democracy and mutual solidarity, but the vehicles for achieving these aims were to be two 'churches' which were not noted for their democracy, and those outside the 'churches' were all too easily branded as deviants.

Finally, Berlinguer's project remained very vague. Throughout these years, he insisted on the unique contribution of the P C I's 'third way' to socialism, a way which followed neither the social-democratic nor the Russian models. In 1978 he explained that, unlike the PCI, European social democracy was not pursuing truly transformative and innovatory policies, but reformist ones; it was trying to attenuate the most strident injustices and contradictions of capitalism, but always within the confines of the capitalist system. However, Berlinguer's own contribution to any transitional programme which could be clearly distinguished from such reformism was minimal. There are references in his speeches to the necessity of introducing 'some elements of the socialist ideal', but these remarks were never accompanied by any theoretical elaboration. The party's 'Proposals for a Medium-term Programme', published in 1977,[26] were a hotch-potch soon to be put quietly to one side. Thus the historic compromise, while bearing witness to the 'rare ethical tension'[27] in Berlinguer's leadership, made no contribution to the distinction between corrective and structural reform. This was to be one of its greatest weaknesses.

Workers' Struggles, Revolutionary Groups, Social Movements, 1973–6

a. THE TRADE UNION MOVEMENT

For the trade unions, 1973–6 were difficult years. The impetus which had sustained them earlier had declined, and the economic situation placed them more on the defensive than in 1971–3. Their agenda was dominated by inflation, the closing of factories and the decentralization of production. As the international crisis deepened, many Italian firms closed and many multinational firms withdrew from an Italy where, in their opinion, the trade unions were too strong and the cost of labour too high. Millions of hours of Cassa Integrazione were announced. In the face of this onslaught, workers often occupied their factories and tried to organize solidarity campaigns at a local and national level.[28]

In 1975 the trade unions, on a national level, were still strong enough to win an agreement on index-linking which adequately protected the real wages of the lowest paid.[29] However, a year later the struggle for the renewal of the metalworkers' and chemical workers' contracts resulted in the first major defeat for the trade unions since the 'hot autumn'. Under the pressure of the economic crisis, the balance of power in the factories was shifting slowly back to the employers.

At the same time, the union movement itself became more institutionalized. The vigorous ebb and flow between base and leadership which had characterized earlier years now coagulated into a more traditional pattern of centralized direction. The factory councils began to decline in importance. Rather than elections to the councils taking place without reference to trade union etiquettes (on the *scheda bianca*), the three trade union federations insisted on nominating more and more delegates. The executive committees of many factory councils became full-time trade union activists within the factory and assumed the role of mediating between the trade union hierarchies and the mass of the membership. One step further up, the trade union leadership increasingly looked to political intervention as the solution to the grave problems of the time. As Lumley has written, 'consultation with institutions was privileged over consultation of the rank and file'.[30]

In spite of these negative developments, the working-class movement in the Centre and North remained very strong. In February 1974, when the government announced sharp increases in the price of petrol, food and oil products, workers in many factories marched out in spontaneous protest. The demonstrations lasted for a week.

Later in the same year, another attempt to combat price increases led to the innovative and organized protest which went under the name of *'autoriduzione'* ('autoreduction'). In August 1974 groups of workers at FIAT Rivalta refused to pay the 25–50 per cent increases demanded by the private bus companies which took them to work. Instead, they offered to pay at the old season-ticket rate. The local metalworkers' union quickly organized the protest and elected 'bus delegates' who collected the season-ticket money at the old rate and sent it to the bus companies. The example of the FIAT workers was then taken up throughout Turin and Piedmont. 'Autoreduction' also spread from transport to electricity. The local electrical unions organized the paying of bills at the old tariff (some 50 per cent of the new), and promised that no one would have their supply cut off for taking such action. As a result, an estimated 150,000 electricity bills were 'auto-reduced' in Piedmont. During the winter of 1974–5 the movement spread rapidly to other cities of the Centre and North; telephone charges were also brought under attack.

This extensive non-payment was supported by some local trade unions and by all the revolutionary groups. However, the trade union leadership was extremely reluctant to be involved in illegal actions, and the PCI also condemned the movement as adventurist. The rank-and-file committees which had been set up to coordinate the protest also found great difficulty in persuading the majority of families to join the action. Inflation was deeply felt, but not to the point of uniting a neighbourhood on the basis of defying the law. By mid-1975 the movement was dead, even though inflation was at its peak.[31]

One last experiment in rank-and-file action, this time institutional, is worthy of mention. In the early 1970s *consigli di zona* (zone councils) were set up as the neighbourhood counterparts of factory councils. They were planned originally to coordinate protest action *outside* the factory, to be elected on a delegate basis and to be the focal point for the building up of solidarity in the neighbourhoods of the great cities. However, the political parties, including the PCI, fearful of losing control over the councils, insisted that they should nominate delegates in strict ratio to the local strength of the parties. As such, the zone councils became merely another level of party control and influence, and not a direct expression of local opinion. Innovation was thus canalized and stifled. The zone councils remained without influence, and the mass of the city population remained apathetic to them or ignorant of their existence.[32]

b. THE REVOLUTIONARY GROUPS

The growing defensiveness of the workers' movement posed new and difficult problems for the revolutionary groups. It became ever less feasible to present the revolution as imminent. In June 1974, Adriano Sofri of Lotta Continua could still claim that 'the masses are at a turning-point of revolutionary significance',[33] but there was little to sustain such faith. The groups had to face the fact that a long, uphill struggle was ahead. The PCI was not going to disappear when faced with the shrill cries of 'revisionists'; nor was there going to be a sudden breakthrough to mass revolutionary politics. New perspectives had to be sought, which took into account the groups' position in the wider context of Italian politics – their relationship to institutions, to the trade unions, to elections and so on.

No very satisfactory answer was produced: the majority of the groups simply accentuated the *party* nature of their organizations. Rather than seeking alternative forms and new models of organization, they aped the traditional structures of the international workers' movement, with centralism triumphing over democracy. As Bobbio writes, in Lotta Continua, from 1973 onwards, 'the possibility of comrades contributing to the formation of the political line was much reduced; the responsibility for the major decisions was ever more concentrated at the top of the pyramid'.[34] The leaders of the groups took themselves increasingly seriously. Sofri became secretary of Lotta Continua in 1973; Aurelio Campi, his counterpart in Avanguardia Operaia, delivered a three-hour opening speech at the congress of the group in the autumn of 1974.

The groups fossilized and became more authoritarian, but their influence did not diminish. The revolutionary left was strong in all the major cities, but Milan, with its vast industrial hinterland, was probably its nerve-centre. These were the years in which the groups could regularly mobilize 20,000–30,000 people in the city; years when the squads of Fascist youths who tried to establish no-go areas, as at San Babila, were beaten off the streets by the groups' highly organized *servizi d'ordine* (para-military stewards' organizations); when an alternative culture both innovatory (the theatre of the famous actor and playwright Dario Fo at the Palazzina Liberty) and derivative (the unquestioning importation of the drug culture and highly commercialized rock music) flourished as never before.[35]

The movement in the universities never regained the force of 1967–8, but that in the secondary schools, controlled by the revolutionary left, was stronger than ever before. In the army too, in the wake of the Chilean coup, all the major groups intensified their activities. Thousands of copies of *Proletari in Divisa* were distributed in the barracks on a monthly basis. The demonstration in Rome in September 1974, commemorating the first anniversary of the Chilean coup, was marked by the presence of some two hundred conscript soldiers in uniform.[36] In the major factories in the North, the revolutionary groups continued to be strongly represented, with their own cells, bulletins and group meetings.

c. RED TERRORISM: ORIGINS AND EARLY ACTIVITIES

For a small number of militants the groups no longer offered any answer. The Red Brigades (Brigate Rosse, BR) were formed as early as 20 October 1970; they described themselves as 'autonomous workers' organizations', prepared to fight the employers on their own terms. In practice, this signified the decision to give pride of place in political action to violent, armed struggle. The Italian red terrorists, like all terrorists before them, wanted to accelerate the course of history. As the early part of the seventies passed, and the revolution came no nearer, their impatience grew. The widespread and largely legal struggle carried out by the revolutionary groups in civil society was, in their opinion, not getting anywhere. What was needed instead was illegal and violent action, which would sharpen the contradictions in Italian capitalism and make inevitable a civil war between exploiters and exploited.

The founder members of the Red Brigades came from diverse social and ideological backgrounds. Some, like Renato Curcio and Mara Cagol, had been students at Trento university and members of Maoist groups. Others, like Alberto Franceschini and his friends in Reggio Emilia, had belonged to the FGCI (the Communist youth movement). Many had strongly Catholic backgrounds, and the transition from adolescent religious idealism to the revolutionary groups (most often Potere Operaio and Lotta Continua) and then to the terrorist bands was a common one. Most of the first terrorists were from working-class or lower-middle-class families. Franceschini's grandmother had been a leader of the peasant leagues, his father a worker and anti-Fascist who had been deported to Auschwitz.[37]

The models for the red terrorists were primarily those of the Latin American urban guerrilla movements. The two volumes on the Tupamaros published by Feltrinelli became a sort of do-it-yourself manual for the early Red Brigades. The other reference point was the Italian partisan movement of 1943–5. The terrorists interpreted the Resistance as a striking example of a youthful minority using violent means for just ends.

It will long be a matter of debate to what degree the social movements and revolutionary groups of '68 onwards were responsible for the growth of terrorism.[38] There is no doubt that the very widespread justification of 'proletarian' and 'revolutionary' violence present in the long 'hot autumn' provided a framework within which terrorism could flourish. It is also true that the continuous violent clashes in a city like Milan between extreme left demonstrators, Fascist groups and the forces of order made violence habitual to many militants. Many of the members of the semi-military *servizi d'ordine* were to populate the terrorist brigades as the decade progressed. The myth of imminent revolution was also a direct emanation from '68. When the revolution did not arrive, it was not surprising that some militants decided that a final, supreme voluntarist act would provide the necessary short cut.

However, the differences between the broad movement and the terrorist bands were greater than their similarities. For all their faults, the revolutionary groups realized that any transformation of Italian society had to derive from action in civil society, from the building of a mass movement, from changing popular consciousness. Success or failure was to be measured in these terms alone. The terrorists, by contrast, by choosing to work clandestinely and to use exemplary violent action, cut themselves off from reality and put in its place their own invented world. Their arid communiqués were the supreme example of abstract ideology replacing social analysis. Incapable, until too late, of measuring the likely effects of their actions, the terrorists reaped a tragic harvest. Not only were they to kill in the most cold-blooded fashion, but they were also to contribute greatly to the destruction of the whole movement for change in Italian society.[39]

The early actions of the Red Brigades, from 1972 onwards, were no more than armed propaganda concentrated in Milan and then Turin. Right-wing trade unionists, managers and foremen, principally in the two Milanese factories of Pirelli and Sit Siemens, were their first targets. Sometimes their victims' cars were set on fire, sometimes they were beaten up. In March 1972, Idalgo Macchiarini, a manager of Sit Siemens, became the first person to be kidnapped by the BR (for some twenty minutes). The terrorists tied a placard around his neck, bearing the following inscription: 'Macchiarini, Idalgo, Fascist manager of Sit Siemens, tried by the BR. The proletarians have taken up arms, for the bosses it is the "beginning of the end".' The Red

Brigades aimed at this time to win over the factory vanguards of Milan and Turin; no one was killed by them.[40]

The other clandestine left-wing group operating, in a manner of speaking, at this time was the GAP (Gruppo di Azione Partigiana) of Giangiacomo Feltrinelli. Feltrinelli, the wealthy publisher and friend of Fidel Castro, was obsessed by the possibility of a right-wing coup in Italy. His GAP was supposed to be the basis for armed resistance against such a coup, but existed more in imagination than in reality. In March 1972, Feltrinelli blew himself up when attempting to attach explosives to an electric pylon at Segrate, near Milan.

From early 1974, the quality of the Red Brigades' actions changed. From now on they announced 'an attack on the heart of the state'. On 18 April the Genoese judge Mario Sossi was kidnapped by the organization. This day had been chosen because Giovanni Agnelli became the president of Confindustria on 18 April, an event which, according to the BR, marked 'the beginning of a Gaullist-style coup in Italy'. Sossi's kidnapping, which lasted for thirty-five days, enabled the BR to achieve national notoriety. At the end of it, after the Red Brigades' request for an exchange of prisoners had been rejected, Sossi was released unharmed.

The recruitment to terrorist groups became more widespread. In 1973 Potere Operaio (see p. 312) dissolved itself, and a part at least of its militants chose the path of clandestine action. The year was also decisive for the movement for prisoners' rights. A long series of revolts took place in Italy's prisons, all demanding the reform of the codes governing prisoners' conditions and rights. In spite of repeated promises, the government did little to improve conditions, and the traditional left-wing forces left the prisoners' movement in isolation. Out of this bitter defeat grew the NAP, the Nuclei Armati Proletari, consisting mainly of ex-prisoners and ex-members of Lotta Continua. The NAP were poorly organized, and after a few actions which imitated those of the BR, they were practically dismantled and destroyed by the police. The remnants of the organization fused briefly with the BR in 1976.[41]

After the Sossi kidnapping the police began systematically to mop up the forces of red terrorism in Italy. Hiding-places were discovered, the Red Brigades were infiltrated, and an increasing number of arrests and shoot-outs occurred. It was in one of these, near Milan in October 1974, that Roberto Ognibene, a member of the Red Brigades, killed the Carabiniere, Marshal Felice Maritano. In another, in June 1976, Mara Cagol, one of the BR's founding members, was killed by the police. By early 1976 Mario Moretti was the only member of the Red Brigades' executive committee still at large. The number of effective members of the organization had been reduced to a dozen.[42]

d. SOCIAL MOVEMENTS IN THE SOUTH

If the early seventies saw the first excursions down the tragic blind alley of red terrorism, they also witnessed one or two extraordinary attempts to turn the tide of history in the South. During the years 1968–73, as we have seen, southern urban protest had been mainly municipal or narrowly corporate in character, led by the extreme right and subordinate to the dominant political culture. From 1973 onwards, sadly out of phase with the northern movement, there were the first attempts to break this mould.

The Neapolitan movement of the *disoccupati organizzati* (the organized unemployed) was the most striking example of this new spirit. In 1973 a cholera epidemic had swept the city, causing many deaths. In the popular quarters of the centre, where the *bassi* (see pp. 36–7) still predominated, neighbourhood committees were set up to demand that a proper sewer system be constructed and that other elementary forms of public and private hygiene be introduced. Out of these committees grew the organization of the unemployed.[43]

Naples had, and still has, one of the worst records of unemployment in Europe. In the absence of a developed industrial structure, many of the poor in this vast city (population 2,700,000 in 1971) still lived in the early seventies as they had done in 1945 – from small trading, contraband, petty thieving, domestic work and so on. In 1977, according to the Camera di Lavoro, only 28.3 per cent of the active population was in regular work. In the same year the official number of unemployed was 170,000. This figure was misleading in two, opposing ways. Nearly all of Naples' poor had *some* work or other, however part-time or precarious. But at the same time the number of *under*-employed was very much greater than the official figures suggested. All the poor were heavily dependent on clientelistic contact and corruption as levers to help them obtain regular jobs.[44]

The 'organized unemployed' tried to break these patterns. In the place of the official and corrupt *collocamento* (labour-exchange lists), the movement drew up lists of unemployed based on the twin criteria of those most in need and those most active in the day-to-day struggle for jobs. The movement was organized on a democratic basis, with delegates from different areas and a city-wide executive committee. The first seven hundred members of the organization succeeded, after a long struggle, in gaining regular jobs as manual workers in the municipality's public works and restorations department. With great difficulty, the movement also gained recognition from the major trade unions, and the CGIL–CISL–UIL banner was unfurled at the head of its many demonstrations. Spurred on by these initial successes, the movement spread rapidly, reaching its peak in 1975–6 when it had between 10,000 and 15,000 active members. Both the Maoists of the 'PCI d'Italia' and Lotta Continua were active in its midst, but the Communist Party always remained suspicious of it.[45]

The movement's principal forms of action were regular protests in the centre of the city, blocking the traffic for many hours and leading to clashes with the police. The unemployed explained that 'as we can't strike or close a factory, for the moment the streets are our factory, and as the workers stop production, so we stop the traffic'.[46] There were also regular occupations of local government offices as well as an ongoing and unsuccessful appeal to the workers of Alfasud to stop working overtime. Perhaps the most telling tactic chosen by the movement was the week long *'sciopero a rovescio'* ('strike in reverse') undertaken at the new Neapolitan Policlinico (hospital). This work-in revived in the heart of the modern urban service sector a form of action which had been used by the rural labourers in the late 1940s. Two hundred people from the organization, of whom sixty were women, went to work alongside the regular employees for one week, in order to draw attention to the dramatic understaffing in the hospital.[47]

The movement had many weaknesses. The criteria on which its lists were drawn up – the subjective one of presence in the struggle and the objective one of need – could be and often were in contradiction with each other. There was also, as was to be expected, some discrimination by the men against unemployed women; those women who took an active part in the movement and its meetings were sometimes denounced as 'whores'. The ignorance and bigotry in what one unemployed Neapolitan called 'this society of wolves' would not disappear overnight. There was more than one case of corruption, and of an individual's desire for a regular job triumphing over his fidelity to the movement.[48]

None the less, in the notoriously difficult area of organizing the unemployed, the Neapolitans built a mass movement second to none in Europe. This was all the more remarkable given the political traditions of the city. The 'organized unemployed' not only attacked the clientelistic and political basis on which employment opportunities were based; they also tried to undermine, as Di Vittorio had tried to do for the southern rural labourers after the war, the employers' control of the labour market. In doing so, they created an extraordinary, albeit temporary, solidarity amongst a section of the Neapolitan underemployed; as one member of the movement wrote: 'we discovered that our most secret problems were the same as those of the others'.[49]

Naples in 1975 and 1976 saw a series of collective struggles of which the movement of the unemployed was only the most significant. *Autoriduzione* spread here too, with thousands of families refusing to pay electricity bills. There were also many housing occupations, both in the public and the private sector. For the first time, the disabled and handicapped of the city, of whom there were many hundreds, organized themselves to fight for their rights. They were among the first groups in the traditional May Day procession of 1976.[50]

The other capital of the South, Palermo, did not witness such extensive mobilization, but even here the tight hold of the D C and the Mafia seemed for a moment to be in doubt. The earthquake which had reduced the Belice to ruins in 1968 also had dire effects upon the centre of Palermo. After the wartime bombing, the city's historic centre had been left in a state of total degradation by successive D C administrations. By 1974 the centre's population, which had stood at around 200,000 in 1945, had declined to some 50,000. After the earthquake of 1968 a first wave of illegal house occupations had forced the prefect to assign empty public housing to the squatters. In the autumn of 1975 a second wave followed. Hundreds of families, mainly from the centre, but also from the shanty towns of the peripheries, occupied both private and public housing. They were supported by members of the revolutionary groups. Women from the poorest quarters of the city were the guiding force behind the action. On 10 November 1975 a general strike was proclaimed, the P C I agreed to a day of action and a massive demonstration marched through the city's centre.

The housing movement did not survive for long or achieve notable victories. It was difficult indeed to organize in a city marked, as Chubb has written, 'by extreme social and economic fragmentation and the absence of any associative structures that could serve as poles of aggregation for the population'.[51] The new public housing on the extreme periphery of the city, the CEP estate completed in 1967 and the ZEN estate (1968–71), only reinforced their inhabitants' sense of despair. In the slums of the city centre there had at least been street communities. On the new estates, which were miles from anywhere, there was no street lighting, no shops, no schools, no rubbish collection and sometimes, because the inhabitants were squatting, no electricity or running water. These estates were the extreme examples of the atomization, alienation and isolation which were the overriding features of public housing construction in contemporary Italy: 'They have sent us here to die ... we have been abandoned in the desert, deported to an island, like in the Stone Age, worse than in a cemetery.'[52]

e. FEMINISM

The last of the collective movements to develop in the early 1970s was that destined to have the greatest influence in the long run. As Mariella Gramaglia has written, feminism in Italy came after the agitations of 1968, and went beyond them.[53]

In the 1960s in Italy, politics was almost exclusively the domain of men. In Turin the male immigrants from the South told Fofi that 'everyone knows that women don't understand anything about politics, and so it's right that they leave these things to the men'.[54] Even in Communist

Bologna in 1972, Kertzer noted a woman activist complaining in her section meeting that time and time again comrades' wives refused to speak to her about joining the P C I, 'asserting that their husbands take care of those things'.[55]

The student movement and 1968 had seen more young women taking part in politics than at any time since 1945–8. Similarly, during the 'hot autumn' and after, thousands of women workers were in the forefront of trade union struggles. Women were the protagonists of some of the most determined battles to prevent sackings and closures – at the Autovox and Luciani factories in Rome, at Marvin Gelber and the Crouzet in Milan, at the Pettinature di Lane in Genoa, and so on. Even so, the male-dominated trade unions were very slow to champion women's rights or change their own practices. It was symptomatic of their attitudes and those of the left-wing parties that in the Workers' Charter of 1973 the article banning unfair discrimination at work did not mention discrimination based on sex.[56]

From the end of 1975 onwards the women's movement assumed national proportions, reaching its peak in the following year. Two processes contributed to the development of this great collective moment in the history of Italian women. First, as inflation and stagnation took their toll, the trend of constant improvement in living standards was brusquely halted. Women, especially working-class women, found it increasingly difficult to balance family budgets. Their own potential for contributing to their families' resources through paid work, either at home or outside it, was constantly menaced by the economic crisis. These pressures on the well-being of the family produced, as Laura Balbo has written, 'subjective tensions in women but also the development of a collective consciousness'.[57] Of course, the forms of this consciousness varied greatly in relation to the women's social class, their age, what part of the country they lived in, etc. But everywhere, in greater or lesser numbers, women became involved in social struggles on an unprecedented scale. The battles for housing, on *autoriduzione*, for improved services in the neighbourhoods, saw women emerge from the private sphere and take a leading role in collective action. In Turin, in September 1974, no less than six hundred families occupied the new Falchera estate in what was one of the largest and best organized of Italian occupations. After a struggle which lasted several months, every single family was guaranteed a home by the Turin council. The women of the occupation set up their own action committee, started a gynaecological centre and forced the commune to open a kindergarten on the estate. 'Rosa', thirty-one years old and married with two children, had moved from Calabria to Turin in 1961. She was a worker in a local factory, had always voted Communist, and became a 'staircase delegate' during the occupation. She told Re and Derossi how she came to take part:

Before the occupation I lived at Falchera Vecchia. The flat was very old and in a bad state. We'd been asking for years for a new house. The day of the occupation I went to work and I didn't know anything about what was happening. I'm not saying that I was against the occupation; only that I always thought that they gave priority to those who were really in need, and so forth. Well, I came back from work and I found the house empty and a note from my mother saying that she'd gone to join the occupation at the Falchera! I have to say I wasn't pleased at all, because, as I've just said, I wasn't sure it was right. So I went to the occupation to look for my mother and to see what flat she'd occupied. When I found her she came towards me rather hesitantly; she thought I was going to be cross and shout at her. She said to me: 'Listen, I came to the occupation because I saw that everyone was going and I thought it was right; four of you live in a kitchen and a bedroom, and then there's me, and that makes five.' There was so little room in that old flat, the toilet was an outside one and unhygienic as well. So I said, 'No, mamma, you did well.' I didn't want to seem to be shouting at her, but deep inside I still wasn't that pleased. But then once this struggle started, I realized they'd been giving flats to people who were better off than us. And so I said to myself, we've done well, and my mother and I began to get to know the other women who were occupying. A lot's changed for me during this occupation. In the factory I've always been in favour of the strikes and I know what it is to fight. But the struggle at the Falchera has been different because so many women have got involved. And we've talked about so much, not just the occupation, but all sorts of things.[58]

The second process, that both preceded the one described above, and fed into it, was the growth of Italian feminist groups from 1970 onwards. These were small groups in the major cities, formed mainly of middle-class women. For them, the influence of the American women's movement, with its emphasis on separatism and consciousness-raising, was all-important. As Anna Rossi-Doria has written, feminism has historically contained within it the themes both of equality (with men) and diversity (of women).[59] For the Italian groups of the seventies, the accent was very much on the second. They concentrated on pooling their experiences of a patriarchal world that was hostile to them; on analysing their own sexuality and women's oppression by men; on formulating demands which were less for parity than for women's rights in an autonomous sphere of their own. As in France, the groups were interested in working together in the fields of psychoanalysis, of theory, of feminist literature.

They also proposed a more general politics. At the heart of it was the slogan, first coined by the American group NOW, that 'the personal is political'. Liberation was not to be postponed until after the revolution, but was to start in the sphere of the private, in everyday relationships between women, men and children. Indeed, only by transforming the here and now, the personal, was there any possibility of achieving a later, more global transformation. This 'prefigurative' politics, as it came to be called, was the antithesis of the praxis of the revolutionary groups, where personal relationships were subordinate to the greater goal of eventual radical change. Different too was the women's emphasis on non-violence and their insistence on loose and non-authoritarian forms of organization. This attempt to redefine the very bases of politics, however Utopian, was strikingly new, in strong contrast to the ancient models of both the traditional and non-traditional left.

Different groups in the Italian feminist movement raised different demands. Rivolta Femminile denounced marriage and the family as the site of male domination; Lotta Femminista raised the slogan of 'wages for house-work'; the UDI, the traditional movement of Communist women, put more emphasis on the intervention of the state to relieve women's oppression. One of the most influential groups was the MLD, the Movimento della Liberazione delle Donne Italiane. This was an organization closely connected with the small Radical Party, which was to become the principal pressure group for civil-rights reform in the mid-1970s. The MLD combined demands for equality (the elimination of gender discrimination in the schools, of sexual discrimination at work, etc.), with those which would increase women's autonomy (i.e. the right to control their own bodies through free contraception and the liberalization of abortion).

The first major demonstration of the women's movement, some 20,000 strong, took place in Rome on 6 December 1975. It was disturbed by a group of men from a Roman section of Lotta Continua who, unable to accept the idea of a 'women's only' demonstration, tried to join it by force. That evening, the headquarters of Lotta Continua were occupied by enraged women members of the group. It was a sign of things to come.[60]

Throughout 1976 the women's movement developed rapidly. Women *delegati* (shop stewards) set up collectives in their different unions and created women's commissions in the factory councils. Through the 150-hour education scheme, women teachers and feminists had a unique opportunity of widening their audience. In the secondary schools feminist ideas and collectives spread very fast indeed. All this created more than a few difficulties. There were tensions between the original founders of the movement and the influx of younger women; there was the danger of the authority of the movement being invoked in mystical fashion to justify a new conformity; there were rivalries between different groups. The 'new politics' was having to fight a hard battle with the old.[61]

However, all these tensions were temporarily rendered secondary in the battle to reform the laws on abortion. This issue successfully united, in a way which was never to be repeated, the very diverse social and theoretical strands of the Italian women's movement. Abortion was illegal in Italy in 1970, and was punishable by up to five years' imprisonment. Tens of thousands of illegal abortions were carried out each year. Those women able to do so flew to clinics abroad; others had to put their health at stake by having recourse to back-street practitioners. There could not have been a greater gap between, on the one hand, the official morality of church and state, and, on the other, social reality.

In 1975 the M L D and the small Radical Party organized the collection of signatures for a referendum on the abortion question. Five hundred thousand signatures were needed; 800,000 were collected. Women's mobilization on this issue was able to transform it from an important civil-rights question into a wide-ranging discussion on women's position in Italian society. In April 1976, 50,000 women marched in Rome. Only the calling of a general election, in June 1976 (to which we must now turn), prevented the referendum from going ahead.[62]

Parties, Reforms and Elections, 1974–6

If these years still witnessed the growth of remarkable, diverse and innovative social movements, like those of feminism and the Neapolitan unemployed, they did not see much in the way of reform. Both the economic crisis and that of the D C seem to have been too severe to allow much space for social legislation. However, two measures are worthy of mention, the first constituting a considerable advance, the second much less so.

In the spring of 1975 Italian family law was finally reformed, with the relevant provisions of the civil code of 1942 and the penal code of 1930 being replaced by new legislation. The battle to change the law had been initiated by Pietro Nenni way back in 1966, but progress had come to a standstill at the committee stage of the Senate. Only the result of the divorce referendum and ensuing pressure from the women's movement succeeded in unblocking the situation.

The most important principle of the new law was that which estab-lished parity between the two partners in marriage. Previous insistence on the supremacy of the male head of household, and of the right of a husband to control his wife's behaviour and activity, was abandoned definitively. In addition, new norms were to govern the relationship between parents and children. Parents had the duty not only to 'maintain, instruct and educate' their children, but also to take into account their 'capacity, natural inclinations and aspirations'. A further provision abolished nearly all legal discriminations against children born out of wedlock. In all, the law marked a major departure from the previous legal conception of the Italian family as a hierarchical, authoritarian and pyramidal structure.[63]

The second reform, which had as its object the school system, was less successful. In 1973 and 1974, the Christian Democrat Minister of Education, Franco Maria Malfatti, attempted to democratize the structures of Italian education, introducing elected bodies at every level in order to give representation to teachers, parents and pupils. However, the legislation erred on the side of caution, giving only consultative rather than real power to the various constituencies. Students boycotted the new elections and parents turned out to vote in very small numbers. Control was left firmly in the hands of the central educational bureaucracy, the local authorities (*provveditori*) and the head teachers.[64]

Reformism stagnated, but just when it looked as if the Italian politicians were once again becalmed, the elections of 1975 and 1976 unexpectedly offered totally new perspectives.

At first, there was little sign of what was to come. Even after the débâcle of the divorce referendum Amintore Fanfani remained at the head of the DC. He was convinced that the DC could still win at the regional and local elections of June 1975 if it appealed to the traditional values and anti-Communism of the electorate. This time the whole party gave him unqualified support; the DC's hold on local and regional power was at stake.

The campaign preceding the June 1975 election was marked by a climate of widespread violence. The strategy of tension had never been abandoned by the extreme right. On 28 May 1974, little more than a fortnight after the divorce referendum, a bomb exploded in the main square at Brescia, during the course of an anti-Fascist demonstration. Eight people were killed. That same summer, on 4 August, another bomb exploded on a train travelling between Florence and Bologna. This time there were twelve victims.[65] Street violence escalated in the first months of 1975. First a Greek student, Giorgio Mantekas, a sympathizer of the MSI, was killed in the course of clashes in Rome between the neo-Fascists and the left groups. Then in Milan, on 15 April 1975, a neo-Fascist killed Claudio Varalli of the student movement. A day later, during the course of the demonstration called in protest at Varalli's murder, a police lorry ran down and killed Giannino Zibecchi, of the anti-Fascist committees.

Fanfani presented his party as the only one that could restore 'law and order' and pointed to the new public-order law (the *legge Reale*) which the DC had forced through in March 1975. The PCI, on the other hand, waged a very effective campaign concentrating on the corruption and disorder of Christian Democrat control of local government. 'We are the party with clean hands' was the message with which the PCI's campaign posters bombarded the electors. The positive experience of local government in the Red Belt was contrasted with the chaos and clientelism of most of the regions under DC control.

The results of the regional and local elections of 15 June 1975 saw a great advance for the PCI: the party increased its vote by 6½ per cent in comparison to 1970 (the previous regional elections), and reached 33 per cent of the vote. The Socialists also did well, polling nearly 12 per cent, an increase of 1.5 per cent. The DC fell back 2 per cent to 35 per cent, though it is important to note that the regions with special status (Sicily, Sardinia, Trentino-Alto Adige, Friuli-Venezia Giulia, Val d'Aosta), where the DC vote was strong, were not called upon to vote in June 1975. The MSI–DN, with 6½ per cent, increased its vote a little compared to 1970, but declined markedly in comparison to the national elections of 1972.

The elections of 1975 signalled an earthquake in regional and local government. With the pro-Communist Francesco De Martino at the head of the PSI, the Socialists quickly agreed to join the PCI in the creation of left-wing local administrations. The regions of Emilia-Romagna, Tuscany and Umbria had been in left-wing hands since 1970. Now they were joined by Lombardy, Piedmont and Liguria. Even more striking was the change of guard in Italy's cities. With the exception of Palermo and Bari, every single major city fell into left-wing hands. At Naples a left-wing council took control for the first time ever. The Communists, boosted by their activism during the 1973 cholera epidemic and by the climate of social mobilization described above, became the largest single party in the city, with 32.3 per cent of the votes compared to the DC's 28.4 per cent. This was a result which would have been unthinkable five years earlier.

At the same time the 1975 elections opened up dramatic perspectives on a national scale. The left as a whole had polled 47 per cent of the votes, more than ever before. The PCI, with its 33 per cent, was just 2 per cent short of becoming the largest party in the country. The dominance of the Christian Democrats, undisputed since 1948, was under serious threat.

The DC responded, much too late, by sacking Fanfani as secretary of the party. In his place they put Benigno Zaccagnini, not one of their leading figures, but an ex-partisan, noted for his honesty and simplicity. The appointment of Zaccagnini, who received the weighty support of Aldo Moro, was intended to serve two purposes: first, to promote a new and more 'decent' image of the party; and second, to open the way for a constructive dialogue with the PCI. It was Moro's intention to respond eventually to Berlinguer's request for an alliance, but on terms which would strengthen the Christian Democrats.

However, no sooner had the 'honest Zac' become secretary than an even more damaging scandal broke over the heads of the DC and its allies. From a Senate inquiry in Washington it emerged that Lockheed, the American aircraft company, had been paying bribes to politicians all over the industrialized world in order to secure orders for its planes. In Italy three ministers were accused of accepting bribes: the Christian Democrats Mariano

Rumor (a former President of the Council of Ministers) and Luigi Gui, and the Social Democrat Mario Tanassi. A parliamentary commission of inquiry voted to remove Tanassi's and Gui's parliamentary immunity and send them to the Constitutional Court for trial. There Gui was found not guilty but Tanassi was sentenced to a brief prison sentence in March 1977. In Rumor's case, the parliamentary commission split 10–10, and the deciding vote of its president, the Christian Democrat Mino Martinazzoli, saved Rumor from standing trial.[66]

In this atmosphere of scandal and crisis, the Christian Democrats organized their thirteenth congress, held in Rome in March 1976. It was to be one of the most anguished and hard fought in the history of the party, to be compared only with the Florence congress of 1959 (see p. 255). Zaccagnini's supporters, who presented themselves as the 'renovators' of the party, just beat off the challenge of the 'moderates' (the Dorotei, and the supporters of Andreotti and Fanfani). However, when it came to drawing up lists for the DC's new national council, the 'renovators' had an all-too-familiar ring about them: Aldo Moro, Mariano Rumor and Emilio Colombo headed the list. The list of 'moderates' saw Andreotti as no. 1, followed by Piccoli, Bisaglia and, in fourth place, Giovanni Gioia of Sicilian fame.[67]

Thus Zaccagnini promised more than he could deliver. He was very much Moro's man, and Moro, as we have seen, was not likely to 'renovate' anything in a hurry, least of all his own party. None the less, Zac's narrow victory gave heart to those sections of the party which had become demoralized and disaffected in the wake of the long series of scandals and the referendum defeat.

The new-look DC was soon put to the test. In the spring of 1976, the political parties, in order to avoid the abortion referendum, tried to reach agreement on a reform of the abortion laws. After some discussion, the Christian Democrats presented a proposal which still defined abortion as a crime, a proposal which could only be approved with the support of the MSI. The PSI immediately withdrew its support from the government of the time (a fragile DC minority government under Moro's tutelage). National elections, once again a year ahead of time, became inevitable.

Not since 1948 was an Italian election fought with such commitment and excitement; nor had one ever acquired such international resonance. The situation in southern Europe in 1975 and 1976 was the cause of considerable disquiet to the United States. Portugal was in the grips of revolution, in Spain the end of Franco's regime was imminent, in France a united left seemed to be on the brink of power, Greece and Turkey were at loggerheads over Cyprus, and now in Italy the DC seemed to be about to lose power to the Communists. It was little wonder that the *Economist* at the time called the Mediterranean the soft underbelly of NATO.

The development of Euro-Communism increased American fears. During 1975 the Spanish, French and Italian parties moved closer together, reiterating their commitment to a democratic road to socialism and their independence from the Soviet Union. The Spanish and Italian parties, for instance, in their joint declaration of 12 July 1975, decided 'solemnly to declare that their conception of the march towards socialism in peace and freedom expresses not a tactical attitude but a strategic conviction'.[68] This new unity of purpose aroused great interest amongst European public opinion. It also posed further problems for the US government. If the Euro-Communists' criticism of the Soviet Union was to be welcomed, their ambition to become a major force in European politics was more than a little disquieting. Euro-Communism, in America's opinion, could only lead to further destabilization.

On 20 September 1975, John Volpe, the American ambassador in Rome, gave an exclusive interview to the Italian magazine *Epoca*.[69] In it he stated, in no uncertain terms, the US opposition to the entry of the PCI into the Italian government. Any such Communist presence would create 'a basic contradiction' at the heart of NATO. Furthermore, détente depended on the maintenance of the delicate equilibrium between the two superpowers; that equilibrium would be seriously threatened if the PCI joined a government coalition. The interview aroused great indignation in Italy, but in the following months Henry Kissinger, the US Secretary of State, reaffirmed the American hostility to the Italian Communists.[70]

Berlinguer did his best to counter the American attitudes. In a famous interview with Giampaolo Pansa of the *Corriere della Sera*, he declared that the Communists would not pull Italy out of NATO if they won the elections. On the contrary, continued Berlinguer with astonishing frankness, 'by leaving it we would upset the international balance. I too feel safer being on this side of the fence.'[71]

In Italy, election fever increased as the opinion polls showed that the 'sorpasso' (the 'overtaking' of the DC by the PCI) was a real possibility. One poll, that in *L'Espresso*, actually gave the PCI 34.5 per cent and the DC only 27.6 per cent.[72] Berlinguer continued to advocate the need for historic compromise. The DC preferred to call on its traditional allies in Italian society to help it in its hour of peril. It filled its lists with respected Catholics and persuaded Umberto Agnelli, the younger brother of Giovanni, to stand as one of its candidates. The time had come to close ranks, to support 'honest Zac', and to fight off the Communist challenge.

The end of the election campaign was marked once again by violence. In May, at the end of an election meeting held by Sandro Saccucci (a candidate of the MSI and a leader of Borghese's coup attempt in

1970), his friends opened fire with pistols and killed the young Communist Luigi Di Rosa. Twelve days before the election, the Red Brigades, marshalling their slim forces, ambushed and killed the senior Genoese judge, Francesco Coco, and his two police escorts. (Coco was the magistrate who refused to negotiate with the BR at the time of Sossi's kidnapping.) The Christian Democrats used these two incidents to strengthen their thesis of the 'opposing extremes' – Fascist on the one hand, 'reds', including the PCI, on the other. On 14 June *Time* magazine put Berlinguer on its cover under the title: 'Italy – the Red Menace'.[73]

The results of the elections of 20 June 1976 surprised nearly all observers. The PCI had done even better than a year earlier, polling 34.4 per cent of the votes. However, the DC's support had held firm, and with 38.7 per cent of the vote it remained comfortably the largest party. All the smaller parties fared badly: the PSI gained less than 10 per cent, and remained at its 1972 level; the PSDI and the PRI got little more than 3 per cent each, and the Liberals with 1.3 per cent practically disappeared. The MSI dropped too, down to 6.1 per cent. The revolutionary groups fielded candidates for the first time, under the umbrella list of Democrazia Proletaria (DP). They fared miserably, polling only 1.5 per cent of the votes. The Radicals also entered Parliament, polling just 1.1 per cent of the vote.[74]

The electorate, whose attention had rightly been dominated by the question of the *'sorpasso'*, had concentrated their votes on the two major parties. PRI, PSDI and PLI all lost votes to the DC, while the PCI had clearly taken votes from the PSI and from DP (the revolutionary groups). The Christian Democrats had done well because the bulk of the *ceti medi* and all the big bourgeoisie had rallied to them. Indro Montanelli, Italy's most famous conservative journalist and editor of *Il Giornale Nuovo*, had urged his readers to 'bung up your noses, but vote DC'. They had obviously taken him at his word. The vast majority of those who feared the national and international consequences of a Communist victory had supported the DC; so too had the Catholic world, in a more concerted way than at any time since the 1950s. A new group, Comunione e Liberazione, standing for militant, youthful and traditionalist Catholic values, had played a small but significant part in mobilizing support.

As for the PCI, the reasons for its success in 1975 and 1976 will long be debated. Berlinguer himself was sure that the strategy of the historic compromise lay at the heart of his party's victory. A substantial section of the *ceti medi*, attracted by the prospect of a grand coalition to save the country in its hour of crisis, and reassured by the PCI's commitment to the Atlantic Pact, had voted Communist for the first time. This was probably the case, but other factors were at least as important. Among them were Berlinguer's own sober but charismatic leadership, and the fact that 18–21-year-olds were voting for the first time. Probably the most important of all was the lengthy process of political action and mobilization in civil society which had been going on ever since 1968. The enormous growth of trade union membership (still on the increase in 1976), the education sessions of the 150-hour scheme, the social movements connected with employment, housing and inflation, the development of left-wing groups in the professions like the CGIL *scuola* and Magistratura Democratica, all these had aroused a new collective consciousness amongst the working classes and some sections of the *ceti medi*. This part of Italy had voted *en masse* for the PCI, hoping that the *'sorpasso'* would lead to a new political dynamic in the history of the Republic. Their support had not been enough for outright victory, but the PCI was in a stronger position than ever before.[75]

The Governments of National Solidarity, 1976–9

a. A TIME FOR DECISIONS

The victory of the PCI and the poor showing of the PSI posed difficult questions for both parties. The answers that they gave to them in the summer of 1976 were in large measure to shape Italian politics for the next decade.

Faithful to the strategy that he had formulated in 1973, Berlinguer remained convinced that all the energy and strength of his party should go towards forging a compromise with the Christian Democrats. The left had polled nearly 47 per cent of the votes, but Berlinguer was not interested in trying to build on this basis. The Italian crisis, he maintained, was too grave for a leftist adventure. The Americans were hostile to the PCI taking power, the country was economically unstable, street violence had reached new levels of savagery. In such a situation, Italian democracy had to be defended. The best way to do this, argued Berlinguer, was to form a coalition of all the main parties and move slowly towards a Communist presence in the government.

The counter-argument was that the country was crying out for change and reform. It would not be possible to achieve either by making an alliance with the DC. Berlinguer, it is argued, should have capitalized upon the enduring movement of protest in civil society in order to forge an alternative to Christian Democrat politics. The PCI could not have taken power immediately, but it could have used the years after 1976 to build a united opposition, and to prepare the terrain for a decisive victory at the next elections. A strong opposition with a clear reforming programme was the best answer to Italy's crisis.

Both positions had much to commend them. Looked at historically, it seems possible to say that the second option (that of a left alternative) was more fraught with danger. The international situation was not favourable to a left-wing reforming government. Any Italian attempt of this sort might well have encountered the sort of international economic sabotage which the French Socialist government (with an overwhelming majority at home) experienced in 1981–2. There was also the danger, very much on Berlinguer's mind, that an eventual left government could push a part of the *ceti medi* and the employers towards authoritarian politics, as had happened in the years 1920–22.

On the other hand, the second option seems in retrospect to have been the *only* convincing reformist strategy. If the pressure from below for change and the mobilizations of 1968–76 were to be sustained, there had to be a convincing opposition to lead them. And if serious corrective reform, like that of the state, was to be envisaged, it could not be undertaken in tandem with the DC. The left alternative was thus both risky and necessary.

The second, fateful decision of the summer of 1976 was that taken at the central committee of the Socialist Party when it met in July at the Midas Hotel in Rome. The party's secretary, Francesco De Martino, paid the price for failure. He was replaced by the young Milanese vice-secretary, Bettino Craxi. Forty-three years old, Craxi was considered to be on the right of the party. He had always been a faithful pupil of Nenni, was an admirer of the German Social Democrats, and soon revealed himself to be a leader of notable character and determination. No profound thinker, Craxi was none the less a formidable strategist for his own party.

In the early 1970s the Socialists had backed a left alternative hoping that, as in France, there would be a gradual redressing of the balance between Socialists and Communists. The 1976 elections had destroyed those hopes. Craxi decided that if the party was to survive and prosper it had to become more autonomous and less philo-Communist than it had been under De Martino. A PCI secretary more attentive than Berlinguer to the question of left unity would have seen the danger. But Berlinguer tended to take for granted the PSI's subordinate position within the left, and concentrated nearly all his attention on the Christian Democrats.[76] Crushed and isolated by this alliance between the two major parties, the PSI never forgave the Communists their arrogance of these years. Craxi was not slow to realize that a new coalition of the centre-left would eventually give him and his party more room and more power than any left alternative under the suffocating 'hegemony' of the Communists.

Thus at a time when the left had received more votes than ever before, the two major left-wing parties grew further and further apart. In the summer of 1976 the opportunity, albeit fraught with difficulty, existed for building an alternative to the Christian Democrats. The opportunity was not taken, and no such chance was to present itself again.

b. THE AIMS OF THE DC AND THE PCI

On 11 August 1976 a new government under the leadership of Giulio Andreotti gained the approval of the Chamber of Deputies. Andreotti named it the government of *'non sfiducia'* ('not no-confidence') because it was based on the abstention of the opposition parties. The Communists and Socialists were not part of the government, but they agreed not to cause its downfall. In return they were to be consulted fully on its programme. Andreotti's government was to survive in this fashion until January 1978. He then resigned but immediately formed another government (his fourth), which was to last until January 1979. In this second period, the Communists edged an inch or two nearer government, being included in the 'government area' in Parliament, voting in favour of the government, but not receiving any ministries. These two governments of Andreotti went under the name of governments of 'national solidarity'.

The strategy of the Christian Democrats in these years seems clear enough. Giulio Andreotti was hardly the new face of the DC to whom Berlinguer had hoped to appeal. A conservative Catholic and pupil of De Gasperi, Andreotti in his time had held practically every ministerial post. In particular, he had been Minister of Defence for many years, at a time when the secret services were being infiltrated by the extreme right wing. His electoral stronghold was Lazio, where he had built up a formidable clientelistic network. Well-liked in the Vatican, Andreotti was subtle and cynical; for the DC he was the ideal man for a slow *'logoramento'* ('wearing down') of the Communists.[77]

Behind him stood Moro. The *'grande tessitore'* ('master weaver'), as Italian political commentators have often called him, hoped to perform gradually on the PCI the same operation that he had performed on the PSI in the 1960s. The Communists were eventually to be brought into the government, without trauma and without challenging the DC state system. In the honoured tradition of Italian *trasformismo*, the PCI, having been the major opposition party, would gradually acquire all the trappings of government. And, as with the Socialists at the time of De Lorenzo, the fear of an authoritarian political solution would work its own restraining magic.

Moro's deeply ingrained attitudes were revealed in his intransigent defence of his DC colleagues involved in the Lockheed scandal. On 9 March 1977, in an atypical outburst in Parliament, Moro proclaimed: 'There must be no scapegoats, no human sacrifices ... The DC stands firm in defence of its men ... You will not judge us on the piazzas, we will not let ourselves be put on trial.'[78] The message, for once, was unequivocal. There was to be no self-criticism, no threat to the unity of the party, no challenge to its dominance of Italian politics. Any alliance with the Communists would be on these bases alone.

This was a message which Berlinguer did not want to hear, and which the day-to-day subtlety and ambiguity of Moro's language helped him not to hear. Berlinguer never thought that the task ahead would be easy. He, too, had seen what had happened to the Socialists, but he thought that the two situations differed greatly. At the beginning of the centre-left, the PSI had been almost completely isolated, with 10 per cent of the vote and the trade unions against it. In 1976, however, the left was immeasurably stronger, both in Parliament and in society. Berlinguer wrote at the time: 'The old ruling classes and the old political élite know by now that they are no longer able to impose sacrifices on the working class and the Italian workers; they must ask us for them, and they will ask us; the time when they merely did what they wanted, as for most of the 1950s and 1960s, has gone for ever.'[79] In return for these sacrifices, which would curb inflation and lift Italy out of the recession, the working class would gradually come to exercise hegemony in Italy society. There would take place 'a profound change in the economic and social structures, in the functioning of the state and the whole public sector, in relations of power, in the way of life and habits of the country'.[80] As for Lombardi in the early 1960s, so for Berlinguer in the mid-1970s: the alliance with the Christian Democrats was not to be a mere vehicle for corrective reform, but rather a springboard for profound structural transformation.

'Anni di Piombo' ('The Years of the Bullet')

a. TERRORISM AND DESPAIR

In the event, the governments of national solidarity came to be dominated by one theme only – that of terrorism. As Lama has said, with his usual frankness: 'In those years Italy ran great risks ... the battle [against terrorism] completely absorbed us, and so we did not see all the rest with the necessary clarity.'[81]

In the last six months of 1976, three factors contributed greatly to the growth of terrorism. The first of these was the crisis of the revolutionary groups. The election results had been a disaster for them and their members were deeply disillusioned. Many of them had been continuously involved in militant politics since 1968; half a million votes and six deputies in Parliament was too meagre a reward for so much effort.

At the end of October Lotta Continua held its second congress at Rimini. It was an extraordinary affair. Hardly had it begun than the workers on the one hand, and the women on the other, decided to hold their own meetings to decide the fate of the group. The rest of the members, as Bobbio has written, waited in the corridors, 'preoccupied and fascinated'.[82] Women's politics won the day: every discussion was turned inwards, the personal became political and the leading members of the group recognized that their whole way of approaching politics had to be rethought. At the end of the congress Lotta Continua dissolved itself as an organization, though its daily newspaper was to continue publication for some years.[83]

Lotta Continua's congress had been moving and startlingly innovative for those who had attended it, but it sounded the death knell for the groups. One by one they fell apart under the weight of self-criticism and demoralization. Soon only a small rump remained, calling itself Democrazia Proletaria and trying with difficulty to adapt to very changed times.

The groups had made many mistakes, but they had at least concentrated on the building of a mass movement to the exclusion of individual terrorist action. Without their lead, the older cadres and the new, often highly politicized generation of the late seventies suddenly found a political vacuum to the left of the P C I. Autonomia Operaia (also known as Autonomia Organizzata), a loose federation of rank-and-file collectives noted for their violence, tried to fill it. Behind them lurked the terrorist bands.

Secondly, the P C I cut itself off increasingly from that part of its base amongst youth in the universities and major cities that had given it crucial support in the June elections. As the party moved closer to government, and its alliance with the D C strengthened, so it tried ever harder to establish its credentials as a 'responsible' government party. Here Belinguer made one of his worst mistakes. In the thirty years of the Republic his party's militants had always been on the receiving end of repressive police measures. But from 1976 onwards, the P C I, instead of championing civil-rights issues, rapidly became a most zealous defender of traditional law and order measures. Its uncritical support for the renewal of the Reale public-order law, against which it had voted in 1975, was a case in point. On crucial issues concerning politicized youth – the right to demonstrate, police powers, preventive detention, prison reform, etc. – the P C I was ominously silent.

The party's more severe critics pointed to its Stalinist past as the explanation of its new-found authoritarianism.[84] Whatever the causes, there was no doubting the effect. Protest against the historic compromise was too often dubbed as deviant behaviour *tout court*. Maria Pia Garibaldo, a shop steward in Bologna and member of the PCI since 1972, wrote to Lotta Continua at this time explaining why she was not renewing her PCI party membership:

I understood that our strategy of opposition to the student movement was absurd, dictated by a policy of conciliation towards the DC which would inevitably lead us to accept repression. One can't hide behind the trite analysis that calls the students 'fascists', paid *provocateurs*, because this movement – the Autonomists, the Metropolitan Indians – expresses real anger, real social disintegration . . . We are supposed to represent 'social-democratic' order, good for the shopkeepers, and bosses big and small, while *they* represent subversion, extremism, the wicked wolf in fairy tales.[85]

A terrible paradox developed. The Communists wanted to prevent the spread of violence, but their policies were creating a more fertile terrain for the terrorists.

In Italy, 1976 did not see a dramatic decline in the activity of the terrorist bands as it did in other European countries. On the contrary, the bands were reorganizing and recruiting. Behind this disquieting development lay not only the increasing political space left to the terrorists, but an inexplicable laxity on the part of the police. The Red Brigades seemed destined to disappear early in 1976, but they were allowed to grow again in the next eighteen months. Quite why the police relaxed their grip is not known. It may have been that they felt that the battle was won; other, more sinister, interpretations have claimed that terrorism was allowed to flourish again in order to condition the PCI still further.[86]

b. THE MOVEMENT OF 1977

The reasons for the gulf that was opening up between the PCI and some sections of Italian youth were not only political, but social and economic as well. The crisis meant increasing unemployment, in both the manual and intellectual sectors of the labour market. Indeed, for youth the gap between the two was contracting. More and more young people were going into higher education; the universities, in the absence of reform, were becoming ever more crowded; and there were ever fewer jobs at the end of the education tunnel. A different type of youth movement developed in the major cities. Disaffected from traditional politics, often unable or unwilling to find more than marginal or occasional work, desiring above all to *'stare insieme'* ('be together') and enjoy themselves, the youth of the movement of 1977 differed radically from their idealistic and ideological predecessors of

1968. The movement began from the needs of its participants; if 'auto-reduction' was to be practised, it was to be of the price of pop-concert tickets, not of family electricity bills. In Milan, youth groups began to occupy buildings and convert them into social centres; by the end of 1977 around fifty such centres had been created, with some 5,000–7,000 participants. Concerts, films, photographic and music workshops, discussion circles, yoga classes, were just some of the activities of the centres. So too were counselling services for drug addicts. These were the years when hard drugs, especially heroin, became widely available in Italian cities, with appalling consequences for an underemployed and disillusioned generation.[87]

In broad terms it is possible to discern two strands in the movement of 1977, even if they often intertwined. The one was 'spontaneous' and 'creative', sympathetic to feminist discourse, ironic and irreverent, seeking to create alternative structures rather than challenge the powers-that-be. The 'Metropolitan Indians', with their warpaint and rejection of industrial society, were the most vivid representatives of this tendency. The other was 'autonomist' and militarist. It aimed to build on the culture of violence of the previous years, and to organize the 'new social subjects' for a battle against the state.[88] Autonomia Operaia sought to dominate this tendency, with former leaders and intellectuals of Potere Operaio, like Toni Negri and Oreste Scalzone, very much in its forefront.

In February 1977 students occupied Rome university to protest against reform proposals made by the Education Minister Malfatti. The occupation quickly became a focal point for disaffection in the capital. Autonomia Operaia, much to the disgust of the feminists, controlled the occupation and limited freedom of speech in it. On 19 February Luciano Lama, head of the CGIL, heavily protected by trade union and PCI stewards, came to address the occupation. Both the 'creative' and 'militarist' wings of the movement mobilized against him. In a tragic scene of mutual incomprehension, Lama was shouted down and violent clashes broke out between the Autonomi and the stewards of the PCI. A fortnight later, a demonstration of some 60,000 young people in the capital degenerated into a four-hour guerrilla battle with police. Shots were fired on both sides, and a part of the demonstrators chanted a macabre slogan in praise of the P 38 pistol, the chosen weapon of the Autonomi.

From Rome, the movement spread to Bologna. On 11 March 1977, after a meeting of Communione e Liberazione had been disrupted by left-wing students, clashes broke out at Bologna university. The Carabinieri were called in. As so often in the past, they opened fire when they had no need to do so. Francesco Lo Russo, an unarmed sympathizer of Lotta Continua, was shot dead. There then followed furious clashes between youth and police, not only in Bologna but in other major cities as well. In Bologna the situation became so serious that armoured cars patrolled the streets. The city that had been the pride and joy of the Communists, hailed widely as one of the best governed in Europe, had suddenly become a battleground, with thousands of young people protesting against the repressive tendencies of the P C I (see also below, pp. 395–7).[89]

In September 1977, a conference was called in Bologna to discuss repression in Italian society, with special emphasis on the role being played by the P C I. Some 20,000–25,000 young people descended on the city for three days. It was an extremely delicate moment, not helped by Berlinguer dubbing members of the movement *'untorelli'* ('plague-bearers'). The Bolognese P C I responded with a supreme example of 'repressive tolerance'. Food, lodging, meeting spaces and the main piazza of the city were all made available by the local council, which knew that it would be denounced whatever it did. The conference itself was a damp squib, marked by opportunist interventions by the French *'nouveaux philosophes'*, and by squalid hand-to-hand fighting for control of the microphone at the mass meeting in the Palasport. The demonstration that marked the end of the three days passed off, mercifully, without incident.

From then on the movement fizzled out. The militarized wing had not made the gains they hoped for. Most people in the movement, however disaffected they felt from the governments of national solidarity, were not prepared to take up arms. The youth centres of Milan and elsewhere gradually disappeared, starved of funds by suspicious local authorities. Most of this section of youth swelled the ranks of the *riflusso*, the great retreat into private life, the abandonment of collective action, the painful coming to terms with failure.[90]

c. THE RED BRIGADES AND THE KIDNAPPING OF ALDO MORO, MARCH 1978

The Red Brigades hoped that the movement of 1977 would be the moment when terrorism broke through to become a mass phenomenon. Had it done so, there seems little doubt that the Republic would not have survived in its present form. It did not happen, but a sufficient number of sympathizers were recruited in 1976 and 1977 to enable the terrorist groups to intensify their activities.

This new phase of the BR's actions, which was to last through 1977 and 1978, was dubbed the 'strategy of annihilation'. Indiscriminate action was announced, aimed at members of the professions and 'servants of the state'. The aim was to terrorize whole sections of the ruling élites and their supporters, so that the state itself would be unable to function properly. As for the political parties, the D C remained the principal target, but some B R bulletins warned that the principal danger was no longer 'Gaullism', but 'social democracy', i.e. the P C I.[91]

In 1976 the Red Brigades and other left-wing terrorist groups killed eight people and seriously wounded sixteen; in 1977 they killed seven and wounded forty. Apart from policemen and magistrates, journalists became a principal target. In June, 1977, Indro Montanelli, editor of *Il Giornale Nuovo*, was wounded in the legs by the BR, and in November Carlo Casalegno, assistant editor of *La Stampa*, was mortally wounded, again by the BR.

By early 1978 the Red Brigades had five columns in action, in Milan, Turin, Genoa, Rome and the Veneto. However, nothing that they had done up to that point presaged the action that they took on 16 March 1978. This was the day on which Andreotti was due to present his new government to the Chamber of Deputies, with the Communists in the 'area of government' for the first time. That morning Aldo Moro's car and his police escort were ambushed in Via Fana on their way to Parliament. All the policemen accompanying Moro, and his chauffeur, were killed. Moro himself was bundled into a waiting car, which disappeared into the Roman traffic.

When news spread of what had happened in Via Fana, the Italians were deeply shocked and demoralized. The trade unions called a general strike; hundreds of thousands of people demonstrated in the main cities. However, there was no unanimity amongst rank-and-file workers. Salvatore Tropea, a journalist from *La Repubblica*, reported on a mass meeting inside the FIAT Spa Stura factory at Turin. Five thousand workers had listened to the Communist trade unionist, Bruno Trentin, denounce the actions of the Red Brigades. The unions had put up a large banner with a slogan on it reading: 'Against all terrorism, to improve the state'. However, speaker after speaker from the floor said something rather different from the official union line:

These institutions don't merit our support.

For thirty years we've suffered terrorism in the factories, with fascist foremen, with pension payments that take months to arrive, with uncontrolled and forced migration . . . I don't condemn the Red Brigades and I don't condemn anyone. I'm against terrorism, but I know that what we need here, immediately, are reforms.

This dramatic situation didn't come about yesterday, it's the result of non-government, of the distortions of this state.

The trial at Turin [of the original leaders of the Red Brigades] must go on, but so must that at Catanzaro [for the bomb in the bank at Piazza Fontana], that of the Lockheed scandal and so many others.

Tropea commented: 'Perhaps at the Spa Stura only the *enragés* spoke up, but certainly no one challenged what they had to say.'[92]

Ten years after the event, there are still many mysteries surrounding Moro's kidnapping. For fifty-four days the BR, headed by Mario Moretti, held Moro prisoner in a secret hiding-place. During this time, the principal question which tormented the politicians and the whole country was the following: should the state stand firm and refuse any pact with the Red Brigades or should it negotiate to save Aldo Moro's life?

Moro himself, who (according to the terrorists' accounts) behaved with dignity and courage during his ordeal, wrote a series of anguished letters to his family and his colleagues, begging them to try to secure his release.[93] The Socialists, with Bettino Craxi very much in the lead, argued strongly in favour of compromise. The democratic state, they said, enjoyed the active support of the population; a humanitarian act, like an exchange of prisoners, would not weaken democracy but strengthen it. The Communists took the opposite view. In their opinion, any yielding to the terrorists would both legitimize them and encourage them to further action of the same sort. There had to be no compromise, as there had been no compromise in the Resistance. Leading opinion-makers, like Eugenio Scalfari, editor of the recently founded newspaper, *La Repubblica*, agreed completely. In a famous leader of 21 April 1978, he wrote: 'the decision that has to be taken is a terrible one because one has to sacrifice the life of a man or forgo the Republic. Sadly, for democrats there can be no doubt as to what to choose.'[94] The Christian Democrats were, understandably enough, divided. Those closest to Moro wanted to save him at all costs. Others were afraid that if they yielded, the PCI would seem to the electorate to be the only party willing to stand firm. Reluctantly, the DC under Andreotti chose the path of no compromise.

Aldo Moro was killed by the Red Brigades on 9 May 1978. His murderers took his body in the boot of a car to the very centre of Rome, to Via Caetani, a road equidistant from the DC and PCI headquarters. They had shown themselves to be ruthless and efficient, but they had not won a victory. Within their ranks there had been grave dissent over the decision to kill Moro. Outside their ranks, there was a very widespread feeling of revulsion over what they had done. The crisis of Italian terrorism, as is generally recognized, dates from the death of Moro. With hindsight, it would thus seem correct to argue that those who advocated intransigence were in the right. Had Moro not been killed but exchanged for one or more imprisoned terrorists, the Red Brigades would have appeared both invulnerable and willing to compromise, with the result that their appeal would almost certainly have widened.[95]

As it was, the killings went on, and indeed increased throughout 1979 and 1980. The Red Brigades and other left-wing groups killed twenty-nine people in 1978, twenty-two in 1979 and thirty in 1980. Among their victims was the Genoese worker and PCI member, Guido Rossa, who was killed because he had denounced to the police a white-collar worker in his factory whom he suspected of terrorist activities; the university professor and leading

Catholic intellectual, Vittorio Bachelet, murdered inside Rome university; and the courageous young journalist of the *Corriere della Sera*, Walter Tobagi, killed on 28 May 1980 by the so-called '28 March' group.

However, the terrorists were becoming ever more isolated, and the defections from their ranks grew. Furthermore, a highly efficient and determined Carabiniere general, Carlo Alberto Dalla Chiesa, had at last been appointed to coordinate the anti-terrorist offensive. He made every effort to persuade disillusioned terrorists to become *'pentiti'* ('repentants'), and to cooperate in unmasking the clandestine organizations. A law was passed which promised *'pentiti'* very reduced prison sentences in return for their cooperation. In 1980, a key Red Brigade member, Patrizio Peci, was arrested and decided to collaborate with Dalla Chiesa. Others followed in his trail, and the BR columns were dismantled one by one. The law on the *'pentiti'* proved very successful, even if it allowed some terrorists like Marco Barbone, one of the killers of Walter Tobagi, to escape with ludicrously light sentences.

Thus, through a combination of political firmness on the one hand and the enticement of weary killers on the other, the democratic state overcame the terrorist threat. The terrorists had never been able to persuade more than a few hundred people that an armed struggle was in any way justified in contemporary Italy. There was much dissatisfaction, as the FIAT Spa Stura workers made clear, but little belief that murderous ambushes and kidnappings were a solution to Italy's problems. After Moro's death, Italian democracy was not only defended but strengthened.

However, it is also important to remember that in this same period alarming violations of democratic rights took place. The state authorities were all too willing to organize witch-hunts and hand out sentences which neither aided the fight against terrorism nor guaranteed impartial justice. The most notorious incident was the case of those arrested on 7 April 1979. Pietro Calogero, a Paduan magistrate close to the PCI, was convinced that Professor Toni Negri and the group around him at Padua university were the moving intellectual and political force behind Italian terrorism. A number of teachers and students at the Faculty of Political Science were arrested; Negri and others were charged with being members of the Red Brigades and Negri's voice was 'recognized' as being that which had telephoned Eleonora Moro during her husband's last days. The '7 April' group languished in prison for a period of years before being brought to trial. One by one the most serious charges against the great majority of them were revealed as false, either at their original trial or on appeal. The politics of the group, which were those of Autonomia, could hardly be called attractive, but too little distinction was ever made by their prosecutors between what had been said and what had been done. As a result there were cases like that of Luciano Ferrari Bravo, a lecturer in politics at Padua university, who, having spent several years in prison awaiting trial, was condemned to ten years' imprisonment for 'membership of an armed band' (on no other evidence than his writings) and was eventually found not guilty on appeal. Meanwhile Antonio Savasta, leading member of the Red Brigades in the Veneto and self-confessed killer, served a very limited prison sentence after he had 'repented' and agreed to help the Carabinieri with their inquiries.[96]

Attempted Reform

The problem of terrorism certainly dominated the governments of national solidarity, but it would be wrong to judge them on this alone. As we have seen, the Communists had considerable expectations of their cooperation with the Christian Democrats. It is to the governments' record in the area of reform, a record by no means to be dismissed out of hand, that we must now turn.

a. THE STATE

In May 1977 the Communist Claudio Petruccioli, in an editorial in *L'Unità*, asked the following question: 'Is it possible to distinguish the democratic state from the system of power (according to some "the regime") which has been in operation for thirty years?' He gave the following answer on behalf of his party: 'We believe that, notwithstanding their profound interlocking, the very close links that tie one to the other, it is possible to make this distinction; furthermore, we believe that Italy's future and salvation are dependent on making this distinction operational. The democratic state must be made more robust by freeing it from the oppressive and parasitic links which constrain and debilitate it.'[97]

These were promising words, even if they risked making of the state an ahistorical entity. In practice, though, the party did not have a concrete programme of state reform. Within Parliament itself (with Ingrao President of the Chamber of Deputies), one or two changes were made. For instance, greater follow-up control was introduced for a number of laws, so that Parliament could check what progress they were making and keep an eye on their funding. Whereas between 1948 and 1976 only 75 laws out of some 8,000 had any regulations of this sort, between 1976 and 1979 44 out of 539 laws had elements of control written into them. However, when Parliament was called upon to use these new powers, it did so in an atmosphere of general indifference.[98]

The most important of the P C I actions with regard to the state was the struggle they undertook to get real powers transferred to the regions. Ever since their introduction, there had been no clear division of responsibilities between central and regional government. In July 1975 law no. 382 made good this deficiency, but it ran the risk of not being put into practice because of fierce opposition from vested interests within the central state. It was only in July 1977, after a long parliamentary battle waged by Communist and Socialist deputies, that the provisions of the law became a reality. A large number of *'enti inutili'* were finally abolished; the regions gained the necessary financial autonomy, and took over full responsibility in such areas as health care and environmental planning.[99]

In their actions in other parts of the state, however, the PCI seemed only to lose ground, not to gain it. As we have seen, their attitudes to civil liberties in a time of emergency left a great deal to be desired. Their desire for respectability and their emphasis on the strong state made them pay lip-service only to areas such as the reform of the prisons, the control of the powers of the police, the speeding up of the law courts, the safeguarding of the right to dissent. These were areas which were not only crying out for reform but which had always been a chosen terrain for the left wing of European social democracy. Only in the tenacious struggle, carried on mainly by the CGIL, for the creation of a democratic police trade union linked with the major confederations did the left make any progress.

Elsewhere, there was disquieting evidence that the PCI, far from 'freeing the democratic state from its oppressive and parasitic links', was itself embracing time-honoured practices. This was particularly true in the area of *lottizzazione* – the distribution of jobs within the state apparatus on the basis of party membership and strength, rather than on that of technical expertise and competence. In the allotment of posts within the RAI (the state television), banks like the wealthy Monte dei Paschi of Siena and other parts of the state, the PCI seemed to be behaving like any other party. The Communists' defence was twofold: first, that belonging to a party should not of itself be an element either in favour or against a particular candidate for a state job; secondly, that if the PCI did not fight to occupy these key posts, everything would stay as it had always been. In July 1977 Eugenio Scalfari of *La Repubblica* warned that these had been the exact arguments of the Socialists some fifteen years earlier: 'we fail to see why the Communists should emerge unscathed from those same marshes into which the Socialists sank'.[100]

b. POLITICAL ECONOMY

The PCI's proximity to government undoubtedly alarmed some elements in the capitalist class, but in general the hysteria and sabotage which had greeted the centre-left in 1962 seemed to be lacking in 1976. With Agnelli at the head of Confindustria, more prudent counsels prevailed. By 1976 it was clear that the face-to-face confrontations of the previous years had not been resolved in capital's favour; rather, in conjunction with the international economic crisis, they had brought Italy to the brink of economic disaster. It was time to try another tack. The more percipient of the employers saw that behind the grandiloquent declarations of the 'working class becoming the ruling class', the PCI seemed willing to cooperate in saving the economy in traditional fashion. Perhaps, they argued, the Communists could be used as firemen, as Labour and social-democratic governments had often been used before in western Europe; the flames of workers' militancy could be doused by Berlinguer's appeals for self-sacrifice and austerity.

This neo-corporatist strategy received invaluable assistance from Luciano Lama as head of the CGIL. Here too the situation differed dramatically from 1962–3, when the CGIL had refused La Malfa's plea for cooperation. On 24 January 1978, in a famous interview in *La Repubblica*, Lama came out in favour of wage restraint, increased productivity and workers' mobility; in return he demanded decreased unemployment and greater attention to the problems of the South. He also denounced both capital and labour for claiming, respectively, that profits and wages were independent variables within the economic system. For Lama there were no such things as independent variables; at a time of crisis employers and employed had to respect each other's interests. In February, at the national assembly of the CGIL at the congress centre in the Roman suburb of EUR, Lama's line triumphed. As never before in the history of the Republic, employers, unions and government sat down to salvage the economy.

What were the results of this cooperation? The economy certainly took a turn for the better. Inflation dropped to 12.4 per cent for 1978, exports boomed and some business confidence returned. The Bank of Italy's major devaluation in the first half of 1976, and the continuing floating downwards of the lira thereafter, played a significant part in this mini-recovery. But so too did the compromises made by the unions. The mechanisms of wage indexing were made less favourable to the workers, strikes were discouraged and agreements over mobility and productivity were signed with the employers.[101]

In return, the unions received very little. Some prices of consumer goods did rise less fast, but unemployment did not diminish and little was done for the South. The much-heralded law on industrial conversion, passed in August 1977, was intended to lay down new norms for state intervention in industry. It turned out to be a fiasco. Nearly every important area of decision-making was excluded from its competence, and even leading members of the PCI denounced it.[102]

Worst of all, the EUR line of the CGIL led to rank-and-file

disillusionment, the falling away of working-class commitment and the consequent weakening of both the trade unions' and the PCI's bargaining position *vis-à-vis* their allies/opponents. Once again, as in 1945–7, the PCI was unable and unwilling to use its considerable powers of mass mobilization to force the DC into making real concessions. Once again, they accepted the internal logic of the capitalist plea to salvage the economy without having an alternative economic strategy of their own.[103]

The old riddles, which were at the heart of any serious discussion of a 'third way' to socialism, remained unanswered: was it possible for the economy to recover and thrive without destroying the victories of the working-class movement? Were profits and increased workers' power in any way compatible? From the experience of 1976–9 in Italy, the answer, if such it can be called, was quite simply 'no'.

c. HOUSING AND TOWN PLANNING

We left housing reform in 1971, with the partially successful reform of October of that year (see pp. 329–30). During the governments of national solidarity, no less than three major laws were passed in the area of housing and town planning: that of 28 January 1977 on the *'edificabilità dei suoli'* (building rights); the *equo canone* (fair rent) act of 27 July 1978; and the ten-year plan for residential housing of 5 August 1978. Taken together, they represented an impressive attempt to come to terms with one of Italy's most intractable problems.

The law on building rights was based on two principles: every building permit brought with it the obligation to contribute to the services installed by local government; and every commune had to adhere strictly to long-term programmes of expansion which took into account the needs of the community and the construction of public housing. Even if the law did not go as far as Sullo had done in monitoring proprietors' rights, it was still an ambitious attempt to control urban growth. Yet as with so much of the legislation that preceded it, the new law was undermined by forces both in the state and in society. The Constitutional Court decided that its most important provisions infringed citizens' rights. Even more seriously, the law was widely ignored, especially in the South. At the beginning of the 1980s a further wave of abusive building swept Sicily and elsewhere, and the municipal authorities did nothing to prevent it.[104]

The second law, the Fair Rent Act of 1978, was the subject of a very protracted parliamentary struggle. The moderate parties wanted to guarantee the rights of proprietors, both large and small; the left wanted to make sure that tenants were not charged an exorbitant rent and that they enjoyed security of tenure. Eventually, the law laid down a series of clearly established norms for evaluating dwellings, and a fair annual rent was fixed at 3.85 per cent of the value of each house or flat. The left had wanted the rent to be fixed at 3 per cent of the value, the DC and its allies at 5 per cent. Landlords were allowed to raise rents to up to 75 per cent of the increase in the cost of living (the DC had wanted 100 per cent). Tenants received security of tenure for only four years, after which landlords were free to evict them. Landlords also received increased powers to evict tenants if they were accumulating rent arrears.[105]

Fruit of a laborious compromise, the Fair Rent Act did represent the first post-war attempt to control rents in both the private and the public sector. It replaced the absurd situation where a minority of rents had been frozen for years, while the majority had been left to the fluctuations of market forces. However, the act did not resolve tenants' problems, especially in the big cities where renting was most common. Many landlords refused to make their properties available under the new conditions, with the result that after 1978 there was a startling decline in the number of dwellings available for 'fair' renting. By contrast, the black market flourished. The building industry was also deterred from constructing new dwellings for renting in the major urban areas and switched much of its attention to second houses in seaside and mountain resorts.[106]

The third law, the ten-year plan for residential housing in the public sector (1978), was intended to take up where the 1971 law had left off. The plan made provision for the construction of 100,000 dwellings per year. Vast amounts of money (4,000bn lire for the period 1976–81) were allocated to the project. Attempts were made to simplify the bureaucratic and technical processes for the construction of the new dwellings. Sadly, once again a gulf separated the law and its realization. By 1984, instead of the 600,000 dwellings projected, less than 125,000 had been built, and of them only half were destined for renting.[107]

All in all, the housing and town-planning reforms of the late 1970s were a valiant attempt to increase the importance of public-sector building and to extend public control in an area best described as a jungle. They failed for two principal reasons. The first was that within the state itself reform proposals concerning housing were, as one qualified commentator has written, 'slowly chewed up and spat out by an apparatus in which the ideology of ownership and that of bureaucracy harmonized perfectly to create a paralysing mediation'.[108] Secondly, even if *within* the state everything had functioned as it ought to have done, *outside* it, in civil society, the state lacked nearly all the necessary instruments, both cultural and material, to enforce its laws.

d. HEALTH

In May 1978 a famous law (no. 180) was passed which changed the state's attitudes to mental illness. It was the fruit of a long battle to close the mental hospitals of Italy, a battle which had been led for many years by Franco Basaglia and the group of doctors around him. Basaglia, first at the mental hospital of Gorizia and then at that of Trieste, had tried to restore the human dignity of the mentally ill, and to make them 'subjects' rather than 'objects' in the process of health care. In so doing, he and his group led the world in changing attitudes to mental illness. The law of May 1978 encapsulated many of their ideas, especially that of freeing mental patients from institutions and reintegrating them as far as possible with their families and into the community. But as so often, the law was not followed by the provisions necessary to guarantee its realization. The mental hospitals were closed, but insufficient new structures were created to look after the mentally ill in society. All too frequently, the burden fell back upon families, sometimes with tragic results.[109]

On 23 December 1978, six months after the law on mental health, the Italian national health system was instituted. The first projects for such a system dated back to 1948. In the intervening years there had been innumerable other projects, and no less than fifteen committees of inquiry had met, proposed and dispersed. To have reached the point of legislation was thus a considerable achievement.

Before the law of 1978, health provision in Italy had relied on a chaotic mixture of social-service agencies and private institutions (see pp. 151–2). By the mid-1970s health care in the North and Centre of the country compared reasonably to the rest of Europe in terms of material provision, even if the standard of medicine remained low. For instance, the North and Centre of Italy had 10.38 beds per 1,000 inhabitants, compared to 10.5 in Britain and 12.00 in France. In the South, though, there were only 5.4 beds available per 1,000 inhabitants.[110] The ordinary citizen gained access to health care by belonging to a health insurance scheme: employees, either in private or public firms, usually belonged to INAM, ENPAS, INADEL or ENPDEP. The self-employed had three great pension and insurance organizations, respectively for peasant proprietors, artisans and *commercianti*. However, there also existed many smaller schemes catering for different corporate groups. All these institutions were the site of political power, clientelism and corruption.

The law of 1978 tried to convert this disparate, autonomous and wasteful system into a single coordinated whole. It established the USL, the Unità Sanitarie Locali (local medical units), as the sovereign organizations for health care in every commune and every quarter of the major cities. The law attributed specific responsibilities to different parts of the state so that duplication of responsibilities and disputes over areas of competence could be eliminated. It also tried to lay down guide-lines for action in all three areas of health care – the prevention of illness, its cure and the consequent rehabilitation of the patient. Prior to 1978 little or nothing had been done in the first area, and the third had always been regarded as the task of the family.

The new law created an ambitious framework which, as Pastori writes, was 'one of the most important acquisitions made by the politics of reform in the whole republican period'.[111] But it was no more than a framework, and above all an institutional one. As the USL came into being, so they revealed great weaknesses in the way they had been conceived. They were in receipt of vast amounts of money, but insufficient criteria had been laid down as to how that money should be spent. In his annual report for 1984, the president of the Corte dei Conti presented a long list of examples of the misspending in which the USL had indulged.[112] Patients and doctors, encouraged by the ticket system, spent their own and the state's money on medicines and tablets as they had never done before. The profits of the multinational chemical companies went completely unchecked. Furthermore, in spite of increased spending and personnel, the USL were often unable, even in the Centre and North, to ensure a rapid and efficient service for the patient. Waiting-lists were often as long as they were in Britain in the eighties, but the fault could not be attributed to cuts in public spending.

Worst of all, the USL became an unrivalled site for *lottizzazione*. Ruffolo and others had called for some form of participation or control of the USL by the general public, an elected assembly to which the administrators would in some way be answerable. This would have been a first, timid step towards structural reform, in that it would have gone beyond the traditional structures of European health systems in which the hierarchy of command, headed by the consultants and hospital administrators, had always gone unchallenged. But under the Italian law of 1978, the assembly with titular control over the USL was simply the local government council, with the result that the most important administrative posts, including that of president, were divided amongst card-carrying members of the parties. In 1985 the DC had 57 per cent of the USL presidents and the PSI 20 per cent. The attractions of controlling vast budgets of this sort were all too obvious.[113]

Finally, the law of 1978 did not succeed in redressing the balance between North and South. Whereas in some northern and central areas, like the Veneto and Emilia-Romagna, the health service was as efficient as any in Europe, in the South the old Italian drama of beds in hospital corridors, of families cooking food for their relatives inside the hospitals, even of payments being made in order to be admitted, all went on and even intensified. In Naples in the 1980s to be poor was bad enough; to be ill and poor was a tragedy.

e. ABORTION

The last of the major reforms of these years was in the field of abortion. Instead of holding the referendum which had been called by the MLD and the Radicals, the parties of the governing majority tried to formulate another compromise. Once again, there was a protracted parliamentary struggle. The bill on abortion was approved by the Chamber of Deputies in January 1977, but it was voted down in the Senate in June, and it only finally became law on 22 May 1978. The DC had agreed to withdraw any provisions which made voluntary abortion a crime. In so doing they incurred the wrath of much of the church hierarchy. The PCI, for its part, infuriated the women's movement and disappointed many of its own women members by agreeing to limitations on a woman's right to choose. Under the new law, women had to consult with a social worker and a doctor, and allow a seven-day 'meditation' period before proceeding. Girls under eighteen required parental permission before having an abortion. This clause, insisted upon by the DC to 'defend the family', had the inevitable effect of making young girls those most likely to continue to seek illegal abortions. Finally, medical staff were given the right of conscientious objection. As the majority of doctors were male and Catholic, women still found great difficulty in procuring abortions in some hospitals and in some parts of the country.[114]

f. A BALANCE SHEET

The 'profound change in economic and social structures' which Enrico Berlinguer had seen as a consequence of the 'historic compromise' was nowhere to be found in the record of reform for the years 1976–8. Once again, as with the PCI's predecessors in the centre-left, a gulf separated the stated aim of structural reform from the reality of what was achieved. Hopes had been raised inordinately, with the result that the quite impressive patchwork of reform resulting from the 'historic compromise' was too easily dismissed out of hand. In reality, the period 1976–8 can be compared with that of 1969–73 for the number and range of its initiatives. Laws were passed, like those on abortion and fair rents, which were the result of elaborate negotiation between political parties with very differing interests. Many of these laws were serious attempts at corrective reform; nearly all of them were poorly executed, and some were not executed at all.

By the end of the 1970s, Italy had a welfare state, but it was very much 'all'italiana'. Money payments, like pensions and subsidies, still took pride of place over services, especially in the South. The services that had been created, and they were often numerous and impressive (from health care, which we have dealt with, to kindergartens, sports facilities, etc., with which we have not), were frequently poorly administered and always the vehicles of party-political interest. The political parties invaded civil society but did little to improve the image or the functioning of the state. The P CI, in its years in the government majority, failed to distance itself from this process or to guarantee sufficient respect for the free choice of citizens.

In one important respect the years of national solidarity differed from those that had preceded them. For the first time, the unions, rather than confronting the government in the hope of winning reform, as in the period 1971–3, decided to experiment with the road of cooperation. The results in terms of the economy were encouraging, but the partial decline of inflation was too meagre a reward for the CGIL's restraint. Neo-corporatism, and this was not only Italy's experience, revealed itself to be all too one-sided at a time of economic crisis.

The Experience of Left-wing Local Government, 1975–80

At a national level, the P CI had always remained on the margins of government in these years. It had been able to condition the actions of the D C, but not to treat with it as an equal. However, at a local level, after the elections of 1975, the Communists were the strongest force in nearly all of the municipal councils of the great cities. No account of the years of national solidarity would be complete without examining the record of at least some of these local governments.

a. BOLOGNA

We must begin with the city that had been in left-wing hands ever since the war (see pp. 203–4 and 295–7). In 1973 life was made more difficult for all local governments by a key clause in the tax-reform law. The right to levy local taxes, already much more limited than in Britain, was taken away from local councils altogether. Instead the central state administration fixed the quotas to be assigned to local councils, and arranged their payment from central state funds. Given the notorious delays of the Treasury, and the sharp rise in inflation and interest rates, the deficits of local government grew dramatically.[115]

In spite of these financial difficulties, the reforming zeal of the new generation of Bolognese Communists showed little sign of abating. In June 1972, the mayor, Renato Zangheri, introduced a radical new traffic plan with strict limitations for private vehicles and a renewed concentration on cheap public transport. Throughout the early and mid-1970s, the city's social services continued to expand: school programming for the whole day (*'iltempo pieno'*) helped working parents, and made afternoon activities for schoolchildren less mindless than the traditional *doposcuola* (after-school activities); handicapped persons were offered training and found suitable jobs; centres for the mentally sick were instituted to help those who had been released from the recently closed psychiatric hospitals.[116]

The most ambitious scheme of all was the restoration of the historic centre of the city as part of the plan for economic and popular housing (see p. 296). The development of most other Italian city centres had been marked by the expulsion of the local working population and the renting or selling of restored houses to the rich, both native and foreign. The whole of Venice, and certain quarters of Rome – Trastevere was one – were clamorous examples of this process. In Bologna, the authorities decided to ensure that local inhabitants were kept *in situ* after restoration had been completed. In this way, the city centre's traditional character and life would be preserved.

The local authorities also tried to go one step further. They proposed the expropriation of landlords in the city centre, with adequate compensation, and then, after restoration, the handing back of buildings to co-operatives of landlords and tenants. This was an attempt, as the planners put it, 'to reverse class relations in the city centre'.[117] The proposal was probably the closest the P C I ever came in Bologna to structural reform. It aroused a storm of protest from the city's middle classes, who saw it, not without reason, as an attempt to limit the unbridled right of the private ownership of housing. Anxious not to alienate the *ceti medi*, the city authorities abandoned the idea of cooperatives in 1973. None the less, other parts of the plan went ahead, and the restoration of Bologna's city centre remained a model which the rest of Italy should have imitated and did not.[118]

The Communists thus continued to take important initiatives in Bologna, but forces were at work which were to undermine their local government strategy, and which led to the grave crisis of 1977. In the first place, the social tensions of 1968–76 tore holes in the P C I's carefully constructed social alliances. When labour relations were relatively tranquil, as for most of the 1960s, it was not difficult for the local authorities to mediate between employer and employed, both of whom probably voted for the Communists. But in the 'hot autumn' such mediation fell apart. In late 1969, the head of the P C I's factory commission in Bologna told Hellman:

Given the kind of industry we have in Tuscany and Emilia, the issue of renewing contracts places the workers' interests and those of the artisan and small producer in direct conflict, and therefore calls the entire line into question. On an idealistic level, many are on our side, but now, with unprecedented militancy all the way down to firms with, say, three members, paternalism and all sorts of other issues have come forward. Tactically, we do all we can, which is to minimize the damage, but . . . the fact is that this is an insoluble contradiction.[119]

Closely related to this were the consequences of the growth in moonlighting and the decentralization of production. Throughout the 1970s, the structure of industry in Emilia-Romagna was becoming not just small-scale but positively pulverized. Home working, second and third jobs, short-term contracts, were becoming ever more dominant features of the productive landscape. The PCI and the CGIL were powerless in the face of them. One indicator of their difficulties was the level of unionization among metalworkers in Bologna in 1975. Practically all the large and medium-scale firms were unionized, but only 3,000 workers out of 30,209 had union cards in firms employing one to nineteen workers. Forty per cent of all metalworkers in Bologna were not in unions even in 1975, at the height of trade union influence.[120] And if this was true of an advanced sector like metalworking, the picture was undoubtedly bleaker still in sectors which were less trade union conscious.

In the very small firms, the workers were the least protected, the most vulnerable to patriarchal patterns of authority, the most likely to work long hours for poor wages. By the late 1970s a marginalized, precarious and heavily exploited sector of the labour force, often very young, existed side by side with the traditional working class. For them, appeals for 'austerity' and 'sacrifice' made no sense at all.[121]

Thus by 1977 the PCI was clearly failing to appeal to important sections of the Bolognese population. Its membership was getting older (more than 60 per cent were over forty in 1974) and more respectable. It prided itself on democratic innovations like the neighbourhood councils, but in reality these were attended more by the party faithful than by the population as a whole. A mass of young people, both students (who paid astronomically high rents in the city) and workers, fell outside the party's influence.[122] The PCI believed that it had built a successful model of hegemony based on class alliances, but the explosion of 1977 showed that it had some serious rethinking to do.

In the period up to 1979, it cannot be said that re-evaluation was taken very far. Indeed, the need to establish alliances with the Christian Democrats on a local as well as a national level meant that great restraint had to be exercised at the very moment when new proposals should have been forthcoming. On more than one occasion, important initiatives in the area of the social services were abandoned after criticism from quarters close to the DC. This was the case with the Ramazzini regional social-research institute, founded in 1976. In 1978, after a number of generic attacks upon it in right-wing newspapers, the institute was mysteriously closed down without even its scientific committee being told why.[123] Under the historic compromise, the exact location of decision-making and its motivation became more, not less, obscure.

b. NAPLES

When the Communist Maurizio Valenzi became mayor of Naples in 1975, and other members of the PCI took over key posts in the local government, they were faced with a much more difficult task than their colleagues in Bologna. Living conditions, possibilities of employment, the location of power, the very instruments of local government differed radically in the two cities. According to the national census, in Naples in 1971 47.3 per cent of dwellings still did not have a shower or bath, and 17.7 per cent still had outside lavatories. Families were larger in Naples than in Bologna, with 20 per cent having six or more members compared to only 4.7 per cent in Bologna. Since the early sixties the Neapolitan population had grown more rapidly than the Bolognese, the housing stock was grossly inadequate and the collapse of jerry-built blocks of flats was a common occurrence. In three months alone, from November 1977 to January 1978, fourteen buildings collapsed, depriving some 3,000 people of their homes. Of 20,000 local government employees in Naples, more than 7,000 were porters or attendants or dustmen. Some key planning offices in the town hall lacked any qualified personnel at all.[124]

Theoretically, with so much to be done, the left had a great opportunity to make its mark. However, the real levers of power in Naples were not in their hands. All the command posts of the local economy — Italsider, Alfasud, the port consortium, the Bank of Naples, the daily newspaper *Il Mattino* — were firmly controlled by their opponents. A local DC councillor estimated that all eighty-eight key economic jobs in the city were held by the DC and 65 per cent of these were in the hands of Antonio Gava's Dorotei.[125]

It proved next to impossible to reverse a situation that had steadily acquired its physiognomy over the previous thirty years. The left-dominated council did manage a few steps forward. For instance, between 1975 and 1979 333 kindergarten classrooms were opened, compared to the 210 constructed in the previous thirty years. Much of the corruption in the affairs of local government, such as that governing the tendering of contracts, was eliminated. However, the initial results, as the local Communist Andrea Geremmica candidly admitted, were to make the situation worse. In February 1978 he told Sandro Viola of *La Repubblica*: 'The general crisis of the country has led to the emergence of a series of key problems that previously, with the politics of clientelism and money hand-outs, had remained hidden. But now that the hand-outs no longer exist, the full impact of so many desperate situations is making itself felt.'[126]

Objective conditions thus made life very hard for the left-wing members of the council, but they were not helped by having to ally with the DC. Indeed, the Neapolitan Communists found themselves in an impossible position. They had to reach agreement with the very people who were responsible for so much of the situation that they were trying to remedy. Worse still, the DC, though still in the council, did everything it could to sabotage it. Local government employees, faithful to the DC and organized in corporate unions, struck against the council's attempt to curb absenteeism. New lists of the unemployed were organized by the DC and the MSI to foment further dissent and make impossible the allocation of the few jobs there were.[127]

The PCI had announced that they would be a party of 'government and struggle' in these years. The first took pride of place over the second. Anxious not to alienate the DC, the council remained suspicious and sometimes hostile to the social movements which had awakened the city from 1974 onwards. Most important of all, the council failed to find a *modus vivendi* with the 'organized unemployed'. The movement declined, and disillusionment with collective action increased.[128]

c. TURIN

Much the same sort of story can be told for Turin. In spite of a well-intentioned and very popular mayor, Diego Novelli, left-wing government of the city proved a great disappointment. Here too the balance between 'government' and 'struggle' tipped heavily in favour of the former. As elsewhere, all the more experienced cadres from the party sections were put into positions of responsibility in local government; the sections were deprived of leadership, with important negative consequencs for the party's role in rank-and-file movements. Agreement with the DC, even though it was in opposition locally, was listed as a top priority.

Nothing illustrates better the consequences of this strategy than the fate of the Torinese *consigli di quartiere* (neighbourhood councils). These had arisen spontaneously and vigorously in the previous years, and by 1976 there were nearly forty of them. Local members of the PCI, dubbed *'quartieristi'* by their comrades, had played an active part in their foundation. In 1975 the PCI in Turin had made the granting of institutional status for the neighbourhood councils, and direct elections to them, important planks of their electoral platform. Yet these elections never took place. In October 1977 the local PCI outlined to its cadres the reasons why; prime amongst them, as Hellman records, was that 'the local party was striving to reach an "accord" with the local DC, and it was felt that direct elections would force all the parties to draw lines, accentuate the differences between themselves and otherwise undermine the kind of *rapprochement* the Communists were seeking'.[129] Seats on the neighbourhood councils were divided on a party basis instead.

Overall, the feeling in Turin grew that the 'new mode of governing' was not so new at all. The values of the 'partitocracy' seemed to predominate over all others. The Communists, for all their good intentions, were unable to break the mould. The traditional ways of using local power, especially those favouring members of one's own party, continued undisturbed. In 1983 a major scandal broke in Turin. Prominent members (mainly Socialist) of the left-wing local council were accused and convicted of receiving bribes. The left-wing council fell, and with it went all hopes of a fresh start in local politics.

Some Conclusions

The day after the death of Aldo Moro, many commentators wrote that the Republic would never be the same again. Giuseppe Saragat, who had been its President, commented that 'side by side with the corpse of Aldo Moro lies that of the first Republic'. Eugenio Scalfari of *La Repubblica* warned that 'if we do not work in unison to re-found the Republic ... there will be only adventurism and civil war'. Luigi Pintor of *Il Manifesto* echoed his sentiments: 'From now on this society and this state cannot remain as they were and are, not even if we wanted them to: if they do not change for the better they will perish.'[130] None of this was true. The Republic went on in much the same way as before. Democracy survived, but no radical change took place in the relationship between state and society.

In the years of national solidarity the Communists played a leading role in defending democracy, as they had done before in the history of the Republic. But their experience of quasi-government at a national level, and their full investiture of power at a local level, proved disappointing. At the time a great many words were spent on the 'problems of transition' to socialism, or 'the transition to the transition', but the 'historic compromise' did not even manage the far less ambitious and more humble tasks of corrective reform. Throughout this crucial period, the PCI was unclear in its aims and unsure of its weapons.

Instead, Giulio Andreotti, and here one cannot help but believe that Aldo Moro would have approved, managed, to quote Luciano Lama again, 'to keep us on our best behaviour'.[131] The Andreotti/Berlinguer cooperation had disconcerting parallels with that between De Gasperi and Togliatti (not for nothing had Andreotti been De Gasperi's under-secretary). On both occasions the Communists had the difficult task of trying to force through reform from a subordinate position; but on both occasions they allowed themselves to be lulled and deflected by the superior statecraft of their opponents. When the experiment of national solidarity finished, Berlinguer acknowledged that 'we have perhaps erred somewhat on the side of ingenuity'.[132] Given what had happened before, both in 1945–7 and 1962–8, this was an extraordinary admission.

The years of national solidarity had three other major consequences. The post-'68 movement of protest had been, almost against its original intentions (which had been revolutionary), principally responsible for the stuttering reformism of 1969 onwards. By 1976, as we have seen, that movement had been pushed back on to the defensive, most of all in the factories. None the less, it remained exuberant in much of Italian society, in the South as well as the North; and organized labour was far from dispersed, as the demonstration of 250,000 metalworkers in November 1977 testified. Between 1976 and 1979 this extraordinary, multi-faceted protest movement was destroyed. Terrorism bore a great deal of responsibility for the abandonment of collective goals and the triumph of the *'riflusso'*. It deprived social protest of any political space, making the choice between the status quo and the armed bands the only one available. But responsibility, on a different level, also rests with the lack of political mediation offered by the left-wing parties and the trade unions. The nexus between protest and reform was one which the left failed to grasp in these years.

Secondly, in its quest for a lasting alliance with the DC, the PCI under Berlinguer seriously overlooked and underestimated the Socialists. If we take the restricted but revealing parliamentary example of proposed amendments to laws in the period 1976–9, we find that the DC's amendments had a 75 per cent success rate, those of the PCI 67 per cent, but those of the PSI only 50 per cent. Furthermore, the times that the Communists supported Socialist initiatives were few and far between.[133] The PSI was accustomed to claim its 'centrality' to Italian politics. This role came under serious threat during the 'historic compromise', and Bettino Craxi, for one, did not forget the lesson.

Finally, to end on a positive note, Aldo Moro's death, and all those that preceded and followed it at the hands of the terrorists, did not 're-found' the Republic, but they may not have gone in vain. The *'anni di piombo'* produced a sea change in the attitudes of a whole generation of Italians towards violence. As one murder followed another, the advocacy of 'revolutionary' violence, so much an integral part of the movement of '68, was hammered out of the heads of Italian youth. By the end of the decade the problems of equity and democracy in the Republic had not been resolved, but one way of confronting them had been discounted.

The End of an Era

By the beginning of 1979 the Communists had had enough. They were no nearer government than they had been two years earlier. The new President of the United States, Jimmy Carter, had at first seemed more flexible about their entry into government, but from January 1978 he adopted a stance of adamant opposition.[134] The compromise with the DC was showing few results, and the base of the PCI was growing increasingly restive. When Lama urged Berlinguer to continue to support the EUR line of the CGIL, Berlinguer warned him that 'without an army we won't be able to fight any battles at all'.[135]

On 31 January 1979 Andreotti resigned. The Communists made it clear that they were going over to the opposition. Andreotti formed a new government with the Republicans and the Social Democrats, but he failed to win a vote of confidence in the Senate. National elections, this time two years ahead of schedule, became inevitable.

The main result of the elections held on 3 June 1979 was the severe loss of votes by the PCI, which declined from 34.4 to 30.4 per cent. The PSI increased its vote marginally, the DC declined very marginally (to 38.3 per cent), and the Radicals registered the best result, moving from 1.1 per cent to 3.5 per cent. Otherwise almost nothing changed. The small centre parties, whose demise had been expected, held on to, or slightly increased their percentage of the vote. The MSI fell to 5.3 per cent.[136]

In the aftermath of the elections, Berlinguer changed tack. The lessons of 1979 were all too clear. The party had lost one and a half million votes. It was down 9 per cent at Mirafiori in Turin, and 10–15 per cent in the popular central quarters of Naples; at a national level 10 per cent fewer young people had voted for it than in 1976. In November of that year, Berlinguer announced that the 'historic compromise' was no more. Its place was to be taken by the 'democratic alternative', which was to see the PCI and PSI at the core of an alliance to wrest power from the DC.

When the Communist leadership finally broke with the DC, there was rejoicing in very many of the PCI sections. 'At last we can stop having to swallow toads' was the comment of one section secretary. But Berlinguer's enforced switch of strategy had come too late, and could offer few fruits. The PSI was already determined to go its own way, back towards a new edition of the centre-left. As a result, the polemics between the two left parties reached new heights. There was no chance whatsoever of the 'democratic alternative' coming into being.

At the same time the employers prepared for a decisive showdown with the labour movement. In the mid-1970s they still feared that the movement was too strong to tackle head-on. By 1979 they were prepared to try. In October 1979 FIAT sacked sixty-one workers at Mirafiori, workers whom they claimed had taken or threatened violent action within the factory. There was no doubt that those workers who belonged to or were sympathetic to Autonomia Operaia had not been slow to menace foremen: 'Do you want to finish your days in a wheelchair?' was all too frequent a threat at FIAT in the late seventies. Nor was it a threat without substance: three FIAT managers had been shot dead, and another nineteen foremen and managers had been wounded or badly beaten up.[137]

However, amongst the sixty-one who had been sacked, FIAT also listed many rank-and-file militants who had had nothing to do with terrorism. Once they were tarred with the same brush, it was difficult to distinguish between the two groups. The unions at first backed the '61', but the response to calls for solidarity action were only lukewarm. By the autumn of 1979 disillusionment and the downturn in the struggle had bitten deep. In addition, many workers loathed the politics and actions of Autonomia Operaia, and were glad to see them go.

A year later FIAT staged the decisive attack. On 8 September 1980 the firm announced that because of falling world car sales, it would have to put 24,000 workers on Cassa Integrazione (see p. 353) for fifteen months. At the end of that time, half of the workers would be allowed back into the FIAT factories, but the other half would have to find new jobs outside the firm. Amongst the 24,000 were nearly all those who had played a leading part in the factory struggles from 1969 onwards. Three days later, FIAT announced even tougher measures: they were going to dismiss 14,000 workers immediately.

The trade unions reacted by calling for something very unusual in the history of Italian labour – a total strike, with the complete blocking of the FIAT factories by pickets. At first, the response to the strike was very enthusiastic. In Poland, Lech Walesa and his fellow workers had recently staged their historic occupation at Danzig. The FIAT workers felt that they were fighting a crucial battle in the history of Italian trade unionism.

On 25 September 1980 Enrico Berlinguer came to the gates of Mirafiori. He promised the workers that if they occupied FIAT the PCI would support them to the hilt, 'so as to enable you to last one hour longer than the *padroni'*.[138] For so cautious a man, it was an extraordinarily incautious speech, open to many interpretations. It caused him the execration of nearly all the commentators of the time, both moderate and not so moderate.

Had the workers' movement been as strong as it had been in the mid-1970s, Berlinguer would have been proved right in saying what he did. Some would argue that he was right in any case, because the factory vanguards had to be defended at all costs. But as it was, the Turin branch of the metalworkers' union (FLM) was no longer strong enough for a total strike, let alone an occupation. In such a situation, Berlinguer's speech left the union leaders little room for manoeuvre; as one of the local leaders of the FLM said afterwards, 'Berlinguer's was an affectionate but mortal embrace.'[139]

On 27 September FIAT announced the suspension of all sackings and only three months of Cassa Integrazione for all 24,000 workers. It was a clever move because it divided the workers. The threat of immediate redundancies had receded, those on Cassa Integrazione would receive 90 per cent of their earnings, and many workers, short of funds after the holidays, were not prepared to go on striking without being paid (the Italian unions have no strike funds to speak of). In vain the FLM pointed out that the Cassa Integrazione was merely the ante-chamber for redundancies. The unity of the workers began to crumble, and militants from other factories had to be brought in to man the pickets.

One evening in early October, Cesare Romiti, the managing director of FIAT, decided to send his bodyguard home early. Accompanied only by a friend, he then drove all the way around the outside of Mirafiori:

Yes, it was a bit of a risky and idiotic thing to do, seeing the position I held at FIAT. But there was more than one reason for doing it. In some way I wanted to charge up my batteries, to give myself courage again, to convince myself of the arguments which had sustained me throughout the dispute . . . I saw that the pickets were made up of people who were cheerful, who were singing and laughing . . . and then I understood. These weren't FIAT workers, because FIAT workers at that moment could only have been worried, tormented, and anguished . . . These were the usual 2,000 trade union professionals, they were playing a political part, the hard men, but it was still a part. So I returned home a little encouraged, thinking perhaps things would work out well for us.[140]

On the thirty-fourth day of the strike, 14 October 1980, a remarkable demonstration marched through the main streets of Turin. It was composed of some thirty to forty thousand FIAT foremen, managers, white- and blue-collar workers. They held placards demanding the right to return to work, and chanted slogans like '*Novelli, Novelli* [the mayor of Turin], *fai aprire i cancelli*' ('Novelli, Novelli, open up the factory gates'). The size of the demonstration took everyone by surprise. The intermediate strata at FIAT had mobilized spontaneously, and had taken with them a substantial number of workers as well. The movement at Turin was irrevocably split. The following day, the trade union leaders signed an agreement with FIAT; it was a capitulation, but few doubted that they had any option. Giovanni Agnelli had won a famous victory and set the pattern of industrial relations for the coming decade.

On 15 October 1980, at the Smeraldo cinema in Turin, the hundreds of workers who formed the enlarged FIAT factory council met with the trade union leaders. It was a bitter moment. Giovanni Falcone, a delegate from the bodywork section at Mirafiori, made the following memorable speech, an epitaph for the hopes of a very particular generation of workers:

FALCONE: A comrade said to me a few evenings ago: 'It's a fact of history: another comrade like us spoke up in 1969, today it's your turn, and in this way an epoch is coming to a close.' Back in '69 it was the beginning, now it's the end . . . I've got to admit that it leaves me with a pretty bitter taste in my mouth. Because for me twelve years of struggle have not only been any old twelve years, but a long political experience, and it's been like that for all of us. Let's go back for a moment. I was an immigrant who came up from the South, from the countryside, like so many others. I couldn't have put two words together if you'd paid me . . . I was shy; I still am in part, even though I've got over most of it now. I wouldn't have dreamed of being able to make a political speech. Do you think FIAT's going to keep on somebody like me in the factory? Do you think they're going to call me back to my shop? [applause and vigorous signs of approval] . . . It's true that it's a minority of workers who have always got things done here. But it's a minority that has always counted for something, that has always acted. If the majority had been willing to participate actively, if they'd all come to Piazza San Carlo, if they'd all been on the picket line, I don't think, comrades, that we would just have refused the sackings; we would of course have done much greater things. Poland teaches us that lesson: have you seen what they've managed to do in Poland since they've got the backing of all the workers?! We know that in Italy, in a country like Italy, that we can never have the backing, and above all the physical and moral participation, of all the workers; within the working class today there are conflicting interests . . .

MARIANETTI (*trade union leader and chairman*): Time, comrade, wind up please.

FALCONE: Don't worry, comrade, but I think that after twelve years and now that they're throwing me out, you'll allow me to speak for a minute more [renewed cheers], because I'm sure that I'll never again have the chance to speak like this [further applause], as a FIAT delegate, as a FIAT worker. But at least I've got the satisfaction of going out in style, and I'm proud of all the struggles that I've taken part in, quite apart from the fact that the bosses will never take me back [ovation].[141]

Chapter 11

Italy in the 1980s

T O ATTEMPT to write the history of a decade that has not yet finished is not a sensible undertaking. What follows, therefore, is no more than a tentative interpretation of some aspects of social, economic and political change in the 1980s. One fact, though, is immediately apparent: the singular dislocation between society and politics which has characterized so much of the history of the Republic has continued in the 1980s. In other words, while society has undergone further rapid transformations, the political system and the form of state have been unable to adapt swiftly or to overcome their historic defects. This brief epilogue will attempt a last survey of Italian society, to serve as a counterpoint to those of the 1940s (Chapter 1) and of the era of the 'economic miracle' (Chapter 7). We shall then turn, for the last time, to politics and ideology.

Italian Society in the 1980s

a. THE ECONOMY

In the first few years of the new decade, the gloom that had hung over the Italian economy continued to persist. Inflation reached its highest ever annual rate of 21.1 per cent in 1980, and was much slower to come down than in other European countries. By 1983 it was still 15 per cent per annum. As for growth, there was a mini-boom in 1980, but 1982 and 1983 were especially black years, with growth rates of − 0.5 per cent and − 0.2 per cent respectively. Only 1975 had been worse.[1]

As the decade progressed, Italy's economy began to pick up very sharply. Behind this recovery lay a global one stimulated by the reflation of the American economy through deficit financing. The falling price of oil also played a crucial role. All over Europe growth rates improved, as did the volume of trade.

Within Italy, various factors combined to make the country's recovery an especially notable one. FIAT's victory of October 1980 had been a watershed of national significance. The balance of power between capital and labour had swung back decisively to the employers. The trade union movement was not routed in quite so explicit or frontal a fashion as in Great Britain. However, when a referendum of 1985 resulted in the reduction of the *scala mobile* (index-linked wage increases), the business classes felt more secure and more willing to invest than at any time since 1963.[2] Their confidence was further increased by the decline of terrorism and by the political stability established by Bettino Craxi's presidency of the Council of Ministers (see below, p. 419). After nearly twenty years of intense social crisis, Italy seemed at last to have been pacified, and on capitalist terms.

The result was a new era of prosperity which some commentators have gone so far as to call a second 'economic miracle'.[3] Inflation declined rapidly to just 4.6 per cent in 1987. Growth rates were very solid from 1984 onwards. Although final figures for the most recent years are not available at the time of writing, it would be safe to say that GDP grew by an average of well over 2.5 per cent per annum in the period 1983–7, compared to 0.85 per cent in the previous four years. The balance of trade, heavily aided by the falling dollar and reduced oil prices, turned in Italy's favour. Italian firms, whose losses and debts had assumed major proportions by the beginning of the eighties, began to improve their performance markedly from 1984 onwards. Major restructuring took place, the number of employees diminished, the cost of labour as a percentage of turnover returned to pre-1968 levels. FIAT, as so often, led the way, assuring itself the leading place amongst European car manufacturers, but also diversifying and internationalizing its affairs still further. Other traditionally strong sectors of Italian industry did well: engineering firms, especially those linked with the boom in Italian design; the clothing and footwear industry, which benefited greatly as Italian fashion acquired renown on the world market. The small firms of the Third Italy continued to prosper, selling their products on an international scale. At the same time the internal market was buoyant as never before, with consumption in the Centre and North on a par with the richest regions of Europe.[4]

In the period 1982–7 the Milan stock-market increased its

capitalization more than fourfold. Shareholding became a mass phenomenon, with some three to four million Italians investing their money on the stock exchange. A direct link had been established between the Italians' notorious saving capacities and the major capitalist firms. The crash of 1987 certainly dampened this enthusiasm, but the market held steady in 1988 and the economy continued to boom.[5]

By the late 1980s Italy claimed to have overtaken Britain, to become the fifth largest industrial nation of the Western world, after the United States, Japan, West Germany and France. Giovanni Goria, then Treasury Minister, first made this claim in January 1987. It has been hotly disputed ever since. In February of the same year Nigel Lawson, the British Chancellor of the Exchequer, told Parliament that the U K's recent growth rate was double Italy's, that its economy was 14 per cent larger and its living standards 15 per cent higher. O E C D figures, published in August 1987, tended to contradict him; in 1986 Italy had a Gross Domestic Product of $599.8bn, compared to the U K's $547.4bn. With the recent revision of Italy's national economic statistics to take the 'black economy' into account, it seems likely that the *'sorpasso'* (overtaking) will be confirmed in future years.[6]

One of the most significant aspects of Italy's startling economic recovery has been the turn-about in the conditions of public-sector industry. At the beginning of the decade, as we have seen, I R I was one of the most crisis-ridden groups in the whole of Europe. The favourable economic conditions of the mid-1980s and the dynamic management of Romano Prodi, a university professor from Bologna, have done much to transform this situation. Prodi, appointed in October 1982, combined controversial privatization (the selling-off of Alfa-Romeo to F I A T) with radical restructuring and heavy investment. The result has been that I R I has now balanced its books for the first time since the 1960s. Prodi's success at I R I has been mirrored by that of Franco Reviglio at E N I, who, from 1983 onwards, has led the company to its most successful period since the time of Mattei.[7]

Finally, the restricted élite of Italian capitalism has been enlarged and reinforced by a number of new arrivals: Raoul Gardini, at the head of one of the largest chemical and fertilizer groups in Europe, Carlo De Benedetti, whose original power base was at Olivetti, Silvio Berlusconi with his vast media empire, Luciano Benetton of clothing fame. All of them are strongly committed to the international expansion of their holdings, so much so that European financial circles have talked of a new age of Italian *'condottieri'*.[8]

This multi-faceted economic revival has led to a new ethos pervading the country, replacing both the collectivist values of the early 1970s and the pessimism of the *riflusso* of the early 1980s. The 'enterprise culture' seems to have found its natural home in Italy. *La Repubblica* and *L'Espresso*, respectively Italy's most influential daily newspaper and weekly journal, have both recently introduced weighty business and financial supplements. In late 1987 William Scobie, the *Observer* correspondent in Italy, accurately caught the mood of the moment: 'Italy finally has become, in 1987, one of Europe's greatest success stories. Suddenly, this is a land of upward mobility, of vital computerized industry, bustling young business managers and slick middle-aged tycoons who have abjured their Sixties ideals in the sacred cause of profit. Class war is passé. Export or die.'[9]

A few qualifications must be made to this optimistic picture. The Italian public-sector deficit has continued to grow throughout the 1980s and successive governments have been able to do little or nothing to bring it under control. By 1985 the Italian public debt had reached 84.6 per cent of the country's Gross Domestic Product, compared to 69.4 per cent in Japan, 53.7 per cent in Britain and 48.5 per cent in the United States. Since then, the Italian situation has worsened, so much so that by the end of 1989 the public debt is expected to exceed GDP for the first time.[10] Ancient ills have combined with new needs: historic inefficiency and waste in the public sector has joined with much increased spending on welfare, especially on health provision, to produce a spiralling deficit. Any long-term continuation of Italy's economic renaissance is threatened by this enormous debt.

Secondly, doubts remain about the fragility of an economy based so heavily on the conversion of imported raw materials into exported manufactured goods. Such a situation makes Italy especially vulnerable to fluctuations in world prices of raw materials. It is also uncertain how well the economy is prepared to meet the challenge of the single European market in 1992: its relative shortage of high-technology industries, its fragmented and sluggish banking system, much of it publicly owned, its plethora of small and medium-sized firms, all give cause for concern.[11]

Lastly, the southern problem remains unresolved. The old story has to be told once again: the South has increased in prosperity, but not at the same rate as the Centre and North. Unemployment north of Rome is static or falling; in the South it has increased to over 20 per cent. As Eugenio Scalfari has written: 'the South is accumulating frustrations, youth unemployment, economic distortions, imbalances between resources consumed and resources produced. The southern question is more open than ever; indeed, economic growth has accentuated its importance.'[12]

b. SOCIAL CLASSES

Recent trends in Italian society contain a number of surprises. In the first place, the active workforce as a percentage of the total population has ceased to decline. The lowest point was reached in 1972 and 1973, when only 35.5 per cent of the population was officially in work. The percentage then climbed, slowly but steadily, to 36.7 per cent in 1985.[13]

Within this general picture, there is a more familiarly European pattern: a continued sharp decrease in agricultural employment, the slow decline of industry, the rapid growth of the tertiary (service) sector. However, there is a further surprise: the level of women's employment has risen sharply since 1972, whereas that of men has remained stagnant. The number of women employees rose by nearly 50 per cent in the period 1970–85. More than ever before in Italy, women are not just working before getting married, but returning to the labour force once their children are of school age. The era of the Italian woman as permanent housewife, so typical of the years of the 'economic miracle', is giving way to one in which women are more active on the labour market.[14] In the Centre and the North, therefore, more families than ever before are enjoying at least two incomes, and sometimes more if adult children are still living at home.

By contrast, the southern labour market does not present anything like so favourable a picture. Here the active workforce is still a declining percentage of the population and women's employment is stagnant. There are, of course, some regional exceptions (parts of Campania, Puglia and eastern Sicily), but the overall picture is a dismal one.[15]

A final overall trend is the increasing differentiation between that part of the workforce which is *'garantito'* (protected, in regular work, covered by social insurance and pension schemes), and that which is not. Although the majority of the *garantiti* are to be found in the Centre and the North, and of the *non-garantiti* in the South, the situation is not so simple. Temporary, casual, part-time and 'black' work are a nation-wide phenomenon, from the metalworking *'boîte'* (small workshops) of Piedmont to the casual agricultural labour of southern Puglia.

If we turn to examine the balance between the different sections of society, the most striking change in the seventies and eighties has been the further sharp growth in the urban *ceti medi* as a percentage of the total active population. According to Sylos Labini's figures, the urban middle classes have risen from 38.5 per cent of the active population in 1971 to 46.4 per cent in 1983. Behind this overall growth lie a number of different trends. White-collar employment in the private sector has increased more slowly than that in the public sector (from 8.7 to 10.2 per cent for the former, from 8.0 to 12.5 per cent for the latter). In the public sector the introduction of the regions and of welfare reforms have both led to a major increase in the number of publicly employed professional, technical and intellectual workers. By the mid-1980s, to take just one example, there were some 900,000 teachers in Italy, or 4.4 per cent of the active population. A similar dramatic growth is to be found amongst health and social workers.[16]

The more traditional sectors of the urban *ceti medi*, the artisans and the shopkeepers, have maintained their numerical weight. Artisans have grown slowly from 5.3 to 5.8 per cent of the active population. Shopkeepers have also increased marginally (10.2 to 10.4 per cent), but here a distinction has to be made between different types of activity. While the number of food shops has remained stationary, that of other categories of retail selling has increased from 398,000 in 1971 to 503,275 in 1981. Far from declining with modernization, the Italian shopkeeping class thus seems as numerous and robust as ever. In 1982 the Lombard regional council carried out a survey of shops in Italy. It found one shop for every eighty inhabitants in Lombardy, one for every sixty-two in central Italy, and one for every fifty-two in the South. These are by far the highest densities to be found in any of the major European countries.[17]

In the South, many shops hover on the brink of viability, but everywhere new consumerism has been responsible for some remarkable fortunes being made. Indeed, a jaundiced view would single out those terrible twins, the butcher and the chemist, as the symbols of the new Italy. Clothing and footwear shops have enjoyed an extravagant boom. The products of the new technologies, tape and video recorders, colour televisions, home computers, have all had no difficulty in finding a mass market.

The urban middle classes are thus well on the road to becoming the dominant section in Italian society. It would be a mistake, though, to view them as other than a very composite stratum, split in many different ways, bound more by corporations than by class. Little research has been done into their constituent nature and attitudes. If we know something about the professions and sections like bank workers, we know next to nothing about the new shop owners, who can with difficulty be called by the old and more modest term of shopkeeper.[18]

As for the working class, here too there have been very significant changes. Its weight in the active population has, according to Sylos Labini, declined from 47.1 per cent in 1971 to 42.7 per cent in 1983. The balance between those working in large factories and those in small has tipped significantly in favour of the latter. Numbers of employees in the service sector (about which, once again, we know very little) have increased rapidly; those in industry have declined.[19]

Most significantly, the subjective evaluation of the working class, both of itself and by other sectors of society, has been transformed. It is no longer viewed as one of the two great protagonists in Italian society. Its position as the collective leader of a project of transformation, around which other sections of society would cluster, has given way to a more defensive and subordinate role.

If we return to FIAT Mirafiori for the last time, outside Gate 2, which in the 1970s had always been a meeting-place for militants, now there are only street traders and the sellers of Puglian grapes for home-made wine. 'The last time we tried to put a picket line there,' recounts Roberto Lasagna of the FIOM, 'was during the renewal of the wage contracts of 1983. It cost us twenty names denounced to the police and one sacking. After that we stopped trying.'[20]

The factory councils still exist, but they are no longer the standard-bearers for a collective strategy. Protest has become fragmented, with sectional interests prevailing. The trade unions have seen their authority increasingly threatened by the rank-and-file organizations of separate categories of workers. The COBAS (*comitati di base*) have mobilized different groups of workers and of the *ceti medi* with notable militancy, but without the ability to achieve (or indeed to seek) a unifying strategy. Producers and consumers have become increasingly divided as public-sector strikes have caused maximum disruption to everyday life.

At the bottom of the social scale, a large number of Italians have still not benefited in any way from the country's new affluence. In 1983 Ermanno Gorrieri was commissioned by the President of the Republic, Sandro Pertini, to carry out an inquiry into poverty. He reported that 6.9 per cent of the population in the Centre and the North of the country were below the official poverty line, while in the South the total was well over 18 per cent.[21] In the country as a whole three groups were at particular risk: the old, who were increasing as a percentage of the total population; the young of the urban peripheries, who found regular work with difficulty, and who were prey to the use of hard drugs;[22] and the ever-increasing number of immigrant workers from other countries.

By the early 1980s Italy had ceased to be a net exporter of labour. Perhaps as many as 600,000 foreign workers, most often from North Africa, are now concentrated in the major Italian cities. Their most visible activity, dominated by the Moroccans, is the selling of poor-quality clothes, bags and trinkets on streets and beaches up and down the peninsula. But they are also engaged in a large number of other poorly paid and irregular jobs: from the Filipino women domestics in the big cities to the Egyptian foundry workers of Emilia, from the Tunisians in the Sicilian fishing industry at Mazara del Vallo to the Eritreans and Ethiopians working as dishwashers, porters and building workers in Milan.[23] The humiliations and suffering of the Italians in northern Europe in the 1950s and 1960s are now those of the Africans in Italy. And if there are no signs telling them to keep out of public gardens (as there were in Switzerland for the Italians), incidents of intolerance and aggression have certainly not been lacking.[24]

c. FAMILIES

One of the themes which has constantly resurfaced in the course of this book has been that of the relationship between family strategies and collective action. It has become apparent that there has been no simple, linear development of familism (the pursuit of exclusively family values and actions). Nor has there been a constant tendency towards the accentuation of the private at the expense of the public.[25] Rather, there have been places and moments when collective and family interests have strongly intertwined: in the northern cities during the Resistance, in the southern peasant movement of the 1940s, in the Catholic north-east in the forties and fifties, in many of the social movements from 1968 onwards, such as that of the Neapolitan unemployed in the period 1974–6. On the other hand, there have been places and periods when family strategies have acquired an overridingly private dimension, and the collective aspect of social life has become secondary: before and during the 'economic miracle', in the *riflusso* of the late seventies, in most of the urban South for most of the time.

In the 1980s, too, there has been no single or simple way of characterizing the relationship between family and society. On the one hand, the decline of collective values and the vigorous new emphasis on the material prosperity of the individual family unit have led to a new age of familism: families have become ever more concerned with their own well-being, and less with the collective problems of society as a whole. This trend has undoubtedly been the dominant one in the 1980s.

On the other hand, there is significant evidence of a new associationism in Italian society: voluntary work, recreation clubs, cooperatives, have all flourished as never before. It has been estimated that over one fifth of the adult population in Italy is now involved in social activities and clubs of some sort, with some four and a half million people active in voluntary work.[26] Furthermore, there is evidence of family members organizing in the public domain on issues that concern essentially private pain and suffering: one example are the 'mothers of Primavalle', who have formed an association in a popular quarter of Rome to combat the spread of hard drugs amongst their children; another are the 110 families of the victims of the terrorist bomb which exploded in Bologna station in August 1980 (see below, p. 423), who have combined to campaign against terrorism and to bring to trial those responsible for the crime. Organizations such as these have led to the coining of a new phrase: the 'moral familism' of the eighties has come to be contrasted to Banfield's famous 'amoral familism' of the fifties.[27]

Great care must be taken not to overestimate these trends in Italian society. 'Moral familism' would appear to be a limited phenomenon, and much of the new associationism is either purely recreational or involved in single-issue campaigns. With the exception of certain elements in the ecological movement, there is no wide-reaching alternative philosophy which can be compared to the very strong world pictures presented by the Communists and the Catholics in the 1940s and 1950s. None the less, the proliferation of societies and collective activities in Italian civil society is in marked contrast to much of what has gone before, and to the traditional dominance of the political parties and the church.

If we turn now to look in detail at the Italian family itself, we find significant changes both with regard to its structure and to its development in the Three Italies. The family in Italy, as elsewhere in Europe, has continued to diminish in size. It averaged just three members at the time of the national census of 1981, an average size which decreased to 2.8 in the north-west and rose to 3.3 in the South; 45.7 per cent of Italian families now had two or three members, 17.8 per cent had only one (thus ceasing to be families), and the number with five or more had declined from 21.5 per cent in 1971 to 14.9 per cent in 1981. Extended families had also decreased from 16.9 per cent of the total in 1971 to 11.2 per cent ten years later. Italian birth rates have declined significantly. From the peak year of 1964, when 1,032,000 babies were born, the rate has declined to 552,000 in 1987. This was the lowest figure for all major European countries.[28]

Italian families are thus getting smaller and more nuclear, but all recent research has pointed to their continuing cohesiveness. The trend towards the abandonment of the old which Pizzorno noted at Rho in 1959 does not seem to have been borne out at a general level. Even in urban contexts, Italian grandparents remain closely involved in the care of grand-children; and once the older generation is threatened by fragility and immobility, it receives considerable assistance and company, especially from daughters and their families. Other relations, too, are frequently involved in the life of the family.[29]

In the 1970s and 1980s the growth in income of the majority of Italian families has been so marked that Giuseppe De Rita has written of this period as a watershed in the history of the Italian family.[30] The Italian family has certainly prospered as never before, becoming both a centre of accumulation and an example of dedication and entrepreneurship. At the same time, Italian youth is as family-oriented as at any period since the war. The autonomy of much of northern urban youth and its partial challenge to the family in the late sixties and early seventies have given way to a new attachment to the family unit. Grown-up children tend to stay at home well into adult life. The family is geared to the production of income and the meeting of needs through the activity of each of its members. Two surveys of young people between the ages of fifteen and twenty-four, published in 1984 and 1988, suggested that all sections of Italian youth put the family at the top of its scale of values. Social and religious commitment, and political activity, came out at the bottom of their lists.[31]

Such family-oriented values should not be allowed to conceal funda-mental shifts in the roles and needs of individuals within the family. There has been an ever-increasing process of 'individualization' (*individuazione*) of the family, of demarcations of activity and consumption by age and by sex: women have radically redefined their roles and responsibilities, youth has increasingly sought its own activities and space at an ever younger age, even the place of children has drastically altered as they have become fewer in number. Any lingering image of the closed nature of the Italian family – all work, rest and socializing with relations – has given way to a reality where individual members of the family relate more and more to their peer groups and the outside world. The family remains united at the level of income and overall strategy, but its individual members often go their own ways at the level of consumption and free time.[32]

If we turn briefly to families in the Three Italies, some sharp distinctions emerge. In the north-west, the classic area of large urban agglomerations, families are both more prosperous and smaller than ever before. There has been a marked increased in women's work, and family savings have risen markedly since 1970; 52.8 per cent of families in this region now own their own houses, compared to 38.7 per cent in 1961.[33]

Families also have access, thanks to the reforms of the 1970s, to a far wider range of state services than ever before: kindergarten schools, proper medical care, subsidies for medicines, recreational and sports facilities, etc. It has been suggested that family and collectivity have been brought closer together in this way, with the state more involved in the life of the citizen than ever before.[34] On one level this is true, but as is so often the case collective provision has been introduced without the creation of collective consciousness.

In their life-styles and in their culture, northern urban families have come a long way from Borgo San Paolo in the 1940s or even the new Falchera estate in the early 1970s. Collective actions and solidarity – tenants' associations, the 150-hour education scheme, active trade unionism – have given way to sophisticated, mobile and essentially familist uses of leisure time. Family strategies now operate largely to the exclusion of collective goals. Beppe Rorvo, a Catholic and trade unionist at FIAT in Turin, put the matter succinctly in a conversation with the journalist Gad Lerner: 'I believed that we weren't fighting only for ourselves, only for the factory, but for something more than either. Even then, in '69, you didn't stop thinking about your family problems. But the family came afterwards, first came our general objectives. Today it's not like that. The family comes in first place.'[35]

In the Centre and north-east of the country, many of the same features and attitudes are to be found. State services are as widespread as in the north-west, and have a reputation for efficiency. The quality of life, though, with its interplay of city and countryside, is higher here than in the northern metropolis. Many families still maintain a close link with the land.

In the Third Italy, the family as *azienda* (as business concern) is at least as frequent a model as the family formed of two workers both in receipt of wages or salaries. There exists a work ethic, geared to the making of family fortunes, which allows self-exploitation and the exploitation of one's relatives at levels which are difficult to find elsewhere in Italy.[36] Local government, both Catholic and Communist, has operated to protect and promote the vitality of this local family capitalism.[37]

In the 1980s it is women's activities that have changed most in the families of the Third Italy. In Emilia-Romagna, for instance, whereas the previous generation of women had remained as housewives or aided their husbands in the setting up of small family firms (see pp. 233–5), the present generation has tended increasingly to establish a work identity of its own. A 'double presence' has been established, both at home and at regular work, most often in white-collar jobs.[38]

The success story of families and businesses in the Third Italy has so often been recounted in glowing terms that it is worth pausing to reflect for a moment on some of the problems that remain. The family as *azienda* cannot help but be a constrictive form of social organization. Parents, children and relatives are engaged in a common enterprise, but the hierarchy of work and command must reproduce many of the authoritarian and patriarchal attitudes of the traditional sharecropping family.

A tragic incident of March 1987 in the port of Ravenna revealed both the seamier side of the Third Italy's 'economic miracle' and the stratum of families that was excluded from its benefits. Thirteen casual labourers lost their lives when they were overcome by fumes while cleaning a ship's hold. The small firm which employed them, MecNavi, was a subcontractor which paid 5,900 lire (under £3) an hour for men to work in conditions where no safety regulations applied. This was 'black' work with a vengeance; no trade union organization was allowed. The men who died were aged between seventeen and sixty. Most of them were local and the youngest was at his first day of work. One of them, Mohamed Mosad, was an Egyptian whose address was given as a beach hut at Marina di Ravenna. In prosperous and Communist Ravenna a great deal of soul-searching took place as to how such conditions continued to exist. A letter to the newspaper, *Il Manifesto*, urged its readers to remember that the Third Italy's new prosperity had been achieved not only by harmonious, hard-working and socially mobile families, but thanks also 'to the "below the stairs" work in the hosiery factories at Carpi, thanks to the artisanal machine workshops with their bevies of super-exploited apprentices, thanks to the Tunisians who have sweated and died in the foundries of Modena and Reggio Emilia'.[39]

If we turn now to the urban South, it is clear that a majority, not a minority, of families still face grave problems. The average size of families in the southern cities has remained much greater than elsewhere in Italy. The concept of maximizing the number of persons available for the labour market is still stronger than any idea of limiting family size in order to conserve resources.

These larger families have to survive in a situation of stagnation on the labour market. Often the male head of the family is not in regular work. Children leave school early and seek jobs of any sort and duration in the service sector. A minority of teenagers, both male and female, continue their studies with the coveted aim of gaining a degree. In Salerno, as Simone Piccone Stella has written, this very often provides only a number of 'truce' years at university before they are forced to confront an almost equally difficult labour market, even if at a higher level.[40]

Southern urban families also face a situation where the services offered by the state are very much less effective than in the Centre or the North. Money payments to families, as we have seen, are a poor substitute for efficient public transport, proper health care, well-run schools. In the absence of honest or prescient local government, the southern cities have for the most part become urban jungles, asphyxiated by traffic and dominated by criminal organizations. The family remains a necessary refuge from a hostile environment; the lack of *fede pubblica* (civic trust) continues to bedevil southern society.[41]

Finally, a glance at families in the rural South. Over the last fifteen years the hill and mountain areas have shown further signs of decline. The rural exodus has been so great and property has remained so divided that there has been an increasing abandonment of agriculture and what has been called 'a disintegration of production structures'.[42] The system of 'agro-assistance' has evolved, whereby the state aids families which can only in a residual sense be defined as peasants. A constant flow of money payments reaches the villages of the internal regions of the South: invalidity pensions, family benefits, pensions reserved for peasant proprietors, subsidies for artisans, regional assistance, etc.

As in the urban areas of the South, these money hand-outs are the dominant form of state intervention. Essential services, like that of running water, long taken for granted elsewhere, are lacking for many months of the year in many parts of the southern interior. In the old agro-towns, women often have washing-machines and the most modern kitchen equipment in their homes, but are forced in the summer months to do the washing by hand or at the public fountain, when a trickle of water arrives at night time.[43]

Throughout the rural South, family life has been disrupted by migration. Even in the 1980s the patterns that we noted for the 1960s – of fathers being absent for many months of the year, of mothers or even grandparents being left to bring up children, of ageing populations – seem to have remained significant phenomena.[44] The money that has flowed back into the villages and the agro-towns has permitted a very marked amelioration of living standards. It has also led to a massive wave of families building their own houses, most often without any sort of building permit. In much of small-town and rural southern Italy, on the coasts even more than in the interior, the landscape resembles one vast building site, with houses constructed, or half-constructed, anywhere and everywhere.[45]

Kinship networks, as Piselli has reiterated, have remained as strong as ever. Yet these, as the landscape of the rural South testifies, are networks without collective projects, without a consciousness that transcends family interest. Neither from civil society nor from the state has there emerged a new and less destructive formulation of the relationship between family and collectivity.

Politics and Ideology in the 1980s

a. A BLOCKED POLITICAL SYSTEM

The 1980s have been a period of great political continuities. After the brief experiment of the years of national solidarity, politics have been dominated by the alliance between the Christian Democrats and the Socialists. For more than twenty-five years, in fact, with very few intervals, the DC–PSI alliance has formed the basis for Italian government. The object of furious polemics and even histrionics on the part of both parties, with 1986–7 being a particularly entertaining period, the alliance has in reality been one of the longest lasting in European politics, and the dominant form of government in the history of the Republic.

Of course, the 1980s have seen variations, both personal and political. The election in 1978 of the noted anti-Fascist and Socialist, Sandro Pertini, as President of the Republic, proved an extraordinarily felicitous choice. This tiny and frail old man reinvigorated the office of President. His outspoken advocacy of democratic values, his constant re-evocation of his anti-Fascist youth, his invitation every year to thousands of schoolchildren to come and meet him in the Quirinale, left an indelible impression on Italian public opinion. Pertini became the most popular President that the Republic ever had. Thirty-five years after Parri's brief government, the Resistance returned memorably to the highest echelons of the state. As a consequence, Italian democracy was much strengthened.

It was Pertini who took the initiative in 1981 to invite the Republican Giovanni Spadolini to become President of the Council of Ministers. This was the first time since Parri that a member of a party other than the DC had led the country. Spadolini's two brief governments, lasting from June 1981 to November 1982, were not much more than an interim period, but the mould had been broken. In 1983 the national elections brought a disastrous result for the Christian Democrats. They fell from 38.3 per cent of the vote to 32.9 per cent, by far their worst result since 1948. Their new secretary, Ciriaco De Mita, had fought the elections on a neo-conservative programme of state spending cuts, renewal of the party and an end to clientelism. Not surprisingly, the traditional Christian Democrat electorate did not like what they heard. Afterwards, the way was open for Bettino Craxi to become the first ever Socialist President of the Council of Ministers.[46]

Craxi's term of office lasted longer than anyone had anticipated, from 1983 to 1987. His assertive personality, tactical skill and innate political ability earned him many admirers and not a few enemies. In 1987 fresh elections brought his party 14.3 per cent of the vote, an increase of 2.9 per cent on 1983. At the same time the Christian Democrats, still under the command of a rather more cautious De Mita, improved marginally on their 1983 performance, gaining 34.3 per cent of the vote. The balance between the two major governing parties had thus shifted during the 1980s. The Socialists had increased their vote by some 4.5 per cent since 1979, the Christian Democrats had lost 4 per cent exactly. Of equal significance, Craxi had come to be seen as the dominant personality in Italian politics.

However, the problems associated with the DC–PSI alliance, endemic since 1963, have shown no signs of disappearing. This is not a political alliance based on mutual trust, parity or programmatic accord. It is, rather, riven by suspicion, by personal rivalry, by an eternal jockeying for position. It makes any strategic planning next to impossible, wastes an extraordinary amount of time and energy and leads inexorably to weak rather than strong government.

As a result, the reformism of the 1980s appears no more consistent, and in many ways less significant, than that of the 1970s. The eighties would seem to have many parallels with the decade prior to 1968. At that time the economy was booming, the material bases for reform clearly existed, but the centre-left politicians let the opportunity slip by. Craxi has been a more able strategist for his party than for the country, and in the absence of pressure from social movements, such as those that existed between 1968 and 1978, the reform record has indeed been a modest one.

Probably its most significant element has been the attempt in October 1984 by the Republican Bruno Visentini, while Minister of Finance, to ensure that shop owners pay their taxes. The ludicrous situation had been reached by which shop owners were declaring taxable incomes inferior to the wages that they paid out to their own employees. None the less, shop owners went on strike, the government five-party coalition (DC, PSI, PSDI, PRI, PLI) was put into crisis and Visentini's fiscal reform was carried only with great difficulty.[47]

The other measure worthy of note was again the work of a Republican, Giuseppe Galasso, who was under-secretary at the strange-sounding Ministry of Cultural Assets (*Beni Culturali*) during the Craxi government. Galasso introduced a law compelling each region to draw up a regional landscape plan (*piano paesistico regionale*). The aim was to defend Italy's coastlines and other aspects of her environment from further ruination. This was certainly a case of shutting the stable door after the horse had bolted, but it was still much better than nothing. The law, as Galasso himself explained, 'has been repeatedly attacked; there were attempts at sabotage in Parliament by requests to revise it, and by inserting clauses in other laws which would contradict it. The opposition that it has aroused derives from the fact that it is difficult in Italy to reverse the tendency by which economic criteria always take precedence over values like the quality of life or the safeguarding of the environment.'[48] All Italian regional governments were supposed to have drawn up their landscape plans by the end of 1986, but by that date only three had done so, and no single plan had yet become operational.[49]

The enduring but rather unproductive DC–PSI alliance is one element in the blocked Italian political system. The other is the absence of any credible alternative. The 1980s have been a dismal decade for the Communists. The end of the collective movements of the 1970s, the defeat at FIAT in November 1980, the decline of their fellow Communist parties in the West, have all taken their toll. But the party has also been bedevilled by bad luck and poor thinking. The sudden death of Enrico Berlinguer in 1984 deprived the Communists of the one man of sufficient political ability and international stature to guide them through the doldrums of the eighties.[50] The extraordinary demonstration at his funeral, with well over a million people in the streets of Rome, was the last moment when the PCI held the centre of the national stage.

The party has been quite unable to renew its political thinking. The 'third way' to Socialism, which for all its vagueness had exercised considerable intellectual and political fascination, has given way to deep uncertainty at a theoretical level. In the day-to-day politics of Italy, the party also appears to have no clear message. Most of the time it entreats the Socialists to abandon their alliance with the DC, and to form a government of the left. Occasionally, it winks an eye at the DC. The result is that the PCI seems to have neither long-term nor short-term political objectives, and consequently fails to appear as a credible opposition. Its electoral decline has been significant, from 30.4 per cent in 1979 to 29.9 per cent in 1983 and 26.6 per cent in 1987. The replacement as party secretary of Alessandro Natta by Achille Occhetto during the course of 1988 may have signalled an end to this long decline, but it is still much too early to pass judgement on Occhetto's 'new course'.

The political system is therefore blocked, with a government which only half succeeds in governing and an opposition which only half opposes. Interest in politics remains extraordinarily high. Turn-out at national elections averages around 90 per cent, and at local and regional elections an astonishing 75–80 per cent. At this level, democratic politics is alive and well in Italy, certainly as much as in any other European country. On another level, though, there is a deep frustration with a political system, based on a very pure version of proportional representation, which is quite obviously not working.[51] The so-called Eurobarometers, opinion polls conducted in the EEC countries ever since 1973, provide dramatic confirmation of this frustration. In reply to the question 'Are you satisfied with the way democracy works in your country?', an average 75 per cent of Italians in the decade 1978–87 replied that they were 'not at all satisfied' or 'not very satisfied'. These levels were far higher than in any other of the major European nations. Comparative figures for France were 45 per cent, for Britain 38 per cent and for West Germany 22 per cent.[52]

b. THE CITIZEN AND THE STATE

One cannot help but suspect that many of those Italians who expressed their dissatisfaction had in mind not only the political system but also the malfunctioning of the state – its inability to meet its citizens' requests and thus resolve one of the central problems of democracy.

This is not to say that no progress has been made during the history of the Republic. From the 1970s onwards, with the great increase of welfare services and provision, the state has intervened to aid the citizen more effectively than ever before. Regional government has furthered this process. It is enough to spend even a little time in one of the prosperous regions of the Centre and the North, whether it be the Veneto or Tuscany or Lombardy, to be aware of the flow of money and services channelled by the state to nearly every part of Italian society.[53]

On the other hand, many of the Italian state's fundamental problems, which have so often surfaced during the course of this book, have not been resolved. Indeed, some of them have become more serious. It is worth examining them in turn.

The deformed relationship between state and citizen, which was first examined in Chapter 5, has remained a constant and entrenched feature of the Republic. The discretionary powers of the public administrator are the real operational criteria of the Italian state. Norms and regulations, of course, exist and are adhered to, but the public official responds *most effectively* to external pressure: to the call of friendship or kinship, to the lure of political favour or financial reward. In August 1988 the journalist Stefano Malatesta went to interview the superintendent of the archaeological site of Pompeii, Baldassare Conticello. In the superintendent's office, alongside his desk, was a large Italian flag. Conticello explained why it was there: 'I am not afflicted by an excessive sense of nationalism. I have had to put it there to make it understood that this office is not my personal market, my stall [*bancarella*]. I am not here to buy and to sell. I represent the state. But since no one here has any sense of the state, but only of the family, of the clan, of the political party or of the criminal band [*cosca*], everyone firmly believes that a superintendent must use his post for his own exclusive advantage, to make money.'[54]

No state bureaucracy is altogether free of corruption. But if an essential criterion of a modern state is the relatively transparent nature of the business conducted between the citizen and the public administration, then Italy remains at the bottom of the list of modern European states.

A second, closely related problem is the inefficiency of the majority of state services. If their quantity and quality increased significantly in the 1970s, there still remains much to be done. The non-functioning of services is the lament of all sections of the Italian population. At the élite level, major figures of the Italian economy like De Benedetti and Prodi warn that unless radical steps are taken soon to combat the inefficiency of services like the post and the telephones, and to reduce the delays inherent in all state transactions, Italy will be unable to meet the European challenge of 1992. At a more modest level, every citizen has his or her own horror story. In November 1987 Giorgio Ruffolo, Enzo Mattina and others founded the 'Movement for the Defence of the Citizen' (Il Movimento per la Difesa del Cittadino). Its aim is to mobilize citizens to protest against what Ruffolo has called 'bureaucratic micro-persecution'.[55] The weekly magazine *L'Espresso*, which supports the venture, received two thousand letters in six months, all recounting the most extraordinary stories of bureaucratic tyranny, ineptitude, or worse. Some were published in a weekly column, and form a historic dossier of the Italian state in action.[56] In spite of this publicity, there are very few signs of any change in the mode of functioning (or non-functioning) of the state apparatuses.

Another area of deficiency, which has become all the more noticeable as reform laws proliferated in the 1970s, was the inability of the public administration to ensure that laws passed are laws enforced. In many areas the state has not been equipped with the apparatus or the personnel necessary to ensure the realization of new legislation. Visentini's fiscal reform of 1984 was widely heralded as one of the most important laws of the 1980s. Yet an inquiry of September 1986 found that the tax officers to whom the task of enforcement had been entrusted were too few in number and too poorly paid. Visentini had stated that 'we need a highly specialized and well-paid corps, able to resist outside pressure'. Instead, in Forcellini's words, 'the fiscal administration is today a jammed mechanism, degraded and falling to pieces: poor organization, insufficient personnel, especially at the higher levels, lack of modern means, ridiculous salaries, rampant corruption'.[57]

Behind these deficiencies lies the continuing 'archipelago' nature of the state (see p. 154). The uninterrupted 'occupation' of the state by the DC and the enduring necessity for coalition has meant that government has become predominantly the conciliation of diverse political and corporate groups. This is the fundamental reason why the public-sector deficit can be reduced only with the greatest difficulty. In July 1988 Giuliano Amato, the Socialist Minister of the Treasury, explained in an unusually frank way why he, as head of the most powerful ministry in Italy, was able to do so little:

I have the sensation of moving in an archipelago . . . Single ministries are much less responsive to the collegial will of the government and much more to that of 'the triangle' which each forms with the corresponding parliamentary commission and the interest groups of the sector: the government decides one thing on the career of brigadiers but the relevant ministry, with this or that under-secretary, goes to the Defence Commission and decides the opposite . . . All in all, the system is centrifugal, everything has to be negotiated, everyone negotiates with everyone else, every procedural step is a negotiation, and at each negotiation either one stops or one loses a part of what one is proposing.[58]

Finally, in certain areas of the country the authority of the state is still in doubt. The twinned menace of terrorism and the strategy of tension gradually declined in the 1980s, but not without further blood being shed and plots being discovered. The most terrible tragedy was that of the deaths caused by a bomb which exploded in Bologna station on 2 August 1980. This was the culmination of the cycle of right-wing terrorism; eighty-five people died. A year later the existence of a subversive masonic lodge, the P2, was discovered. Its members included prominent figures in the armed forces, in business and in the world of politics. The precise objectives of the lodge have remained obscure, but there is little doubt that its head, Licio Gelli, was seeking to construct an anti-Communist network within the highest echelons of the Italian state.[59]

It is in the South, though, that the greatest danger to the authority of the state has come to the fore. On 3 September, General Alberto Dalla Chiesa and his wife were assassinated by the Mafia in Palermo. Dalla Chiesa was the Carabiniere officer who had played the leading role in the unmasking of the Italian terrorist groups. He had been sent by the government to combat the Mafia and had been in Sicily only a few months before he was killed.[60]

From the 1960s onwards, the Mafia, far from disappearing as its rural bases were depopulated, had transferred its activities to lucrative urban markets — drugs above all, but also the monopoly of control over certain trades and institutions. At the same time other major criminal organizations, like the Camorra at Naples and the 'Ndrangheta in Calabria, had increased their influence in southern civil society. The state, especially in the wake of the killing of Dalla Chiesa and the earlier assassination of the Sicilian Communist, Pio La Torre, has tried to wage a sterner war on these criminal elements than ever before. In 1987 the *'maxi-processo'* ('maxi-trial') of 456 *mafiosi* took place in Palermo. Amongst the accused were the legendary Mafia leaders Luciano Liggio and Michele Greco. Of the accused, nineteen were sentenced to life imprisonment.[61]

However, the outcome of this anti-Mafia battle is far from certain. At the end of 1988 the anti-Mafia commissioner Domenico Sica warned that three regions of Italy — Campania, Calabria and Sicily — were no longer under the full control of the state. The real links between Mafia power and political power have never been allowed to emerge into the limelight. And in one sense the battle is already lost. In 1986 it was estimated that some 12.5 per cent of the Italian Gross Domestic Product was the fruit of criminal activity; nearly half of this was from the commerce of drugs, and the rest from extortion, thefts, kidnappings and illegal payments for favours.[62]

Changing Values

In a seminal article written in 1971, the sociologist Alessandro Pizzorno pointed to the success of the Italian ruling élite in gaining support from the *ceti medi* by a strategy of 'individualist attraction'.[63] In the fifties and sixties the *ceti medi*, attracted by the bright lights of consumerism and the possibility of individual advancement, had become the firm supporters of the moderate, democratic status quo. In the 1980s it is possible to suggest that this consensus, first established amongst the *ceti medi*, has become generalized to society as a whole. In other words, the traditional values of the family have become wedded to those of parliamentary democracy and consumer capitalism. Such values have, with very few exceptions, become predominant in all sectors of society. Italy's great transformation, then, has been in keeping with the model of modernity which first emerged at the time of the 'economic miracle'; a model with strong American influences, which was heavily contested between 1968 and 1973, but which seems to have entered a golden age in the 1980s.

In a recent interview the Socialist Gianni De Michelis, at the time the Vice-President of the Council of Ministers, referred to 1968 as the 'twilight of the Gods', the last great collective moment in Italian history, the end of all dreams of a new era.[64] Sidney Tarrow has maintained that the 'transition to mature capitalism' has resulted in the 'ultimate assimilation of the working class'.[65] Both judgements would seem to be somewhat premature. There is no reason to believe that the strong traditions of collective action in recent, and not so recent, Italian history have died a sudden death. Nor can there be much foundation to the belief that consumer capitalism has solved the 'riddle of history'. As Hirschman has pointed out, consumerism probably has its own stock of disappointments in store for us all.[66] It remains to be seen, therefore, whether the values of the 1980s will acquire permanency, or whether alternative visions can still find more than an exiguous place in the history of the Italian Republic.

Statistical Appendix

Compiled by
Giulio Ghellini and Paul Ginsborg

Our intention in this appendix is to present a brief statistical overview of the changes in Italian society during the last four decades. The tables are not intended to be exhaustive, but aim to provide the reader with further information on some of the principal themes discussed in the book. In particular the tables should aid the understanding of three aspects of the Italian Republic: the social evolution of the country since the war, changes in political attitudes and behaviour, and developments in the economy. We have tried to use consistent and homogeneous series of historical data, even though on occasion this has meant not being able to extend the series to cover the most recent years.

For the social aspects of the appendix we have decided, as was noted in the preface, to adopt a territorial division of the data into four geographical areas : the North-West, the North-East and Centre, Lazio, the South and islands.[1] Lazio has been treated as a case apart because of the predominance of Rome in that region, with its consequent distorting effect upon regional statistics. It thus seemed sensible not to combine the data from Lazio with data from other central or southern regions.

For the other two themes we have mainly used national statistics. Often the data had more relevance in this form, and in any case there were difficulties in collating satisfactorily historical series from different regions; this was especially the case for the economic tables.

The map on p. 428 shows the territorial divisions chosen, and provides the shading key used to distinguish the four regions in the subsequent graphs. We have listed the sources for the tables and explanations of them, where appropriate, in the Notes to the Appendix on pp. 452–4.

1. The regions contained in the three agglomerated geographical areas are the following: for the North-West, the regions of the Val d'Aosta, Piedmont, Lombardy and Liguria; the North-East and Centre comprises the Trentino-Alto Adige, Veneto, Friuli-Venezia Giulia, Emilia-Romagna, Marches, Tuscany, Umbria, the Abruzzi; and the South and islands is made up of Molise, Campania, Puglia, Basilicata, Calabria, Sicily and Sardinia.

 North-West

North-East and Centre

Lazio

South and islands

1 Average number of family members by geographical area, 1936–81

	Italy	North-West	North-East and Centre	Lazio	South and islands
1936	4·3	3·8	4·7	4·3	4·3
1951	4·0	3·4	4·2	4·0	4·2
1961	3·6	3·2	3·8	3·7	3·9
1971	3·3	3·0	3·4	3·4	3·7
1981	3·0	2·8	3·0	3·0	3·3

2 Extended families by geographical area, 1951–81

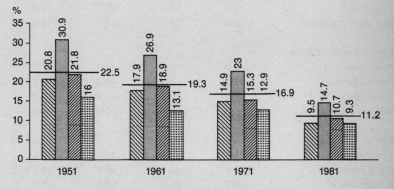

The horizontal line shows the average for the whole of Italy

3 Indices of the concentration of extended families by geographical area, 1951–81

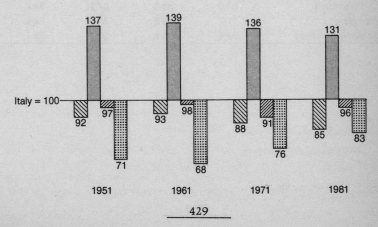

4   Family size by geographical area, 1951–81 (percentages)

	1951	1961	1971	1981
Italy				
1 member	9·5	10·6	12·9	17·8
2 or 3 members	38·1	42·0	44·4	45·7
4 members	19·0	20·4	21·2	21·5
5 or more members	33·3	27·0	21·5	14·9
North-West				
1 member	12·5	13·7	16·1	21·3
2 or 3 members	45·9	49·7	49·9	49·6
4 members	19·2	19·4	20·1	19·9
5 or more members	22·4	17·2	13·9	9·2
North-East and Centre				
1 member	8·0	9·4	11·8	17·2
2 or 3 members	35·7	41·0	45·3	48·6
4 members	19·8	21·5	21·8	21·0
5 or more members	36·5	28·1	21·0	13·2
Lazio				
1 member	8·8	8·3	10·7	16·0
2 or 3 members	36·4	40·6	43·3	44·9
4 members	20·7	24·0	25·3	25·3
5 or more members	34·0	27·1	20·7	13·8
South and islands				
1 member	8·5	9·6	11·4	15·6
2 or 3 members	34·0	36·3	37·9	39·2
4 members	17·7	19·2	20·6	22·5
5 or more members	39·8	34·9	30·1	22·7

5 Composition of families in Italy, 1951–81

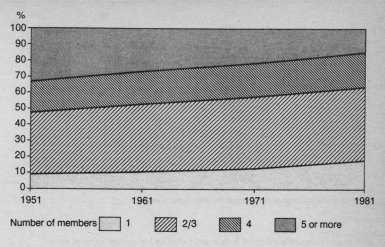

Number of members: 1 ☐ 2/3 ▨ 4 ▨ 5 or more ■

6 Single-person households and families with five or more members by geographical area, 1951–81

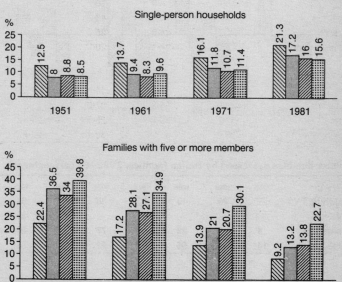

Single-person households

	1951	1961	1971	1981
	12.5	13.7	16.1	21.3
	8	9.4	11.8	17.2
	8.8	8.3	10.7	16
	8.5	9.6	11.4	15.6

Families with five or more members

	1951	1961	1971	1981
	22.4	17.2	13.9	9.2
	36.5	28.1	21	13.2
	34	27.1	20.7	13.8
	39.8	34.9	30.1	22.7

7   Home-ownership by geographical area, 1951–81

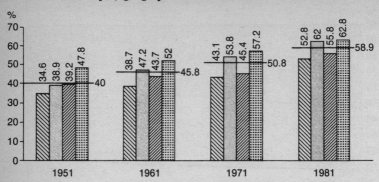

The horizontal line shows the average for the whole of Italy

8   Indices of concentration of home-ownership by geographical area, 1951–81

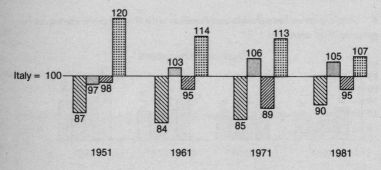

9   Consumer durables possessed by Italian families, 1953–85 (percentages)

	1953	1960	1965	1971	1975	1980	1985
Black and white TV	–	20	49	82	89	85	64
Colour TV	–	–	–	–	–	22	58
Washing-machine	4	5	23	63	77	86	89
Refrigerator	14	17	55	86	93	98	99

10   Cars per thousand inhabitants in Italy, 1950–85

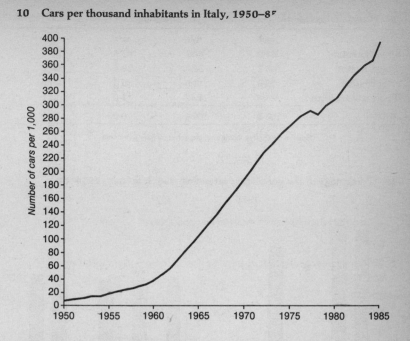

11   Composition of the working population by social class in Italy, 1951–83

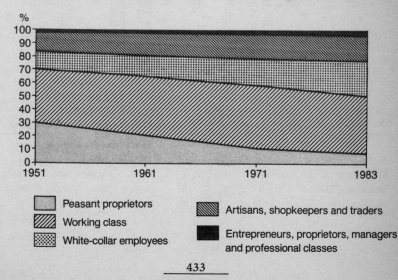

Peasant proprietors

Working class

White-collar employees

Artisans, shopkeepers and traders

Entrepreneurs, proprietors, managers and professional classes

12   Composition of white-collar employment in Italy, 1951–83 (percentages)

	1951	1961	1971	1983
Private sector	41·9	42·7	43·6	39·1
Public sector	36·7	38·1	39·4	48·2
education	13·0	13·8	15·0	20·9
Special categories *a*	21·4	19·2	17·0	12·7
Total	100·0	100·0	100·0	100·0

*a*Special categories include religious and military personnel.

13   Percentage of the population attending church in Italy, 1954–88

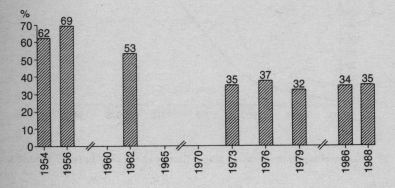

14   Principal flows of inter-regional migration, 1955–61

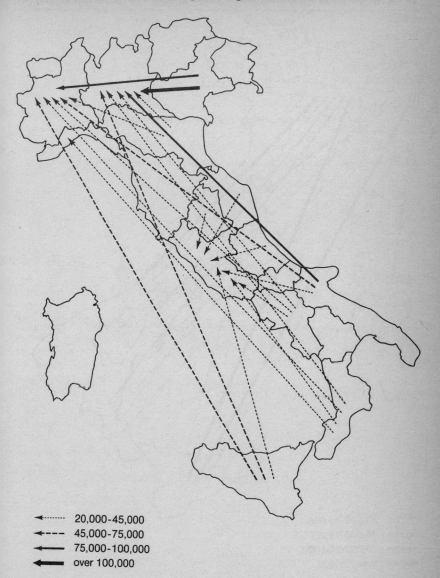

◄·········	20,000-45,000
◄- - - -	45,000-75,000
◄———	75,000-100,000
◄▬▬▬	over 100,000

15   Principal flows of inter-regional migration, 1962–71

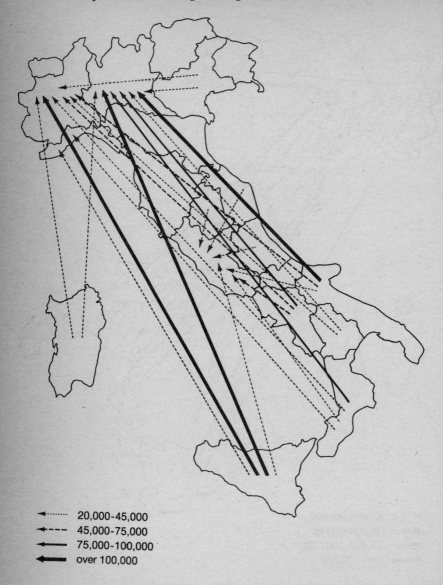

◄······   20,000-45,000
◄-----   45,000-75,000
◄──────   75,000-100,000
◄██████   over 100,000

16   Principal flows of inter-regional migration, 1972–81

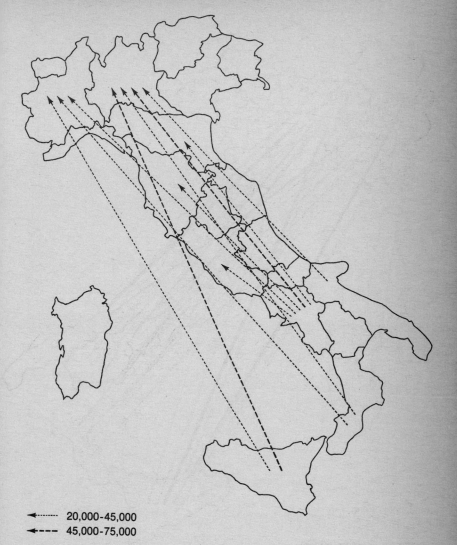

◄------- 20,000-45,000
◄---- 45,000-75,000

17   Principal flows of inter-regional migration, 1955–81

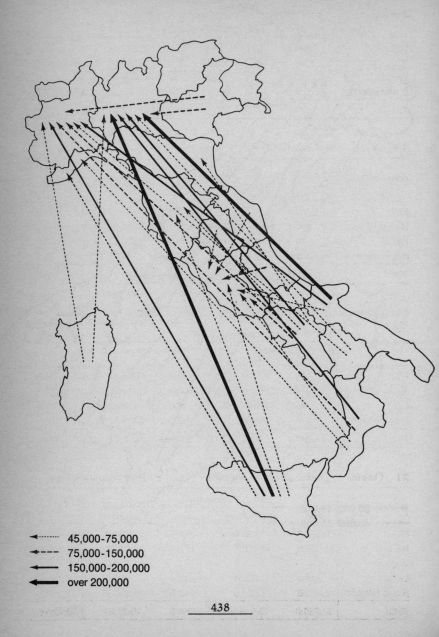

◄········   45,000-75,000
◄----   75,000-150,000
◄────   150,000-200,000
◄━━━   over 200,000

18 Origins and destinations of migratory flows, 1955–61 (thousands)

Area of origin	Destination					Residents, 1961	
	NW	NE and Centre	Lazio	S and islands	Total	No.	%
NW	2,324·5	199·8	36·6	101·5	2,662·4	13,157	26·0
NE and Centre	595·3	2,955·1	193·9	120·9	3,865·2	16,182	32·0
Lazio	43·5	85·6	306·1	64·2	499·4	3,959	7·8
S and islands	568·3	237·1	196·6	2,085·9	3,087·9	17,326	34·2
Total	3,531·6	3,477·6	733·2	2,372·5	10,114·9	50,624	100·0

19 Origins and destinations of migratory flows, 1962–71 (thousands)

Area of origin	Destination					Residents, 1971	
	NW	NE and Centre	Lazio	S and islands	Total	No.	%
NW	3,884·4	405·7	96·8	478·6	4,869·5	14,938	27·6
NE and Centre	591·1	3,990·7	266·8	217·4	5,066·0	16,802	31·0
Lazio	91·3	159·7	568·8	149·2	969·0	4,684	8·7
S and islands	1,409·0	415·0	325·5	3,175·0	5,324·5	17,708	32·7
Total	5,979·8	4,971·1	1,257·9	4,020·2	16,229·0	54,132	100·0

20 Origins and destinations of migratory flows, 1972–81 (thousands)

Area of origin	Destination					Residents, 1981	
	NW	NE and Centre	Lazio	S and islands	Total	No.	%
NW	3,128·4	351·1	80·2	544·7	4,104·4	15,291	27·0
NE and Centre	271·1	2,993·9	142·9	204·5	3,612·4	17,429	30·8
Lazio	70·2	153·1	557·5	141·4	922·2	5,002	8·9
S and islands	877·7	398·4	223·8	2,939·7	4,439·6	18,835	33·3
Total	4,347·4	3,896·5	1,004·4	3,830·3	13,078·6	56,557	100·0

21 Origins and destinations of migratory flows, 1955–81 (thousands)

Area of origin	Destination				Total
	NW	NE and Centre	Lazio	S and islands	
NW	9,341·3	956·6	213·6	1,124·8	11,636·3
NE and Centre	1,457·5	9,939·7	603·6	542·8	12,543·6
Lazio	205·0	398·4	1,432·4	354·8	2,390·6
S and islands	2,855·0	1,050·5	745·9	8,200·7	12,852·1
Total	13,858·8	12,345·2	2,995·5	10,223·1	39,422·6

22 Educational qualifications of Italians over six years of age, by geographical area, 1951–81 (percentages)

	1951	1961	1971	1981
Italy				
Degree	1·0	1·3	1·8	2·8
Secondary school	3·3	4·3	6·9	11·5
Middle school	5·9	9·6	14·7	23·8
Elementary school, or literate but without qualifications	76·9	76·5	71·4	58·8
Illiterate	12·9	8·3	5·2	3·1
North-West				
Degree	1·1	1·4	1·8	2·7
Secondary school	3·9	4·8	7·0	12·1
Middle school	8·6	12·7	17·4	26·6
Elementary school, or literate but without qualifications	83·6	79·3	72·5	57·8
Illiterate	2·8	1·8	1·3	0·8
North-East and Centre				
Degree	0·8	1·1	1·6	2·6
Secondary school	3·0	3·9	6·4	11·3
Middle school	5·3	8·8	14·5	23·8
Elementary school, or literate but without qualifications	81·6	80·3	74·1	60·4
Illiterate	9·3	5·9	3·4	1·9
Lazio				
Degree	2·2	2·6	3·4	4·5
Secondary school	5·4	7·0	10·2	15·6
Middle school	9·0	13·7	18·2	25·9
Elementary school, or literate but without qualifications	73·2	70·2	64·4	51·9
Illiterate	10·2	6·5	3·8	2·1
South and islands				
Degree	0·9	1·2	1·7	2·6
Secondary school	2·6	3·5	6·4	10·0
Middle school	4·0	6·9	11·5	20·9
Elementary school, or literate but without qualifications	67·7	72·1	69·6	60·1
Illiterate	24·8	16·3	10·8	6·4

23 Educational qualifications of Italians over six years of age, 1951–81

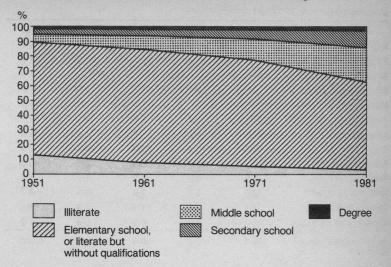

Legend:
- Illiterate
- Elementary school, or literate but without qualifications
- Middle school
- Secondary school
- Degree

24 Illiterates and those with degrees or secondary-school diplomas by geographical area, 1951–81 (percentages)

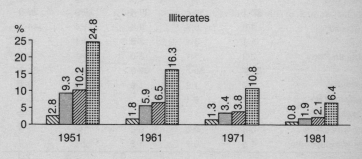

Illiterates

	1951	1961	1971	1981
	2.8	1.8	1.3	0.8
	9.3	5.9	3.4	1.9
	10.2	6.5	3.8	2.1
	24.8	16.3	10.8	6.4

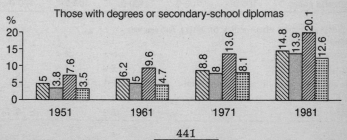

Those with degrees or secondary-school diplomas

	1951	1961	1971	1981
	5	6.2	8.8	14.8
	3.8	5	8	13.9
	7.6	9.6	13.6	20.1
	3.5	4.7	8.1	12.6

25 Valid votes cast in elections to the Chambers of Deputies, 1948–87 (percentages)

	1948	1953	1958	1963	1968
PSIUP, PDUP, DP[a]	–	–	–	–	4·4
PCI	–	22·6	22·7	25·3	26·9
Popular Front	31·0	–	–	–	–
PSI	–	12·7	14·2	13·8	–
PSU	–	–	–	–	14·5
PSDI	7·1	4·5	4·6	6·1	–
Republican Party	2·5	1·6	1·4	1·4	2·0
DC	48·5	40·1	42·4	38·3	39·1
Liberal Party	3·8	3·0	3·5	7·0	5·8
Monarchist Party	2·8	6·9	4·9	1·7	1·3
MSI, MSI–DN[b]	2·0	5·8	4·8	5·1	4·4
Others with seats	1·1	0·5	1·1	0·5	0·5
Others without seats	1·3	2·3	0·5	0·8	1·0
Total of valid votes	100·0	100·0	100·0	100·0	100·0

	1972	1976	1979	1983	1987
PSIUP, PDUP, DP[a]	1·9	1·5	1·4	1·5	1·7
Greens	–	–	–	–	2·5
Radical Party	–	1·1	3·4	2·2	2·6
PCI	27·1	34·4	30·4	29·9	26·6
PSI	9·6	9·6	9·8	11·4	14·3
PSDI	5·1	3·4	3·8	4·1	3·0
Republican Party	2·9	3·1	3·0	5·1	3·7
DC	38·7	38·7	38·3	32·9	34·3
Liberal Party	3·9	1·3	1·9	2·9	2·1
MSI and PMN	8·7	6·1	–	–	–
MSI, MSI–DN[b]	–	–	5·3	6·8	5·9
Others with seats	0·6	0·6	0·8	1·2	1·6
Others without seats	1·5	0·2	1·8	2·1	1·9
Total of valid votes	100·0	100·0	100·0	100·0	100·0

[a]PSIUP in 1968 and in 1972; PDUP in 1979; DP in 1976, 1983 and 1987.
[b]MSI–DN in 1979

26 Elections to the Chamber of Deputies, percentages of voters and non-voters, 1948–87

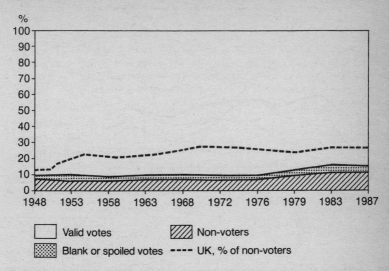

27 Percentage of those 'not very', or 'not at all' satisfied with the way democracy is working in four EC countries, 1970–87

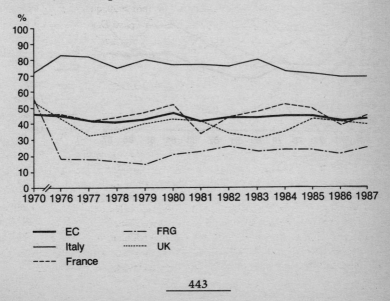

28 Attitudes towards society: agreement with the choice 'support for existing institutions' in four E C countries, 1970–87

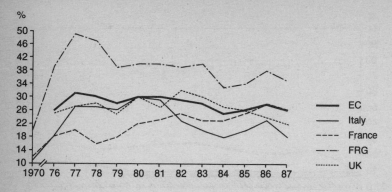

29 Attitudes towards society: agreement with the choice 'need for reform' in four E C countries, 1970–87

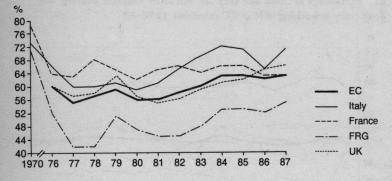

30 Attitudes towards society: agreement with the choice 'need for revolutionary change' in four EC countries, 1970–87

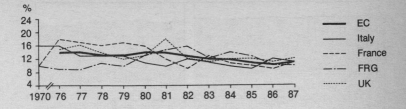

31 Annual increase in Gross Domestic Product in Italy, 1948–85

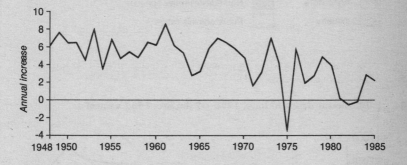

32 Gross Domestic Product per head in Italy, 1951–85 (thousands of lire, 1987 values)

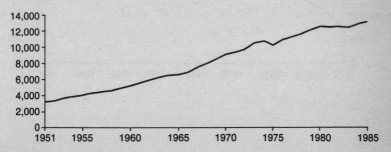

33   Composition of added value by sector in Italy, 1951–85

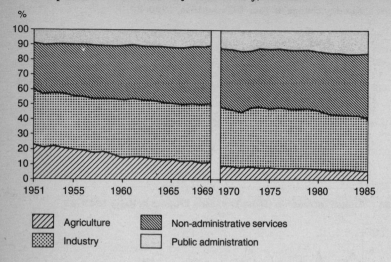

Agriculture

Industry

Non-administrative services

Public administration

34   Public-sector deficit in Italy, 1970–87 (bn lire, 1987 values)

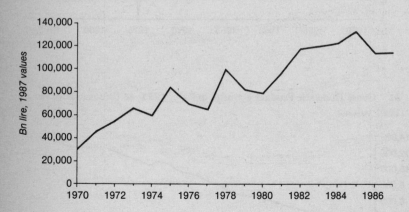

35   Annual rate of inflation in Italy, 1948–87

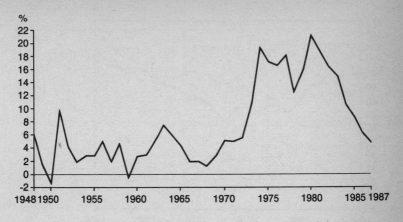

36   Levels of economic activity, employment and extent of unemployment by gender in Italy, 1959–85

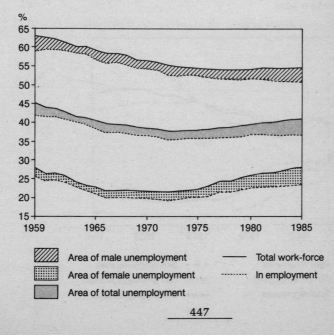

37 Indices of employment by sex in Italy, 1959–85 (1959=100)

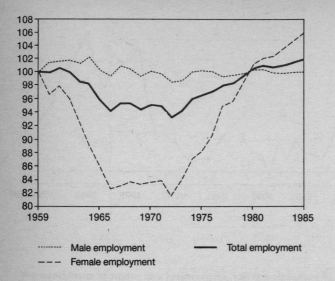

.... Male employment   ——— Total employment
——— Female employment

38 Indices of employment by type of employment and by sex in Italy, 1959–85 (1959 = 100)

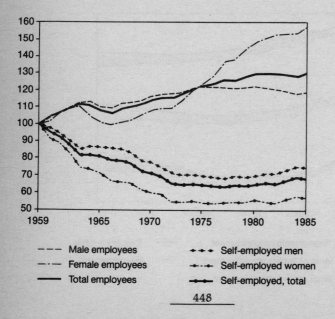

——— Male employees   ⋯•⋯ Self-employed men
—·—· Female employees   —·—· Self-employed women
——— Total employees   —●— Self-employed, total

39 **Indices of employment by economic sector in Italy, 1959–85 (1959 = 100)**

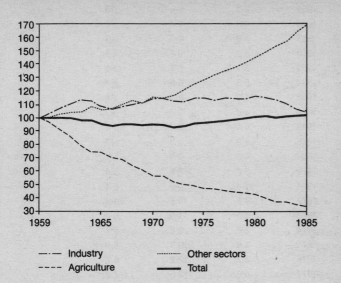

- —·— Industry
- – – – Agriculture
- ·········· Other sectors
- ▬▬▬ Total

40   Unemployment in Italy, 1959–85 (percentage)

	Men	Women	All
1959	6·1	8·8	7·0
1960	4·8	7·4	5·6
1961	4·2	7·3	5·1
1962	3·5	6·8	4·5
1963	3·1	5·7	3·9
1964	3·3	6·8	4·3
1965	4·3	8·1	5·4
1966	4·6	8·9	5·9
1967	4·1	8·7	5·4
1968	4·2	9·5	5·7
1969	4·0	9·9	5·7
1970	3·7	9·6	5·4
1971	3·8	9·5	5·4
1972	4·6	10·9	6·4
1973	4·2	11·6	6·4
1974	3·6	9·6	5·4
1975	3·8	10·7	5·9
1976	4·2	12·2	6·7
1977	4·6	12·6	7·2
1978	4·7	12·6	7·2
1979	4·9	13·3	7·7
1980	4·8	13·1	7·6
1981	5·4	14·4	8·4
1982	6·1	14·9	9·1
1983	6·6	16·2	9·9
1984	6·8	17·1	10·4
1985	7·0	17·3	10·6

41   Numbers in search of employment in Italy, 1959–85

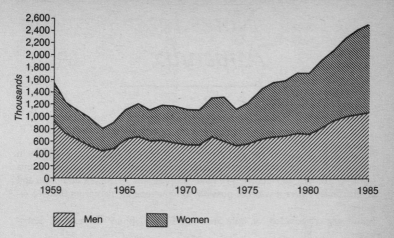

42   Number of hours lost through labour disputes in Italy, 1949–86

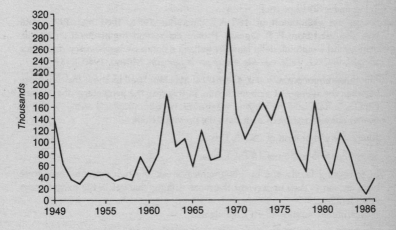

Notes to
Appendix

1   As the data for 1936 for the Abruzzi and Molise was only available in aggregate form, it was decided to include both regions in the geographical area of the North-East and Centre. We have adopted this procedure both here and in later tables where it was not possible to have separate data from the two regions.
    Source: our elaboration of data from IST AT (Istituto Centrale di Statistica).

2   It should be noted that for the years 1951, 1961, and 1971 the Molise data is again combined with that from the Abruzzi. An extended family consists of the head of family and his or her partner, their child or children, grandparent(s) and/or other relations. Extended families are often both multiple and vertical, in the sense of having more than one couple and more than two generations living under the same roof.
    Source: our elaboration of IST AT data. For 1951, 1961 and 1971, data was also used from P. P. Donati, 'Profilo dei recenti cambiamenti strutturali, demografici e culturali della famiglia italiana e connesse implicazioni di politica sociale', in C. G. Vella, ed., *Un sinodo per la famiglia*, Milano, 1980, p. 59.

3   The index of concentration is a statistical indicator used to show the difference between the average of a phenomenon, in this case the percentage of extended families in Italy, and the varying subgroups, here geographical areas.
    Source: our elaboration of data from the previous chart.

4   *Source*: our elaboration of IST AT data.

5   *Source*: our elaboration of IST AT data.

6   In comparing family size by geographical areas, the two extreme cases have been chosen as they underwent the most striking changes in the period under consideration.
    Source: our elaboration of IST AT data.

7   The 1961 data for Molise was combined with that for the Abruzzi.
    Source: our elaboration of IST AT data.

8   *Source*: our elaboration of IST AT data.

9   The data is drawn from non-continuous surveys. From 1980 the ownership

of colour and of black and white television sets has been listed separately. The percentages of the two add up to more than 100 since families who owned both types of television were counted twice.

Source: Doxa (opinion-poll organization) surveys for the years listed.

10 *Source*: ISTAT.

11 There are obviously enormous obstacles to achieving a homogeneous classification of the working population by social class. What is presented here is far from satisfactory, but constitutes a partial reworking of data calculated by P. Sylos Labini in two successive studies (1976, 1986). The methodological corrections introduced by the author in 1986 implied a marginal revision of the data for 1951 and 1961, which had not been re-calculated by the author. For a further discussion of these issues, see pp. 235–9 and pp. 505–6, notes 94–6.

Source: our elaboration of data from P. Sylos Labini, *Saggio sulle classi sociali* and *Le classi sociali negli anni '80*.

12 *Source*: as 11.

13 This uses data from different and not always homogeneous sources. In particular for the years 1954–73 the age group is that of 18 years and over, while for the later period it is that of 14 years and over. In addition, the data sometimes refers to the frequency of church attendance on a Sunday, and in other cases to church attendance on at least one day during the week.

Source: Doxa surveys for the years 1954–73, Eurisko (another opinion-poll organization) for the years 1976–88.

14–17 The maps show the net migrations from one region to another, in other words the balance of migration (immigrants minus emigrants) from one region to another. Also, in order to keep the maps as uncluttered as possible, only balances above 20,000 persons have been shown.

Source: our elaboration of forthcoming ISTAT data to which we were kindly given access by the Institute.

18 It is important to remember that ISTAT migration figures are based on notified changes of residence from one commune to another. For the possible distortions to which this gives rise, see p. 218, and p. 501, n. 34. To aid the reader in understanding this and the subsequent three tables, it may be of use to take the first line of table 18 as an example. Reading the first line horizontally, from left to right, gives us the following information: that between 1955 and 1961 2,324,500 persons changed their place of residence *within* the north-west; 199,800 moved from the north-west to the north-east and Centre; 101,500 moved from the north-west to the South and islands; giving a total of changes of residence of 2,662,400. In 1961 13,157,000 people were resident in the north-west, 26 per cent of the total Italian population. If the table is read vertically, then the column gives us details of the *influx* of population to the north-west from other parts of Italy, as well as the changes of residence within the north-west itself.

Source: as 14.

19–21 *Source*: as 14.

22 Elementary school in Italy lasts for five years, from the ages of six to eleven; middle school (*scuola media inferiore*) for three years, from eleven to fourteen; and secondary school (*scuola media superiore*) for five years, from fourteen to nineteen.
Source: our elaboration of ISTAT data.

23 *Source*: our elaboration of ISTAT data.

24 Here, as with chart 6, we have taken the two extreme cases, as they were the ones which registered the greatest changes in the period under consideration.
Source: our elaboration of ISTAT data.

25 *Source*: our elaboration of ISTAT data.

26 In addition to showing the percentage breakdown of the Italian data, the graph also shows the percentage of non-voters in United Kingdom general elections since the war.
Source: our elaboration of ISTAT data.

27 The data is taken from a questionnaire which formed part of a survey conducted by various European research institutions from 1970 onwards. The interview sample numbered approximately one thousand in each country, and the interviewees were asked to express their opinion about the functioning of democracy in their own country. Various degrees of satisfaction could be expressed: very (satisfied), fairly, not very, not at all.
Source: our elaboration of Eurobarometer data.

28 The question, which appeared in the survey cited above, asked the interviewee to express his or her preference for one of three principal attitudes towards society: support for existing institutions, the need for reform, the need for revolutionary change.
Source: see 27.

29–30 *Source*: see 27.

31 Although in the last chapter of this book (see above pp. 407–8) details were given of Italy's GDP after 1985, and thus after the revision in the method of its calculation, we have decided here to maintain the homogeneity of this series of statistics, which comes to an end in 1985.
Source: our elaboration of ISTAT data.

32 *Source*: our elaboration of ISTAT data.

33 Although presented in a single graph, the data actually comes from two separate historical series. The first, from 1951 to 1969, draws on data prior to the introduction of the European Community system of Integrated Economic Accounting; the second, from 1970 to 1985, utilizes data compiled after the introduction of the IEA.
Source: our elaboration of ISTAT data.

34 *Source*: our elaboration of Bank of Italy data.

35 *Source*: ISTAT.

36 The graph represents the Italian activity rate (the labour force as a percentage

of the total population) and the employment rate (the employed as a percentage of the total population). Thus the top horizontal band on the graph gives details of the activity and employment rates for men, the middle band for both men and women, and the bottom band for women only. The shaded areas between the two rates represent in each case the incidence of unemployment.

It should be noted that in this and the five tables which follow, it has not been possible to include data for the later years of the 1980s, even though it is available, due to the change in the definition of unemployment introduced by ISTAT from 1986 onwards.

Source: our elaboration of ISTAT data.

37   *Source*: our elaboration of ISTAT data.

38   It should be noted that the substantial decrease in the numbers of self-employed men and women is to be attributed in large measure to the decline of peasant proprietor families.

Source: our elaboration of ISTAT data.

39   *Source*: our elaboration of ISTAT data.

40   The rate of unemployment represents the percentage of people actively seeking work, calculated with respect to the total number of people in the labour force.

Source: our elaboration of ISTAT data.

41   *Source*: ISTAT.

42   *Source*: ISTAT.

Notes

Preface

1 Memorandum of I. M. Willart, 'Anglo-Italian relations', n.d. (Nov.–Dec. 1943); National Archives, Washington (NAW), RG 331, 10000/132/330, nos. 6484–8.

2 E. Banfield, *The Moral Basis of a Backward Society*, Glencoe, Ill., 1958, p. 10.

3 C. Tullio-Altan, *La nostra Italia*, Milano, 1986, p. 83.

4 D. Dolci, *Inchiesta a Palermo*, Torino, 1956, p. 166.

5 ibid.

6 A. Bagnasco, *Tre Italie: la problematica territoriale dello sviluppo italiano*, Bologna, 1977.

Chapter 1

1 S. Hood, *Carlino*, Manchester, 1985 (first published as *Pebbles from My Skull*, London, 1963), pp. 15–16.

2 ibid., p. 38.

3 ibid., pp. 33–4. Franco's real name was Maurilio Franchi.

4 ibid., pp. 52–3.

5 On British escaped prisoners of war in Italy at this time, see R. Absalom, 'Per una storia di sopravvivenze. Contadini italiani e prigionieri britannici evasi', *Italia Contemporanea*, vol. XXXII (1980), no. 140, pp. 105–22. Other first-hand accounts include: G. Lett, *Rossano*, London, 1955; E. Newby, *Love and War in the Apennines*, London, 1971.

6 F. W. Deakin, *The Brutal Friendship. Mussolini, Hitler and the Fall of Italian Fascism*, London, 1962.

7 Traditional accounts of the March stoppages have always afforded pride of place to FIAT Mirafiori. For a convincing demolition of this myth and a re-evaluation of the Turin strikes, see T. Mason, 'Gli scioperi di Torino del marzo 1943', in F. Ferratini Tosi, G. Grassi and M. Legnani, eds., *L'Italia nella seconda guerra mondiale e nella Resistenza*, Milano, 1988, pp. 399–422.

8 N. Gallerano *et al.*, 'Crisi di regime e crisi sociale', in G. Bertolo *et al.*, *Operai e contadini nella crisi italiana del 1943–1944*, Milano, 1974, pp. 42–7 and 50–54. For Vittorio Valletta, managing director of FIAT, see P. Bairati, *Vittorio Valletta*, Turin, 1983, pp. 99–101. For Vittorio Cini, the Venetian financier and industrialist, see M. Reberschak, 'Vittorio Cini', *Dizionario biografico degli italiani*, vol. XXV, Roma, 1981, p. 631.

9   See the remarks of Giorgio Amendola in a discussion with G. C. Pajetta and L. Basso, *Rinascita*, vol. XXII (1965), no. 29, pp. 15–19.

10   For Genoa, see A. Gibelli, *Genova operaia nella Resistenza*, Genova, 1968, p. 45; for Milan, see the unsigned internal Communist report in V. Foa, *Sindacati e lotte operaie (1943–1973)*, Torino, 1975, pp. 36ff.; for Rome, see the police informer's report of 30 July 1943 cited in S. Colarizzi, *La seconda guerra mondiale e la Repubblica*, Torino, 1984, pp. 191–2.

11   A detailed account of the Allied project to save Rome can be found in A. M. Garland and H. McGaw Smyth, *Sicily and the Surrender of Italy*, Washington, DC, 1965, pp. 477–509. For the armistice negotiations, Colarizzi, *La seconda guerra mondiale*, pp. 212–19.

12   The text of Badoglio's announcement is printed in G. Candeloro, *Storia dell'Italia moderna*, vol. X, Milano, 1984, p. 222. Candeloro's treatment of the 'Forty-five Days' (ibid., pp. 162–229) is as balanced and masterly as much else in his outstanding history of Italy.

13   C. R. S. Harris, *Allied Military Administration in Italy 1943–1945*, London, 1957, p. 75. For a dramatic and sympathetic account of the king's journey, A. Degli Espinosa, *Il regno del Sud*, Roma, 1946, pp. 1–7.

14   H. Michel, *The Shadow War*, London, 1972, p. 14. For Andrea Romano in Turin, R. Luraghi, *Il movimento operaio torinese durante la Resistenza*, Torino, 1958, p. 103; but see also C. Dellavalle, 'Torino', in Bertolo *et al.*, *Operai e contadini*, pp. 195–6, for a rather more sober view.

15   L. Picciotto Fargan, 'La persecuzione antiebraica in Italia', in Ferratini Tosi *et al.*, eds., *L'Italia nella seconda guerra mondiale*, pp. 197–213; S. Zuccotti, *The Italians and the Holocaust*, London, 1987. The classic description of the Nazis' raid on the Roman ghetto is G. Debenedetti, *16 ottobre 1943*, Milano, 1959.

16   G. Quazza, *Resistenza e storia d'Italia*, Milano, 1976, pp. 115–16.

17   The programme is reprinted in M. Legnani, *L'Italia dal 1943 al 1948*, Torino, 1973, pp. 24–6. The most thorough and recent work on the Action Party is G. De Luna, *Storia del Partito d'Azione*, Milano, 1982.

18   Legnani, *L'Italia dal 1943 al 1948*, pp. 27–9. See also P. Nenni, *Intervista sul socialismo italiano* (ed. G. Tamburrano), Bari, 1977, pp. 60–62.

19   B. Fenoglio, *Il partigiano Johnny*, Torino, 1968, p. 40.

20   See C. Pavone, 'Tre governi e due occupazioni', *Italia Contemporanea*, vol. XXXVII (1985), no. 160, pp. 57–79.

21   Luraghi, *Il movimento operaio torinese*, pp. 21ff. Luraghi gives the figure of 192,186 workers in the industrial sector, of whom less than 30,000 were white-collar workers.

22   M. Gribaudi, *Mondo operaio e mito operaio*, Torino, 1987, pp. 68ff. Gribaudi writes (p. 71): 'If relations no longer shared, as in the countryside, the same domestic spaces and activities, none the less their persons populated the daily lives of every family, characterizing their histories and identities.'

23 Oral testimony collected for, and reproduced in, *Torino fra le due guerre* (exhibition catalogue), Torino, 1978.

24 B. Guidetti Serra, *Compagne*, Torino, 1977, vol. 1, p. xii.

25 *Torino fra le due guerre*, p. 2.

26 A typical exchange which Gribaudi cites is that of a wardrobe constructed for one family in return for shoes made as a 'favour' for another; *Mondo operaio e mito operaio*, pp. 107ff.

27 ibid., p. 111.

28 C. Saraceno, 'La famiglia operaia sotto il fascismo', *Annali della Fondazione G. G. Feltrinelli*, vol. XX (1979–80), p. 227; for symbolic protests, see L. Passerini, *Fascism in Popular Memory*, Cambridge, 1987, pp. 65–126; and Guidetti Serra, *Compagne*, vol. 1, pp. 235–6, testimony of Antizarina Cavallo.

29 G. Levi *et al.*, 'Cultura operaia e vita quotidiana in Borgo San Paolo', *Torino fra le due guerre*, p. 20. For the new pastimes, Passerini, *Fascism in Popular Memory*, p. 59; for the new myths, M. Gribaudi, *Mondo operaio e mito operaio*, p. xxviii.

30 L. Ganapini, 'Milano', in Bertolo *et al.*, *Operai e contadini*, p. 147, n. 6; see also G. Consonni and G. Tonon, 'Aspetti della questione urbana a Milano dal fascismo alla ricostruzione', *Classe*, vol. VIII (1976), no. 12, pp. 49–53.

31 Gibelli, *Genova operaia nella Resistenza*, pp. 74–5, 95–7.

32 For Turin, Luraghi, *Il movimento operaio torinese*, p. 72; for Milan, Ganapini 'Milano', in Bertolo *et al.*, *Operai e contadini*, p. 145; and especially N. Gallerano, 'Gli italiani in guerra. Apunti per una ricerca', in Ferratini Tosi *et al.*, ed., *L'Italia nella seconda guerra mondiale*, pp. 308–16.

33 C. Cederna, M. Lombardi and M. Somaré, *Milano in guerra*, Milano, 1979, p. 6.

34 Dellavalle, 'Torino', in Bertolo *el al.*, *Operai e contadini*, pp. 210–12.

35 In Turin, at the end of November 1943, the German authorities made important concessions over food and pay; in Milan in December, most of the major factories took strike action from 13 December onwards. Here strike leaders were arrested but at least on one occasion, at the Breda factory, a mass demonstration of workers forced their release; see Dellavalle, 'Torino', in Bertolo *et al.*, *Operai e contadini*, p. 219 and L. Ganapini, *Una città, la guerra*, Milano, 1988, pp. 73–80.

36 Mussolini, in a radio broadcast of 18 September 1943, had proclaimed: 'our postulates are the following: ... to annihilate the parasitic plutocracies and at last to make labour the theme of our economy and the indestructible basis of the state'; Deakin, *The Brutal Friendship*, p. 565; see also pp. 665–77 for the failure of socialization.

37 G. Salvemini, 'Partigiani e fuorusciti', *Il Mondo*, 6 December 1952; quoted in C. Pavone, 'Le idee della Resistenza: antifascisti e fascisti di fronte alla tradizione del Risorgimento', *Passato e presente*, vol. II (1959), no. 7, p. 870.

38 The outstanding article on this theme is C. Pavone, 'La guerra civile', *Annali della Fondazione Luigi Micheletti*, vol. II (1986), pp. 395–415. See also the testimony of Rini Bastia in Guidetti Serra, *Compagne*, vol. II, p. 647.

39 Gibelli, *Genova operaia*, pp. 82–6.

40 R. Battaglia, *Storia della Resistenza italiana*, Torino, 1964 (1st ed., 1953), pp. 185–95; C. Delzell, *Mussolini's Enemies: the Italian Anti-Fascist Resistance*, Princeton, 1961, p. 371; A. Gibelli and M. Ilardi, 'Genova', and Dellavalle, 'Torino', in Bertolo *et al.*, *Operai e contadini*, pp. 124–7, 249–53 (the strike failed almost completely at Genoa); Ganapini, *Una città, la guerra*, pp. 87ff.; for Florence, Foa, *Sindacati e lotte operaie*, pp. 43ff.

41 Ganapini, *Una città, la guerra*, pp. 116–20.

42 Gibelli and Ilardi, 'Genova', in Bertolo *et al.*, *Operai e contadini*, pp. 127–8.

43 Bairati, *Valletta*, pp. 138–9.

44 C. Pazzagli, 'Dal paternalismo alla democrazia', *Annali dell'Istituto Alcide Cervi*, vol. VIII (1986), p. 19. See also his fundamental work, *L'agricoltura toscana nella prima metà dell'800*, Firenze, 1973.

45 See the remarks by Col. Kennedy at the Allied/Italian Agricultural Conference, 30 Nov.–3 Dec. 1944: 'In Tuscany there is the very good system of land tenure and mezzadria. This system has stood the test of many 100 [*sic*] of years and I hope that it may be extended to other parts of Italy' (NAW, RG 331/10000/1131, no. 6433, minutes of the conference). On the landowner's power over the sharecropping family, see F. M. Snowden, 'From sharecropper to proletarian: the background to Fascism in rural Tuscany, 1880–1920', in J. A. Davis, ed., *Gramsci and Italy's Passive Revolution*, London, 1979, p. 138.

46 INEA (Istituto Nazionale di Economia Agraria), *Monografie di famiglie agricole*, vol. V, *Mezzadri e piccoli proprietari coltivatori in Umbria*, Milano–Roma, 1933, pp. 66–97.

47 Snowden, 'From sharecropper to proletarian', p. 154 and p. 169, n. 64.

48 INEA, *Monografie di famiglie agricole*, vol. V, p. 78.

49 M. Barbagli, *Sotto lo stesso tetto*, Bologna, 1984, pp. 436–7.

50 INEA, *Monografie di famiglie agricole*, vol. V, p. 78.

51 S. F. Silverman, 'Agricultural organisation, social structure, and values in Italy: amoral familism reconsidered', *American Anthropologist*, vol. LXX (1968), no. 1, p. 9.

52 F. Mugnaini, 'A veglia; monografia breve su un "abitudine"', *Annali del'Istituto Alcide Cervi*, vol. IX (1987), pp. 119–44. See also Barbagli, *Sotto lo stesso tetto*, pp. 461ff.

53 G. Contini has written a fascinating article on the subject: 'Natalino Carrai: il mondo di un bambino contadino (toscano) alla fine degli anni '30', forthcoming.

54 Sir J. Bowring, 'Report on the statistics of Tuscany, Lucca, the Pontifical and the Lombardo-Venetian states, with a special reference to their commercial relations', *Parliamentary Papers*, vol. XVI (1839), 'Reports from Commissioners', p. 40. For Bowring it was the peasants' isolation which was responsible for this state of affairs: 'Where there is no association there must be much ignorance.'

55 See S. Soldani, 'La grande guerra lontano dal fronte', in G. Mori, ed., *Storia d'Italia . . . La Toscana*, Torino, 1986, pp. 345–452.

56 G. Bertolo and L. Guerrini, 'Le campagne toscane e marchigiane durante il fascismo. Note sulla situazione economica e sociale dei ceti contadini', *Il Movimento di Liberazione in Italia*, vol. XXII (1970), no. 101, pp. 111–60. See also P. Corner, 'Fascist agrarian policy and the Italian economy in the inter-war years', in J. A. Davis, ed., *Gramsci and Italy's Passive Revolution*, pp. 249ff.

57 R. Absalom, 'Terre desiderate, terre sognate: alcuni fattori economici e no del comportamento politico degli ex mezzadri', *Annali dell'Istituto Alcide Cervi*, vol. VIII (1986), p. 186.

58 I. Origo, *War in Val d'Orcia*, London, 1985 (1st ed., 1947), p. 75.

59 Absalom, 'Terre desiderate, terre sognate', pp. 186–7.

60 Hood, *Carlino*, p. 137.

61 L. Guerrini, 'La Toscana', in Bertolo *et al.*, *Operai e contadini*, pp. 364ff.

62 ibid., pp. 378ff.

63 M. Rossi-Doria, 'Struttura e problemi dell'agricoltura meridionale' (1944), in his *Riforma agraria e azione meridionalista*, Bologna, 1948, pp. 1–49; see also his later article, 'Il Mezzogiorno agricolo e il suo avvenire: "l'osso e la polpa"', in Fondazione L. Einaudi, *Nord e Sud nella società e nell'economia di oggi*, Torino, 1968, pp. 285–99.

64 INEA, *Monografie di famiglie agricole*, vol. IV, *Contadini siciliani*, Milano–Roma, 1933, pp. 19–42.

65 ibid., p. 23.

66 ibid., p. 24. The major feast day of Lentini was that of S. Giuseppe. An orphan girl dressed up as the Madonna sat on a throne erected in the main piazza. Around her were gifts which had been sent to the organizing committee and which were to be auctioned off. If the girl smiled during the ceremony it was the portent of a good harvest (ibid., p. 32).

67 M. Rossi-Doria, *Riforma agraria e azione meridionalista*, pp. 5ff. For a fine description of conditions on the Tavoliere in the first decades of the twentieth century, see F. M. Snowden, *Violence and Great Estates in the South of Italy. Apulia, 1900–1922*, Cambridge, 1986.

68 G. Russo, *Baroni e contadini*, Bari, 1979 (1st ed., 1955), p. 47. Russo had taken the well-known American journalist Theodore White with him on part of his journey throughout the South: 'Nor will I forget the memory of that hotel at Potenza, where a half-broken stove filled the bedroom with smoke and where the ingenuous American, on entering the hotel, had asked ' "s'il y a le téléphone dans la chambre?" ' (ibid., p. 18).

69   M. Rossi-Doria, *Riforma agraria e azione meridionalista*, pp. 14–25. See also D. Mack Smith, 'The Latifundia in modern Sicilian history', *Proceedings of the British Academy*, vol. LI (1965), pp. 85–124.

70   A. Rossi-Doria, *Il ministro e i contadini*, Roma, 1983, pp. 75–9.

71   M. Rossi-Doria, *Riforma agraria e azione meridionalista*, pp. 35–6.

72   See S. Gentile, 'Mafia e gabelloti in Sicilia: il PCI dai decreti Gullo al lodo De Gasperi', *Archivio Storico per la Sicilia Orientale*, vol. LXIX (1973), no. 3, p. 505, n. 30.

73   P. Arlacchi, *Mafia, Peasants and Great Estates*, Cambridge, 1983, pp. 132ff. Even so, the *latifondisti* were facing increasingly severe problems by 1943: see R. Villari, 'La crisi del blocco agrario', in Istituto Gramsci, *Togliatti e il Mezzogiorno*, vol. 1, Roma, 1977, pp. 3–35.

74   P. Cinanni, *Lotte per la terra nel Mezzogiorno, 1943–53*, Venezia, 1979, p. 114. In an inland area less typical of the traditional *latifondo*, the province of Taranto in southern Puglia, an enterprising New Zealand officer calculated the annual income of the estate on which he was billeted in the summer of 1944 (*New Statesman*, 8 July 1944). The 940-acre estate, given over to olive production and carrying 12,000 trees, was owned by an absentee Spanish nobleman, the Marquis de Arruaga. Out of an estimated gross annual income of £24,000, the nine permanent labourers on the estate were paid £650 in all, and the 150 girls employed on a casual basis to pick the olives received another £1,500. The administrator of the Marquis's seven estates in Puglia was paid £1,000 annually, and the *fattore*, the local farm manager, another £300, which 'permits him the luxury of a FIAT Balilla, for which he used to cadge petrol from us'. With the fertilizer and the replacement of farm equipment costing another £2,000, 'I should say that the Marquis would be unlucky if he did not clear £15,000 from this one farm. I should put the correct figure at nearer £20,000.'

75   C. Levi, *Christ Stopped at Eboli*, London, 1948, p. 75.

76   A. Blok, *The Mafia of a Sicilian Village*, New York, 1975 (1st ed., 1974), p. 48.

77   INSOR (Istituto Nazionale di Sociologia Rurale), *La riforma fondiaria: trent'anni dopo*, Milano, 1979, vol. 1, pp. 428–30, for a long extract from the speech.

78   E. De Martino, *Sud e magia*, Milano, 1959, and *La terra del rimorso*, Milano, 1961; A. Rossi, *Le feste dei poveri*, Bari, 1969. See also C. Levi, *Christ Stopped at Eboli*, p. 76: 'The deities of the State and the city can find no worshippers here on the land, where the wolf and the ancient black boar reign supreme, where there is no wall between the world of men and the world of animals and spirits, between the leaves of the trees above and the roots below.'

79   See the oustanding article by G. Gribaudi, 'Mito dell'eguaglianza e individualismo: un comune del Mezzogiorno', in G. Chianese *et al.*, *Italia 1945–1950*, Milano, 1985, p. 467. See also, although for a later period, J. Davis, *Land and Family in Pisticci*, London, 1973, pp. 67–9.

80   By 1919 the peasant league at Cerignola had 18,000 members, with virtually

every adult labourer in its ranks. The prefect reported that 'the organization of the working-class is perfect'; Snowden, *Violence and Great Estates*, p. 167.

81 P. Bevilacqua, 'Quadri mentali, cultura e rapporti simbolici nella società rurale del Mezzogiorno', *Italia Contemporanea*, vol. XXXVI (1984), no. 154, p. 69.

82 See the suggestive article by A. Pagden, 'The destruction of trust and its economic consequences in the case of eighteenth-century Naples', in D. Gambetta, ed., *Trust: Making and Breaking Cooperative Relations*, Oxford, 1988, pp. 127–41.

83 Quoted in Bevilacqua, 'Quadri mentali', p. 62; see also Tullio-Altan, *La nostra Italia*, pp. 27–8 for a long list of similar proverbs.

84 D. Gambetta, 'Mafia: the price of distrust', in Gambetta, ed., *Trust*, pp. 158–75.

85 See the section on the Piana di Gioia Tauro in Arlacchi, *Mafia, Peasants and Great Estates*, pp. 67–121.

86 L. Franchetti, 'Condizioni politiche e amministrative della Sicilia', in L. Franchetti and S. Sonnino, *Inchiesta in Sicilia*, vol. 1, Firenze, 1974 (1st ed., 1876), p. 129.

87 P. Bevilacqua, *Le campagne del Mezzogiorno tra fascismo e dopoguerra. Il caso della Calabria*, Torino, 1980, p. 6, n. 7.

88 For the restriction of emigration abroad in this period, see A. Treves, *Le migrazioni interne nell'Italia fascista*, Torino, 1976, pp. 110ff. Emigration abroad dropped from an annual average of 303,442 between 1921 and 1925 to 48,901 between 1936 and 1940. While it is clear from Treves's work that Fascist laws limiting internal migration were massively ignored, it also seems true that the major interregional migrations of the time took place in the North, not the South, of the country (see her Appendix, map 3).

89 C. Duggan, *La mafia durante il fascismo*, Soveria Mannelli, 1986. In the 1930s Fascist party reports from Sicily spoke invariably of the destitution of the population: 'Here in Sicily there is no industry nor work, and very many families for days at a time have to go to bed on empty stomachs' (ibid., p. 250).

90 N. Gallerano, 'La disgregazione delle basi di massa del Fascismo nel Mezzogiorno e il ruolo delle masse contadine', in G. Bertolo *et al.*, *Operai e contadini*, pp. 458ff.; Bevilacqua, *Le campagne del Mezzogiorno*, pp. 306–52; M. Talamo and C. De Marco, *Lotte agrarie nel Mezzogiorno 1943–44*, Milano, 1976, pp. 38–9.

91 Harris, *Allied Military Administration*, pp. 87ff.

92 On 3 August 1943 in the House of Commons Aneurin Bevan described AMGOT (Allied Military Government) as 'an ugly word to cover an uglier deed'; *Parliamentary Debates*, House of Commons, 5th Series, vol. 391, cols. 2201–66 for the debate on the political situation in Italy. For the widespread expectations that the arrival of the Allies would alleviate the extreme hardships of the population, see the autobiography of a working-class woman from southern Sicily: M. Occhipinti, *Una donna di Ragusa*, Milano, 1976, pp. 66–9. See also the article 'Sicily Today', *New Statesman*, 5 Feb. 1944, written by 'a

British soldier who was there from the landing on 10 July 1943 until his recent return to this country': 'The invasion of Sicily was not only a military rehearsal for the invasion of the rest of Europe, but obviously a political one as well. Our political tasks in Sicily were clear. We had to win the sympathy and cooperation of the Sicilians, and to prove to them, and to the world, that the Atlantic Charter and similar democratic promises are a reality. We could achieve these aims by ameliorating the life of the war-stricken peasantry, rehabilitating bombed towns and battle areas, reorganizing and developing the social services, importing and distributing food and vital clothing, and destroying the influence of Fascism . . . The cruellest indictment of our failure to foresee and prepare for the food shortage is the startling appearance of the casual prostitution of women whose husbands are in the Italian army. "Liberated" women have offered their bodies for a tin of bully beef.'

93   For the killings at Montesano, Gallerano, 'La disgregazione delle basi di massa', in Bertolo *et al.*, *Operai e contadini*, p. 486. For land occupations E. Ciconte, *All'assalto delle terre del latifondo*, Milano, 1981, pp. 11–18, and Cinanni, *Lotte per la terra nel Mezzogiorno*, pp. 17ff. In some of the villages of Basilicata and Calabria, once the Germans had left and the Allies had marched through, the peasants declared their own republics. Thus in September 1943 at Calitri, the republic of Battocchio, called after its leader, was proclaimed. At a meeting of 29 September it was decided 'to resolve the ancient injustices of land tenure by the generalized expropriation of the *latifondo*'. A few days later the Carabinieri, aided by American troops, suppressed the republic; Talamo and De Marco, *Lotte agrarie nel Mezzogiorno*, pp. 43–7.

94   M. A. Macciocchi, *Letters from inside the Italian Communist Party to Louis Althusser*, London, 1973, p. 91.

95   P. A. Allum, *Politics and Society in Post-war Naples*, Cambridge, 1973, p. 48.

96   NAW, RG 331, 10000/132/330, no. 6500, letter from Colonel Fiske to the Regional Commissioner, Southern Region, 28 Sept. 1944. For conditions in Naples see also P. De Marco, 'Il difficile esordio del governo militare e la politica sindacale degli Alleati a Napoli, 1943–44', *Italia Contemporanea*, vol. XXXI (1979), no. 136, pp. 39–66; N. Lewis, *Naples '44*, London, 1978; A. Moorehead, *Eclipse*, London, 1945, pp. 62–9.

97   *Sunday Chronicle*, 12 Dec. 1948, quoted in A. Sampson, *Macmillan, a Study in Ambiguity*, London, 1967, pp. 69–70.

Chapter 2

1   PRO, Private Secretary's Papers, FO 800/414, quoted in D. W. Ellwood, *Italy 1943–1945*, Leicester, 1985, p. 117. Ellwood's is the best and most detailed account of Allied attitudes in Italy. The minutes of the meeting report Churchill as follows: 'The Italians were in a miserable condition. He [Churchill] did not think much of them as a people, but they had a good many votes in New York State. This was off the record [*sic*].'

2   W. S. Churchill, *The Second World War*, vol. V, *Closing the Ring*, London, 1952, p. 48.

3   C. Pavone, 'La continuità dello Stato. Istituzioni e uomini', in *Italia 1945–48. Le origini della Repubblica*, Torino, 1974, p. 192.

4   *Parliamentary Debates*, 5th series, vol. 397, 22 Feb. 1944.

5   Ellwood, *Italy 1943–1945*, p. 104; for Alexander's remark, ibid., p. 208.

6   ibid., p. 105. However, Macmillan was no freer than the others from habitual British condescension towards the Italians. See for example his comments on Pietro Longhi, non-party chairman of the CLNAI (H. Macmillan, *War Diaries*, London, 1984, p. 737 (16 April 1945)): 'He is a banker; fat, genial, good-tempered, educated at London University, and seems a sensible and patriotic fellow, without the usual swank, panache, blather and overweening vanity which seems the chief Italian characteristic. In fact, he struck me favourably. He was almost (but of course not quite) like an Englishman.'

7   Quoted in the earlier, Italian, edition of Ellwood's book, *L'alleato nemico*, Milano, 1977, p. 317. On American attitudes see also E. Collotti, 'Collocazione internazionale dell'Italia dall'armistizio alle premesse dell'alleanza atlantica (1943–1947)', in G. Quazza et al., *L'Italia dalla Liberazione alla Repubblica*, Milano, 1977, p. 37. He writes: 'It was not only the American democratic tradition which enabled them to look at institutional problems in a less prejudiced way . . .; there was undoubtedly in Roosevelt a greater anti-Fascist sensibility.' Indeed, elements of progressive Democrat and New Deal thinking were often present in the opinions and actions of the Americans in Italy at this time.

8   H. Macmillan, *The Blast of War, 1939–1945*, London, 1967, p. 670.

9   P. Togliatti, 'Le istruzioni alle organizzazioni di partito nelle regioni occupate', *Opere scelte*, Roma, 1974, pp. 331–2. The debate on the formation of Communist strategy has been very extensive. For an exegesis, see D. Sassoon, *Togliatti e la via italiana al socialismo*, Torino, 1980, pp. 1–62. For a critical view, L. Cortesi, 'Palmiro Togliatti, la "svolta di Salerno" e l'eredità gramsciana', *Belfagor*, vol. XXX (1975), pp. 1–44.

10 P. Togliatti, 'Per la libertà d'Italia, per la creazione di un vero regime democratico', *Opere*, vol. V, Roma, 1984, p. 76. See also F. Sbarberi, *I comunisti italiani e lo stato, 1929–1956*, Milano, 1980, pp. 240–53; G. Amyot, *The Italian Communist Party*, London, 1981, pp. 37, 45–6; E. Hobsbawm, 'Gli intellettuali e l'antifascismo', in *Storia del marxismo*, vol. III, pt 2, Torino, 1981, p. 487, and the explanation which the *Quaderno dell'Attivista*, the journal for Communist cadres, offered in August 1947: 'Progressive democracy is a new road to socialism. It is a road which unites all the healthy elements of the population behind an advanced democratic regime which is open to every possible progressive development. Precisely for this reason, it is a strategy for socialism which is less painful, less costly and less bloody than that which in Russia, because of historical circumstances, had to be the way of the dictatorship of the proletariat' (M. Flores, ed., *Il Quaderno dell'Attivista*, Milano, 1976, p. 56).

11 P. Togliatti, 'Per la libertà d'Italia', *Opere*, vol. V, p. 73.

12 A. Gramsci, *Selections from the Prison Notebooks*, ed. Q. Hoare and D. Nowell-
    Smith, London, 1971, p. 238.

13 S. J. Gundle, 'Gramsci, Togliatti, and the "Italian road to Socialism"', unpublished
    research paper, 1983. This is, of course, a most controversial area. Most Italian
    Communist Party commentaries have assumed a complete convergence be-
    tween Gramsci's and Togliatti's thought. For the other extreme, which separates
    Gramsci the revolutionary from Togliatti the reformist, see C. Boggs, 'Gramsci
    and Eurocommunism', *Radical America*, vol. XIV (1980), no. 3, pp. 7–23.

14 P. Togliatti, *I compiti del partito nella situazione attuale*, Roma, 1945, p. 37, quoted
    in Istituto di Studi e Ricerche Carlo Cattaneo, *L'organizzazione politica del PCI e
    della DC*, Bologna, 1968, pp. 32–3.

15 For a heroic but ultimately unsuccessful attempt to defend Gramsci's view of
    the party as elaborated in the Prison Notebooks, see J. Femia, *The Political
    Theory of Antonio Gramsci*, Oxford, 1981, pp. 130–89.

16 Benedetto Croce was swift to realize the tactical advantage which Togliatti's
    proposals had given the PCI; see his diary of the time in B. Croce, *Quando
    l'Italia era tagliata in due*, Bari, 1948, p. 99. For a poorly substantiated critique of
    the PCI from the left, see F. Claudin, *The Communist Movement from
    Comintern to Cominform*, London, 1975, pp. 344–69, section entitled 'The
    Revolution Frustrated (Italy)'.

17 Quazza, *Resistenza e storia d'Italia*, p. 337. However wide of the mark their other
    criticisms, the Yugoslav Communists made this point very clearly in their
    criticism of Togliatti in 1947. The PCI, according to them, had not known
    how to conquer key positions at the very moment when the masses were at
    their greatest strength; ibid., p. 334, and the accounts of the first meeting of
    Cominform in E. Reale, *La nascita del Cominform*, Milano, 1958, pp. 17, 119–20,
    and V. Dedijer, *Tito Speaks*, London, 1953, p. 305.

18 See above all Pavone, 'La continuità dello Stato', *passim*.

19 For the intellectual environment at the Catholic university in Milan at this time,
    see R. Moro, *La formazione della classe dirigente cattolica (1929–37)*, Bologna,
    1979. For the founding of the DC and its ideology, G. Baget-Bozzo, *Il partito
    cristiano al potere. La DC di De Gasperi e di Dossetti, 1945–1954*, vol. 1, Firenze,
    1974, pp. 9–69.

20 'La parola dei democratici cristiani' (Jan. 1944), in Legnani, ed., *L'Italia dal 1943
    al 1948*, p. 37. See also De Gasperi's 'Idee ricostruttive della Democrazia
    Cristiana' (July 1943), in P. G. Zunino, ed., *Scritti politici di Alcide De Gasperi*,
    Milano, 1979, pp. 256–63.

21 E. Forcella, *Celebrazione di un trentennio*, Milano, 1974, p. 189, article of 1–15
    March 1934, and p. 196 (article of 16–31 Jan. 1937).

22 G. Galli, *Storia della Democrazia Cristiana*, Bari, 1978, p. 28.

23 A Psychological Warfare Branch report (no. 29 of 5 August 1944) told of how
    certain Calabrian clergy, previously ardent Fascists, 'are now active propagan-

dists of the official Church party, the DC, through which they hope to maintain their influence on public life, control of the schools and the formation of a large mass that will vote in the future elections on their bidding' (PRO, FO 371/43946/R 13191). For the development of Catholic Action see G. F. Poggi, *Catholic Action in Italy*, Stanford, 1967, pp. 14–29.

24 G. Pasini, *Le ACLI delle origini, 1944–48*, Roma, 1974; G. Ciranna, 'Un gruppo di pressione: la Confederazione Nazionale Coltivatori Diretti', *Nord e Sud*, vol. V (1958), no. 38, pp. 9–39. For an extended discussion of the two organizations, see above, pp. 171–3.

25 M. Reberschak, 'La proprietà fondiaria nel Veneto tra Fascismo e Resistenza', in *Società rurale e Resistenza nelle Venezie*, Milano, 1978, pp. 135–58.

26 G. Pintor, *Il sangue d'Europa (1939–43)*, ed. V. Gerratana, Torino, 1950, p. 187.

27 Ellwood, *Italy 1943–1945*, p. 96. Churchill did not forgive General N. Mason-Macfarlane, head of the Allied Control Commission in Italy, for having allowed this change of government, and he was replaced by the American Captain (later Rear-Admiral) Ellery Stone.

28 The Council of Ministers, in its meeting of 1 September 1944, promised that it would undertake an immediate reform of the bureaucracy, so as 'to establish the number of civil servants in proportion to real needs, and to introduce into the administration, along with the necessary guarantees, a greater rapidity and swiftness of execution' (ACS, 'Verbali del consiglio dei ministri', b.3, meeting of 1 Sept. 1944). Little was done. The problem was both one of personnel and of institutional structure. For example, the Consorzi Agrari were semi-autonomous agencies which under the Fascist regime had the tasks of collecting agricultural commodities and distributing agricultural supplies, such as fertilizer, etc. As such they wielded enormous economic power in the countryside. They were not abolished in the period 1943–5, and their personnel was little changed; see NAW, OSS, R and A, report no. 2540, pp. 14ff.

29 Luigi Longo, one of the foremost leaders of the PCI in the North, estimated that whereas in early 1945 the PCI had 4,000–5,000 cadres in the North, the PSIUP had only one thousand, who did not form a homogeneous group at all; see Quazza, *Resistenza e storia d'Italia*, p. 320.

30 See the anonymous article 'Rivoluzione, ordine e brigantaggio', in *L'Italia Libera*, Piedmontese edition, vol. II, no. 1 (n.d., but of early 1944). The article continued: 'We are far from making democracy synonymous with a bourgeois parliamentary system to be received as a gracious gift from the Allies. Nor do we identify democracy with a preconceived scheme which attributes to a fraction of the masses or to a party the right to initiate and to decide from on high on behalf of the rest of the population.'

31 In Arezzo, for example, the Psychological Warfare Branch reported: 'The Communist Party seems to have become the strongest, and to have remained the strongest party in Arezzo; the reason given is that this party always has been the best organized ... The support of the majority of the people who

style themselves Communists seems to derive from the success of the Russians against the Germans. People say that Communism must have something in it if it can produce such results' (report no. 29, 5 Aug. 1944, PRO, FO 371/43946/R 13191).

32 It is worth noting that Longo and Secchia in the North gave a more radical interpretation to 'progressive democracy' than did the other leaders of the party, but without ever imperilling the PCI's unity of action. The northern leaders in fact contributed greatly to the growth of the party. They showed great sensibility to the real needs of the working class and considerable ability in reflecting these in their propaganda. Massimo Salvadori, a Liberal, has left this description of Longo and Emilio Sereni, another of the PCI's leaders in the North in the early summer of 1945: 'Both of them, but especially Longo, personified the idea I had had for years of Communist leaders: admirable in their spirit of self-sacrifice and their devotion to their ideals; ready for any personal sacrifice if it served the Party; inflexible in all their dealings with non-Communists. Fascists used the expression "souls of steel" referring to themselves, but it was the Communists who had them' (M. Salvadori, *The Labour and the Wounds*, London, 1958, p. 217).

33 Quazza, *Resistenza e storia d'Italia*, pp. 256ff.; see also D. Travis, 'Communism in Modena: the provincial origins of the Partito Comunista Italiano (1943–1945)', *Historical Journal*, vol. XXIX (1986), pp. 886ff.

34 For the spirit of solidarity in Florence at this time, see P. Calamandrei, *Uomini e città della Resistenza*, Bari, 1977 (1st ed., 1955), pp. 139–201; G. Francovich, *La Resistenza a Firenze*, Firenze, 1961. On the AMG/CTLN clash, R. Absalom, 'Il ruolo politico ed economico degli Alleati a Firenze (1944–1945)', in E. Rotelli, ed., *La ricostruzione in Toscana dal CLN ai partiti*, Bologna, 1980, esp. pp. 254ff.; see also Ellwood, *Italy, 1943–1945*, pp. 152–7.

35 L. Arbizzani, 'Notizie sui contadini della pianura bolognese durante la Resistenza', *Il Movimento di Liberazione in Italia*, vol. XVI (1964), no. 75, pp. 30–67.

36 N. S. Onofri, *Marzabotto non dimentica Walter Reder*, Bologna, 1985.

37 For a good summary of this debate, A. Gambino, *Storia del dopoguerra dalla Liberazione al potere DC*, Bari, 1975, pp. 11–14, but above all E. Aga-Rossi, 'La politica angloamericana verso la Resistenza italiana', in Ferratini Tosi *et al.*, eds., *Italia nella seconda guerra mondiale*, pp. 150–54.

38 Fenoglio, *Il partigiano Johnny*, pp. 268–9.

39 F. Catalano, 'La missione del CLNAI al Sud', *Il Movimento di Liberazione in Italia*, vol. VIII (1955), no. 36, pp. 3–43 (p. 24 for Parri on Maitland Wilson). Macmillan had a rather different view of the general: 'Poor Jumbo – he agrees to everything with anybody. My job is really acting as a long-stop, otherwise these generals let a terrible lot of balls go by to the boundary' (*War Diaries*, p. 575, entry for 6 Nov. 1944). The full English text of the agreement is published in H. L. Coles and A. K. Weinberg, *Civil Affairs: Soldiers Become Governors*, Washington, DC, 1964, pp. 541–2.

40 For Pertini's remark, Catalano, 'La missione del CLNAI al Sud', p. 40. The full discussion in the CLNAI is to be found in the minutes of the meeting of 12 Jan. 1945, in G. Grassi, ed., 'Verso il governo del popolo'. Atti e documenti del CLNAI, 1943–1946, Milano, 1977, pp. 222–7. However, Candeloro is of the opinion that the agreement was probably the most that the CLNAI could have obtained at that moment, 'granted the general and particular difficulties of the situation in Italy' (Candeloro, Storia dell'Italia moderna, vol. X, p. 316).

41 Coles and Weinberg, Civil Affairs, p. 545.

42 Candeloro, Storia dell'Italia moderna, vol. X, p. 317. Bonomi had promised Stone, the head of the Allied Control Commission, that he would ensure that the CLNAI 'remains in a subordinate position and does not have the least character of a de facto government' (Coles and Weinberg, Civil Affairs, pp. 542–3, letter of 23 Dec. 1944).

43 For the exchange of letters between the parties, see the texts published in P. Secchia, Il Partito comunista e la guerra di Liberazione, 1943–1945, Annali dell'Istituto G. G. Feltrinelli, vol. XIII (1971), pp. 768–8.

44 ibid., p. 785, letter of 12 Jan. 1945; p. 788 for the Socialist reply of 20 Jan. 1945.

45 For Lucio Tasca, see U. Santino, 'Fine dell'unità antifascista e ricomposizione del blocco dominante', in Centro Siciliano di Documentazione, Ricomposizione del blocco dominante, lotte contadine e politica delle sinistre in Sicilia (1943–1947), Palermo, 1977, pp. 13–14. In 1941 Tasca had written an Elogio del latifondo, in which he praised the millenary history of the latifondo and spoke of the 'Sicilians' great love of cereal farming'. See also G. Giarrizzo, 'La Sicilia politica 1943–1945. La genesi dello statuto regionale', Archivio Storico per la Sicilia Orientale, vol. LXVI (1970), nos. 1–2, pp. 9–136. For the Separatists and their leader Andrea Finocchiaro Aprile, G. C. Marino, Storia del separatismo siciliano, Roma, 1979.

46 Santino, 'Fine dell'unità antifascista', pp. 24–8.

47 See Occhipinti, Una donna di Ragusa, and the preface to it by E. Forcella, 'Un altro dopoguerra', pp. 5–34. For a detailed account of the economic situation in Sicily at this time, C. Spingola, 'Crisi alimentare e problemi di ordine pubblico in Sicilia nel secondo dopoguerra', in N. Gallerano, ed., L'altro dopoguerra. Roma e il Sud 1943–1945, Milano, 1985, pp. 341–54.

48 A. Rossi-Doria, Il ministro e i contadini, passim.; P. Ginsborg, 'The Communist party and the agrarian question in southern Italy, 1943–48', History Workshop Journal, no. 17 (1984), pp. 81–101.

49 The text of the Pact of Rome is published in Foa, Sindacati e lotte operaie, pp. 50–52; see also S. Turone, Storia del sindacato in Italia, Bari, 1973, pp. 102–4. The Socialist Bruno Buozzi, one of the principal architects of trade union unity, had been shot by the Germans as they retreated from Rome. By the time of the first congress of the CGIL, in January 1945, the trade union already had more than one million members in southern and central Italy. At this congress the

Christian Democrat leader Achille Grandi made a long speech in favour of the liquidation of the *latifondo*.

50 This strategy had close similarities with that pursued by the peasant movement after the First World War; see, for example, P. Corner, *Fascism in Ferrara, 1919–25*, Oxford, 1975, pp. 85ff. It is necessary to distinguish between the two forms of *imponibile* and *collocamento*: the one *'di classe'* (class-controlled), which Di Vittorio was trying to institute; the other *'di stato'* (state-controlled), which presented no great threat to the landowners. Indeed, the *imponibile di stato* had been instituted by the Fascist regime.

51 'Relazione della segretaria federale al II° congresso provinciale del PCI di Cosenza, Ott. 1945', Archivio PCI, Calabria 1943–45, 1944 Cosenza, 063/416–449; quoted in A. Rossi-Doria, *Il ministro e i contadini*, p. 47.

52 Cinanni, *Lotte per la terra nel Mezzogiorno*, p. 52.

53 C. Levi, Preface to M. Pantaleone, *The Mafia and Politics*, London, 1966, p. 13 (my translation is slightly different from the one published there).

54 P. Spriano, *Storia del Partito Comunista Italiano*, vol. V, Torino, 1975, p. 494. Gullo's willingness to acquiesce to Togliatti on major strategic decisions was never in question.

55 See pp. 106–8.

56 C. Cederna *et al.*, *Milano in guerra*, p. 18.

57 Gibelli, *Genova operaia*, pp. 153–7.

58 Luraghi, *Il movimento operaio torinese*, pp. 223ff.

59 Gibelli, *Genova operaia*, pp. 248–9.

60 See esp. ibid., pp. 167–74, but also L. Ganapini, *Una città, la guerra*, p. 184.

61 See Parri's report in P. Secchia and F. Frassati, *La Resistenza e gli Alleati*, Milano, 1962, p. 353.

62 Spriano, *Storia del PCI*, vol. V, p. 534.

63 *Atti della Commissione d'inchiesta sul salvataggio del porto di Genova*, ed. Istituto Storico della Resistenza in Liguria, Genova, 1951.

64 G. Vaccarino, C. Gobetti and R. Gobbi, *L'insurrezione di Torino*, Parma, 1968. For what it was like to be inside FIAT Mirafiori during the insurrection, see the testimony of Anna Fenoglio in Guidetti Serra, *Compagne*, vol. 1, pp. 144–5.

65 This figure is based on the estimate given by G. Bocca, *La Repubblica di Mussolini*, Bari, 1977, p. 339.

66 Ellwood, *L'alleato nemico*, p. 375 (quote not included in English version).

67 On 8 March 1945 Macmillan warned the Allied authorities that 'the possibility cannot be overlooked that the Committees of Liberation or the component political parties will not abide by this agreement [that of 26 Dec. 1944 between the Rome government and the CLNAI] if circumstances seem favourable for a political upheaval which would either bring the Committees out as the

Government of Italy or would wrest from the Government in Rome a measure of autonomy which might be in effect complete independence from Rome . . .'; NAW, RG 331/10000/473 (11). After Liberation Macmillan noted in his Diary: 'I had a talk with Bonomi. He improves on acquaintance. He has considerable political flair. Whether he has the "guts" to go through a difficult and semi-revolutionary period, I do not know' (*War Diaries*, p. 747, entry for 30 April 1945).

68 See the article by Ernesto Rossi, 'Il vento del Nord', in *L'Italia Libera*, Lombard edition, vol. III, no. 8, 27 April 1945.

69 Quoted in Spriano, *Storia del PCI*, vol. V, p. 523.

70 R. Lombardi, 'Problemi di potere in Milano liberata', in *La Resistenza in Lombardia*, Milano, 1965, p. 262.

71 Harris, *Allied Military Administration*, p. 278.

72 ibid., p. 358.

73 Ellwood, *Italy 1943–1945*, p. 279, n. 29.

74 Harris, *Allied Military Administration*, p. 363; Ellwood, *Italy 1943–1945*, p. 228.

75 Quoted in R. Battaglia, *Risorgimento e Resistenza*, Torino, 1964, p. 332. M. Clark, *Modern Italy, 1871–1982*, London, 1984, p. 315, has rightly warned against exaggerating the military achievements of the Resistance.

76 Newby, *Love and War in the Apennines*, p. 220.

77 Spriano, *Storia del PCI*, vol. V, p. 541.

Chapter 3

1 The insurrection in the northern cities had done much in this respect, but the major reason was the successful negotiations conducted between Germans, clergy, employers and the forces of the Resistance; see M. Fini, 'Oligarchia elettrica e Resistenza di fronte al problema della difesa degli impianti', in G. Bonvini and A. Scalpelli, eds., *Milano fra guerra e dopoguerra*, Bari, 1979, pp. 231ff.

2 C. Daneo, *La politica economica della ricostruzione, 1945–49*, Torino, 1975, pp. 328–30. There is no proper study of the important question of the relationship between industrial and financial capital in Italy in these years. One or two relevant points are to be found in R. Balducci, 'Capitale finanziario e struttura industriale', in F. Vicarelli, ed., *Capitale industriale e capitale finanziario: il caso italiano*, Bologna, 1979.

3 Ministero per la Costituente, *Rapporto della Commissione economica*, pt II, *Industria*, vol. II, Appendice alla Relazione (Interrogatori), Roma, 1946, p. 90. For the attitude of the industrial employers towards the working class, see also Mariuccia Salvati, *Stato e industria nella ricostruzione*, Milano, 1982, p. 444.

4 Guido Carli, the long-serving governor of the Bank of Italy, told Eugenio Scalfari in 1977: 'The Italian entrepreneurs have never considered the state as a social organization for which they were responsible, even together with the other groups in society. This was probably a defect that goes back to our

origins. It is of the utmost gravity, and is responsible for more than one of the evils and structural weaknesses from which we suffer today' (G. Carli, *Intervista sul capitalismo italiano*, ed. E. Scalfari, Bari, 1977, p. 71).

5   Ministero per la Costituente, *Rapporto della Commissione economica*, pt II, vol. II, pp.107 and 110.

6   Three thousand textile firms employed 14 per cent of Italy's industrial workforce in 1938. At the end of the war the major Italian textile mills had suffered little damage, whereas competitors in Germany and Japan had been wiped out. William Clayton, the US Assistant Secretary of State, who was also the chief stockholder in the world's largest cotton export firm (Anderson, Clayton and Co.), took a special interest in the Italian textile industry. In May 1945 he wrote: 'I do not need to stress the great importance of getting these mills going'; the problem was shortage of raw cotton, 'of which we have plenty'; Clayton to William Phillips, 26 May 1945, quoted in J. L. Harper, *America and the Reconstruction of Italy, 1945–1948*, Cambridge, 1986, p. 45.

7   See S. Setta, *Croce, il liberalismo e l'Italia postfascista*, Roma, 1979.

8   G. Gonella, 'La D.C. per la nuova Costituzione', speech at the first congress of the DC, 24–7 April 1945, *I Congressi nazionali della Democrazia Cristiana*, Roma, 1959, p. 52. Gonella went on to say that the middle stratum was 'courted by many, helped by none . . . it is this very middle stratum of honest savers systematically robbed by the state, of upright men who with dignity wear their worn-out suits, of fathers who go without meals to keep their children at school, it is exactly this *ceto medio* whom today we need to save from a pressing and professed poverty' (ibid., p. 53).

9   NAW, RG 331, 10000/132/318, no. 6000, letter from Colonel C. H. French, 8 Feb. 1945.

10 From the Milan programme of the DC, July 1943, in A. Damiliano, ed., *Atti e documenti della Democrazia Cristiana 1943–67*, vol. I, Roma, 1968, p. 10. See also the appeal to the *ceti medi* at the Rome 'assembly' of the DC (July–Aug. 1945), in Baget-Bozzo, *Il partito cristiano al potere*, vol. I, p. 82. De Gasperi told the Roman cadres of his party at this time: 'We must not be numbered amongst the arrogant or the swindlers. There is a single law for us, that of morality, which we must put into practice . . .; in your neighbourhoods you must behave irreproachably both in your private and your public life, so that it can be said: that man is a gentleman [*galantuomo*], and he is a gentleman because he is a Christian'; quoted in G. Miccoli, 'Chiesa, partito cattolico e società civile', in V. Castronovo, ed., *L'Italia contemporanea 1945–1975*, Torino, 1976, pp. 207–8. For De Gasperi's general political strategy, see P. Scoppola, *La proposta politica di De Gasperi*, Bologna, 1977.

11 See, for example, the working-class children who were looked after on the Origo estate in the Val d'Orcia; Origo, *War in Val d'Orcia, passim*.

12 A. Oddone, 'Ricostruzione morale', *La Civiltà Cattolica*, vol. XCVII (1946), vol. 1, 5 Jan., p. 15.

13 Gonella, 'La D.C. per la nuova Costituzione', p. 43.

14 G. Chianese, *Storia sociale della donna in Italia (1800–1980)*, Napoli, 1980, p. 102.

15 Oddone, 'Ricostruzione morale', p. 17.

16 Dossetti was born in 1913 and educated at the Università Cattolica in Milan. He took part in the Resistance, was a member of the CLN for the province of Reggio Emilia, and was the guiding force behind the influential journal *Cronache sociali*, which began publication in May 1947 and ceased in October 1951 (see Baget-Bozzo, *Il partito cristiano al potere*, vol. 1, pp. 149–51). For Dossetti's anti-capitalism, see his circular of 27 March 1945 to the parish priests of the mountain villages of the province of Reggio Emilia: 'Christian Democracy does not want to, and cannot be a conservative movement. It wishes to be a movement permeated by the conviction that in choosing between the ideology and experience of liberal capitalism on the one hand, and the experience, if not the ideology, of the mass anti-capitalist movements on the other, it is the first, not the second, which is more radically anti-Christian' (cited in P. Pombeni, *Il gruppo dossettiano e la fondazione della democrazia italiana (1943–1948)*, Bologna, 1979, p. 187). A useful summary of the principal ideas of Dossetti's group is to be found in G. Galli and P. Facchi, *La sinistra democristiana*, Milano, 1962, pp. 295–353.

17 De Gasperi's words were noted by E. Sereni, *Il Mezzogiorno all'opposizione*, Torino, 1948, pp. 20–21.

18 W. Reitzel, M. Kaplan and C. Coblenz, *United States Foreign Policy 1945–1955*, Washington, DC, 1956, p. 115.

19 C. Keyder, 'The American recovery of southern Europe: aid and hegemony', in G. Arrighi, ed., *Semiperipheral Development*, London, 1985, pp. 139–41. Keyder dubs American economic strategy of the time as 'international Keynesianism', because (p. 140) it 'raised the demand-creating functions of the Keynesian national state to the international level ... At the same time, its policies serve to legitimate the authority of the hegemonic power.' See also J. and G. Kolko, *The Limits of Power*, New York, 1972, pp. 375ff.

20 Quoted in G. Warner, 'Italy and the Powers, 1943–1949', in S. J. Woolf, ed., *The Rebirth of Italy, 1943–1950*, London, 1972, p. 47.

21 Harper, *America and the Reconstruction of Italy*, pp. 74–5, 90ff., and 183, n. 47. UNRRA aid to Italy reached its peak in 1946, with a grant of $450m. This was designed to supply the following percentages of total Italian imports: 70 per cent of food, 40 per cent of fuel, 82 per cent of agricultural and 22 per cent of industrial materials and machinery, 100 per cent of medical supplies (ibid., p. 75).

21a See N. Gallerano, 'L'altro dopoguerra', in Gallerano, ed., *L'altro dopoguerra*, pp. 43–5; and the famous novel of C. Malaparte, *The Skin*, London, 1962.

22 M. Mafai, *L'apprendistato della politica*, Roma, 1979, pp. 101ff.

23 G. Manzini, *Una vita operaia*, Torino, 1976, pp. 57–8.

24 P. Rugafiori, 'Genova', in F. Levi, P. Rugafiori and S. Vento, *Il triangolo industriale tra ricostruzione e lotta di classe, 1945–1948*, Milano, 1974, p. 67, n. 9.

25 C. Federici, 'La ricostruzione a La Spezia', tesi di laurea, Facoltà di lettere, Università di Pisa, 1976–7.

26 V. Foa, 'La ricostruzione capitalistica e la politica delle sinistre', in *Italia 1945–48. Le origini della Repubblica*, Torino, 1974, p. 125.

27 Quoted in Rugafiori, 'Genova', p. 48.

28 Testimony of Brogi, an anarchist worker at the SIMA factory, cited in L. Lanzardo, *Classe operaia e partito comunista alla FIAT*, Torino, 1971, p. 53, n. 1.

29 See his intervention at the second National Council of the PCI, 8–11 April 1945, quoted in C. Daneo, *La politica economica della ricostruzione*, p. 102.

30 Interview with Camilla Ravera, in G. Bocca, *Palmiro Togliatti*, Bari, 1973, p. 445.

31 Pavone, 'Le idee della Resistenza', p. 914.

32 V. Foa, 'Introduzione' to F. Levi *et al.*, *Il triangolo industriale*, p. xix. Elsewhere he writes: 'What was decisive was the refusal to place democratic objectives – control from above and below over industry, agrarian reform, a rigorous financial policy geared to reconstruction, abolition of the old repressive apparatus of the prefects and career policemen, self-government extended as far as possible – at the centre of action and direct conquest: everything was proposed instead in an electoral key, with the programme delegated to the parties for future legislative assemblies' ('La ricostruzione capitalistica', p. 131).

33 Testimonies of Gullo and Secchia to Gambino, *Storia del dopoguerra*, p. 104 (Gullo), p. 141 (Secchia).

34 For the PCI's attempts to woo the *ceti medi* see the excellent article by S. Hellman, 'The PCI's alliance strategy and the case of the middle classes', in D. Blackmer and S. Tarrow, *Communism in Italy and France*, Princeton, 1975, pp. 373–412. For the PCI and peasant proprietors, see A. Rossi-Doria, 'La politica agraria del movimento operaio e la questione dei coltivatori diretti', in *Il ministro e i contadini*, pp. 171–240. The dilemma was not, of course, peculiar to the PCI. It was that faced by all social democratic parties in the West in the twentieth century; see A. Przeworski, *Capitalism and Social Democracy*, Cambridge, 1986.

35 The letter of 16 Aug. 1947 is cited in Gambino, *Storia del dopoguerra*, p. 387. The building of the mass party was not, as Giorgio Bocca has written, 'the political revolution hoped for by so many, but it was a cultural revolution that changed the face of Italy' (Bocca, *Togliatti*, p. 401).

36 Manzini, *Una vita operaia*, p. 51.

37 G. Ascoli, 'L'UDI tra emancipazione e liberazione (1943–64)', in G. Ascoli *et al.*, *La questione femminile in Italia dal '900 ad oggi*, Milano, 1977, p. 124. See also Mafai, *L'apprendistato della politica*, pp. 123ff.

38 R. Lombardi, 'Il programma politico comunista', *La Civiltà Cattolica*, vol. XCVII (1946), vol. 2, 18 May, pp. 276–84. The reference to divorce is on p. 282, that to 'free love' on p. 283.

39 Quoted in S. Merli, 'La costituente socialista', in S. Sechi and S. Merli, *Dimenticare Livorno*, Milano, 1985, p. 102.

40 For Saragat's intervention, see ibid., pp. 148–66.

41 G. Arfé, 'Prefazione', to F. Taddei, *Il socialismo italiano del dopoguerra: correnti ideologiche e scelte politiche (1943–1947)*, Milano, 1984, p. 18.

42 *I congressi della CGIL*, vol. I, Roma, 1949, p. 109.

43 H. Stuart Hughes, *The United States and Italy*, Cambridge, Mass., 1979 (1st ed., 1963), p. 141.

44 See the interview which Parri gave to Manlio Cancogni, 'I ragazzi di Maurizio', *L'Espresso*, vol. XI (1965), no. 50. However, all the evidence from the Allied archives shows that the top levels of the Allied Commission were in favour of agrarian reform in the South. When Lt Col. W. Hartman, the head of the agricultural sub-commission, tried to impose a veto on the Gullo decrees, he was overruled by A. G. Antolini, the acting Deputy Chief of Staff, Economic Section, with the support of Ellery Stone, the head of the Commission; see the letter of 23 October 1944 from Antolini to Gullo, NAW, RG 331, 10000 159 1127, no. 626 (the letter begins: My dear Minister Gullo . . .').

45 R. Lombardi, 'Problemi di potere in Milano liberata', p. 266.

46 Letter of 29 May 1945, quoted in Pavone, 'La continuità dello Stato', p. 180.

47 See Parri's speech in *Unire per costruire* (numero unico sul primo congresso dei CLN dell'Alta Italia), Milano, 1945, pp. 24–32; cited in Legnani, *L'Italia dal 1943 al 1948*, p. 76.

48 P. Nenni, *Tempo di guerra fredda. Diari 1943–56*, ed. G. Nenni and D. Zucaro, Milano, 1981, p. 191; but see also M. Flores, 'Il regime transitorio', in *Dalla Liberazione alla Costituente*, Milano, 1981, p. 13. The Constituent Assembly still retained the final say over the Peace Treaty and the electoral law.

49 Pavone, 'La continuità dello Stato', p. 282, n. 292.

50 ibid., pp. 244–5 (for Orano), p. 248 (for Ricci).

51 ibid., p. 252. For a detailed study of judicial activity in Piedmont in this period, L. Bernardi, G. Neppi-Modona and S. Testori, *Giustizia penale e guerra di Liberazione*, Milano, 1984. For the history of the failure of *epurazione* see M. Flores, 'L'epurazione', in G. Quazza et al., *L'Italia dalla Liberazione alla Repubblica*, pp. 413–67.

52 C. Daneo, *La politica economica della ricostruzione*, p. 106; ibid., p. 105, for the quotation from Togliatti's speech.

53 ibid., p. 150. No plan for the construction of new public housing was approved by the Council of Ministers in this period. For the sorry story of the lack of initiatives in this field, see below, pp. 246–7.

54 A. Graziani, ed., *L'economia italiana: 1945–1970*, Bologna, 1971, p. 25.

55   ibid., pp. 27–9. A detailed treatment of this intricate question is E. Piscitelli, 'Del cambio o meglio del mancato cambio della moneta del secondo dopoguerra', *Quaderni dell'Istituto Romano per la Storia d'Italia dal Fascismo alla Resistenza*, vol. I (1969), No. 1, pp. 3–89. See also Scoccimarro, *Il secondo dopoguerra*, Milano, 1956, vol. II, pp. 29–33, and Mariuccia Salvati, *Stato e industria*, pp. 190–200. At the same time no overhauling of Italy's antiquated and unjust tax system was attempted. According to the Socialist newspaper *Avanti!* (27 July 1946), two thirds of the state's annual income in 1946 was still coming from indirect taxes on popular consumption; see Gambino, *Storia del dopoguerra*, p. 243. For a detailed study of the tax system at this time, S. Steve, *Il sistema tributario e le sue prospettive*, Milano, 1947, pp. 94–159.

56   Foa, *Sindicati e lotte operaie*, pp. 30ff. For details of the move towards greater wage equality see table 36 in C. Daneo, *La politica economica della ricostruzione*, p. 186.

57   Quoted in ibid., p. 94.

58   See Legnani, *L' Italia dal 1943 al 1948*, p. 94.

59   The details of Morandi's bill are to be found in R. Morandi, *Democrazia diretta e riforme di struttura*, Torino, 1975, pp. 88–97; see also pp. 219–25 for Morandi's views on the role the councils could play in the transition to socialism.

60   Foa, 'Introduzione' to F. Levi *et al.*, *Il triangolo industriale*, p. xxii. See also the very useful two-page insert on the *scala mobile* in *Il Manifesto*, 27 Sept. 1974. For the employers' attitudes, Mariuccia Salvati, *Stato e industria*, pp. 444–5.

61   As Manlio Rossi-Doria commented in 1967: 'Alongside the Catholic peasants of the Trentino, who followed De Gasperi, we can certainly say that it is to the *cafoni* [yokels] of Basilicata and Calabria that we owe those few million votes which mean that today we live under a republic and not a monarchy' (Fondazione L. Einaudi, *Nord e Sud nella società e nell'economia italiana di oggi*, Torino, 1968, p. 308).

62   G. Amendola, 'Prime considerazioni sulle elezioni del Mezzogiorno', *Rinascita*, vol. III, (1946), nos. 5–6.

63   Gambino, *Storia del dopoguerra*, p. 131.

64   See S. Setta, *L'Uomo qualunque, 1944–1948*, Bari, 1975.

65   The Constitution has been the source of a very extensive bibliography. See, among many others, U. Terracini, *Come nacque la Costituzione*, Roma, 1978; P. Calamandrei and P. Levi, *Commentario sistematico alla Costituzione italiana*, Firenze, 1950; P. Scoppola, *Gli anni della Costituente fra politica e storia*, Bologna, 1980; Pavone, 'La continuità dello Stato', pp. 216–28.

66   Terracini, *Come nacque la Costituzione*, p. 54; G. F. Poggi, 'The church in Italian politics from 1945 to 1950', in Woolf, ed., *The Rebirth of Italy*, p. 150. As Candeloro points out, the Lateran Pacts, as they were introduced into the Constitution, were in open contradiction with several of its other articles,

especially that which established the equality before the law of all citizens, regardless of sex, language or religion. On the other hand, he defends Togliatti's action on the grounds that article 7 would have been approved anyway (if only by an estimated five votes), and that the P C I's decision helped to make sure that politics in Italy 'did not assume the dimensions of a religious war or degenerate into such bitterness as to render impossible the survival of the democratic regime'; G. Candeloro, *Storia dell'Italia moderna*, vol. XI, Milano, 1986, pp. 127–9.

67 Terracini, *Come nacque la Costituzione*, pp. 56–7.

68 Daneo, *La politica economica della ricostruzione*, pp. 160–61.

69 Gambino, *Storia del dopoguerra*, p. 258.

70 ibid., p. 259. The apocalyptic way in which Pius XII viewed these years is nowhere better expressed than in his address of 20 April 1946 to the young men of Catholic Action. Taking up their battle-cry of 'Let us save the children', Pius spoke of 'the spiritual ruin of children and adolescents, of six, ten, fifteen years old, produced almost inevitably by the effect of an a-religious schooling; by the dangers of the streets; by the morally unhealthy and perhaps corrupt climate of the factory and the workshop. In the natural order of things – or better, according to the dispositions of divine Providence – a child must be born and grow up in the healthy climate of a Christian family and society, and there, step by step, develop and grow … For more than fifteen centuries the Italian people has remained faithful to this order of things, which appeared to them normal and unchallenged. Such an order was their comfort, their salvation in days of peril, their support in the face of transformations, crises, social and political conflicts and agitations. But over the course of the last hundred years or more, an insidious, constant and systematic battle has been waged to undermine, more profoundly than by means of violent action, the Christian culture of the Italian people. Today our adversary has decided that his work has reached such a point that the final assault can begin' ('Allocuzione di S.S. Pio XII alla gioventù maschile di A.C.I. sulle gravi necessità dell'ora presente', *La Civiltà Cattolica*, vol. XCVII (1946), vol. 2, 4 May, p. 170).

71 R. Orfei, *L'occupazione del potere*, Milano, 1976, pp. 76ff.

72 Harper, *America and the Reconstruction of Italy*, pp. 108–16.

73 Scoccimarro, *Il secondo dopoguerra*, vol. 1, pp. 239–40.

74 The problem of Trieste has recently been examined in considerable detail by G. P. Valdevit, *La questione di Trieste, 1941–1954*, Milano, 1986.

75 For the Socialist split, see above all Taddei, *Il socialismo italiano del dopoguerra*, pp. 303–65.

76 Daneo, *La politica economica della ricostruzione*, p. 125. It is worth noting that the C G I L made strenuous efforts in this period to recruit and organize amongst civil servants, and to negotiate agreements to protect them against the effects of inflation. On the other hand, as Foa has pointed out, these efforts probably constituted an obstacle to the left's formulation of a radical

programme for restructuring the civil service and ridding it of its many inefficient and parasitical elements; Foa, 'Introduzione' to F. Levi *et al.*, *Il triangolo industriale*, p. xix.

77 Quazza, *Resistenza e storia d'Italia*, pp. 344–5.

78 Gambino, *Storia del dopoguerra*, pp. 248–9; Daneo, *La politica economica della ricostruzione*, pp. 190–94.

79 A. Rossi-Doria, *Il ministro e i contadini*, p. 155. For Sicily, see F. Renda, 'Il movimento contadino Sicilia', in *Campagne e movimento contadino nel Mezzogiorno d'Italia*, vol. I, Bari, 1979, pp. 592–658; for Calabria (by far the most studied area), Ciconte, *All'assalto delle terre del latifondo*; P. Cinanni, *Lotte per la terra e comunisti in Calabria 1943–53*, Milano, 1977; P. Bevilacqua, '1945: luci ed ombre del movimento contadino', *Rivista Storica Calabrese* (New series), vol. 1 (1980), pp. 131–63; for Lazio, G. Crainz, 'Il movimento contadino e l'occupazione delle terre dalla Liberazione alle lotte dell'autunno 1946', *Quaderni della Resistenza Laziale*, vol. IV (1977), pp. 7–72.

80 It is necessary to treat the figures concerning peasant demands with some caution, in that different communes or cooperatives sometimes asked for the same piece of land, thus inflating the number of rejections; see Renda, 'Il movimento contadino in Sicilia', pp. 619–26.

81 G. Cortese, 'Il cataclisma Gullo', *Il Giornale*, 25 April 1946.

82 For further details of the legal fate of this decree, see A. Rossi-Doria, *Il ministro e i contadini*, pp. 69–72.

83 For Calabria see the testimony of F. Calderazzo in G. Mottura and U. Ursetta, *Il diritto alla terra*, Milano, 1978, pp. 96–7. For Sicily, the many anonymous testimonies in G. Saladino, *Terra di rapina*, Torino, 1977, pp. 10–42.

84 After the First World War, Gramsci had been scathing in his condemnation of the assignment of uncultivated land to the peasants without proper aid; see the article 'Operai e contadini', *L'Ordine Nuovo*, 3 Jan. 1920: 'What can a poor peasant achieve by occupying uncultivated or poorly cultivated lands? He is quite likely, long before harvest time, to hang himself from the strongest bush or the least unhealthy looking wild fig in the undergrowth of his uncultivated land. And even if he doesn't, without machinery, without accommodation at the place of work, without credit to tide him over until harvest time, without cooperative institutions to acquire the harvest and preserve him from the usurers – without all these things, what can a poor peasant achieve by possession?'; A. Gramsci, *Selections from Political Writings 1910–1920*, ed. Q. Hoare, London, 1977, p. 147. For the arrival and eventual fate of one of the fifteen tractors, see G. Gribaudi, 'Mito dell'eguaglianza e individualismo', pp. 480–81 and 504: 'That symbol of "real socialism", the Soviet tractor, finished badly as well. It disappeared and was never found again. Some say that a member of the cooperative dismantled it and sold its parts. Anyway, there's no official version.'

85 A. Orlandini and G. Venturini, *Padrone arrivedello a battitura*, Milano, 1980, pp. 98–9. Gullo had wanted to extend his decree on agrarian contracts to central

Italy as well, but in the autumn of 1944 the DC and PLI representatives in the Council of Ministers had expressly vetoed any such idea.

86 ibid., p. 51. In the province of Siena alone, the union had 33,556 members by 1947. Though the exact statistics are not available, the great majority of members were undoubtedly sharecroppers.

87 Anonymous testimony in P. De Simonis, ' "Il grano era la forma dove s'era più forti" ', *Annali dell'Istituto Alcide Cervi*, vol. VIII (1986), pp. 296–7.

88 D. Tabet, 'I consigli di fattoria', *Annali dell'Istituto Alcide Cervi*, vol. VIII (1986), p. 287–92. The composition of the councils varied, sometimes incorporating landless labourers as well. For an enlightened and paternalist view, see Origo, *War in Val d'Orcia*, where the central buildings on the Origo estate included a school and infirmary.

89 Orlandini and Venturini, *Padrone arrivedello a battitura*, p. 126.

90 E. Piscitelli, *Da Parri a De Gasperi*, Milano, 1975, pp. 153–7. Piscitelli interprets the *lodo* De Gasperi as a major concession to the *mezzadri*.

91 Gambino, *Storia del dopoguerra*, p. 334. Harper, *America and the Reconstruction of Italy*, p. 119 and pp. 131–4, is at pains to stress that the US could offer more moral than economic aid at this critical moment, coming as it did between UNRRA and ERP.

92 Pantaleone, *Mafia and Politics*, p. 133; Centro Siciliano di Documentazione, *Portella delle Ginestre: una strage per il centrismo*, Palermo, 1977; see also the testimony in Saladino, *Terra di rapina*, p. 24: ' "The law! You've stuffed your heads full of this law. It's we who make the law here, *da che mondo è mondo*." That's what a *mafioso* told me and it was true. They made the law and to enforce it in 1947 alone there were twenty-three workers killed. Eleven on the first of May at Portella di Ginestra, the others were heads of peasant leagues, trade unionists, secretaries of the Federterra, all killed *sulle trazzere*.' And ibid., p. 25: 'Rizzotto was twenty-six years old, a landless labourer, a socialist, the secretary of the Camera di Lavoro of Corleone. They snatched him on the evening of 10 March 1948 and bundled him into a car. "Where is Rizzotto?": I shudder every time I remember that cry, roared with the full force of his lungs by Di Vittorio in Palermo to a packed Piazza Politeama. He shouted those words in syllables: *"do-vè Ri-zzo-tto"*, time after time, as if he expected a reply, and the echo came back, went round and was lost in that piazza frozen into silence, with tens of thousands of people who held their breath and held back their tears.'

93 Harper, *America and the Reconstruction of Italy*, p. 140. Einaudi also cut government subsidies on bread, electricity, the railways and the post; see Candeloro, *Storia dell'Italia moderna*, vol. XI, p. 166.

94 For the debate on Einaudi's measures, see, among others, A. O. Hirschman, 'Inflation and deflation in Italy', *American Economic Review*, vol. XXXVIII (1948), pp. 598–606; M. De Cecco, 'Sulla stabilizzazione economica del 1947', in his *Saggi di politica monetaria*, Milano, 1968, pp. 109–41; Mariuccia Salvati, *Stato e*

industria, pp. 338–54; U. Ruffolo, 'La linea Einaudi', *Storia Contemporanea*, vol. V (1974), no. 4, pp. 637–71. P. Barucci, *Ricostruzione, pianificazione, Mezzogiorno*, Bologna, 1978, pp. 135ff., points out how Einaudi's triumph was simultaneously the defeat of the left and of Catholic economists like Saraceno and Vanoni, who were closely tied to the social doctrines of Dossetti. Nearly all commentators (and the US officials of the time) criticize Einaudi for continuing deflationary policies after mid-1948; Harper, *America and the Reconstruction of Italy*, p. 138.

95 Reale, *Nascita del Cominform, passim.*

96 In November 1947 Scelba gave instructions for one of the last of the CLN prefects, Ettore Troilo of Milan, to be replaced. Gian Carlo Pajetta, secretary of the Communist Party in Lombardy, ordered the prefecture in Corso Monforte to be occupied in protest. Workers flocked into the centre of the city, road-blocks were set up and armed partisans took over operations. Togliatti was nearly as alarmed and furious as De Gasperi. For him actions of this sort, even if only intended as a show of force, as Pajetta always maintained, would quickly condemn the PCI to the realm of illegality. The Milanese Communists were ordered to withdraw and a face-saving formula, which amounted to a postponed victory for Scelba, was quickly agreed upon; Bocca, *Togliatti*, pp. 486–7.

97 G. Crainz, 'I braccianti padani', in G. Chianese *et al.*, *Italia 1945–50*, pp. 223–6. On the *collocamento* the landowners maintained the right to name the landless labourers they wanted. See also E. Tortoreto, 'Lotte agrarie nella valle padana nel secondo dopoguerra, 1945–50', *Movimento Operaio e Socialista*, vol. XIII (1967), nos. 3–4, p. 263.

98 Gambino, *Storia del dopoguerra*, pp. 446ff. Gambino's is the best overall account of the 1948 campaign. See also, for American activities, J. E. Miller, 'Taking off the gloves: the United States and the Italian elections of 1948', *Diplomatic History*, vol. VII (1983), no. 1, pp. 34–55.

99 R. Gannon, *The Cardinal Spellman Story*, Garden City, 1962, p. 347, cited in Warner, 'Italy and the Powers', in Woolf, ed., *The Rebirth of Italy*, p. 54. See also J. and G. Kolko, *The Limits of Power*, pp. 438–9.

100 Gambino, *Storia del dopoguerra*, pp. 468ff.

101 ibid., pp. 457ff.

102 For Cardinal Siri, ibid., p. 442. For Pius XII, Miccoli, 'Chiesa, partito cattolico e società civile', p. 220. Pius also had recourse to cycling metaphors: 'Take your example from Gino Bartali [one of the most famous Italian cyclists of the time] who is a member of Catholic Action. He has many times won the sought-after yellow jersey. You too must pedal fast in this championship of ideals'; 'Discorso agli uomini di Azione Cattolica', *La Civiltà Cattolica*, vol. XCVIII (1947), vol. 3, 20 Sept., p. 553. On the theme of cyling see the letter of 29 Oct. 1947 from J. Ward of the British Embassy in Rome: 'Both parties are making great efforts to get hold of the youth of the country, but whereas the Communists would put their money on the "Dance Halls of the People", beauty competitions and

suchlike efforts reminiscent of Hollywood, the CDs have been more clever by capturing the world of sport, particularly football and bicycling, the two great passions of the Italians' (Archives Centre, Churchill College, Cambridge, papers of P. Noel-Baker, 4/410).

103 C. Falconi, *Gedda e l'Azione Cattolica*, Firenze, 1958, pp. 125–40.

104 DC poster reproduced in *L'Unità*, 15 Jan. 1978. See also the book of DC posters and propaganda, *C'era una volta la D.C.*, Roma, 1975.

105 Gambino, *Storia del dopoguerra*, p. 467. A few days before the elections, the government created 'special transitional categories' for temporary office workers in the Roman ministries; in this way more than 200,000 clerks were given secure jobs; R. Romanelli, 'Apparati statali, ceti burocratici e modo di governo', in Castronovo, ed., *L'Italia contemporanea*, p. 155.

106 Rugafiori, 'Genova', in F. Levi *et al.*, *Il triangolo industriale*, p. 93. On the left's attitude to the Marshall Plan, see Daneo, *La politica economica della ricostruzione*, pp. 254–6.

107 *Corriere della Sera*, 22 April 1948.

108 W. Tobagi, *La rivoluzione impossibile*, Milano, 1978. For the events at Abbadia San Salvatore see G. Serafini, *I ribelli della montagna*, Montepulciano, 1981, and A. Orlandini, *L'insurrezione proletaria nella provincia di Siena in risposta all'attentato a Togliatti*, Firenze, 1976, pp. 113–20.

109 Rugafiori, 'Genova', in F. Levi *et al.*, *Il triangolo industriale*, pp. 96–7.

110 Quoted in Bocca, *Togliatti*, p. 524.

111 For details of the trial and sentences, see Serafini, *I ribelli della montagna*, p. 119. See also the testimony of Fortunato Avanzati, in Orlandini, *L'insurrezione proletaria*, p. 119. Avanzati was sent by the PCI from Siena to restore order in Abbadia San Salvatore. He arrived there on the morning of 16 July 1948: 'Here he had a heated discussion with his comrades, including his father and his brother. They maintained that to demobilize was to do the same as in 1921, that the workers could no longer bear the exploitation and poverty, that they could not run away and hide as during Fascism. Rather than accept these things they said it was better to go the whole way, once and for all, even if that meant to die.'

Chapter 4

1 R. Lombardi, *Scritti politici*, ed. S. Colarizi, vol. I (1945–63), Venezia, 1978, *passim*; R. Morandi, *Democrazia diretta e riforme di struttura*, *passim*; Sassoon, *Togliatti e la via italiana*, pp. 241–88; Amyot, *The Italian Communist Party*, pp. 43–4, 54–5. For a more detailed discussion of the nature of reformism, see below, pp. 265–7.

2 For Dossetti's intervention, see *I congressi nazionali della Democrazia Cristiana*, p. 252.

3 A. Rossi-Doria, *Il ministro e i contadini*, pp. 151–3.

4   Cinanni, *Lotta per la terra e comunisti in Calabria*, pp. 105–6.

5   Speech of 11 April 1947 to the Messina Federation, in P. Togliatti, 'Separatismo e autonomia', *Cronache Meridionali*, vol. IV (1957), nos. 7–8, p. 428. For an extended discussion of the PCI's alliance strategy in the South, see S. G. Tarrow, *Peasant Communism in Southern Italy*, New Haven, CT, 1967, pp. 253ff.

6   There was a constant tension between the peasant cadres and the urban-based regional leadership. In October 1946 the Cosenza Federation reported: 'We have even heard it said that comrades from the province, after having undertaken a journey of many kilometres, were greeted in the Federation just as the poor peasant is greeted when he goes to a government office in the city, and finds the clerk sitting behind his desk, with no time or words to waste on the poor ignoramus who understands nothing about the law or anything else' (Archivio PCI, Calabria 1946–1948, 1946, Cosenza, 114/1454–1457, cited in A. Rossi-Doria, *Il ministro e i contadini*, p. 51). The national Communist organization, Alleanza dei Contadini, was only finally to be founded in 1955. See also G. Maione, 'Mezzogiorno, 1946–1950. Partito Comunista e movimento contadino', *Italia Contemporanea*, vol. XXXVIII (1986), no. 163, pp. 31–64.

7   Cinanni, *Lotte per la terra e comunisti in Calabria*, pp. 85–6.

8   See the eye-witness accounts collected in Mottura and Ursetta, *Il diritto alla terra*, pp. 201–6; Cinanni, *Lotte per la terra nel Mezzogiorno*, pp. 58–63; Bevilacqua, *Le campagne del Mezzogiorno*, pp. 447–9.

9   V. Gorresio, *La Stampa Nuova*, 2 Nov. 1949.

10   Saladino, *Terra di rapina*, pp. 8–9.

11   G. Modica, 'Il ruolo delle donne nelle lotte contadine', in Centro Siciliano di Documentazione, *Ricomposizione del blocco dominante*, pp. 53–6.

12   G. Gribaudi, 'Mito dell'eguaglianza e individualismo', p. 470.

13   Partito Comunista Italiano, Federazione Regionale della Sicilia, *Lettera al compagno siciliano*, Palermo, 1945, p. 5.

14   G. Gribaudi, 'Mito dell'eguaglianza e individualismo', pp. 461–2 and 496–7. See also the eloquent judgement of Ernesto De Martino: 'He who has experience of the peasant movement in the South knows very well that in this struggle for emancipation something is fermenting which goes beyond the predominant demand for land. It is something which involves a new way of being, the first experiment with a higher morality and with a more active participation in politics, the rejection of ancient ideological servitudes, and in their place the illumination of sudden flashes of a new and civilized vision of life and of the world' ('Postilla a considerazioni storiche sul lamento funebre lucano', *Nuovi Argomenti*, vol. VIII (1955), no. 12, p. 39).

15   For division and dissent, Saladino, *Terra di rapina*, p. 31. Anna Rossi-Doria makes this telling judgement on the problem of rural alliances: 'To favour the "peasants without land" meant on the one hand to undermine the local power equilibrium between the classes, but on the other to reinforce the alliance

between large and small proprietors which guaranteed that very equilibrium's permanence', *Il ministro e i contadini*, p. 142.

16   Cinanni, *Lotte per la terra nel Mezzogiorno*, pp. 65–8. See also 'Bollettino della sezione comunista di Montescaglioso', *Rinascita*, vol. VII (1950), no. 3, p. 139.

17   Cinanni, *Lotte per la terra nel Mezzogiorno*, pp. 91ff.; Russo, *Baroni e contadini*, pp. 7ff.; and the anthropological study of C. White, *Patrons and Partisans*, Cambridge, 1980.

18   Cited in F. Renda, 'Il movimento contadino in Sicilia', in *Compagne e movimento contadino nel Mezzogiorno d'Italia*, 2 vols., Bari, 1979–80, p. 665, n. 10.

19   For the peasants' actions at Bronte in 1950, see Renda, 'Il movimento contadino in Sicilia', p. 666, and also his article 'La Ducea di Nelson', *Il Siciliano Nuovo*, 1 July 1950. Carlo Levi visited Bronte in 1952 and noted the appalling poverty of its inhabitants and the rapacity of the stewards of the Duchy; C. Levi, *Le parole sono pietre*, Torino, 1955, pp. 78–85. For one of the original disputes between the Nelson administration and the peasants of Bronte, see the copy of the letter from Palermo of Philip Thorez to Earl Nelson, 10 March 1827 (Archivio di Stato, Palermo, Archivio Nelson, b. 585): 'It is with the greatest pleasure that I do myself the honour of communicating to your Grace the happy result of our suit against the Brontesi before the Supreme Court of Accounts, ... not-withstanding all the manoeuvre [*sic*] of our opponents, and a strong feeling compassion [*sic*] artfully excited in the breast of every judge in favour of the Brontesi, who were represented as actually dying for want of fuel in a cold and inhospitable region ... The importance of the success gained over the Brontesi, while it rescues the woods from their insatiable rapacity, opens a new road to augment the revenues of the Bronte Estate.'

20   In Sardinia, for example, in the province of Sassari, the poorly cultivated olive groves of Antonio Segni, the Minister of Agriculture, were occupied, and the peasants mobilized in many other areas of the island. Sardinian landless labourers could find usually no more than one hundred days' work in the whole year, and the shepherds' remunerations were the worst in all Italy. Strong tensions existed between peasants and shepherds, who often wanted the same land for different purposes; G. Sotgiù, 'Lotte contadine nella Sardegna del secondo dopoguerra', in *Campagne e movimento contadino nel Mezzogiorno d'Italia*, vol. I, pp. 721–814.

21   Tortoreto, 'Lotte agrarie nella valle padana', pp. 277–85; Crainz, 'I braccianti padani', pp. 260–64. The strike of May and June 1949, involving hundreds of thousands of landless labourers, lasted thirty-six days, but gained very few con-cessions.

22   Crainz, 'I braccianti padani', p. 248. On conditions in the Po delta, R. King, *Land Reform: the Italian Experience*, London, 1973, pp. 90–92; and T. Merlin, 'Le radici storiche del socialismo nella Bassa Padana', *Schema*, vol. V (1982), nos. 9–10 p. 139.

23   For 1946, 'Le linee programmatiche della D.C.', in *I congressi nazionali della DC*, p. 23; for 1947, Damiliani, ed., *Atti e documenti della DC*, vol. 1, pp. 331–2.

24 G. Mottura, 'La D.C. e lo sviluppo del moderatismo nelle campagne', in F. Vianello *et al.*, *Tutto il potere della D.C.*, Roma, 1975, p. 180; R. Piazza, 'Dibattito teorico e indirizzi di governo nella politica agraria della Democrazia Cristiana (1944–1951)', *Italia Contemporanea*, vol. XXVI (1974), no. 117, pp. 49–92.

25 *Corriere della Sera*, 29 Aug. and 20 Oct. 1948, quoted by Galli, *Storia della DC*, pp. 111–12.

26 For the generic nature of the commitment of *Cronache Sociali* to agrarian reform, Piazza, 'Dibattito teorico', pp. 57–8.

27 NAW, RG 59/865.52/12–549, NA; cited in Harper, *America and the Reconstruction of Italy*, p. 164. More work needs to be done both on American attitudes and on how far De Gasperi was influenced by them at this moment; A. Tarchiani, in his book *Dieci anni tra Roma e Washington*, Verona, 1955, does not mention this problem.

28 For the debate in the Sicilian assembly, Renda, 'Il movimento contadino in Sicilia', pp. 669–75; see also Baget-Bozzo, *Il partito cristiano al potere*, vol. II, p. 232.

29 Renda, 'Il movimento contadino in Sicilia', p. 687. For landowner evasion techniques in Sicily, see Blok, *The Mafia of a Sicilian Village*, p. 77, for the Corleone district; C. Levi, *Le parole sono pietre*, p. 84, for Bronte; for Calabria, P. Pezzino, *La riforma agraria in Calabria*, Milano, 1977, pp. 90–91.

30 A. M. Seronde, 'La réforme agraire', in J. Meyriat, *La Calabre*, Paris, 1960, p. 118. In Basilicata Davis recounts that out of 1,158 'valid' applications, only 449 peasants received land in the villages of Pisticci and Montalbano; J. Davis, *Land and Family in Pisticci*, pp. 147–8. For Sicily, Renda, 'Il movimento contadino in Sicilia', p. 687.

31 Pezzino, *La riforma agraria in Calabria*, pp. 96–100. His figure for the Calabrian cooperatives is for December 1946, and it should perhaps be borne in mind that, as has already been mentioned, considerable amounts of land were lost by the cooperatives in 1948. In the various regions of the South it is by no means clear how many of the members of the cooperatives formed since 1944 actually received land under the reform. In Calabria, Pezzino (p. 100) claims that none did; in Basilicata, though, there is evidence from the Melfese district that the interests of the cooperative members were safeguarded; Talamo and De Marco, *Lotte agrarie del Mezzogiorno*, p. 39, n. 46. At 'Velia' in Campania, the land of the cooperative was reassigned, despite vigorous initial protests from the local PCI; G. Gribaudi, 'Mito dell'eguaglianza e individualismo', p. 485. In Sicily, according to Renda, the cooperatives were farming 86,000 hectares at the time of the reform, while only 74,290 hectares were distributed by the reform itself. However, he does not give details of how much of the first figure was reabsorbed into the second; 'Il movimento contadino in Sicilia', p. 688.

32 Pezzino, *La riforma agraria in Calabria*, p. 95; see also G. Galasso, *La riforma agraria in Calabria*, Roma, 1958, p. 52.

33 King, *Land Reform*, pp. 84ff.

34   For the quadripartite division of the reform area, Pezzino, *La riforma agraria in Calabria*, pp. 82ff., and his case studies of S. Giovanni in Fiore, pp. 140–51, Isolo di Capo Rizzuto, pp. 151–7, Corigliano Calabro, pp. 158–66, and Santa Severina, pp. 166–72.

35   For explanation of the difference between this figure and that cited earlier of 76,011 hectares of land actually distributed, see Pezzino, *La riforma agraria in Calabria*, p. 105, n. 30. The rest of the land was either unsuitable for cultivation, or else woods, or was retained by the reform board for experimental farms.

36   In the Marchesato, for instance, a group of experts opposed to the board's decision had calculated that a minimum of thirty hectares was needed for self-sufficiency; see also the comments of L. Gambi, *Calabria*, Torino, 1965, pp. 458–60.

37   Pezzino, *La riforma agraria in Calabria*, p. 109.

38   ibid., pp. 136–8.

39   ibid., p. 129.

40   King, *Land Reform*, pp. 95ff. But for a rather more negative view, L. Bartolotti, 'L'evoluzione del territorio', in Mori, ed., *Storia d'Italia . . . La Toscana*, p. 807. The reform in the Po delta also fared reasonably well. This was the only reform area where large estates already being run as fairly efficient capitalist enterprises were subject to expropriation. The amount of land confiscated, mainly from large sugar companies, was small in extent, some 49,000 hectares in all. However, those fortunate enough to receive a farm had a viable economic entity at their disposal. With the help of extensive land reclamation, the production of wheat, maize and sugar-beet, as well as dairy farming, soon exceeded pre-reform levels. Under the stimulus of the reform, the pattern of land ownership in the Polesine changed notably. Peasant property of 2–10 hectares increased from 12.5 per cent of cultivable land in 1946 to 20.7 per cent in 1962, while estates of over 100 hectares declined from 42.8 per cent to 29.9 per cent; M. Paci, *Mercato del lavoro e classi sociali in Italia*, Bologna, 1973, pp. 171ff.; King, *Land Reform*, p. 93.

41   Blok, *The Mafia of a Sicilian Village*, p. 80; King, *Land Reform*, pp. 110–13.

42   C. Barberis, 'Avvio al dibattito', in INSOR, *La riforma fondiaria: trent'anni dopo*, vol. I, Milano, 1979, p. 50.

43   King, *Land Reform*, pp. 110–111.

44   *Dal latifondo al potere, Atti del Convegno degli assegnatari DC delle terre di riforma fondiaria*, Roma, 1955, p. 37, cited in Tarrow, *Peasant Communism in Southern Italy*, p. 353.

45   Barberis, 'Avvio al dibattito', p. 36.

46   ibid., p. 56; for Einaudi, L. Einaudi, *Lo scrittoio del Presidente*, Torino, 1976, p. 476; for Segni, Cinanni, *Lotte per la terra nel Mezzogiorno*, p. 99.

47   M. Rossi-Doria, 'La riforma agraria sei anni dopo', in his *Dieci anni di politicia agraria nel Mezzogiorno*, Bari, 1958, p. 135.

48 Rosario Villari notes that 'while 100,000 families received land, millions of peasants were from then on forced to emigrate'; R. Villari, 'La crisi del blocco agrario', p. 31. Renato Zangheri compares the modest amount of land confiscated in the Italian case with the very much greater amounts expropriated in Poland, Yugoslavia and Romania between the two world wars; R. Zangheri, 'A trent'anni dalla legge di riforma agraria', in *Campagne e movimento contadino nel Mezzogiorno d'Italia*, vol. II, pp. 651–2.

49 Tortoreto, 'Lotte agrarie nella valle padana', pp. 266–77.

50 For Sicily, Nocifora has highlighted recently the process by which old and absentee landowning families sold considerable amounts of their estates at the time of the reform to local landowners, who proceeded to make more rational use of the land. Such exchanges, he argues, exceeded in importance those of the land reform itself; E. Nocifora, 'Riforma agraria e classi sociali in Sicilia', *Nuovi Quaderni del Meridione*, vol. XIX (1981), no. 73, pp. 73–89.

51 See the model case history of 'Gerardo Pastore' cited in G. Gribaudi, 'Mito dell'eguaglianza e individualismo', pp. 507–8. Pastore was an active PCI member at 'Velia' in the 1940s. He took part in the land occupations, gained a *podere* thanks to the reform and persuaded others to sell him their land; he then left the PCI for the PSI. Today, recounts Gribaudi, he is a wealthy and politically very influential agricultural entrepreneur. See also, from a different perspective, the comments of Manlio Rossi-Doria: 'In particular, the social services of the reform boards, which could have done a great deal for the education of the peasants and to help them develop a healthy cooperative life, have in fact become political instruments to increase the electoral strength of the DC in these areas'; 'La riforma agraria sei anni dopo', p. 139.

52 R. Villari, 'La crisi del blocco agrario', p. 27.

53 Pezzino, *La riforma agraria in Calabria*, p. 31, n. 68; G. Mottura and E. Pugliese, *Agricoltura, Mezzogiorno e mercato del lavoro*, Bologna, 1975, p. 28, n. 14.

54 For the growth of the Coldiretti, see below, pp. 171–2; for the Federconsorzi, M. Rossi-Doria, *Rapporto sulla Federconsorzi*, Bari, 1963; E. Rossi, P. Ugolini and L. Piccardi, *La Federconsorzi*, Milano, 1963.

Chapter 5

1 In 1952 Pius XII was afraid that the left would gain control of Rome's local government. He therefore ordered Don Sturzo, the veteran leader of the Partito Popolare, to propose formally an alliance at a local level between the DC and the neo-Fascists of the MSI. Sturzo complied reluctantly, but De Gasperi was very much more evasive. The alliance was not formed, but in the event proved unnecessary because the left failed to win sufficient votes in Rome to take control. In June 1952 De Gasperi requested an audience with the Pope for himself and his family. It was the thirtieth anniversary of his wedding, and his daughter Lucia had just taken her vows to become a nun. Pius XII refused to receive the De Gasperi family. De Gasperi wrote to Giorgio Mameli, the Italian ambassador to the Vatican: 'As a Christian I accept this humiliation,

although I do not know how to justify it. But as President of the Council of Ministers and Minister for Foreign Affairs, a certain dignity and authority are conferred upon me. I cannot rid myself of these, even in private matters. They impose upon me the necessity to express my astonishment at so exceptional a refusal'; M. R. Catti De Gasperi, *De Gasperi, uomo solo*, Milano, 1964, p. 335.

2   G. Scarpari, *La Democrazia Cristiana e le leggi eccezionali, 1950–1953*, Milano, 1977, *passim*. For Dossetti's retirement from political life and an assessment of his political influence, see Baget-Bozzo, *Il partito cristiano al potere*, vol. II, pp. 349–55.

3   Letter of March 1952, published in *De Gasperi scrive* (ed. M. R. De Gasperi), vol. I, Brescia, 1974, pp. 114–15. For the failure of De Gasperi's 'centrism' of these years, see also the introduction by P. G. Zunino to *Scritti politici di Alcide De Gasperi*, pp. 77–88.

4   Rosenbaum, *Il nuovo fascismo*, Milano, 1975, pp. 106ff., and above all Colarizzi, *La seconda guerra mondiale*, pp. 610–21.

5   D. Hine, 'Italy', in F. F. Ridley, ed., *Government and Administration in Western Europe*, London, 1979, pp. 179–80.

6   G. Salvemini, 'L'elefantiasi burocratica', *L'Unità*, 30 May 1913, reprinted in S. Cassese, ed., *L'amministrazione pubblica in Italia*, Bologna, 1974, p. 72. Carocci traces the development of the use of state power to satisfy personal favours back to the period 1876–82, after the fall of the *Destra storica*: G. Carocci, 'Un difetto di egemonia', in *Il vizio d'origine* (ed. G. Zincone), *La Biblioteca della Libertà*, vol. XVII (1980), nos. 77–8, p. 103. Most commentators agree that the Fascist period saw a marked increase in clientelism, with membership of the party a prerequisite for state employment.

7   S. Cassese, *Il sistema amministrativo italiano*, Bologna, 1983, p. 32. For a slightly different set of figures, but which show the same general trends, F. Ferraresi, *Burocrazia e politica in Italia*, Bologna, 1980, tab. 3.1, p. 98. For some European comparisons (though only for the post-war period), see Cassese, *Il sistema amministrativo italiano*, tab. 13.1, p. 304. By 1960 7.7 per cent of all those employed in Italy were state employees; in Germany the corresponding figure for the same year was 8.0 per cent, for France 12.9 per cent, and for the UK 16.4 per cent. These figures would tend to contradict any superficial description of the especially 'bloated' nature of the Italian public sector.

8   Ferraresi, *Burocrazia e politica*, tab. 3.5, p. 114.

9   A. De Stefani, *Una riforma al rogo*, Roma, 1963, pp. 12–13, cited in S. Cassese, *Questione amministrativa e questione meridionale*, Milano, 1977, pp. 90–91.

10   Cassese, *Il sistema amministrativo italiano*, pp. 34–8.

11   E. Cerquetti, *Le forze armate italiane dal 1945 al 1975*, Milano, 1975, especially pp. 87ff. and p. 101.

12   For a revealing testimony of police life in the 1940s and 1950s, see S. Medici, *Vite di poliziotti*, Torino, 1979, pp. 19ff. In 1948 one of Medici's interviewees, a

Neapolitan who was unemployed at that time, became an auxiliary policeman at Imperia in Liguria: '[Our officers] told us that the area was full of partisans, that during the war of Liberation unspeakable things had happened there: churches had been sacked, police headquarters and prefectures had been burnt down, "Italians" had fought each other in a bloody civil war. Their message was to distrust the population and not to be taken in by the city's outward appearance of calm. And to cap it all they appealed in the most objectionable way to our solidarity as southerners, contrasting us to the people of the city – rich, mean, communist, and northerners to boot'; ibid., p. 23. See also G. Boatti, *L'arma*, Milano, 1978, chapter 1 and the preface by G. Rochat; and S. Bertocci, 'Indagine sull'arma dei Carabinieri', *Il Ponte*, vol. XVI (1960), no. 7, pp. 1060–77.

13   C. Rodotà, *La corte costituzionale*, Roma, 1986, pp. 44–5.

14   For the attitudes and values of the Associazione Nazionale Magistrati in the post-war period see R. Canosa and P. Federico, *La magistratura in Italia dal 1945 a oggi*, Bologna, 1974, pp. 79–95.

15   For a lively journalistic denunciation of the workings (or lack of them) of the ministerial bureaucracy, see G. Bianchi, *L'Italia dei ministeri: lo sfascio guidato*, Roma, 1981, *passim*.

16   P. Allum, *Italy: Republic without Government?*, London, 1973, p. 165. For a historical perspective on the organizational criteria of the public administration, R. Romanelli, 'Apparati statali, ceti burocratici e modo di governo', in Castronovo, ed., *L'Italia contemporanea*, pp. 159ff.

17   Article of 2 June 1949 by R. De Caterini, quoted in R. Cavarra and M. Sclavi, *Gli statali, 1923–1978*, Torino, 1980, p. 46.

18   V. Emiliani, *L'Italia mangiata*, Torino, 1975, p. 5.

19   Mariuccia Salvati, *Stato e industria*, pp. 372–82; for Finmeccanica, M. V. Posner and S. J. Woolf, *Italian Public Enterprise*, London, 1967, pp. 56–7; for employment in 1948, *IRI, '33–'73*, Roma, 1973, tab. 1.

20   The *parastato* does not just consist of social-service agencies but also those dealing with sport, tourism, leisure, etc.; see Cassese, *Il sistema amministrativo italiano*, p. 18.

21   For the D'Aragona commission, see A. Cherubini, *Storia della previdenza sociale*, Roma, 1977, pp. 365–72, and pp. 412–17 for the condition of the social-security institutions by 1960. For their respective budgets, M. Bonaccorsi, 'Gli enti pubblici del settore della sicurezza sociale', in F. Cazzola, ed., *Anatomia del potere democristiano*, Bari, 1979, tab. 7, pp. 90–91. For their overlapping nature, with its attendant problems, L. Conti, *L'assistenza e la previdenza sociale*, Milano, 1958, p. 83 and pp. 173–82.

22   Emiliani, *L'Italia mangiata*, pp. 9–11.

23   Although Italian prefects could effectively suffocate local autonomy, they did not enjoy the extensive powers of their French counterparts, who were the heads of all state agencies in their locality. The laws governing the powers of

local communes had last been adjusted in Italy under Fascism in 1934 and were not changed in the post-war period. The whole structure of centre–periphery relations was in direct contrast with Article 5 of the Constitution, which stated that the Republic 'would adapt the principles and methods of its legislation to the requirements of autonomy and decentralization'; Cassese, *Il sistema amministrativo italiano*, pp. 163ff.; Allum, *Republic without Government*, pp. 112–25; Romanelli, 'Apparati statali', pp. 151–2; R. C. Fried, *The Italian Prefects*, Yale, 1963, *passim*. Most prefects, as Fried shows, came from lower-middle-class southern families.

24　See the work of the Catholic scholar, R. Orfei, *L'occupazione del potere*, Milano, 1976, *passim*; for 'colonization', J. Meynaud, *Rapporto sulla classe dirigente italiana*, Milano, 1966, p. 184; for 'symbiosis', C. Donolo, 'Social change and transformation of the state in Italy', in R. Scase, ed., *The State in Western Europe*, London, 1980, p. 178.

25　For a fascinating combination of these two elements, a combination which in practice left the road wide open for the consumer revolution, see Amintore Fanfani's speech as party secretary at the VIth congress of the D C held at Trento on 14–18 October 1956: 'When we encourage technological progress we are acting politically in favour of the second industrial revolution, which is personalistic, solidaristic and thus Christian. This second revolution, by multiplying the number of goods, reduces human toil and will reduce the harshness of the struggle for existence, the distress in economic life, the gravity of poverty and the temptations connected with it. The greater abundance of goods will make it easier to alleviate depression, whether it is of an individual, a group or a people' (*I congressi nazionali della DC*, p. 601).

26　See A. S. Zuckerman, *The Politics of Faction*, New Haven, CT, 1979; see also table 1 in G. Pasquino, 'Italian Christian Democracy: a party for all seasons?', in P. Lange and S. Tarrow, *Italy in Transition*, London, 1980, p. 91.

27　Donolo, 'Social change and transformation of the state', p. 165.

28　On Andreotti's tenure at the Ministry of Defence see J. Walston, *The Mafia and Clientelism: Roads to Rome in Post-war Calabria*, London, 1988, p. 76.

29　F. Cazzola, 'I pilastri del regime', *Rassegna Italiana di Sociologia*, vol. XVII (1976), tab. 13, p. 446. The president of INAM was a member of the DC from 1944 to 1974, and that of INAIL a member of the Liberal Party from 1949 to 1964. See also G. Pridham, ed., *Coalition Behaviour in Theory and Practice*, Cambridge, 1986, especially pp. 198–231.

30　A. Predieri, 'Parlamento "75"', in A. Predieri, ed., *Il parlamento nel sistema politico italiano*, Milano, 1975, p. 18 and p. 31. During the first five legislatures (1948–72) over 75 per cent of all laws were passed at committee stage; between 1948 and 1968 71 per cent of all laws were 'micro-sectional' or 'individual'; this percentage increased to 76 in the fifth legislature (1968–72).

31　S. Cassese, *Esiste un governo in Italia?*, Roma, 1980, p. 72.

32　A. De Gasperi, 'Nella lotta per la democrazia', speech at the fifth congress of the D C, Napoli, 26–29 June 1954, *I congressi nazionali della DC*, p. 502.

33 G. Galli, *Fanfani*, Milano, 1975, p. 61. For Fanfani and the new party, see below pp. 167–8.

34 See G. Provasi, *Borghesia industriale e Democrazia Cristiana*, Bari, 1976, pp. 140–41 and 166–71; and G. Pirzio Ammassari, *La politica della Confindustria*, Napoli, 1976, pp. 71–4.

35 The exact degree of autonomy of the Bank of Italy has been the subject of heated debate. For an interesting exchange of opinions on this point see Carli, *Intervista sul capitalismo italiano*, pp. 39–45; see also G. Puccini, *L'autonomia della Banca d'Italia*, Milano, 1978.

36 G. Di Capua, *Come l'Italia aderì al Patto Atlantico*, Roma, 1969, pp. 97–100; for the whole debate see pp. 87–121. The most complete account of how Italy joined N A T O is to be found in R. Quartararo, *Italia e Stati Uniti. Gli anni difficili (1945–1952)*, Napoli, 1986, pp. 246–328.

37 Cited in Di Capua, *Come l'Italia aderì al Patto Atlantico*, pp. 148–9.

38 ibid., pp. 165–88. For the humours of the Catholic base, see G. Rumi, 'Opportunismo e profezia. Cultura cattolica e politica estera italiana, 1946–63', *Storia Contemporanea*, vol. XI (1981), nos. 4–5, pp. 813–19.

39 Cf. N. Kogan, *A Political History of Italy*, New York, 1983, pp. 119–20.

40 See the remarks of G. Toniolo, 'L'utilizzazione dei fondi E R P nella ricostruzione italiana: alcune ipotesi di lavoro', in E. Aga-Rossi, ed., *Il piano Marshall e l'Europa*, Roma, 1983, pp. 189–92. For an overall survey of E R P funds for Italy, Candeloro, *Storia dell'Italia moderna*, vol. XI, pp. 199–203.

41 D. Ellwood, 'Il piano Marshall e il processo di modernizzazione in Italia', in Aga-Rossi, ed., *Il piano Marshall*, p. 154. The principal sections of Hoffman's 'country study' are reprinted in L. Villari, ed., *Il capitalismo italiano del Novecento*, vol. II, Bari, 1975, pp. 616–43.

42 P. P. D'Attorre, 'Aspetti dell'attuazione del piano Marshall in Italia', in Aga-Rossi, ed., *Il piano Marshall*, pp. 163–80. D'Attorre charts how much the E R P programme contributed to the modernization of Italian industry, through the new machines and techniques it introduced, the exchange visits it arranged, the specialized knowledge it imparted. Journals like *Produttività* and *Metodi, Tecnica e Organizzazione* were full of technical information on American products as well as advice on relatively new areas like marketing.

43 M. R. Catti De Gasperi, *La nostra patria Europa*, Milano, 1969, p. 24. For De Gasperi's commitment to Europe, see G. Petrilli, *La politica estera ed europea di De Gasperi*, Roma, 1975, *passim*.

44 S. Pistone, ed., *L'Italia e l'unità europea*, Torino, 1982, p. 162, n. 36.

45 L. Cafagna, 'In tegrazione europea', in B. Bongiovanni, G. C. Jocteau and N. Tranfaglia, *Storia d'Europa*, vol. IV, Firenze, 1981, p. 1673. See also L. Graziano, *La politica estera italiana nel dopoguerra*, Padova, 1968, p. 142. For Spinelli's influence on De Gasperi, see Pistone, *L'Italia e l'unità europea*, pp. 175–7.

46 Cassese, *Il sistema amministrativo italiano*, pp. 63–84. For the survey of 1965, see

La burocrazia centrale in Italia. Analisi sociologica, Milano, 1965, pp. 283ff. For the journal *Burocrazia*, founded in 1946, see G. Melis, 'La cultura e il mondo degli impiegati', in S. Cassese, ed., *L'amministrazione centrale*, Torino, 1984, p. 397.

47 E. Gorrieri, *La giungla retributiva*, Bologna, 1972, *passim*. For the details of Fanfani's provisions of 1954, Cavarra and Sclavi, *I statali*, pp. 63ff. See also Clark, *Modern Italy*, pp. 338–9. The emphasis on sectionalism destroyed any possibilities of trade union solidarity within the civil service; in addition, many hundreds of CGIL activists in the civil service lost their jobs between 1948 and 1952; this latter date was marked by a wholesale purge in the Ministry of Defence (Cavarra and Sclavi, *I statali*, p. 60).

48 G. Pescatore, 'Dai complessi organici ai progetti speciali', *Notiziario IRFIS*, no. 29, April 1971; quoted in G. Gribaudi, *Mediatori*, Torino, 1980, p. 52.

49 M. Rossi-Doria, 'L'intervento straordinario dopo vent'anni', in his *Scritti sul Mezzogiorno*, Torino, 1982, p. 21.

50 Some idea of the extent of the Cassa's interventions can be gained by browsing through the six volumes of Centro Studi della Cassa per il Mezzogiorno, *Cassa per il Mezzogiorno. Dodici anni, 1950–1962*, Bari, 1976.

51 For a breakdown of the Cassa's spending in its first ten years, see S. Petriccione, *Politica industriale e Mezzogiorno*, Bari, 1976, tab. 1, p. 7.

52 G. Galli, *Storia della DC*, pp. 137–8. For the new political élite in the South, G. Gribaudi, *Mediatori*, pp. 26–7 and 78–80.

53 G. Bocca, *Storia della Repubblica italiana*, Milano, 1981–2, no. 24, p. 216. For biographical details on Mattei, D. Votaw, *The Six-Legged Dog*, Berkeley, 1964, pp. 9ff.

54 *Il Popolo*, 23 April 1950, quoted in G. Galli, *La sfida perduta*, Milano, 1976, p. 81.

55 Votaw, *The Six-Legged Dog*, p. 15.

56 G. Galli, *La sfida perduta*, pp. 83–4. Galli ascribes to Mattei (ibid., p. 250) the responsibility of having been the first person within the DC to use state funds systematically in this way.

57 This phrase is put into Mattei's mouth by Francesco Rosi in his film *Il caso Mattei* (1971).

58 For a detailed discussion of the circumstances surrounding Mattei's death see G. Galli, *La sfida perduta*, pp. 223–48. Galli points out that this was the period when the CIA was busy organizing assassination attempts against those judged to be America's enemies.

59 G. Gribaudi, *Mediatori*, p. 50. See also P. Spanò, 'Gli enti del settore creditizio. Aspetti economici e politici dello sviluppo del credito speciale all'industria nel secondo dopoguerra', in Cazzola, ed., *Anatomia del potere DC*, pp. 253–326; for the dominance of Christian Democrat presidents of these institutions, tab. 2, pp. 272–3. Zuckerman, *The Politics of Faction*, p. 85, gives a breakdown of party control of all credit institutions, though for the later period of 1969–71.

60 Ferraresi, *Burocrazia e politica*, pp. 261–2; see also F. Cavazzuti, 'La DC e il blocco dominante', in *Tutto il potere della DC*, p. 71.

61 M. Carabba, *Un ventennio di programmazione, 1954–74*, Bari, 1977, p. 4.

62 ibid., p. 6 and pp. 16–17; and G. Amato, ed., *Il governo dell'industria in Italia*, Bologna, 1972, p. 37.

63 Michele Salvati, *Economia e politica in Italia dal dopoguerra a oggi*, Milano, 1984, p. 56.

64 See, for instance, Cavarra and Sclavi, *Gli statali*, p. 54.

65 A. Moro, 'La DC per la donna nella famiglia e nella società', in Movimento Femminile della DC, *La famiglia e le trasformazioni della società italiana*, Roma, 1963, p. 69.

66 See the inquiry published in *Tempi Moderni*, Jan.–March 1961, quoted by G. Galli, *Storia della DC*, pp. 193–4. For the Palermo figures, see J. Chubb, *Patronage, Power and Poverty in Southern Italy*, Cambridge, 1982, p. 65.

67 A. Fanfani, *Relazione al consiglio nazionale della DC, 12–14 marzo 1955*, Roma, 1955, p. 22; cited in Istituto di Studi e Ricerche Carlo Cattaneo, *L'organizzazione politica del PCI e della DC*, p. 401.

68 C. Falconi, *La chiesa e le organizzazioni cattoliche in Italia (1945–1955)*, Torino, 1956, p. 335; for other details of parish life, see pp. 329–57. For figures of church attendance see Statistical Appendix, table 13.

69 Falconi, *La chiesa e le organizzazioni cattoliche*, pp. 399–408. For the birth and growth of Azione Cattolica, L. Ferrari, 'Il laicato cattolico fra Otto e Novecento; dalle associazioni devozionali alle organizzazioni militanti di massa', in *Storia d'Italia. Annali IX: la Chiesa e il potere politico dal Medioevo all'età contemporanea*, ed. G. Chittolini and G. Miccoli, Torino, 1986, pp. 931–74.

70 Istituto di Studi e Ricerche Carlo Cattaneo, *La presenza sociale del PCI e della DC*, Bologna, 1968, p. 352.

71 Falconi, *La chiesa e le organizzazioni cattoliche*, p. 407. There were 983 in central Italy and 514 in the South.

72 Istituto di Studi e Ricerche Carlo Cattaneo, *La presenza sociale*, pp. 516 and 518.

73 I. Bianco, *Il movimento cooperativo italiano*, Milano, 1975, pp. 24–5. The Catholic cooperative movement was not known for its political activism, and leading members of the DC did not hold posts in it. The CCI maintained very good relations with the *Confagricoltura*, the landowners' organization, so much so that ACLI preferred to organize its cooperatives independently; Istituto di Studi e Ricerche Carlo Cattaneo, *La presenza sociale*, pp. 102ff.

74 Falconi, *La chiesa e le organizzazioni cattoliche*, pp. 439–68.

75 Allum, *Politics and Society in Post-war Naples*, Appendix A, p. 346.

76 Pio XII, 'Esortazione del Sommo Pontefice all'episcopato d'Italia, 25 gennaio 1950', in *Discorsi e radiomessaggi di Sua Santità Pio XII*, vol. XI, Città del Vaticano, 1961, p. 408; quoted in S. Lanaro, 'Società civile, "mondo" cattolico e Democrazia Cristiana nel Veneto', in S. Lanaro and M. Isnenghi, eds., *La Democrazia Cristiana dal Fascismo al 18 aprile*, Venezia, 1978, p. 12.

77 ibid., p. 17.

78   Ciranna, 'Un gruppo di pressione; la Confederazione Nazionale Coltivatori Diretti', p. 28.

79   ibid., p. 29.

80   ibid., p. 35.

81   ibid., p. 34. Both the above quotations are taken from Bonomi's speeches to the annual congresses of the Coldiretti in 1956 and 1957.

82   *Il libro del militante aclista*, Roma, n.d. (4th ed.), p. 248; quoted in Istituto di Studi e Ricerche Carlo Cattaneo, *La presenza sociale*, p. 465.

83   ibid., p. 467 and pp. 471–2 for the calendar of a typical ACLI circle. For a detailed account of the development of the organization, M. C. Sermanni, *Le ACLI: dal ruolo formativo all'impegno politico sindacale (1944–1961)*, Napoli, 1978.

84   For Fanfani's bill, see Foa, *Sindacati e lotte operaie*, pp. 83–4.

85   ibid., p. 81; and V. Foa, 'Sindacato e corporazione' in his *La cultura della CGIL*, Torino, 1984, p. xi. For the history and development of the organization, G. Baglioni, *Il sindacato dell'autonomia*, Bari, 1977.

86   E. Colombo, 'La famiglia a Montecitorio', in L. Gedda, ed., *Spiritualità della famiglia*, Milano, 1952, p. 136.

87   M. Marazziti, 'Cultura di massa e valori cattolici: il modello di "Famiglia Cristiana"', in A. Riccardi, ed., *Pio XII*, Bari, 1984, p. 310.

88   See the entry 'Famiglia' in *Enciclopedia cattolica*, vol. V, Roma, 1950, p. 994.

89   T. Goffi, *Morale familiare*, Brescia, 9th ed., 1962, p. 264.

90   Quoted in ibid., p. 265.

91   *Enciclopedia cattolica*, vol. V, pp. 994–5.

92   Goffi, *Morale familiare*, p. 266.

93   The young Franca Falcucci admitted that 'our conception of the family, as we have tried to outline it, has been accused of a tendency towards isolation, or rather as being counterposed to the wider horizons that open up to humanity beyond the family'. She vigorously denied that this was the case: 'We are not for a family that is "devoutly" closed, but for a family that is "devoutly" open'; F. Falcucci, 'La famiglia, società naturale fondata sul matrimonio', in Movimento Femminile della DC, *La famiglia e le trasformazioni*, pp. 24–5.

94   E. Ruffini, 'La teologia di fronte alle problematiche della famiglia nella tensione tra "pubblico" e "privato"', in Università Cattolica del Sacro Cuore, *La coscienza contemporanea tra 'pubblico' e 'privato'*, Milano, 1979, pp. 144–5, 149, 154–5, 158.

95   For the introduction of the term 'integralismo' into Italy and its variegated uses, see Baget-Bozzo, *Il partito cristiano al potere*, vol. II, p. 359, n. 6.

96   See above, p. 77.

97   Unione Donne di Azione Cattolica Italiana, *Matrimonio e famiglia. Nozioni e informazioni culturali per propagandiste e delegate di Azione Familiare*, Roma, 1958, p. 120.

98 Goffi, *Morale familiare*, p. 286.

99 While there is no full-length study of the Christian Democrats in the Veneto, the southern cities have been the object of a number of major works: Allum, *Politics and Society in Post-war Naples*; M. Caciagli *et al.*, *Democrazia Cristiana e potere nel Mezzogiorno*, Firenze, 1977 (Catania); L. Graziano, *Clientelismo e sistema politico. Il caso dell'Italia*, Milano, 1979 (Salerno); Chubb, *Patronage, Power and Poverty* (Palermo).

100 For Marghera in the period 1945–55, C. Chinello, *Classe, movimento, organizzazione*, Milano, 1984; for the last great strike of the *braccianti* in May–June, 1954, ibid., pp. 447–60.

101 P. Allum, 'La DC Vicentina nel secondo dopoguerra: appunti per una ricostruzione', *Strumenti*, vol. III (1984), nos. 3–4, p. 21; Lanaro, 'Società civile, "mondo cattolico" e Democrazia Cristiana nel Veneto', in Lanaro and Isnenghi, eds., *La Democrazia Cristiana*, p. 48.

102 *La Voce dei Berici*, 4 May 1958, quoted in Allum, 'La DC Vicentina nel secondo dopoguerra', p. 23.

103 M. Isnenghi, 'Alle origini del 18 aprile. Miti, riti, mass media', in Lanaro and Isnenghi, eds., *La Democrazia Cristiana*, p. 283.

104 I owe these details to a conversation with Piero Brunello, who remembers the arrival of the *Madonna pellegrina* in his street in San Polo di Piave. See also C. Ginzburg, 'Folklore, magia, religione', in *Storia d'Italia*, vol. I, Torino, 1972, p. 672.

105 A. Cittante, *Memorie di un sindacalista rurale*, Rovigo, 1973, p. 228.

106 A. Bagnasco and C. Trigilia, eds., *Società e politica nelle aree di piccola impresa: il caso di Bassano*, Venezia, 1984, tab. 3.17, p. 113. In the province of Vicenza at the same date the DC had only 18,000 members; ibid., tab. 3.14, p. 110.

107 For Palermo and Gioia, Chubb, *Patronage, Power and Poverty*, p. 63. These new leaders did not have any pre-existing resources at their disposal, unlike the old notables, and state clientelism was therefore essential to their survival; see Caciagli *et al.*, *Democrazia Cristiana e potere nel Mezzogiorno*, p. 93. In Naples in the 1950s the monarchist Achille Lauro ruled supreme.

108 See the detailed breakdown in ibid., pp. 273–92.

109 Allum, *Politics and Society in Post-war Naples*, p. 37.

110 Caciagli *et al.*, *Democrazia Cristiana e potere nel Mezzogiorno*, p. 273.

111 ibid., p. 326. For further details on the hospital, pp. 323–31.

112 On jobs in local industry, Allum, *Politics and Society in Post-war Naples*, p. 167; on the ISTICA scandal at Catania, Caciagli *et al.*, *Democrazia Cristiana e potere nel Mezzogiorno*, pp. 76ff.

113 *Italia sotto inchiesta. Corriere della Sera, 1963–1965*, Firenze, 1965, p. 708.

114. Allum, *Politics and Society in Post-war Naples*, pp. 170ff. For variations at Catania, Caciagli *et al.*, *Democrazia Cristiana e potere nel Mezzogiorno*, pp. 151–8.

115 Allum, *Politics and Society in Post-war Naples*, p. 165.

116 ibid., p. 162.

117 See *Il Vittorioso*, vol. XV (1951), no. 12 and *Il Pioniere*, vol. II (1951), no. 13. However, it should be noted that *Il Vittorioso* in this period was surprisingly free of Catholic moralizing and was certainly less ideological than its Communist counterpart.

118 *Noi Uomini*, 17 March 1952, quoted in Falconi, *Gedda e l'Azione Cattolica*, p. 302.

119 See above, p. 488, n. 25.

120 A. Pizzorno, 'I ceti medi nel meccanismo del consenso', in his *I soggetti del pluralismo*, Bologna, 1980, p. 82.

121 See M. C. Belloni *et al.*, 'I commercianti e la mobilitazione politica', in C. Carboni, ed., *I ceti medi in Italia*, Bari, 1981, pp. 247–9; and G. Vicarelli, 'Famiglia e sviluppo economico nell'Italia centro-settentrionale', in U. Ascoli and R. Catanzaro, eds., *La società italiana degli anni Ottanta*, Bari, 1987, pp. 137–8.

122 P. Allum and I. Diamanti, '*50–'80. Vent'anni*, Roma, 1986, p. 160; see also the whole section, pp. 143–66.

Chapter 6

1 For an overview of these years, G. Rasi, 'La politica economica e i conti della nazione', *Annali dell'economia italiana*, vol. XI (1953–8), Milano, 1982, pt 1, pp. 63–177.

2 A. Gibelli, 'I grandi costruttori', in A. Micheli, *Ansaldo 1950*, Torino, 1981, p. xii. Some areas of Italian industry, like textiles, practised what became known at the time as '*supersfruttamento*' (hyper-exploitation). Teresa Noce, secretary of the textile section of the CGIL, reported in 1951 that while there had been very little investment in new machinery, three workers were now being asked to do the work of eight, that the working day often amounted, with overtime, to twelve to fifteen hours and that the incidence of child labour (under fourteen years of age) had dramatically increased. The effect of these conditions on workers' health was very marked; *Notiziario CGIL*, Roma, 1951, pp. 200–211, quoted in Foa, *Sindacati e lotte operaie*, p. 95.

3 Paci, *Mercato del lavoro e classi sociali in Italia*, pp. 296–7 and 322ff. For the growth of small firms in the 1950s see the comments of L. Ganapini and P. Rugafiori, 'Per una rilettura degli anni '50', *Movimento Operaio e Socialista*, vol. VII (1984), no. 2, pp. 163–70.

4 L. Casali and D. Gagliani, 'Movimento operaio e organizzazione di massa. Il PCI in Emilia-Romagna (1945–1954)', in P. P. D'Attore, ed., *La ricostruzione in Emilia-Romagna*, Parma, 1980, p. 265.

5 *Atti della Commissione parlamentare di inchiesta sulla miseria e sui mezzi per combatterla*, 15 vols., Milano–Roma, 1953–8. For a useful selection of extracts see P. Braghin, ed., *Inchiesta sulla miseria in Italia*, Torino, 1978.

6 *Atti della Commissione parlamentare . . . sulla miseria*, vol. VI, pp. 80–85. See also the descriptions in P. P. Pasolini, *A Violent Life*, London, 1968. It is worth mentioning that the Fascist regime had exacerbated the housing problem by destroying a number of popular quarters in the centre so as to construct a 'truly imperial' city.

7 *Atti della Commissione parlamentare . . . sulla miseria*, vol. VI, p. 82.

8 *L'Unità*, Milan edition, 8 Feb. 1950, quoted by P. Santi, 'Il piano del lavoro nella politica della CGIL: 1949–1952', in F. Vianello, ed., *Il piano del lavoro della CGIL, 1949–1950*, Milano, 1978, p. 24. For Di Vittorio's announcement of the plan, *I congressi della CGIL*, vol. III, Roma, 1952, pp. 54–9.

9 One of the favourite tactics was the work-in, or the 'strike in reverse', which was used to such effect in the occupation of the Fucino basin (see p. 128). In dozens of villages in the Veneto and Emilia, as well as in Sardinia and Calabria, labourers began to build dykes and canals, and to reclaim land; Santi, 'Il piano del lavoro', pp. 37–8. Probably the most successful struggle connected with the plan took place in the Val Vomano, in the Abruzzi. There the local Camera di Lavoro under the leadership of Tom Di Paolantonio organized two thousand unemployed to begin work again on the construction of a power station and reservoir which had been abandoned for six years. After direct negotiations between the CGIL and the government, 100 million lire were assigned to the project, and the power station and reservoir were completed in three years; see the contribution of T. Di Paolantonio, in Vianello, ed., *Il piano del lavoro*, pp. 159–64.

10 V. Foa, 'Intervento', in Vianello, ed., *Il piano del lavoro*, p. 177. For the remarks of De Gasperi and Costa, see respectively, B. Manzocchi, *Lineamenti di politica economica in Italia (1945–1949)*, Roma 1960, p. 75; and *Annuario CGIL 1950*, p. 227, speech of 6 Dec. 1949; both cited in Santi, 'Il piano del lavoro', p. 16.

11 Foa, 'Intervento', p. 178.

12 G, Fabiani, 'Il piano del lavoro e le lotte per la riforma', in Vianello, ed., *Il piano del lavoro*, pp. 117ff.

13 Cited by R. Amaduzzi, 'Intervento', in Vianello, ed., *Il piano del lavoro*, p. 151.

14 Gibelli, 'I grandi costruttori', pp. xxxiv-xxxv.

15 Santi, 'Il piano del lavoro', p. 39.

16 A. Accornero, *Gli anni '50 in fabbrica*, Bari, 1976, pp. 66ff.; C. Daneo, *La politica economica della ricostruzione*, pp. 320–21; Santi, 'Il piano del lavoro', pp. 43–4, with the figures for FIAT and Olivetti.

17 Gibelli, 'I grandi costruttori', p. xlviii. See also G. Contini, *Memoria e storia: le officine Galileo nel racconto degli operai, dei tecnici, dei manager, 1944–1959*, Milano, 1985, pp. 58–9.

18 A. Accornero and V. Rieser, *Il mestiere dell' avanguardia*, Bari, 1981, p. 21. Note also Rieser's warning (ibid. p. 8) against accepting certain commonplaces about this period, such as that the CISL and UIL were nothing but bosses' unions, and that the CGIL was super-centralized and nothing more than a transmission belt for the politics of the PCI.

19 G. Della Rocca, 'L'offensiva politica degli imprenditori nelle fabbriche', in *Annali dell'Istituto G. G. Feltrinelli*, vol. XVI (1974–75), pp. 620–21 and 626.

20 G. G. Migone, 'Stati Uniti, FIAT e repressione antioperaia negli anni Cinquanta', *Rivista di Storia Contemporanea*, no. 2 (1974), p. 258.

21 ibid., pp. 263–5. See also E. Pugno and S. Garavini, *Gli anni duri della FIAT*, Torino, 1975, *passim*.

22 Foa, *Sindacato e lotte operaie*, p. 80, and his article 'La svolta del 1955' (first published 1955), in his *La cultura della CGIL*, pp. 16–20.

23 Foa, *Sindacato e lotte operaie*, pp. 113ff.

24 For Cattani, see 'Il PSI negli anni del frontismo', *Mondoperaio*, vol. XXX (1977), nos. 7–8 (1977), pp. 63–5. Pasquale Amato has noted how the Institute for Socialist Studies closed in 1950, how few young people joined the party in these years and how dogma reigned supreme. Much of the responsibility for this state of affairs must be ascribed to Rodolfo Morandi and his insistence on 'Frontism' at all costs; P. Amato, *Il PSI tra frontismo e autonomia*, Cosenza, 1978, pp. 160–62.

25 *L'Unità*, Milan ed., 20 Jan. 1951, quoted in N. Ajello, *Intellettuali e PCI, 1944–58*, Bari, 1979, p. 286.

26 N. Bobbio, 'Pace e propaganda di pace' (1952), in his *Politica e cultura*, Torino, 1955, p. 79.

27 See V. Foa, 'I socialisti italiani', in his *Per una storia del movimento operaio*, Torino, 1980, p. 279.

28 For the speeches of Nenni, Basso and Lombardi at the thirty-first congress of the PSI, see *Il socialismo italiano di questo dopoguerra*, Milano, 1968, pp. 404, 409–10, 421, quoted in G. Galli, *Storia del socialismo italiano*, Bari, 1980, pp. 217–18.

29 P. Ingrao, 'Il XX congresso del PCUS e l'VIII congresso del PCI', in *Problemi di storia del PCI*, Roma, 1971, p. 136.

30 G. Baldi, *Vita e lotte delle case del popolo in provincia di Firenze, 1944–1956*, Firenze, 1956, pp. 15–19.

31 ibid., pp. 34ff.

32 For some notes on the early history of the *feste*, see C. Bernieri, *L'albero in piazza*, Milano, 1977, pp. 7–36. For the celebration in Rome in September 1948, see the notable PCI documentary film, *È tornato Togliatti*.

33 See the section on these organizations in Istituto di Studi e Ricerche Carlo Cattaneo, *La presenza sociale del PCI e della DC*, pp. 177–329.

34 'Inauguriamo l'anno sociale del nostro circolo', *La Voce della Donna*, no. 16–17, 1 Dec. 1954, republished in M. Michetti *et al.*, *UDI: laboratorio di politica delle donne*, Roma, 1984, pp. 145–53; the quotation is on p. 147.

35 *Famiglia e società nell'analisi marxista*, *Critica Marxista*, Quaderno no. 1, published as a supplement to no. 6, 1964. There seemed little agreement on basic themes.

Emilio Sereni polemicized with Umberto Cerroni and others for suggesting that the family might disappear under Communism. On the contrary, said Sereni, 'a new, superior and fully humanized type of family (and one that is of productive relations in as much as they are the basis of a particular social grouping) will necessarily exist also in the Communist society for which we are struggling'; ibid., pp. 164–5.

36   U D I, *Donna, vota per la dignità della tua vita, per il benessere della tua famiglia, per la pace*, Roma, 1953, p. 3.

37   *Famiglia e società nell'analisi marxista*, 'Intervento' of R. Rossanda, p. 212.

38   L. Ganapini, ed., '. . . *Che tempi, però erano bei tempi . . .*', Milano, 1986, p. 179.

39   In 1953 A. Valli of the P CI central committee warned the party's cadres that because they were always out of the home engaged in political activities, there was a real danger that their wives, listening to well-meaning neighbours and the parish priest, would vote for the Christian Democrats. What was the solution to this problem? Not, according to Valli, that the militant should spend less time on politics and more on family life, but rather than he should spend more time on political propaganda in the home. In this way the wives of Communists would vote Communist and 'of each of our families we will make a firm and secure nucleus of struggle for democracy and socialism'; A. Valli, 'Per chi voterà tua moglie?', article of 16 April 1953, in Flores, ed., *Il 'Quaderno dell'Attivista'*, pp. 153–6.

40   L. Lombardo Radice, 'La battaglia delle idee', *Rinascita*, vol. V (1948), no. 3, p. 326.

41   P. Togliatti, 'Sviluppo e trionfo del marxismo', *Rinascita*, vol. VI (1949), no. 12, p. 517.

42   A. Natoli, 'Improvvisamente ci sentimmo tutti orfanelli', *La Repubblica*, 5–6 March 1978.

43   Cited in Ajello, *Intellettuali e PCI*, p. 303.

44   L. Longo, 'Costruendo il socialismo si son fatti degli errori, ma la vostra non è democrazia', *Rinascita*, Vol. XIII (1956), no. 3, p. 136.

45   Testimony of Ignazio Silone in Bocca, *Togliatti*, p. 586.

46   P. Togliatti, 'Discorso agli operai di Belgrado' (1964), *Rinascita*, vol. XXVII (1970), no. 34, p. 32; cited in Bocca, *Togliatti*, p. 598.

47   Dolci, *Inchiesta a Palermo*, p. 143.

48   'Nel 1951 il Kremlino voleva sostituire Togliatti e la direzione del P CI approvò', *L'Espresso*, vol. XIV (1970) no. 13.

49   E. Collotti, 'Introduzione all'archivio Pietro Secchia, 1945–1973', *Annali della Fondazione G. G. Feltrinelli*, vol. XIX (1978), pp. 7–135; see also M. Mafai, *L'uomo che sognava la lotta armata*, Milano, 1984, pp. 109–47.

50   P. Togliatti, 'Ceto medio e Emilia rossa', in his *Opere scelte*, p. 466.

51   A. Colombi, 'I comunisti emiliani al lavoro', in P. P. D'Attorre, ed., *I comunisti in Emilia-Romagna*, Bologna, 1981, p. 55.

52 V. Ferretti, 'Cooperazione e partito comunista a Reggio Emilia', in D'Attorre, ed., *La ricostruzione in Emilia-Romagna*, pp. 195–210; and S. Nardi, 'Il movimento cooperativo emiliano nel secondo dopoguerra', in ibid., pp. 173–94. For a general survey of the Italian cooperative movement, I. Bianco, *Il movimento cooperativo italiano*, Milano, 1975.

53 For a lively denunciation of Communist activities in the cooperatives, see the report on Emilia-Romagna by I. Montanelli, in *Italia sotto inchiesta*, esp. pp. 381–6 and 401–6. On p. 384 he describes the Communists as the 'mice in the cheese' of cooperation. The left's views on cooperatives in the 1950s are discussed by G. Sapelli, 'La cooperazione come impresa: mercati economici e mercato politico', in G. Bonfante *et al.*, *Il movimento cooperativo in Italia*, Torino, 1981, pp. 268–71. For the maintenance of rural alliances in the dairy cooperatives of Reggio Emilia, see Ferretti, 'Cooperazione e partito comunista a Reggio Emilia', pp. 206–7. A useful introduction in English to the history of the National League of Cooperatives is J. Earle, *The Italian Cooperative Movement*, London, 1986.

54 P. P. D'Attorre, 'I comunisti in Emilia-Romagna nel secondo dopoguerra: un'ipotesi di lettura', in *I comunisti in Emilia-Romagna*, pp. 15–16. On women and the Emilian party, Casali and Gagliani, 'Movimento operaio e organizzazione di massa', pp. 272–3. At Bologna the percentage of housewives in the party increased from 10.7 to 16.8 between 1948 and 1954.

55 In Modena for example, in the early 1950s, G. D'Alema was sent to steer the Modena federation on to the correct lines, but he was far from successful; see Amyot, *The Italian Communist Party*, pp. 134–7. For the history of the Modena federation from 1943 to 1954, D. Travis, 'Communism in Modena: the Development of the PCI in Historical Context (1943–1952)', unpublished PhD thesis, University of Cambridge, 1984.

56 R. Nicolai, 'Realizzazioni dell'amministrazione democratica della città di Bologna', *Rinascita*, vol. XIII (1956), no. 3, pp. 150–54. See also V. Tarozzi, 'Le lavanderie meccaniche, nuovo servizio sociale', in *Comunisti. I militanti bolognesi del PCI raccontano*, Roma, 1983, pp. 262–7; and L. Arbizzani, 'Nuova amministrazione senza riforme', in Comune di Bologna, *Giuseppe Dozza a dieci anni dalla morte*, Bologna, 1985, pp. 55ff.

57 Democrazia Cristiana, *Libro bianco su Bologna*, Bologna 1956; A. Borselli, 'Come sorsero i quartieri', in Comune di Bologna, *Giuseppe Dozza a dieci anni dalla morte*, p. 91. For the Dozza–Dossetti contest, see the comments of P. P. D'Attorre, 'La politica', in R. Zangheri, ed., *Bologna*, Bari, 1985, p. 174; also N. Matteucci, 'Dossetti a Bologna', *Il Mulino*, vol. V (1956), no. 56, pp. 382–90. For the 'free commune' of Bologna, F. Piro, *Comunisti al potere*, Bologna, 1983, p. 139.

58 P. Togliatti, 'Intervista', in *Nuovi Argomenti*, no. 20 (May–June 1956), reprinted in his *Opere scelte*, pp. 702–28. The quotation is on p. 727.

59 Quoted in Sassoon, *Togliatti e la via italiana*, p. 184.

60 Togliatti, 'Intervista', in *Nuovi Argomenti*, pp. 705–6 for the USSR, p. 709 for China.

61 E. Vallini, *Operai del Nord*, Bari, 1957, pp. 114–15.

62 From *L'Unità*, 1–2 July 1956, cited in Ajello, *Intellettuali e PCI*, pp. 389–90.

63 Testimony of Davide Lajolo in ibid., p. 402.

64 See the speeches of Giuseppe Prestipino and Valerio Bertini in *Partito Comunista Italiano, VIII Congresso. Atti e risoluzioni*, Roma, 1957, pp. 93–101 and 131–6. Bertini said (p. 132): 'Comrades, there [in the Eastern bloc] the hens used to lay more eggs and the cows had more calves; such was the climate of paradise that was depicted for those countries. And if there was an obstacle by the name of Raik [*sic*], Raik was eliminated, and everything went back to how it was before, to the best of all possible worlds ... only now does *L'Unità* discover that [in Hungary] the salaries of the police and the state officials were too high, that the "red Saturdays" and compulsory Russian in the schools were a mistake, that the party leaders toured the cities in extra-luxurious cars with the blinds drawn down.' Bertini was a worker in the Officine Galileo in Florence; for the reactions of Italian workers to the events of 1956, G. Contini, 'Gli operai comunisti e la svolta del 1956', *Annali della Fondazione Giacomo Brodolini*, vol. I (1987), pp. 433–53.

65 *Partito Comunista Italiano, VIII° Congresso*, pp. 229–34.

66 L. Longo, *Revisionismo nuovo e antico*, Torino, 1957, p. 39.

67 G. Galli, *Storia del socialismo italiano*, p. 221.

Chapter 7

1 M. Cacioppo, 'Condizione di vita familiare negli anni Cinquanta', *Memoria*, no. 6 (1982), p. 88.

2 C. Daneo, *Breve storia dell'agricoltura italiana*, Milano, 1980, p. 179. The amount of land owned in plots between half a hectare and ten hectares increased in the period 1947–55 from 8,116,100 hectares to 8,891,600. The decline of share-cropping has been as yet little studied; see the observations of M. Paci, *La struttura sociale italiana*, Bologna, 1982, pp. 114–15: see also, for the province of Volterra, E. Bianchi, *Il tramonto della mezzadria toscana e i suoi riflessi geografici*, Milano, 1983. For the comparison of Italian agriculture with that of Yugoslavia and Greece, V. Castronovo, 'La storia economica', *Storia d'Italia*, vol. IV, Torino, 1975, p. 442.

3 *Minifundia* of between half a hectare and two hectares, often incapable of supporting a peasant family, covered some four million hectares by 1961, nearly 20 per cent of land under cultivation; see G. Medici, U. Sorbi, and A. Castrataro, *Polverizzazione e frammentazione della proprietà fondiaria in Italia*, Milano, 1962, p. 20.

4 F. Piselli, *Parentela ed emigrazione*, Torino, 1981, p. 85. For emigration overseas, U. Ascoli, *Movimenti migratori in Italia*, Bologna, 1979, pp. 36ff. and p. 43, tab. 1.7.

5   U. Ascoli, *Movimenti migratori*, p. 47, tab. 1.8.

6   Banfield, *The Moral Basis of a Backward Society*, pp. 52ff.; Italian translation, *Le basi morali di una società arretrata*, ed. D. De Masi, Bologna, 1976, pp. 75ff. This Italian edition is strongly recommended as it contains an excellent selection of articles from the debate that Banfield's book aroused (pp. 207–330), as well as an extensive bibliography. See also D. S. Pitkin's admirable *The House that Giacomo Built*, Cambridge, 1985, pp. 80–123.

7   Michele Salvati, *Economia e politica*, pp. 32–3.

8   For FIAT's strategy in these years, see Bairati, *Valletta*, pp. 254ff. and pp. 269ff. For developments in the chemical and petrochemical industry, E. Scalfari, *Rapporto sul neo-capitalismo in Italia*, Bari, 1961, pp. 17–30.

9   P. Rugafiori, 'I gruppi dirigenti della siderurgia "pubblica" tra gli anni Trenta e gli anni Sessanta', in F. Bonelli, ed., *Acciaio per l'industrializzazione*, Torino, 1982, pp. 358–66; Scalfari, *Rapporto sul neo-capitalismo*, pp. 59–68.

10 Graziani, ed., *L'economia italiana*, pp. 42–3; for fiscal and lending policies, G. Ackley, 'Lo sviluppo economico dal 1951 al 1961', in ibid., pp. 191–2; for 'external economies', Castronovo, 'La storia economica', p. 427.

11 Scalfari, *Rapporto sul neo-capitalismo*, p. 101.

12 For a good discussion in English of the relationship between exports and other factors contributing to Italian growth in this period, see D. Sassoon, *Contemporary Italy*, London, 1986, pp. 31ff.; see also Michele Salvati, *Economia e politica*, pp. 57ff. For growth rates, Statistical Appendix, table 31.

13 K. Kaiser, 'Le relazioni transnazionali', in F. L. Cavazza and S. R. Graubard, eds., *Il caso italiano*, Milano, 1974, tab. 1, p. 406 for a breakdown of the direction of Italy's exports from 1955 to 1970. Other statistics are taken from Michele Salvati, *Economia e politica*, pp. 60–61. However, it should be noted that income from tourism and emigrant savings continued to increase as well: the first from 6.6 per cent of national income in 1953 to 11.7 per cent in 1961, the second from 5.7 to 7.4 per cent; P. Saraceno, *L'Italia verso la piena occupazione*, Milano, 1963, p. 142.

14 P. Santi, 'Un esempio dello sviluppo capitalistico in Italia: il settore degli elettrodomestici', *Problemi del Socialismo*, vol. X (1968), no. 31, pp. 710–35. In 1951 FIAT manufactured 70 per cent of Italian fridges, but then chose to concentrate on automobile construction, leaving market space for new firms. By the mid-1960s the six major companies in the field were Zanussi, Ignis, Indesit, Zoppas, Castor and Candy (the last two specializing in washing-machines).

15 ibid., pp. 714–22 and 726–31 (pp. 730–31 for Zanussi at Pordenone).

16 Castronovo, 'La storia economica', p. 430.

17 For Adriano Olivetti and his model factory at Ivrea, see G. Berta, *Le idee al potere*, Milano, 1980, and D. Ronci, *Olivetti, anni 50*, Milano, 1980.

18 See Statistical Appendix, table 39.

19 Graziani, ed., *L'economia italiana*, pp. 45–9. Pasquale Saraceno has commented:

'The formation of social capital and in general the political economy of public spending has in great part followed the process of development rather than being one of its determinants. This has meant that the structure of public spending has come to reflect a process of development which has to a great extent acted autonomously; public intervention has not oriented it towards reducing existing imbalances' (Saraceno, *L'Italia verso la piena occupazione*, p. 153). In similar terms Predieri has referred to 'macroeconomic freedoms allowed to private firms, which were aided but not directed' (Predieri, 'Parlamento 1975', p. 35).

20 The classic study of dualism is that by V. Lutz, *Italy: a Study in Economic Development*, Oxford, 1962. For an excellent introduction to the problem, Graziani, ed., *L'economia italiana*, pp. 35–41.

21 A. Antonuzzo, *Boschi, miniera, catena di montaggio*, Roma, 1976, p. 42.

22 ibid., p. 47.

23 ibid., p. 52.

24 ibid., pp. 150–51.

25 ibid., p. 158.

26 ibid., p. 157.

27 U. Ascoli, *Movimenti migratori*, p. 111. See also Treves, *Le migrazioni interne*, pp. 77–8.

28 See Statistical Appendix, tables 14, 15, 18 and 19.

29 A. Corsi, 'L'esodo agricolo dagli anni '50 agli anni '70 in Italia e nel Mezzogiorno', *Rassegna Economica*, vol. XLI (1977), no. 3, p. 723.

30 Paci, *Mercato del lavoro e classi sociali*, p. 110.

31 Corsi, 'L'esodo agricolo', tab. 5, p. 737.

32 The number of registered labourers in the South increased in the period 1957–63, with women and children taking the place of the men who had left, which did not happen in the North; ibid., p. 732.

33 U. Ascoli, *Movimenti migratori*, pp. 53–4. In the period 1958–63 emigration overseas diminished considerably; net emigration (the number of those emigrating less the number of those returning) amounted overall to 246,000 persons, but the latter part of the period (1961–3) witnessed a dramatic decline; ibid., tab. 1.9, p. 48.

34 ibid., pp. 117ff. In 1978 the 'Centro di specializzazione e ricerche economico-agrarie per il Mezzogiorno' of the University of Naples at Portici carried out a survey, commune by commune, of emigration from the South. It did so on the basis of persons actually present rather than on that of residence, which it found to be frequently deceptive. The survey found that between 1951 and 1971 4,200,000 persons had emigrated from the South, out of a total population at that time of some eighteen million; M. Rossi-Doria, *Scritti sul Mezzogiorno*, p. 11, note.

35 L. Meneghetti, *Aspetti di geografia della popolazione. Italia 1951–67*, Milano, 1971, tab. 51, p. 190, for Rome; tab. 48, p. 178, for Milan; tab. 47, p. 174, for Turin.

36 Castronovo, 'La storia economica', p. 443.

37 Corsi, 'L'esodo agricolo', pp. 747–8. For details of the increase in the number of tractors, R. Stefanelli, 'Il mercato del lavoro nell'agricoltura italiana, 1948–1968: strutture e politiche dell'occupazione', in *I braccianti. 20 anni di lotte*, Roma, 1969, p. 127. For 'tractor mania', N. Revelli, *Il mondo dei vinti*, Torino, 1977, pp. xxii–xxiii. For the end of the *imponibile*, U. Ascoli, *Movimenti migratori*, p. 76, n. 60.

38 D. L. Norcia, *Io garantito*, Roma, 1980, p. 36.

39 G. Russo, *Chi ha più santi in paradiso*, Bari, 1965, pp. 123ff.; and G. Fofi, *L'immigrazione meridionale a Torino*, Milano, 1964, p. 78. For the attractions of urban life for the peasantry, see the comments of Sirio Lombardini in 1967: 'the peasant wants security with regard to income, to prospects of employment, to hours of work. These are the peasantry's traditional aspirations, and they become all the more relevant as the number of employment alternatives increase'; 'Intervento', in Fondazione L. Einaudi, *Nord e Sud nella società e nell'economia di oggi*, p. 473.

40 Fofi, *L'immigrazione meridionale*, pp. 99–104.

41 ibid., p. 106.

42 ibid., pp. 102–4.

43 ibid., pp. 249.

44 Paci, *Mercato del lavoro e classi sociali*, pp. 89 and 92–3.

45 F. Alasia and D. Montaldi, *Milano, Corea*, Milano, 1975 (1st ed., 1960), p. 14. For building workers, Paci, *Mercato del lavoro e classi sociali*, pp. 17 and 46; Fofi, *L'immigrazione meridionale*, pp. 119–20, 135–6, 166.

46 Fofi, *L'immigrazione meridionale*, pp. 121ff.

47 Testimony in Alasia and Montaldi, *Milano, Corea*, pp. 364–5.

48 Fofi, *L'immigrazione meridionale*, p. 142.

49 ibid., pp. 140 and 165.

50 C. Canteri, *Immigrati a Torino*, Milano, 1964, p. 64.

51 Alasia and Montaldi, *Milano, Corea*, p. 130; see also A. Baglivo and G. Pellicciari, *La tratta dei meridionali*, Milano, 1973, pp. 169–77.

52 Fofi, *L'immigrazione meridionale*, pp. 178ff. More generally for the Industrial Triangle, G. Albertelli and G. Ziliani, 'Le condizioni alloggiative della popolazione immigrata', in G. Pellicciari, ed., *L'immigrazione nel triangolo industriale*, Milano, 1970, pp. 283–303.

53 Interview in Alasia and Montaldi, *Milano, Corea*, pp. 183–4.

54 ibid., pp. 60 and 78.

55 Fofi, *L'immigrazione meridionale*, p. 231. See also his very interesting section on education and integration (pp. 207ff.), based on interviews in forty schools in Turin. As for hospitals, G. Tamburrano, *Storia e cronaca del centro-sinistra*, Milano, 1971, p. 87, gives the following national statistics: whereas in 1933 there were 2,090 hospitals and health-care institutions, by 1960 their numbers had only increased by 317. In the same period the number of days spent per year by patients in hospitals had nearly doubled, from 65,500,000 to 127,700,000.

56 For figures on consumer durables, see below, p. 239.

57 Russo, *Chi ha più santi*, p. 132.

58 ibid., p. 136. See also Piselli, *Parentela ed emigrazione*, p. 332.

59 Russo, *Chi ha più santi*, pp. 125–6.

60 ibid., p. 128.

61 A. Riboldi, *I miei 18 anni nel Belice*, Assisi, 1977, pp. 27–8. See also the letter from an Italian emigrant in Switzerland in *Mondo Nuovo*, vol. IV (1962), no. 1, 14 January, p. 2.

62 P. Saraceno, *L'Italia verso la piena occupazione*, p. 193.

63 P. Saraceno, 'Il vero e il falso sugli aiuti al Sud', *Corriere della Sera*, 14 July 1974. In this article Saraceno examines the distribution of spending between the various sectors of the Cassa's activity in the years between 1951 and 1973.

64 For some remarks on the technocratic vision of development in the South and the forces behind the law of 1957, G. Gribaudi, *Mediatori*, pp. 104–8 and 130; see also Castronovo, 'La storia economica', p. 428. For Emilio Colombo at Potenza, L. Sacco, *Il cemento del potere*, Bari, 1982.

65 E. Scalfari and G. Turani, *Razza padrona*, Milano, 1974, p. 372. They point out that it was very easy for firms to find funds for the remaining 10 per cent of their 'risk capital' either from some other state fund or by 'over-estimating' their needs. In this way 'more than one petrochemical plant has been financed to the tune of 115–120 per cent'. See also G. Addario, *Una crisi del sistema*, Bari, 1982, p. 52.

66 Russo, *Chi ha più santi*, pp. 126–7.

67 ibid., pp. 111–12. For Gela, E. Hytten and M. Marchioni, *Industrializzazione senza sviluppo*, Milano, 1970. For Nino Rovelli's activities in Sardinia, where his company came to dominate the island, Scalfari and Turani, *Razza padrona*, pp. 325ff.; M. Lelli, *Proletariato e ceti medi in Sardegna*, Bari, 1975.

68 For an overall view of the 'development zones', Castronovo, 'La storia economica', pp. 447ff. For the depopulated villages, especially of the mountain areas, A. Baglivo and G. Pellicciari, *Sud amaro: esodo come sopravvivenza*, Milano, 1970, pp. 15–37.

69 Chubb, *Patronage, Power and Poverty*, p. 34; for net emigration, 1961–71, U. Ascoli, *Movimenti migratori*, p. 134.

70   Allum, *Politics and Society in Post-war Naples*, pp. 32–7.

71   Russo, *Chi ha più santi*, pp. 15–16 and 21. The upper city of Naples was where the richer part of the population (some 200,000 people) lived; separated from the historic centre by a 'Chinese wall made of cement'; ibid., p. 33.

72   Fondazione L. Einaudi, *Nord e Sud*, p. 325.

73   ibid., p. 331.

74   ibid., pp. 460–63. In a conversation with the author in January 1988, Rossi-Doria said that he realized soon after he had made these proposals that they were impracticable because the abandonment of the *latifondo* areas had already taken too firm a grip.

75   Corsi, 'L'esodo agricolo', p. 733.

76   Daneo, *Breve storia dell'agricoltura*, p. 212. For the two 'Green Plans' see ibid., pp. 205–7 and 210–11; and G. Mottura and E. Pugliese, *Agricoltura, Mezzogiorno e mercato del lavoro*, Bologna, 1975, pp. 29–31 and 66–70. It should be noted that in the first 'Green Plan' considerable amounts of state money were still being dedicated to social rather than productive investment. Of the 403 bn lire allocated for farm improvement, Daneo estimates (p. 206) that only 250 bn were effectively used to increase productivity. Even in the second 'Green Plan', a more restricted number of farms continued to enjoy considerable state subsidies in the form of grants, credits and the maintenance of price levels for agrarian products.

77   Daneo, *Breve storia dell'agricoltura*, pp. 209–11; Mottura and Pugliese, *Agricoltura, Mezzogiorno*, p. 113. For the damaging results for Italy of the first EEC policy negotiations, held in 1960–61, see R. Galli and S. Torcasio, *La partecipazione italiana alla politica agraria comunitaria*, Bologna, 1976, pp. 21–45. For later failures to make Italian agricultural interests prevail, ibid., pp. 246–60.

78   Paci, *La struttura sociale*, pp. 115–16. It should be noted that in the Emilian plains the pattern was somewhat different. There a significant stratum of peasant proprietors was producing for the market; 'push' factors were therefore less significant than in other central regions.

79   See Statistical Appendix, diagrams 14 and 15.

80   C. Trigilia, *Grandi partiti e piccole imprese*, Bologna, 1986, tab. 3.3, p. 167.

81   See G. Nigro, 'Il "caso" Prato', in Mori ed., *Storia d'Italia . . . La Toscana*, pp. 821–65.

82   A. Bagnasco, 'Borghesia e classe operaia', in U. Ascoli and R. Catanzaro, eds., *La società italiana degli anni Ottanta*, Bari, 1987, pp. 40ff. For the Veneto, see also B. Anastasia and E. Rullani, 'La nuova periferia industriale', *Materiali Veneti*, nos. 17–18 (1981–2), pp. 7–203.

83   Trigilia, *Grandi partiti e piccole imprese*, pp. 214–15. See also the other two volumes resulting from this research: A. Bagnasco and C. Trigilia, eds., *Società e politica nelle aree di piccola impresa: il caso di Bassano*, Venezia, 1984; A. Bagnasco and C. Trigilia, eds., *Società e politica nelle aree di piccola impresa: il caso di Valdelsa*, Milano, 1985.

84 The sharecropping family, as Bagnasco has written, was 'in many cases large enough to constitute an organism capable of controlling its own destiny, autonomous enough to test its innovative and organizational capacities, stable enough on its land over time to have acquired sufficient experience . . .; it will be this type of family which will push its aspiring members on to the labour market, and will provide aid in the form of wage work which, at least to start with, would be poorly paid and irregular'; Bagnasco, 'Borghesia e classe operaia', p. 41. See also Statistical Appendix, tables 2 and 3.

85 For national or local government reactions and actions, Trigilia, *Grandi partiti e piccole imprese*, pp. 177ff.

86 See Statistical Appendix, tables 36, 37 and 38.

87 See Statistical Appendix, table 37. Taking 1959 as a base of 100, women's work in industry rose to 104 by 1961, but slipped back to 95 in 1964; the figures for agriculture were 100 in 1959, falling rapidly to 72 in 1964. Overall there is a decline in the number of women *registered* in work from 100 in 1959 to 89 in 1964. The 1959 level was only to be reached again in 1980.

88 P. Sylos Labini, *Saggio sulle classi sociali*, Bari, 1974, tab. 1.6, p. 160. Because the national census takes place in Italy at the beginning of every decade, and because the 1961 census fell in the middle of the boom, I have thought it useful to give the figures for both 1961 and 1971.

89 For Confindustria in these years, see Pirzio Ammassari, *La politica della Confindustria*, pp. 91–122. For a good overall impression, Castronovo, 'La storia economica', p. 432.

90 L. Gallino, 'L'evoluzione della struttura di classe in Italia', *Quaderni di Sociologia*, vol. XIX (1970), no. 2.

91 G. Bocca, *Miracolo all'italiano*, Milano, 1980 (1st ed., 1962), p. 20. See also A. Martinelli, 'Borghesia industriale e potere politico', in A. Martinelli and G. Pasquino, eds., *La politica nell'Italia che cambia*, Milano, 1978, p. 273.

92 M. Barbagli, *Disoccupazione intellettuale e sistema scolastico in Italia*, Bologna, 1974.

93 A. Dina, 'I tecnici nella società contemporanea', *Problemi del Socialismo*, vol. IX (1967), nos. 24–5, p. 1409.

94 Sylos Labini, *Saggio sulle classi sociali*, tab. 1.2, p. 156, and tab. 2.2, p. 164. Contrast his remarks about the 'pathological expansion of the bureaucracy', ibid., p. 49 and pp. 66ff., with Cassese's figures; between 1960 and 1976, according to Cassese (*Il sistema amministrativo*, p. 304), state employees as a percentage of all those employed increased by 6.2 per cent in Germany, 5.3 per cent in the UK, 4.6 per cent in Italy and 1.4 per cent in France. Sylos Labini's book gave rise to an extended debate in Italy, centring on the accuracy of his statistics, and the relative weight of the working class and the *ceti medi*: see L. Ricolfi, 'A proposito del "Saggio" di Sylos Labini: la base statistica', *Quaderni Piacentini*, vol. XIV (1975), no. 57, pp. 60–76; L. Ricolfi, P. Sylos Labini and L. D'Agostini, 'Discussione', *Quaderni Piacentini*, vol. XV (1976), nos.

60–61, pp. 129–42; L. Maitan, *Dinamica delle classi sociali in Italia*, Roma, 1975; C. Trigilia, 'Sviluppo, sottosviluppo e classi sociali in Italia', *Rassegna Italiana di Sociologia*, vol. XVII (1976), no. 2, pp. 249–96; L. Zappella, 'Evoluzione del territorio e classi medie in Italia', *Critica Marxista*, vol. XIII (1975), no. 6, p. 147–67. In his later book, *Le classi sociali negli anni '80*, Bari, 1986, Sylos Labini accepted that not all peasant proprietors (*coltivatori diretti*) could be automatically classified as 'middle class' and listed them as a separate category. See also the pertinent remarks on this subject by E. Pugliese, 'Le classi sociali nel Mezzogiorno', *Sviluppo*, no. 16 (1979), p. 8 (extracted version): 'Membership of the peasant proprietors' national insurance scheme and the cultivation of a quarter of a hectare of rented land may be sufficient for a semi-proletarian peasant to declare himself "independent" in the I S T A T forms, but they do not authorize an economist or a sociologist to consider him part of the *ceto medio*.'

95 Sylos Labini, *Saggio sulle classi sociali*, tabs. 1.4, 1.5, 1.6 and 2.2, pp. 158–60 and 164. See also Chapter 5 above, p. 183, where the figures refer to *all* those involved in commerce and not just those 'practising commerce from a fixed abode'. However, it is worth noting the discrepancies between Sylos Labini's figures and those of Belloni *et al.* even for 'commerce from a fixed abode'; according to the first, this category accounted for 6.7 per cent of the workforce in 1951, 7.6 per cent in 1961, 8.7 per cent in 1971; according to the second, the corresponding figures are 4.76 per cent (1957), 7.20 per cent (1961), 8.65 per cent (1971).

96 See Statistical Appendix, table 11; also Sylos Labini, *Saggio sulle classi sociali*, p. 45, and tabs. 1.1 to 1.4, pp. 155ff., and tab. 2.2, p. 164.

97 G. Salierno, *Il sottoproletariato in Italia*, Roma, 1972.

98 S. Gundle, 'Communism and Cultural Change in Post-war Italy', unpublished PhD thesis, Cambridge University, 1985, p. 121.

99 M. D'Antonio, *Sviluppo e crisi del capitalismo italiano 1951–1972*, Bari, 1973, tab. 2, p. 57.

100 See Statistical Appendix, table 9.

101 Gundle, 'Communism and Cultural Change', p. 142.

102 Bocca, *Miracolo*, p. 29.

103 L. Balbo, *Stato di famiglia*, Milano, 1976, pp. 82–3.

104 See Statistical Appendix, table 9.

105 S. Gundle, 'L'americanizzazione del quotidiano. Televisione e consumismo nell'Italia degli anni Cinquanta', *Quaderni Storici*, vol. XXI (1986), no. 62, pp. 574–5.

106 O. Calabrese, *Carosello o dell'educazione serale*, Firenze, 1975.

107 Telegram of the Pope sent by his Secretary of State to the 'Secondo convegno nazionale dei consiglieri ecclesiastici diocesani della CNCD', in Confederazione Nazionale dei Coltivatori Diretti, *Aspetti sociali e religiosi del mondo rurale italiano*, Roma, 1958, p. 7.

108 P. P. Pasolini, *Scritti corsari*, Milano, 1975, pp. 69–70, article of 11 July 1974.

109 M. Calamandrei, 'La città in campagna', *L'Espresso*, vol. V (1959), no. 4, p. 13; cited in Gundle, 'L'americanizzazione del quotidiano', p. 576.

110 Antonuzzo, *Boschi, miniera, catena di montaggio*, pp. 68–9.

111 M. Caesar and P. Hainsworth, *Writers and Society in Contemporary Italy*, London, 1984, pp. 17–19.

112 See Statistical Appendix, tables 1–6.

113 On the individual family's isolation and its attempts to satisfy needs in this period, see the pertinent remarks of Laura Balbo: 'It is clear which definitions of privatization derived from these premises: private as competitive (each family gathered resources for itself, in competition with other families); private as opposed to collective (in the sense that for each single case a "particular" solution was sought, whereas in fact the needs were general); private, finally, in the sense of non-political (needs and problems are referred to the closed and isolated ambience of each family unit, according to a logic which prevents solidarity and collective actions)'; Balbo, *Stato di famiglia*, p. 31. For the new privacy at Rho, A. Pizzorno, *Comunità e razionalizzazione*, Milano, 1960, pp. 184–5.

114 ibid., p. 183.

115 Balbo, *Stato di famiglia*, pp. 85–6.

116 V. Gorresio, 'Durante e dopo il boom: sesso, matrimonio, famiglia', in *I Problemi di Ulisse*, vol. XV, (1981), no. 91, pp. 33ff.

117 See Statistical Appendix, table 13, and S. Burgalassi, *Il comportamento religioso degli italiani*, Firenze, 1968, p. 27.

118 ibid., p. 19. Comparative figures for parishes in the centre of major cities were not that much more encouraging: 16 per cent for men and 27 per cent for women.

119 A. Monelli and G. Pellicciari, 'Comportamenti di voto e pratica religiosa', in Pellicciari, ed., *L'immigrazione nel triangolo industriale*, p. 334.

120 L. Milani, *Esperienze pastorali*, Firenze, 1957, pp. 464–5: quoted by Ginzburg, 'Folklore, magia, religione', p. 674.

121 On the town-planning law of 1942, see F. Ferraresi and A. Tosi, 'Crisi della città e politica urbana', in L. Graziano and S. Tarrow, *La crisi italiana*, Torino, 1979, vol. 2, pp. 561–2; and G. Ruffolo, *Riforme e controriforme*, Bari, 1977, p. 44. For the slowness with which the *piani regolatori particolareggiati* came into force, see L. Bortolotti, 'L'evoluzione del territorio', in Mori, ed., *Storia d'Italia . . . La Toscana*, p. 815. By 1957 only one commune in Tuscany, Chianciano, had had its plan approved.

122 For the numbers of houses built per annum, G. Rochat, G. Sateriale and L. Spano, *La casa in Italia, 1945–80*, Bologna, 1980 p. 17; for the organization of the construction industry, ibid., pp. 8ff.

123 ibid., pp. 17–18; G. Campos Venuti, 'Programmare: perché è più difficile, perché è necessario', *Rinascita*, vol. XL (1984), no. 43, p. 13.

124 M. Cancogni, 'Cicicov in Campidoglio', *L'Espresso*, vol. II (1986), no. 4.

125 Ruffolo, *Riforme e controriforme*, p. 34. See also, for the sack of Rome, A. Cederna, *Mirabilia urbis*, Torino, 1965; and I. Insolera, *Roma moderna*, Torino, 1963.

126 M. McLuhan, 'American advertising', *Horizon*, nos. 93–4 (1947), p. 132; quoted in Gundle, 'L'americanizzazione del quotidiano', p. 579.

127 For some fine examples of American concepts of the benefits of modernization, Ellwood, 'Il piano Marshall e il processo di modernizzazione in Italia', *passim*.

128 See the remarks by D. I. Kertzer, 'Urban research in Italy', in M. Kenny and D. I. Kertzer, eds., *Urban life in Mediterranean Europe*, Urbana, IL, 1983, p. 67; F. Crespi and F. Martinelli, 'La dinamica delle relazioni sociali nel contesto urbano', *Rivista di Sociologia*, vol. VI (1968), no. 16, pp. 5–62; and for an extreme case, Judith Chubb's description of the new housing estates on the periphery of Palermo, *Patronage, Power and Poverty*, p. 198.

129 G. Siri, 'Tendenze contemporanee e valori permanenti della famiglia cristiana', in *Famiglie di oggi e mondo sociale in trasformazione* (XXVIII Settimana sociale dei Cattolici d'Italia, Pisa, sett. 1954), Roma, 1956, p. 20.

130 Damiliano, ed., *Atti e documenti della DC*, vol. 2, p. 1819.

131 Direttivo Nazionale di Gioventù Aclista, *Incontri sulla famiglia*, Roma, n.d., p. 4.

132 Istituto di Studi e Ricerche Carlo Cattaneo, *La presenza sociale del PCI e della DC*, p. 277.

133 *Vie Nuove*, 1 January 1956, p. 11; quoted in Gundle, 'L'americanizzazione del quotidiano', p. 578.

134 T. Seppilli, 'Intervento', in *Famiglia e società nell'analisi marxista*, pp. 177–9.

135 Pasolini, *Scritti corsari*, p. 157, article of 1 Feb. 1975. For an interesting discussion of the connection between modernization and *'virtù'*, see T. Mason, 'Moderno, modernità, modernizzazione: un montaggio', in *Movimento Operaio e Socialista*, New series, vol. X (1987), nos. 1–2, pp. 45–63.

136 Foa, 'Sindacato e corporazione', in his *La cultura della CGIL*, p. xiii.

137 Fofi, *L'immigrazione meridionale*, p. 157.

138 D. Lanzardo, *La rivolta di Piazza Statuto*, Milano, 1979, p. 101.

139 ibid., pp. 84–100.

140 ibid., pp. 95–9 and 108.

141 See the testimony of G.C. in ibid., p. 130. For a fascinating account of a group of youngsters in Turin in the early 1960s, see the testimony of D.B., aged fourteen at the time of Piazza Statuto; ibid., p. 155.

Chapter 8

1 P. Ottone, *Fanfani*, Milano, 1966, p. 110.

2 ibid., pp. 120–23. See also the detailed description in G. Baget-Bozzo, *Il partito cristiano e l'apertura a sinistra*, Firenze, 1977, pp. 150–63.

3 G. Galli, *Storia della DC*, pp. 194ff.

4 A. Coppola, *Moro*, Milano, 1976, pp. 16–18. This short political biography remains the most reliable guide to Moro's career. Much of what has been published after Moro's death has been hagiographical in character. An interesting impression of Moro at the time he became secretary of the party is that conveyed by James E. King, who in May 1961 was sent by Arthur Schlesinger, Jr, to meet various Italian political leaders. King noted: 'What struck me about Moro was his intelligence, his sense of calm, his self-confidence ... On a personal level he is very cold and at every moment he gave me the impression that he was thinking about something else, even when we were talking about things in which he showed some interest' (memorandum of King to W. Rostow, 1 May 1961, quoted in Italian in R. Faenza, *Il malaffare*, Milano, 1978, p. 280).

5 Cited in P. G. Murgia, *Il luglio 1960*, Milano, 1960, p. 53.

6 Rosenbaum, *Il nuovo fascismo*, p. 202.

7 Murgia, *Il luglio 1960*, pp. 99–140.

8 R. Leonardi and A. A. Platt, 'La politica estera americana nei confronti della sinistra italiana', *Il Mulino*, vol. XXVI (1977), no. 252, p. 554.

9 Faenza, *Il malaffare*, pp. 264ff.

10 Leonardi and Platt, 'La politica estera', p. 561.

11 See E. Forcella, 'Il "mito" di Kennedy', in A. Schlesinger Jr *et al.*, *Gli anni di Kennedy*, Milano, 1964, p. 62. Kennedy visited Italy from 30 June to 2 July 1963, and at that stage made his support for the centre-left quite explicit. For an entertaining account of the visit, based on American documents and CIA bugging, Faenza, *Il malaffare*, pp. 352–8.

12 Quoted in V. Gorresio, *La nuova missione*, Milano, 1968, p. 48.

13 ibid., p. 73.

14 ibid., pp. 66–7 and 197.

15 S. Magister, *La politica vaticana e l'Italia, 1943–78*, Roma, 1979, pp. 241–60.

16 Gorresio, *La nuova missione*, p. 104.

17 For a debate on the encyclical, see *Mater et magistra. Contenuto e valore dell'enciclica di Giovanni XXIII in un incontro alla televisione*, Roma, 1962. Those taking part were A. Butte, F. Vito, A. C. Jemolo, G. Lazzati and G. La Pira. The encyclical is reproduced in the appendix, pp. 59–126.

18 Gorresio, *La nuova missione*, p. 181.

19 For the long-term effects of the encyclical, see the essays, by both Catholics and non-Catholics, collected by G. C. Zizola, *Risposte a Papa Giovanni*, Roma, 1973. For an excellent account in English of the papacy of John XXIII, P. Hebblethwaite, *John XXIII*, London, 1984.

20 Partitio Socialista Italiano, *34° congresso nazionale, Milano, 15–20 marzo 1961*, Milano, 1961, p. 41.

21 ibid., p. 50.

22 ibid., pp. 163 and 165.

23 Quoted in Tamburrano, *Storia e cronaca*, p. 110. Dean Rusk, the American Secretary of State, was deeply alarmed by Lombardi's statements and his position in the party. How was it possible, asked Rusk, for the USA to support the PSI when Lombardi demanded the recognition of Communist China, the withdrawal of all American troops from Italy and a continuing fight against capitalism and imperialism?; see the telegram from Rusk to the American embassy, 18 Oct. 1961, quoted in Faenza, *Il malaffare*, p. 311.

24 *Primo congresso nazionale di studio della Democrazia Cristiana, San Pellegrino Terme, 13–16 settembre 1961*, Roma, 1961. For a summary of Ardigò's speech, pp. 27–36; for Saraceno's, pp. 39–44. Saraceno recalled the words of John XXIII in *Mater et magistra* to the effect that the state had to perform in the economic field a 'greater, more organic and multiform role'.

25 *Atti dell'VIII congresso della Democrazia Cristiana (Napoli, 27–31 gennaio 1962)*, Roma, 1963, p. 97.

26 Bairati, *Valletta*, p. 328.

27 Tamburrano, *Storia e cronaca*, p. 73. For Mattei, see the article by L. Libertini, 'Facciamo il punto sulla DC', *Mondo Nuovo*, vol. IV, no. 10, 20 May 1962.

28 Tamburrano, *Storia e cronaca*, p. 132.

29 Gigliobianco and Salvati make the important point that in post-war Italy there was no natural interchange between the political élites and the personnel of private industry as there was in France; their separation was to have negative consequences for both; A. Gigliobianco and M. Salvati, *Il maggio francese e l'autunno caldo italiano: la risposta di due borghesie*, Bologna, 1980, pp. 44–5. See also Guido Carli's remarks above, pp. 470–71, n. 4.

30 For corrective reforms see, for example, Saraceno's intervention at the San Pellegrino Terme conference (*Primo congresso nazionale di studio della DC*, pp. 39–44); and U. La Malfa, *Verso la politica di piano*, Napoli, 1962. On the problem of the public administration, see La Malfa's remarks of 1977: '[In De Gasperi's time] there was already a degeneration of political and administrative practice, and afterwards it became more extensive. So much so that when I returned to the government in 1962, as Minister of the Budget, I observed that I had found the state in worse conditions than those in which I had left it in 1953'; U. La Malfa, *Intervista sul non-governo*, ed. A. Ronchey, Bari, 1977, p. 54.

31 R. Lombardi, 'Una nuova frontiera per la sinistra', in V. Parlato, ed., *Spazio e ruolo del riformismo*, Bologna, 1974, p. 66. For structural reform in Togliatti's thought, see Sassoon, *Togliatti e la via italiana*, pp. 241–88. For the concept of 'non-reformist reforms' see A. Gorz, *Strategy for Labour: A Radical Reappraisal*, Boston, Mass., 1971, pp. 7ff.

32 For a striking and pessimistic view of the possibility of structural reform in Italy, see C. Napoleoni, 'Riforme del capitale e capitale riformato', in Parlato, ed., *Spazio e ruolo del riformismo*, pp. 87–94. For some further reflections, Ginsborg, 'The Communist Party and the agrarian question in southern Italy', pp. 98–9. For an interesting attempt to provide a primarily economic typology of reforms, G. Esping-Andersen, R. Friedland and E. O. Wright, 'Modes of class struggle and the capitalist state', *Kapitalistate*, nos. 4–5 (1976), pp. 186–220.

33 *Mondo Nuovo*, vol. IV, no. 10, 20 May 1962, p. 8.

34 Ministero del Bilancio, *Problemi e prospettive dello sviluppo economico italiano* (Nota presentata al parlamento dal Ministro del Bilancio, U. La Malfa, 22 maggio 1962), Roma, 1962.

35 A. Baldassare and C. Mezzanotte, *Gli uomini del Quirinale*, Bari, 1985, pp. 111–17. For Gronchi's presidency, ibid., pp. 62–104.

36 E. Rossi, *Elettricità senza baroni*, Bari, 1962.

37 Scalfari and Turani, *Razza padrona*, pp. 14–15 and 21–2. See also La Malfa's account (*Intervista sul non-governo*, p. 57): 'From one day to the next the scheme prepared by us (Riccardo Lombardi and I were working closely together at the time) was rejected by Guido Carli, the governor of the Bank of Italy, and by various Christian Democrat leaders. They presented us with a scheme which replaced the guarantees for shareholders with the payment of compensation directly to the ex-trusts. And we, at that point, made the mistake of giving way.'

38 For a good explanation of the background to this law, F. Magistrelli and R. Ragozzino, 'La cedolare "mista": vincitori e perdenti', *Problemi del Socialismo*, vol. IX (1967), no. 16, pp. 287–8.

39 See Statistical Appendix, table 22. For teachers' attitudes to the new law, see M. Barbagli and M. Dei, *Le vestali della classe media*, Bologna, 1969, pp. 73–157. There was also significant opposition to the introduction of the *doposcuola*, afternoon activities organized by the schools (Italian school hours were usually from 8.30 a.m. to 1.30 p.m. six days a week). Under the new law the *doposcuola* was introduced, but only for an optional ten hours a week. A major reason for this limitation was the fear of undermining family bonds. As one woman teacher explained, in a fascinating attack on what she perceived to be American family life: 'I am against the *doposcuola*. We don't have the same mentality as the Americans, who see each other at 7 a.m. and then again at midnight. We have a different way of doing things. The Italian child needs the influence of its family and to see what takes place within it. In American families, the less you see of each other the better it is; in Italian families the more you see of each other the better it is, if families behave as they should behave. Children should be at home for parents to guide them. The child who is out of the house all day loses its love for the family and does not acquire a family consciousness. Now they want to introduce divorce; we're certainly on the right road!' (ibid., p. 123). See also A. L. Fadiga Zanatta, *Il sistema scolastico italiano*, Bologna, 1971, pp. 76–98.

40 Tamburrano, *Storia e cronaca*, p. 131 and p. 145, n. 1.

41 Graziani, ed., *L'economia italiana*, pp. 69ff.; for hours lost in strikes, Statistical Appendix, table 42.

42 See the editorial in *24 Ore*, 29 March 1963; See also Provasi, *Borghesia industriale e Democrazia Cristiana*, pp. 185–6.

43 C. Giustiniani, *La casa promessa*, Torino, 1981, p. 66. See also A. Fubini, *Urbanistica in Italia*, Milano, 1978, pp. 245–8. In April 1962, law no. 167 gave municipal authorities considerable powers to initiate public housing schemes but very limited finances with which to carry them through; M. Marchi *et al.*, *Il volto sociale dell'edilizia popolare*, Roma, 1975, pp. 33–6.

44 Sullo recounted afterwards how his relatives had asked him, aghast, if he really meant to take away their householders' rights; F. Sullo, *Lo scandalo urbanistico*, Firenze, 1964, p. 17. For the power and composition of the Italian building industry, V. Parlato, 'Il blocco edilizio', in F. Indovina, ed., *Lo spreco edilizio*, Venezia, 1978, pp. 189–200.

45 See Statistical Appendix, table 25.

46 Tamburrano, *Storia e cronaca*, pp. 249–50.

47 Quoted in M. Legnani, *Profilo politico dell'Italia repubblicana, 1943–74*, Napoli, 1974, p. 44. For a brief history of the new party, see S. Miniati, *PSIUP, 1943–72. Vita e morte di un partito*, Roma, 1981.

48 G. Galli, *Storia della DC*, p. 228. Emilio Colombo was to remain at the Treasury for no less than eight years, from June 1963 until August 1970. He was then President of the Council of Ministers until Jan. 1972, after which he returned to the Treasury for a brief spell in 1972, and again from March 1974 until March 1976 (I am grateful to Dr James Walston for this information).

49 Interview with G. Tamburrano in *Storia e cronaca*, pp. 283–4. For the failures of Moro's government, see also Foa, 'I socialisti italiani', pp. 285–6.

50 *Atti della Commissione parlamentare d'inchiesta sugli eventi del giugno–luglio 1964*, 2 vols., Roma, 1971.

51 There is considerable evidence of CIA–SIFAR collusion in the compilation of these files; see Faenza, *Il malaffare*, pp. 315ff.

52 Article published in *L'Astrolabio*, 21 May 1967, reprinted in Legnani, *Profilo politico*, pp. 194–204 (p. 196).

53 R. Collin, *The De Lorenzo Gambit*, London, 1976, *passim*.

54 *Atti della Commissione parlamentare d'inchiesta*, vol. I, p. 743. It should be pointed out that all the other Carabinieri officers present at the meeting strenuously denied Aurigo's version of what had happened.

55 The exact nature of the conversation between Segni and De Lorenzo has never been revealed. For the July crisis seen from the viewpoint of the CIA, Faenza, *Il malaffare*, pp. 364–73. It is clear that while Kennedy was in favour of the centre-left and made that support explicit when visiting Rome at the end of June 1963, the CIA office in Rome, under William Harvey, was doing its best to

sabotage the new political coalition. Throughout this period close links were maintained between the CIA and De Lorenzo.

56 *Avanti!*, 26 July 1964.

57 Tamburrano, *Storia e cronaca*, pp. 309ff.

58 Baldassare and Mezzanotte, *Gli uomini del Quirinale*, pp. 135–44.

59 See Statistical Appendix, table 42.

60 Ferrari and Tosi, 'Crisi della città', p. 566; Rochat *et al.*, *La casa in Italia*, p. 23.

61 Quoted in Tamburrano, *Storia e cronaca*, p. 159.

62 Mancini was accused both from the left by the deputy Rocco Minasi of PSIUP, and from the extreme right (by the weekly magazine *Candido*); see Walston, *Mafia and Clientelism*, pp. 165ff.

63 Michele Salvati, *Economia e politica*, pp. 68–9; see also his article 'Quattro punti facili', *L'Indice*, vol. II (1985), no. 2, p. 26.

64 G. Alzona, 'Grande industria: sviluppo e strutture di controllo, 1963–72', in A. Graziani, ed., *Crisi e ristrutturazione dell'economia italiana*, Torino, 1975, tab. 5, p. 264 and pp. 279–81. See also G. Amato, *Economia, politica e istituzioni in Italia*, Bologna, 1976, pp. 96–7; Scalfari and Turani, *Razza padrona*, pp. 54–5 and p. 179; G. Maggia and G. Forengo, *Appunti sul sistema delle partecipazioni statali*, Torino, 1976, pp. 229–40.

65 Michele Salvati, *Economia e politica*, p. 78: 'if, at the beginning of the sixties, the connection between merit and competence on the one hand, and decision-making powers on the other, was still robust, in the following years it became ever more slender'.

66 A. Mutti, 'Elementi per un' analisi della borghesia di stato', *Quaderni di Sociologia*, vol. XXVII (1979), no. 1, pp. 24–70; A. Nannei, *La nuovissima classe*, Milano, 1978.

67 Quoted in Scalfari and Turani, *Razza padrona*, p. 278.

68 Cefis's rise to power is charted in detail in ibid., *passim*.

69 R. D. Putnam, 'Atteggiamenti politici dell'alta burocrazia nell'Europa occidentale', *Rivista Italiana di Scienza Politica*, vol. III (1973), no. 1, pp. 172–5.

70 Cassese, *Il sistema amministrativo*, p. 76.

71 Galli and Torcasio, *La partecipazione italiana*, pp. 246 and 256. See also Ruffolo, *Riforme e controriforme*, p. 102, and his *Rapporto sulla programmazione*, Bari, 1975, esp. pp. 91–106. The letter from A. Voci, director-general at the Ministry of the Interior, to S. Cassese (*Il sistema amministrativo*, p. 83), gives a revealing picture of the labyrinth which a new law had to negotiate.

72 Quoted in Caciagli *et al.*, *Democrazia Cristiana e Mezzogiorno*, p. 227. For Gullotti at Messina see L. Mattina, 'Il sistema di potere democristiano a Catania e Messina', *Quaderni della Fondazione G.G. Feltrinelli*, no. 21 (1982), pp. 155–77.

73 Chubb, *Patronage, Power and Poverty*, pp. 132 and 134.

74 ibid., pp. 144ff. See also U. Baduel, 'Il DC Ciancimino', *L'Unità*, 11 Nov. 1984.

75 Chubb, *Patronage, Power and Poverty*, p. 157.

76 G. Gribaudi, *Mediatori*, pp. 122–3; G. Bonazzi, A. Bagnasco and S. Casillo, *Industria e potere politico in una provincia meridionale*, Torino, 1972, pp. 404–18.

77 G. Galli, *Storia della DC*, pp. 272ff.

78 Chubb, *Patronage, Power and Poverty*, pp. 168–9. According to Sylos Labini's figures, in 1951 in the South only 4.5 per cent of the active population were white-collar civil servants; by 1971 this number had increased to 8.1 per cent. However, it is interesting to note that the percentage increase was no greater in the decade 1961–71 than in 1951–61, and that the numerical increase was actually more marked in the earlier decade; see *Saggio sulle classi sociali*, p. 158, tab. 1.5.

79 Chubb, *Patronage, Power and Poverty*, p. 283, n. 2. See also N. Boccella, *Il Mezzogiorno sussidiato*, Milano, 1982

80 G. Gribaudi, *Mediatori*, p. 116.

81 Amyot, *Italian Communist Party*, pp. 76ff.

82 See above, pp. 45–6.

83 P. Togliatti, *Memoriale di Yalta*, Roma, 1970, p. 10.

84 Until very recently, it has not been possible to establish with any precision Togliatti's role in the purging of the international Communist movement in the 1930s. The opening of the Comintern archives now offers new possibilities to historians. In July 1988, the Soviet historian Frederik Firsov, having read some of the Comintern papers for the 1930s, gave this first, extremely balanced judgement: 'All the leaders of the Comintern in that period had a responsibility for what happened. But I must add, so as not to state only a half truth, that they could do nothing different. That is not to absolve them; if anything it renders their tragedy even greater ... The leaders wrote and signed what they were forced to sign. That in itself was terrible enough. It was as if they were on an escalator of the Underground, which brought them down to the furthest depths of horror ... I know of Tasca's case and now, reading his critique of Stalin, one understands without any shadow of doubt that he was right. But for someone with Togliatti's make-up it was different. For him the decisive problem was the life of his party, its relationship with the Comintern and with the USSR. For that reason he chose the way he did' (*La Repubblica*, 26 July 1988, interview with Ezio Mauro).

There remains the question of Togliatti's behaviour on returning to Italy. In 1944 the libertarian Communist, Victor Serge, wrote him an anguished letter, asking him to tell the world about the fate of a number of Italian comrades who had fled from Fascism to Russia and who had not been heard of since; Togliatti never replied. (M. Guarnaschelli and V. Serge, 'Il morbo di Stalin', *Belfagor*, vol. XXXVIII (1983), pp. 85–90.)

85   G. Amendola, *Classe operaia e programmazione democratica*, Roma, 1966, esp. pp. 535—615. It should be noted that Amendola's liberal social-democratic tendencies were tempered by rigid and orthodox views on the leadership's control of the party.

86   P. Ingrao, *Masse e potere*, Roma, 1980; Amyot, *Italian Communist Party*, pp. 58—64 and p. 168.

87   Amyot, ibid., pp. 67—72 and pp. 162ff.

88   Piro, *Comunisti al potere*, pp. 137—9.

89   G. Fanti, 'Relazione introduttiva', Prima conferenza regionale del PCI (Bologna, 1959), in D'Attorre, ed., *I comunisti in Emilia-Romagna*, p. 127.

90   G. Fanti and R. Zangheri, 'Classe operaia e alleanze in Emilia', in *Cinquantesimo del PCI* (*Critica Marxista*, Quaderno no. 5, 1972), p. 259.

91   Piro, *Comunisti al potere*, p. 170; D'Attorre, 'I comunisti in Emilia-Romagna' in *I comunisti in Emilia-Romagna*, p. 20.

92   I. Montanelli, 'Il comunismo imprenditoriale', in *Italia sotto inchiesta*, p. 383; Marchi *et al.*, *Il volto sociale*, pp. 45ff., who point out, however, that the areas of popular housing had attracted more white-collar than blue-collar workers in percentage terms (ibid., p. 58).

93   M. Jäggi, R. Müller and S. Schmid, *Red Bologna*, London, 1977, pp. 37ff. (First published as *Das röte Bologna*, Zürich, 1976.)

94   Quoted in Ferraresi and Tosi, 'Crisi della città', p. 577. See also Zangheri's interview with the all-too-credulous Jäggi, Müller and Schmid: 'our policy sheds much clearer light than any other policy on the contradictions of capitalism and thus helps to overcome it. And overcome it with reforms that induce the largest numbers of people to mobilize – that is the point – and bring genuine solutions to the problems of the system. We do not believe these solutions remain within the capitalist system' (Jäggi *et al.*, *Red Bologna*, p. 199).

95   P. Togliatti, *Discorsi sull'Emilia*, Bologna, 1964, p. 88.

Chapter 9

1   For educational reform and the increase in school and university numbers, see R. Lumley, 'Social Movements in Italy, 1968–1978', unpublished PhD thesis, Centre for Contemporary Cultural Studies, University of Birmingham, 1983, pp. 145ff.

2   R. Rossanda, *L'anno degli studenti*, Bari, 1968, p. 14.

3   G. Viale, 'Contro l'università', in L. Baranelli and M. G. Cherchi, eds., *Quaderni Piacentini. Antologia 1962–68*, Milano, 1977, p. 432.

4   *I lavoratori studenti. Testimonianze raccolte a Torino* (introduction by V. Foa), Torino, 1969; see also G. Martinotti, *Gli studenti dell'università di Milano*, Milano, 1973; nearly a third of Milan state university's population were worker-students at this time.

5   From a conversation with the author. See also L. Passerini, *Autoritratto di*

gruppo, Firenze, 1988, p. 33; and Luigi Bobbio: 'We no longer wanted supinely to play the role of the ruling class, to become zealous and obtuse judges, conformist journalists, inventors of machines to improve productivity at the expense of the workers, doctors set on making money to the detriment of their poorest patients. Something had broken down in the transmission of values between the generations' (L. Bobbio, 'Arroganza e sacchi a pelo', *Panorama*, vol. XXV (1987), no. 1128, p. 231).

6 Scuola di Barbiana, *Lettera a una professoressa*, Firenze, 1967, pp. 112 and 116; published in English as School of Barbiana, *Letter to a Teacher*, London, 1970.

7 Viale, 'Contro l'università', p. 429.

8 For Trento, Rossanda, *L'anno degli studenti*, pp. 44ff.

9 'Mozione approvata dall'assemblea generale degli studenti occupanti, 19 Nov. 1967', quoted in Lumley, 'Social Movements', p. 189.

10 See S. Mobiglia, 'La scuola: l'onda lunga della contestazione', to be published in the *Annali della Fondazione L. Micheletti*. It was not until the autumn of 1968 that the movement spread outwards from a handful of schools, and that thousands of school students became involved. Amongst their demands were the freedom to hold meetings in school time, the right of everyone to education and to a student grant, the end of individual exams and marking, the accountability of teachers to students.

11 Lumley, 'Social Movements', pp. 174–8.

12 E. Scalfari, *L'autunno della Repubblica*, Milano, 1969, p. 195. Scalfari is referring here to his trial for defamation, of which he and Raffaele Jannuzzi, both at that time of *L'Espresso*, had been accused by General De Lorenzo.

13 Quoted in Passerini, *Autoritratto di gruppo*, p. 46.

14 L. Castellina, in *Famiglia e società capitalistica*, Quaderni de 'Il Manifesto', no. 1, Roma, 1974, pp. 14–37. See the Turin leaflet of 27 Feb. 1968 containing the students' answers to their parents' standard criticisms, reprinted in Passerini, *Autoritratto di gruppo*, pp. 105–6.

15 L. Passerini, 'Non solo maschio. La presenza ambivalente delle donne nel movimento', in *Marzo 1968* (supplement to *Il Manifesto*, no. 76, 30 March 1988), pp. 16–17.

16 For the architecture faculty at Venice, Rossanda, *L'anno degli studenti*, pp. 57–64.

17 Viale, 'Contro l'università', p. 441.

18 Lumley, 'Social Movements', p. 180.

19 L. Longo, 'Il movimento studentesco nella lotta anticapitalistica', *Rinascita* (supplement *Il Contemporaneo*) vol. XXV (1968), no. 8, p. 15; G. Amendola, 'Necessità della lotta su due fronti', in ibid., pp. 3–4.

20 *L'Espresso*, vol. XIV (1968), no. 4, 16 June.

21 ibid. There was further discussion of the poem in the issue of 23 June, and a long reply by Pasolini on 30 June.

22 For a discussion of the strengths and weaknesses of direct democracy as it was manifested in the international student movement, see P. Ortoleva, *Saggio sui movimenti del 1968 in Europa e in America*, Roma, 1988, pp. 121ff.

23 M. Boffi *et al.*, *Città e conflitto sociale*, Milano, 1972, pp. 128ff. For migration, see Statistical Appendix, tables 15, 16, 19 and 20, and U. Ascoli, *Movimenti migratori*, pp. 128ff.

24 Fofi, *L'immigrazione meridionale*, pp. 303–4; for 'Altopiano', Piselli, *Parentela ed emigrazione*, p. 326.

25 Fofi, *L'immigrazione meridionale*, pp. 308–11; Paci, *Mercato del lavoro e classi sociali*, pp. 207ff., and p. 334.

26 Lumley, 'Social Movements', pp. 92–3.

27 The thesis of inadequate representation is argued most strongly by A. Pizzorno and his collaborators in their four-volume work, *Lotte operaie e sindacato in Italia (1968–1972)*, Bologna, 1974.

28 Foa, *Sindacato e lotte operaie*, pp. 164ff.; G. Pupillo, 'Classe operaia, partiti e sindacati nella lotta alla Marzotto', *Classe*, vol. II (1970), no. 2, pp. 37ff.; N. Zandegiacomi, 'Marzotto, un monumento nella polvere', in *Marzo 1968* (supplement to *Il Manifesto*, no. 76, 30 March 1988), pp. 29–30. After 19 April an agreement was hastily signed between management and the CISL, but by the beginning of 1969 tension was again running high. From 24 January 1969 onwards the factory was occupied by the workers for a month, at the end of which management agreed to the majority of their requests.

29 Foa, *Sindacato e lotte operaie*, p. 163. For the pension reform which ensued, see below, p. 328.

30 L. Bobbio, *Lotta Continua*, Roma, 1979, pp. 29–30.

31 The best single history of any of these groups is Bobbio, *Lotta Continua*. See also A. Garzia, *Da Natta a Natta. Storia del Manifesto e del PDUP*, Bari, 1985; and D. Degli Incerti, ed., *La sinistra rivoluzionaria in Italia*, Roma, 1976 (a collection of documents). For two useful introductions in English, S. Hellman, 'The "New Left" in Italy', in M. Kolinsky and W. E. Paterson, eds., *Social and Political Movements in Western Europe*, London, 1976, pp. 243–75; V. Spini, 'The new left in Italy', *Journal of Contemporary History*, vol. VII (1972), nos. 1–2, pp. 51–72.

32 I. Regalia, M. Regini and E. Reyneri, 'Labour conflicts and industrial relations in Italy', in C. Crouch and A. Pizzorno, eds., *The Resurgence of Class Conflict in Western Europe since 1968*, London, 1978, vol. I, p. 109; see also A. Luppi and E. Reyneri, *Autobianchi e Innocenti*, Bologna, 1974 (vol. I of Pizzorno *et al.*, *Lotte operaie e sindacato in Italia*), pp. 175–6.

33 Foa, *Sindacati e lotte operaie*, pp. 166ff.; M. Mosca, 'I CUB alla Bicocca', in *Marzo 1968* (supplement to *Il Manifesto*, no. 76, 30 March 1988), pp. 33–4; G. Bianchi *et al.*, *I CUB: comitati unitari di base*, Roma, 1971; *1968–72: Le lotte alla Pirelli*, Milano, 1972.

34 Foa, *Sindacati e lotte operaie*, pp. 154ff. and pp. 171–2.

35 Regalia *et al.*, 'Labour conflicts', pp. 112–14.

36 R. Del Carria, *Proletari senza rivoluzione*, vol. V, Roma, 1977, p. 115.

37 Regalia *et al.* 'Labour conflicts', p. 112.

38 Quoted in L. Bobbio, *Lotta Continua*, p. 34.

39 G. Viale, 'Cinquanta giorni di lotta alla FIAT', in his *S'avanza uno strano soldato*, Roma, 1973, p. 57. For the 'battle of Corso Traiano', Foa, *Sindacato e lotte operaie*, pp. 183ff., and L. Bobbio, *Lotta Continua*, p. 35.

40 Quoted in L. Bobbio, *Lotta Continua*, p. 48.

41 Quoted in Luppi and Reyneri, *Autobianchi e Innocenti*, p. 148. For the FIM–CISL, G. P. Cella, B. Manghi and P. Piva, *Un sindacato italiano negli anni Sessanta*, Bari, 1972.

42 P. Lange, G. Ross and M. Vannicelli, *Unions, Change and Crisis: French and Italian Union Strategy and the Political Economy, 1945–1980*, London, 1984, pp. 136ff.

43 Foa, *Sindacato e lotte operaie*, p. 187.

44 For the development of white-collar radicalism, J. R. Low-Beer, *Protest and Participation*, Cambridge, 1978.

45 Regalia *et al.*, 'Labour conflicts', p. 110.

46 See G. Giugni *et al.*, *Gli anni della conflittualità permanente*, Milano, 1976.

47 Quoted in Foa, *Sindacati e lotte operaie*, pp. 208–9. For the development of the councils, see G. Romagnoli, *Consigli di fabbrica e democrazia sindacale*, Milano, 1976.

48 Regalia *et al.*, 'Labour conflicts', pp. 149–50.

49 A typical defensive struggle of these years was the one in which Antonio Antonuzzo (see above, pp. 217–18) was involved at the Superbox factory at Lesmo (Brianza) in the winter of 1972–3. The British Metal Box company, which owned the factory, wanted to close it down. Antonuzzo, who had become a full-time trade unionist in the FIM–CISL, helped to organize the occupation of the factory, which lasted for some three months: 'On Christmas Eve the midnight mass was celebrated in the factory by Don Luigi Oggioni, with some 1,500 people taking part. Don Oggioni, in his sermon, said that if Jesus had still to be born, God would have chosen an occupied factory as his birthplace.' Metal Box refused to reconsider, the factory was closed, and some 250 jobs were lost; Antonuzzo, *Boschi, miniere, catena di montaggio*, pp. 230ff.

50 Foa, *Sindacati e lotte operaie*, p. 203.

51 See the slightly longer Italian version of the article by Regalia *et al.*, 'Labour conflicts': 'Conflitti di lavoro e relazioni industriali in Italia, 1968–75', in C. Crouch and A. Pizzorno, *Conflitti in Europa*, Milano, 1977, App. 1, p. 69. See also Statistical Appendix, table 42.

52 Mosca, 'I CUB alla Bicocca', p. 34.

53 Testimony in Alasia and Montaldi, *Milano, Corea*, pp. 366 and 368–9.

54 Norcia, *Io garantito*, p. 59. Compare this testimony with the very similar one of the CGIL militant at Magneti Marelli in the mid-1950s (see above, p. 197).

55 ibid., p. 64.

56 A fine regional study of this experience is V. Capecchi *et al.*, *Le 150 ore nella regione Emilia-Romagna. Storia e prospettive*, 6 vols., Bologna, 1982. For an overview, see E. Guerra, 'Per una storia delle 150 ore in Emilia-Romagna', ibid., vol. 1, pp. 11–42. For the 1973 contract, Foa, *Sindacati e lotte operaie*, pp. 201–3.

57 R. Canosa, *Storia di un pretore*, Torino, 1979, p. 70. See also M. Ramat ed., *Storia di un magistrato. Materiali per una storia di Magistratura Democratica*, Roma, 1986.

58 L. Bobbio, *Lotta Continua*, p. 84.

59 ibid., p. 79. After the autumn of 1969, Lotta Continua, while not abandoning the factory struggle, shifted its attention towards the city and towards its poorest elements. The unemployed and underemployed, the migrants, the most marginal and oppressed members of the proletariat, seemed those most willing to take direct action.

60 Lumley, 'Social Movements', p. 258.

61 F. Di Ciaccia, *La condizione urbana. Storia dell'Unione Inquilini*, Milano, 1974, pp. 57–8.

62 For an account of the Milanese squats in Via MacMahon and Via Tibaldi in 1971, see Boffi *et al.*, *Città e conflitto sociale*, pp. 151–5. For a summary of housing struggles in the major Italian cities up to 1974, A. Daolio ed., *Le Lotte per la casa in Italia*, Milano, 1974, esp. pp. 19–22. See also M. Mattei, A. Morini and V. Simoni, *Le lotte per la casa a Firenze*, Roma, 1975.

63 Boffi *et al.*, *Città e conflitto sociale*, pp. 75–145.

64 ibid., p. 135.

65 For the full details of these election results, see Statistical Appendix, table 25.

66 G. Galli, *Storia della DC*, pp. 309ff. In the pre-congress period there had been eight factions at work: the Dorotei, the Fanfaniani, the Morotei (the supporters of Aldo Moro), the Tavianei (the supporters of P. E. Taviani), the 'Centristi Popolari', Base, Forze Nuove, and the 'new left' of F. Sullo.

67 Quoted in Tamburrano, *Storia e cronaca*, pp. 322–3.

68 G. Galli, *Storia del socialismo italiano*, pp. 269ff.

69 Allum, *Italy: Republic without Government?*, pp. 225–38.

70 Turone, *Storia del sindacato*, pp. 444–8; O. Castellino, *Il labirinto delle pensioni*, Bologna, 1976.

71 For the passage of the Workers' Charter through Parliament, and Brodolini's role in it, E. Stolfi, *Da una parte sola*, Milano, 1976. For the assessment of one of the Milanese magistrates most involved in applying the Charter, Canosa, *Storia di un pretore*, pp. 35–47. See also the detailed studies edited by T. Treu, *L'uso politico dello Statuto dei lavoratori*, Bologna, 1975, and *Lo Statuto dei lavoratori: prassi sindacali e motivazioni dei giudici*, Bologna, 1976.

72 A. Coletti, *Il divorzio in Italia*, Roma, 1974, pp. 133–51.

73 Ferraresi and Tosi, 'Crisi della città', p. 567; G. Ruffolo, *Riforme e controriforme*, pp. 53–5. For a study of the complicated passage of the law, S. Potenza, 'Riforma della casa e movimento sindacale', in Indovina, ed., *Lo spreco edilizio*, pp. 252–303; see also M. Achilli, *Casa: vertenza di massa*, Padova, 1972.

74 Regalia *et al.* 'Conflitti di lavoro', pp. 41–2 and n. 19.

75 Daolio, *Le lotte per la casa*, p. 27; M. Regini, *I dilemmi del sindacato*, Bologna, 1981, p. 113. See also the remarks of Vittorio Foa: 'In my experience every time that the institutional voice of the trade unions became more important, and their role as co-decision-maker on a national level increased, so their real force diminished, because their links with their social base became less strong. This was a repeated and disillusioning experience' (Foa, 'Sindacato e corporazione', in his *La cultura della CGIL*, p. xx.)

76 For a detailed exposition of this point in relation to the housing law of Oct. 1971, see G. Ruffolo, *Riforme e controriforme*, pp. 54–5.

77 R. Valiani, *La tassazione diseguale*, Roma, 1983, p. 39; see also G. Tremonti and G. Vitaletti, *Le cento tasse degli italiani*, Bologna, 1986.

78 See, above all, A. Graziani, 'Il Mezzogiorno nel quadro dell'economia italiana', in A. Graziani and E. Pugliese, eds., *Investimenti e disoccupazione nel Mezzogiorno*, Bologna, 1979, pp. 7–65.

79 P. Armstrong, A. Glyn and J. Harrison, *Capitalism since World War II*, London, 1984, pp. 269–308.

80 Gigliobianco and Salvati, *Il maggio francese e l'autunno caldo italiano*, p. 21.

81 ibid., p. 23.

82 'La malattia: profitto zero' (interview of E. Scalfari with G. Agnelli), *L'Espresso*, vol. XVIII (1972), no. 47; see also Provasi, *Borghesia industriale e Democrazia Cristiana*, p. 258.

83 Pirzio Ammassari, *La politica della Confindustria*, pp. 172ff.

84 G. Rasi, 'La politica economica e i conti della nazione', in *Annali dell'economia italiana*, vol. XIV, pt 1 (1971–77), Milano, 1985, p. 145.

85 *La strage di stato*, Roma, 1970, pp. 29ff.

86 M. Del Bosco, *Da Pinelli a Valpreda*, Roma, 1972, pp. 54–7.

87 Giorgio Galli makes the distinction between a minority wing who wanted the strategy of tension to lead to a coup, and a majority who would have been content with a government that put the emphasis on anti-left-wing measures and greater law and order. He argues that the orchestration of the strategy was fundamentally the work of the *'corpi separati'* – secret services, both Italian and foreign, and politicized sectors of the officer corps of the tank and parachute regiments, as well as sectors of the navy and air force; G. Galli, *Storia della DC*, pp. 322–4.

88 M. Magrone and G. Pavese, *Ti ricordi di Piazza Fontana?*, vol. 1, Bari, 1986.

89 G. De Lutiis, *Storia dei servizi segreti in Italia*, Roma, 1984, pp. 100–107.

90 Faenza, *Il malaffare*, pp. 315ff.

91 Baldassare and Mezzanotte, *Gli uomini del Quirinale*, pp. 163ff.

92 See *Statistical Appendix*, table 25.

93 G. Ruffolo, *Riforme e controriforme*, p. xxxiii.

94 For a good analysis of class structure in the South in these years, C. Donolo, 'Sviluppo ineguale e disgregazione sociale. Note per l'analisi delle classi nel meridione', *Quaderni Piacentini*, vol. IX (1972), no. 47, pp. 101–28. For the 'hot autumn' in the South, E. Mattina, 'Il Mezzogiorno e l'autunno caldo', in *L'autunno caldo dieci anni dopo, 1969–1979*, Lerici–Roma, 1979.

95 S. Moretti, 'Avola 1968', in *I braccianti*, pp. 366–79.

96 Piselli, *Parentela ed emigrazione*, esp. pp. 112–16 and 204–5.

97 M. Rossi-Doria, 'Dopo i fatti di Battipaglia', in his *Scritti sul Mezzogiorno*, p. 6.

98 For another, less renowned incident, see Collettivo Marxista di Lavoro Politico di Napoli, 'Castellamare di Stabia: analisi di una rivolta (nov. 1971)', *Inchiesta*, vol. II (1972), no. 5, pp. 21–5.

99 For the socio-economic background, P. Ferraris, 'I cento giorni di Reggio: i presupposti della rivolta e la sua dinamica', *Giovane Critica*, 1971, pp. 2–43.

100 F. D'Agostino, *Reggio Calabria. I moti del luglio 1970–febbraio 1971*, Milano, 1972, p. 140.

101 For Catania, G. Galli, *Storia della DC*, p. 342; Walston, *Mafia and Clientelism*, p. 213, table 5.5.

102 V. Guerrazzi, *Nord e Sud uniti nella lotta*, Padova, 1974, p. 106.

103 *1968–72: le lotte alla Pirelli*, p. 13.

104 For Milan, Boffi *et al.*, *Città e conflitto sociale*, p. 133. It should be added, in fairness, that the high turnover rate of the immigrant population must have accounted, at least in part, for their lack of knowledge of neighbourhood politics.

105 Regalia *et al.*, 'Conflitti di lavoro', p. 3.

106 For wages and social expenditure, P. Lange, 'Semiperiphery and core in the European context', in Arrighi, ed., *Semiperipheral Development*, p. 187. For housing and consumer goods, Statistical Appendix, tables 7–9.

107 Rossanda, *L'anno degli studenti*, pp. 121–2.

108 Maggia and Fornengo, *Appunti sul sistema delle partecipazioni statali*, pp. 221ff.; see also their table on p. 235. Taking the major 150 Italian companies in the period 1969–73, the *partecipazioni statali* increased their percentage of total employment from 19.9 to 25.2, of turnover from 21.3 to 29.8, and of fixed capital from 31.0 to 39.2.

109 F. Reviglio, *Spesa pubblica e stagnazione dell'economia italiana*, Bologna, 1977, p. 13.

110 For a good summary of the malfunctioning of the state bureaucracy, Cassese, *Il sistema amministrativo*, pp. 273–87.

111 A. Cederna, 'I terremotati a vita del Belice', 'Quanti monumenti inutili nel Belice' and 'Il Belice rinasce malgrado i padrini', *Corriere della Sera*, 17, 21 and 29 Aug. 1978.

112 A. Riboldi ed., *Lettere dal Belice e al Belice. Le speranze tradite*, Milano, 1977, pp. 46–7.

Chapter 10

1 G. Galli, *Storia della DC*, p. 372.

2 G. Pasquino, 'Crisi della DC ed evoluzione del sistema politico', *Rivista Italiana di Scienza Politica*, vol. V (1975), pp. 443–72.

3 For details of the scandal, and the legislation favouring the petrol companies, G. Galli, *L'Italia sotterranea*, Bari, 1983, pp. 134–8.

4 De Lutiis, *Storia dei servizi segreti*, pp. 107ff. The SID had replaced the SIFAR (of De Lorenzo fame) in 1966. In November 1972, Arnaldo Forlani, one of the younger and more sober Christian Democrat leaders, warned in a public speech at La Spezia that there was evidence of 'probably the most dangerous plot that the reactionary right has developed and organized in the whole post-war period'. Forlani never elaborated on this statement. Vito Miceli was from Trapani in Sicily, and members of the extended Miceli family had frequently been cited in the reports of the parliamentary anti-Mafia commissions.

5 G. Galli, *Fanfani*, Milano, 1975, p. 6.

6 Magister, *La politica vaticana e l'Italia*, p. 426. The most detailed and illuminating treatment of the church's various positions and of the whole debate on divorce is to be found in P. Furlong, 'The Catholic Church and the Question of Divorce in Italy', unpublished PhD thesis, University of Reading, 1981.

7 See the speech of Feb. 1974 by F. Di Giulio to a workers' conference of the party (Partito Comunista Italiano, *VI^a conferenza operaia del PCI, Genova, 8–10 febbraio 1974*, Roma, 1974, p. 41): 'We know that for the great majority of workers the personal problem of divorce does not exist. For the Italian worker the family is a deeply serious project, to be appreciated and to defend. In the family he has found a bulwark and a defence in the most difficult moments of his life and of his struggles. The family constitutes the memory of so many sacrifices undertaken so as to be able to educate one's children. We appeal to this worker, for whom the family means so much, to be seriously involved, as much as possible, in the struggle for divorce. Not for himself, for whom there will not be and will never be a problem of divorce, but for his fellow worker, for his fellow citizen, for whom life has reserved a different destiny.' Compare these views with those of a thirty-five-year-old Communist worker at the Ansaldo Meccanico Nucleare plant at Genoa (May 1974): 'divorce is certainly a greater victory for the workers than the well-to-do, because the latter have

always had the economic resources to seek other solutions, like the Sacra Rota [the church courts]' (no. 24 of sixty-eight replies to V. Guerrazzi, ed., *L'altra cultura. Inchiesta operaia*, Venezia, 1975, p. 161).

8   Lange, 'Semiperiphery and core in the European context', p. 205.

9   Armstrong *et al.*, *Capitalism since World War II*, pp. 309ff.; Rasi, 'La politica economica e i conti della nazione', *Annali dell'economia italiana*, vol. XIV, pt 1, p. 98.

10 Armstrong *et al.*, *Capitalism since World War II*, p. 310.

11 Michele Salvati, *Economia e politica*, p. 112.

12 Rasi, 'La politica economica', p. 111.

13 For a valuable analysis of why Italian inflation remained higher than that elsewhere in Europe, see Michele Salvati, *Economia e politica*, pp. 119–21. The determined defence of the *scala mobile* throughout most of the seventies, argues Salvati, linked wages and prices more closely than in other countries; profits were not recouped through slashing real wages, and employers continued to pass wage costs on in prices. Two possible ways out of this spiral – the growth of productivity at work, and the containment of the incomes of other groups in society, especially in public administration – were not realized.

14 Ascoli, *Movimenti migratori*, p. 57.

15 R. Cornwall, 'Italy grows fat on its underground economy', *Financial Times*, 10 February 1979. See also p. 408 for ISTAT's decision to take the 'black economy' into account in the statistics.

16 Michele Salvati, *Economia e politica*, pp. 124ff.

17 D. J. Coyle, 'The economy', *Financial Times*, 'Survey of Italy', 12 April 1976.

18 For a good comparison of the personalities of Togliatti and Berlinguer, see V. Gorresio, *Berlinguer*, Milano, 1976, p. 30.

19 E. Berlinguer, 'Riflessioni sull'Italia dopo i fatti del Cile', *Rinascita*, 28 Sept., 5 and 9 Oct. 1973; reprinted in E. Berlinguer, *La 'Questione comunista', 1969–75*, ed. A. Tatò, Roma, 1975, vol. II, pp. 609–39.

20 ibid., p. 621.

21 ibid.

22 ibid., p. 635.

23 ibid., pp. 638–9.

24 E. Berlinguer, *Austerità, occasione per trasformare l'Italia*, Roma, 1977, p. 13.

25 ibid., p. 51.

26 Partito Comunista Italiano, *Proposta di un progetto a medio termine*, Roma, 1977.

27 A. Asor Rosa, 'La cultura politica del compromesso storico', *Laboratorio Politico*, vol. II (1982), nos. 2–3, p. 19. For a very critical review of the PCI's strategy, T. Abse, 'Judging the PCI', *New Left Review*, no. 153 (1985), pp. 5–40.

28 One of the most famous and hard-fought of these struggles was at the Leyland–

Innocenti factory in Milan. British Leyland had bought the Innocenti car factory in 1972 and produced a glamorous version of the Mini there. But falling car sales and BL's own ever-growing problems at home caused management to announce, in the summer of 1975, 1,700 redundancies out of a workforce of 4,700. Three months later, Leyland made it clear that they wanted to sell the factory. The workers replied by occupying on 26 Nov. 1975. The occupation lasted all winter, with an average of 1,000 workers present in the factory every day. As the weeks passed, some of the younger immigrant workers were forced for lack of funds to return home to the South to await the reopening of the factory. All the working-class institutions of the city were mobilized in support of the Innocenti workers. However, the occupation still ended in defeat. BL were determined to go, and in February 1976 a face-saving compromise was reached. The Italo-Argentinian entrepreneur De Tomaso took over the factory with Italian state aid, but continued to employ only some 2,500 workers there, with the promise of taking more back later. Not even the strength of the massive Milanese FLM (the metalworkers' union) had been able to prevent defeat.

29   L. Lama, *Intervista sul mio partito*, Bari, 1986, p. 29. As Lama pointed out, this agreement brought its own problems, because skilled workers' real wages were constantly diminishing in comparison with the semi-skilled, and there was growing disillusionment amongst the higher grade workers with trade union policy.

30   Lumley, 'Social Movements', p. 470.

31   *Autoriduzione. Cronache e riflessioni di una lotta operaia e popolare, settembre/ dicembre 1974*, Milano–Roma, 1975; E. Cherki and M. Wieviorka, 'Autoreduction movements in Turin', *Semiotext[e]*, no. 3 (1980), pp. 72–80; Lumley, 'Social Movements', pp. 466–8.

32   Daolio, *Le lotte per la casa*, p. 14. For the Turin experience of the councils, see below, p. 399

33   Quoted in L. Bobbio, *Lotta Continua*, p. 137.

34   ibid., p. 130.

35   For the culture of the new left, Gundle, 'Communism and Cultural Change', pp. 276–87.

36   Bobbio, *Lotta Continua*, pp. 131–3. In November 1975 the first national assembly of the soldiers' movement took place in Rome; 220 delegates were present, representing 133 barracks. The new left at this time had three national daily newspapers: *Il Manifesto, Lotta Continua*, and *Il Quotidiano dei Lavoratori* (the organ of Avanguardia Operaia).

37   G. Bocca, *Noi terroristi*, Milano, 1985, pp. 28 ff., G. Galli, *Storia del partito armato, 1968–1982*, Milano, 1986, pp. 5–19; see also P. Furlong, 'Political terrorism in Italy', in J. Lodge, ed., *Terrorism: a Challenge to the State*, Oxford, 1981, pp. 57–90; and the interesting article by N. Tranfaglia, 'La crisi italiana e il problema storico del terrorismo', in his *Labirinto italiano*, Torino, 1984, pp. 227–82.

38   See in particular N. Dalla Chiesa, 'Del sessantotto e del terrorismo; cultura e politica tra continuità e rottura', *Il Mulino*, vol. XXX (1981), no. 273, pp. 53–94.

39 G. G. Migone, 'Il terrorismo che stabilizza', *L'Indice*, vol. III (1986), no. 8, p. 4. See also C. Pavone, 'Sparo dunque sono. Il nodo della violenza', *Il Manifesto*, 6 May 1982.

40 For the first period of the Red Brigades' activity, G. C. Caselli and D. Della Porta, 'La storia delle brigate rosse: strutture organizzative e strategie d'azione', in D. Della Porta and G. Pasquino, eds., *Terrorismi in Italia*, Bologna, 1984, pp. 156ff.

41 Soccorso Rosso Napoletano, ed., *I NAP*, Milano, 1976; L. Bobbio, *Lotta Continua*, p. 139.

42 Caselli and Della Porta, 'Storia delle BR', pp. 170ff. For Mara Cagol and other women in the Red Brigades, I. Faré and F. Spirito, *Mara e le altre*, Milano, 1979.

43 G. Esposito, ed., *Anche il colera*, Milano, 1973.

44 V Capecchi and E. Pugliese, 'Due città a confronto: Bologna e Napoli', *Inchiesta*, vol. VIII (1978), nos. 35–6, pp. 3 and 12.

45 See F. Ramondino, ed., *Napoli: i disoccupati organizzati*, Milano, 1977.

46 ibid., p. 21.

47 ibid., pp. 182–204. This is an extraordinary account.

48 For some of these difficulties, V. Dini, 'Il movimento dei disoccupati organizzati a Napoli', *Inchiesta*, vol. VIII (1978), nos. 35–6, pp. 88–91.

49 Ramondino, ed., *Napoli: i disoccupati organizzati*, p. 35.

50 Capecchi and Pugliese, 'Due città a confronto', pp. 48–9.

51 Chubb, *Patronage, Power and Poverty*, pp. 162–3; for the housing movement, ibid., pp. 180ff.

52 *L'Ora*, 25 May 1973; quoted by Chubb, *Patronage, Power and Poverty*, p. 196.

53 M. Gramaglia, 'Il 1968. Il venir dopo e l'andar oltre del movimento femminista', *Problemi del Socialismo*, vol. XVII (1976), no. 4, pp. 179–201.

54 Fofi, *L'immigrazione meridionale*, p. 267.

55 D. I. Kertzer, *Comrades and Christians*, Cambridge, 1980, p. 61.

56 A. Vinci and A.Vettore, 'Le donne, il '69 e il sindacato', in *L'autunno caldo 10 anni dopo*, p. 189; for the factory struggles mentioned above, E. De Grandis and I. Spezzano, 'L'autunno caldo e la questione femminile', in ibid., pp. 180–81.

57 Balbo, *Stato di famiglia*, p. 91.

58 G. Re and G. Derossi, *L'occupazione fu bellissima*, Roma, 1976, pp. 100–101.

59 A. Rossi-Doria, 'Una tradizione da costruire', in M. L. Odorizio *et al.*, *Donna o cosa?*, Torino, 1986, pp. 200ff.

60 Odorizio *et al.*, *Donna o cosa?*, pp. 187–8; Bobbio, *Lotta Continua*, pp. 161ff.

61 A. Rossi-Doria, 'Una tradizione da costruire', p. 206.

62 For an interesting study of the feminist movement in Italy, J. Adler Hellman, *Journeys among Women*, Oxford, 1987.

63   C. and S. Rodotà, 'Il diritto di famiglia', in *Ritratto di famiglia degli anni '80*, Bari, 1981, pp. 159–204.

64   G. Ruffolo, *Riforme e controriforme*, pp. 119–20.

65   G. Flamini, *Il partito del golpe*, vol. III, pt 2, Bologna, 1983, pp. 562–80.

66   G. Galli, *L'Italia sotterranea*, pp. 177–80.

67   G. Galli, *Storia della DC*, pp. 415–21.

68   The text of this declaration and that of the French and Italian parties of 15 Nov. 1975 are to be found in P. Filo Della Torre, E.Mortimer and J. Story, *Eurocommunism: Myth or Reality?*, London, 1979, pp. 330–38. See also Giorgio Napolitano's lengthy interview with Eric Hobsbawm, in G. Napolitano, *The Italian Road to Socialism*, London, 1977, pp. 76ff.

69   S. Bonsanti, 'Perché siamo contrari ad un governo con il PCI', *Epoca*, vol. XXVI (1975), no. 1302, 20 Sept; see also R. Brancoli, *Spettatori interessati*, Milano 1980, pp. 76–7.

70   B. Olivi, *Carter e l'Italia*, Milano, 1978, pp. 113–15.

71   G. P. Pansa, 'Berlinguer conta "anche" sulla NATO per mantenere l'autonomia da Mosca', *Corriere della Sera*, 15 June 1976.

72   *L'Espresso*, vol. XXII (1976), no. 23, 6 June, opinion poll by the Pragma Institute.

73   *Time*, 14 June 1976, and the article therein, 'Don Enrico bids for power', pp. 12–18.

74   See Statistical Appendix, table 25.

75   The most detailed analysis of voting patterns in 1976 is G. Pasquino and A. Parisi, eds., *Continuità e mutamento elettorale in Italia*, Bologna, 1977, esp. pp. 11–65.

76   Luciano Lama later described Berlinguer's view of the Socialists as follows: 'He believed that the PSI was a party almost beyond repair. According to him, the only thing that we could do was to conduct a bitter, hard and insistent polemic with the Socialists to see whether, by means of a drastic cure, we could persuade them to change their ways' (Lama, *Intervista sul mio partito*, pp. 121–2).

77   For a short biography, R. Orfei, *Andreotti*, Milano, 1972.

78   P. Guzzanti, 'La difesa di Moro', *La Repubblica*, 10 March 1977.

79   Berlinguer, *Austerità, occasione per trasformare l'Italia*, p. 52.

80   ibid., p. 41.

81   Lama, *Intervista sul mio partito*, p. 68

82   L. Bobbio, *Lotta Continua*, p. 177.

83   ibid., pp. 179 ff.

84   See for instance S. Timpanaro, 'PCI, riformismo, socialdemocratizzazione', *Praxis*, no. 13 (1977), pp. 4–7. For the party abandoning its tradition of defending and guaranteeing citizens' liberties, R. Gagliardi, 'Quarantuno anni di partito comunista', *Il Manifesto*, 12 June 1984.

85 M. Kunzle, ed., *Dear Comrades. Readers' Letters to Lotta Continua*, London, 1980, pp. 9–10.

86 G. Galli, *Storia del partito armato*, pp. 130–54: 'The security forces who, as we have seen, had always been able, right from the beginning, to deal with the terrorist groups, apparently lost this capacity at a stroke, just when the BR were preparing the most clamorous operation in the entire history of the armed struggle' (ibid., p. 152).

87 G. Arnao, *Rapporto sulle droghe*, Milano, 1976. For the growth of social centres in Milan, Lumley, 'Social Movements', pp. 522–5.

88 L. Bobbio, *Lotta Continua*, p. 183.

89 F. Mussi, *Bologna '77*, Roma, 1978. For interviews with some participants in the movement, G. Salierno, *La violenza in Italia*, Milano, 1980, pp. 16–17.

90 For the parabola of the movement of 1977, see Lumley, 'Social Movements', pp. 532–3.

91 Caselli and Della Porta, 'Storia delle BR', pp. 184ff. See also D. Della Porta and M. Rossi, 'I terrorismi in Italia tra il 1969 e il 1982', *Cattaneo*, vol. III (1983), no. 1, pp. 1–44.

92 *La Repubblica*, 28 April 1978; see also M. Cavallini, ed., *Il terrorismo in fabbrica*, Roma, 1978.

93 Most of Moro's prison letters were published in G. Bocca, *Moro: una tragedia italiana*, Milano, 1978. The content of the letters was disowned by the DC leadership, who insisted that they had been dictated by the terrorists and not written by the 'real' Moro. The DC disclaimers were subject to savage attack by Leonardo Sciascia in his famous pamphlet, *L'affaire Moro*, Palermo, 1978.

94 *La Repubblica*, 21 April 1978.

95 Recent accounts of Moro's kidnapping and death include M. Scarano and M. De Luca, *Il mandarino è marcio*, Roma, 1985. The authors attempt to show that discredited members of the secret services and organized crime also played a role in the kidnapping.

96 G. Bocca, *Il caso 7 aprile*, Milano, 1980.

97 *L'Unità*, 15 May 1977; see also the further article by Petruccioli, 'Uno stato all'altezza della vita democratica', *L'Unità*, 14 May 1978.

98 F. Cazzola, 'La solidarietà nazionale de parte del parlamento', *Laboratorio Politico*, vol. II (1982), nos. 2–3, pp. 192–3.

99 A. Barbera, *Governo locale e riforma dello Stato*, Roma, 1978, pp. 14–102.

100 *La Repubblica*, 31 July 1977.

101 Michele Salvati, *Economia e politica*, pp. 146ff. For economic recovery, Statistical Appendix, tables 31 and 35.

102 See Cazzola, 'La solidarietà nazionale', p. 205, n. 25; and the leader by C. Napoleoni, *La Repubblica*, 25 March 1978.

103 For the difficulties that the PCI suffered from being half in and half out of the government, see G. Napolitano, *In mezzo al guado*, Roma, 1979.

104 Rochat *et al.*, *La casa in Italia*, pp. 29–30; for *'abusivismo'* see below, p. 418.

105 ibid., pp. 30–31.

106 See L. Libertini, 'La casa perduta', *Rinascita*, vol. XL (1984), no. 43, p. 12.

107 Campos Venuti, 'Programmare: perché è più difficile, perché è necessario', p. 13.

108 G. Ruffolo, *Riforme e controriforme*, p. 67.

109 F. Ongaro Basaglia, '180, quel debito di solidarietà ancora da saldare', *L'Unità*, 15 May 1988.

110 G. Ruffolo, *Riforme e controriforme*, p. 7.

111 G. Pastori, 'L'attuazione del servizio sanitario nazionale', *Il Mulino*, vol. XXX (1981), no. 278, p. 838. See also U. Ascoli, ed., *Welfare State all'italiana*, Bari, 1984, pp. 5–52; and A. Piperno, 'La politica sanitaria', in ibid., pp. 153–80. For some comparisons of preventive care in Britain and Italy, R. C. R. Taylor, 'State intervention in postwar European health care: the case of prevention in Britain and Italy', in S. Bornstein, D. Held and J. Krieger, eds., *The State in Capitalist Europe*, London, 1984, pp. 91–117.

112 See A. Stabile, 'Le mani dei partiti sulla sanità', *La Repubblica*, 2 April 1985.

113 ibid. See also P. Guzzanti, 'Gli ospedali terra di conquista', *La Repubblica*, 7 April 1985; G. Ruffolo, *Riforme e controriforme*, p. 21.

114 For problems in Caserta, for instance, J. A. Hellman, *Journeys among Women*, pp. 178–82. For a good overall view, L. Caldwell, 'Abortion in Italy', *Feminist Review*, no. 7 (1981), pp. 49–65.

115 Ferraresi and Tosi, 'Crisi della città', pp. 572–3.

116 Capecchi and Pugliese, 'Due città a confronto', p. 41; for traffic policies, Jäggi *et al.*, *Red Bologna*, pp. 63ff.

117 M. Marcelloni, 'Bologna: il conflitto politico fa arretrare il piano', in P. Cecarelli and F. Indovina, eds., *Risanamento e speculazione nei centri storici*, Milano, 1974, p. 58.

118 For a detailed exposition of this revealing story, Ferraresi and Tosi, 'Crisi della città', pp. 587ff.

119 S. Hellman, 'The PCI's alliance strategy', pp. 399–400.

120 Capecchi and Pugliese, 'Due città', tab. 4, p. 10.

121 S. Sechi, 'L'albero, la foresta e la nuova peste', *Il Mulino*, vol. XXVI (1977), no. 250, pp. 291–2. See also F. Murray, 'Flexible specialisation in the "Third Italy"', *Capital and Class*, no. 33 (1987), pp. 84–95.

122 For the university, Sechi, 'L'albero, la foresta', pp. 285–6; for the PCI's ageing membership, Capecchi and Pugliese, 'Due città', pp. 17ff.

123 Capecchi and Pugliese, 'Due città', pp. 45–6.

124 *La Repubblica*, 9 Nov. 1977, interview by G. Bocca with A. Bassolino, at that

time the new regional secretary of the PCI in Campania; for families and living conditions, Capecchi and Pugliese, 'Due città', pp. 21ff.

125 Quoted in M. Valenzi, *Sindaco a Napoli*, Roma, 1978, pp. 141–2. Valenzi recounted how the left-wing *giunta* was unable to negotiate a loan with the Banco di Napoli and had to apply instead to the Istituto Bancario S. Paolo of Turin.

126 *La Repubblica*, 8 Feb. 1978. For kindergartens, Chubb, *Patronage, Power and Poverty*, p. 282, n. 31.

127 Chubb, *Patronage, Power and Poverty*, pp. 226–8. See also the article by Carlo Franco in *La Repubblica*, 1 Feb. 1978, reporting on fighting breaking out between rival groups of the organized unemployed.

128 Dini, 'Il movimento dei disoccupati organizzati', pp. 49ff.

129 S. Hellman, 'A new style of governing: Italian Communism and the dilemmas of transition in Turin, 1975–1979', *Studies in Political Economy*, vol. 1 (1979), no. 2, pp. 159–97.

130 For Saragat and Scalfari, *La Repubblica*, 10 May 1978; for Pintor, *Il Manifesto* of the same date.

131 See his interview with S. Gatti in *L'Espresso*, vol. XXX (1984), no. 50, 16 Dec.

132 Interview with G. P. Pansa in *La Repubblica*, 30 May 1979.

133 Cazzola, 'La solidarietà nazionale', pp. 189–90.

134 See the State Department declaration of 12 Jan. 1978, reprinted in *La Repubblica*, 13 Jan. 1978.

135 Lama, *Intervista sul mio partito*, p. 85.

136 See Statistical Appendix, table 25.

137 G. P. Pansa in *La Repubblica*, 11 Oct 1979.

138 S. Tropea in *La Repubblica*, 27 Sept. 1980.

139 Conversation with the author.

140 C. Romiti, *Questi anni alla Fiat* (interview with G. P. Pansa), Milano, 1988, pp. 123–4.

141 I am grateful to M. Revelli for sending me the unpublished transcription of the tape of the meeting of 15 Oct. 1980. Falcone's speech is to be found on pp. 109–23. For a documentary account of the dispute, P.Perotti and M. Revelli, *Fiat autunno 80. Per non dimenticare*, Torino, 1986 (for 15 Oct., pp. 112–19).

Chapter 11

1 See Statistical Appendix, tables 31 and 35.

2 For a good introduction to the background to the reduction of the *scala mobile*, and the consequent referendum, see A. Di Gioia, *La scala mobile*, Roma, 1984.

3 G. Turani, *1985–1995. Il secondo miracolo economico italiano*, Milano, 1986.

4   For inflation rates and GDP annual growth, Statistical Appendix, tables 31 and 35. For the upturn in Italian industry from 1984, Turani, *1985–1995*, pp. 52–72; for FIAT, ibid., pp. 72–85; Romiti, *Questi anni alla FIAT*, pp. 143–64; A. Friedman, *Tutto in famiglia*, Milano, 1988, pp. 92ff.

5   C. Tyler, 'Time of uncertainty for the Milan bourse', *Financial Times*, 'Survey on the Italian economy', 17 Nov. 1978.

6   C. Tyler, 'The statisticians remain coy', ibid. In view of the bitter competition for economic primacy between the governments of the two countries, readers may find it ironical to note that the revision upwards of Italian statistics was based on the recommendations of a committee headed by Sir Claus Moser, former head of the UK's own Central Statistical Office, and appointed by the Italian government.

7   A. Friedman, 'State industries grapple with privatisation', *Financial Times*, 'Survey on Italy', 18 April 1988; S. Gatti, 'Prodi, sani e forti', *L'Espresso*, vol. XXXIII (1987), no. 8, pp. 180–88. IRI was losing nearly 3,000bn lire in 1982, but by 1986 it had balanced its books.

8   Turani, *1985–1995*, pp. 11–19; R. Di Rienzo, 'Affari Loro', *L'Espresso*, vol. XXXIII (1987), no. 21, pp. 214–17. In May 1987 the capitalization on the Milan stock-market of the three major private Italian groups was as follows: Agnelli, 44,620bn lire; Ferruzzi (Gardini) 24,729bn; De Benedetti, 13,709bn.

9   W. Scobie, 'La dolce Italia', *Observer*, 15 Nov. 1987.

10 Figures for 1985 are from OECD statistics quoted in *Financial Times*, 'Survey on the Italian economy', 17 Nov. 1987; see also J. Wyles, 'Deficit looms as an EC Problem', *Financial Times*, 'Survey on Italy', 18 April 1988; and M. Valentini, 'La forbice non taglia più', *L'Espresso*, vol. XXXV (1989), no. 9, pp. 222–4.

11 J. Wyles, 'The word is not the deed', *Financial Times*, 'Survey on Italian industry', 4 July 1988; D. Lane, 'Trade balance sliding further into deficit', *Financial Times*, 'Survey on Italy', 18 April 1988. Romano Prodi also pointed out two further deficiencies: the lack of long-term planning, which had led Italy for instance to lose its leading position in the world market for household electrical appliances; and the absence of Italian business schools, with the single exception of the Bocconi at Milan; Gatti, 'Prodi, sani e forti', p. 183.

12 E. Scalfari, 'Un paese diviso tra le Alpi e le Piramidi', *La Repubblica*, 'Affari e Finanze', 9 Jan. 1987. In the South in 1988 45 per cent of all those between 14 and 29 years of age, and 58.1 per cent of women in the same age group, were seeking work; see the SVIMEZ report for 1988 quoted by S. Livadiotti, 'Buio a Mezzogiorno', *L'Espresso*, vol. XXXV (1989), no. 10, pp. 259–61.

13 Michele Salvati, *Economia e politica*, pp. 139ff.; Statistical Appendix table 38.

14 Vicarelli, 'Famiglia e sviluppo economico', p. 143.

15 A. Bagnasco, 'Borghesia e classe operaia', in Ascoli and Catanzaro, *La società italiana degli anni Ottanta*, p. 47.

16   L. Gallino, 'Le classi sociali in Italia; trent'anni dopo', in his *Della ingovernabilità*, Milano, 1987, tab. 2, p. 105. Rather than analysing social classes in traditional terms, Gallino suggests a new division based on the four major systems of Italian society: the political, the economic, that of 'socio-cultural reproduction', and that of 'bio-psychic reproduction'; see also P. Sylos Labini, *Le classi sociali negli anni '80*, Bari, 1986, p. 207, tab. 1.1.2.

17   F. Recanatesi, 'Compro, vendo, evado', *La Repubblica*, 17 Jan. 1984; A. Talamanca, 'Il bottegaio mangia l'operaio', *L'Espresso*, vol. XXIV (1978), no. 6, 12 Feb., pp. 124–6, where the following European comparisons are cited: there is one shop for every 67 inhabitants in Italy, one for every 90 in France, one for every 105 in Great Britain and one for every 115 in Germany. See also F. Bugno and G. F. Modolo, 'Il bottegaio', *L'Espresso*, vol. XXVIII (1982), no. 37, pp. 160–66, who cite a D O X A opinion poll of 1980 on the voting preferences of Italian shopkeepers. Their choices departed from the figures for all voters in only two respects: the P C I was under-represented with 21.8 per cent of shopkeeper preferences; the P S I was over-represented with 19.4 per cent.

18   For white-collar workers in the public sector, C. Sebastiani, *Pubblico impiego e ceti medi*, Roma, 1975: see also G. Gasparini, *Gli impiegati*, Milano, 1979, which analyses white-collar work in the chemical and engineering industries, in banks and the *parastato*. For teachers, M. Dei and M. Rossi, *Sociologia della scuola italiana*, Bologna, 1978.

19   Sylos Labini, *Le classi sociali*, p. 207, tab. 1.1.2. These figures are for all workers, not just for industrial and building workers, as in 1971 (see above, p. 238).

20   G. Lerner, *Operai*, Milano, 1988, p. 92.

21   *La povertà in Italia. Rapporto conclusivo della commissione di studio istituita presso la Presidenza del Consiglio dei Ministri*, Roma, 1986, tab. 2.6, p. 51.

22   For the situation in a quarter like Quarto Oggiaro on the periphery of Milan, G. Lerner, 'I senza niente', *L'Espresso*, vol. XXX (1984), no. 45, 11 Nov; for the despair, cynicism and *qualunquismo* of a group of Roman unemployed in the labour exchange (Ufficio di Collocamento) on the Via Appia Nuova, see the report by G. P. Pansa in *La Repubblica*, 1 Feb. 1978; for the situation in the capital eleven years later, L. Villoressi, 'Una capitale con la miseria dentro il cuore', *La Repubblica* (Roman edition), 28 March 1989.

23   It is extremely difficult to estimate the exact numbers of immigrant workers in Italy. Ministry of Interior statistics of December 1985 listed 423,000 foreigners in Italy, but as many as a third of these were from the other European countries. Numbers have certainly risen sharply since 1985, and the number of illegal immigrants can only be guessed at. For some of the difficulties in this field, O. Casacchia, 'La dimensione quantitativa dell'immigrazione straniera in Italia', in N. Sergi, ed., *L'immigrazione straniera in Italia*, Roma, 1987, pp. 9–34; for a typology of immigration and the possibilities of employment, F. Carchedi

and G. B. Ranuzzi, 'Tra collocazione nel mercato del lavoro secondario ed esclusione dal sistema della cittadinanza', ibid., pp. 35–80.

24 One of the most notorious recent incidents was that of an Eritrean woman being forced off a Roman bus, simply because she was Eritrean; 'Giù dal bus, "negra". Ora si nasconde per paura' (*L'Unità*, 17 May 1988).

25 This is the thesis of P. P. Donati, who writes of the spiralling process from the 'accumulative privatization' (*privatismo accumulativo*) in the fifties to the 'consumerist privatization' (*privatismo consumistico*) of the sixties and the 'anti-crisis privatization' of the seventies (*un privatismo di ripiegamento anti-crisi*); P. P. Donati, *Pubblico e privato, fine di una alternativa?*, Bologna, 1978, p. 290.

26 These figures refer to 1986, and are based on the second report on '*associazionismo sociale*', compiled by IREF (Istituto di Ricerche Educative e Formative of the ACLI); see M. R. Calderoni, 'Otto milioni di uomini di "buona volontà"', *L'Unità*, 10 April 1989. Bepi Tomai, the director of IREF, was at pains to point out the path-breaking aspects of these new experiences, even in the South: 'We interviewed twenty of these southern organizations, and do you know what emerged? . . . a great affinity with the popular, mutual aid and cooperative movement of the late nineteenth century, with the emphasis placed strongly on moral and cultural values.'

27 G. Turnaturi and C. Donolo, 'Familismi morali', in C. Donolo and F. Fichera, *Le vie dell'innovazione*, Milano, 1988, pp. 164–85.

28 See Statistical Appendix, tables 1 to 6. For a review of the development of Italian studies on the family, C. Saraceno, 'La sociologia della famiglia tra crisi delle teorie e innovazione tematica', *Quaderni di Sociologia*, vol. XXXII (1985), nos. 4–5, pp. 307–34. For the declining birthrate, E. Occorsio, 'Per l'Europa è scattato l'allarme grigio', *La Repubblica*, 12 May 1989. It is estimated that at present rates the Italian population will have shrunk by some 300,000 by the year 2008, and that those over sixty-five years of age will have increased from 13.4 per cent of the population in 1987 to 18.6 per cent in 2007.

29 F. Bugarini and G. Vicarelli, 'Interazione e sostegno parentale in ambiente urbano', *Rassegna Italiana di Sociologia*, 1979, no. 3, pp. 461–93; L. Balbo, M. Cacioppo and M. P. May, *Struttura urbana, sistema di orari, bisogni*, Bologna, 1984; Paci, *La struttura sociale italiana*, pp. 69–79 and in particular tab. 5, p. 76, which suggests that this type of modified extended family, to use Litwak's expression, is more common in Italy than elsewhere in Europe.

30 G. De Rita, 'L'impresa famiglia', in P. Melograni and L. Scaraffia, eds., *La famiglia italiana dall'Ottocento a oggi*, Bari 1988, pp. 383–4 and 393–4.

31 A. Cavalli and A. De Lillo, *Giovani oggi*, Bologna, 1984 and *Giovani anni '80*, Bologna, 1988. For the scale of values see *Giovani anni '80*, tab. IV, 1, p. 71. Religious commitment had marginally improved its standing in the later survey. The scale in both 1984 and 1988 read in the following order (from top to bottom): family, work, girl or boyfriend and friends in general, pastimes, studying and cultural interests, sport, social commitment, religious commitment,

political activity. For 'fatalistic' youth, pp. 65ff., for girls in southern families, pp. 109ff. The survey published in 1988 found that out of every 100 young people aged twenty-three or twenty-four, 79 still lived at home.

32   C. Saraceno, 'Interdipendenze e spostamenti di confini tra "pubblico" e "privato"', *Il Mulino*, vol. XXXII (1983), no. 289, pp. 784–97. For an interesting discussion of changes in Italian men's and women's roles from the second half of the nineteenth century to the present day, L. Scaraffia, 'Essere uomo, essere donna', in Melograni and Scaraffia, *La famiglia italiana*, pp. 193–258. The surveys of Cavalli and De Lillo bear testimony to the greater autonomy of Italian youth within the family, but have also revealed the continuing limitations placed upon daughters' freedoms in poorer families in the South; *Giovani anni '80*, pp. 109ff.

33   Statistical Appendix, table 7. Family savings in the 1970s were characterized predominantly by investment in houses, state bonds and deposit accounts. In the 1980s they have diversified somewhat, into the ownership of shares, investment in life insurance and private pension schemes, etc.; De Rita, 'L'impresa famiglia', pp. 402–5.

34   G. Vicarelli, 'Famiglia e sviluppo economico', p. 144.

35   Lerner, *Operai*, p. 31. See also C. Saraceno, 'Modelli di famiglia', in *Ritratto di famiglia degli anni' 80*, p. 67–80, and B. Barbero Avanzini and C. Lanzetti, *Problemi e modelli di vita familiare*, Milano, 1980, pp. 194–223 and 244–5. This last study, based on interviews carried out in 1976 with 997 married persons in Milan between the ages of 26 and 45, reveals the very low levels of social participation even in the middle of the 1970s. The only involvement which the authors deem 'minimally significant' was that in schools, in which more than a third of those interviewed, mostly women, took an active interest.

36   C. Saraceno, 'Modelli di famiglia', p. 88. See also P. Giudicini, G. Scidà, eds., *Il familismo efficiente*, Milano, 1981.

37   Trigilia, *Grandi partiti e piccole imprese*, pp. 183ff. Trigilia notes that local government councils can give little direct economic support to small industry, but can create a 'local social salary' made up primarily of efficent social services. In this field the communes of the 'Red Belt' have been particularly successful. For the success story of the Third Italy see also A. Bagnasco, 'Borghesia e classe operaia', p. 43; his fascinating study of Tuscan development, 'Le classi e la formazione sociale regionale', in Mori, ed., *Storia d'Italia ... La Toscana*, pp. 733–68; and that of G. Becattini, 'Riflessioni sullo sviluppo socio-economico della Toscana in questo dopoguerra', ibid., pp. 899–924. For statistics on the increase in the number of small firms between 1971 and 1981, De Rita, 'L'impresa famiglia', p. 387.

38   L. Balbo, 'La doppia presenza', *Inchiesta*, vol. VIII (1978), no. 32, pp. 3–6; V. Capecchi, 'La famiglia interclassista: geografia attuale delle diseguaglianze', *Il Manifesto*, 15 May 1986.

39   Letter from D. Troiano, *Il Manifesto*, 11 April 1987. See also M. Mafai, 'Superprotetti e lavoro nero', *La Repubblica*, 17 March 1987.

40   S. Piccone Stella, *Ragazze del Sud*, Roma, 1979, pp. 40ff.

41   E. Mingione, 'Economia informale, strategie familiari e Mezzogiorno', *Inchiesta*, vol. XVI (1986), n. 74, pp. 2–3.

42   M. Rossi-Doria, 'Limite e prospettive della trasformazione agraria nel Mezzogiorno', *Ulisse*, vol. XVI (1983), no. 95, pp. 65–7.

43   Saraceno, 'Modelli di famiglia', p. 98. For 'residual' peasant families, E. Pugliese, 'Per l'analisi delle classi subalterne nel Meridione', in C. Donolo *et al.*, *Classi sociali e politica nel Mezzogiorno*, Torino, 1978, p. 92. For the flow of money payments, Boccella, *Il Mezzogiorno sussidiato, passim*.

44   For an important study of an emigration zone in the Sicilian interior, E. Reyneri, *La catena migratoria*, Milano, 1978.

45   See, for example, A. Stabile, 'Ecco il volto della Sicilia abusiva', *La Repubblica*, 20 Feb. 1986.

46   For the elections of 1983, Statistical Appendix, table 25.

47   G. Pasquino, 'Mediazione e opportunismo', *Rinascita*, vol. XLI (1984), no. 43, 3 Nov. p. 9. See also the menacing remarks about the electoral power of the shopowners, made by Giuseppe Orlando, the veteran leader of the major shopowners' federation, the Confcommercio, in an interview with G. P. Pansa (*La Repubblica*, 18 Oct. 1984): 'Let's do some sums. The small businesses affected by Visentini's measures number four million. To these we must add another one million self-employed professionals (*liberi professionisti*). Total: five million. Multiply by at least two. New total: ten million electors, perhaps more. As you see, the problem is of enormous proportions. Certainly not all of them will spoil their ballot papers. But it is still a biblical flux that we're talking about!' In the event, the elections of 1987 saw no such electoral protest.

48   D. Pasti, 'Regione "bella addormentata"', *La Repubblica*, 24 Oct. 1986.

49   F. Miracco, 'In morte della legge Galasso', *Il Manifesto*, 15 Jan. 1989.

50   P. Ginsborg, 'Berlinguer's legacy', *London Review of Books*, vol. VI (1984), no. 18, 4 Nov.

51   For an opposite view J. La Palombara, *Democracy, Italian Style*, New Haven, CT, 1987.

52   Statistical Appendix, tables 26 and 27.

53   U. Ascoli, 'Il sistema italiano di welfare', in U. Ascoli, *Welfare State all'italiana*, pp. 39ff.

54   S. Malatesta, 'Il santuario dell'amore pietrificato del Vesuvio', *La Repubblica*, 20 Aug. 1988.

55   G. Ruffolo, 'Aux armes les citoyens!', *Micromega*, no. 4 (1986), p. 7.

56   P. Di Nicola, 'Cittadini in marcia', *L'Espresso*, vol. XXXIII (1987), no. 47, pp. 22–3. The weekly column was called 'Diritti smarriti' (Lost Rights), and was published from Feb. 1987 onwards.

57   P. Forcellini, 'La macchina in panne', *L'Espresso*, vol. XXXII (1986), no. 35, 7 Sept., pp. 185–6.

58 G. Amato, 'Conto poco e lo so, vi racconto perché . . .', *La Repubblica*, 23 July 1988. The title of the letter is *La Repubblica*'s, not Amato's.

59 G. De Lutiis, ed., *La strage. L'atto d'accusa dei giudici di Bologna*, Roma, 1986, pp. 3–92 for the bomb at Bologna station, pp. 303–80 for Licio Gelli and the P2. See also *L'Italia della P2*, Milano, 1983.

60 For the background to Dalla Chiesa's assassination, see N. Dalla Chiesa, *Delitto imperfetto*, Milano, 1984; P. Arlacchi *et al.*, *Morte di un generale*, Milano, 1982.

61 C. Staiano, ed., *L'atto di accusa dei giudici di Palermo*, Roma, 1986: for the development and transformation of the Mafia, R. Catanzaro, 'Mafia, economia e sistema politico', in U. Ascoli and Catanzaro, *La società italiana degli anni Ottanta*, pp. 255–79.

62 CENSIS, *A metà decennio. Riflessioni e dati sull'Italia dall'80 al'85*, Milano, 1986, pp. 87–8. For Domenico Sica's remarks, S. Bonsanti, 'Quei prefetti non sono all'altezza', *La Repubblica*, 16 Nov. 1988.

63 Pizzorno, 'I ceti medi nel meccanismo del consenso'.

64 See the debate between G. De Michelis and L. Colletti, 'Socialismo: nuova sinistra', *L'Espresso*, vol. XXXII (1986), no. 42, 26 Oct.

65 S. Tarrow, 'The crisis of the late 60s in Italy and France', in Arrighi, *Semi-peripheral development*, p. 238.

66 A. O. Hirschman, *Shifting Involvements*, Princeton, NJ, 1982, p. 46: 'I have come across much evidence that, in the West, each time economic progress has enlarged the availability of consumer goods for some strata of society, strong feelings of disappointment in, or of hostility toward, the new material wealth have come to the fore. Along with appreciation, infatuation and even addiction, affluence seems to produce its own backlash, almost regardless of what *kinds* of goods are newly and more abundantly marketed.'

Bibliography

of Works Cited in the Text

* Particularly useful as introductory reading.

Absalom, R., 'Per una storia di sopravvivenze. Contadini italiani e prigionieri britannici evasi', *Italia Contemporanea*, vol. XXXII (1980), no. 140, pp. 105–22.

'Il ruolo politico ed economico degli Alleati a Firenze (1944–1945)', in Rotelli, ed., *La ricostruzione in Toscana dal CLN ai partiti*, q.v., pp. 233–43.

'Terre desiderate, terre sognate: alcuni fattori economici e no del comportamento politico degli ex mezzadri', *Annali dell'Istituto Alcide Cervi*, vol. VIII (1986), pp. 181–9.

Abse, T., 'Judging the P C I', *New Left Review*, no. 153 (1985), pp. 5–40.

Accornero, A., *Gli anni '50 in fabbrica*, Bari, 1976.

Accornero, A., and Rieser, V., *Il mestiere dell'avanguardia*, Bari, 1981.

Achilli, M., *Casa: vertenza di massa*, Padova, 1972.

Addario, G., *Una crisi del sistema*, Bari, 1982.

Aga-Rossi, E., 'La politica angloamericana verso la Resistenza italiana', in Ferratini Tosi *et al.*, eds., *Italia nella seconda guerra mondiale*, q.v., pp. 141–54.

Aga-Rossi, E., ed., *Il piano Marshall e l'Europa*, Roma, 1983.

Agnelli, G., 'La malattia: profitto zero' (Interview with E. Scalfari), *L'Espresso*, vol. XVIII (1972), no. 47.

Ajello, N., *Intellettuali e PCI, 1944–58*, Bari, 1979.

Alasia, F., and Montaldi, D., *Milano, Corea*, Milano, 1975 (1st ed., 1960).

Albertelli, G., and Ziliani, G., 'Le condizioni alloggiative della popolazione immigrata', in Pellicciari, ed., *L'immigrazione nel triangolo industriale*, q.v., pp. 283–303.

Allum, P., 'La D C Vicentina nel secondo dopoguerra: appunti per una ricostruzione', *Strumenti*, vol. III (1984), nos. 3–4, pp. 19–34.

Italy: Republic without Government?, London, 1973.

* *Politics and Society in Post-war Naples*, Cambridge, 1973.

Allum, P., and Diamanti, I., *'50–'80. Vent'anni*, Roma, 1986.

Alzona, G., 'Grande industria: sviluppo e strutture di controllo, 1963–72', in Graziani, ed., *Crisi e ristrutturazione nell'economia italiana*, q.v., pp. 248–87.

Amaduzzi, R., 'Intervento', in Vianello, ed., *Il piano del lavoro*, q.v., pp. 147–51.

Bibliography

Amato, G., *Economia, politica e istituzioni in Italia*, Bologna, 1976.

Amato, G., ed., *Il governo dell'industria in Italia*, Bologna, 1972.

Amato, P., *Il PSI tra frontismo e autonomia*, Cosenza, 1978.

Amendola, G., *Classe operaia e programmazione democratica*, Roma, 1966.

'Necessità della lotta su due fronti', *Rinascita*, (supplement, *Il contemporaneo*). vol. XXV (1968), no. 18.

'Prime considerazioni sulle elezioni del Mezzogiorno', *Rinascita*, vol. III (1946), nos. 5–6.

'Unità e socialismo' (a discussion with G. C. Pajetta and L. Basso), *Rinascita*, vol. XXII (1965), no. 29.

* Amyot, G., *The Italian Communist Party*, London, 1981.

Anastasia, B., and Rullani, E., 'La nuova periferia industriale', *Materiali Veneti*, nos. 17–18 (1981–2), pp. 7–203.

Antonuzzo, A., *Boschi, miniera, catena di montaggio*, Roma, 1976.

Arbizzani, L., 'Notizie sui contadini della pianura bolognese durante la Resistenza', *Il Movimento di Liberazione in Italia*, vol. XVI (1964), no. 75, pp. 30–67.

'Nuova amministrazione senza riforme', in Comune di Bologna, *Giuseppe Dozza a dieci anni dalla morte*, q.v., pp. 55–78.

Arfé, G., 'Prefazione', in Taddei, *Il socialismo italiano*, q.v., pp. 9–19.

Arlacchi, P., *Mafia, Peasants and Great Estates*, Cambridge, 1983.

Arlacchi, P., *et al.*, *Morte di un generale*, Milano, 1982.

* Armstrong, P., Glyn, A., and Harrison, J., *Capitalism since World War II*, London, 1984.

Arnao, G., *Rapporto sulle droghe*, Milano, 1976.

Arrighi, G., ed., *Semiperipheral Development*, London, 1985.

Ascoli, G., 'L'UDI tra emancipazione e liberazione (1943–64)', in Ascoli, G., *et al.*, *La questione femminile*, q.v., pp. 105–59.

Ascoli, G., *et al.*, *La questione femminile in Italia dal '900 ad oggi*, Milano, 1977.

Ascoli, U., *Movimenti migratori in Italia*, Bologna, 1979.

'Il sistema italiano di Welfare', in Ascoli, U., ed., *Welfare State all'italiana*, q.v., pp. 5–52.

Welfare State all'italiana, Bari, 1984.

Ascoli, U., and Catanzaro, R., eds., *La società italiana degli anni Ottanta*, Bari, 1987.

Asor Rosa, A., 'La cultura politica del compromesso storico', *Laboratorio Politico*, vol. II (1982), nos. 2–3, pp. 5–43.

Atti della Commissione d'inchiesta sul salvataggio del porto di Genova, ed. Istituto Storico della Resistenza in Liguria, Genova, 1951.

Atti della Commissione parlamentare d'inchiesta sugli eventi del giugno–luglio 1964, 2 vols., Roma, 1971.

Bibliography

Atti della Commissione parlamentare d'inchiesta sulla miseria e sui mezzi per combatterla, 15 vols., Milano–Roma, 1953–8.

Atti dell'VIII congresso della Democrazia Cristiana (Napoli, 27–31 gennaio 1962), Roma, 1963.

Autoriduzione. Cronache e riflessioni di una lotta operaia e popolare, settembre–dicembre 1974, Milano–Roma, 1975.

L'autunno caldo dieci anni dopo, 1969–1979, Lerici–Roma, 1979.

Baget-Bozzo, G., *Il partito cristiano al potere. La DC di De Gasperi e di Dossetti, 1945–54*, 2 vols., Firenze, 1974.

 Il partito cristiano e l'apertura a sinistra, Firenze, 1977.

Baglioni, G., *Il sindacato dell'autonomia*, Bari, 1977.

Baglivo, A., and Pellicciari, G., *Sud amaro: esodo come sopravvivenza*, Milano, 1970.

 La tratta dei meridionali, Milano, 1973.

Bagnasco, A., 'Borghesia e classe operaia', in Ascoli, U., and Catanzaro, eds., *La società italiana degli anni Ottanta*, q.v., pp. 30–49.

 'Le classi e la formazione sociale regionale', in Mori, ed., *Storia d'Italia . . . La Toscana*, q.v., pp. 735–68.

 Tre Italie. La problematica territoriale dello sviluppo italiano, Bologna, 1977.

Bagnasco, A., and Trigilia, C., *Società e politica nelle aree di piccola impresa: il caso di Bassano*, Venezia, 1984.

 Società e politica nelle aree di piccola impresa: il caso di Valdelsa, Milano, 1985.

Bairati, P., *Vittorio Valletta*, Torino, 1983.

Balbo, L., 'La doppia presenza', *Inchiesta*, vol. VIII (1978), no. 32, pp. 3–6.

 Stato di famiglia, Milano, 1976.

Balbo, L., Cacioppo, M., and May, M. P., *Struttura urbana, sistema di orari, bisogni*, Bologna, 1984.

Baldassare, A., and Mezzanotte, C., *Gli uomini del Quirinale*, Bari, 1985.

Baldi, G., *Vita e lotte delle case del popolo in provincia di Firenze, 1944–1956*, Firenze, 1956.

Balducci, R., 'Capitale finanziario e struttura industriale', in Vicarelli, F., ed., *Capitale industriale e capitale finanziario: il caso italiano*, q.v., pp. 357–404.

* Banfield, E., *The Moral Basis of a Backward Society*, Glencoe, Ill., 1958.

Baranelli, L., and Cherchi, M. G., eds., *Quaderni Piacentini. Antologia, 1962–68*, Milano, 1977.

Barbagli, M., *Disoccupazione intellettuale e sistema scolastico in Italia*, Bologna, 1974.

 Sotto lo stesso tetto, Bologna, 1984.

Barbagli, M., and Dei, M., *Le vestali della classe media*, Bologna, 1969.

538

Bibliography

Barbera, A., *Governo locale e riforma dello Stato*, Roma, 1978.

Barbera Avanzini, B., and Lanzetti, C., *Problemi e modelli di vita familiare*, Milano, 1980.

Barberis, C., 'Avvio al dibattito', in INSOR, *La riforma fondiaria*, q.v., pp. 31–57.

Barucci, P., *Ricostruzione, pianificazione, Mezzogiorno*, Bologna, 1978.

Battaglia, R., *Risorgimento e Resistenza*, Torino, 1964.

    Storia della Resistenza italiana, Torino, 1964 (1st ed., 1953).

Becattini, G., 'Riflessioni sullo sviluppo socio-economico della Toscana in questo dopoguerra', in Mori, ed., *Storia d'Italia . . . La Toscana*, q.v., pp. 901–26.

Belloni, M. C., *et al.*, 'I commercianti e la mobilitazione politica', in Carboni, ed., *I ceti medi in Italia*, q.v., pp. 234–50.

Berlinguer, E., *Austerità, occasione per trasformare l'Italia*, Roma, 1977.

    La 'Questione comunista', 1969–1975, ed. A. Tatò, 2 vols., Roma, 1975.

    'Riflessioni sull'Italia dopo i fatti del Cile', in Berlinguer, E., *La 'Questione comunista', 1969–75*, q.v., Vol. II, pp. 609–39.

Bernardi, L., Neppi-Modona, G., and Testori, S., *Giustizia penale e guerra di Liberazione*, Milano, 1984.

Bernieri, C., *L'albero in piazza*, Milano, 1977.

Berselli, A., 'Come sorsero i quartieri', in Comune di Bologna, *Giuseppe Dozza a dieci anni dalla morte*, q.v., pp. 87–96.

Berta, G., *Le idee al potere*, Milano, 1980.

Bertelli, S., *Il gruppo*, Milano, 1984.

Bertocci, S., 'Indagine sull'arma dei carabinieri', *Il Ponte*, vol. XVI (1960), no. 7, pp. 1060–77.

Bertolo, G., and Guerrini, L., 'Le campagne toscane e marchigiane durante il fascismo. Note sulla situazione economica e sociale dei ceti contadini', *Il Movimento di Liberazione in Italia*, vol. XXII (1970), no. 101, pp. 111–60.

Bertolo, G., *et al.*, *Operai e contadini nella crisi italiana del 1943–1944*, Milano, 1974.

Bevilacqua, P., *Le campagne del Mezzogiorno tra fascismo e dopoguerra. Il caso della Calabria*, Torino, 1980.

    '1945: luci ed ombre del movimento contadino', *Rivista Storica Calabrese* (New series), vol. I (1980), pp. 131–63.

    'Quadri mentali, cultura e rapporti simbolici nella società rurale del Mezzogiorno', *Italia Contemporanea*, vol. XXXVI (1984), no. 154, pp. 51–70.

Bianchi, E., *Il tramonto della mezzadria toscana e i suoi riflessi geografici*, Milano, 1983.

Bianchi, G., *L'Italia dei ministeri: lo sfascio guidato*, Roma, 1981.

Bianchi, G., *et al.*, *I CUB: Comitati unitari di base*, Roma, 1971.

Bianco, I., *Il movimento cooperativo italiano*, Milano, 1975.

Blackmer, D., and Tarrow, S., eds., *Communism in Italy and France*, Princeton, 1975.

Bibliography

* Blok, A., *The Mafia of a Sicilian Village*, New York, 1975 (1st ed., 1974).

Boatti, G., *L'arma*, Milano, 1978.

Bobbio, L., 'Arroganza e sacchi a pelo', *Panorama*, vol. XXV (1987), no. 1128.

    Lotta Continua, Roma, 1979.

Bobbio, N., 'Pace e propaganda di pace' (1952) in N. Bobbio, *Politica e cultura*, Torino, 1955, pp. 72–83.

Bocca, G., *Il caso 7 aprile*, Milano, 1980.

    Miracolo all'italiana, Milano, 1980 (1st ed., 1962).

    Moro: una tragedia italiana, Milano, 1978.

    Noi terroristi, Milano, 1985.

    Palmiro Togliatti, Bari, 1973.

    La Repubblica di Mussolini, Bari, 1977.

    Storia della Repubblica italiana, Milano, 1981–2.

Boccella, N., *Il Mezzogiorno sussidiato*, Milano, 1982.

Boffi, M., *et al.*, *Città e conflitto sociale*, Milano, 1972.

Boggs, C., 'Gramsci and Eurocommunism', *Radical America*, vol. XIV (1980), no. 3, pp. 7–23.

'Bollettino della sezione comunista di Montescaglioso', *Rinascita*, vol. VII (1950), no. 3.

Bonaccorsi, M., 'Gli enti pubblici del settore della sicurezza sociale', in Cazzola, ed., *Anatomia del potere democristiano*, q.v., pp. 57–159.

Bonazzi, G., Bagnasco, A., and Casillo, S., *Industria e potere politico in una provincia meridionale*, Torino, 1972.

Bonelli, F., ed., *Acciaio per l'industrializzazione*, Torino, 1982.

Bonfante, G., *et al.*, *Il movimento cooperativo in Italia*, Torino, 1981.

Bongiovanni, B., Jocteau, G. C., and Tranfaglia, N., eds., *Storia d'Europa*, 4 vols., Firenze, 1981.

Bonsanti, S., 'Perché siamo contrari ad un governo con il PCI', *Epoca*, vol. XXVI (1975), no. 1302.

Bonvini, G., Scalpelli, A., eds., *Milano fra guerra e dopoguerra*, Bari, 1979.

Bornstein, S., Held, D., Krieger, J., eds., *The State in Capitalist Europe*, London, 1984.

Bortolotti, L., 'L'evoluzione del territorio', in Mori, ed., *Storia d'Italia . . . La Toscana*, q.v., pp. 773–820.

Bowring, Sir J., 'Report on the statistics of Tuscany, Lucca, the Pontifical and the Lombardo-Venetian States, with a special reference to their commercial relations', *Parliamentary Papers*, vol. XVI (1839), 'Reports from Commissioners', pp. 1–159.

I braccianti. Venti anni di lotte, Roma, 1969.

Braghin, P., ed., *Inchiesta sulla miseria in Italia*, Torino, 1978.

Brancoli, R., *Spettatori interessati*, Milano, 1980.

Bugarini, F., and Vicarelli, G., 'Interazione e sostegno parentale in ambiente urbano', *Rassegna Italiana di Sociologia*, no. 3 (1979), pp. 464–93.

Bugno, F., and Modolo, G. F., 'Il bottegaio', *L'Espresso*, vol. XXVIII (1982), no. 37.

Burgalassi, S., *Il comportamento religioso degli italiani*, Firenze, 1968.

La burocrazia centrale in Italia. Analisi sociologica, Milano, 1965.

Caciagli, M., *et al.*, *Democrazia Cristiana e potere nel Mezzogiorno*, Firenze, 1977.

Cacioppo, M., 'Condizione di vita familiare negli anni Cinquanta', *Memoria*, no. 6 (1982), pp. 83–90.

* Caesar, M., and Hainsworth, P., *Writers and Society in Contemporary Italy*, London, 1984.

Cafagna, L., 'Integrazione europea', in Bongiovanni *et al.*, eds., *Storia d'Europa*, q.v., vol. IV, pp. 1665–87.

Calabrese, O., *Carosello o dell'educazione serale*, Firenze, 1975.

Calamandrei, M., 'La città in campagna', *L'Espresso*, vol. V (1959), no. 4.

Calamandrei, P., *Uomini e città della Resistenza*, Bari, 1977 (1st ed., 1955).

Calamandrei, P., and Levi, P., *Commentario sistematico alla Costituzione italiana*, Firenze, 1950.

Caldwell, L., 'Abortion in Italy', *Feminist Review*, no. 7 (1981), pp. 49–65.

Campagne e movimento contadino nel Mezzogiorno d'Italia, 2 vols., Bari, 1979–80.

Campos Venuti, G., 'Programmare: perché è più difficile, perché è necessario', *Rinascita*, vol. XL (1984), no. 43.

Cancogni, M., 'Cicicov in Campidoglio', *L'Espresso*, vol. II (1956), no. 4.

'I ragazzi di Maurizio', *L'Espresso*, vol. XI (1965), no. 50.

Candeloro, G., *Storia dell'Italia moderna*, vol. X, Milano, 1984, vol. XI, Milano, 1986.

Canosa, R., *Storia di un pretore*, Torino, 1979.

Canosa, R., and Federico, P., *La magistratura in Italia dal 1945 a oggi*, Bologna, 1974.

Canteri, C., *Immigrati a Torino*, Milano, 1964.

Capecchi, V., and Pugliese, E., 'Due città a confronto: Bologna e Napoli', *Inchiesta*, vol. VIII (1978), nos. 35–6, pp. 3–54.

Capecchi, V., *et al.*, *Le 150 ore nella regione Emilia-Romagna. Storia e prospettive*, 6 vols., Bologna, 1982.

Carabba, M., *Un ventennio di programmazione, 1954–74*, Bari, 1977.

Carboni, C., ed., *I ceti medi in Italia*, Bari, 1981.

Carchedi, F., and Ranuzzi, G. B., 'Tra collocazione nel mercato del lavoro secondario ed esclusione del sistema della cittadinanza', in Sergi, ed., *L'immigrazione straniera in Italia*, q.v., pp. 35–80.

Carli, G., *Intervista sul capitalismo italiano*, ed. E. Scalfari, Bari, 1977.

Carocci, G., 'Un difetto di egemonia', in *Il vizio d'origine*, ed. G. Zincone, *La Biblioteca della Libertà*, vol. XVII (1980), nos. 77–8, pp. 99–114.

Casacchia, O., 'La dimensione quantitativa dell'immigrazione straniera in Italia', in Sergi, ed., *L'immigrazione straniera in Italia*, q.v., pp. 9–34.

Casali, L., and Gagliani, D., 'Movimento operaio e organizzazione di massa. Il PCI in Emilia-Romagna (1945–1954)', in D'Attorre, ed., *La ricostruzione in Emilia-Romagna*, q.v., pp. 255–84.

Caselli, G. C., and Della Porta, D., 'La storia delle brigate rosse: strutture organizzative e strategie d'azione', in Della Porta and Pasquino, eds., *Terrorismi in Italia*, q.v., pp. 153–221.

Cassese, S., *Esiste un governo in Italia?*, Roma, 1980.

> *Questione amministrativa e questione meridionale*, Milano, 1977.

> *Il sistema amministrativo italiano*, Bologna, 1983.

Cassese, S., ed., *L'amministrazione centrale*, Torino, 1984.

> *L'amministrazione pubblica in Italia*, Bologna, 1974.

Castellino, O., *Il labirinto delle pensioni*, Bologna, 1976.

Castronovo, V., 'La storia economica', in *Storia d'Italia*, q.v., vol. IV, pt 1, pp. 5–506.

Castronovo, V., ed., *L'Italia contemporanea 1945–75*, Torino, 1976.

Catalano, F., 'La missione del CLNAI al Sud', *Il Movimento di Liberazione in Italia*, vol. VIII (1955), no. 36, pp. 3–43.

Catanzaro, R., 'Mafia, economia e sistema politico', in Ascoli, U., and Catanzaro, *La società italiana negli anni Ottanta*, q.v., pp. 255–82.

Catti De Gasperi, M. R., *De Gasperi, uomo solo*, Milano, 1964.

> *La nostra patria Europa*, Milano, 1969.

Cavalli, A., and De Lillo, A., *Giovani anni '80*, Bologna, 1988.

> *Giovani oggi*, Bologna, 1984.

Cavallini, M., ed., *Il terrorismo in fabbrica*, Roma, 1978.

Cavarra, R., and Sclavi, M., *Gli statali, 1923–1978*, Torino, 1980.

Cavazza, F. L., and Graubard, S. R., eds., *Il caso italiano*, Milano, 1974.

Cazzola, F., 'I pilastri del regime', *Rassegna Italiana di Sociologia*, vol. XVII (1976), pp. 421–47.

> 'La solidarietà nazionale dalla parte del parlamento', *Laboratorio Politico*, vol. II (1982), nos. 2–3, pp. 5–43.

Cazzola, F., ed., *Anatomia del potere democristiano*, Bari, 1979.

Cecarelli, P., and Indovina, F., eds., *Risanamento e speculazione nei centri storici*, Milano, 1974.

Cederna, A., *Mirabilia urbis*, Torino, 1965.

Cederna, C., Lombardi, M., and Somaré, M., *Milano in guerra*, Milano, 1979.

Cella, G. P., Manghi, B., and Piva, P., *Un sindacato italiano negli anni Sessanta*, Bari, 1972.

CENSIS, *A metà decennio. Riflessioni e dati sull'Italia dall'80 all'85*, Milano, 1986.

Centro Siciliano di Documentazione, *Portella delle Ginestre: una strage per il centrismo*, Palermo, 1977.

Ricomposizione del blocco dominante, lotte contadine e politica delle sinistre in Sicilia (1943–1947), Palermo, 1977.

Centro Studi della Cassa per il Mezzogiorno, *Cassa per il Mezzogiorno. Dodici anni, 1950–1962*, 6 vols., Bari, 1976.

C'era una volta la D.C., Roma, 1975.

Cerquetti, E., *Le forze armate italiane dal 1945 al 1975*, Milano, 1975.

Cherki, E., and Wieviorka, M., 'Autoreduction movements in Turin', *Semiotext(e)*, no. 3 (1980), pp. 72–80.

Cherubini, A., *Storia della previdenza sociale*, Roma, 1977.

Chianese, G., *Storia sociale della donna in Italia (1800–1980)*, Napoli, 1980.

Chianese, G., *et al.*, *Italia 1945–50. Conflitti e trasformazioni sociali*, Milano, 1985.

Chinello, C., *Classe, movimento, organizzazione*, Milano, 1984.

Chittolini, G., and Miccoli, G., eds., *Storia d'Italia, Annali, IX: la Chiesa e il potere politico dal Medioevo all'età contemporanea*, Torino, 1986.

* Chubb, J., *Patronage, Power and Poverty in Southern Italy*, Cambridge, 1982.

Churchill, W. S., *The Second World War*, vol. V, *Closing the Ring*, London, 1952.

Ciconte, E., *All'assalto delle terre del latifondo*, Milano, 1981.

Cinanni, P., *Lotte per la terra e comunisti in Calabria, 1943–53*, Milano, 1977.

Lotte per la terra nel Mezzogiorno, 1943–53, Venezia, 1979.

Ciranna, G., 'Un gruppo di pressione: la Confederazione Nazionale Coltivatori Diretti', *Nord e Sud*, vol. V (1958), no. 38, pp. 9–39.

Cittante, A., *Memorie di un sindacalista rurale*, Rovigo, 1973.

* Clark, M., *Modern Italy, 1871–1982*, London, 1984.

Claudin, F., *The Communist Movement from Comintern to Cominform*, London, 1975.

Colarizzi, S., *La seconda guerra mondiale e la Repubblica*, Torino, 1984.

Coles, H. L., and Weinberg, A. K., *Civil Affairs: Soldiers Become Governors*, Washington, DC, 1964.

Coletti, A., *Il divorzio in Italia*, Roma, 1974.

Collettivo Marxista di Lavoro Politico di Napoli, 'Castellamare di Stabia: analisi di una rivolta (nov. 1971)', *Inchiesta*, vol. II (1972), no. 5, pp. 21–5.

Collin, R., *The De Lorenzo Gambit*, London, 1976.

Collotti, E., 'Collocazione internationale dell'Italia dall'armistizio alle premesse dell'alleanza atlantica (1943–1947)', in Quazza *et al.*, *L'Italia dalla Liberazione alla Repubblica*, q.v., pp. 27–118.

Bibliography

'Introduzione all'archivio Pietro Secchia, 1945–1973', *Annali della Fondazione G. G. Feltrinelli*, vol. XIX (1978), pp. 7–135.

Colombi, A., 'I comunisti emiliani al lavoro', in D'Attorre, ed., *I comunisti in Emilia-Romagna*, q.v., pp. 52–61.

Colombo, E., 'La famiglia a Montecitorio', in Gedda, ed., *Spiritualità della famiglia*, q.v., pp. 136–41.

Comune di Bologna, *Giuseppe Dozza a dieci anni dalla morte*, Bologna, 1985.

Comunisti. I militanti bolognesi del PCI raccontano, Roma, 1983.

Confederazione Nazionale dei Coltivatori Diretti, *Aspetti sociali e religiosi del mondo rurale italiano*, Roma, 1958.

I congressi della CGIL, vol. I, Roma, 1949; vol. III, Roma, 1952.

I congressi nazionali della Democrazia Cristiana, Roma, 1959.

Consonni, G., and Tonon, G., 'Aspetti della questione urbana a Milano dal fascismo alla ricostruzione', *Classe*, vol. VIII (1976), no. 12, pp. 43–101.

Conti, L., *L'assistenza e la previdenza sociale*, Milano, 1958.

Contini, G., *Memoria e storia: le officine Galileo nel racconto degli operai, dei tecnici, dei manager, 1944–1959*, Milano, 1985.

'Natalino Carrai: il mondo di un bambino contadino (toscano) alla fine degli anni '30' (forthcoming).

'Gli operai comunisti e la svolta del 1956', *Annali della Fondazione Giacomo Brodolini*, vol. I (1987), pp. 433–53.

Coppola, A., *Moro*, Milano, 1976.

Corner, P., *Fascism in Ferrara, 1915–25*, Oxford, 1975.

'Fascist agrarian policy and the Italian economy in the inter-war years', in Davis, J. A., ed., *Gramsci and Italy's Passive Revolution*, q.v., pp. 239–74.

Corsi, A., 'L'esodo agricolo dagli anni '50 agli anni '70 in Italia e nel Mezzogiorno', *Rassegna Economica*, vol. XLI (1977), no. 3, pp. 721–53.

Cortesi, L., 'Palmiro Togliatti, la "svolta di Salerno" e l'eredità gramsciana', *Belfagor*, vol. XXX (1975), pp. 1–44.

Crainz, G., 'I braccianti padani', in Chianese *et al.*, *Italia 1945–1950*, q.v., pp. 173–326.

'Il movimento contadino e l'occupazione delle terre dalla Liberazione alle lotte dell'autunno 1946', *Quaderni della Resistenza Laziale*, vol. IV (1977), pp. 7–72.

Crespi, F., and Martinelli, F., 'La dinamica delle relazioni sociali nel contesto urbano', *Rivista di Sociologia*, vol. VI (1968), no. 16, pp. 5–62.

Croce, B., *Quando l'Italia era tagliata in due*, Bari, 1948.

Crouch, C., and Pizzorno, A., eds., *Conflitti in Europa*, Milano, 1977.
The Resurgence of Class Conflict in Western Europe, 2 vols., London, 1978.

D'Agostino, F., *Reggio Calabria. I moti del luglio 1970–febbraio 1971*, Milano, 1972.

Bibliography

Dal latifondo al potere. Atti del Convegno degli assegnatari DC delle terre di riforma fondiaria, Roma, 1955.

Dalla Chiesa, N., 'Del sessantotto e del terrorismo; cultura e politica tra continuità e rottura', *Il Mulino*, vol. XXX (1981), no. 273, pp. 53–94.

Delitto imperfetto, Milano, 1984.

Dalla Liberazione alla Costituente, Milano, 1981.

Damiliano, A., ed., *Atti e documenti della Democrazia Cristiana 1943–67*, 2 vols., Roma, 1968–9.

Daneo, C., *Breve storia dell'agricoltura italiana*, Milano, 1980.

La politica economica della ricostruzione 1945–49, Torino, 1975.

D'Antonio, M., *Sviluppo e crisi del capitalismo italiano 1951–1972*, Bari, 1973.

Daolio, A., ed., *Le lotte per la casa in Italia*, Milano, 1974.

D'Attorre, P. P., 'Aspetti dell'attuazione del piano Marshall in Italia', in Aga-Rossi, *Il piano Marshall*, q.v., pp. 163–80.

'I comunisti in Emilia-Romagna nel secondo dopoguerra: un'ipotesi di lettura', in D'Attorre, *I comunisti in Emilia-Romagna*, q.v., pp. 7–29.

D'Attorre, P. P., ed., *I comunisti in Emilia-Romagna*, Bologna, 1981.

La ricostruzione in Emilia-Romagna, Parma, 1980.

Davis, J., *Land and Family in Pisticci*, London, 1973.

Davis, J. A., ed., *Gramsci and Italy's Passive Revolution*, London, 1979.

Deakin, F. W., *The Brutal Friendship. Mussolini, Hitler and the Fall of Italian Fascism*, London, 1962.

Debenedetti, G., *16 ottobre 1943*, Milano, 1959.

De Cecco, M., *Saggi di politica monetaria*, Milano, 1968.

Dedijer, V., *Tito Speaks*, London, 1953.

De Gasperi, A., 'Idee ricostruttive della Democrazia Cristiana', in Zunino, ed., *Scritti politici di Alcide De Gasperi*, q.v., pp. 256–63.

'Nella lotta per la Democrazia' (discorso al V Congresso della DC Napoli, 26–29 giugno 1954), in *I Congressi nazionali della DC*, q.v., pp. 478–503.

De Gasperi, M. R., ed., *De Gasperi scrive*, 2 vols., Brescia, 1974.

De Gasperi, M. R., See also Catti De Gasperi, M. R.

Degli Espinosa, A., *Il regno del Sud*, Roma, 1946.

Degli Incerti, D., ed., *La sinistra rivoluzionaria in Italia*, Roma, 1976.

De Grandis, E., and Spezzano, I., 'L'autunno caldo e la questione femminile', in *L'autunno caldo dieci anni dopo*, q.v., pp. 178–86.

Dei, M., and Rossi, M., *Sociologia della scuola italiana*, Bologna, 1978.

Del Bosco, M., *Da Pinelli a Valpreda*, Roma, 1972.

Del Carria, R., *Proletari senza rivoluzione*, vol. V, Roma, 1977.

Della Porta, D., and Pasquino, G., eds., *Terrorismi in Italia*, Bologna, 1984.

Della Porta, D., and Rossi, M., 'I terrorismi in Italia tra il 1969 e il 1982', *Cattaneo*, vol. III (1983), no. 1, pp. 1–44.

Della Rocca, G., 'L'offensiva politica degli imprenditori nelle fabbriche', *Annali dell'Istituto G. G. Feltrinelli*, vol. XVI (1974–75), pp. 609–38.

Dellavalle, C., 'Torino', in Bertolo *et al.*, *Operai e contadini*, q.v., pp. 193–253.

De Luna, G., *Storia del Partito d'Azione*, Milano, 1982.

De Lutiis, G., *Storia dei servizi segreti in Italia*, Roma, 1984.

De Lutiis, G., ed., *La strage. L'atto di accusa dei giudici di Bologna*, Roma, 1986.

Delzell, C. F., *Mussolini's Enemies: the Italian Anti-Fascist Resistance*, Princeton, NJ, 1961.

De Marco, P., 'Il difficile esordio del governo militare e la politica sindacale degli Alleati a Napoli, 1943–44', *Italia Contemporanea*, vol. XXXI (1979), no. 136, pp. 39–66.

De Martino, E., 'Postilla a considerazioni storiche sul lamento funebre lucano', *Nuovi Argomenti*, vol. VIII (1955), no. 12, pp. 1–42.

    Sud e magia, Milano, 1959.

    La terra del rimorso, Milano, 1961.

De Michelis, G., and Colletti, L., 'Socialismo: nuova sinistra', *L'Espresso*, vol. XXXII (1986), no. 42.

Democrazia Cristiana, *Libro bianco su Bologna*, Bologna, 1956.

De Rita, G., 'L'impresa famiglia', in Melograni and Scaraffia, eds., *La famiglia italiana dall'Ottocento a oggi*, q.v., pp. 383–416.

De Simonis, P., 'Il grano era la forma dove s'era più forti', *Annali dell'Istituto Alcide Cervi*, vol. VIII (1986), pp. 293–306.

De Stefani, A., *Una riforma al rogo*, Roma, 1963.

Di Ciaccia, F., *La condizione urbana. Storia dell'Unione Inquilini*, Milano, 1974.

Di Capua, G., *Come l'Italia aderì al Patto Atlantico*, Roma, 1969.

Di Gioia, A., *La scala mobile*, Roma, 1984.

Dina, A., 'I tecnici nella società contemporanea', *Problemi del Socialismo*, vol. IX (1967), nos. 24–5, pp. 1406–16.

Dini, V., 'Il movimento dei disoccupati organizzati a Napoli', *Inchiesta*, vol. VIII (1978), nos. 35–6, pp. 88–91.

Di Nicola, P., 'Cittadini in marcia', in *L'Espresso*, vol. XXXIII (1987), no. 47.

Direttivo Nazionale di Gioventù Aclista, *Incontri sulla famiglia*, Roma, n.d.

Di Rienzo, R., 'Affari loro', in *L'Espresso*, vol XXXIII (1987), no. 21.

Dolci, D., *Inchiesta a Palermo*, Torino, 1956.

Donati, P. P., 'Profilo dei recenti cambiamenti strutturali, demografici e culturali della famiglia italiana e connesse implicazioni di politica sociale', in Vella, ed., *Un sinodo per la famiglia*, q.v., pp. 51–93.

Pubblico e privato, fine di una alternativa?, Bologna, 1978.

Donolo, C., 'Social change and transformation of the state in Italy', in Scase, ed., *The State in Western Europe*, q.v., pp. 164–96.

'Sviluppo ineguale e disgregazione sociale. Note per l'analisi delle classi nel meridione', *Quaderni Piacentini*, vol. XI (1972), no. 47, pp. 101–28.

Donolo, C., and Fichera, F., *Le vie dell'innovazione*, Milano, 1988.

Donolo, C., ed., *Classi sociali e politica nel Mezzogiorno*, Torino, 1978.

Duggan, C., *La mafia durante il fascismo*, Soveria Mannelli, 1986 (English ed., *Fascism and the Mafia*, New Haven, CT, and London, 1989).

* Earle, J., *The Italian Cooperative Movement*, London, 1986.

Einaudi, L., *Lo scrittoio del Presidente*, Torino, 1976.

Ellwood, D., *L'alleato nemico*, Milano, 1977.

    * *Italy 1943–1945*, Leicester, 1985.

'Il piano Marshall e il processo di modernizzazione in Italia', in Aga-Rossi, ed., *Il piano Marshall*, q.v., pp. 149–62.

Emiliani, V., *L'Italia mangiata*, Torino, 1975.

Enciclopedia cattolica, 12 vols., Roma, 1948–54.

Esping-Andersen, G., Friedland, R., and Wright, E. O., 'Modes of class struggle and the capitalist state', in *Kapitalistate*, nos. 4–5 (1976), pp. 186–220.

Esposito, G., ed., *Anche il colera*, Milano, 1973.

Fabiani, G., 'Il piano del lavoro e le lotte per la riforma', in Vianello, ed., *Il piano del lavoro*, q.v., pp. 100–124.

Fadiga Zanatta, A. L., *Il sistema scolastico italiano*, Bologna, 1971.

Faenza, R., *Il malaffare*, Milano, 1978.

Falconi, C., *La chiesa e le organizzazioni cattoliche in Italia (1945–1955)*, Torino, 1956.

Gedda e l'Azione Cattolica, Firenze, 1958.

Falcucci, F., 'La famiglia, società naturale fondata sul matrimonio', in Movimento Femminile della DC, *La famiglia e le trasformazioni*, q.v., pp. 7–35.

Famiglia e società capitalistica (Quaderni de *Il Manifesto*, no. 1), Roma, 1974.

Famiglia e società nell'analisi marxista, in *Critica Marxista*, Quaderno no. 1, supplement to no. 6, 1964.

Famiglie di oggi e mondo sociale in trasformazione (XXVIII Settimana sociale dei cattolici d'Italia, Pisa, sett. 1954), Roma, 1956.

Fanfani, A., 'Relazione al VI° Congresso della D.C.', in *I congressi nazionale della DC*, q.v., pp. 579–624.

Bibliography

Relazione al consiglio nazionale della D.C., 12–14 marzo 1955, Roma, 1955.

Fanti, G., 'Relazione introduttiva', Prima conferenza regionale del PCI (Bologna 1959), in D'Attorre, *I comunisti in Emilia-Romagna*, q.v., pp. 121–44.

Fanti, G., and Zangheri, R., 'Classe operaia e alleanze in Emilia', in *Cinquantesimo del PCI* (*Critica Marxista*, Quaderno no. 5, 1972), pp. 259–71.

Faré, I., and Spirito, F., *Mara e le altre*, Milano, 1979.

Federici, C., 'La ricostruzione a La Spezia', tesi di laurea, Facoltà di lettere, Università di Pisa, 1976–7.

Femia, J., *The Political Theory of Antonio Gramsci*, Oxford, 1981.

Fenoglio, B., *Il partigiano Johnny*, Torino, 1968.

Ferraresi, F., *Burocrazia e politica in Italia*, Bologna, 1980.

Ferraresi, F., and Tosi, A., 'Crisi della città e politica urbana', in Graziano and Tarrow, eds., *La crisi italiana*, q.v., pp. 559–605.

Ferrari, L., 'Il laicato cattolico tra Otto e Novecento: dalle associazioni devozionali alle organizzazioni militanti di massa', in Chittolini and Miccoli, eds., *Storia d'Italia, Annali', IX*, q.v., pp. 931–74.

Ferraris, P., 'I cento giorni di Reggio: i presupposti della rivolta e la sua dinamica', *Giovane Critica*, 1971, pp. 2–43.

Ferratini Tosi, F., Grassi, G., and Legnani, M., eds., *L'Italia nella seconda guerra mondiale e nella Resistenza*, Milano, 1988.

Ferretti, V., 'Cooperazione e partito comunista a Reggio Emilia', in D'Attorre, ed., *La ricostruzione in Emilia-Romagna*, q.v., pp. 195–210.

Filo Della Torre, P., Mortimer, E., and Story, J., *Eurocommunism: Myth or Reality?*, London, 1979.

Fini, M., 'Oligarchia elettrica e Resistenza di fronte al problema della difesa degli impianti', in Bonvini and Scalpelli, eds., *Milano fra guerra e dopoguerra*, q.v., pp. 231–85.

Flamini, G., *Il partito del golpe*, 4 vols., Bologna, 1980–84.

Flores, M., 'L'epurazione', in Quazza *et al.*, *L'Italia dalla Liberazione alla Repubblica*, q.v., pp. 413–67.

'Il regime transitorio', in *Dalla Liberazione alla Costituente*, q.v., pp. 1–75.

Flores, M., ed., *Il 'Quaderno dell'Attivista'*, Milano, 1976.

Foa, V., *La cultura della CGIL*, Torino, 1984.

'Intervento' in Vianello, ed., *Il piano del lavoro della CGIL*, q.v., pp. 174–82.

'Introduzione' to *I lavoratori studenti. Testimonianze raccolte a Torino*, q.v., pp. 9–48.

'Prefazione', in Levi, F., *et al.*, *Il triangolo industriale*, q.v., pp. vii–xxvii.

Per una storia del movimento operaio, Torino, 1980.

'La ricostruzione capitalistica e la politica delle sinistre', in *Italia 1945–48*, q.v., pp. 99–136.

Sindacati e lotte operaie (1943–1973), Torino, 1975.

Fofi, G., *L'immigrazione meridionale a Torino*, Milano, 1964.

Fondazione L. Einaudi, *Nord e Sud nella società e nell'economia di oggi*, Torino, 1968.

Forcella, E., 'Un altro dopoguerra', in Occhipinti, *Una donna di Ragusa*, q.v., pp. 5–34.

  Celebrazione di un trentennio, Milano, 1974.

  'Il "mito" di Kennedy', in Schlesinger *et al.*, *Gli anni di Kennedy*, q.v., pp. 54–67.

Forcellini, P., 'La macchina in panne', *L'Espresso*, vol. XXXII (1986), no. 35.

Franchetti, L., 'Condizioni politiche e amministrative della Sicilia', in L. Franchetti, S. Sonnino, *Inchiesta in Sicilia*, vol. 1. Firenze, 1974 (1st ed., 1876), pp. 3–271.

Francovich, C., *La Resistenza a Firenze*, Firenze, 1961.

Fried, R. C., *The Italian Prefects*, Yale, 1963.

Friedman, A., *Tutto in famiglia*, Milano, 1988 (original English ed., *Agnelli and the Network of Italian Power*, London, 1988).

Fubini, A., *Urbanistica in Italia*, Milano, 1978.

Furlong, P., 'The Catholic Church and the Question of Divorce in Italy', unpublished PhD thesis, University of Reading, 1981.

  * 'Political terrorism in Italy', in Lodge, ed., *Terrorism: a Challenge to the State*, q.v., pp. 57–90.

Galasso, G., *La riforma agraria in Calabria*, Roma, 1958.

Gallerano, N., 'L'altro dopoguerra', in Gallerano, ed., *L'altro dopoguerra*, q.v., pp. 31–49.

  'La disgregazione delle basi di massa del Fascismo nel Mezzogiorno e il ruolo delle masse contadine', in Bertolo *et al.*, *Operai e contadini*, q.v., pp. 435–96.

  'Gli italiani in guerra. Appunti per una ricerca', in Ferratini Tosi *et al.*, eds., *L'Italia nella seconda guerra mondiale*, q.v., pp. 308–16.

Gallerano, N., ed., *L'altro dopoguerra. Roma e il Sud 1943–1945*, Milano, 1985.

Gallerano N., *et al.*, 'Crisi di regime e crisi sociale', in Bertolo *et al.*, *Operai e contadini*, q.v., pp. 3–78.

Galli, G., *Fanfani*, Milano, 1975.

  L'Italia sotterranea, Bari, 1983.

  La sfida perduta, Milano, 1976.

  Storia della Democrazia Cristiana, Bari, 1978.

  Storia del partito armato, 1968–1982, Milano, 1986.

  Storia del socialismo italiano, Bari, 1980.

Galli, G., and Facchi, P., *La sinistra democristiana*, Milano, 1962.

Galli, R., and Torcasio, S., *La partecipazione italiana alla politica agraria comunitaria*, Bologna, 1976.

Galli della Loggia, E., 'Ideologie, classi e costume', in Castronovo, ed., *L'Italia contemporanea*, q.v., pp. 379–434.

Gallino, L., *Della ingovernabilità*, Milano, 1987.

'L'evoluzione della struttura di classe in Italia', *Quaderni di Sociologia*, vol. XIX (1970), no. 2.

* Gambetta, D., 'Mafia: the price of distrust', in Gambetta, ed., *Trust*, q.v., pp. 158–75.

Gambetta, D., ed., *Trust: Making and Breaking Cooperative Relations*, Oxford, 1988.

Gambi, L., *Calabria*, Torino, 1965.

Gambino, A., *Storia del dopoguerra dalla Liberazione al potere DC*, Bari, 1975.

Ganapini, L., *Una città, la guerra*, Milano, 1988.

'Milano', in Bertolo *et al.*, *Operai e contadini*, q.v., pp. 145–92.

Ganapini, L., ed., '. . . Che tempi, però erano bei tempi . . .', Milano, 1986.

Ganapini, L., and Rugafiori, P., 'Per una rilettura degli anni 50', *Movimento Operaio e Socialista*, vol. VII (1984), no. 2, pp. 163–70.

Gannon, R., *The Cardinal Spellman Story*, Garden City, NY, 1962.

Garland, A. M., and McGaw Smyth, N., *Sicily and the Surrender of Italy*, Washington, D C, 1965.

Garzia, A., *Da Natta a Natta. Storia del Manifesto e del PDUP*, Bari, 1985.

Gasparini, G., *Gli impiegati*, Milano, 1979.

Gatti, S., 'Intervista con Lama', *L'Espresso*, vol. XXX (1984), no. 50.

'Prodi, sani e forti', *L'Espresso*, vol. XXXIII (1987) no. 8.

Gedda, L., *Spiritualità della famiglia*, Milano, 1952.

Gentile, S., 'Mafia e gabelloti in Sicilia: Il P C I dai decreti Gullo al lodo De Gasperi', *Archivio Storico per la Sicilia Orientale*, vol. LXIX (1973), no. 3, pp. 491–508.

Giarrizzo, G., 'La Sicilia politica 1943–1945. La genesi dello statuto regionale', *Archivio storico per la Sicilia orientale*, vol. LXVI (1970) nos. 1–2, pp. 9–136.

Gibelli, A., *Genova operaia nella Resistenza*, Genova, 1968.

'I grandi costruttori', in Micheli, *Ansaldo 1950*, q.v.

Gibelli, A., and Ilardi, M., 'Genova', in Bertolo *et al.*, *Operai e contadini*, q.v., pp. 95–143.

Gigliobianco, A., and Salvati, M., *Il maggio francese e l'autunno caldo italiano: la risposta di due borghesie*, Bologna, 1980.

Ginsborg, P., 'Berlinguer's legacy', *London Review of Books*, vol. VI (1984), no. 18.

'The Communist party and the agrarian question in southern Italy 1943–48', *History Workshop Journal*, no. 17 (1984), pp. 81–101.

Ginzburg, C., 'Folklore, magia, religione', in *Storia d'Italia*, vol. 1, Torino, 1972, pp. 603–76.

Giudicini, P., and Scidà, G., eds., *Il familismo efficiente*, Milano, 1981.

Giugni, G., *et al.*, *Gli anni della conflittualità permanente*, Milano, 1976.

Giustiniani, C., *La casa promessa*, Torino, 1981.

Bibliography

Goffi, T., *Morale familiare*, Brescia, 1962 (1st ed., 1958).

Gonella, G., 'La D.C. per la nuova Costituzione', in *I congressi nazionali della DC*, q.v., pp. 29–64.

Gorrieri, E., *La giungla retributiva*, Bologna, 1972.

Gorresio, V., *Berlinguer*, Milano, 1976.

'Durante e dopo il boom: sesso, matrimonio, famiglia', *I problemi di Ulisse*, vol. XV (1981), no. 91, pp. 33–40.

La nuova missione, Milano, 1968.

Gorz, A., *Strategy for Labour: a Radical Reappraisal*, Boston, Mass., 1971.

Gramaglia, M. 'Il 1968. Il venir dopo e l'andar oltre del movimento femminista', *Problemi del socialismo*, vol. XVII (1976), no. 4, pp. 179–201.

Gramsci, A., *Selections from Political Writings 1910–1920*, ed. Q. Hoare, London, 1977.

Selections from the Prison Notebooks, ed. Q. Hoare and D. Nowell-Smith, London, 1971.

Grassi, G. ed. 'Verso il governo del popolo.' *Atti e documenti del CLNAI, 1943–1946*, Milano, 1977.

Graziani, A., 'Il Mezzogiorno nel quadro dell'economia italiana', in Graziani and Pugliese, eds., *Investimenti e disoccupazione nel Mezzogiorno*, q.v., pp. 7–65.

Graziani, A., ed, *Crisi e ristrutturazione dell'economia italiana*, Torino, 1975.

L'economia italiana: 1945–1970, Bologna, 1971.

Graziani, A., and Pugliese, E., eds., *Investimenti e disoccupazione nel Mezzogiorno*, Bologna, 1979.

Graziano, L., *Clientelismo e sistema politico. Il caso dell'Italia*, Milano, 1979.

La politica estera italiana nel dopoguerra, Padova, 1968.

Graziano, L,, and Tarrow, S., eds., *La crisi italiana*, 2 vols., Torino, 1979.

Gribaudi, G., *Mediatori*, Torino, 1980.

'Mito dell'eguaglianza e individualismo: un comune del Mezzogiorno', in Chianese *et al.*, *Italia 1945–1950*, q.v., pp. 455–575.

Gribaudi, M., *Mondo operaio e mito operaio*, Torino, 1987.

Guarnaschelli, M., and Serge, V., 'Il morbo di Stalin', *Belfagor*, vol. XXXVIII (1983), no. 1, pp. 85–90.

Guerra, E., 'Per una storia delle 150 ore in Emilia-Romagna', in Capecchi *et al.*, *Le 150 ore nella regione Emilia-Romagna*, q.v., vol. I, pp. 11–42.

Guerrazzi, V., *Nord e Sud uniti nella lotta*, Padova, 1974.

Guerrazzi, V., ed., *L'altra cultura. Inchiesta operaia*, Venezia, 1975.

Guerrini, L., 'La Toscana', in Bertolo *et al.*, *Operai e contadini*, q.v., pp. 319–88.

Guidetti Serra, B., *Compagne*, 2 vols., Torino, 1977.

Gundle, S. J., 'L'americanizzazione del quotidiano. Televisione e consumismo nell'Italia degli anni Cinquanta', *Quaderni Storici*, vol. XXI (1986), no. 62, pp. 561–94.

Bibliography

'Communism and Cultural Change in Post-war Italy', unpublished PhD thesis, Cambridge University, 1985.

'Gramsci, Togliatti and the "Italian road to Socialism" ', unpublished research paper, 1983.

Harper, J. L. *America and the Reconstruction of Italy, 1945–1948,* Cambridge, 1986.

Harris, C. R. S., *Allied Military Administration in Italy, 1943–1945,* London, 1957.

* Hebblethwaite, P., *John XXIII,* London, 1984.

* Hellman, J. Adler, *Journeys among Women,* Oxford, 1987.

Hellman, S., 'The "New Left" in Italy', in Kolinsky and Paterson, eds., *Social and Political Movements in Western Europe,* q.v., pp. 243–75.

'A new style of governing: Italian Communism and the dilemmas of transition in Turin, 1975–1979', *Studies in Political Economy,* vol. 1 (1979), no. 2, pp. 159–97.

* 'The PCI's alliance strategy and the case of the middle classes', in Blackmer and Tarrow, *Communism in Italy and France,* q.v. pp. 373–419.

* Hine, D., 'Italy', in Ridley, ed., *Government and Administration in Western Europe,* q.v., pp. 156–203.

Hirschman, A. O., 'Inflation and deflation in Italy', *American Economic Review,* vol. XXXVIII (1948), pp. 598–606.

Shifting Involvements, Princeton, NJ, 1982.

Hobsbawm, E., 'Gli intellettuali e l'antifascismo', in *Storia del Marxismo,* vol. III, pt 2, Torino, 1981, pp. 443–90.

* Hood, S., *Carlino,* Manchester, 1985 (first published as *Pebbles from My Skull,* London, 1963).

Hughes, H. Stuart, *The United States and Italy,* Cambridge, Mass., 1979 (1st ed., 1963).

Hytten, E., and Marchioni, M., *Industrializzazione senza sviluppo,* Milano, 1970.

Indovina, F., ed., *Lo spreco edilizio,* Venezia, 1978.

INEA (Istituto Nazionale di Economia Agraria), *Monografie di famiglie agricole,* vol. IV, *Contadini siciliani,* Milano–Roma, 1933.

Monografie di famiglie agricole, vol. V, *Mezzadri e piccoli proprietari coltivatori in Umbria,* Milano–Roma, 1933.

Ingrao, P., *Masse e potere,* Roma, 1980.

'Il XX congresso del PCUS e l'VIII congresso del PCI' in *Problemi di storia del PCI,* q.v., pp. 131–68.

Insolera, I., *Roma moderna,* Torino, 1963.

INSOR (Istituto Nazionale di Sociologia Rurale) *La riforma fondiaria: trent' anni dopo,* 2 vols., Milano, 1979.

Isnenghi, M., 'Alle origini del 18 aprile. Miti, riti, mass media', in Lanaro and Isnenghi, eds., *La Democrazia Cristiana,* q.v., pp. 277–344.

Istituto di Studi e Ricerche Carlo Cattaneo, *L'organizzazione politica del PCI e della DC*, Bologna, 1968.

La presenza sociale del PCI e della DC, Bologna, 1968.

Istituto Gramsci, *Togliatti e il Mezzogiorno*, 2 vols., Roma, 1977.

Italia 1945–48. Le origini della Repubblica, Torino, 1974.

Italia sotto inchiesta. Corriere della sera, 1963–1965, Firenze, 1965.

Jäggi, M., Müller, R., and Schmid, S., *Red Bologna*, London, 1977 (first published as *Das röte Bologna*, Zürich, 1976).

Kaiser, K., 'Le relazioni transnazionali', in Cavazza and Graubard, eds., *Il caso italiano*, q.v., pp. 401–19.

Kenny, M., and Kertzer, D. I., eds., *Urban Life in Mediterranean Europe*, Urbana, IL, 1983.

Kertzer, D. I., *Comrades and Christians*, Cambridge, 1980.

'Urban research in Italy', in Kenny and Kertzer, eds., *Urban Life in Mediterranean Europe*, q.v., pp. 53–75.

Keyder, C., 'The American recovery of southern Europe: aid and hegemony', in Arrighi, ed., *Semiperipheral Development*, q.v., pp. 135–48.

King, R. *The Industrial Geography of Italy*, London, 1988.

Land Reform: the Italian Experience, London, 1973.

* Kogan, N., *A Political History of Italy*, New York, 1983.

Kolko, J. and G., *The Limits of Power*, New York, 1972.

Kolinsky, M., and Paterson, W. E., eds., *Social and Political Movements in Western Europe*, London, 1976.

Kunzle, M., ed., *Dear Comrades. Readers' Letters to Lotta Continua*, London, 1980.

La Malfa, U., *Intervista sul non-governo*, ed. A. Ronchey, Bari, 1977.

Verso la politica di piano, Napoli, 1962.

Lama, L., *Intervista sul mio partito*, Bari, 1986.

Lanaro, S., 'Società civile, "mondo cattolico" e Democrazia Cristiana nel Veneto', in Lanaro and Isnenghi, eds., *La Democrazia Cristiana*, q.v., pp. 3–71.

Lanaro, S., and Isnenghi, M., eds. *La Democrazia Cristiana dal Fascismo al 18 aprile*, Venezia, 1978.

Lange, P., 'Semiperiphery and core in the European context', in Arrighi, ed., *Semiperipheral Development*, q.v., pp. 179–214.

Lange, P., Ross, G., and Vannicelli, M., *Unions, Change and Crisis: French and Italian Union Strategy and the Political Economy, 1945–80*, London, 1984.

* Lange, P., and Tarrow, S., eds., *Italy in Transition*, London, 1980.

Bibliography

Lanzardo, D., *La rivolta di Piazza Statuto*, Milano, 1979.

Lanzardo, L., *Classe operaia e partito comunista alla Fiat*, Torino, 1971.

* La Palombara, J., *Democracy, Italian Style*, New Haven, CT, 1987.

I lavoratori studenti. Testimonianze racolte a Torino, Torino, 1969.

Legnani, M., *L'Italia dal 1943 al 1948*, Torino, 1973.

  Profilo politico dell'Italia repubblicana, 1943–74, Napoli, 1974.

Lelli, M., *Proletariato e ceti medi in Sardegna*, Bari, 1975.

Leonardi, R., and Platt, A. A., 'La politica estera americana nei confronti della sinistra italiana', *Il Mulino*, vol. XXVI (1977), no. 252, pp. 546–73.

Lerner, G., *Operai*, Milano, 1988.

  'I senza niente', *L'Espresso*, vol. XXX (1984), no. 45.

Lett, G., *Rossano*, London, 1955.

* Levi, C., *Christ Stopped at Eboli*, London, 1948 (1st Italian ed., *Cristo si è fermato a Eboli*, Torino, 1945).

  Le parole sono pietre, Torino, 1955.

  'Preface' to Pantaleone, *The Mafia and Politics*, q.v. pp. 9–16.

Levi, F., Rugafiori, P., and Vento, S., *Il triangolo industriale tra ricostruzione e lotta di classe, 1945–1948*, Milano, 1974.

Levi, G., *et al.*, 'Cultura operaia e vita quotidiana in Borgo San Paolo', in *Torino fra le due guerre*, q.v., pp. 2–45.

* Lewis, N., *Naples '44*, London, 1978.

Libertini, L., 'La casa perduta', *Rinascita*, vol. XL (1984), no. 43.

  'Facciamo il punto sulla D.C.', *Mondo Nuovo*, vol. IV (1962), no. 10, 20 May.

Il libro del militante aclista, Roma, n.d. (4th ed.).

Livadiotti, S., 'Buio a Mezzogiorno', *L'Espresso*, vol. XXXV (1989), no. 10.

Living with an Earthquake, London, 1978.

Lodge, J., ed., *Terrorism: a Challenge to the State*, Oxford, 1981.

Lombardi, R., 'Una nuova frontiera per la sinistra', in Parlato, ed., *Spazio e ruolo del riformismo*, q.v., pp. 65–74.

  'Problemi di potere in Milano liberata', in *La Resistenza in Lombardia*, q.v., pp. 257–67.

  Scritti politici, ed. S. Colarizzi, 2 vols., Venezia, 1978.

Lombardi, R. (padre), 'Il programma politico comunista', *La Civiltà Cattolica*, vol. XCVII (1946), vol. 2, 18 May.

Lombardini, S., 'Intervento', in Fondazione L. Einaudi, *Nord e Sud*, q.v., pp. 472–5.

Bibliography

Lombardo Radice, L., 'La battaglia delle idee', *Rinascita*, vol. V (1948), no. 3.

Longo, L., 'Costruendo il socialismo si son fatti degli errori, ma la vostra non è democrazia', *Rinascita*, vol. XIII (1956), no. 3.

'Il movimento studentesco nella lotta anticapitalistica', *Rinascita* (supplement *Il contemporaneo*), vol. XXV (1968), no. 18.

Revisionismo nuovo e antico, Torino, 1957.

Low-Beer, J. R. *Protest and Participation*, Cambridge, 1978.

Lumley, R., 'Social Movements in Italy, 1968–78', unpublished PhD thesis, Centre for Contemporary Cultural Studies, University of Birmingham, 1983.

Luppi, A., and Reyneri, E., *Autobianchi e Innocenti*, Bologna, 1974. (vol. 1 of Pizzorno *et al.*, *Lotte operaie e sindacato in Italia*, q.v.).

Luraghi, R., *Il movimento operaio torinese durante la Resistenza*, Torino, 1958.

Lutz, V., *Italy: a Study in Economic Development*, Oxford, 1962.

* Macciocchi, M. A., *Letters from inside the Italian Communist Party to Louis Althusser*, London, 1973.

McLuhan, M., 'American advertising', *Horizon*, nos. 93–4 (1947), pp. 132–41.

Macmillan H., *The Blast of War, 1939–45*, London, 1967.

War Diaries: Politics and War in the Mediterranean, January 1943–May 1945, London, 1984.

Mafai, M., *L'apprendistato della politica*, Roma, 1979.

L'uomo che sognava la lotta armata, Milano, 1984.

Maggia, G., and Fornengo, G., *Appunti sul sistema delle partecipazioni statali*, Torino, 1976.

Magister, S., *La politica vaticana e l'Italia, 1943–1978*, Roma, 1979.

Magistrelli, F., and Ragozzino, R., 'La cedolare "mista": vincitori e perdenti', *Problemi del socialismo*, vol. IX (1967) no. 16, pp. 285–98.

Magrone, M., and Pavese, G., *Ti ricordi di Piazza Fontana?*, Bari, 1986.

Maione, G., 'Mezzogiorno, 1946–1950. Partito Comunista e movimento contadino', *Italia Contemporanea*, vol. XXXVIII (1986), no. 163, pp. 31–64.

Maitan, L., *Dinamica delle classi sociali in Italia*, Roma, 1975.

Malaparte, C., *The Skin*, London, 1962 (1st Italian ed., *La pelle*, Roma–Milano, 1949).

Mangini G., *Una vita operaia*, Torino, 1976.

Manzocchi, B., *Lineamenti di politica economica in Italia (1945–1959)*, Roma, 1960.

Marazziti, M., 'Cultura di massa e valori cattolici: il modello di "Famiglia Cristiana"', in Riccardi, ed., *Pio XII*, q.v. pp. 307–33.

Marcelloni, M., 'Bologna: il conflitto politico fa arretrare il piano', in Cecarelli and Indovina, eds., *Risanamento e speculazione nei centri storici*, q.v., pp. 49–82.

555

Marchi, M., *et al.*, *Il volto sociale dell'edilizia popolare*, Roma, 1975.

Marino, G. C., *Storia del separatismo siciliano*, Roma, 1977.

Martinelli, A., 'Borghesia industriale e potere politico', in Martinelli and Pasquino, eds., *La politica nell'Italia che cambia*, q.v., pp. 254–95.

Martinelli, A., and Pasquino, G., eds., *La politica nell'Italia che cambia*, Milano, 1978.

Martinotti, G., *Gli studenti dell'università di Milano*, Milano, 1973.

Mason, T., 'Moderno, modernità, modernizzazione: un montaggio', *Movimento Operaio e Socialista*, New Series, vol. X (1987), nos. 1–2, pp. 45–63.

'Gli scioperi di Torino del marzo 1943', in Ferratini Tosi *et al.*, eds., *L'Italia nella seconda guerra mondiale*, q.v. pp. 385–408.

Mater et magistra. Contenuto e valore dell'enciclica di Giovanni XXIII in un incontro alla televisione, Roma, 1962.

Matteucci, N., 'Dossetti a Bologna', *Il Mulino*, vol. V (1956), no. 56, pp. 382–90.

Mattina, E., 'Il Mezzogiorno e l'autunno caldo', in *L'autunno caldo dieci anni dopo*, q.v., pp. 166–77.

Mattina, L., 'Il sistema di potere democristiano a Catania e Messina', *Quaderni della Fondazione G. G. Feltrinelli*, no. 21 (1982), pp. 155–77.

Medici, G., *Politica agraria*, Bologna, 1952.

Medici, G., Sorbi, U. and Castrataro, A., *Polverizzazione e frammentazione della proprietà fondiaria in Italia*, Milano, 1962.

Medici, S., *Vite di poliziotti*, Torino, 1979.

Melis, G., 'La cultura e il mondo degli impiegati', in Cassese, ed., *L'amministrazione centrale*, q.v., pp. 301–402.

Melograni, P., and Scaraffia, L., eds., *La famiglia italiana dall'Ottocento a oggi*, Bari, 1988.

Meneghetti, L., *Aspetti di geografia della popolazione. Italia 1951–67*, Milano, 1971.

Merlin, T., 'Le radici storiche del socialismo nella Bassa Padana', *Schema*, vol. V (1982), nos. 9–10, pp. 137–52.

Meynaud, J., *Rapporto sulla classe dirigente italiana*, Milano, 1966.

Meyriat, J., *La Calabre*, Paris, 1960.

Miccoli, G., 'Chiesa, partito cattolico e società civile', in Castronovo, ed., *L'Italia contemporanea 1945–1975*, q.v., pp. 191–252.

Michel, H., *The Shadow War*, London, 1972 (original French ed., *La Guerre de l'ombre*, Paris, 1970).

Micheli, A., *Ansaldo 1950*, Torino, 1981.

Michetti, M., Repetto, M., and Viviani, L., *UDI: laboratorio di politica delle donne*, Roma, 1984.

Migone, G. G., 'Stati Uniti, FIAT e repressione antioperaia negli anni Cinquanta', *Rivista di Storia Contemporanea*, no. 2 (1974), pp. 232–81.

'Il terrorismo che stabilizza', *L'Indice*, vol. III (1986), no. 8.

Bibliography

Milani, L., *Esperienze pastorali*, Firenze, 1957.

1968–72: Le lotte alla Pirelli, Milano, 1972.

Miller, J. E., 'Taking off the gloves: the United States and the Italian elections of 1948', *Diplomatic History*, vol. VII (1983), no. 1, pp. 34–55.

Mingione, E., 'Economia informale, strategie familiari e Mezzogiorno', *Inchiesta*, vol. XVI (1986), no. 74, pp. 1–3.

Miniati, S., *PSIUP, 1963–72. Vita e morte di un partito*, Roma, 1981.

Ministero del Bilancio, *Problemi e prospettive dello sviluppo economico italiano* (Nota presentata al Parlamento dal Ministro del Bilancio, U. La Malfa, 22 maggio 1962), Roma, 1962.

Ministero per la Costituente, *Rapporto della Commissione economica presentato all' Assemblea Costituente*, 17 vols., Roma, 1946–7.

Mobiglia, S., 'La scuola: l'onda lunga della contestazione', *Annali della Fondazione L. Micheletti* (forthcoming).

Modica, G., 'Il ruolo delle donne nelle lotte contadine', in Centro Siciliano di Documentazione, *Ricomposizione del blocco dominante*, q.v., pp. 53–6.

Montanelli, I., 'Emilia-Romagna', in *Italia sotto inchiesta*, q.v., pp. 373–446.

Moorehead, A., *Eclipse*, London, 1945.

Morandi, R., *Democrazia diretta e riforme di struttura*, Torino, 1975.

Monelli, A., and Pellicciari, G., 'Comportamenti di voto e pratica religiosa', in Pellicciari, ed., *L'immigrazione nel triangolo industriale*, q.v., pp. 324–38.

Moretti, S., 'Avola 1968', in *I braccianti*, q.v., pp. 366–79.

Mori, G., ed., *Storia d'Italia. Le regioni dall'Unità a oggi. La Toscana*, Torino, 1986.

Moro, A., 'La D.C. per la donna nella famiglia e nella società', in Movimento Femminile della D.C., *La famiglia e le trasformazioni della società italiana*, q.v., pp. 67–108.

L'intelligenza e gli avvenimenti (testi 1959–1978), Milano, 1979.

Moro, R., *La formazione della classe dirigente cattolica (1929–37)* Bologna, 1979.

Mosca, M., 'I CUB alla Bicocca', in *Marzo 1968* (supplement to *Il Manifesto*, no. 76, 30 March 1988).

Mottura, G., 'La D.C. e lo sviluppo del moderatismo nelle campagne', in Vianello *et al.*, *Tutto il potere della D.C.*, q.v., pp. 173–92.

Mottura, G., and Pugliese, E., *Agricoltura, Mezzogiorno e mercato del lavoro*, Bologna, 1975.

Mottura, G., and Ursetta, U., *Il diritto alla terra*, Milano, 1978.

Movimento Femminile della DC, *La famiglia e le trasformazioni della società italiana*, Roma, 1963.

Mugnaini, F., 'A veglia: monografia breve su un' "abitudine"', *Annali dell'Istituto Alcide Cervi*, vol. IX (1987), pp. 119–44.

Murgia, P. G. *Il luglio 1960*, Milano, 1960.

Murray, F., 'Flexible specialisation in the "Third Italy"', *Capital and Class*, no. 33 (1987), pp. 84–95.

Mussi, F., *Bologna '77*, Roma, 1978.

Mutti, A., 'Elementi per un'analisi della borghesia di stato', *Quaderni di Sociologia*, vol. XXVII (1979), no. 1, pp. 24–70.

Nannei, A., *La nuovissima classe*, Milano, 1978.

Napoleoni, C., 'Riforme del capitale e capitale riformato', in Parlato, ed., *Spazio e ruolo del riformismo*, q.v., pp. 87–94.

Napolitano, G., *In mezzo al guado*, Roma, 1979.

    The Italian Road to Socialism, ed. E. J. Hobsbawm, London, 1977.

Nardi, S., 'Il movimento cooperativo emiliano nel secondo dopoguerra', in D'Attorre, ed., *La ricostruzione in Emilia-Romagna*, q.v., pp. 173–94.

'Nel 1951 il Kremlino voleva sostituire Togliatti e la direzione del PCI approvò', *L'Espresso*, vol. XIV (1970), no. 13.

Nenni, P. *Intervista sul socialismo italiano*, ed. G. Tamburrano, Bari, 1977.

    Tempo di guerra fredda. Diari 1943–56, eds. G. Nenni and D. Zucaro, Milano, 1981.

* Newby, E., *Love and War in the Apennines*, London, 1971.

Nicolai, R., 'Realizzazioni dell'amministrazione democratica della città di Bologna', *Rinascita*, vol. XIII (1956), no. 3.

Nigro, G., 'Il "caso" Prato', in Mori, ed., *Storia d'Italia ... La Toscana*, q.v., pp. 823–68.

1968–72: le lotte alla Pirelli, Milano, 1972.

Nocifora, E., 'Riforma agraria e classi sociali in Sicilia', *Nuovi Quaderni del Meridione*, vol. XIX (1981), no. 73, pp. 73–89.

Norcia, D. L., *Io garantito*, Roma, 1980.

Notiziario CGIL, Roma, 1951.

Occhipinti, M., *Una donna di Ragusa*, Milano, 1976.

Oddone, A., 'Ricostruzione morale', *La Civiltà Cattolica*, vol. XCVII (1946), vol. 1, 5 Jan.

Odorizio, M. L., *et al.*, *Donna o cosa?*, Torino, 1986.

Olivi, B., *Carter e l'Italia*, Milano, 1978.

Onofri, N. S., *Marzabotto non dimentica Walter Reder*, Bologna, 1985.

Orfei, R., *Andreotti*, Milano, 1975.

    L'occupazione del potere, Milano, 1976.

* Origo, I., *War in Val d'Orcia*, London, 1985 (1st ed., 1947).

Orlandini, A., *L'insurrezione proletaria nella provincia di Siena in risposta all'attentato a Togliatti*, Firenze, 1976.

Orlandini, A., and Venturini, G., *I giudici e la Resistenza*, Milano, 1983.

   Padrone arrivedello a battitura, Milano, 1980.

Ortoleva, P. *Saggio sui movimenti del 1968 in Europa e in America*, Roma, 1988.

Ottone, P., 'Campania', in *Italia sotto inchiesta*, q.v., pp. 681–735.

   Fanfani, Milano, 1966.

Paci, M., *Mercato del lavoro e classi sociali in Italia*, Bologna, 1973.

   La struttura sociale italiana, Bologna, 1982.

Pagden, A., 'The destruction of trust and its economic consequences in the case of eighteenth-century Naples', in Gambetta, ed., *Trust*, q.v., pp. 127–41.

* Pantaleone, M., *The Mafia and Politics*, London, 1966.

Parlato, V., 'Il blocco edilizio', in Indovina, ed., *Lo spreco edilizio*, q.v. pp. 189–200.

Parlato, V., ed., *Spazio e ruolo del riformismo*, Bologna, 1974.

Partito Comunista Italiano, *VI^a conferenza operaia del PCI, Genova, 8–10 febbraio 1974*, Roma, 1974.

   VIII° Congresso. Atti e risoluzioni, Roma, 1957.

   Proposta di un progetto a medio termine, Roma, 1977.

Partito Comunista Italiano, Federazione Regionale Della Sicilia, *Lettera al compagno siciliano*, Palermo, 1945.

Partito Socialista Italiano, *XXXIV° Congresso nazionale, Milano, 15–20 marzo 1961*, Milano, 1961.

Pasini, G., *Le ACLI dalle origini, 1944–48*, Roma, 1974.

Pasolini, P. P., 'Poesia' in *L'Espresso*, vol. XIV (1968), no. 24.

   Scritti corsari, Milano, 1975.

   A Violent Life, London, 1968.

Pasquino, G., 'Crisi della D C ed evoluzione del sistema politico,' *Rivista Italiana di Scienza Politica*, vol. V (1975), pp. 443–72.

   'Italian Christian Democracy: a party for all seasons?', in Lange and Tarrow, eds., *Italy in Transition*, q.v., pp. 88–109.

   'Mediazione e opportunismo', *Rinascita*, vol. XLI (1984), no. 43.

Pasquino, G., and Parisi, A., eds., *Continuità e mutamento elettorale in Italia*, Bologna, 1977.

Passerini, L. *Autoritratto di gruppo*, Firenze, 1988.

   Fascism in Popular Memory, Cambridge, 1987.

   'Non solo maschio. La presenza ambivalente delle donne nel movimento', in *Marzo 1968* (supplement to *Il Manifesto*, no. 76, 30 March 1988).

Pastori, G., 'L'attuazione del servizio sanitario nazionale', *Il Mulino*, vol. XXX (1981), no. 278, pp. 838–49.

Pavone, C., 'La continuità dello Stato. Istituzioni e uomini', in *Italia 1945–48. Le origini della Repubblica*, q.v., pp. 137–289.

Bibliography

'La guerra civile', *Annali della Fondazione Luigi Micheletti*, vol. II (1986), pp. 395–415.

'Le idee della Resistenza: antifascisti e fascisti di fronte alla tradizione del Risorgimento', *Passato e Presente*, vol. II (1959), no. 7, pp. 850–918.

'Tre governi e due occupazioni', *Italia Contemporanea*, vol. XXXVII (1985), no. 160, pp. 57–79.

Pazzagli, C. *L'agricoltura toscana nella prima metà dell'800*, Firenze, 1973.

'Dal paternalismo alla democrazia', *Annali dell'Istituto Alcide Cervi*, vol. VIII (1986), pp. 13–35.

Pellicciari, G., ed., *L'immigrazione nel triangolo industriale*, Milano, 1970.

Perotti P., and Revelli, M., *Fiat autunno '80. Per non dimenticare*, Torino, 1986.

Pescatore, G., 'Dai complessi organici ai progetti speciali', *Notiziario IRPIS* 29, April 1971.

Petriccione, S., *Politica industriale e Mezzogiorno*, Bari, 1976.

Petrilli, G., *La politica estera ed europea di De Gasperi*, Roma, 1975.

Pezzino, P., *La riforma agraria in Calabria*, Milano, 1977.

Piazza, R., 'Dibattito teorico e indirizzi di governo nella politica agraria della Democrazia Cristiana (1944–1951)', *Italia Contemporanea*, vol. XXVI (1974), no. 117, pp. 49–92.

Picciotto Fargan, L., 'La persecuzione antiebraica in Italia', in Ferratini Tosi *et al.*, eds., *L'Italia nella seconda guerra mondiale*, q.v., pp. 197–213.

Piccone Stella, S., *Ragazze del Sud*, Roma, 1979.

Pintor, G., *Il sangue d'Europa (1939–43)*, ed. V. Gerratana, Torino, 1950.

Pio XII, 'Allocuzione di S. S. Pio XII alla gioventù maschile di A.C.I. sulle gravi necessità dell'ora presente', *La Civiltà Cattolica*, XCVII (1946), vol. 2, 4 May.

'Discorso agli uomini di Azione Cattolica, 7 sett. 1947', *La Civiltà Cattolica*, XCVIII (1947), vol. 3, 20 Sept.

'Esortazione del Sommo Pontefice all'episcopato d'Italia, 25 gennaio 1950', in *Discorsi e radiomessaggi di Sua Santità Pio XII*, vol. XI, Città del Vaticano, 1961.

Piperno, A., 'La politica sanitaria', in Ascoli, U., ed., *Welfare State all'Italiana*, q.v., pp. 153–84.

Piro, F., *Comunisti al potere*, Bologna, 1983.

Pirzio Ammassari, G., *La politica della Confindustria*, Napoli, 1976.

Piscitelli, E., *Da Parri a De Gasperi*, Milano, 1975.

'Del cambio o meglio del mancato cambio della moneta nel secondo dopoguerra', *Quaderni dell'Istituto Romano per la storia d'Italia dal Fascismo alla Resistenza*, vol. I (1969), no. 1, pp. 3–89.

Piselli, F., *Parentela ed emigrazione*, Torino, 1981.

Pistone, S., ed., *L'Italia e l'unità europea*, Torino, 1982.

Bibliography

Pitkin, D. S., *The House that Giacomo Built*, Cambridge, 1985.

Pizzorno, A., 'I ceti medi nel meccanismo del consenso', in Pizzorno, *I soggetti del pluralismo*, Bologna, 1980, pp. 67–98.

Comunità e razionalizzazione, Milano, 1960.

Pizzorno, A., et al., *Lotte operaie e sindacato in Italia (1968–72)*, 4 vols., Bologna, 1974.

Poggi, G. F., *Catholic Action in Italy*, Stanford, 1967.

'The church in Italian politics, 1945–50', in Woolf, ed., *The Rebirth of Italy*, q.v., pp. 135–55.

Pombeni, P., *Il gruppo dossettiano e la fondazione della democrazia italiana (1943–1948)*, Bologna, 1979.

* Posner, M. V., and Woolf, S.J., *Italian Public Enterprise*, London, 1967.

Potenza, S., 'Riforma della casa e movimento sindacale', in Indovina, ed., *Lo spreco edilizio*, q.v., pp. 270–306.

La povertà in Italia. Rapporto conclusivo della commissione di studio istituita presso la Presidenza del Consiglio dei ministri, Roma, 1986.

Predieri, A., 'Parlamento '75', in Predieri, ed., *Il parlamento nel sistema politico italiano*, Milano, 1975, pp. 11–89.

Pridham, G., ed., *Coalition Behaviour in Theory and Practice*, Cambridge, 1986.

Primo congresso nazionale di studio della Democrazia Cristiana, San Pellegrino Terme, 13–16 settembre 1961, Roma, 1961.

Problemi di storia del PCI, Roma, 1971.

Provasi, G., *Borghesia industriale e Democrazia Cristiana*, Bari, 1976.

Przeworski, A., *Capitalism and Social Democracy*, Cambridge, 1986.

'Il PSI negli anni del frontismo', *Mondoperaio*, vol. XXX (1977), nos. 7–8.

Puccini, G., *L'autonomia della Banca d'Italia*, Milano, 1978.

Pugliese, E., 'Le classi sociali nel Mezzogiorno', *Sviluppo*, no. 16 (1979), pp. 5–16.

'Per l'analisi delle classi subalterne nel Meridione', in Donolo ed., *Classi sociali e politica nel Mezzogiorno*, q.v., pp. 79–100.

Pugno, E., and Garavini, S., *Gli anni duri della FIAT*, Torino, 1975.

Pupillo, G., 'Classe operaia, partiti e sindacati nella lotta alla Marzotto', in *Classe*, vol. II (1970), no. 2, pp. 37–65.

Putnam, R. D., 'Atteggiamenti politici dell'alta burocrazia nell'Europa occidentale', *Rivista Italiana di Scienza Politica*, vol. III (1973), no. 1, pp. 145–86.

Quartararo, R., *Italia e Stati Uniti. Gli anni difficili (1945–1952)*, Napoli, 1986.

Quazza, G., *Resistenza e storia d'Italia*, Milano, 1976.

Quazza, G., et al., *L'Italia dalla Liberazione alla Repubblica*, Milano, 1977.

Bibliography

Ramat, M., ed., *Storia di un magistrato. Materiali per una storia di Magistratura Democratica*, Roma, 1986.

Ramondino, F., ed., *Napoli: i disoccupati organizzati*, Milano, 1977.

Rasi, G., 'La politica economica e i conti della nazione', in *Annali dell'economia italiana*, vol. XI (1953–8), Milano, 1982, pt 1, pp. 63–177, and vol XIV (1971–7), Milano, 1985, pt 1, pp. 89–216.

Re, G., and Derossi, G., *L'occupazione fu bellissima*, Roma, 1976.

Reale, E., *La nascita del Cominform*, Milano, 1958.

Reberschak, M., 'La proprietà fondiaria nel Veneto tra Fascismo e Resistenza', in *Società rurale e Resistenza nelle Venezie*, Milano, 1978, pp. 135–58.

'Vittorio Cini', in *Dizionario biografico degli italiani*, vol. XXV, Roma, 1981, pp. 626–34.

Regalia, I., *et al.*, 'Conflitti di lavoro e relazioni industriali in Italia, 1968–75', in Crouch and Pizzorno, *Conflitti in Europa*, q.v.

Regalia, I., Regini, M., and Reyneri, E., 'Labour conflicts and industrial relations in Italy,' in Crouch and Pizzorno, eds., *The Resurgence of Class Conflict*, q.v., vol. 1, pp. 101–58.

Regini, M., *I dilemmi del sindacato*, Bologna, 1981.

Reitzel, W., Kaplan, M., and Coblenz, C., *United States Foreign Policy, 1945–1955*, Washington, D C., 1956.

Renda, F., 'Il movimento contadino in Sicilia', in *Campagne e movimento contadino nel Mezzogiorno d'Italia*, q.v., vol. I, pp. 592–658.

La Resistenza in Lombardia, Milano, 1965.

Revelli, N., *Il mondo dei vinti*, 2 vols., Torino, 1977.

Reviglio, F., *Spesa pubblica e stagnazione dell'economia italiana*, Bologna, 1977.

Reyneri, E., *La catena migratoria*, Milano, 1978.

Riboldi, A., *I miei 18 anni nel Belice*, Assisi, 1977.

Riboldi, A., ed., *Lettere dal Belice e al Belice. Le speranze tradite*, Milano, 1977.

Riccardi, A., ed., *Pio XII*, Bari, 1984.

Ricolfi, L., 'A proposito del "Saggio" di Sylos Labini: la base statistica', *Quaderni Piacentini*, XIV (1975), no. 57, pp. 60–76.

Ricolfi, L., Sylos Labini, P., and D'Agostini, L., 'Dibattito', *Quaderni Piacentini*, XV (1976), nos. 60–61, pp. 129–42.

Ridley, F. F., ed., *Government and Administration in Western Europe*, London, 1979.

Ritratto di famiglia degli anni '80, Bari, 1981.

Rochat, G., Sateriale, G., and Spano, L., *La casa in Italia*, Bologna, 1980.

Rochat, G., 'Prefazione', in Boatti, *L'arma*, q.v., pp. 9–13.

Rodotà, C., *La corte costituzionale*, Roma, 1986.

Rodotà, C. and S., 'Il diritto di famiglia', in *Ritratto di famiglia degli anni '80*, q.v., pp. 159–204.

Romagnoli, G., *Consigli di fabbrica e democrazia sindacale*, Milano, 1976.

Romanelli, R., 'Apparati statali, ceti burocratici e modo di governo', in Castronovo, ed., *L'Italia contemporanea*, q.v., pp. 145–90.

Romiti, C., *Questi anni alla Fiat*, ed. G. Pansa, Milano, 1988.

Ronci, D., *Olivetti anni '50*, Milano, 1980.

Rosenbaum, P., *Il nuovo fascismo*, Milano, 1975.

Rossanda, R., *L'anno degli studenti*, Bari, 1968.

Rossi, A., *Le feste dei poveri*, Bari, 1969.

Rossi, E., *Elettricità senza baroni*, Bari, 1962.

Rossi, E., Ugolini, P., and Picciardi, L., *La Federconsorzi*, Milano, 1963.

Rossi-Doria, A., *Il ministro e i contadini*, Roma, 1983.

'Una tradizione da costruire', in Odorizio *et al.*, *Donna o cosa?*, q.v., pp. 198–209.

Rossi-Doria, M., 'Limite e prospettive della trasformazione agraria del Mezzogiorno', in *Ulisse*, vol. XVI (1983), no. 95, pp. 62–70.

'Il Mezzogiorno e il suo avvenire: "l'osso e la polpa"', in Fondazione L. Einaudi, *Nord e Sud*, q.v., pp. 285–99.

Rapporto sulla Federconsorzi, Bari, 1963.

Riforma agraria e azione meridionalista, Bologna, 1948.

'La riforma agraria sei anni dopo', in M. Rossi-Doria, *Dieci anni di politica agraria nel Mezzogiorno*, Bari, 1958, pp. 135–46.

Scritti sul Mezzogiorno, Torino, 1982.

'Struttura e problemi dell'agricoltura meridionale', in M. Rossi-Doria, *Riforma agraria e azione meridionalista*, q.v., pp. 1–49.

Rotelli, E., ed., *La ricostruzione in Toscana dal CLN ai partiti*, Bologna, 1980.

Ruffini, E., 'La teologia di fronte alle problematiche della famiglia nella tensione tra "pubblico" e "privato"', in Università Cattolica del Sacro Cuore, *La coscienza contemporanea*, q.v., pp. 141–75.

Ruffolo, G., 'Aux armes les citoyens!', *Micromega*, no. 4 (1986), pp. 5–10.

Rapporto sulla programmazione, Bari, 1975.

Riforme e controriforme, Bari, 1977.

Ruffolo, U., 'La linea Einaudi', *Storia Contemporanea*, vol. V (1974), no. 4, pp. 637–71.

Rugafiori, P., 'Genova', in Levi, F., *et al.*, *Il triangolo industriale*, q.v., pp. 3–102.

'I gruppi dirigenti della siderurgia "pubblica" tra gli anni Trenta e gli anni Sessanta', in Bonelli, ed., *Acciaio per l'industrializzazione*, q.v., pp. 335–68.

Rumi, G., 'Opportunismo e profezia. Cultura cattolica e politica estera italiana, 1946–63', *Storia Contemporanea*, vol. XI (1981), nos. 4–5, pp. 813–19.

Bibliography

Russo, G., *Baroni e contadini*, Bari, 1979 (1st ed., 1955).

    Chi ha più santi in paradiso, Bari, 1965.

Sacco, L., *Il cemento del potere*, Bari, 1982.

Saladino, G., *Terra di rapina*, Torino, 1977.

Salierno, G., *Il sottoproletariato in Italia*, Roma, 1972.

    La violenza in Italia, Milano, 1980.

Salvadori, M., *The Labour and the Wounds*, London, 1958.

Salvati, Mariuccia, *Stato e industria nella ricostruzione*, Milano, 1982.

Salvati, Michele, *Economia e politica in Italia dal dopoguerra ad oggi*, Milano, 1984.

    'Quattro punti facili', *L'Indice*, vol. III (1986), no. 2.

Salvemini, G., 'L'elefantiasi burocratica', *L'Unità*, 30 May 1913, republished in Cassese, ed., *L'amministrazione pubblica in Italia*, q.v., pp. 71–4.

Sampson, A., *Macmillan, a Study in Ambiguity*, London, 1967.

Santi, P., 'Un esempio dello sviluppo capitalistico in Italia: il settore degli elettro-domestici', *Problemi del Socialismo*, vol. X (1968), no. 31, pp. 710–35.

    'Il piano del lavoro nella politica della CGIL, 1949–1952', in Vianello, ed., *Il piano del lavoro della CGIL, 1949–1950*, q.v., pp. 11–57.

Santino, U., 'Fine dell'unità antifascista e ricomposizione del blocco dominante', in Centro Siciliano di Documentazione, *Ricomposizione del blocco dominante*, q.v., pp. 1–32.

Sapelli, G., 'La cooperazione come impresa: mercati economici e mercato politico', in Bonfante *et al.*, *Il movimento cooperativo in Italia*, q.v., pp. 253–349.

Saraceno, C., 'La famiglia operaia sotto il fascismo', *Annali della Fondazione G.G. Feltrinelli*, vol. XX (1979–80), pp. 189–229.

    'Interdipendenze e spostamenti di confini tra "pubblico" e "privato"', *Il Mulino*, vol. XXXII (1983), no. 289, pp. 784–97.

    'Modelli di famiglia', in *Ritratto di famiglia degli anni '80*, q.v., pp. 45–111.

    'La sociologia della famiglia tra crisi delle teorie e innovazione tematica', *Quaderni di Sociologia*, vol. XXXII (1985), nos. 4–5, pp. 307–34.

Saraceno, P., *L'Italia verso la piena occupazione*, Milano, 1963.

* Sassoon, D., *Contemporary Italy*, London, 1986.

    Togliatti e la via italiana al socialismo, Torino, 1980.

Sbarberi, F., *I comunisti italiani e lo stato, 1929–1959*, Milano, 1980.

Scalfari, E., *L'autunno della Repubblica*, Milano, 1969.

    Rapporto sul neo-capitalismo in Italia, Bari, 1961.

Scalfari, E., and Turani, G., *Razza padrona*, Milano, 1974.

Scaraffia, L., 'Essere uomo essere donna', in Melograni, Scaraffia, eds., *La famiglia italiana*, q.v., pp. 193–258.

Bibliography

Scarano, M., and De Luca, M., *Il mandarino è marcio*, Roma, 1985.

Scarpari, G., *La Democrazia Cristiana e le leggi eccezionali, 1950–1953*, Milano, 1977.

Scase, R., ed., *The State in Western Europe*, London, 1980.

Schlesinger, A. M., Jr, *et al.*, *Gli anni di Kennedy*, Milano, 1964.

Sciascia, L., *L'affaire Moro*, Palermo, 1978. (English ed., *L'affaire Moro*, Manchester, 1987.)

Scoccimarro, M., *Il secondo dopoguerra*, 2 vols., Milano, 1956.

Scoppola, P., *Gli anni della costituente fra politica e storia*, Bologna, 1980.

> *La proposta politica di De Gasperi*, Bologna, 1977.

> ' "Pubblico e privato": aspetti storico-politici', in Università Cattolica del Sacro Cuore, *La coscienza contemporanea*, q.v., pp. 24–43.

Scuola di Barbiana, *Lettera a una professoressa*, Firenze, 1967. (English trans., School of Barbiana, *Letter to a Teacher*, London, 1970).

Sebastiani, C., *Pubblico impiego e ceti medi*, Roma, 1975.

Secchia, P., *Il Partito comunista e la guerra di Liberazione, 1943–1945*, in *Annali dell'Istituto G.G. Feltrinelli*, vol. XIII (1971).

Secchia, P., and Frassati, F., *La Resistenza e gli Alleati*, Milano, 1962.

Sechi, S., 'Il PCI: l'albero, la foresta e la nuova peste', *Il Mulino*, vol. XXVI (1977), no. 250, pp. 274–302.

Sechi, S., and Merli, S., *Dimenticare Livorno*, Milano, 1985.

Seppilli, T., 'Intervento', in *Famiglia e società nell'analisi marxista*, q.v., pp. 177–9.

Serafini, G., *I ribelli della montagna*, Montepulciano, 1981.

Sereni, E., *Il Mezzogiorno all'opposizione*, Torino, 1948.

Sergi, N., ed., *L'immigrazione straniera in Italia*, Roma, 1987.

Sermanni, M. C., *Le ACLI: dal ruolo formativo all'impegno politico sindacale (1944–1961)*, Napoli, 1978.

Seronde, A. M., 'La réforme agraire', in J. Meyriat, *La Calabre*, q.v., pp. 85–136.

Setta, S., *Croce, il liberalismo e l'Italia postfascista*, Roma, 1979.

> *L'Uomo qualunque (1944–1948)*, Bari, 1975.

Silverman, S. F., 'Agricultural organisation, social structure, and values in Italy: amoral familism reconsidered', *American Anthropologist*, vol. LXX (1968), no. 1, pp. 1–20.

Siri, G., 'Tendenze sociali contemporanee e valori permanenti della famiglia cristiana', in *Famiglie di oggi e mondo sociale in trasformazione* (XXVIII Settimana sociale dei Cattolici d'Italia, Pisa, sett. 1954), q.v., pp. 17–32.

Smith, D. Mack, 'The Latifundia in modern Sicilian history', *Proceedings of the British Academy*, vol. LI (1965), pp. 85–124.

Snowden, F. M., 'From sharecropper to proletarian: the background to Fascism in

rural Tuscany, 1880–1920', in Davis, ed., *Gramsci and Italy's Passive Revolution*, q.v., pp. 136–171.
Violence and Great Estates in the South of Italy. Apulia, 1900–1922, Cambridge, 1986.

Soccorso Rosso Napoletano, ed., *I NAP*, Milano, 1976.

Il socialismo italiano di questo dopoguerra, Milano, 1968.

Soldani, S., 'La grande guerra lontano dal fronte', in Mori, ed., *Storia d'Italia . . . La Toscana*, q.v., pp. 345–452.

Sotgiù, G., 'Lotte contadine nella Sardegna del secondo dopoguerra', in *Campagne e movimento contadino nel Mezzogiorno d'Italia*, q.v., vol. I, pp. 721–814.

Spanò, P., 'Gli enti del settore creditizio. Aspetti economici e politici dello sviluppo del credito speciale all'industria nel secondo dopoguerra', in Cazzola, ed., *Anatomia del potere DC*, q.v., pp. 253–326.

Spingola, C., 'Crisi alimentare e problemi di ordine pubblico in Sicilia nel secondo dopoguerra', in Gallerano, ed., *L'altro dopoguerra*, q.v., pp. 341–54.

Spini, V., 'The new left in Italy', *Journal of Contemporary History*, vol. VII (1972), nos. 1–2, pp. 51–72.

Spriano, P., *Storia del Partito Comunista Italiano*, 5 vols., Torino, 1975.

Staiano, C., *Africo*, Torino, 1979.

Staiano, C., ed., *L'atto di accusa dei giudici di Palermo*, Roma, 1986.

Stefanelli, R., 'Il mercato del lavoro nell'agricoltura italiana, 1948–1968: strutture e politiche dell'occupazione', in *I braccianti. Venti anni di lotte*, q.v., pp. 107–84.

Steve, S., *Il sistema tributario e le sue prospettive*, Milano, 1947.

Stolfi, E., *Da una parte sola*, Milano, 1976.

Storia d'Italia, 6 vols., Torino, 1972–6.

La strage di stato, Roma, 1970.

Sullo. F., *Lo scandalo urbanistico*, Firenze, 1964.

Sylos Labini, P., *Le classi sociali negli anni '80*, Bari, 1986.
    Saggio sulle classi sociali, Bari, 1974.

Tabet, D., 'I consigli di fattoria', *Annali dell'Istituto Alcide Cervi*, vol. VIII (1986), pp. 287–92.

Taddei, F., *Il socialismo italiano del dopoguerra: correnti ideologiche e scelte politiche (1943–1947)*, Milano, 1984.

Talamanca, A., 'Il bottegaio mangia l'operaio', *L'Espresso*, vol. XXIV (1978), no. 6.

Talamo, M., De Marco, C., *Lotte agrarie nel Mezzogiorno, 1943–44*, Milano, 1976.

Tamburrano, G., *Storia e cronaca del centro-sinistra*, Milano, 1971.

Tarchiani, A., *Dieci anni tra Roma e Washington*, Verona, 1955.

Tarozzi, V., 'Le lavanderie meccaniche, nuovo servizio sociale', in *Comunisti. I militanti bolognesi del PCI raccontano*, q.v., pp. 262–7.

* Tarrow, S. G., 'The crisis of the late 60s in Italy and France', in Arrighi, ed., *Semiperipheral Development*, q.v., pp. 215–42.

Peasant Communism in Southern Italy, New Haven, CT, 1967.

Tasca, L., *Elogio del latifondo*, Palermo, 1941.

Taylor, R. C. R., 'State intervention in postwar European health care: the case of prevention in Britain and in Italy', in Bornstein *et al.*, eds., *The State in Capitalist Europe*, q.v. pp. 91–117.

Terracini, U., *Come nacque la Costituzione*, Roma, 1978.

Timpanaro, S., 'PCI, riformismo, socialdemocratizzazione', *Praxis*, no. 13 (1977), pp. 4–7.

Tobagi, W., *La rivoluzione impossibile*, Milano, 1978.

Togliatti, P., 'Ceto medio e Emilia rossa', in Togliatti, *Opere scelte*, q.v., pp. 456–84.

I compiti del partito nella situazione attuale, Roma, 1945.

Discorsi sull'Emilia, Bologna, 1964.

'Discorso agli operai di Belgrado', *Rinascita*, vol. XXVII (1970), no. 34.

'Intervista', *Nuovi Argomenti*, no. 20, May–June 1956 (reprinted in Togliatti, *Opere scelte*, q.v., pp. 702–28).

'Le istruzioni alle organizzazioni di partito nelle regioni occupate', in Togliatti, *Opere scelte*, q.v., pp. 331–33.

Memoriale di Yalta, Roma, 1970.

Opere, 5 vols., Roma, 1970–84.

Opere scelte, Roma, 1974.

'Per la libertà d'Italia, per la creazione di un vero regime democratico', in *Opere*, vol. V, q.v.

'Separatismo e autonomia', *Cronache Meridionali*, vol. IV (1957), nos. 7–8.

'Sviluppo e trionfo del marxismo', *Rinascita*, vol. VI (1949), no. 12.

Toniolo, G., 'L'utilizzazione dei fondi ERP nella ricostruzione italiana; alcune ipotesi di lavoro', in Aga-Rossi, ed., *Il piano Marshall e l'Europa*, q.v., pp. 189–92.

Torino fra le due guerre (exhibition catalogue), Torino, 1978.

Tortoreto, E., 'Lotte agrarie nella valle padana nel secondo dopoguerra, 1945–50', *Movimento Operaio e Socialista*, vol. XIII (1967), nos. 3–4, pp. 225–85.

Tranfaglia, N., 'La crisi italiana e il problema storico del terrorismo', in Tranfaglia, *Labirinto italiano*, Torino, 1984, pp. 227–82.

Travis, D., 'Communism in Modena: the Development of the PCI in Historical Context (1943–1952)', unpublished PhD thesis, University of Cambridge, 1984.

'Communism in Modena: the provincial origins of the Partito Comunista Italiano (1943–1945)', Historical Journal, vol. XXIX (1986), pp. 875–95.

Tremonti, G., and Vitaletti, G., *Le cento tasse degli italiani,* Bologna, 1986.

Treu, T., ed., *Lo Statuto dei lavoratori: prassi sindacali e motivazioni dei giudici,* Bologna, 1976.

L'uso politico dello Statuto dei lavoratori, Bologna, 1975.

Treves, A., *Le migrazioni interne nell'Italia fascista,* Torino, 1976.

Trigilia, C., *Grandi partiti e piccole imprese,* Bologna, 1986.

'Sviluppo, sottosviluppo e classi sociali in Italia', *Rassegna Italiana di Sociologia,* vol. XVII (1976), no. 2, pp. 249–96.

Tullio-Altan, C., *La nostra Italia,* Milano, 1986.

Turani, G., *1985–1995. Il secondo miracolo economico italiano,* Milano, 1986.

Turnaturi, G., and Donolo, C., 'Familismi morali', in Donolo and Fichera, *Le vie dell'innovazione,* q.v., pp. 164–84.

Turone, S., *Storia del sindacato in Italia,* Bari, 1973.

UDI, *Donna, vota per la dignità della tua vita, per il benessere della tua famiglia, per la pace,* Roma, 1953.

Unione Donne di Azione Cattolica Italiana, *Matrimonio e famiglia. Nozioni e informazioni culturali per propagandiste e delegate di Azione Familiare,* Roma, 1958.

Università Cattolica del Sacro Cuore, *La coscienza contemporanea tra 'pubblico' e 'privato',* Milano, 1979.

Vaccarino, G., Gobetti, C., and Gobbi, R., *L'insurrezione di Torino,* Parma, 1968.

Valdevit, G. P., *La questione di Trieste, 1941–1954,* Milano, 1986.

Valentini, M., 'La forbice non taglia più', *L'Espresso,* vol. XXXV (1989), no. 9.

Valenzi, M., *Sindaco a Napoli,* Roma, 1978.

Valiani, R., *La tassazione diseguale,* Roma, 1981.

Vallini, E., *Operai del Nord,* Bari, 1957.

Vella, C. G., ed., *Un sinodo per la famiglia,* Milano, 1980.

Viale, G., 'Contro l'università', in Baranelli and Cherchi, eds., *Quaderni Piacentini. Antologia, 1962–68,* q.v., pp. 429–52.

S'avanza uno strano soldato, Roma, 1973.

Vianello, F., ed., *Il piano del lavoro della CGIL, 1949–1950,* Milano, 1978.

Vianello, F., *et al., Tutto il potere della D.C.,* Roma, 1975.

Vicarelli, F., ed., *Capitale industriale e capitale finanziario: il caso italiano,* Bologna, 1979.

Vicarelli, G., 'Famiglia e sviluppo economico nell'Italia centro-settentrionale', in Ascoli, U., and Catanzaro, eds., *La società italiana degli anni Ottanta,* q.v., pp. 127–56.

Bibliography

Villari, L., ed., *Il capitalismo italiano del Novecento*, 2 vols., Bari, 1975.

Villari, R., 'La crisi del blocco agrario', in Istituto Gramsci, *Togliatti e il Mezzogiorno*, q.v., vol. 1, pp. 3–35.

Vinci, A., and Vettore, A., 'Le donne, il '69 e il sindacato', in *L'autunno caldo 10 anni dopo*, q.v., pp. 187–94.

Votaw, D., *The Six-Legged Dog*, Berkeley, CA, 1964.

* Walston, J., *The Mafia and Clientelism: Roads to Rome in Postwar Calabria*, London, 1988.

Warner, G., 'Italy and the Powers, 1943–1949', in Woolf, ed., *The Rebirth of Italy*, q.v., pp. 30–56.

White, C., *Patrons and Partisans*, Cambridge, 1980.

* Woolf, S. J., ed., *The Rebirth of Italy, 1943–1950*, London, 1972.

Zandegiacomi, N., 'Marzotto, un monumento nella polvere', in *Marzo 1968* (supplement to *Il Manifesto*, no. 76, 30 March 1988).

Zangheri, R., 'A trent'anni dalla legge di riforma agraria', in *Campagne e movimento contadino nel Mezzogiorno d'Italia*, q.v., vol. II, pp. 647–57.

Zangheri, R., ed., *Bologna*, Bari, 1985.

Zappella, L., 'Evoluzione del territorio e classi medie in Italia', *Critica Marxista*, vol. XIII (1975), no. 6, pp. 147–67.

Zizola, G. G., ed., *Risposte a Papa Giovanni*, Roma, 1973.

* Zuccotti, S., *The Italians and the Holocaust*, London, 1987.

Zuckerman, A. S., *The Politics of Faction*, New Haven, CT, 1979.

Zunino, P. G., ed., *Scritti politici di Alcide De Gasperi*, Milano, 1979.

Index

Index

Associazione Nazionale Magistrati, 149
Asti, 105
Aurigo, General Remo, 277
Australia, 211
Austria, 283
Autonomia Operaia, 380, 382, 386, 403
Autonomia Organizzata, 382
Avanguardia Operaia, 312, 314, 360
Avola, 337

Bachelet, Vittorio, 386
Badoglio, Marshal Pietro, 12, 13, 16, 40, 41, 44, 47, 48, 52, 53
Bagnasco, Arnaldo, 3
Balbo, Laura, 367
Banfield, Edward, 2, 127, 212, 413
Bank of Italy, 94, 95, 102, 157, 159, 214, 269, 274–5, 353, 389
Barberis, Corrado, 137
Barbone, Marco, 386
Bari, 12, 115, 141, 220, 229, 231, 372
Basaglia, Franco, 392
Basile, Carlo Emanuele, 256
Basilicata, 35, 98, 122, 127, 131, 212, 290
Basso, Lelio, 16, 104, 115, 194, 195, 261, 263, 266, 273, 274, 281
Battaglia, Pietro, 338
Battipaglia, 338, 343
Belelli, Arturo, 202
Belgium, 211
Belice earthquake, 345–7, 366
Bellafiore, Giovanna, 346–7
Benetton, Luciano, 408
Berlingieri, Baron, 124
Berlinguer, Enrico, 294, 330, 379, 389, 400–401; historic compromise, 350–51, 354–8, 372, 374, 375–6, 394, 402; and civil rights, 380, 383; 'democratic alternative', 402; and the FIAT strike, 403–4; death, 420
Berlusconi, Silvio, 408
Bertini, Valerio, 206
Bevilacqua, P., 34
Birindelli, Admiral Gino, 336

Bisaglia, Antonio, 284, 373
Bislini, Antonio, 328
'black' economy, 352, 353, 408
Blok, A., 136
Bobbio, Luigi, 360, 380
Bobbio, Norberto, 194
Bocca, Giorgio, 163, 237, 240
Bologna, 22, 187, 203–4, 212, 216, 295, 296–7, 382–3, 395–7, 413, 423
Bonaparte, Joseph, 32
Bonomi, Ivanoe, 53, 58, 91
Bonomi, Paolo, 50, 53, 140, 171–2, 275
Bordiga, Amadeo, 199
Borletti factory, Milan, 311
Borghese, Prince Junio Valerio, 334–5, 374–5
Boves, 17
Bowring, Sir John, 26
Bravo, Luciano Ferrari, 387
Brescia, 105, 371
Britain: occupation of Italy, 39–42, 51–2, and the Resistance, 56–8; post-war conditions, 78; and Trieste, 115; workforce, 236, 237, 238; living standards, 239; reform, 267
Brodolini, Giacomo, 328
Bronte, 128–9, 217
building speculation, 246–7, 271–2, 280, 287–8 390
bureaucracy, 145–7, 149–52, 161, 285–6, 345, 422
Burgalassi, Silvano, 245
Buscetta, Tommaso, 288

Cadorna, General Raffaele, 57
Cafagna, L., 160
Cagol, Mara, 361, 363
Calabresi, Luigi, 333
Calabria, 33, 34, 106, 122, 124–5, 126, 131–5, 137, 211, 338–9, 424
Calamandrei, M., 241
Calamandrei, Piero, 143
Calogero, Pietro, 386
Calvino, Italo, 207
Camorra, 180, 338, 424

Index

583